THE NEW INTERNATIONAL COMMENTARY ON
THE OLD TESTAMENT—R. K. HARRISON, *Editor*

THE BOOK OF ISAIAH

THE BOOK OF ISAIAH

THE ENGLISH TEXT, WITH INTRODUCTION,
EXPOSITION, AND NOTES

by

EDWARD J. YOUNG
LATE PROFESSOR OF OLD TESTAMENT
WESTMINSTER THEOLOGICAL SEMINARY

VOLUME III

Chapters 40 through 66

WILLIAM B. EERDMANS PUBLISHING COMPANY
GRAND RAPIDS, MICHIGAN

First printing, May 1972
Second printing, November 1974

TABLE OF CONTENTS

The Book of Isaiah

Preface to Volume Three

As was the case in the first two volumes of this commentary, the purpose of the present volume is to allow the prophet to speak for himself. Above all else an attempt has been made to bring out the message of Isaiah. In order to accomplish this purpose it has been necessary to omit discussion of much else. It is simply not possible to take account of all that has been written on these chapters.

In adopting the view that Isaiah of the eighth century B.C. was the author of chapters 40–66 as well as of the remainder of the book that bears his name, I do not believe that I have acted lightly. For nearly thirty-five years I have been reading everything I could obtain that pertained to this prophecy, and I believe that I am thoroughly familiar with the arguments advanced by those who deny Isaianic authorship. Frankly, I am not satisfied with their argumentation, for they ride roughshod over the explicit testimony of Scripture itself, and such a procedure is really but a form of rationalism. Throughout the commentary I have endeavored to point out evidences for the unity of authorship of the book, and in a brief appendix I have sought to list the principal arguments that may be adduced in defense of that unity.

Some will complain that I have not taken advantage of the so-called gains of scholarship made during the last hundred years. I have sought to employ historical and linguistic material where this seemed relevant; but I have not adopted the principles of form criticism as these are commonly employed, for I do not believe that these are necessarily gains. Of what real advantage is it to be told that the *riv* motif, for example, is found at a certain place in the prophecy? I am not convinced that form criticism has really been an aid in the interpretation of the prophecies.

Although it is not possible to refer to all the works written on these particular chapters, I would nevertheless call attention to the following.

Paul Volz: *Jesaja II.*
Charles C. Torrey: *The Second Isaiah.*
Franz Feldmann: *Das Buch Isaias.*
Christopher North: *The Second Isaiah,* Oxford, 1964.

Rachel Margalioth: *The Indivisible Isaiah,* New York, 1964.

James D. Smart: *History and Theology in Second Isaiah,* Philadelphia, 1965.

George A. F. Knight: *Deutero-Isaiah,* New York, 1965.

Karl Elliger: *Deuterojesaja in seinem Verhältnis zu Tritojesaja,* Stuttgart, 1933.

Karl Elliger: *Die Einheit des Tritojesaja,* Stuttgart, 1928.

Aug. Pieper: *Jesaias II,* Milwaukee, 1919.

This last-named work in particular has been of great help in understanding the prophet's message. Throughout the commentary reference has been made to other works.

It is a pleasure to express my gratitude to Mrs. Carl Spackman for the careful manner in which she prepared the typescript. Mrs. Robert Meeker read over the entire manuscript and made many helpful suggestions. My deepest gratitude is due her.

In placing emphasis upon the content of Scripture I fully realize that I am going counter to the prevailing current, which is to stress the form of the writings. Nevertheless, I am convinced that the great need of the Church is for an understanding of what God says, not primarily an attempt to label and classify every utterance found in the Bible. Among the many charges that may be levelled against the prevailing form-critical studies is this fact, that they tend to draw attention away from the proper study of the message of Scripture to an overemphasis upon its form.

This entire work is based upon the fact that the one living and true God is the primary Author of all Scripture and so of this Scripture. Hence, I regard the entirety of Isaiah as the revealed Word of God and have sought so to expound it. One who devotes his attention to this work must at once feel his own inadequacy. He is in the presence of the sublime and the majestic. He is in the presence of the holy Word of the God of truth. May all who read this commentary be drawn to greater love and adoration for Him who commanded, "Look unto me, and be ye saved, all the ends of the earth: for I am God, and there is none else."

—EDWARD J. YOUNG

LIST OF ABBREVIATIONS

acc. accusative
Akk. Akkadian
ANEP Pritchard, *Ancient Near East in Pictures,* Princeton, 1954
ANET Pritchard, *Ancient Near Eastern Texts,* Princeton, 1950
AOTB Gressmann, *Altorientalische Texte und Bilder zum Alten Testament,* Tübingen, 1909
Aq Aquila
Ar. Arabic
BASOR *Bulletin American Schools of Oriental Research*
B Codex Vaticanus
BDB Brown, Driver, Briggs, *Hebrew Lexicon,* Oxford, 1907
BH *Biblia Hebraica*
CBQ *Catholic Biblical Quarterly*
CMAL Driver, *Canaanite Myths and Legends,* Edinburgh, 1956
com. commentary
col. column
COT E. W. Hengstenberg, *Christology of the Old Testament*
DOTT D. Winton Thomas, ed., *Documents from Old Testament Times,* London, 1958
Egy. Egyptian
E.T. English Translation
ExT *Expository Times*
f. feminine
GKC Gesenius, Kautzsch, Cowley, *Hebrew Grammar,* Oxford, 1910

GTT *Gereformeerd Theologisch Tijdschrift*
Heb. Hebrew
HS Brockelmann, *Hebräische Syntax,* Neukirchen, 1956
HTR *Harvard Theological Review*
IB *The Interpreter's Bible*
ILCH Sidney Smith, *Isaiah Chapters xl-lv; Literary Criticism and History,* 1944
imp. imperfect
inf. infinitive
1Q First Isaiah Scroll, Qumran
JAOS *Journal of the American Oriental Society*
JBL *Journal of Biblical Literature*
JNES *Journal of Near Eastern Studies*
KAT Schrader, *Die Keilschriften und das Alte Testament*
KJV King James Version
M Masoretic Text
m. masculine
mss. manuscripts
MSTP Young, *My Servants The Prophets,* Grand Rapids, 1952
ND A. Haldar, *Notion of the Desert in Sumero-Accadian and West Semitic Religions,* Uppsala, 1950
NT New Testament
OTS *Oud-testamentische Studien*
OT Old Testament
part. participle
perf. perfect

9

PIAI	J. Lindblom, *Prophecy in Ancient Israel,* Oxford, 1962	*TII*	Rachel Margalioth, *The Indivisible Isaiah,* New York, 1964
PL	Migne, *Patrologia Latina*	*TT*	Driver, *A Treatise on the Usage of the Tenses in Hebrew,* Oxford, 1892
pl.	plural		
RB	*Revue Biblique*		
RSV	Revised Standard Version	Ug.	Ugaritic
S	Symmachus	*UH*	Cyrus Gordon, *Ugaritic Handbook,* 1947
s.	singular		
SII	Young, *Studies in Isaiah,* Grand Rapids, 1954	*VAB*	*Vorderasiatische Bibliotek*
		VBW	*Views of the Biblical World*
Syr.	Syriac	*VT*	*Vetus Testamentum*
		Vulg.	Vulgate
SZD	Begrich, *Studien zu Deuterojesaja,* München, 1963	*WThJ*	*Westminster Theological Journal*
Targ.	Targum	*ZAW*	*Zeitschrift für die alttestamentliche Wissenschaft*
T	Theodotion		

Outline

The first two volumes of this three-volume commentary on the book of Isaiah dealt with the following material:

III. TRUE DELIVERANCE IS FOUND NOT IN EGYPT BUT IN THE LORD (28:1–35:10)

A. THE LORD'S PURPOSE (28–29)
1. Samaria Ripe for Judgment (28:1-29)
2. The Iniquity of Jerusalem and the Announcement of Deliverance (29:1-24)

B. THE JUDEAN ALLIANCE WITH EGYPT (30–31)
1. To Trust in Egypt Is to Be Deceived (30:1-33)
2. Egypt Is No Help, but the Lord Will Protect Jerusalem (31:1-9)

C. THE CERTAINTY OF THE COMING SALVATION (32–33)
1. A Condition of True Blessedness Will Come (32:1-20)
2. Oppression Will End, and God's Kingdom Will Be Established (33:1-24)

D. GOD'S SOVEREIGNTY MANIFESTED IN JUDGMENT AND SALVATION: CONCLUSION TO CHAPTERS 28–33 (34–35)
1. God's Sovereignty Manifested in Judgment (34:1-17)
2. God's Sovereignty Manifested in Salvation (35:1-10)

IV. THE CONNECTING BRIDGE BETWEEN CHAPTERS 1–35 and 40–66 (36–39)

A. THE CONCLUSION OF THE ASSYRIAN PERIOD (36–37)
1. Sennacherib and the First Attempt of the Empire of Man to Destroy the Kingdom of God (36:1-22)
2. The Failure of the First Attempt to Destroy the Kingdom of God (37:1-38)

B. INTRODUCTION TO THE BABYLONIAN PERIOD (38–39)
1. The Godly Hezekiah (38:1-22)
2. The Babylonian Exile Announced (39:1-8)

The present volume begins with point V.

V. THE SALVATION AND FUTURE BLESSING OF THE TRUE ISRAEL OF GOD (40–66)

A. THE PROLOGUE (40:1-11)
1. The Threefold Comfort (40:1, 2)
2. The Revelation of the Lord's Glory (40:3-5)

3. The Enduring Word of God (40:6-8)
4. The Coming of the Lord God (40:9-11)

B. JERUSALEM'S WARFARE IS ACCOMPLISHED (40:12—48:22)

C. JERUSALEM'S INIQUITY IS PARDONED (49:1—57:21)

D. JERUSALEM HAS RECEIVED OF THE LORD'S HAND DOUBLE FOR ALL HER INIQUITY (58:1—66:24)

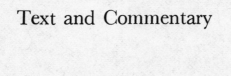

Text and Commentary

V. The Salvation and Future Blessing of the True Israel of God (40–66)

A. THE PROLOGUE (40:1-11)

1. The Threefold Comfort (40:1, 2)

1 Comfort ye, comfort ye my people, saith your God.
2 Speak upon the heart of Jerusalem and cry unto her, that her warfare is accomplished, that her iniquity is pardoned; that she hath received of the hand of the LORD double for all her sins.

When one turns from the thirty-ninth to the fortieth chapter it is as though he steps out of the darkness of judgment into the light of salvation. The contrast is great, and yet it is evident that thirty-nine is a preparation for forty. In thirty-nine Babylon had been brought to the fore as the nation that would receive God's people in captivity, and upon this tragic note that chapter concludes. There will be peace and truth in Hezekiah's own day (the period of Assyrian supremacy), but the descendants of Hezekiah were to go into exile. There had been earlier hints in Isaiah that Babylon would be the power of opposition to the theocracy (cf. chap. 14), and subsequent history makes clear that the Mesopotamian world power that began with Assyria did indeed culminate and reach its zenith in Babylon under Nebuchadnezzar. Thus in the book of Daniel, Babylon is the head of gold and the lion with eagle's wings, the first and great part of the human kingdom whose purpose was the overthrow of the people of God.

Chapters 40ff. serve to answer the dark picture that the thirty-ninth chapter had created. They see the people of God in human bondage, yet they go far deeper and look to the people as being in bondage spiritually, subject to the taskmaster sin. From this bondage there is to be a deliverer, the Servant of the Lord. As they face the future the people are assured that God will be with them in the vicissitudes of their existence.

It is not accurate, however, to say that chapter forty and the following chapters are directed to the people in exile, for they are not yet in Babylon. Isaiah, rather, through the spirit of prophecy

17

sees the time when his people will suffer bondage, for the exhorta-
tions to patience and faith found in these chapters show that the
final fulfillment of the promise was in the future.

In this second major portion of the prophecy there are certain
similarities to the prophet's original call. As once the prophet had
heard the majestic Lord declare, "Go and thou shalt say unto this
people," so again, taken up from sense and earthly life, and looking forward to the changes through which God's people are to
pass, the prophet hears the voice of the same Lord commanding
with respect to His people. In that first commission the prophet
had been charged with the proclamation of a judgment that would
endure until the exile. Now, however, he is to go to *my people* and
proclaim to them a message of comfort and consolation, exalting
the Lord their God as their only hope and redeemer.

Another comparison is in place. As the first part of the prophecy
began with a command (1:2), so also does this one. Furthermore,
both in 1:2 and in the present verse the command is connected
with the speaking of the Lord. In 1:2 heaven and earth are ordered
to listen, for Yahweh has spoken; and here a command is given as
spoken by the people's God. Also, both at the beginning of the
prophecy (1:3) and here (40:1), Israel is addressed as *my people*.
It was this people that had to hear the message of Isaiah as a
prophet of judgment and now could hear him as a messenger of
comfort.

1 Immediately the prophet begins with a command, *Comfort ye*.
It is God who speaks and who commands men to accomplish His
purpose. Instead of saying, "I shall comfort my people," he says
"Comfort ye my people." This work of comforting is to be carried
out by those to whom the command is addressed. Among them
must be included Isaiah himself, but also the other prophets who
are charged to speak God's word. It appears to be a command
directed to the prophets in general, but probably with Isaiah
particularly in mind, for it is actually he who in the words of the
following chapters brings the comfort of the announcement of
salvation.[1]

---

[1] Volz and others, however, think that the pl. is not to be understood
logically but according to mood (*Stimmungsmässig*) and so refers not to a
number of persons but simply to the abundance of comfort. Targ. adds *prophets,
prophesy comforts,* but B supplies ἱερεῖς at the beginning of v. 2. Cf. 2 Kings
21:10; 2 Chron. 33:18, 19. For the idea of comfort in Isaiah cf. 12:1; 22:4; 49:13;
51:3, 12, 19; 52:9; 54:11; 61:2; 66:11, 13.

The repetition serves to bring to the fore the great significance of the command and the fullness and richness of the comfort offered. Such repetitions are quite common throughout the entire book of Isaiah (cf. 24:16; 26:3; 29:1; 38:11, 17, 19; 43:11, 25; 48:11-15; 51:8, 12, 17; 52:1, 11; 57:6, 14, 19; 62:10; 65:1). The command was to be carried out by the proclamation of good and comforting words (cf. Zech. 1:13). As the subsequent chapters show, true comfort consists in setting forth the entire truth concerning the people's tragic condition and in causing them to see God as their only hope. When the heinousness of sin is faced, then the announcement of deliverance may be made. For the reception of these words of grace the people have already been prepared through the earlier announcement of judgment to come. The declaration and threatening of the judgment (e.g. 39:7) is the presupposition for the words of comfort to follow. Indeed, apart from that preceding declaration of judgment, the words of comfort are without much point.

Isaiah designates the object of comfort as *my people*. These words, therefore, are to be understood as accusative, the object of the verb, and not as a vocative as the Vulgate construes them.[2] The people belong to God, for He has chosen them. Hence, even though they may forsake Him, He will not abandon them. It was necessary that He punish them through the judgment of the exile, for Israel must learn humility. At the same time God does not forsake His own. There is no conflict here with what had been stated earlier in chapter six. Those described in that chapter are the reprobate, among whom Ahaz stands out as an example. The nation as such, however, must also be punished for its sins and go into exile. Yet the ancient promises will not be forgotten, and God will now speak to the nation through His prophet words of consolation for the judgment that is to befall it.

We are to construe the verb as present, rather than as future, for it represents the message God is then and there speaking through the mouth of the prophet. At the same time the frequentative force of the word has often been pointed out. Not merely once, but over and over God speaks these gracious words. The particular or-

---

[2] *popule meus* — B has τὸν λαόν. *My people* is a favorite designation in Isaiah, occurring 12 times in 1–39, 9 times in 40–55, and 6 times in 56–66. If the term here includes the idea of perfect reconciliation between God and the exiles (Penna), it should have the same connotation elsewhere, e.g. 1:3.

thography of the verb is a characteristic feature of the book of Isaiah and an evidence for its unity.[3]

In tender covenantal language the speaker is identified as *your God*.[4] The two possessive suffixes present the two aspects of the relationship. There is a notable contrast—*my* people and *your* God. To whom, however, does the possessive *your* refer? It might refer to the ones who are to do the comforting. *Their* God commands them to comfort *His* people. It is better, however, to refer the possessive to the people. "Your God," Isaiah on this construction is saying, "has commanded us to comfort you, His people."

2 The present verse states how the comfort of verse 1 is to be presented, namely, by means of proclamation. Isaiah and the other prophets are to speak, for it is by the declaration of God's truth that comfort is brought to those who are in need thereof. The imperatives of this and the preceding verse accentuate the Lord's almighty power to dispense the rich blessings of the new age as He will. It is in God's wondrous forgiveness and His plan of redemption that we find the basis and reason for this message of consolation. The manner of proclamation is described with the words, *upon the heart of Jerusalem*.[5] The preposition *'al* (upon) seems to suggest that the comfort will come down upon the heart of Jerusalem. The comfort consists in the speaking of words that will fall upon the heart with pleasure, comfort, and refreshment, to encourage and cheer the heart like gentle rain falling upon the ground (cf. Hos. 2:14). Stress falls more upon the effect produced upon the heart than upon the manner of speaking. In Judges 19:3 and Genesis 34:3 the expression is used of words uttered for the purpose of winning someone over, and in Genesis 50:21 it is employed by Joseph to produce confidence in his brethren. To

---

[3] *saith* — not future, as Calvin (*dicet*), but present. The imp. expresses an action that is now being performed and will continue into the future. It is not the beginning of the action in the past that is in view (Kennedy wrongly proposes to read the perf.), but the extension into the future. Thus, the action is not to be regarded as single or momentary but as repeated. The divine word has begun but is not finished. In this sense יאמר occurs in the middle of a speech, a characteristic usage of Isaiah really not paralleled by the extra-Isaianic occurrences of the word. Dillmann thinks that the word is no evidence of Isaianic authorship, but that a phrase such as "and it shall be afterward that God will say" would be required. With the view of the composition of these chapters presented in this work, such an argument loses its weight.

[4] *your God* — the phrase is found only 4 times in Isaiah—35:4; 40:1, 9; 59:2.

[5] *upon the heart* — note *Tzere* in the construct state; cf. Gen. 34:3; 50:21; Judg. 19:3; Ruth 2:13; 2 Sam. 19:7; 2 Chron. 30:22; Hos. 2:14.

speak to the heart, therefore, is to speak the things the heart desires to hear and to speak so as to affect the heart by bringing to it a message of comfort. As is usual in Scripture, man's heart is conceived as the center of his emotions.

In speaking of Jerusalem the prophet has in mind its inhabitants, applying to them the geographical name.[6] The actual city, however, stands for those who dwell therein, and these are the people of God. In this sense, Calvin and others are correct when they assert that Jerusalem represents the Church, the elect of God. At the outset Jerusalem is made prominent and is thus regarded as in existence. It is Jerusalem and not Babylon that is the heart of chapters 40–66. This is also in accordance with the heading of the prophecy (1:1), which identifies the vision of Isaiah as having to do with Judah and (specifically) Jerusalem (cf. the comments on 1:1).

If one were to assume that these chapters came from the time of the exile he would be compelled to interpret Jerusalem in a figurative sense as referring only to the exiles in Babylon. Why, however, would the prophet so designate these exiles when the actual city was in ruins? It is understandable how Isaiah could thus address them when the city was yet in existence and the center of the theocracy, but it is difficult to believe that a prophet with any understanding of the theocracy would address exiles in Babylon as Jerusalem, when the city was no longer the center of the theocracy. This would be a theocratical blunder of the first magnitude. Once the Temple had been destroyed and God's dwelling among men removed, the people could no longer appropriately be designated Jerusalem.

The speaking unto the heart is not to be done by some quiet, obscure method, but by means of vigorous proclamation. Those commanded are to call out to Jerusalem in bold, decisive manner, so that there will be no uncertainty as to the message.[7] By this

---

[6] The conception of Jerusalem as an idea rather than a place has already begun with 28:16. But Volz is beyond the evidence when he says that through "Deutero-Isaiah" the words *Jerusalem, Zion, Israel,* and *Jacob* have been raised from their earthbound reference *("aus ihrem festumrissenen irdischen Boden")* and transformed into figurative words for "the people of God" and "the kingdom of God." The usage of these words must be determined with each particular occurrence. Volz does acknowledge that the geographical sense is not completely lost.

[7] קרא אל — *to cry unto*; for an illustration of the force cf. 6:3; also Zech. 1:4; Jer. 7:27.

crying aloud all doubts will be removed and all will know the surety of the comfort proclaimed.

By means of three clauses introduced by *that* (*ki*), Isaiah presents the threefold content of the message. Grammatically it is also possible to understand the threefold *ki* as causal, giving the reason for the proclamation. On such a construction, however, we are left with no content to the message itself but only with a threefold statement of the reasons for the proclamation of the message. Hence it is better to interpret *ki* as in each instance introducing indirect discourse and as setting forth the content of the words of comfort that fall upon Jerusalem's heart.

Isaiah first declares that Jerusalem's warfare has become full and so is completed. There will no longer be any warfare for her. The word refers to military service, but the prophet uses it here in a figurative sense as indicating a period of hardship and misery generally (cf. also Num. 4:23; Job 7:1; 14:14; Dan. 10:1).[8] The period of time in which Israel must suffer has now been filled and so has come to an end. Thus, Paul also speaks of the fullness of time (Gal. 4:1). There is no warrant for limiting the phrase to the Babylonian exile. Those who believe that these words were uttered directly to the exiles by a prophet living in the exile are compelled to assert either that they must have been spoken at a time when the exile was over (note the force of the verbs) or else that they were uttered shortly before the conclusion of the exile, when it could truly be said that the period of restraint was complete. If, however, this latter was the case, they could only have been spoken by a true prophet who had infallible (hence divinely revealed) knowledge that the exile was about to be ended. The words could not be the mere guess of a man unaided by special divine revelation, for, even in the most propitious of instances, such a guess could not be a message of divinely revealed comfort.

What Isaiah refers to is the long period of bondage and misery brought on the nation by its sin and apostasy, and culminating in the period of wrath and indignation known as the exile. When this

---

8 צבא occurs frequently in the OT and in some contexts must refer to a period of misery or suffering. Generally it is m. but here feminine. An interesting usage is found in Mari (*Archives Royales de Mari*, Paris, 1950, Vol. III, Text 18:20) : *a-di ṣa-ba-am šu-nu-ti be-li* [*a u-s*] *a-an-ni-qu-ma* (as long as my master had not strangled?) . Here the word seems to refer merely to a period of time, possibly of military service. In the deepest sense the "warfare" is the OT dispensation, conceived, as Alexander says, as a period of restriction and constraint.

period was completed, the true theocracy would be revealed; then the kingdom of God would have come. To burdened sinners there can be no more comforting declaration than that the time of burden has ended.

Not only is the period of misery completed but, furthermore, the iniquity of Jerusalem has been pardoned. The verb employed signifies *to receive favorably, to be regarded favorably,* or *to be regarded with satisfaction.* To say that the iniquity is accepted with favor is to say that the punishment meted out for that iniquity is satisfactory or that the sacrifice made for that iniquity is received favorably. In this present passage the thought is either that a sacrifice sufficient to atone for the iniquity has been accepted, or else that the nation's suffering for its iniquity has been regarded as sufficient. On this latter interpretation the thought is not that Israel by its suffering has actually atoned for its sins, but that God regards the nation as having suffered sufficiently. In the light of Pentateuchal passages, however (cf. Lev. 1:4; 7:18; 19:7; 22:23, 25, 27), it would seem that the first interpretation is to be preferred. The iniquity is received with favor, for a sacrifice on behalf of that iniquity has been offered, and the sacrifice offered is acceptable. This interpretation is supported in particular by Leviticus 26:41, 43. Hence it is best to translate, *the debt of her iniquity is paid.* Here is the first intimation of the truth to be more fully revealed in the fifty-third chapter of the book.

In the third point of comfort the prophet makes a statement that is twice as long as each of the previous two statements. Again he employs a verb in the past. Actually, at the time when Isaiah spoke, these blessings had not been realized, for he was looking into the future and through the Spirit of prophecy predicting the time of blessing and salvation ushered in by the Servant of the Lord. Yet, as Alexander wisely remarks, "The verbs are *preterita prophetica,* but for that very reason should not be exchanged for futures, as we have no right to depart without necessity from the descriptive form in which it pleased the Holy Ghost to clothe this prophecy."

From the Lord's hand Jerusalem had received the cup of wrath which had been poured out. Now, from that same hand she has received double blessing.[9] The word *double* stands alone, and for

---

[9] כפלים — not characteristic Oriental exaggeration (Muilenburg), although it need not be taken in a strict numerical sense. But cf. W. Tom (*GTT*, Vol. 59,

that reason the exegetical question is whether this *double* refers to punishment and suffering or whether it indicates blessing and mercy received from the Lord. On either interpretation, however, the exact force of *double* is not to be pressed. Rather, like *mishneh* in Job 42:10ff. and Zechariah 9:12, it simply points to an abundance. If the word refers to suffering and punishment, it indicates that in God's sight Jerusalem has suffered sufficiently because of her sins. Although she has not been punished as much as she deserved, nevertheless her punishment has been sufficient to accomplish its purpose. As against this, however, the idea of receiving double after suffering usually refers to the reception of blessing (cf. Isa. 61:7; Job 11:6). At the same time it fits in better with the thought of the verse as expressing the content of the blessing to refer these words to the punishment and misery that Jerusalem has received. Great has been her suffering, but it has not been sufficient to satisfy the Law she had offended — indeed, no human suffering or misery could satisfy that Law; nevertheless, in His goodness God would bring an end to her misery. His own have been in bondage long enough; the time for blessing and deliverance has come. The chastening rod will be lifted, and the light of salvation will dawn.

Yet Jerusalem's suffering has not been arbitrarily inflicted but came because of her sins. The preposition thus serves to denote the means employed of God to bring about the punishment. It is also possible to construe the preposition as expressing price, and to render, *for all her sins*, i.e. *as the price*, or *in recompense for all her sins*. On this construction the thought is that the sins of Jerusalem have brought about her sufferings. The price she has had to pay for her sins is the receiving of double punishment. Isaiah's use of *all* is not without significance, for it points to the entire mass of sin committed by Jerusalem. The sins were many and they were enormous, so that they would bring upon Jerusalem an abundant punishment.

SPECIAL NOTE

It has been pointed out that the threefold message of comfort, so succinctly stated in this verse, corresponds in actuality to the threefold

1959, pp. 122-123) who suggests that we begin with the sense *to fold together*, i.e. a folding double, so that the word would here indicate that with which the sin is completely covered. Von Rad (*ZAW*, Vol. 79, No. 1, 1967, pp. 80-82) takes the word in the sense of *equivalent*. Cf. also Rev. 18:6.

declaration or preaching of that comfort unfolded in the subsequent chapters. Thus, in 40:2–48:22 the prophet announces to Jerusalem her redemption and deliverance from the judgment. In 49:1–57:21 Isaiah preaches of God's bringing salvation to Israel in place of her sins, and finally in 58:1–66:24 there is pictured the abundant and wondrous salvation that will come to Israel. Note too that in 61:7 the word *mišneh* corresponds to the *kiplayim* of 40:2c.

2. THE REVELATION OF THE LORD'S GLORY (40:3-5)

3 A voice crying, In the wilderness prepare the way of the LORD; make straight in the desert a highway for our God.

4 Every valley shall be exalted, and every mountain and hill shall be brought low; and the crooked shall become straight and the rough places a plain.

5 And the glory of the LORD shall be revealed; and all flesh shall see it together, for the mouth of the LORD hath spoken.

The first two verses are often regarded as a prologue to the prologue (40:1-11). They have presented the consolation from a negative viewpoint; but what is the positive side of the salvation? The following nine verses answer that question. These nine verses again divide themselves into three divisions of three verses each, and we may now note the first of these divisions. In verses 3-5 the prophet is concerned with the wondrous, all-embracing change that the Lord's coming produces in the world.

3 Introducing both the first and the second division (vv. 3, 6) is the word *qol* (*voice*), and this same word appears also in the third division (v. 9) although not at the beginning of the verse. Its introduction in verse 3 is abrupt, as though the prophet were to say, "Hark, a voice." The voice is not that of God, for the message itself speaks of *our God*. The voice must therefore belong to a creature. Yet it is not an angel voice or that of one of the heavenly court, but a human voice, a messenger of God declaring His commands.[10] Further than that, however, we cannot identify the voice from this present passage, for the prophet purposely leaves the identification vague. Grammatically the following word *qore'* (*crying*) may be a predicate or it may be a genitive. We may render either *a voice crying*, or *the voice of one crying*. The Greek

---

[10] Volz identifies the voice as that of invisible powers. He thinks prophets had access to divine councils and so knew of the preparations for earthly events. We are not told, however, in what manner the content of this revelation was made known to Isaiah.

26

versions adopted this latter construction as did the New Testament (Matt. 3:3; Mark 1:3; Luke 3:4; John 1:23). This also places more emphasis upon the one who cries than upon the voice, and so agrees well with the command of verse 2, *cry unto her*.

Not without reason is the identity of the speaker left unrevealed. His identity must fall behind the glorious message he proclaims. The manner of statement is an illustration of the truth, "He must increase but I must decrease." Only from the New Testament do we learn that the reference is to John the Baptist. In Isaiah's language there is a strange mystery as the speaker is kept in the background and only his magnificent message sounds forth. Nevertheless, it is an effective voice, as though resounding over all the country where God's people are. To this voice all men must give ear and hearken.

If we follow the Masoretic accentuation—and for the sake of the parallelism this must be done—we must construe *in the wilderness* with what follows and not with what precedes.[11] The parallelism will then present a chiastic arrangement:

> In the wilderness prepare the way of the Lord,
> Make straight in the desert a way for our God.

Yet, in construing the words with what precedes, the New Testament is not in error, for it applies the language of the Old Testament to its own time, when John the Baptist was crying in the wilderness. Indeed, one is tempted to ask whether, despite the parallelism, this may not have been the manner in which these words were understood by the Jews from the very first.[12]

The first imperative suggests the idea of turning aside obstacles that may be in the way as well as setting in order or arranging, and the second calls to mind the necessity for straightening the way so that it may be viable.[13] The prophet employs two words, *way* and *highway*. The latter refers to a road artificially constructed by

---

[11] *crying* — with *Zaqef Qaton*, a disjunctive accent, and so the word is to be construed with the preceding rather than with the following.

[12] φωνὴ βοῶντος ἐν τῇ ἐρήμῳ; Vulg. *vox clamantis in deserto*.

[13] Penna suggests that the thought may reflect upon an ancient practice whereby the inhabitants of a region, in times of necessity, were summoned to prepare a road so that war troops and chariots might pass over it. Note the language of Esarhaddon (Wiseman, *The Vassal Treaties of Esarhaddon*, London, 1958, line 54), *kaskal sig₅ ina GÌR.II-šú la ta-šá-kan-a-ni*, "you shall indeed place a fair path at his feet."

means of casting up the earth.[14] Isaiah elsewhere makes similar references (45:2; 57:14 and 62:10). What, however, is the purpose of the prophet's commands and to whom are they issued? It is sometimes said that the Lord is here pictured at the head of His people, leading them back across the desert from exile. Or it is claimed that the prophet is picturing the exiles making their way home through the desert. Even Calvin held that the command was issued to Cyrus and the Persians, who had kept the people in captivity. Such interpretations, however, are out of keeping with the language of the text.

When Israel had been in bondage in Egypt, God went through the desert to deliver her (Deut. 33:2; Ps. 68:7). Again at their time of need God came from Sinai to be present with His people (Judg. 5:5). Isaiah's command is addressed to the *my people* of verse 1. They are to prepare the way for the Lord, and this they are to do by means of repentance. It was their iniquity that had kept God from them and had brought the bondage of Babylon and the termination of the theocracy. Hence, the exile came to be known as the period of indignation when the anger of the Lord blazed forth against His people. Now, however, He will come to His own again; but they must prepare the way. If the reference were to a journey of the people, then God Himself would clear and prepare the way; but inasmuch as the picture is that of God coming to His people, it is the people who must prepare. The desert therefore is a

---

[14] *a highway* — Smith (*ILCH*) regards this as a characteristic word in the book of Isaiah, referring to roads artificially raised along a depression, alluding to the natural main route followed by the Assyrian armies. He goes on to conclude, however, that here in 40:3 is probably the earliest known allusion to Persian highroads raised over the plain and driven through a cutting in the hills, such roads being unknown until the time of the Achaemenid kings. But Smith derives this interpretation from the late date he attributes to chap. 40. Why should *mesillāh* have a connotation here different from that which it has in 11:16; 19:23; 33:8? Nor in 49:11; 59:7 or 62:10 is the reference necessarily different. The word also occurs in line 56 of the Moabite Stone (cf. Francis Andersen, "Moabite Syntax," *Orientalia*, Vol. 35, Fasc. 2, 1966, p. 95): *hmslt.b'rnn*. Cf. the fine discussion in Martin Noth, *The Old Testament World*, E.T., Philadelphia, 1966, p. 85. For cuneiform "parallels" to Isa. 40:3-5 (Marduk's return to Babylon from Elam), cf. Friedrich Stummer, "Einige Keilschriftliche Parallelen zu Jes. 40–66," *JBL*, Vol. 45, 1926, pp. 172-173. But whereas a mere statue of Marduk is led to Babylon, in Isaiah the sovereign Yahweh comes, not from one city to another in festal procession, but eschatologically and with redemption, transforming all nature before Him and displaying His glory that all flesh may see it. The cuneiform "parallels" are at best only formal. The differences far outweigh the resemblances.

figure of the obstacles and impediments as well as the difficulties that have kept God from His people.[15] As in times past He had come through the desert to their aid, so will He this time.[16] John the Baptist brings out the fundamental meaning of the prophecy with his cry, "Bring forth therefore fruits meet for repentance" (Matt. 3:8).

4 The prophet now explains in detail how the general command of the previous verse is to be carried out. What is presented in verse 4 is a simple description of what will occur in the future. While it is possible from a grammatical standpoint to regard this verse as continuing the command, nevertheless the simple form of the verbs suggests rather that it is to be taken as expressing what will be in the future. The wondrous changes in nature are figurative of the preparation of the way for the Lord to come to His own.

Whenever a deep obstructing valley is encountered, it will be raised so that it will become even ground and will no longer be an obstacle.[17] Likewise, whenever the way should encounter a mountain or even a hill, these will be brought low in that they will be levelled off and become even, so that they too will no longer constitute obstacles to travel. In the first half of the verse the change is indicated by means of the verb. In the second half, however, the line is introduced by the phrase *and it shall be,* and

15 That *desert* is an excellent figure for the tragic condition of the people is seen in that it is waterless (41:18; 43:19, 20; 48:21), not fertile (41:19; 51:3; 55:13; 60:13), without paths (43:19), and uninhabited (64:10). The word *desert* does not apply to the Babylonian desert, for there is not a word in this section about a return of exiles from Babylon to Palestine.

16 ערבה — the word signifies a *steppe*, i.e. dry land. It is applied to southern Judah west of the Dead Sea (e.g. 1 Sam. 23:24), to the Jordan valley west of the river (e.g. 2 Sam. 2:29), and east thereof (2 Sam. 4:7). It may also refer to the eastern part of the Jordan valley and to the Ghor itself (i.e. the entire Jordan valley). There is no evidence that it here refers to the Babylonian or even the northern Arabian desert. Modern exegetes have appealed to the Babylonian processional way, the great *masdaḫu*, along which the images of the gods were carried during the festivals. Smith rightly rejects the view that the ערבה lies in the Syrian desert but applies the term to the Wadi Arabah (p. 169), and thinks that the road is essentially that which Nabonidus took through Edom and Transjordan. The word, however, is a parallel to מדבר, both terms suggesting that the way for God is to be prepared in a hostile, uninhabited, uninviting region.

17 גיא — *a steep, narrow valley*; as pointed the word reflects *-ay*, as opposed to the normal *gay-'>gēy'*. The verb *yin-nā-śē'* is declarative, and may also imply command. *Let it be raised* is a possible rendering.

this is followed twice by the preposition *to*. Thus, it is stated that the crooked will become straight, and the rough places a plain.

There is a difference of opinion as to the precise significance of the words in this second half of the verse. The first noun is generally rendered *crooked* or *jagged, uneven*. It is the opposite of *mishor*, which indicates something *even* or *smooth*. The thought would either be that the uneven, jagged, rocky places will be smoothed out so that travel over them will be possible, or that the tortuous road will be straightened so that it will lie direct. Finally, there is again question as to the precise significance of *r^ekasim*. Possibly it refers to the steep places or narrow gorges that form an obstacle to journeying. At any rate, these *r^ekasim*, whatever they may be, will be turned into their opposite; they will become a plain.

Isaiah employs a wealth and variety of figures to set forth the truth that the preparation for the Lord's coming will be complete. Inwardly and outwardly all will be in readiness for Him. Whatever had been a hindrance will be entirely removed. The sins of the nation, which had brought about the period of indignation and had kept God from His people, will be removed so that they will no longer stand in the way of His appearance among His own. The way stands clear and straight so that travel over it may be with no impediment whatever.

5 When the way has been fully prepared, then will be revealed the glory of the Lord in His appearance among men; and this glory will be universally witnessed. It will be made plain for all to see, for it has been long hidden. With the destruction of the Temple under Nebuchadnezzar the glory would depart from Jerusalem, and the theocracy would come to an end. No longer would Jerusalem be the holy city, for the people's sins would keep their God from them. Now, however, there is to be a full reversal of the situation. God will again appear among men. This time, however, it will be an eschatological coming, a revelation of the glory of God that will display itself in His salvation (cf. 1 Pet. 4:13b). In all the majesty of His power and grace God will be manifest to His people.[18]

[18] For the concept *glory of the Lord*, cf. com. on chap. 6, note 23. In the Psalms the term describes the splendor and magnificence of the creation (cf. Ps. 19:1; 57:5; 79:9; 96:3). At the time of the exodus also God's glory manifested itself (Ex. 16:10; 24:16ff.; 33:18; 40:34). Christ's redemption is a new exodus in which the glory of God will be revealed. The reference is not to an exodus

This revelation will not take place in a corner but will be seen by all men.[19] It is true that a man will die if he sees God, for man is sinful. Yet, with the revelation of God's glory, a strange thing happens. He that is flesh, indeed, all that are flesh, do what they supposedly cannot do. They see God, and they live. When the incarnate Christ was upon earth He said, "He that hath seen me, hath seen the Father." It is of interest to note that Isaiah does not speak of all men, but of all flesh. And it is of interest also to note that he uses the word *together*, a word so characteristic of his prophecy.[20] Altogether, as a unity, all flesh will see the glory of the Lord.

Of the truth and trustworthiness of this strange and blessed message there can be no doubt, for the very mouth of the Lord Himself has spoken it. This concluding phrase is characteristic of Isaiah (cf. 1:20 and note also 21:17; 22:25; 24:3; 25:8; 58:14, etc.). It was a message that came by verbal revelation, God-breathed, spoken by God's mouth. In place of Jerusalem's period of misery will be the revelation of the glory of the Lord. Thus, the content of verses 3-5 corresponds to the proclamation of comfort in verse 2.

---

from Mesopotamia (Penna thinks there might have been a manifestation of glory at that time), for, among other reasons, at that time all flesh did not behold God's glory.

[19] וראו — *and will see.* B adds τὸ σωτήριον τοῦ θεοῦ, which is preserved in Luke 3:6. In Heb. the object is not expressed, but is probably *the glory of the Lord* understood. It is incorrect to construe *they shall see* with *that the mouth,* etc.

[20] *together* — appears 10 times in 1–39, and 17 times in 40–66. *all flesh* — restricted to mankind (cf. John 17:2; Rom. 3:20; Gen. 7:21). All flesh may see the glory of God, manifested in the sending of Christ, but only His own will truly rejoice therein.

3. The Enduring Word of God (40:6-8)

6 The voice saying, Cry, and he says, What shall I cry? All flesh is grass and all its loveliness like a flower of the field.
7 The grass withereth, the flower fadeth, for the breath of the LORD bloweth against it; surely the people is grass.
8 The grass withereth, the flower fadeth; but the word of our God will stand for ever.

6 Corresponding to the second proclamation of comfort, namely, that Jerusalem's iniquity is pardoned, is the thought (vv. 6-8) that man is frail like the grass, and only the Word of the Lord endures forever. The first word is anarthrous in Hebrew and hence to be construed as indefinite. Who the speaker is we are not told. Drechsler reasons that inasmuch as the word *saying* reflects upon the *says* of verse 1 (a correct observation) the speaker is the Lord Himself. This conclusion, however, does not necessarily follow. Others have suggested that there is a dialogue, as it were, between an angel and the prophet. Again, this cannot be demonstrated. Hitzig has pointed out that in the dialogue between the speakers there is a pleasing mystery, which is lost when one seeks to probe too closely into their identity. Nor is it necessary to identify the speakers. What is of importance is the content of their message, not the personality of the criers.

Whether we construe the first word as construct and render, *the voice of one saying*, as consistency with the rendering in verse 2 would seem to demand, or whether we simply render, *a voice says*, makes little difference as far as the meaning is concerned. In one case the emphasis falls upon the voice; in the other upon the one who speaks.

By means of an imperative the proclamation of the message is presented. One word stands alone: *cry!* It reflects upon the plural imperative *cry* of verse 2. That imperative was addressed to all who should speak unto Jerusalem; this imperative, on the other hand, is singular, and is directed to the principal speaker or messenger to bring the Word of the Lord, namely, Isaiah himself. The command to cry is expressed not only generally but in particular to the prophet.

In response to the command there is a question. We are not told explicitly who asks the question, but it is clear that he is the one who expected to proclaim the message.[21] The questioning calls to mind the scene at Isaiah's initial call (chap. 6) when, before discharging his task, he interrogated the Lord concerning his work. Of significance is the indefiniteness, which is preserved by a use of the third person, *and one said*. This corresponds to the objectivity expressed in *the voice of one crying* in verse 3.[22] It is a mysterious dialogue, carried out by two anonymous voices; and the very indefiniteness of the identity of the speakers brings into bolder relief the message itself.

Different constructions of the language of the second half of the verse have been proposed, but the one that appears to be most free of difficulty and to fit in best with the general context is that which regards these words as expressing the content of the message itself. What the speaker is to cry is that all flesh is grass, etc. He is also to proclaim the imperishable nature of the Word of God.

The words *all flesh* call to mind the similar phrase in verse 5, but here the article accompanies the phrase.[23] If there is any particular force to the article (and this is questionable) it would be to bring out the thought, *all that which is flesh*. Men of flesh are weak and mortal; their life is brief and soon comes to an end. In this respect it is like the grass, for under the burning rays of the sun the grass may soon dry up. In Scripture comparisons with the grass are fairly frequent (cf. Isa. 37:27; 51:12; Ps. 37:2; 90:5; 103:15; 129:6; Job 8:12).

Isaiah is speaking, however, not merely of the frailty of human existence. His thought penetrates as well to the inner life of man. The mind with all its qualities and attributes as well as the

---

21 *cry* — one is reminded by 6a of Mohammed's call. "And he (i.e. Gabriel) said, Read (*'iq-ra'*); I said, What shall I read (*mâ' 'aq-ra-'u*)?" (Ibn Hisham, *The Life of Mohammed*.) The similarity, however, extends only to the form of the expression.

22 *and one said* — B, Vulg., and 1Q read the 1st person. Saadia interestingly inserts a subject, *'al ma'-mûr (the one who was commanded)*. The combination of *voice* and *saying*, אמר, is found here and in 6:8 and nowhere else in the Old Testament. The similarity is stronger if the 1st person is read in 40:6.

23 *flesh* — the appearance of this word here and in v. 5 ties together the two strophes.

spiritual life are included in the prophet's thought. This he designates by the word *its strength*.[24] All that constitutes the glory of man can be compared only with the flower in the field, which exists but a short time and then perishes. Following the Greek, Peter interprets the reference to the Gospel and rightly brings out the true meaning: "For all flesh is as grass, and all the glory of man as the flower of grass" (1 Pet. 1:24a).

7 To give strength to his comparison Isaiah first makes a general statement concerning the nature of grass and flowers. He uses two verbs in the perfect and thus gives expression to what is accepted as true because of general and widespread observation. "It is a well-known fact," so we may paraphrase, "that grass withers and flowers fade."[25] The prophet employs both *grass* and *flower* anarthrously, for he is speaking of grass and flowers generally. Isaiah had earlier used such a comparison in speaking of the waters of Nimrim: "... For the hay is withered away, the grass faileth, there is no green thing" (15:6b). Likewise he had described the drunkards of Ephraim as a fading flower (28:1).

There is a reason for these widely observed facts, namely, that the *breath of the Lord* blows upon the grass and the flower. The introductory *ki*, therefore, is causal, giving the reason for what has been described in the first part of the verse. Other renderings, such as *when* or *as soon as*, although expressing what is true, nevertheless do not seem to be sufficiently precise grammatically. Isaiah employs a picture of someone blowing upon the grass and flowers[26] with the result that all moisture is taken from them and they become dried up and wither. In May, before the rainy season, the Hamsin or Sirocco blows over Palestine, having come from the hot, dry desert regions of Arabia. It is a pernicious wind and blows often for several days without intermission, filling the atmosphere with fine dust and rendering it sultry and oppressive. Possibly it is

---

24 חסדו — *its strength*. L. J. Kuyper ("The Meaning of Isa. XL 6," *VT*, Vol. 13, No. 4, 1963, pp. 489-492) makes out a good case for the translation *its strength*. Cf. Ps. 59:10, 11; 69:16; 143:12; Jon. 2:8 and 2 Kings 20:20 compared with 2 Chron. 32:32. This is supported by Targ., which reads "their strength," תקפהון. Cf. also Snaith, "The Exegesis of Isaiah xl. 5, 6," *ExT*, Vol. 52, 1941, pp. 394-96.

25 נבל — *there fadeth*. Cf. 28:1. The accent has been thrown back to the penult, but *Meteg* still remains with the ultima.

26 בּן — inasmuch as the preceding word concluded with a vowel letter, the *Dagesh* is probably conjunctive *Dagesh forte*.

of this wind that the prophet is thinking when he speaks of the breath (ru*a*ḥ) of the Lord, for the wind is an elemental manifestation of the Lord's breath.

A contemplation of the transitory and temporal character of the grass and flowers leads the prophet to exclaim that what is true of them is also true of the people. In using the definite article *the people*, Isaiah would seem to refer in particular to the people mentioned in verse 1. On this point, however, the commentators differ, and there is no reason for dogmatism.[27]

8 Isaiah now takes up the first part of the preceding verse, omitting the comparison of the people with grass. Thus he brings to the fore the characteristics of transitoriness and weakness to bring out more sharply the contrast with the permanence and enduring quality of the word of God.[28] By referring to the word of God the prophet means every word that proceeds out of the mouth of God (cf. Deut. 8:3; Matt. 4:4). It is possible that there is a specific emphasis upon the promise of verse 2, and the New Testament rightly applies this passage to the Gospel itself (1 Pet. 1:25). In the present passage, however, the emphasis falls upon the vivid contrast between the permanence of God's word and the transitory character of human flesh.

To God's word there is a permanent character. Unlike the flesh of man, which withers and fades, it stands forever. It rises up, stands, and endures. In contrast to all flesh with its perishable nature, the word of God is imperishable and endures forever. The thought is similar to that of our Lord's, "The Scripture cannot be broken." When God speaks, His word expresses the truth; and that truth cannot be annulled or changed.

27 The last three words are not a gloss. They appear in 1Q, although the first word is written והן. The distinction between *He* and *Aleph* in 1Q, however, is very fine.

28 *our God* — the messenger speaks as a representative of his people, and so the suffix *our* points to the covenantal relationship between God and the people.

4. The Coming of the Lord God (40:9-11)

> 9 Upon a high mountain get thee up, bringer of good news,
> Zion! lift up with strength thy voice, bringer of good news,
> Jerusalem! lift *it* up, fear not, say to the cities of Judah, Behold!
> your God!
>
> 10 Behold! the Lord God will come with strength and his arm
> ruling for him; behold! his reward is with him and his work
> before him.
>
> 11 Like a shepherd he will feed his flock, with his arm he will
> gather the young ones, in his bosom he will lift up; the nursing
> ewes he will lead.

9 The announcement of God's presence must be proclaimed far
and wide so that all will know thereof—hence the command to go
up, not merely to a mountain, but to a high mountain. The words
Upon a high mountain occur first in the sentence, in the position
of emphasis. Zion, who brings the good news, is commanded to
ascend this mountain for her own benefit.[29]

There are three possible constructions of the following words.
We may speak of the one that brings good tidings to Zion, or of the
one who brings good tidings, even Zion, or else of Zion's bringer of
good tidings.[30] The first view does not take sufficient account of
the contrast with the cities of Judah, mentioned later in the
verse.[31] Nor does it really offer a satisfactory explanation of the

---

[29] There is no change of scene here from the desert. For the thought cf.
Judg. 9:7 and Matt. 5:1. *for thyself* — ethical dative of advantage.

[30] מבשׂרת — *one who proclaims*, from בשׂר, *to proclaim*, usually of victory,
salvation, etc. Cf. 1 Sam. 31:9; 2 Sam. 18:19; Ps. 68:11. B renders εὐαγγελιζόμενος
and thus prepares for the NT εὐαγγέλιον. Cf. 41:27; 52:7; 60:6; 61:1. Cf. Ug. *bšr*
and *bšrt*, e.g. Driver, *CMAL*, 1956, p. 164; Gordon, *UH*, 1947, p. 220; and *ANET*,
p. 332, for the Lachish Letters.

[31] Cf. KJV "O thou that bringest good tidings to Zion." Vulg. *tu qui
evangelizas Zion, etc.*

feminine form *bringer of good tidings*. This latter objection also applies to the third view, "Zion's bringer of good tidings."[32] Perhaps the second view has the most to commend it.[33] Zion and Jerusalem are then identified as the messengers of peace who announce the coming of the Lord. They are personified as proclaimers of the truth. This is in keeping with the thought of 2:3 that the law of the Lord will go forth from Zion and His word from Jerusalem. It is the duty of the Church to declare the whole counsel of God, and whenever God comes to His people, it is Zion and Jerusalem that must proclaim that fact. This particular coming is eschatological; it is the coming that will bring salvation to His people; it is a message worthy of the most dignified proclamation, and its proclamation lies in the hands of the Church.

A second imperative sets forth the manner in which the proclamation is to be made. Corresponding to *get thee up upon a mountain* is the command *lift up*; corresponding to the adjective *high* is the phrase *with strength* (cf. 13:2; 37:23; 58:1). The language, it may be noted, is Isaianic. Further to encourage Zion and Jerusalem, the command *lift up* is repeated, although the second time the object is not stated. The words constitute a true picture of the manner in which the word of God is to be pro-

---

[32] Gesenius regards the f. as a collective for the m. pl., and adopts the Targ. interpretation, *the prophets who proclaim to Zion.* Hahn renders, *Verkünderin Zions.*

[33] This position is supported by Aq T S Syr. The objections generally offered against this view are: (1) In vv. 1 and 2 Jerusalem is said to be the one to whom the proclamation is made, and vv. 3-9 are said to be the carrying out of the command. Hence, Jerusalem could not here be the one who herself proclaims. It is by no means certain, however, that vv. 6-9 are part of the proclamation. Jerusalem is to be comforted, but Jerusalem also is to fulfill her task of proclaiming good news. Indeed, part of the comfort is the command to preach. (2) It is also argued that it is not suitable to place Jerusalem over against the cities of Judah inasmuch as Jerusalem was one of the latter. In 1:1 and elsewhere, however, such a disjunction is made. The cities of Judah receive the good news from Jerusalem, which is in their midst. The thought is the same as in 2:2-4. The Holy City is thus seen to be not only the seat of true religion but also the center of the Church. (3) To proclaim future salvation is said to be the prophets' task, not Jerusalem's. The community can only proclaim an experienced salvation. Such reasoning, however, is overly refined. When Jerusalem proclaims *Behold! your God*, He will indeed be present with His salvation, for by Zion and Jerusalem Isaiah means not the Jerusalem of the 8th century B.C. nor of the 6th, but the people of God who behold the coming of the Messiah.

claimed to the world.[34] The messenger is to be bold; he is to raise his voice that all may hear. The Church is not to keep this message to herself but is to present it to Judah's cities with a holy boldness. She is not to pose as a seeker after truth, unsure of her message, but to declare in clear, firm, and positive voice that her message is true. She must be vigorously and militantly evangelistic. Hesitation, timorousness, and trembling are out of place. There is no need to fear as though the word of God would not be fulfilled, or as though the message would prove to be untrue and embarrassment would result.

Isaiah states the content of the message in simple terms, *Behold! your God!* The interjection arrests the attention, drawing it to the message itself. The cities of Judah are stopped, as it were, that they might see their God before them. After the long night of sin and warfare, the time of darkness brought on by the sins of the people, at last God Himself is coming again to His own. In these words is found the heart of the Gospel, "the sum of our happiness," as Calvin puts it, "which consists solely in the presence of God." This is the great theme of the remainder of the prophecy; it is the very center of the Gospel. If we have not God, we have nothing; and if we have Him, we have all things.

10 The language of this verse is explanatory of *Behold! your God!* and does not itself constitute a part of that message. Zion and Jerusalem are to call the cities of Judah to look to their God, for He is coming to His people. Two clauses are introduced by *behold!* and these ejaculatory words reveal how God will come and how we are to behold Him. The first designation of God is one Isaiah delights to use, for it characterizes God as the sovereign master, the God of power. He it is who is also the Lord, Yahweh, the covenant God of the people. He is to come as a Strong One. The preposition is probably best understood as *Beth essentiae*, and thus the prophet sets forth the nature of God's coming as consisting in *strength*.[35] There is reflection upon the deliverance from Egypt, when God

---

[34] Alexander aptly appeals to an illustration of the thought in Caesar (*Bellum Gallicum* vii.3), "*Celeriter ad omnes Galliae civitates fama perfertur; nam ubi maior atque illustrior incidit res, clamore per agros regionesque significant; hunc alii deinceps excipiunt et proximis tradunt.*"

[35] Or, the preposition may denote the sphere or character; *in the character of a strong one*; cf. Ex. 6:3; Ps. 39:7. The ancient versions took the word as a substantive, e.g. Vulg. *in fortitudine veniet.* Vitringa (supported by Löwth), *against the powerful one*, i.e. the enemy.

came to His people in bondage for the purpose of delivering them. Again He comes, this time also to bring deliverance, comfort, and blessing. The work is such that only a Strong One can perform it.

God has not yet come to His people, for Isaiah uses the future, *will come*. The work of salvation is still to be accomplished. Supporting the interpretation just given is the phrase, *and his arm is ruling for him*, a phrase subordinate to the main clause and with circumstantial force. The circumstances under which God will come are with *his arm ruling for him*. The *arm* is the symbol of strength and power; hence this is but another way of saying that God will rule in power.[36] The arm will rule for God's benefit, bringing into subjection whatever stands in the way of His coming, or casting down all opposition (cf. 63:19).

What is the *hire* of which the prophet speaks? The word *śakar* refers to a remuneration that has been earned by means of work; and the second word, *p^e'ullah*, indicates work, but also the reward or pay that comes from the performance of the work. The two words are here virtually synonymous.[37] Is God depicted here as dispensing a reward to others or as Himself receiving a remuneration for His own work? Most interpreters appear to prefer the former view, applying the first word to the penal recompense of His enemies and the other to the reward the righteous will receive from His hands. Calvin, for example, states that the words do not refer to a reward due because of human merit, but merely point to the justice of God, who is a rewarder of all who diligently seek Him. May it not be, however, that the second view is far more in keeping with the context?[38] It is God Himself to whom a recompense is due, for He has merited it. Penna is quite right, it seems, in finding the allusion to a mighty act of God performed in war.[39] The reference, however, need not be to the Babylonian captivity as such, but rather to the far more wondrous deliverance from the bondage of sin. A workman has earned his hire as the

36 Cf. 48:14; 51:5, 9; 52:10; 53:1; 59:16; 62:8; 63:5, 12.

37 שכרו — *his hire*. The two words together have the force *the reward of the worker*. When these words have the sense of *hire*, the reference is not to that dispensed by the person, but rather to the hire or wages paid to him.

38 The reference is not to the spoil obtained in war, but to the wages paid for work done (Volz).

39 *"Dio l'ottiene, nel caso presente, con un atto di forza contro l'oppressore babilonese"* (Penna). Cf. BDB, p. 821. The concept of the arm as a manifestation of strength was well known in the ancient Near East. Muilenburg appeals to Amarna Tablet No. 288 and to a Ugaritic statue of Baal.

fruits or reward of his work, but God is deserving of His reward for His great victory against the enemy, the deliverance of man from his sin and its consequences. This is His great work. The hire, then, is found in the redeemed of the Lord, the little ones who are mentioned in the following verse. Although He comes as a strong one, yet it is as a shepherd that He feeds His sheep. His recompense is with Him, in His very sight and possession. Our Lord Himself connected the two thoughts of the Strong One and the reward when He identified Himself as the Good Shepherd who laid down His life for the sheep. Thus He comes, the Strong One, bringing with Him the reward that is His due, even the sheep whom He will carry tenderly in His arms.

11 In former times God's face had, as it seemed, been hidden from the people, and they had suffered through the period of their warfare. Now, however, He will come as a Strong One and will be a Shepherd to His own. Emphasis falls upon the introductory words, *Like a shepherd.* Involved is all the tender care and sacrifice that the shepherd gives to his sheep. He is not like the hireling, who flees in time of danger (cf. John 10:12). As a Shepherd He will shepherd His people.[40] The verb generally translated *feed* also involves the entire work of the shepherd, and may perhaps best be rendered *will shepherd.*[41] Whatever the shepherd must do for his sheep, that the Lord will do for His own, for He is the Good Shepherd.

The Lord possesses a flock, and toward this flock He exercises the office of Shepherd. This flock consists of sheep, i.e. those who are tender and humble and of sheeplike nature. In the language of the New Testament we may say that this flock is His elect, those whom before the foundation of the world He had chosen to save and who in the course of time have received the tender grace of the Shepherd, manifested in the salvation of their souls and in the

---

40 Other possible constructions are: *as a shepherd his sheep will he shepherd* (Stier) ; *like a shepherd who shepherds his sheep* (Hahn) .

41 Cf. Gen. 33:13. In the ancient world the shepherd played an important role. In the temple of the Elamite god Shushinak in Susa, excavators found the statue of a man holding a sheep in his left arm with the right arm extended protectively in front of it. Note *ANET*, 443b. Indeed the role of the shepherd was so noble that God Himself is presented as the Shepherd of His people. The concept of shepherd brings us into the realm of royalty. Cf. Hammurabi's designation of himself as *ri-ia-um* (shepherd) and Sennacherib's *ri-e-um it-pe-šu* (prudent shepherd) . Such examples could easily be multiplied.

constant nourishing and cherishing of them throughout their lives. They are not the strong and powerful, as the world apart from God regards strength and power, but those who without the Shepherd would perish.

It is the function of the remainder of the verse to indicate how the Shepherd cares for His sheep. By means of His arms He gathers them.[42] In verse 10 there had already been mention of His arm as ruling for Him. This *arm* is the symbol of His might and power and is sufficiently strong to gather up the sheep for protection and care. When they are in the Shepherd's arm, nothing can harm or come near to separate them from Him.[43] Those whom He gathers are described as lambs, i.e. the young lambs recently born.[44] They are the weakest members of the flock, which cannot possibly defend themselves against attack and which are in need of the Shepherd's constant protection. By means of His arm He will gather them up, and in His bosom He will carry them so that they will recline in His arm against His bosom. Thus they will not have to walk themselves nor stumble nor go astray.

As for the lambs that are giving suck, the ewes that are nursing, these the Shepherd does not drive, but leads.[45] These ewes need particular care; they cannot be forced along by driving, and so the Shepherd tenderly leads them. Hitherto, God's people had received double at the Lord's hand for their sins; now they find that the Lord is a tender Shepherd to them. Thus in its conclusion the prologue returns to the thought of comfort with which it began.

[42] The preposition expresses means; not *in his arm*.

[43] According to the punctuation the text should read, *With his arm he will gather the lambs, and in his bosom he will lift (them) up. BH* proposes: *the lambs in his bosom he will lift up.* But as the text stands it offers a chiasm that is very forceful: *his flock he will feed—he will gather the lambs.* Also *BH's* proposal requires deletion of the conjunction.

[44] טלאים — lambs; from this word came the designations *talya* (boy) and *talitha* (girl) ; cf. Mark 5:41.

[45] *those who give suck* — f. part. pl.; cf. Gen. 33:13; Ps. 78:71.

B. JERUSALEM'S WARFARE IS ACCOMPLISHED (40:12–48:22)

CHAPTER FORTY

12 Who hath measured in the hollow of his hand the waters, and
meted out heaven with the span, and comprehended in a measure the dust of the earth; and weighed in a balance the mountains and the hills in scales?

13 Who hath meted out the spirit of the LORD, and as the man of
his counsel will cause him to know?

14 With whom did he take counsel, and he made him to understand, and taught in the path of judgment; and taught him
knowledge, and the way of understanding will cause him to
know?

15 Lo! nations as a drop from a bucket, and as dust on scales
are reckoned; lo! islands as an atom he will take up.

16 And Lebanon is not enough for burning, and its beasts are not
enough for a burnt offering.

In the prologue (vv. 3-11) and particularly in verses 3-5 Isaiah
had prepared for the first part of the message of this portion of his
book. He desires to show the matchless and wondrous power of the
God of Israel, Yahweh, the God of heaven and earth who alone is
able to redeem His people from the spiritual bondage their sin had
imposed upon them. The first section, 40:12–48:22, deals with the
conversion of Israel and the revelation of the glory of God which
has brought Israel's period of misery to an end. The language of
the section is striking and beautiful. J. Gresham Machen writes of
the King James translation of this chapter,

> The simplest means are employed in the production of the effect;
> common, homely English words are used; and some of the grandest
> sentences are written in words of one syllable. After the lapse of three
> centuries there is nothing strange or archaic in the language of this
> chapter; the words are those that form our common English speech
> in the twentieth century just as in 1611. But if the materials used are
> simple, the total effect is sublime. There is in this chapter a rhythm
> that never degenerates into metre, a combination of simplicity with

42

grandeur, which uplifts the soul. It is quite impossible, the wondering reader will say, for prose style ever to attain heights greater than these.[46]

12 What kind of God is He whose coming the prophet has announced? In answer a number of questions are raised that immediately reveal that this God is the mighty Creator. The language reflects upon the vastness and majesty of the creation and suggests the care with which creation was accomplished. The mighty waters, for example, were measured. Who, however, has done so mighty a thing?[47] When Isaiah asks, "Who has measured, etc.," he does not mean that no one has measured, but simply asks a rhetorical question designed to show that none but the God of Israel, the Lord, has measured the waters.[48] The stress upon *who* and *whom* in these verses prepares for the emphasis upon "It is I" in the subsequent chapters.

Isaiah uses the term *waters* to designate the waters of the seas generally.[49] Who has measured the waters in the hand full, or, in the hollow of the hand?[50] The two words, taken together, form a striking contrast: the *hand* of man—the *waters* of the sea. Obviously, for man to measure the water in his hand would be an impossibility.

For the sake of vividness the prophet expresses himself chiastically. Having referred to the waters, an element of the earth, he now

---

46 *God Transcendent*, Grand Rapids, 1949, p. 17.

47 The use of the perf. in vv. 12-14 should be noted. Some commentators believe that the perf. serves to designate the impossible as unreal (cf. 65:1, 2; see Jouon, *Grammatica*, 112 J) and bring out the sense, *who would have been able, etc.*? It is better, however, to maintain the normal force of the perf. (cf. Job 28:25ff.; 38:4ff.; Prov. 30:4). To translate by the present is incorrect (Budde). Cf. W. H. Green, *A Grammar of the Hebrew Language*, New York, 1892, § 266:1a.

48 I cannot agree with the usual formulation of the exegetical question, namely, whether *man* or *God* is the subject of *has measured*, for it seems to raise a false disjunction. It is better to ask whether the question expects the answer *no one* or *God*? The thought is simply, *Who has measured*, and the answer, *none but God*. The interrogative is exclusive, designed to show that only God has measured. At the same time God is not named in this context. Note that whereas vv. 1-12 stressed the eschatological salvation, the background for the day of the Lord, the present context harks back to the creation. There can be no true salvation unless it is grounded in and based upon the historical fact of creation.

49 *the waters* — the word is anarthrous. In the Marduk liturgy, Marduk is described as measuring the waters. Cf. Stummer, *op. cit.*, pp. 173-176.

50 *šoʿolô* — *his hollow hand, hand full* (1 Kings 20:10; Ezek. 13:19).

turns to the *heavens*, i.e. the skies. Who has taken his hand and used it as a span for measure, and thus measured out the heavens?[51] The very question again reveals the impossibility of man's doing such a thing.

A third question points to the same thing. Who has comprehended, or grasped, the dust of the earth *in a measure?*[52] The *measure* is a *shalish*, which means a third part.[53] Such a measure is not sufficient to hold the innumerable dust particles. Nor has anyone been able to weigh *the mountains in a balance* or *the hills in scales*. For man the universe is unmeasurable; not, however, for God. The very asking of these questions points out on the one hand the impotence of man by reason of the fact that he is a creature. By the same token, even though God is not named, they also stress the omnipotence of the God of Israel, who in creating the world assigned to the seas, the heavens, and the soil of earth their proper position. "Who hath laid the measures thereof, if thou knowest? or who hath stretched the line upon it?" (Job 38:5ff.). The contemplation of these things should lead the mind directly to the consideration of the greatness and grandeur of the everlasting God, who will come in glory to visit His people.

13 As the glance into the created universe had emphasized God's omnipotence, so a glance into history brings to mind His omniscience. The first verb, *tikken*, has the same significance as in the preceding verse, and indicates the measuring or meting out of something. God alone has measured the waters in the hollow of His hand, but He Himself is unmeasurable. He who has measured the creation cannot be measured by the creation. The Spirit of the Lord is the Spirit of intelligence and understanding who hovered above the waters at the creation (cf. Isa. 34:16; Gen. 1:2; Job 33:4, etc.). It is the Spirit that brings life and makes alive, who brought order out of chaos.[54] No one has brought this Spirit into line

---

[51] *span* — i.e. the distance between the thumb and the tip of the little finger of the outstretched hand; cf. Egy. *dr't, hand*. In Heb. the word refers to a span used as a measure. Lambdin suggests that in Old Kingdom Egyptian the absolute was *ğărät*, and this was apparently borrowed by the northwestern Semites as *ğărtŭ>zeret*.

[52] וכל — *and has comprehended*; only here in the *Qal*; cf. 1 Kings 8:27. The root is כול.

[53] Compare a "quart," the fourth part of a gallon. Some have suggested that the term is used for the *se'āh*, the third part of an ephah (5:10). The Babylonians sometimes measured by thirds. Cf. *ILCH*, p. 97, Note 83.

[54] Volz believes that *rûaḥ* denotes the all-embracing and spiritual essence

44

with a measure so that He must be subjected to the control and direction of man.

The second half of the verse stands in chiastic relation to the first. Thus, the object comes first and is emphasized, and the verb and suffix conclude this half of the verse. These words are probably to be construed as follows: "And a man of His counsel, will He cause Him to know?" The thought then is that no one can act as a counsellor and cause God to know the things that He should know. On this construction, the latter half of the verse really continues the question introduced by the first interrogative pronoun. Objections have been brought forward against this interpretation, but they are not valid.[55] In ancient times it was the duty of citizens to counsel the king. Thus, Esarhaddon in his treaty commands the citizens upon whom the treaty is imposed: "You swear that in the truth of your heart you will talk with him, sound advice of the fullness of your heart you will give him."[56] The man of God's counsel is the man who gives God counsel. No one, the prophet is declaring, can serve as a counsellor of God to cause Him to know what is necessary, inasmuch as He is omniscient.[57]

14 Isaiah now binds together the basic thoughts expressed in the two preceding verses. Thus, 14a takes up verse 13, and 14b verse 12. The interrogative is placed first as an object, and like the preceding interrogatives implies a negative answer. *With whom* refers to men, so that the answer is, "With no man did He consult."[58] The verb is reflexive, *Whom did he consult?* and calls to mind the *man of his counsel* of verse 13 (cf. also 45:21). Inasmuch as in His counselling He is a wonder (9:6), there is no need for Him to counsel with others. The second verb may be rendered, *and he instructs him* (God), so that He may exercise discernment in His acting.[59] The second clause of the first line is difficult, but

---

of Yahweh. Some commentators would here give the verb (*tikkēn*) the sense of *direct, regulate.*

55 Hahn interprets, *and a man of His counsel, does He let him know* (*it*)? Hahn declares the construction adopted herein *unstatthaft.*

56 Cf. Wiseman, *op. cit.*, lines 51b-53.

57 Cf. Rom. 11:34; 1 Cor. 2:16.

58 Note that in v. 14 the subject is not mentioned. It is suggested, however, by the genitive, *Lord,* in the preceding verse.

59 The *waw* consecutive with the imp. expresses result; *with whom did God consult, that he (man) might cause him (God) to understand?* The following verbs are also to be understood as expressing result.

probably the whole may be rendered, *and teaches him (that he may go) in the path of judgment.*

To introduce the second half of the verse the verb is repeated, *who teaches him knowledge?* As *judgment* is the revelation of God's counsel in the wondrous disposal of the creation and formation of the universe, so *knowledge* has reference in particular to the creation. In the created universe the wisdom and judgment of God are displayed. Creation required knowledge, but no one taught God this knowledge, for no creature possesses such knowledge.

Lastly, the thought is strengthened by calling attention to the *way of understanding* which the creation reveals.[60] No man causes God to know this, for it is a secret that belongs to Him alone. The creation reveals the true penetration into the nature of all things that God as the Creator possesses. Job 28:1ff. is a commentary upon this thought. "The Lord by wisdom hath founded the earth; by understanding hath he established the heavens" (Prov. 3:19).

One cannot read these verses without rejoicing in the remarkable manner in which, by means of a few rhetorical questions, Isaiah has exalted the Lord as the omnipotent and omniscient Creator of heaven and earth. And yet these profound thoughts did not originate in the mind of the prophet. Unaided, apart from divine revelation, no sinful man, not even an Isaiah, could have attained to such sublime belief. None of the greatest thinkers of ancient Greece, the keenest intellects of the time, ever succeeded in reaching heights such as these. Whence then did the prophet learn these truths? He was taught of God; these are the truths of revelation. "For since the beginning of the world *men* have not heard, nor perceived by the ear, neither hath the eye seen, O God, beside thee, *what* he hath prepared for him that waiteth for him" (Isa. 64:4).

15 God is the Creator of all things and hence not dependent upon them. He needs not the counsels of man, and He is also independent of nations themselves. To introduce this thought the prophet employs the ejaculation *See!* and thus turns to the heart of his message. Attention is focused immediately upon *nations.* The

---

[60] *understanding* — the pl. of an abstract noun serves to intensify the idea (*keen* or *intense understanding*).

word is anarthrous, for the thought seems to be not so much that the nations of earth are as a drop of the bucket before Him, but that even nations, in contrast with individual men, are as nothing. Thus, having made clear that no one was the counsellor of God, the prophet points out that even nations, those powerful human entities that seem to be able to act according to their own will in human history, are really of no moment in the eyes of God.

In the first half of the verse there is but one verb, hence the verse is to be rendered, *Nations are reckoned as a drop of the bucket and as a dust of the scales.* By separating the subject from the verb by means of two intervening comparative clauses, the author produces a strong rhetorical effect. Furthermore, this arrangement of the words also brings the subject *nations* into closer connection with the objects of comparison. The word translated *drop* is a *hapax legomenon.* The context, however, and the versions, support this rendering. One little drop from a bucket — such is the estimate the Almighty God places upon the nations. He no more needs their counsel than He does that of the individual.

A minor exegetical question must be noticed. What is the relation in which the drop of water stands to the bucket? Are the nations of no more significance than a mere drop of water taken from a bucket?[61] Perhaps it is not possible to settle this question positively, nor is it of import. The prophet is stressing the mere drop of water in comparison with the bucket. A bucketful of water in itself is considerable, but a drop is infinitesimal. Such are nations in the eyes of God.

A second comparison is equally striking and forceful, *the fine dust of the scales.* Even the slightest weight will move the scales, but the fine dust that rests upon them does not affect them. Isaiah is not declaring that God has no concern over the nations; the entirety of Scripture is gracious testimony to the contrary. And the individuals of the nations have been so loved by Him that He has sent His Son to die for them. What Isaiah means, rather, is that in comparison with God the nations are of no significance. He needs them not, for He is their Creator.

To introduce the third comparison the prophet again makes use

---

61 *drop* — those who believe the figure to be the drop hanging from a bucket appeal to the Ar. *marra,* "to flow, pass by," and *mamarrun,* "water-course," and to the preposition *min, from,* "like one from the many drops in the bucket" (Feldmann). König points out that the expression is used in Klopstock's poem, *Die Frühlingsfeier.*

of the word *see!* and thus calls attention to the significance of the expression to follow. Not only are nations insignificant, but also isles. Again, the subject *isles* is anarthrous. The reference is to the islands of the Mediterranean but in particular to its coastlands. In the second part of the book Isaiah often uses this word to designate those districts that are far from Palestine (41:1, 5; 42:4, 10, 12; 49:1; 60:9; 66:19). It is an appropriate word for one who is residing in Palestine, but its appropriateness would be greatly weakened if the author were in Mesopotamia.

With what may the isles be compared? The prophet employs a word that indicates a small or minute part of some substance, a very small particle of dust or a very fine grain of sand. It is the word *daq*, which some commentators render *atom*. Although the imperfect is employed, the text does not describe what God does but what He can do. He does not actually lift up the isles, but, should He desire to do so, it would be no more difficult for Him than to lift up a dust particle or an atom.[62] Great, imposing, magnificent as the isles appear to man, to God they are as nothing.

16 Having stated the utter supremacy of God over the whole creation, the prophet now points out that even in a religious sense He is not dependent upon man. This is done by means of an example, the reference to Lebanon. If Lebanon, with all its wooded glory, is not sufficient for an offering to God, then nothing indeed is sufficient. "The imagery here used," says Alexander, "is justly described by Umbreit as magnificent: nature the temple; Lebanon the altar; its lordly woods the pile; its countless beasts the sacrifice."

By mentioning it first, Isaiah brings emphasis to the word *Lebanon*. At the same time the conjunction *and,* although connecting the word with what precedes, singles it out for special notice, as though the prophet had said, *and even Lebanon.* To bring out the precise force of the original, we may render: *And Lebanon—not is there sufficiency for burning.*[63] Perhaps there is reflection not only upon the quantity but also upon the quality of what is to be

---

[62] *he lifts up* — cf. Syr. *neṭal.* Following Rabbi Jonah, Knobel derives the form from *ṭûl,* and translates, *he casts away;* so Hahn. Maurer, however, is correct in deriving the word from *nāṭal* rather than *ṭûl.*

[63] י֥ד is construct; lit., *sufficiency of burning* (Piel verbal noun) and *sufficiency of burnt offering.* Note, however, the disjunctive *Tiphha* with the construct.

offered, for the cedars of Lebanon were much prized. Not all of Lebanon, filled with wood as it is, is sufficient to keep burning the fire of offering to the Lord.

Parallel in position at the head of their clause are the words *and its beasts.* Thus, the two concepts emphasized *Lebanon* on the one hand and *its beasts* on the other. The forests of mountainous Lebanon teemed with roaming wild animals; but all of these would not provide a sacrifice, for they were not sufficient. Yahweh, the God of Israel, is so high and exalted above man that man is in no way able to present unto Him a sacrifice or offering worthy of Him. The noun *animals* is a collective in Hebrew and includes all those animals that might ordinarily be suitable for an offering. As to the word rendered *burnt offering,* its root idea seems to be that of ascending. Whether this refers to the ascending of the smoke or to the ascent of the animal to the altar is perhaps not possible to say. The thought is that the entirety of the animals of Lebanon is not sufficient to form an offering unto the Lord.

17 All the nations are as nothing before him, less than nothing and vanity are counted to him.

18 And unto whom will ye liken God? and what likeness will ye compare to him?

19 The image a carver has wrought, and a gilder with gold will overlay it; and chains of silver he is casting.

20 The one impoverished in his offering, a tree that will not rot he chooses; a wise carver he seeks for it, to set up an image that will not be moved.

21 Will ye not know? will ye not hear? has it not been told you from the first? Have ye not understood the foundations of the earth?

17 Again the prophet takes up the thought of verse 15 but strengthens and intensifies it. Now he speaks not merely of nations but of all nations, actually denying to them any existence. With the first clause we are to understand the copula *are,* i.e. *All the nations are as nothing before him.* The thought is not essentially different from that of verse 15, but in that verse it had been expressed in picturesque fashion by means of the comparison with a drop from a bucket. By the words *before him* the prophet is not asserting that in God's estimation the nations are nothing, for it is not God's evaluation of the nations that is in view. Rather, the preposition *before* suggests the presenting before one for purposes of making a comparison. In comparison with God the nations are as nothing. The reason for this truth is not stated in this verse, but will soon be presented. God is the Creator who has brought all else into existence. He is infinite, whereas the creation is finite. The creature can never comprehend Him, but must ever bow in wonder before Him.

The English translation *nothing* does not really bring out the force of the Hebrew word *'ayin,* which may be rendered *there is not.* Perhaps we may get at the thought by translating *as not existing.* In comparison with God all the nations are not.

Verse 17b strengthens the thought of 17a. At the same time the details are not particularly simple. In the Hebrew text we have a preposition, *from nothing.* This is simplified by the great Qumran scroll, which reads *like nothing,* an easier reading which removes the difficulty. If the preposition *from* be retained—and is there genuine warrant for not retaining it?—how is it to be interpreted? It would seem that the particle may be taken as a partitive, *a part of nothing,* in the sense that the nations are nothing at all; or else to designate origin, *from nothing,* i.e. originating or produced from nothing.[64] It is difficult to decide positively, but probably the thought is that the nations are to be reckoned as a part of nothing, and inasmuch as the part is less than the whole, as *less than nothing.*

As for the word *nothing,* it simply denotes the end at which something ceases, i.e. nonexistence. The following word, *tohu,* appears in Genesis 1:2 to designate the waste and uninhabitable condition of the earth before God's work of forming and fashioning the cosmos began. This was a condition of desolation in which the earth was the opposite of a well-ordered world. So are the nations with respect to God. We may take the last clause impersonally or as a passive. Thus *with respect to him they are reckoned,* or *with respect to him one reckons.*

18 All the comparisons Isaiah has been introducing lead to the unavoidable and inevitable conclusion that God is the true God and that beside Him there is no other. There is nothing with which He can be compared, for He is the Creator and all else is the creation, the work of His hands. To bring out this truth the

---

[64] Gesenius interprets *from* like the Ar. expletive *min,* i.e. *nothing.* Hahn objects that the concept *less than nothing* is not possible, and that *min* must denote either separation or origin. The idea of comparison is not necessarily to be rejected, for the language is poetical, not mathematical.

prophet asks a question, for the asking of a question is more forceful than the statement of the truth in a simple declaratory sentence.

A conjunction begins the question and at the same time shows the connection with what precedes. To bring out the full force we may paraphrase *and so,* or *and therefore,* for the question follows what has preceded as a natural conclusion.[65] It is a question addressed not to the Israelites in particular but to all men. Without a doubt it does have particular relevance for the Israelites, but it seems to be a restriction of its force to limit it to them. A negative answer is demanded: God can be likened to no one. The comparison has to do not merely with dumb idols but with all that is not God. Is there anything apart from God with which He may be compared? The answer is, "There is not." At the same time it should be noted that the question is *unto whom* and not *unto what will ye liken God?* Perhaps the thought is that there is no human creature to whom God may be likened. No man, be he ever so powerful and exalted, can be compared with God. If all the nations before Him are but as a drop of the bucket, how much less can He be compared with any mere man! It is significant that Isaiah uses the designation *'el* (*God*), which always points to God in distinction from the creature.

Isaiah's question brings us to the heart of genuine theism. There can be no comparison between the living, eternal God (*'el*) and any man, for man is but a creature. Man is limited, finite, temporal; God is infinite, eternal, and unchangeable in all His attributes and perfections. In our thinking about God the infinite distance between God and the creature must ever be kept in mind. To break down this distinction is to fall into the sin of idolatry.

Isaiah now begins his fulmination against the idols, for to compare God with the idols is blasphemy. A parallel question brings out the same thought, *and what likeness will ye compare to him?* The verb implies a setting out or arranging in order. "How then," we may paraphrase the thought, "will ye lay things out so that there will be a comparison with God?" One cannot compare God with the creature, for between the creature and God there is an infinite distance; hence, to make such a comparison is to bring God down to the level of the creature.

---

[65] Gesenius, however, takes the conjunction in its ordinary sense, *and,* and asserts that the argument merely continues. Dillmann rightly compares it with Ar. *fa,* the strong conjunction.

In speaking as he does the prophet does not conflict with the
statement in Genesis that God created man in His image and
likeness. Man is the image of God and in that sense is like God.
But Isaiah here has reference to the absolute distinction between
Creator and creature, a distinction also present in Genesis. Man is
in the image of God, but it does not follow that God can be
compared with man. To make an image of God is to regard Him as
a finite being, and hence is idolatry. "... Ye heard the voice of the
words, but saw no similitude; only ye *heard* a voice" (Deut. 4:12;
cf. also v. 15). Would we see God's "lively image," declares Calvin,
"we must not frame a likeness of Him according to our own fancy,
but we must the rather betake ourselves to His Word."

19 The question of the previous verse leads the prophet to
mention idols. Certainly God cannot be compared with idols, indeed, least of all with them. To bring down the eternal God into
the temporal is the result of comparing Him with the form of a
man. Even the material used in the manufacture of an idol was
created by God Himself. The hands of man created in God's image
employ materials placed in the earth by God to represent God in
the form of a creature. This is to deny God's eternity and infinity.

Isaiah uses the word *idol* first in the sentence, supplying it with
the definite article, and thus pointing to the genus itself. The *pesel*
(*idol*) may be a piece of wood that has been carved or shaped by
carving. In this context, however, particularly in light of the verb
nasak, it refers to a metal statue formed by melting (cf. 44:10).
The words serve as a *casus pendens*: *as for the image, a carver has
cast it*. The work is that of a specialist; *harash* denotes an artisan
such as a carpenter, stonecutter, carver, or blacksmith. It is not
necessary, therefore, to insist upon rendering the verb *cast*, or
poured out. The thought is well brought out if we say that a
skilled workman has formed the metal image.

The second half of the line stands in chiastic relation to the first.
It begins, therefore, with the subject rather than the object.
Whether the *tzoreph* is a different person from the *harash* is
difficult to tell. Usually *tzoreph* refers to a smelter, and inasmuch as
the material with which he works is mentioned, is generally rendered *gilder* or *goldsmith*. Quite possibly, then, *tzoreph* refers to a
different person, the prophet speaking first of the work of the
harash and then of the *tzoreph*.

Of significance also is the usage of the verbal forms. In the first clause there is a perfect, and this is followed in the second by the imperfect. "After the artisan has completed his work of molding the image," so we may paraphrase, "the gilder then overlays it with gold." With *gold*, the definite article is employed, referring to the well-known amount of gold to be used, as though Isaiah had said, "with the amount of gold that you know." The verb itself means *to beat* or *stamp out*. From the root comes the word used in Genesis 1, the *raqiaʻ*, *expanse*. The work the prophet is describing is the taking of the image, already formed from wood or stone, and overlaying it with gold, spreading that gold on it and beating it out so that the entire image will be gilded.[66]

By means of a participial clause the prophet completes the verse. First he mentions the chains of the idol. It is not clear whether these were for decorative purposes or whether they were to suspend the idol. At any rate, the workman overlays them with silver. The exact force of the last word in the verse is difficult to determine; but inasmuch as it is written in a slightly different manner from the similar word in the second clause, we are probably to take it as a participle.[67] But if it is a participle, it can hardly be an example of anaphora, as suggested by Delitzsch. Furthermore, what then is the subject? Probably it is the similar sounding word *tzoreph* (*the gilder*). It is the second artisan then, the one who gilds the image, that also melts the chains of silver. The construction is not without difficulty, but it is not necessary to emend the text. On the interpretation herein adopted two different artisans are mentioned by the prophet; one casts the metal image, the other both gilds it and melts its chains of silver.

20 The language of this verse is quite difficult. Many have interpreted the first word as *he who is rendered poor* or *who is*

---

[66] Cf. *ANET*, 331b, for the translation of a text found in Thureau-Dangin, *Rituels accadiens*, Paris, 1921, pp. 127-154. Lines 190ff. describe the making of two images for the 6th day of Nisan. First a metalworker is given precious stones and gold to make the images. Then a woodworker is given cedar and tamarisk. Finally, when their usefulness is over on the 6th day, they shall be cast into the fire. Smith suggests that the reference to technique may have been because of special comment aroused by the statue of Sin (cf. *Persian Verse Account*, 1:19-32). As Smith himself says, however, the description may have been influenced by the practice of hollow casting for large figures, initiated by Sennacherib, a contemporary of Isaiah.

[67] *casting* — the word is employed without a subject expressed, and denotes action that is actually in progress.

impoverished. This is questionable. Assuming that the word may be rendered *impoverished,* many commentators wish to construe it with the following word by treating the latter as an accusative of specification: *he who is impoverished with respect to his offering, etc.* On this construction the thought is that the man is himself too impoverished to bring a rich oblation.[68] Alexander suggests the rendering *impoverished by oblations,* which has the merit of preserving for *terumah* its true sense. Alexander brings out the force of this rendering in the following words: ". . . The man who has already reduced himself to want by lavish gifts to his idol, still continues his devotions, and as he can no longer afford an image of the precious metals, is resolved at least to have a durable wooden one." But even if a man has impoverished himself by lavish gifts to his idol, why does he need another idol? Does he not already possess an idol; and if he has impoverished himself by giving oblations to this idol, would he simply not bring lesser gifts in the future?

There is therefore another explanation worthy of consideration. It is to take the word *terumah (oblation)* as second accusative of the verb *he chooses.* Thus, *as an oblation, he chooses wood that will not rot.* It is then for emphasis' sake that the word *terumah* is placed first. On this construction the word does not refer to the idol itself but to the wood used in its construction. We should then conceive of the wood as dedicated or offered for the construction of the idol. Whereas this interpretation would be more in keeping with the general sense of *terumah,* at the same time it is contrary to the Masoretic accentuation, which connects the first two words of the sentence and separates *terumah* from what follows.

Our choice, it would seem, must lie between these two latter interpretations; and despite difficulties, the latter construction is probably to be preferred. On this view the impoverished man is choosing wood for his idol and the choice of this wood amounts to an oblation that he brings. The wood that he chooses, however,

---

[68] It may be that (despite Torrey's severe strictures) Jerome pointed to the correct view of this difficult word, *"AMSUCHAN: quod genus ligni est imputribile, quo vel maxime idola fiunt"* (*PL,* Vol. XXIV, Col. 422) . It is possibly to be connected with Sumerian *giš MIS. MA.KAN.NA.* (i.e. wood of the land of Magan = Kirman) . Smith believes that it is mulberry wood. The passage would then be rendered, *mulberry of the offering does the skillful artificer choose.* Cf. also Joseph Reider, *VT,* Vol. 2, 1952, pp. 117f., and the suggestions of A. R. Millard and I. R. Snook in *Tyndale House Bulletin,* No. 14, June 1964, pp. 12, 13.

must be durable, and not wood that will rot. Many were the durable woods to be found in Palestine; we cannot say what particular kind is intended; the emphasis falls merely upon the fact that it is wood that will not rot.[69] The poor man goes into the forest and makes a choice of wood; he shows care and concern in the preparation of his idol. In all this serious description, as Delitzsch remarks, there is true satire.

Having found the wood, the poor man seeks out an artisan who is skilled in his art and has him prepare the idol. Probably the preposition and suffix *lo* have reference to the idol rather than to the impoverished man, so that the thought is: *he seeks out for it a skilled artisan.* It is the task of this artisan to erect an image in such a way that it will not totter (cf. Isa. 41:7). Actually, the last verb is passive, *will not be moved.* To erect the image in such a manner, the artisan would have to make a secure base, larger than the upper part of the statue. Thus, wind would not blow it over nor would it easily topple if anything struck against it. There were actually those who bowed down to this rather than to the eternal and immutable God. Here the temporal would create the eternal, the weak the strong, the finite the infinite, the changeable the unchangeable. Man seeks to create God — and all in the image of man! Isaiah could not more clearly have placed in the open the utter folly and pointlessness of idolatry.

21 To employ materials such as gold, silver, or wood in the construction of idols is folly, for God has created them. The earth is His and all its fullness. These truths the prophet now brings out by means of four questions arranged in chiastic order. He uses the imperfect in the first two questions and the perfect in the last two, and in translation their force should be preserved, *Do ye not know* or *Will ye not know?*[70] Perhaps the voluntative is to be preferred, for then the question is not a mere exclamation of surprise at the people's ignorance, but also includes the thought that the ignorance will continue. "Instead of representing the Godhead in graven images, which are made by temporal hands of temporal material, why will ye not know that God is the creator of all things?"

---

[69] לא־ירקב — the imp. with the negative practically has the force of an adjective.

[70] תדעו — the imp. may express the present when it is conceived as extending into the future. Here, "are ye ignorant, and is this ignorance to continue?"

Parallel to this first question is the second, *Will ye not hear?* It may be that the prophet has in mind his own declaration of the truth. "The truth about God is proclaimed to you by the living voice of the prophets. Why do ye continue in darkness and deafness, unwilling to hear the actual state of the case?" In the four questions Isaiah puts the subject matter in chiastic order, namely, knowing-hearing—hearing-knowing. The third question is expressed in the perfect, taking up the thought, "Is the reason that ye will not hear that the truth has not been told to you?[71] That God is the Creator is not a hidden truth which has never been declared." Over and over again by the mouth of the prophets the truth of creation has been proclaimed to the nation. Indeed, it has been presented from the very beginning of the world. Throughout the history of the entire race, God's revelation was in the world and was proclaimed to man. And while it is true that His eternal power and Godhead are seen from the creation of the world, nevertheless Isaiah seems to refer to a message that has been spoken to man. It is special revelation, in other words, that is here in view.

The last question, however, does refer in particular to general revelation. Similar to the *knowing* mentioned in the first question is the *understanding* of the fourth, *Have ye not understood?* The Masoretes have inserted a disjunctive accent with the verb and so separate it from what follows. In what sense then is the verb to be construed with the noun that follows it? It is possible to take the word *foundations* as an object, but this does violence to the punctuation. Perhaps the word may simply be construed as an accusative and rendered *with respect to the foundations* or *from the foundations*. The prophet employs a figure to show that the earth has been founded, and hence the word simply denotes the creation of the earth. From the creation of the earth men should understand that God is the Creator. "For the invisible things of him from the creation of the world are clearly seen, being understood by the things that are made, even his eternal power and Godhead, so that they are without excuse" (Rom. 1:20).

According to this verse there are two reasons why men who practice idolatry are without excuse. On the one hand, the very foundation of the earth is a testimony that God is the Creator. On

---

71 The preterites (perfects) imply that the action continues to the present and even suggest futurity.

the other, from the beginning the truth has been taught by word of mouth, so that those who have not been willing to hear it are without excuse.

22 He that sitteth upon the circle of the earth, and its inhabitants are as grasshoppers; who stretcheth out the heavens as a curtain, and spreadeth them out as a tent to dwell in.

23 Who giveth rulers to nothing, the judges of the earth like desolation he has made.

24 Not even planted were they, not even sown, not even rooted in the ground their stock; and also he bloweth upon them, and they withered, and a whirlwind like the chaff will take them up.

22 There now follows a series of three clauses introduced by participles with the definite article, and in each case the article practically has the force of a demonstrative pronoun.[72] Thus, the King James Version is correct in rendering, *It is he that sitteth, etc.*, for this brings out the strength of the original. The phrase is in apposition to a subject which is not expressed but which seems to be implied. What is stated in this and the following verses is what the people must have known. "What they have heard and what they have seen in the creation should have taught them that it is God who sitteth, etc."

The phrase *sitting upon the circle of the earth* is a figurative expression for God's providential upholding and maintaining of creation. One would not be impressed with the knowledge that God is the Creator, unless God continually upheld His creation. At the same time, the participle refers to God's being seated upon a throne. Seated as a king, He constantly upholds His creation, and governs it. Isaiah mentions the circle of the earth as the place where God sits. Job 22:14 speaks of the circle of heaven, but this is the only passage of Scripture in which the circle of the earth is mentioned.[73] Probably the phrase has reference to the horizon. Inasmuch as the expression in Job seems to point to the highest

[72] *he who sitteth* — i.e. *it is he who*; the part. with the article stands in apposition to an unexpressed subject which is implicit in the thought of the prophet.

[73] Cf., however, Prov. 8:27, which speaks of "a circle upon the face of the deep." It does not seem warrantable to conclude that Scripture here teaches that the earth is round. Cf. *ANET*, p. 102, for a reference to heaven's zenith in the Adapa legend.

part of the heavens, so here we may understand it of the highest part of the horizon or the zenith. God then sits over the highest part of the earth, the zenith, as enthroned to watch over His creation.

To God seated upon His high throne, men appear as grasshoppers (cf. Num. 13:33). In their actions and activities men are as weak and powerless as the grasshoppers, which, multitudinous as they are, cannot hold the world in its course; and if grasshoppers cannot do it, how much less anything that is made by grasshoppers? The forceful comparison shows the folly of idolatry.

In the second line there is another statement introduced by a participle with the definite article, which shows not only that God controls the earth but also that He has created and controls the heavens. It is God who has spread out (the participle is practically equivalent to a past) the heavens like a curtain. The word rendered *curtain* (*doq*) is a *hapax legomenon*, and seems to denote something very thin. Isaiah's purpose is to show the ease with which God spread out the heavens. For Him it was no greater a task than to spread out a very light and thin veil.

The last clause, *and he spread them out like a tent for dwelling*, introduces a figure taken from nomadic life.[74] The heavens are to extend over the earth so that they will cover it like a tent. It seems best to follow the Masoretic accentuation and construe *for dwelling* with *heavens*. God has spread out the heavens to dwell in like a tent.

23 The language is a strong denial of deism. God has created the world but He has not abandoned it. All the created universe is in His hands and under His control. This applies not alone to the inanimate creation but to man as well. Moreover, it applies to the nations, and even to their rulers. With the present verse, therefore, the prophet attains a climax in his description of the power of God, and this he does by again introducing the thought with a participle and the definite article.[75] No one can resist the power of God, not even the human authorities who exercise lordship over man. God alone gives princes over to nothingness, so that they, as

---

[74] The parts. have characterized God by His actions, *sitting* and *spreading*, and the characterization is continued by means of *waw* consecutive with the imperfect.

[75] Note that the part. is continued by a finite verb in the perf.; cf. 30:2.

it were, partake of the nature of nothingness. The same thought is expressed by a writer of the exile (cf. Dan. 2:21). To give princes to nothingness is to remove them from their positions of power so that they have no power whatever.

As with the first half of verse 22, so in this verse also there is a chiastic arrangement. Isaiah speaks of the judges of the earth, and declares that God has made them into nothingness. It is a succinct statement of what is presented in Job 12:17-21. The verb is in the past, yet serves here to describe a general action without respect to time. It may, therefore, in parallel with the first half of the verse, be rendered in English by the present.

Reference is made in this verse to the *roz^{e}nim*, which word signifies the rulers and potentates of the earth, the men of great power and authority, and to the *shoph^{e}ṭim*, *judges*, who have the power both to rule and to pronounce judgment. God brings these latter into a state of *tohu*, i.e. *desolation*, a word used in Genesis 1:2. This was a condition of the earth that rendered it uninhabitable. As long as the earth was a *tohu* it was not fulfilling the purpose for which it was created. When the judges were rendered a *tohu*, they too were placed in such a condition that they could no longer function as judges.

24 Isaiah now carries out the thought of the preceding verse by showing the suddenness of God's action with respect to the rulers and judges. Even before the princes and judges have been established in their positions God acts and they are removed. Introducing the first three clauses is the word *'aph*, which by itself may be translated *surely*.[76] In each case, however, it is followed by a negative *bal*. Thus, the first clause is to be rendered, *surely, not have they been planted*, i.e. they have scarcely been planted. Isaiah compares the princes and judges to a tree. A tree or sapling that has just been planted does not yet have its roots firmly in the earth, and so it is with the rulers of nations. They are scarcely in the place of power and authority when God removes them.

Using a figure that would apply only to seed sown, the prophet declares that the rulers have not even been sown. Nor even if the tree itself has been felled and only the stump remains does this

---

[76] אַף בֹּל — lit., *surely, not are they planted*, etc.; Hahn, König, *neither, nor*, which is also possible; Targ. *though*; Kimchi, Luther, Calvin, *as if*.

stump possess a root from which new life might come.[77] In the first two statements the passive is employed as though to imply that even the rulers do not ascend the throne in their own power. The tree must be planted, and the seed sown, and so also the rulers must be placed in their positions of authority and power. Perhaps by the usage of the passives the prophet has in mind that the one who is really active in permitting rulers to occupy seats of authority is God Himself.

It is difficult to bring out in English the force of Isaiah's second line. We may render literally, *and even*, the thought being that these rulers were scarcely in power when God breathed upon them. A mere breathing on God's part, in other words, was sufficient to remove them from the scene. No strenuous exertion is required. Isaiah uses a perfect which may be translated by the present, for it is applicable to God's action whenever He performs it. An imperfect follows and sets forth the result of God's action, namely, *that they dry up*. Again, the figure from vegetable life is carried out, for as the light breath causes the plants to wither, so when God acts the princes and rulers are no more.

Perhaps by the *whirlwind* the prophet has in mind the breath of the Lord mentioned in verse 7. Inasmuch as the word stands first in its clause, it probably receives a certain amount of emphasis. It is of little moment whether the verb be rendered in English by the present or the future, for in either case it expresses the consequences of God's blowing. The Psalmist used the figure of the chaff to describe the transitory character of the wicked (cf. Ps. 1:4). When the grain is winnowed, the true seed falls to the ground; but the chaff, being lighter, is easily carried away by the wind. A wind that the Lord sends, therefore, perhaps a stronger wind than a mere breeze, will simply carry the chaff away so that it disappears. Rulers are one moment upon the throne; the next they are gone.

25 And unto whom will ye liken me and (to whom) shall I be equal? saith the Holy One.
26 Lift up on high your eyes, and see; who hath created these? He who causes to come forth by number their host; he calls all of them by name, from abundance of might and because strong in power, not one is found wanting.

---

[77] שֹׁרֵשׁ. — *rooted* (*Poel*), lit., *not has taken root*; the *Holem* with the first radical is not common in the intensive (factitive-causative) stem apart from *Ayin-waw* verbs.

25 In bringing his argument to a conclusion the prophet reverts to the thought of verse 18. Indeed, the first clause is identical with 18a, save that here God Himself is the speaker. The introductory words *And unto whom* govern two verbs, although some take the second verb as expressing result, *that I should be like*. While this is grammatically possible, the first construction is simpler and for that reason adopted here. To be noted is the introductory conjunction, which serves to sum up the thought. By means of the questions the conclusion is drawn: "Ye can liken me to nothing, and I am equal to nothing," i.e. "there is nothing that is equal to me."

As customary, Isaiah employs the pausal form.[78] In referring to God as *Holy One*, he omits the definite article in accordance with the exalted style in which he is writing. Here the aspect of holiness that sees Him as separate from the creature is prominent. God is holy, for He is to be distinguished from His creatures. Only God can ask these questions, for only God is holy. The creature is finite, temporal, and, because of sin, mortal; God is infinite, eternal, and unchangeable.

26 Isaiah elsewhere also employs the concept of lifting up the eyes. It had been used figuratively in 37:23 of Sennacherib in order to portray his presumption. Here, however, it is intended in a physical sense, as also in 49:18; 51:6; 60:4. The eyes are not merely to be raised, but lifted up on high, i.e. to the very height of heaven, in order to see the wondrous works of God, the host of heaven (24:21). As Calvin has so beautifully pointed out, man is formed by God to contemplate the heavens, "for while God formed other animals to look downwards for pasture, he made man alone erect, and bade him look at what may be regarded as his own habitation."

Whenever man in seriousness contemplates the heavens he is met with God's handiwork, for the marvelous bodies of heaven point him to the Creator. That man does not see God as Creator is due to his own blindness. Isaiah's command (for it is the prophet who speaks in this verse) is particularly applicable to the Jews, who were in danger of falling into idolatrous worship of the stars (cf. Amos 5:26; Jer. 7:18; 8:2; 44:17). Against this danger of worship-

---

[78] As in many languages, so in Heb., a verb of saying is inserted into direct speech.

ping the heavenly bodies Moses had given warning long before (cf. Deut. 4:19) .[79]

The heavenly bodies are not gods but creatures, brought into existence by God Himself. Isaiah uses the same word for *created* that had been used in the first verse of Genesis. In the Genesis account the heavenly bodies, the sun, moon, and stars, were made on the fourth day. From this it does not necessarily follow that on that day they were created out of nothing. Actually the creation of the heavens is mentioned in Genesis 1:1, where the word *bara'* is employed. The material of the heavenly bodies was brought into existence at the very beginning. Genesis, however, does not relate the course of these bodies until it declares that on the fourth day God made the sun, etc. From this we may assume that on the fourth day He formed the material, created at the beginning, into the heavenly bodies.[80] What Isaiah is concerned to stress is the fact that these bodies are true creations; they do not exist in their own right, and they are not deserving of worship.

The interrogative pronoun *who* is not the object of the verbs. Isaiah is not commanding, *see who hath created these?* Rather, his words may be better construed, *lift up your eyes on high and see—Who hath created these?* The question then is distinct and independent. It is a direct, not an indirect question. When one looks at the heavens the question of their origin should come into mind. Indeed, one cannot adequately describe the created phenomena of heaven and earth unless first he has answered this question.

The words *who bringeth out, etc.* do not form an answer to the question just asked. Isaiah's thought is not, "He who bringeth them out is the one who rules the heavenly bodies and is their creator." Rather, with these words, *who bringeth out*, we have a new beginning. Isaiah uses the participle with the definite article: *It is he that bringeth out, etc.* Note the similar usage in verses 22, 23a. The prophet is referring to Yahweh, the God of His people, who was constantly in his own thoughts.

God brings out the host *by number*, i.e. counting them one by

---

[79] It is true that Babylonia was the home of star worship, but the danger of such idolatry was present also in Palestine. Gesenius points out that Christian apologetes have employed arguments similar to Isaiah's (e.g. Minucius Felix; Arnobius *Against the Gentiles*) .

[80] Cf. Young, *Studies in Genesis One*, Philadelphia, 1964, pp. 93-97.

one.[81] Isaiah employs a term that has military connotations, for the words *to bring them out* are used in 2 Samuel 5:2 and Isaiah 43:17 of military matters. To bring forth the heavenly host, however, is a work that only God can perform (cf. Job 38:32). The sun, moon, and stars are God's host, created by Him and appointed for His service. Among other functions, they serve Him by declaring His glory and showing forth His handiwork.

Not only has God created and appointed His army, but He has also given to each member a name. Inasmuch as the name indicates the essential nature of a being or object, the thought is that God has assigned to each member of His army its particular nature, characteristics, and function. For the sake of emphasis the words *all of them* appear first. Although to man the stars appear innumerable (cf. Gen. 15:5), yet God knows not merely the number but also the name of each one. The phrase *by name* is to be construed with the verb.

The purpose of the last line is to explain why none of the stars is missing. In what manner, however, are the words to be construed? Some would connect the first words of the line with the verb of the preceding line and render, "He calls them all by name by reason of the abundance of His might and the strength of His power." If this construction is adopted, the final words, *not one is missing*, seem merely to form an appendage. Furthermore, the accentuation is against this construction. If the last line is a unit in itself the question arises, What strength is referred to? Is it the strength of the stars or of God? Do the stars not fail because they themselves are strong, or do they not fail because the power of God upholds them? In keeping with the context we should prefer the latter construction. The word *from* has the force *by reason of* or *on account of*. Not merely is there strength in God, but there is an abundance of strength, more than is needed to call the stars by name. The word *strength* is plural to express intensity. Before the word *'ammitz* (*a strong one*) the preposition is to be understood, so that the force is, *because as a strong one with respect to*

---

81 במספר — others interpret, *in the entire number of them*, or *in great numbers*. The interpretation adopted in the exposition is favored both by the military form of the description and also by the parallel *by name*. The Commander calls out His army by number and by name. Cf. *ANET*, p. 429. The emphasis upon the stars is not necessarily a conscious opposition to the astral worship of Babylonia but is to exalt the wonder of the mighty God as Creator.

power[82] (cf. Job 9:4). He who has brought out the host is able to preserve it in its entirety. Not one of all His innumerable host will fail or cease, for His mighty power can both call it forth and keep it in its appointed place.

27 Why sayest thou, O Jacob, and speakest, O Israel, My way is hid from the LORD, and from my God my judgment will pass over.

28 Hast thou not known, or hast thou not heard, the everlasting God, the LORD, Creator of the ends of the earth, he does not faint, nor does he become weary; there is no searching with respect to his understanding.

29 Giving to the weary strength, and to the one without power he increaseth might.

30 And the youths shall be weary and faint, and the young men shall surely stumble.

31 And those who wait upon the LORD will renew strength, they shall mount up with wings like eagles; they shall run and not be weary, they shall walk and not be faint.

27 Inasmuch as God is not only the Creator but also the Preserver of all things, even the heavenly bodies, nations, and individual men, how can the people of God complain that He has forsaken them? No information is given as to the precise circumstances under which this complaint is uttered, and there is no warrant for the widespread view that it represents a complaint of the exiles in Babylon. It is a universal complaint, raised in times of difficulty and adversity. This is supported by the force of the verbs, which should be rendered by the future, *Why wilt thou say?*[83] Isaiah's implication is that the people had already said this, that they are saying it now and will go on saying it. It was a continual complaint; and the question is designed by way of rebuke, as though to say, "Why dost thou so complain when there is no ground for complaint?" (cf. Ps. 2:1).

Isaiah addresses the people as *Jacob* and *Israel*, for his purpose is to call attention to the nation's ancestor. Conceivably there is also present an allusion to the fact that throughout his lifetime Jacob was out of his homeland, and in a distant country. Hence, it is a

---

82 1Q reads *w'mpz kwhw*, i.e. *and (from) the strength of his power.*

83 *wilt thou say* — note that the 2nd imp. is introduced by weak *waw*, which serves to give emphatic combination to substantially equivalent expressions. The imp. is employed because the matter of which the complainer speaks appears to him to continue indefinitely onward.

suitable word to apply to those who themselves must suffer bondage. One cannot deny that in these chapters there does appear to a
certain extent a Babylonian background, yet this does not mean
that the people are actually in bondage at the time of the prophet's writing. It does mean, however, that he looks forward to the
time when they will be in bondage, and he uses this bondage as a
symbol of the greater, spiritual bondage in which they are engulfed. The designation "Jacob" can hardly be said to characterize
Isaiah 40–55, for the word occurs about thirteen times in chapters
1–39 and twenty-six times in chapters 40–66. By this combination of
the two names of the patriarch his offspring are described. Possibly
Jacob calls attention to the nation as resisting and recalcitrant,
whereas *Israel* brings to mind the thought of prevailing with God,
and hence shows that the nation is an Israel to whom the promises
of God will be fulfilled.

In the second line of the verse the content of the complaint
appears. Israel's *way* is simply her course of life, and there may in
this context be a particular emphasis upon the difficulties that are
found in that way. "The difficult way that I must travel," so we
may paraphrase the thought, "is hidden from my God." Israel
acknowledges that Yahweh is her God, but the pathos is that even
the One whom she will designate "my God" is supposedly ignorant
of what she is suffering. Israel does not believe that the God who
chose her in covenant is omniscient. Parallel to the first member of
the complaint is the second, which is also stated in chiastic manner. In a position of emphasis Isaiah places the words *and from my
God,* for Yahweh, the God of the covenant, is the personal God of
the Israelites. In that personal pronoun there is a certain sadness;
He who is *my* God should not neglect *my* cause.

By the words *my judgment,* Isaiah, as in 1:23, has reference to a
legal case, and in particular to the pronouncing of judgment. The
idea that is implied is that one's cause will be declared to be
righteous or right. It is as though Israel were to say, "I have a
right, and that right is that I be vindicated before all accusers. The
judgment, however, in which I should be vindicated, is one that
my God does not notice." The prophet pictures the judgment as
itself active and passing over or away from God, as though God
does not regard it. It goes without saying that the complaint is
unjustifiable, for it represents a state of mind in which despondency of heart is uppermost and there is an unbelief both in God's
goodness and in His ability to fulfill His promises.

28 By means of a double question Isaiah sets forth the folly of such despondent thoughts. We may translate the first verb by the present and the second by the past, *Dost thou not know and hast thou not heard?* although both verbs may equally well be rendered into English by the past. The questions are designed to call Israel's attention to the folly of her despondent attitude. The Israelites should know, as the result of long experience, and they should have heard, for it had been declared to them over and over again by the prophets what they now deny.

In the following words the prophet sets forth the content of what the Israelites should have known and heard. This is not done by means of indirect discourse; Isaiah does not ask, "Have ye not heard that the Lord, etc.?" Rather, the questions are left without containing answers in themselves. An answer is indeed given, but it consists of separate and independent statements which are more forceful than indirect discourse. The first of these may be rendered, *the God of eternity is Yahweh* (cf. Gen. 21:33). Isaiah uses a common Hebrew idiom which in English is best expressed by means of an adjective, *the eternal God*. To Him there is no beginning or ending, for He is in no sense circumscribed by time. And, as He is eternal in all His attributes, so He eternally watches over His people.

By way of proving or exhibiting the fact that He is eternal, the prophet states that He is the *Creator of the ends of the earth*, i.e. the limits or bounds of the creation. The thought might also be expressed by saying that God is the Creator of the entirety of the earth. Thus, He is eternal and not limited by time, and He is the Creator of all things and not limited by space.

If Israel's way is hid from her God it is not because He is weary. In doing good and in blessing man He does not become weary like a man who grows faint through lack of nourishment or weary through lack of rest. God's ways are right; but men may not understand them, for they are incomprehensible. The understanding or insight that characterizes God's ways and is the basis of His acting is such that man cannot fathom or comprehend it. By means of the negative statement, *there is no searching to his understanding,* Isaiah has reference to men. God of course can fathom His own understanding; He is not incomprehensible to Himself; to man, however, He is incomprehensible. Man cannot search out His understanding. The prophet uses a noun that means *searching out, investigating,* and refers to a searching through or exploring of God's understanding.

This is not to deny that God may be known. If God were unknowable, then Isaiah's appeal would be meaningless. The whole condemnation and criticism of the people in which the prophet is engaging is based upon the assumption that God and His ways may be known. Indeed, if the people knew God and His ways, they would not doubt Him. If God were unknowable, Isaiah's denunciation would be without point. The entire context is a strong argument against such an interpretation.

The language can only be understood as referring to the incomprehensibility of God. The people, while they might to a certain extent understand the ways of God, could never fully understand them. In bringing His promises of salvation and deliverance to fulfillment God exhibited a wisdom the Israelites could never wholly grasp. When God's redeemed people behold His understanding, they may to a degree understand that wondrous insight of God, but they cannot comprehend it. The understanding of man is the understanding of a creature; it is therefore circumscribed and finite; the understanding of God is that of the Creator, and is therefore infinite. The finite mind cannot comprehend the infinite. Whereas, therefore, the finite mind can know God and can apprehend Him as He has revealed Himself, nevertheless it cannot comprehend Him. In His understanding there is a depth and length and breadth that man's mind cannot grasp. God in all His attributes is incomprehensible. The insight that is to bring salvation to Israel is not that of a mere man; it is God's insight. Though he should live forever, man, inasmuch as he is but a creature, will never comprehend it (cf. Rom. 11:33-36).

29 Far from being weary Himself, God is the One who gives strength to those who are weary. The subject of the participle is *the Lord.* Those who may be exhausted through their sufferings are the weary ones, and they receive strength from the God of Israel. The reference need not be restricted to those who believed that God had passed them by, but may well apply to weary people generally. The only source of true strength, in other words, is the eternal God. In a chiastic manner the prophet completes the verse. To those who have no *power* God *increaseth might.* The thought is the same as that expressed in the first half of the verse. The second verb is stronger, for whereas the participle may be rendered *giving*,[84] the imperfect suggests multiplying or giving abundantly.

30 The prophet now sets forth the counterpart of what he had stated in verse 28. God does not become weary, but men do. Furthermore, not merely do men become tired out but even the strongest and most choice become weary. The imperfect may be rendered, *and even the youths may be weary, etc.* The youths are the choicest, those most fit for athletic contests or for military service. Despite their strength and training, they nevertheless become weary. Their strength is not available at all times, and hence, due to exhaustion, they stumble.[85] Isaiah gives to the verb a particular emphasis, for he uses it with the infinitive absolute, *they do indeed stumble.* Youths of robust strength are often cut off even in early life. It may be that, as Calvin suggests, this is due to overexertion. Whatever be the cause, however, it is a fact of experience, which brings before the eyes the transitoriness of human life.

31 On the other hand, what may happen to strong young men does not happen to those who wait on the Lord. The contrast is between the *youths* and *the waiters upon the Lord,* those who fully believe in God's power to deliver, and manifest their confidence in Him by patiently waiting for Him to bring His promise to fulfillment. During the Old Testament dispensation this designation would apply to those who longed for the fulfillment of the promises and in patience waited for them (cf. Luke 2:25, 38). Nevertheless, what the prophet sets forth is also a general truth, applying to the strength that comes to those who at any time wait in patience for God's purposes to be carried out.

The verb used to describe those who wait on the Lord may be rendered *they shall change* or *exchange.* In this context the thought is of changing the strength one has for a better strength, hence the common rendering, *they shall renew strength*, is satisfac-

---

[84] The part. seems to stand in apposition to the general thought about God mentioned in the preceding verse. Note that the negative and imp. continue the idea of present action set forth by the participle.

[85] The coordination of the two imps. in a frequentative sense with weak *waw* is somewhat uncommon; cf. v. 27; 44:16ff. and 59:7. As the verbs are written, the Ḥireq under the preformative must be naturally long, but defectively written.

tory. Implied is a condition of weakness or lack of strength. What strength is possessed by those who wait upon the Lord will be exchanged for strength that is real indeed. Instead of stumbling they will grow stronger and stronger.

Various interpretations are given of the second clause, but that which is most natural and most free from difficulty is, *they shall lift up (the) wing like eagles*. Not to be overlooked is the definite article with *eagles*, the force of which is, "as eagles are wont to do," or "as is well known with eagles." Scripture itself gives examples of the sense in which the words are intended; see Proverbs 23:5b; 30:19; Job 39:27. With apparently no effort the eagle mounts high into the sky; so the people of God will mount up from the depths of their griefs and difficulties. They will not stumble, falling to the earth because they have no strength, but rather, with the ease of the eagle, they will soar on high.

Two further figures complete the description. Those who wait upon the Lord will not only fly, they will also run and they will walk. Thus, the entirety of their life will be one in which they will prevail and go on from strength to strength. We may notice that for the third time Isaiah now brings together the two verbs, *yiga‘* and *ya‘aph* (*be weary* and *faint*).[86] In verse 28 he had employed them of God, in verse 30 of the youths, and in the present verse of those who wait upon the Lord. One figure is apparently derived from the runners in a race and the other from the daily walk of a man. Running does not bring tiredness, nor do they become faint when they walk on and on.

---

[86] With respect to v. 30, the verbs are arranged chiastically.

1 Keep silence before me, O islands, and the people, let them regain strength; let them draw near, then let them speak together, to judgment let us draw near.

2 Who hath aroused from the east, righteousness calls him to its feet; he gives before him the nations, and causeth him to subdue kings, he giveth his sword as the dust, his bow as the driven stubble.

3 He will pursue them, he will pass in peace; he will not go on a path with his feet.

4 Who hath wrought and done it, calling the generations from the beginning? I the Lord, the first and with the last, I am He.

5 The islands have seen and they feared, the ends of the earth tremble; they have approached and come.

6 Each his neighbor they help, and to his brother one says, Be strong!

7 And the carver has strengthened the goldsmith, the smoother with the hammer, the smiter on the anvil; he says of the solder, It is good; and he has strengthened it with nails; it will not be moved.

1 The chapter begins with an address on God's part to the heathen nations, and in particular to the inhabitants of the coastlands and islands of the Mediterranean. The Lord has already spoken directly to Israel, pointing out the impotence of the idols, and now He turns to the worshippers of those idols. The verse begins with an imperative followed by the preposition *unto* — *Turn in silence unto* or *Direct your silence unto*. The opposite thought of turning in silence from a person is found in Job 13:13.

Penna comments that here we have a literary genre frequently found in the second part of Isaiah. He would call it a "debate at trial" in which two people or classes of people are engaged in a contest before judges who must pronounce their sentence.[1] But it is questionable whether such a description accurately fits the text. God does not appear as a party before a judge, waiting to hear a verdict pronounced. Rather, He addresses the isles with the voice of absolute authority; He commands them to turn unto Him in silence. They are to listen to Him and not to the verdict of some "third party." Before His words there can be no answer. For that reason, they are not merely to be silent but are actually to direct their silence unto Him.[2]

The *islands* stand for the coasts of the eastern Mediterranean and its islands. The definite article is missing, for the language is poetical. In 40:15 the prophet had already made clear how insignificant the isles were; when these isles must hear God and His judgment, it will again be manifest that before Him they are as nothing.

Continuing his address, the prophet speaks to nations generally, employing an imperfect form of the verb which continues the force of the first imperative. The second member of the line is thus parallel to the first, and the entire line is constructed chiastically. For this reason it is better to take the introductory *and* of the second member as correlative to the first rather than as introducing the result.[3] Thus, instead of rendering *and the nations will exchange strength*, which is grammatically possible, it is better to render the second clause, *and the nations, let them exchange strength*. Isaiah takes over the expression from 40:31 and uses it in

[1] So also North, but note the similarity in form of expression with 1:2. North does call attention to the absence of mention of judges, and suggests that there can hardly be judges where Yahweh is concerned. Begrich classifies 41:1-5 as a *Gerichtsrede* (*SZD*, pp. 26ff.) . According to a number of modern scholars this verse is an example of a covenant lawsuit, in which the divine judge summons the accused to give an account of his actions. Cf. H. B. Huffmon, "The Covenant Lawsuit and the Prophets," *JBL*, Vol. 78, 1958, pp. 285-295; J. Harvey, "Le '*rîb*-Pattern', requisitoire prophétique sur la rupture de l'alliance," *Biblica*, Vol. 43, 1962, pp. 172-196; G. E. Wright, "The Lawsuit of God: A Form-Critical Study of Deuteronomy 32," *Muilenburg Festschrift*, 1962, pp. 26-27; Dennis J. McCarthy, "Covenant in the Old Testament," *CBQ*, Vol. 37, No. 3, 1965, pp. 231ff.

[2] B ἐγκαινίζεσθε rests upon a substitution of ד for ר. It has no object, and is not to be preferred to M, which is supported by Aq S Vulg. and 1Q.

[3] Hahn, however, maintains that 1b is not a continuation of 1a, but rather sets forth the result of the action of the first verb. This result is said to be a renewing of strength from the fullness of Yahweh's strength.

the same sense in which it was earlier employed.[4] The nations, i.e. all the heathen peoples, are to renew their strength that they may stand in contest with Yahweh, the God of Israel. In these words there is a vigorous challenge, such as can be uttered only by One whose cause is right. "Let the nations renew their strength to plead their cause before Me, it will be of no avail."

Hahn takes the words *they shall draw near* as an example of what is intended in Psalm 2, "they take counsel together." On this interpretation the verb is an indicative, describing the action of the nations in drawing near to one another in order to prepare for speaking their case against the Lord. Whereas from the grammatical point of view this construction is possible, it seems more in keeping with the context to take the verb as a jussive and to render *let them draw near.* It is the Lord who speaks, and the summons is for the nations to draw near to Him to present their case. The sovereignty of God is thus beautifully exemplified. It is He who speaks and commands; His is the voice of authority and He demands that the nations approach Him. He does not go to them, for it is not a contest of equals; they must come to Him, and then they may speak forth their case. They are to speak together, presenting a united voice in their own defense.

The purpose of commanding the nations is that there may be a judgment. Isaiah uses the word in the sense of a pronouncement of sentence by a judge. It is the idea of a court in which a sentence is to be passed. Delitzsch, following Rosenmüller, thinks that the sentence is to be passed by reason, which is the "deciding authority."[5] Such a concept, however, is unscriptural. It is God and He alone who is the Judge, and the sentence to be pronounced is one that He alone utters. Nowhere in the Bible is there warrant for the view that reason is an arbiter between God and man.

2 The Lord now presents His cause, introducing it with a question that calls attention to the activity of Yahweh alone. "Who

[4] "They that wait upon the Lord will renew their strength, let those nations that refuse to wait upon Him renew their strength as best they can." The steps of such renewing are then set forth. Feldmann argues that the elderly renew strength only when they are worn out (*erlahmt*), and there is no mention here of being worn out (*Erlahmung*). In the light of the interpretation herein offered, it is not necessary to assume that the nations are worn out (Dillmann).

[5] "The deciding authority is reason, which cannot fail to recognize the facts, and the consequences to be deduced from them" (Delitzsch). But who is to judge what is and what is not in accord with reason?

other than I? It is I the Lord alone, and no other, who awakes, etc." The verb is in the perfect, and yet refers to something that has not yet taken place. This is clear from the closing words of verse 1, where the nations are summoned to come and hear a judgment that has not yet been pronounced. It is the present verse that gives the content of the judgment. The expression "to awaken," used here and in 13:17, signifies to arouse to action, to bring upon the scene of history. Isaiah completes the first clause with the words *from the east*, designating the place from which the one aroused originates. In verse 25 the direction is given as "north," perhaps to indicate the direction from which one would approach Palestine, and also as "the rising of the sun." Note also 46:11.

The prophet does not answer his question but breaks off the interrogation and describes what will come to pass. Different constructions of the following words have been proposed, but possibly the one most free from difficulty is to render, *(whom) righteousness calls to its foot*. On this construction the suffix of the verb refers to the one whom the Lord awakens. "Who is it that the Lord awakes?" we may paraphrase, "It is the one whom righteousness calls to its foot."

Righteousness, however, is impersonal. In what sense may it be said to call someone to its foot? In answering this question we must seek to ascertain what connotation the word *righteousness* here bears. It would seem to have reference to the purposes of God in raising up one from the east. This one is to do the things that are mentioned in the remainder of the verse, and to do them at the behest of righteousness. The word is not then to be restricted to the sense of a condition of righteousness, but rather includes all God's providential dealings in the carrying out of His righteous purposes. If the righteous purposes of salvation are to be accomplished, they must be carried out by one whom God raises up, and the carrying out of these purposes is the work of righteousness. It is, says Alexander, "the righteousness of God as manifested in his providence, his dealings with his people and their enemies."

Righteousness, which is here personified, summons to come to its service. To come to one's foot simply means to engage in one's service. The one whom God raises up from the east is summoned by righteousness to do the service of righteousness.

It is difficult to determine what the subject of the following verbs is. It may be that righteousness is still personified, and if so it may be taken as the subject. On this construction righteousness is set forth as accomplishing all that is here described. On the other hand, it may be that the prophet simply reverts to the question with which he began the verse and makes further asseverations concerning the Lord Himself. If this is the case, the first line is to be taken as a unit complete in itself, describing one whom God arouses and whom righteousness calls to its service. The prophet then reverts to his subject and depicts what God does with respect to this one.

God therefore is the One who sets before him the nations. Actually the clause is to be understood as a relative sentence; *it is God who.* The word *nations* is anarthrous, for the reference is not to any particular nation but is for the purpose of showing the significance of the one raised up. In his journey from the east this one whom God raises up will face the nations God places before him. More than that, God will cause him to exercise the rule over kings, for he himself is to be a conquering king.[6] The language brings to the fore the essential thought that this one in the entire scope of his conquests is in the hand of God, and that it is Yahweh, the covenant God, who directs his course of march.

The last line consists of two clauses, and the principal exegetical question centers about the identity of the subject of the verb. At first glance it might seem that the same subject is to be continued throughout, namely Yahweh. If this construction be adopted, it is necessary to translate, *He* (Yahweh) *will give his* (the conqueror's) *sword as dust,* a rendering that conflicts with all that has been presented of the victorious career of the conqueror. Alexander seeks to take the word *his sword* as an adverbial accusative, *it shall give (them) as dust to his sword.* Thus by means of the sword the enemy are made like the dust. Nevertheless, this construction is attended with great difficulty. First, it is necessary to understand the object *them,* which is not expressed in the Hebrew. Second, whereas the words *his sword* may be taken in an adverbial sense, this does not appear to be a natural reading. Third, the change of subject is striking: *God* gives the enemy ... with *his* (the conqueror's) sword. Grammatically this is possible but not natural. It is better to take *his sword* as the subject. This involves a change of

---

6 ירד — *he causes to subdue.* In the *Hiphil* the apocopated form of the *Lamed-He* verb often omits the helping vowel, and assumes its original *Qaṭl* form. It may, however, take a helping vowel, e.g. *yeḡel.* Both are really segolate forms. 1Q reads *ywryd—he causes to bring down.*

subject from the preceding clause, but it yields a free and natural sense. It is the sword of the conqueror that gives men over to the dust. Likewise, in the second clause *his bow* also serves as subject. The bow of the conqueror renders men like the chaff that is driven. It is not even necessary to supply *them* as an object of the verb. The very conciseness of expression lends to the language great vividness: *his sword appoints to dust, his bow to driven stubble.*

There remains the question who it is that God raises up from the east. Of whom is the prophet speaking? To this question various answers have been given. It has been suggested that the reference is to Christ, to the Apostle Paul, or to Abraham. For reasons that we have set forth in the Special Note, we believe that the prophet is alluding to Cyrus the Persian. At this point he does not mention Cyrus by name, but merely introduces him gradually and in a somewhat mysterious manner. Soon, however, he will speak more clearly concerning the deliverer of Israel, mentioning him by name and stating what his great work is to be. From the east righteousness will summon that one whom God is to bring against nations in victory.

3 This present verse is speaking of Cyrus and his advances, and hence the subject of the verbs is Cyrus, and not the Lord nor righteousness. The first verb declares the truth that the one whom God awakens will pursue his enemies. These enemies are not named, but are designated by the verbal suffix, which is an object and may be rendered *them*. Before the onrush of Cyrus the enemies will flee, and he will pursue after them, for to him victory is assured. God has roused him up, and he is serving as God's servant to accomplish His will.

Although Cyrus will pursue others, he himself will not be pursued. Rather he will pass over the land in safety and peace.[7] A statement of the reason for this is given in the final clause of the verse. The purpose of this clause is to show the ease with which the conqueror will come. By means of the phrase *with his feet* Isaiah means to suggest that he will not use the ordinary method

---

7 *in peace* — i.e. *peacefully*; the noun describes the moral state, and is to be construed as a circumstantial accusative. The verb *come*, יבוא, is used almost in the sense of *enter*; cf. Judg. 18:18; 2 Kings 11:19; Ps. 100:4.

of march.[8] He will not employ his normal strength, trodding along a path as conquerors often must do. He will not come plodding along, trudging in a weary manner over a difficult road. By way of illustration appeal is often made to Daniel 8:5, which speaks of a he-goat that "came from the west on the face of the whole earth, and touched not the ground. . . ."

4 Having set forth the ease with which the conqueror will come, the prophet now seeks to exalt God and His power by asking a rhetorical question that will focus attention upon the One who brings the conqueror. The prophet employs two verbs that are practically synonyms. The first verb (*pa'al*) may be rendered in English by *work* or *wrought*, and the second (*'asah*) by *accomplish*.[9] God has not only begun this work, but has also decisively completed it; He is its Author and He its Finisher.

In translating the second clause we shall retain the participle, *calling*. The clause then serves to describe the One who has done the wondrous things of which the prophet speaks. By the word *calling* the prophet either means that God predicts the nations, declaring that they shall come into existence, or else that he calls the nations into existence. As God will arouse from the east one to do His bidding in the carrying out of His righteous purposes, so also He from the beginning calls the nations. When taken in comparison with what is said about God's arousing Cyrus, it would seem that the calling is that of proclaiming or summoning the nations, so that they will come into existence. This God has done *from the head*, i.e. from the beginning (cf. 40:21). No nation exists apart from God.

In the last line of the verse there is a sublime affirmation of the eternity of the God of Israel. "It is," writes Delitzsch, "the full meaning of the name Jehovah which is unfolded here; for God is called Jehovah as the absolute I, the absolutely free Being, pervading all history, and yet above all history, as He who is Lord of His own absolute being, in revealing which He is purely self-determined; in a word, as the unconditionally free and unchange-

---

[8] *with his feet* — this does not imply that the one from the east was mounted (*ILCH*), and we are certainly not warranted in concluding that if Cyrus does not tread the path with his feet the passage is mythical (Gressmann, *Ursprung der israelitisch-jüdischen Eschatologie*, pp. 305-06). Cf. also *Iliad* xx.226-230 and *Aeneid* vii.807ff.

[9] The two perfs. are connected by *waw* conjunctive, as in Isa. 1:2; 9:7; 44:8.

ably eternal personality." That there are statements in the Avesta
and Plato that present a formal resemblance to what is stated here
in no sense detracts from the truthfulness of the prophecy.[10]
When Plato speaks of God as having in his hands the beginning,
end and middle of all beings, his words are formally true, but they
are not a divine revelation. What Isaiah is here affirming is a
special revelation from God; it is an affirmation of what is true,
and for that reason is a message of good news and blessing.

In answer to the questions raised in the first line of the verse,
God replies that He is Yahweh. The personal pronoun appears in
an emphatic position at the beginning of the line. This tremendous word *I,* appearing so frequently in these chapters, seems to
answer the rhetorical questions introduced by "Who?" in chapter
forty. The word Yahweh is in apposition to the pronoun, *I, Yahweh.*
He is the first, i.e. the One who exists before all else. Calvin states
that this does not relate to the eternity of essence but to the government God exercises upon earth. The meaning is not that God is the
first to come into existence or that He is the first one of those beings
that have existed. Such a thought is counter to all that the Bible
teaches. Rather, we must understand the language in reference to
the idols and gods that are being condemned. God is the first in
that He antedates all these; inasmuch as He is the director of
human history, He antedates all history. God, therefore, is the first
in the sense that before all human history began to run its course,
He IS. The language stresses His independence of human history
and movements. He is above history; He is above His creation.

By the word *last* the prophet probably refers to the last generations of men. Men of the last generations cannot escape the
presence of Yahweh, for He is eternal. Generation succeeds generation; before them all God is, and when the last ones come into
existence He is present. Yahweh is He, i.e. the God who throughout all ages is the same as to His being.[11] As Buhl pointed out,

[10] Zarathustra says (*Gatha* 31:8), "I recognized, O Mazda, that thou art the
first and also the last"; Koran 57:3, "He (*huwa*) is the first and the last." Cf.
Plato *Laws* 715e. To maintain that Yahweh is here presented merely as contemporary with all history, and not as eternal, does not do justice to the
language or the context.

[11] Thus, a striking contrast appears in 4b, which begins with *I* and concludes with *He.* Alexander takes the pronoun as answering the question, *Who
has wrought and done it?* Cf. Montgomery, *JBL,* Vol. 63, 1944, pp. 161-63; and
Morgenstern, *JBL,* Vol. 62, 1943, pp. 269-280.

this is a pregnant predicate (cf. 43:10; 48:12). To say that God is HE is to say that He is the eternal One. Herein is found the definition of the word Yahweh — He who appeared to Moses as the eternal One, who changes never, "I am that I am." Thus the prophet gives an answer to the questions that have been asked. It is the eternal God, the One who alone can call forth the generations, who has called Cyrus from the east in order that His purposes of righteousness may be carried out.

5 In this verse the argument is continued and the effects of Cyrus' advance depicted. A play revolving around the words *they have seen* (*ra'u*) and *they have feared* (*yira'u*), which cannot well be brought out in English, introduces the verse. Such word plays are frequent in Isaiah, particularly in the latter half of the book. As a result of having seen what Yahweh has done in arousing one from the east, the isles have fallen into fear. They fear not so much because of the approach of Cyrus as because of the God who placed him upon the stage of history. Here is a God unlike the idols of the heathen, a God who can truly move the course of nations. The first verb is perfect, but is a prediction of what will occur in the future; the second verb is future, and strengthens the idea of futurity expressed by the first. "The isles will see," we may render, "and as a result of having seen, will be in fear."

Indeed, as far as there are lands, stretching to the very ends of the earth, fear will produce trembling among the nations, wherever they are, when they learn of what the Lord has done. With this second expression only a verb in the future is employed, but a verb of seeing may be understood. Two verbs, one perfect and the other future, complete the verse, and describe the approach of the nations to one another to bring mutual encouragement. *They will draw near* and *they will come*, for they will be terrified at the work of the God of Israel. Nations do not come to the God of Israel, who has accomplished such a wonder, but to one another, to seek help at the hand of the idols they themselves have made.

6 The prophet describes the manner in which the ends of the earth approach one another and how they proceed to give mutual encouragement.[12] One nation will help another. The thought is

---

[12] The imps. assert facts of definite occurrence, lit., *each his neighbor they keep helping*, i.e. *each one helps his neighbor*, and *to his brother keeps saying*.

that this will be done individually. Here is no thought of repentance or of turning from the idols. Rather, encouragement is given to abide firm in the condition in which the nations already find themselves.

7 Although the judgment approaches fast, and the nations have seen it, they nevertheless do not turn unto God but remain in their idolatry, depending upon the idols they themselves have constructed. To show the folly of idolatry, the prophet points out that the idols are dependent upon the nation's ordinary workmen and upon the smallest details of construction. Even the nails are necessary to prevent the idol from moving; its strength lies not in itself, but in the nails that hold it together.

The introductory *And* connects the verse with the preceding and introduces an example of the manner in which encouragement is given. The carver who has poured out the image (cf. 40:19) has strengthened or encouraged the goldsmith who refines or smelts the gold. It may seem that the order of the nouns should be reversed, and that the refiner or smelter should encourage the caster of the image. But the prophet's purpose is simply to point out that there is encouragement given among the workmen without necessarily implying that one group of workmen alone encourages the other. A second type of workman is he who *makes smooth with the forge hammer*, probably another designation for the smelter.[13] This designation, however, calls attention to the manner in which the workman carries out his task. He is to beat out the gold with his hammer so that it lies over the idol smoothly. He himself has been encouraged, and so in turn gives encouragement to the man who strikes the anvil.[14] Possibly this was the one who fashioned the chains of silver (cf. 40:19b). Yet the designation may simply imply

---

13 *a forge hammer* — 1Q reads *pltys*; possibly this is an instance where *Lamed* shares the characteristics of *Nun*, being assimilated when it closes an unaccented syllable and represented by *Dagesh forte*.

14 *hólem pā'am* — the one striking the anvil (lit., *foot*). In accordance with *Nasôg Aḥor*, the accent is thrown back to *Milel*. Inasmuch as the ultima is now a closed, unaccented syllable, the short *i* vowel must appear as *Segol*. In Ug. *p'n* (Heb. *p'm*) is used in parallelism to *ḥrz*, possibly to designate a weapon of Baal. Cf. *UH*, text 75, lines 40f. Haldar (*ND*, pp. 36-38) suggests that *p'n* may designate a hammer or club with which Baal smashes the heads of his enemies. On p. 38 he reproduces an illustration from *Syria*, Vol. 14, 1933, showing Baal in such action.

one who acted as a smith generally. Perhaps the word is but a synonym for smelter. With respect to soldering, this latter, having inspected it, declares that it is good, i.e. in satisfactory condition. This is the soldering that fastens the gold to the form of the idol. What a god he must be that needs a common laborer to pass inspection and declare that he is in good condition! Finally, the man who smites the anvil makes the idol firm by means of nails. These he apparently uses to fasten the idol firm into the wall so that it will not fall over.[15] Possibly he drives the nails into a wall and attaches the chains to them. When all is completed, the idol stands firm, ready for use. To such folly were the nations driven when God aroused his servant from the east.

8 And thou, Israel, art my servant; Jacob, it is thee whom I have chosen: the seed of Abraham, my friend.

9 Thou whom I have grasped from the ends of the earth, and from its remote parts have called thee, and said to thee, My servant art thou, I have chosen thee and not rejected thee.

10 Fear not, for I am with thee, be not dismayed, for I am thy God; I have strengthened thee, yea! I have helped thee, surely I have upheld thee with the right hand of my righteousness.

8 God has commanded the nations to hear, but the prophet does not say whether they make any response. The appearance of the one whom the Lord has aroused in the east has sent the nations to their idols. Israel, however, is the Lord's servant and will receive salvation from that very region in which God has aroused Cyrus.

The introductory *And* sets forth Israel in contrast to the nations. They resort to their man-made idols, but Israel will find comfort in her God. Thus the *And* sets forth a significant contrast. Isaiah employs the singular *thou* with emphasis, for God addresses the people as an individual. God now turns to His own servant, the nation that is to be the recipient of His blessings. In 40:27 the prophet had first mentioned Jacob and then Israel; here the order is reversed. Thus, the two names of the patriarch are combined and applied to his descendants.

Israel is *my servant*. This is not a term of disdain, anymore than when Paul calls himself the bondservant of Jesus Christ. A servant

---

15 *it will not be moved* — or, *that it be not moved*. When there is no preceding conjunction the imp. and negative may express purpose, as in Ex. 28:32; Ps. 10:18.

of the Lord is one, whether an individual or a nation, that has been honored by God in being chosen to perform a specific task. Israel as the servant of the Lord had the task of living in the world as a kingdom of priests, a peculiar nation, to show forth the glories of her covenant God, who had called her into the marvelous light of His salvation.

Jacob was chosen to serve.[16] He is the servant of the Lord, but he occupies that position because of God's choice. Not of its own volition did the nation become the Lord's servant, but only through sovereign grace. The choice was on God's part, and in that He chose Israel He did not choose other nations but passed them by. By a calling of grace God chose Israel and set her apart to be His servant. At the same time, although the designation *servant* is one of honor, it nevertheless brings into clear focus the position Israel is to occupy and does occupy with respect to God. As a nation Israel may not guide her own destiny nor plot her own course, for she is a servant and must do the bidding of her master, her covenant God. Having been chosen of God, Israel in her national life must express this condition of servitude by its works.

This is the first occurrence in Isaiah of the term *servant* to designate someone as a servant of the Lord. It is particularly appropriate that the term be introduced at this point, both for the sake of Israel herself and for the remaining world. First Israel must learn the meaning of the term. Up to this point she had acted in haughty disdain of the true meaning of the covenant and the theocracy. Isaiah's earlier messages (e.g. chap. 5) were filled with denunciations of the wickedness and haughtiness of this nation. Israel behaved as though she were the master of her own fate, the arbiter of her own destiny, exhibiting a frame of mind that had come to particularly bald expression in the act of Ahaz in which he rejected the promised Messiah and turned for help to the world empire of man, as represented at the time by Tiglath-pileser III.

Such an attitude of haughtiness, however, was inimical to the best interests of the theocracy, and indeed, if permitted to go on to its logical conclusion would have destroyed the theocracy and obliterated the promises of salvation. A lesson therefore must be

---

[16] *I have chosen thee* — when the relative pronoun is governed by a verb as here, the accusative of the object affected by the verb is expressed by appending the pronominal suffix to the verb. *Jacob, thou art the one whom I have chosen*, lit., *Jacob, whom I have chosen thee*.

learned by Israel. In her there must be inculcated the truth that although the promises had been hers, she was nevertheless but a servant, who must do not her own will but the will of her covenant and electing God. To learn this lesson she must pass through the humiliation of the exile, from which she would be delivered only by God's grace and His appointed instrument Cyrus. She must also learn that from the bondage of sin, which was the root of her misfortunes, she could be delivered only by One who, in a far truer sense than she herself, was a Servant of the Lord, to whom no other could be compared.

We may therefore view the exile as a period in which the wrath and indignation of God were revealed against His chosen people, and also as a time of instruction in which Israel must learn that she is to be a servant, obedient to God. That she may the better learn this lesson, she is told of the unique Servant of the Lord who through substitutionary suffering will bring about for her a redemption from her sin and a reconciliation with her God.

Although the people are named for their ancestor, Jacob-Israel, the promise was made to the patriarch Abraham, whose seed the nation is. In the mention of Abraham there is a note of tender comfort, for the people who are to suffer the wrath of the exile and to learn the lesson therefrom are reminded that they are the seed of one who stood in close relationship to God as a friend. Abraham was a "lover of God," as shown in Genesis 18:17-19; and to Abraham God would manifest the mercy of deliverance (cf. Deut. 4:37; 7:6-8). In speaking of Abraham by the designation *'oh^{a}vi* (lit., *my lover*), God is greatly honoring the patriarch, for this is an even higher designation than that of servant (cf. John 15:14, 15). In 2 Chronicles 20:7 and James 2:23 the same designation is applied to Abraham, as also in Arab tradition.[17] Those who have received the fulfillment of the promises have also been adopted by God and are heirs of the promises. They too are no longer servants but friends.

9 The introductory relative pronoun refers to Jacob-Israel, the

---

[17] Cf. Koran 4:125: "And who is better in respect to religion than he who has submitted himself (lit., his face) to Allah, while he is doing good and he follows the faith (lit., word) of Abraham the Upright, and God took Abraham as a friend (*ḥalīl*)". Actually, the word means *he who loves me*, the suffix being objective. For extrabiblical parallels cf. *ANET*, pp. 143ff., and *CBQ*, Vol. 25, 1963, pp. 77-87.

nation. "Thou art Israel whom I have grasped, etc."[18] The picturesque verb signifies more than "to take," and is better rendered by "grasp" or "seize." God has taken strong hold on Israel with His hand; He has seized Israel so that it cannot escape His grasp. The idea of removing is not actually expressed in the verb, but in the light of the context is implied. Thus, "I have grasped thee from the ends of the earth" means, "I have grasped thee and brought thee from the ends of the earth." It refers to a resolute action on God's part.

It is possible to take the preposition *min* in a partitive sense, and to obtain the thought, "From among all the ends of the earth I have grasped thee only." However, in the light of the parallel expression, *its remote parts,* this interpretation is unlikely. It is far better, because in keeping with the parallelism, to construe the phrase as indicating the distant lands from which God had brought His people. To one living in Palestine, Ur of the Chaldees would seem to be at so great a distance that it might be called the ends of the earth. In itself the phrase *ends of the earth* simply indicates places that are most distant. When applied to the call of Israel in Abraham, the standpoint from which these words are spoken is definitely Palestinian. If at the time Israel was actually in Babylon, would God have designated the call of Abraham as having been from the ends of the earth?

Parallel to the expression *the ends of the earth* is *and from its remote parts.* The basic idea in both expressions is remoteness. Whether they are to be taken only in a purely local sense, however, is questionable. It is possible that the prophet is giving expression to the same idea as that of the apostle, "And you who were sometime afar off have been made nigh" (Eph. 2:13). The first line contains a chiasm which should not be overlooked, *I have grasped thee from the ends of the earth, and from its most remote parts I have called thee.* The first verb suggests the efficacious grace that brought the people to God; the second points to the effectual calling that summoned them to be His people.

In calling Israel God identified her as His servant. This He did when He formed her into a nation at Sinai. As God's servant, Israel was to serve Him and not herself, for He had chosen her and not rejected her. Passing by other nations, which He

---

18 The relative pronoun should not be deleted, but the relative clause is practically resolved into a separate sentence.

rejected, God chose Israel.[19] Looking back to her very beginnings, Israel could say that her existence as a nation flowed from
God's grace. She did not deserve to be chosen, and yet, of all the
nations, God set His affection upon Israel and called her to be
His servant.

10 This verse forms the conclusion of the address to Israel to
which verses 8 and 9 served as an introduction. Inasmuch as Israel
has been chosen of God to be His servant, she is not to fear as
the nations round about her were doing. In not fearing, Israel
would show herself distinct. The nations had seen what God was
doing and consequently feared (41:5). Israel was to be unlike
them; she was not to fear.[20] In the first place Israel was not to fear
when she saw the mighty workings of God in the earth. God had
aroused one in the east who was coming in power so that other
nations trembled; for Israel, however, his coming was not a cause
for fear. The meaning of the passage is far deeper, however. Israel
is not to fear at all; there is no enemy, no sudden change upon the
scene of history, nothing that should cause her to fear, for her
God is with her. She is the seed of Abraham, and to Abraham
God had once spoken, "Fear not, Abram: I am thy shield, and thy
exceeding great reward" (Gen. 15:1). This was the first of the
mighty "fear not's" to be found in redemptive history. To Isaac
also the same prohibition was given, "Fear not"; and in its utterance reference was made to Abraham (Gen. 26:24). And in
Jacob's time of doubt and difficulty, there came the divine word,
"Fear not." The seed of Abraham is to act in faith, nothing
doubting, trusting in the God of the patriarchs, even her own
God, Yahweh.

Parallel to the expression *Fear not* is one that means *do not gaze
about in anxiety*. The verb has reference to those who are fearful
and hence look about in all directions to see whether there is

---

[19] The words *I have not rejected thee* do not apply to some point in Israel's
earthly history. Rather, they form a contrast to *I have chosen thee*. Israel was
the object of God's election, not of His rejection.

[20] As Hahn points out, with the nations were idols and against them was
the Eternal One; Israel, however, had the almighty God as her Helper. The
expression *fear not* is frequent in these chapters (40:9; 41:10, 13, 14; 43:1, 5;
44:2, 8; 51:7; 54:4). It is an appropriate counterpart to the description of
Christ's work of salvation, and leads to the New Testament message, "Fear not,
for behold! I bring you good tidings of great joy."

anything that can harm them. This is not for Israel, for God is with her. The order of the words is striking, *with thee am I!* With Israel is the Lord, her God. Greater resources than this she could not have. Of all peoples she is the richest. (Cf. 40:9; 43:2, 5 and Acts 18:9, 10; note the language, "Be not afraid . . . for I am with thee. . . .")

In the last line the prophet exhibits in what manner the Lord will show Himself to be with the people and be their God. In the three verbs there is a certain gradation of the thought, although it is difficult to distinguish precisely the connotation of each. The first verb may be rendered *I strengthen thee* or *I have strengthened thee.* The verbs are actually perfects and should be translated by either the past or the present. God will give to Israel whatever firmness or strength is needed to meet the events of the future. In the second place God has helped Israel. The verb is strengthened by the particle *'aph (surely).* When Israel is in need, God is present with His aid. Lastly, God upholds Israel. The last verb is almost a synonym of the first, but possibly points out more directly God's protection and sustaining power. By sustaining Israel, God prevents her from stumbling (cf. 40:30). This He does by means of the right hand of His righteousness, i.e. His righteous right hand. The word for *right hand* signifies the power and might of God. This is a right hand that works by means of *righteousness,* manifested in God's providential dealings. To Israel this righteousness will be a blessing; but to the nations who know Him not, the righteousness will appear in the punitive and retributive justice meted out for their wickedness.

11 Lo! ashamed and confounded shall be all those incensed against thee; they shall be as nothing, and destroyed will be the men of thy strife.

12 Thou shalt seek them, and not find them, thy men of quarrel; they shall be as nothing and as naught, thy men of war.

13 For I am the LORD, thy God, who strengtheneth thy right hand; who saith to thee, Fear not, I have helped thee.

11 Isaiah deals in contrasts, and thus makes the truth stand out in clearer focus. Although the righteousness of God's right hand will sustain Israel, the enemies will be completely confounded. Indeed, the negative aspect of Israel's help will be found in the destruction of her enemies. The language is to be taken generally; it does not refer to the Babylonians or to any other peoples in particular. The truth that the prophet sets forth is that in the coming to realization of God's kingdom, the kingdom of evil will be subdued.

By means of an introductory *Behold!* the prophet directs attention to his message. Two verbs immediately follow, the first of which may be rendered *they will be ashamed,* and the second *they will be confounded.* Both are imperfects and are connected by weak *waw.*[21] Shame will come when the objects of divine wrath realize their true condition, and confusion will result when they seek for help from their idols. Haughty and confident they had been, for they had despised the working of Israel's God, Yahweh, and had been incensed against Israel; now, however, when He has acted, they have no counsel or plan.

In the second line the prophet describes the enemies as *the men of thy quarrel,* i.e. *the men against whom thou hast a quarrel.* Whether this is a parallel description of the enemies of the first line, or whether it designates a second class of enemies, is perhaps not possible to decide.[22] In the first line their own attitude was mentioned; here it is simply said that they are the ones who have a quarrel against Israel. By *quarrel* an actual lawsuit is intended. In the light of the preposition and suffix in line one (*bak*) we may understand the suffix with *quarrel* as objective. If this is correct, the words *thy quarrel* mean *the quarrel against thee.* It is perfectly possible, however, to construe the suffix as subjective, in which case the thought is that Israel has a quarrel. If the suffix be taken as objective, then the class of enemy referred to is one that not merely is enraged against Israel but also engages in active litigation against her. In any case, the outcome of this enemy is sure. It will be like nothing, and will perish.

12 The prophet now carries on further the thought of the latter half of the previous verse.[23] To convince Israel of the truth of his message, he informs her that the nation may seek for her enemies but will not find them. In the first line he describes the enemies as *the men of thy struggle,* i.e. *the men who struggle against thee,* and

21 The second verb indicates the result of the previous action.
22 The expression elsewhere applies to adversaries in a tribunal; cf. Job 31:35; Jer. 15:10. It is apparently similar to the Hittite *bel dini.*
23 The first half of v. 12 is not found in 1Q. It was probably obliterated.

in the second line as *the men of thy war*.[24] By saying that these enemies will be like nothing, the prophet strengthens what he had earlier asserted in the second line of verse 11.

13 There is a reason why the declaration of verses 11 and 12 is trustworthy. God has strengthened Israel's right hand. *I who am Yahweh am also thy God.* The Lord takes hold of Israel's right hand, so that the hand will not fall and Israel will not stumble.[25] If anyone other than the Lord had said to Israel, *Fear not*, the words would have been meaningless; but He who thus speaks to His people has helped them. God who has commanded the nation not to fear has already given to her His help.

> 14 Fear not! thou worm of Jacob, ye men of Israel; I have helped thee, saith the LORD, and thy Redeemer is the Holy One of Israel.
> 15 Behold! I have placed thee for a threshing sledge, sharp, new, possessed of teeth; thou shalt thresh mountains and beat them small, and hills thou shalt place like the chaff.
> 16 Thou shalt fan them, and a wind will take them up, and a whirlwind will scatter them; and thou shalt joy in the LORD, in the Holy One of Israel shalt thou boast.

14 Verses 14-16 are a compact unit, complete in itself, a fact that appears not merely from the content but also from the appearance of the phrase *the Holy One of Israel* in both verses 14 and 16. The prophet again proceeds to comfort the nation, and emphasizes the comfort by means of a reminder of the nation's deep humiliation. Using verbs taken from verse 10, he again commands the people not to fear. He addresses them, however, as the *worm of Jacob*, reflecting upon the statement of Job 25:6.[26] Possibly also there is reflection upon the Messianic Psalm 22:6, for it is true, as Delitzsch points out, that these passages stand under a Messianic light. He who is the true Servant is also a worm and no man, and He reflects the true heart and essence of the servant nation. The designation itself, however, is not used in a disrespectful sense, but

---

[24] The genitive following a construct may be used periphrastically to express the idea of material or attribute; *thy struggling men*, i.e. *the men who struggle against thee.*

[25] Cf. 42:6; 45:1; 51:18.

[26] *worm of Jacob* — the genitive serves to render a general concept more specific.

rather calls attention to the sad plight and distressful condition into which the nation had fallen and from which only the power of God could bring help. Such a designation would remind the nation of its state and would be more suitable for consolation than if the prophet had heaped upon it epithets of praise and honor.

The second designation is *men of Israel*; but many critics prefer to emend the text, for they think there should be some word parallel in thought to the *worm* of the first clause. Some have taken the word in its strict sense as *dead ones*; thus Jerome, *qui mortui estis in Israel*, which is approved by Calvin. Ewald changed the word to *rimmath (worm of)*, which has led to some unfortunate translations. Penna renders *vermiciattolo (small worm, maggot)* and Kissane *maggot*. Ewald himself had translated *gekrummtes Israel*. These renderings, however, make Israel appear despicable and lend a tone to the language that the word *worm* alone did not have.

Maurer, on the other hand, makes the suggestion that a strict parallelism of thought is not always found, and suggests that we retain the rendering *men*. This is by far the best procedure. This rendering seems to reflect upon the phrase "men of number" (i.e. "few men") found in Genesis 34:30 and Deuteronomy 4:27. But the ideas of fewness and mortality are really secondary and are perhaps suggested by the mere presence of the word. The thought is that the men of Israel, few and weak, are really but a helpless worm and in utter need of help. The words *men of Israel* are in apposition to the phrase *worm of Jacob,* but they do not form a complete parallel thereto.[27]

The prophet gives the reason why Israel should not fear, namely that God has helped her; and this is strengthened by the assertion *saith the Lord*. A new designation of God also appears, namely *Redeemer*. The word is used of a near kinsman (Lev. 25:24, 25) and also of one who delivers from bondage by the payment of a ransom. God had redeemed His people from the bondage of Egypt and now was to redeem them from the great bondage of sin in which they found themselves (cf. 43:14; 44:6, 24; 47:4; 48:17; 49:7, 26; 54:5, 8; 59:20; 60:16; cf. also 43:1; 44:22, 23;

---

[27] *men of Israel* — for one thing, the words constitute the entire second half of 14a. If there is to be complete parallelism we should expect something corresponding to the *fear not* of the first half of 14a. Corresponding to *fear not* is *I have helped thee* in 14b.

88

48:20; 52:9; 63:9). He whom Isaiah saw in the Temple, whose glory fills the whole earth, who is of purer eyes than to behold iniquity, is the One who pays the price to buy back His people, Jacob and Israel, from the bondage into which they had been sold. "The reference to the Son of God, although it might not be perceptible of old, is now rendered necessary by the knowledge that this act, even under the old dispensation, is always referred to the same person of the Trinity" (Alexander).

15 Not only will the Holy One redeem Israel but He will also cause her to prevail over her enemies and all obstacles. This is a new and important element of their salvation, and to call attention to its dignity Isaiah uses the word *Behold!* By this means he arouses the attention to face the comfort and consolation of which he proceeds to speak. God has placed (*appointed, set*) Israel as a *threshing sledge*. This was a flat plank or board, with rollers underneath studded with iron or basalt spikes. This instrument is *sharp*, and *new*, so it is effective in its working (cf. 28:27). Furthermore it is *possessed of mouths* (edges?) so that it will cut sharply.[28]

In the second line the prophet addresses Israel, and tells her that she will be such an instrument as will thresh even mountains and pulverize them.[29] The language is figurative to show that no peoples, be they ever so great or powerful, even as mighty as the kingdom of man that was then overshadowing the world, could stand in the way of Israel. Not that Israel in herself had the strength to withstand and destroy her enemies, but as the redeemed people of God she would in the strength of her God do valiantly. The parallel thought lends strength to the idea, *Israel will render the hills like chaff*. Israel, weak and downtrodden, a worm, will overcome obstacles far greater than herself, and that with the help of God.

16 The prophet continues the figure of Israel's victorious actions. Having threshed the mountains and reduced the hills to

---

[28] Tiglath-pileser III, "I trampled down Beth-Amukkan as in threshing," Nimrud slab inscription. Cf. J. Reider, *VT*, Vol. 2, 1952, pp. 116ff.; Haldar, *ND*, p. 36.

[29] *and thou shalt pulverize* — weak *waw* with imp. expresses result. *Thou shalt thresh*, and consequently, thou shalt pulverize. Hamlin (*JNES*, Vol. 13, 1954, pp. 185-190) thinks that the mountains represent cultic centers with allusion to the Babylonian ziggurat.

chaff, the nation will winnow them and a strong wind will carry them away. On the other hand, Israel will not only continue to exist but will rejoice in her God. Once the mountains have been ground to dust, Israel in the normal way will winnow them, casting the dust into the air, so that the strong wind may carry it away. It is questionable whether we are to see here a sifting among the unbelieving nations, so that some from among them, the good grain, falling to the ground and hence not being carried away like the chaff, will be preserved. The thought rather is that the wicked nations are to be winnowed and, inasmuch as they are chaff, will be carried away (cf. Ps. 1:4). Emphasis falls upon their removal. For that reason a storm wind is mentioned. Actually such a wind would carry away both chaff and good grain, but the prophet's purpose is to point out the forcefulness of the removal. Indeed, a certain gradation appears, in that the prophet first mentions the ru^ah (wind) as lifting up the mountains, i.e. what is left of the mountains after they have been reduced to dust, and then the $s^e'arah$ (whirlwind, or storm wind), which scatters the particles of dust so that they are completely removed from the scene.

Although the obstacles will be completely removed, Israel will rejoice in her God.[30] By means of and thou the prophet brings out the contrast. As a victor Israel will rejoice, but this rejoicing will be in Yahweh the Holy One of Israel. She will not boast as though the victory had been wrought in her own power, but will acknowledge that all was of the Lord; this she will do not grudgingly but with rejoicing.

17 The afflicted and the poor are seeking water, and it is not; their tongue is parched with thirst. I the LORD will answer them, I the God of Israel will not forsake them.

18 I will open upon the bare hills streams, and in the midst of valleys fountains; I will place the desert for a pool of water, and a dry land for springs of water.

19 I will give in the desert cedar, acacia and myrtle, and oil tree: I will place in the wilderness cypress, elm and box together.

20 To the end they may see and know and consider and understand together, for the hand of the LORD hath done this; and the Holy One of Israel, he hath created it.

17 The prophet now takes up again the description of the people as needy, which he had introduced in chapter forty and again in the word worm of 41:14, to show that no matter how great

30 Note the chiasm in 16b.

that need might be, God would meet and answer it. To describe the people he employs two words frequently used together, *ʿaniyyim* (*afflicted*) and *ʾevyonim* (*poor*), which represent Israel in the state of affliction and poverty that had come upon it (cf. 32:7). Such affliction and poverty, however, are not to be understood merely in a material sense; rather these words appear to refer to the devout and pious who endure suffering patiently, trusting in the Lord (cf. Ps. 40:17; 70:5; 86:1; 109:22; Jer. 20:13; 22:16, etc.).[31] If this latter connotation is prominent here, it would call attention to the nation as chosen of God, waiting patiently for Him to bring His deliverance. The description is that of men in a dry land, looking for water, a figure that would be all too well understood by the prophet's countrymen. The desperate need of the afflicted ones is stated in two clauses: *they seek water*, yet that water is not at hand, and *their tongue faints for thirst*.[32] These latter words heighten the description. By means of a striking assonance (*mayim waʾayin*) the prophet indicates the lack of water: *it is not*. When the poor and needy are in such condition God will answer their need.[33] The cry of His people's need has come unto Him, and He will answer. Perhaps there is also present the thought of God's answering the specific prayers of the people. His action, however, in the fullest sense may be termed an answer to the people.

The language describes a condition of severe need. The people are in a condition from which they cannot by human means extricate themselves. Salvation must come to them from without. The picture is that of a journey through the wilderness such as is

---

31 On the other hand, Volz thinks that the words are not to be taken in a spiritual sense but refer to those who on the return home from Babylon to Palestine suffered thirst, difficulty, and danger in the intervening desert. The context, however, refers to a spiritual salvation. Furthermore, the supposed dangers of the desert are greatly overemphasized. Ezra had the returning exiles camp for three days at "the river that runs to Ahava" (Ezra 8:15, 21) and proclaimed a fast. This would have been a foolish thing to do if the people were suffering from hunger and thirst.

32 *are seeking* — despite the omission of the article the part. may be construed as relative; cf. 1 Kings 11:8; 2 Kings 10:6. It is better, however, to construe the part. as expressing present action. The whole of 17a may then have the force of a temporal clause, and is thus correctly translated in the common English versions. 1Q adds the article.

33 נָשָׁתָּה — *Dagesh forte affectuosum* in ת emphasizes the *Qametz* in the principal pause. I interpret the form as 3 f. s. *Qal* perf. from נשׁת (not from שׁתת). The *Niphal* occurs in 19:5 and Jer. 18:14.

91

described in 40:3, not through the desert lying between Mesopotamia and Palestine. The language is a general description of affliction that comes to God's people when they have felt His judgment. In this sense it may apply to the exile, but the application is not to be so restricted. God's people, because of their deep sin, have fallen into a desperate plight. When their cry comes to Him and He sees their affliction, He will answer and bring His deliverance. As in verse 13, both *Yahweh* and the *Holy One of Israel* are in apposition to the personal pronoun *I*. In the remarkable work of redemption it is the covenant God of Israel, the I AM of Mt. Sinai, who is active; and He is the Holy One whom Isaiah had seen in the vision when he was called to preach to *this people*.[34]

18 The prophet now proceeds to point out how God will answer the cry of the people. In figurative language he shows that God will introduce a complete reversal of conditions. Under the figure of *dry hills, valleys, desert* and *dry land* he characterizes the present condition of God's people. All these things are to be changed by God Himself. Wherever there are bare places (possibly sand dunes; cf. Jer. 12:12) God will open streams, i.e. will cause water to flow where none has been before, with the result that in place of barrenness there will be fruitful, fertile land. In the midst of dry river beds, mere wadis where there was no water, there will be springs of water. Even the desert will become pools of water, and the dry land will send forth water (cf. 43:2). Everywhere in the wilderness, whether on the heights or in the wadis, there is to be a radical and all-embracing change. The desert will no longer be dry; it will be as a garden (cf. 43:19, 20; 44:3, 4; 48:21 and 35:7; Ps. 107:35, which is similar to the last line of the present verse; 114:8). The figure of water symbolizes life, for in a dry land the people were in a land of death. The picture calls attention to the supernatural character and the complete radicalness of the salvation the Lord will provide for His people.[35]

[34] The 1st person pronoun *I* casts its shadow over the entirety of vv. 17b-19. Following this pronoun there are 6 verbs in these verses that are 1 s.

[35] Volz remarks that the prophet believes in an actual transformation (*eine wirkliche Umwandlung*) of nature for the purpose of Israel's return home through the wilderness. If "second" Isaiah thought that this return (*Rückwanderung*) was actually to be accompanied by miracles such as characterized the exodus from Egypt, he was deceived, and in proclaiming such things he was a deceiver. For a discussion of שְׁפָיִים cf. G. R. Driver in *Occident and Orient*, 1936, pp. 78-80.

19 Not only will there be water where it had not been previously, but also, inasmuch as there is water, trees will grow where formerly they had not grown. In the wilderness of her misery Israel will seek shade but will not find it. Hence God will also provide for this need. The *'erez* is a cedar (cf. 9:9) ; the *shittah* an acacia; the *hadas* a myrtle tree. The *'etz shemen* (*oil tree*, lit., tree of oil) is possibly the wild olive in distinction from the *zayith* (the cultivated olive tree). In the Arabah God will place the cypress, the *tidhar* (hard oak?) and the *te'ashshur* (fir tree?) together.[36] All these trees together will give an appearance of luxuriousness and beauty. As Delitzsch suggests, it is a sevenfold glory that shines forth. The trees named are common to Syria and Palestine, and Isaiah delighted in using such figures (cf. 5:7; 6:13; 27:6; 37:31). One may well wonder how a writer who lived in Mesopotamia all his life would have possessed such a knowledge of the trees of Palestine. That Isaiah, on the other hand, should have had such knowledge is easily understandable.

The emphasis upon water and trees had also been found in the account of Eden in Genesis 3. Through the entrance of sin into the world, however, the garden was forfeited, and man entered a world where thorns and thistles would grow and he would labor by the sweat of his brow. In picturing the future age of blessing, the eschatological period when the restoration will occur, Isaiah uses the combined figures of water and trees. It is as though a bit of heaven had come down to earth; and indeed, those who one day will be blessed of these rivers and these trees are in the heavenlies in Christ Jesus.

20 The prophet now gives the reason why God will accomplish

---

[36] Not only do these trees offer shade and beauty, but, as Penna states, the idea of utility is also not lacking. The cedar (characteristic of Lebanon) is used for building (cf. 9:9). The acacia (*shittāh*) is a hard wood used for cabinetmaking (cf. Ex. 25:5, 10, 13, etc.) and is to be identified with Egy. *šnq*; cf. Akk. *samṭu*. For the myrtle, cf. Akk. *hadaššatu*, and Isa. 55:13. The olive is one of Palestine's principal trees. The *tidhār* is thought to be the hard oak. Bochart thought that the *te'aššûr* was an evergreen, about 20 feet in height, which grows in Lebanon. Others identify it with *sherbin*, a species of cedar. Cf. the discussions in H. and A. Moldenke, *Plants of the Bible*, Waltham, Mass., 1952. The use of יחדו combining three nouns also occurs in 11:6 and 60:13 and apparently nowhere else in the Old Testament. The concept of reviving the wilderness (מדבר) and desert (ערבה) also seems to be peculiarly Isaianic; cf. 35:1, 6; 40:3; 41:19; 51:3.

the promised salvation, namely that men may know that He is the true God. Do the subjects of the verbs refer to Israel alone or to men generally? Volz suggests that the subject is identical with those mentioned in verse 17. On this construction the purpose is to convince the poor and afflicted that their God is the true God. Others believe that the subject is more general and that the blessings given to Israel are for the purpose of convincing the entire world that Israel's God Yahweh is the very God of creation. On this interpretation the prophet is carrying out what he had said of "all flesh" in 40:5. It is perhaps not possible to decide definitely in favor of one or the other of these interpretations, but quite possibly the reference is general and includes all men, both Israelites and others. God's action of salvation thus will produce an effect upon all men, and all men will know that He is the true God.

Four verbs, connected by the weak *waw,* express the purpose of God's acting.[37] Men will *see* that the desert is to become a well-watered land. They will *know,* in that they will possess the knowledge that what has occurred is the work of God's own power. Such knowledge will not be fleeting, but men will actually *place* in their hearts (i.e. will give themselves over to serious reflection and meditation upon) the fact that God has worked. Lastly they will *understand* the meaning of what they have seen. Their contemplation will be based upon understanding.

What forms the object of their sensory and spiritual perception is the fact that the *hand* (i.e. the *power*) of Israel's God, Yahweh, has acted. The unbelievable change, in which the dead are brought to life, will be seen to be the work of God's might. Those who see will not be like the blind and ignorant who seek to explain the regenerating work of God upon naturalistic presuppositions of one kind or another. Rather, their own blindness and ignorance will be removed, and they will understand this supernatural regeneration for what it actually is, a manifestation of the power of Israel's God.

More than that, they will understand that Yahweh, the God of Israel, is also the Holy One who dwells in Israel's midst, and that He has created these things. In the usage of the verbs Isaiah introduces a certain gradation, proceeding from *'aśah* to *bara'.* This latter verb, employed in Genesis 1:1, points to the utterly new and marvelous character of the work God will accomplish. It is a

[37] The imps., connected by *waw* conjunctive, give distinctness to the recital of separate particulars.

work so radical and all-changing that it may be described with the very verb that depicted God's first work of creation. This work is fundamentally new and marvelous, a new creation.

21 Bring near your cause, saith the LORD; bring forward your defenses, saith the King of Jacob.
22 Let them bring forward and make known to us the things that will happen; the former things, what they were, show forth, that we may set our heart, and know their issue; or cause us to hear the coming things.
23 Cause to make known the coming things hereafter that we may know that ye are gods; yea, ye shall do good or evil, and we shall look about and see together.
24 Behold! ye are of nothing, and your work of naught; an abomination is the one choosing you.

Having shown that the God of Israel possesses wondrous power to create a new and marvelous thing, even the redemption of His people, the prophet now introduces a challenge uttered by the Lord Himself to the idols of paganism. The challenge is expressed in four closely knit verses. Verses 21 and 22 are tied together by the presence in both of the words *haggishu* (*draw near*) and *yaggishu* (*let them draw near*). Verses 22 and 23 are connected by the presence in each of the word *haggidu* (*make known*), which is found in the middle of 22 and at the beginning of 23. Again 23 and 24 are formally connected by the presence of *'attem* (*ye*) in the middle of verse 23 and at the beginning of 24 (*hen 'attem*). There is probably also a formal connection between verses 21 and 24 in that in both of them the plural suffix *kem* (*your*) is found.

21 The Lord has declared what He will do; He will perform a work that only God can accomplish. It is now the turn of the idols to show what power they have. The opportunity is theirs to present their case and to defend themselves.[38] God addresses the idols and idol worshippers generally and not merely the Israelites who had worshipped idols. All who have depended upon idols as their help are now ordered to present a defense of their actions. The case for idolatry is to be pleaded. How weak and inept it will

---

38 *your defenses* — עצמה (s.). In the Mishnah, the root is used of those who dispute in judgment. Cf. also Ar. *'isma*. The proposed emendations of this verse are not satisfactory. The picture is future and hence not to be understood against the background of Cyrus' initial activities.

sound in the light of the mighty acts of salvation that the God of Jacob has performed!

He who speaks with this absolute authority is the *King of Jacob*. He is a King who is able to do what a king should do. He can truly protect His own when their time of need comes. At the time, Jacob was but a worm; and the stump from which the Branch would go forth was underground. The promises were sure, however; and the true King of Jacob would bring these promises to reality. The King alone was in a position to command the idolaters and the idols.

22 The command in the second person now shifts over to a jussive in the third, *Let them* (the idols) *bring near* their messages. The second verb also refers to the idols themselves, "let the idols declare to us and thereby show that they possess the strength attributed to them by the idolaters."[39] The idols can prove their divinity by predicting what will take place in the future. The God of Israel had predicted the future, declaring that judgment would come and that His own people would be delivered. He had also raised up Cyrus in the east. Thus He had carried out what He had predicted. If the idols are truly gods, let them now come forward with their messages and declare the future. They are not even challenged to control the future; it is sufficient merely to state what it will be.

In the first line of the verse the prophet has spoken of the things that will happen. Now, however, in the second line he becomes more specific, and mentions both the former things and the things to come. With respect to the former things he commands the idols to make known what they are in order that men may know what their outcome will be. There are two principal interpretations of these words: (1) They refer to prophecies already uttered and fulfilled. This is said to preserve the contrast between the former things and the latter. If the idols are truly divinities, they should know the things that have already occurred and be able to state what they were. (2) On the other hand, some hold that the terms former and latter are to be taken within the limitation imposed by the general statement, *the things that will happen*. On this inter-

---

[39] The jussive with weak *waw* probably expresses intention, *let them bring near that they may declare*, etc. 1Q also has the *Hiphil*. Iwry (*JAOS*, Vol. 81, No. 1, 1961, p. 34) interprets the *Hiphil* of נָּגַשׁ as meaning *to divine, to make contact with the deity.*

pretation the former things refer to the near future, and the latter things are those events that were to occur in the far distant future. Thus, the contrast between *former* and *latter* is preserved, yet both phrases refer to what will still take place. The *first things* will shortly occur, and their signs or indications may already be discerned by the events at hand. Can the idols tell even those things that will shortly come to pass? "These are events that we ourselves will see; they are to take place in our lifetime. If the idols will predict these events we can direct our attention to them and know how they will eventuate. Their issue will then be before our eyes, and we shall know that it accords with what the idols have predicted." Those who adopt this second interpretation assert that:

(1) It preserves a proper contrast between the *former* and the *latter*, inasmuch as both are embraced under the general concept of *the things that will happen*.

(2) The language seems to imply that the latter part of the former things has not yet taken place. Idols are commanded to declare the former things so that we may know what their issue is. If the former things referred to events that had already taken place, would not their *latter part* also have already occurred?

(3) The command to the idols to declare things that have already occurred seems somewhat out of place when we have just been told that the challenge to the idols has to do with *the things that will happen*. It should also be noted that it would be difficult for the speaker and those whom he represents to set their hearts (i.e. apply the attention) and to know (i.e. understand) the latter part of the things that had already occurred. In this connection it is to be noted that the suffix with *latter part* refers to the feminine word, *the first things*. Isaiah is speaking of the first things and the latter part of the first things. If, however, this second position be adopted, it should be noted that this is the only place in the prophecy where it may be admitted. Elsewhere, "the former things" always refers to what is past.

Lastly, the prophet mentions *things that are to come*, by which he has in mind events that lie in the future. He commands the idols to cause us to hear what these things will be. Attention should be directed to the particle *or*, which presents a mighty choice. It is as though the prophecy said: "Declare the former things, or, if you wish, the things in the distant future. If the one is not pleasing, choose the other; only predict something, so that we shall know that you are a god."

Two comments are in order: (1) The challenge here laid down to the idols is to predict the future. It is not enough that false religion engage in its vague prophecies, which are not prophecies at all. (2) This verse illustrates the true method of Christian apologetics. Falsehood is here placed upon the defensive; it is commanded in the name of the God of Israel to defend its cause and to point out its justification for existence. There are difficulties in the acceptance of Christianity, but the Christian need not be expected to answer every difficulty. Rather, he must challenge the very right of unbelief to a hearing. The cause of God is best defended by means of a challenging offensive such as is here offered.

23 In this verse the command continues, the first clause being a practical equivalent of the last clause of the preceding verse. At the same time it returns to the generality of the first line of verse 22. It is a command to declare *the things that will come*, but this is strengthened by an additional qualifying word, *hereafter*.[40] The language appears to be redundant, but it may be that the prophet is reflecting upon both the *former things* and *the coming things* which he had just mentioned. If the idols can do this, he reasons, it will be possible to recognize that they are divine.[41] Isaiah employs the word *'elohim*, in the sense of *that which is divine*. His argument is: "Only God can declare what the future will be. If the idols can declare the future, it follows that they are the same kind of beings as God. If they cannot, they are not God, and hence can lay no claim upon a man's worship."

Hahn prefers another construction of the words, one the Masoretic accentuation could support. He would render *ki* as *for*, thus, "Declare the future things, and we shall know, for ye are gods." On this construction, the prophet is addressing the idols ironically. Hahn thinks that the usual construction contradicts both verses 22 and 26, but such is not the case. The challenge is bona fide; if in accordance with this command anyone can predict the future, he shows that he possesses the qualifications of deity. Hahn's construction really breaks the symmetry of the first line, dividing it into two unequal parts.

[40] לְאָחוֹר — *hereafter,* the opposite of *mēr̄ōʾš*; cf. 42:23.

[41] וְנִרְא — *that we may see* (1Q *wnr'h*.), an apocopated form in the 1st pl., from רָאָה, not from וְרָא, as is shown by the *Seʿgol*. BH gives the *Keʿtiv* as *weniraʾ*; but I find no evidence for this, and Duhm comments that it does not fit in with Yahweh's speech.

In the second line the prophet narrows down the general command, enjoining the idols either to do good or to do evil, i.e. the idols are to proclaim messages either of deliverance or of judgment, as Yahweh the God of Israel had done.[42] Although it is not certain that the reference is to be limited to prediction, nevertheless, in this context the activity of the idols is thus restricted.

"If the idols can truly predict, then the result will be that we who behold will gaze astonished, and we will see together both the good and the bad that the idols perform." Isaiah's language is difficult, but a good case can be made for taking the word *yaḥdaw (together)* as referring to things seen rather than to the subject of the verb (but cf. 40:5).[43]

24 This verse forms the conclusion of the argument just presented and also serves as a transition to what follows. God has challenged the idols and they have made no reply; hence, the conclusion follows, introduced by the word *Behold!* This word, actually possessing the force of a command, draws the attention again to the nothingness of the idols and to the tragic condition of those who are their worshippers. Addressing the idols the prophet declares that they are *from nothing*, i.e. they possess no reality.[44] The language is similar to 40:17. Calvin calls attention to the objection that might be raised, namely, that the idols were indeed material in their composition. How then can it be said that they are of nothing? It may be replied that the prophet has in mind the same thought as that of the apostle Paul, "an idol is nothing" (1 Cor. 8:4). He does not deny that there is material substance to an idol; he has himself given a description of their manufacture. What he denies is that the idol can act as God. As to predicting the

---

[42] Thus, the thought is not, "Do at least something, whether it be good or evil."

[43] Alexander thinks it more natural to apply the *together* to the two contending parties united in the same act. Hahn applies the word to the object seen, the good and evil to be announced by the idols. Jehovah will see whether the future will bring both what is promised and what is threatened. *Together*, argues Hahn, cannot refer to the subject of *we shall see*, for in the entire passage Jehovah alone speaks in the plural. It is also possible to refer the word to the two verbs, we shall gaze and see together, i.e. these actions will be performed in conjunction one with the other.

[44] The preposition *min* is used in a partitive sense; cf. 40:17. It is also possible that *min* is comparative, in which case a preceding adjective would have to be understood, *ye are worse than nothing.*

future, the idol can do nothing. Just as in 40:17 there was no denial of the existence of the nations, so here there is no denial of the material substance of idols. But the idols are not what they are supposed to be. In this sense they are from nothing.

Likewise, the work the idols perform is nothing, for they cannot do anything.[45] Predicting the future is impossible for them, inasmuch as they are unable to speak a word. Idols can say and do nothing, for they themselves are nothing.

From this fact the inescapable conclusion follows that the man who chooses an idol to be his god is an abomination. To be sure, he is foolish, for he is doing something that is itself foolish; but his action is more than foolish; it is wicked and despicable, and for that reason the one who does it is an abomination. The word is strong, and was used, for example, by Moses in describing the idolatries and superstitious practices of the Canaanites as well as those who engaged in such practices. Such a one is an abomination not merely in the eyes of man but before God. The idolater is said to *choose* the idols (cf. Judg. 5:8), an action that betrays the depravity of his own heart.[46] In speaking of him as "morally the most degraded of beings" Delitzsch is not incorrect. For only a wicked and depraved heart would reject the true Lord of hosts to do obeisance to an idol. John 3:19, 20 gives the divine interpretation of such abominable actions. When fallen man exercises his will, he chooses not the truth but the vain and dark imaginations of his own heart; he turns to idolatry.

25 I have raised up one from the north, and he has come, from the rising of the sun will he call upon my name; and he shall come upon princes as mortar, and as a potter treadeth clay.

26 Who hath declared from the beginning, that we might know,

---

[45] אפס — *naught*, omitted in 1Q. Several rabbis derived the word from *'ep'eh*, *viper* or *adder*, and rendered, *worse than the adder*, which would refer to the wickedness of action, whereas here the reference is to the powerlessness of the idols. Hence, it has been explained as a mere parallel to *'epes, nothingness* (cf. 40:17; 41:12, 29), for ע and ס are said to be related (Gesenius, Hahn). Delitzsch derives the word from *pā'āh, to breathe*, and takes it as a synonym of *rûah, breath*. Cf. *VT*, Vol. 1, 1951, p. 299.

[46] *an abomination* — note ellipsis of the relative or the subject. Hahn suggests that the word denotes the subject as regarded by men. Through the disaster into which one falls by means of idolatry, he is regarded by men as an abomination. Cf. *ANET*, p. 315, with respect to Cyrus' action upon Marduk worship.

and from beforehand, that we might say, It is right? Yea, none
makes known; yea, none causes to hear; yea, none heareth
your words.

27 First to Zion, Behold! behold them! and to Jerusalem a messenger of good tidings I give.

28 And I will look, but there is no man, and of these but there
is no one counselling; and I will ask them, and they will return
a word.

29 Lo! they are all naught, nothing their works; wind and emptiness their molten images.

25 Isaiah now expresses directly and affirmatively what had
been suggested in verse 2 by means of a question. Having challenged the idols and declared that they are nothing, he now
returns to the subject matter of verses 1-4. It is God who speaks
and who declares positively that He will raise up one from the
north. Although a definite object is not expressed, it is implied in
the following clause, so that we may bring out the force by rendering, *one who will be from the north.*[47]

In verse 2 the direction *east* had been given, but here it is *north*.
Those who apply this language to Abraham refer the east to Ur
and the north to Haran, an interpretation that definitely implies a
standpoint in Palestine. Those who apply the language to Cyrus
find a difficulty, but it is not insurmountable. It is not necessary to
say that east refers to Persia and north to the land of the Medes,
which Cyrus conquered. The designation *east* is general, and denotes the place of origin of the invader. On the other hand *north* is
the common designation of the place from which invasions into
Palestine are made. Probably it means no more than that the
invader will come from afar (cf. Jer. 1:14; 6:22; 25:9; 46:20; 47:2;
50:3, etc.). The language applies admirably if spoken in Palestine,
but it is difficult to understand how it would fit the situation of a
"second Isaiah" in Babylon.

In the second half of the first line the prophet refers to the east
under the language, *the place of the rising of the sun.* Possibly
then the use of *tzaphon* (north) is intentional in order to avoid
the repetition of *mizraḥ* (east). The one whom God raises up

---

47 ויאת — *and he has come,* for *way-ya'-t.* Here *Aleph* loses its consonantal
power. The perfects express the future. The reference is not to the past; rather,
whereas the idols cannot predict the future, the Lord will even perform an act
in the future.

does come from the east; but inasmuch as he comes as an invader, he like other invaders of Palestine is said to come from the north.

This one from the east will call upon the name of Yahweh.[48] The phrase may mean, "call by means of My name," in the sense of calling upon the name (cf. Zeph. 3:9; Jer. 10:25), or it may mean calling out or pronouncing the name (cf. Isa. 43:1; 44:5; 45:3, 4). Perhaps the latter is to be preferred, for it appears to be exemplified in the proclamation recorded in the opening verses of Ezra.

In the second line the prophet describes the manner of coming. Ruthlessly will this conqueror come. He will come against $s^e gan$-im (governors of districts or provinces)[49] as though they were *mortar*. They will have no more power to resist his approach than does mortar. Changing the figure the prophet points out that just as the potter is able to trample upon the clay with which he works, so will this conqueror trample under foot his enemies.[50]

26 As in verse 25 the prophet reverted to his first argument (vv. 2-7) in which the omnipotence of God was seen, so now he takes up the second argument, relating to God's omniscience. And this is done by means of a question. *Who,* the verse begins, implying, Who among all the gods that Israel worships? We should probably translate the first verb by the past, *Who has made known,* referring it to oracles already uttered, and implying that Yahweh, the God of Israel, has made such predictions.

The verb has a qualifying clause, *from the head,* i.e. from the beginning. It would seem that the reference is to the beginning of the course of history that is unfolding. It is as though the question read, "Who has declared what we now see before it actually began to take place? If any of the idols had done that, we could know the meaning of what is occurring."

As earlier suggested, this question not only implies that none of the idols has made such a prediction, but it also implies that Yahweh the God of Israel has so predicted. Those who do not

48 The imp. in 25b after the *perfecta prophetica* in 25a suggests that 25b is to be rendered as a relative clause, *one who calls by my name.*

49 סגנים — *rulers* (cf. Akk. *šaknu, šakin*), a governor of a district or province (Jer. 51:23, 28; Ezek. 23:6; Ezra 9:2; Neh. 2:16). Cf. *Journal of Theological Studies,* Vol. 10, 1959, pp. 84-87.

50 In its preparation the potter would knead the clay by treading upon it with his feet (Nah. 3:14). A tomb painting from Thebes (2nd millennium B.C.) depicts a workman standing in the clay, kneading it with his feet. Cf. *VBW,* Vol. III, p. 69; also *ANEP,* pp. 309, 314, 330, 345.

believe that this chapter speaks of Cyrus point to this fact and claim that no such predictions concerning Cyrus were made before his appearance, and some defenders of the Cyrus interpretation declare that we are not able to point to any such predictions.[51] If, however, we assume that the entire prophecy is the work of Isaiah, we find that there are indeed very definite prophecies concerning the appearance of Cyrus, and these even speak of him as coming in the distant future (cf. 44:24-28 and 45:1-4). The present passage itself is a prophecy of Cyrus, even though it does not name him.

In the parallel section the prophet states essentially the same thought. In place of *from the head* he now says, *from before*, i.e. earlier. "Had the idols spoken earlier we could have passed judgment upon their messages when we saw them fulfilled. We could have declared that their predictions were justified." When the prophecy has been fulfilled it will be possible to say that its fulfillment is in accord with the prediction (cf. 43:9).

The questions can be answered with confidence; there was no idol at all that made known these things that came to pass. To strengthen the answer the prophet employs an asseverative particle, *surely*, and thus brings emphasis to the truthfulness of what he declares. Isaiah expresses the answer by means of participles. There is no one that causes to make known, there is no one that causes to be heard; and then, as a response to these two statements, he concludes with another participle, there is no one that hears your words. It is not that people disregard the words of the idols; they do not even hear such words.

27 The first part of this verse is difficult and by many considered in need of emendation. Textual difficulty, however, is not sufficient reason for emendation; hence we shall endeavor to interpret the text as it stands. The word *ri'shon*, standing at the beginning of the verse, may be rendered *As a first one*, the thought being that Yahweh is the first to have spoken to Zion. We may then understand the verb *I have spoken* as following. At the same time we may legitimately connect *to Zion* with the verb *I give* at the close of the sentence. The whole may then be rendered: *As a first one to Zion, Behold! behold them! and to Jerusalem a messenger I give.*[52]

51 Penna gives a good discussion of these questions (*loc. cit.*).
52 Less satisfactory is the rendering, "See! there they are (thy children)," or "see, there it is," and "to Jerusalem I gave a messenger." *Behold!* is a

A principal difficulty is the meaning of the words *Behold! behold them!* The following interpretation at least has the merit of consistency. If we understand a verb *I have said* after the first word, then the interjection calls attention to the words that God has spoken. The idols have not been able to speak a word of prediction; they know nothing of future events. On the other hand, Yahweh is the first to have spoken of what would come to pass. His words are before all, and so the prophet commands his hearers to look at them. This interpretation fits in well with the second half of the verse, which asserts that God gives to Jerusalem an announcer. This announcer is the prophet, even Isaiah himself by whom God speaks forth the things that are to occur.

28 To strengthen the argument God Himself continues to speak. The first verb may be taken as an apocopated form and regarded as forming the protasis of a conditional sentence, *And should I see,* i.e. look inquiringly, for the sake of examination. The remainder of the first line serves as the apodosis. The result of God's investigating is that there is no man whatsoever who could or who had announced anything similar to what God Himself had declared. Furthermore, from among these (the idols), there was none giving counsel. For the purpose of emphasis the prophet places first the phrase *and from these,* perhaps in a depreciatory sense, as though to say, "and from among all of these idols, not even one could give counsel." In the great work of redemption, there was need of counsel. For that reason the Messiah Himself is called a wonder of a counsellor (9:6), but in this essential task the idols were of no help. Multitudinous as they were, not even one from among them could give counsel (cf. 44:26).

In the last clause there are two verbs introduced by weak *waw.* The translation is difficult, but the procedure that appears most free from difficulty is to take the first verb in a sense parallel to that of the first verb of the sentence, *and should I ask them?*[53] The second verb may either express purpose, *that they should*

---

favorite expression of Isaiah. Its usage to announce a particular subject can be paralleled in Babylonian at least as early as the Amarna texts, e.g. no. 8, line 41. Smith (*ILCH*) points out that it is also found in Hittite; cf. E. F. Weidner, *Politische Dokumente aus Kleinasien,* p. 114, lines 11, 18, 19. In vv. 27, 29 it prepares for the triumphant *Behold!* of 42:1.

[53] Note that, as in v. 23, the jussive appears here in the 1st person.

return a word, or may be a question, *and do they return a word?* Thus we may either render, *and should I ask them that they may return a word?* or *and I ask them and will they return a word?* On the first construction the sentence is an anacoluthon, the apodosis being omitted. In any case the verse clearly teaches that the idols were unable to speak concerning the future deliverance. Just as the raising up of Cyrus showed the omnipotence of the God of Israel, so also the fact that He had predicted the deliverance revealed His omniscience. The expression *to return a word* means merely *to answer*.

29 *Behold!* now directs attention to the conclusion of the whole matter (cf. v. 24). It is a conclusion that Israel needs to take to heart and not forget. Furthermore, it is a conclusion of wide scope. All of the idols, declares the Lord, are vanity. The words *all of them* are placed first for emphasis' sake; there are no exceptions, idols of all kinds, wherever they are, whoever their worshippers, all of them are nothingness. In fact their works are also said to be nothingness. Here again, the word *'ephes* (*nothingness*) receives the emphasis by its position. To what, however, do the words *their works* refer? If we take the words as a parallel to *all of them*, they would appear to refer to the works the idols themselves perform. On the other hand, if the words be taken as a parallel to the following *their molten images*, then they would seem to refer to the idols themselves as the products of those who make them. To insist upon a change of reference of the suffixes in the verse itself introduces an element of clumsiness. It is more natural in each instance to refer the suffixes to the idols. On this interpretation the works of the idols would refer to the things the idols are supposed to do and say. Inasmuch as they do and say nothing, their work is nothingness.

Likewise the molten images belong to the idols in the sense that they are the visible representation of the idol. It cannot be denied that this interpretation contains difficulties. On the whole, however, it would seem to be the most free from difficulty. To the usual terms employed for nonentity Isaiah here adds two more, *wind* and *desolation*. Wind is an effective term for expressing emptiness of thought, and *tohu* (desolation), used in Genesis 1:2 to designate the uninhabitable condition of the earth, here stresses the fact that the idols cannot accomplish what is profitable. Their work results in emptiness or desolation, so that it is to no purpose. The emphatic position of the words *wind* and *desolation* must be noticed. No god can stand under the withering challenge of the one living and true God, the God of Israel. He alone directs the course of history, and what He does cannot be duplicated by gods made by human hands.

THE ONE FROM THE EAST (ISA. 41:1-4, 25, 26)

In the commentary we have proceeded upon the assumption that the one whom God raises from the east is Cyrus. As early as the Targum, however, a different interpretation appeared. The Targum renders 41:2, "Who brought in haste (openly, *bgly*) from the east Abraham, the chosen of righteousness in truth." Jerome applied the passage to Christ, although not many have followed him in this.[54]

Both Kissane and Torrey adopted the targumic interpretation, for the following reasons.

(a) In 41:25 the one whom God brings is said to call upon God's Name. Hence, if this applies to Cyrus we should either have to hold that he was a monotheist or that the text is corrupt. Neither of these alternatives is supported by other evidence.

(b) There is a similarity between the language that describes the one from the east and that which describes Israel. If the prophet is making a comparison between the life of Abraham and Israel's future history the term "seed of Abraham" takes on new significance.

(c) The clauses "I the Lord called thee in righteousness" and "I will hold thy hand and protect thee" (42:6) are said to be virtually a combination of 41:26 and 41:10cd, which indicates that both of the latter passages refer to Israel.

(d) Cyrus could not be described as coming from the north, whereas Abraham could be said to have come from the east (Ur) or from the north (Haran).

(e) It is implied in 4b that between the promise and its fulfillment there were many generations, and this would not apply to Cyrus.

(f) The "former things" refer to events in the past which had been foretold and which had been fulfilled. Usually, argues Kissane, there is an analogy between the "former things" and the "latter things"; and inasmuch as the "latter things" here include the choice of Israel as a messenger to the nations, what more appropriate parallel could there be than the original election of Israel in the person of Abraham?

Credit must be given to Kissane for adducing these arguments. Torrey also adopts the same position, for it fits in well with his general inter-

---

[54] "Neque enim Iudaeorum tantum Deus, sed et gentium, qui vocavit Christum Dominum Salvatorem, qui factus est nobis sapientia a Deo, institia et sanctitas, et redemptio" (*In Isaiam Prophetam, ad loc.*) .

pretation of the prophecy.[55] Before proceeding to consider these arguments one by one we shall set forth what appears to be the general emphasis of these chapters, for that in itself constitutes the basic reason why we believe the reference is to Cyrus rather than to Abraham. Inasmuch as this position appears in detail in the commentary proper, it is necessary here only to set it forth in brief compass.

Beginning with chap. 40 the prophet writes of the conditions of the people in bondage. He is to be a messenger of comfort to them. They are in physical servitude in that they are removed from their homeland. To deliver them God will send Cyrus. In chap. 41 this deliverer is depicted only in general terms; in chap. 44 he is named. In these early chapters of the second part of the prophecy the nation Israel is also prominent as a servant, the word calling attention to the contrast between what Israel actually was and what it was destined to be.

At the same time, no sooner had intimations been given of a human deliverer than the prophet, rising from consideration of the nation as a servant, focuses attention upon the Servant *par excellence*, who will perform for Israel a work that neither they themselves nor Cyrus can accomplish.[56] Whereas Cyrus will set the people free from Babylonia, the Servant will deliver them from the spiritual bondage of sin in which they find themselves.

In the light of these brief remarks we may comment on the particular arguments of Kissane.

(a) 41:25 probably means *to call by means of God's Name*. If this is correct the proclamation of Cyrus given in Ezra 1:1-4 would be an example of what is intended.

(b) There is indeed similarity between the language describing the one from the east and that describing Israel, but similarity does not prove identity.

(c) These phrases in 42:6 refer to the Servant *par excellence* and not to the historical Israel alone. Hence, the conclusions Kissane draws from them are not warranted (see comments on 42:6).

(d) This question of the direction or provenience is considered in the commentary. Cf. comments on 41:25.

(e) In reply to this argument consult the comments on 41:4. The verse says nothing about generations intervening between the promise and its fulfillment.

(f) Again, this argument can be answered only by a consideration of the phrases "former things" and "latter things." See the comments on 41:22.

---

[55] C. C. Torrey, *The Second Isaiah*, Edinburgh, 1928. I have evaluated Torrey's work in *SII*, pp. 87, 89.

[56] The Babylonians believed that Marduk had called Cyrus (*ANET*, pp. 315ff.; and cf. *Biblica*, Vol. 48, Fasc. 1, pp. 57ff.).

CHAPTER FORTY-TWO

1 Behold! my servant, I hold him fast, my chosen one (in whom) my soul delighteth. I have given my Spirit upon him; judgment to the nations he will bring out.

2 He will not cry and he will not lift up (his voice), and not will he cause to be heard in the street his voice.

3 A reed bruised he will not break and flax smoking he will not quench it; for truth he will cause judgment to go out.

4 He will not be dim and he will not be crushed until he place in the earth judgment, and for his law the isles will wait.

1 With the word *Behold* we are again upon the threshold of a great message. It stands in contrast to the "Behold" that introduced the last verse of chapter forty-one, and calls attention to the greatest of all themes, the work of the Lord's servant. To whom, however, is it addressed? Some think that the audience consists of supramundane beings, others that it is Israel herself. At least the readers of the prophecy are included; indeed, all to whom the message comes. They are to turn their thoughts away from the idols of vanity to the One who can bring salvation to His people.

The word *servant* is emphatic, for it expresses the central theme. Isaiah had already identified Israel as God's servant (41:8). Why then is there a special introduction at this point? It would seem that the word is here used in a different sense from 41:8, and is not merely an identification of Israel. In particular if the prophecy is addressed to the nation, it would be unlikely that Israel is the servant. It is true that Codex Vaticanus identifies the servant as Israel, and Skinner remarks that this shows how easily readers might make this identification. But the Targum equates the servant with the Messiah.

The very atmosphere of the passage suggests something distinctive about this servant. He belongs to God, and God willingly acknowledges him. As Torrey remarks, the strain here is loftier and the picture more impressive. We have taken a step beyond 41:8.

The designation is one of honor, as is shown by the parallel word *elect*. He who is the servant, with all that word implies, is also the elect of God; and he whom God has chosen is also God's servant. Far from being a term of depreciation, the term points to one who stands in a peculiar relationship to God.[1] Extrabiblical usages seem to suggest the same thing.[2] The title presupposes a special election.

It is not necessary to take the following clause, *I hold him fast*, as a relative, although many commentators do so.[3] The language does not mean that God leans upon the servant. Nor does it mean that God holds him fast despite his present unworthiness, nor simply that God holds him. And there is no warrant for saying that the prophet has deliberately adopted high court style and that the phrase refers to the appointment of the servant to his ministry.

When construed with the preposition, the verb simply means "to sustain," "to hold fast," and here refers to the divine aid vouchsafed to the servant. The fact that God thus sustains the servant shows that God holds him in the deepest affection.

---

[1] In an exegetical commentary there is not enough space to engage in a thorough discussion of the identity of the Servant of the Lord. The reader is referred to the following works as an introduction to the subject: C. R. North, *The Suffering Servant in Deutero-Isaiah*, London, 1956; H. H. Rowley, *The Servant of the Lord*, Oxford, 1965; V. de Leeuw, *De Ebed Jahweh-Profetieen*, Assen, 1956; Edward J. Young, *SII*; Otto Eissfeldt, *The Old Testament: An Introduction*, E.T. New York, 1965, pp. 330-336. The position adopted in this commentary is as follows: The servant is the Messiah (Jesus Christ) conceived as the Head of His people, the Church (or the redeemed Israel). At one time the body is more prominent, at another (e.g. chap. 53) the Head. That the servant points to the Messiah is seen in that his work is spiritual in nature, the redemption of his people from the guilt and power of their sins. That the Messiah is not exclusively intended is seen from the fact that (1) imperfection is attributed to the servant, 42:19; (2) he is designated Israel, 41:8; 44:1; 49:3; (3) other passages of Scripture apply these passages to the Church: Jer. 11:19; Acts 13:47; 2 Cor. 6:2. Cf. de Leeuw, *De koninglijke Verklaring van de Ebed-Jahweh-Zangen*, 1952, pp. 456, 457.

[2] Cf. *DOTT*, p. 123; Lindhagen, *The Servant Motif in the Old Testament*, Uppsala, 1950, and note the designation of Cyrus as the young servant (*aradsu ṣaḫri*) of Marduk; cf. Langdon, *VAB*, IV, Nabonidus I, Col. 1:28ff. In Ug. Danel and Krt are both designated *'bd il*; cf. *Krt*, lines 153, 155, 299-300 and Aqht ii.1.35; Gordon, *UH*, pp. 182, 185, 187. Nebuchadnezzar is designated the servant of Šamaš, Azitawadu the servant of Baal, etc.

[3] Two simple sentences are here coordinated, instead of using a relative clause; and the connection with the preceding is thus suggested merely by the juxtaposition; cf. also 1 Kings 11:14; Jer. 5:15; 49:31.

A second designation of honor is the phrase *my chosen one*. In the Hebrew the form of the word points to one who has been chosen and continues in the character of a chosen one. Hence, we must reject the old interpretation, set forth by Calvin and others, that the word simply means "choice" or "excellent." Perhaps he who is chosen may be regarded as a choice one, but this is not the principal connotation. The servant's work is not such that anyone can perform it. He who is to carry it out must be chosen of God Himself.

The one whom God has chosen is also one in whom God delights with the fullness of His being.[4] God has so found acceptance in him that even His soul delights in him. The word is employed in the Mosaic law of God's delight in the sacrifices. The verb, although perfect, need not necessarily refer only to one act, namely the moment of the servant's call, but may just as well express the continued delight God finds in His servant. The New Testament uses this expression of Christ Himself (cf. Matt. 3:17 and 17:5).

To endue the servant for his work, God has placed His Spirit upon him.[5] The Spirit is a divine force and supernatural power who equips the recipient to perform his task. He was given not only to prophets but also to others. The Spirit is said to come *upon him*, as though He came down from heaven to rest upon the servant. Whether the verb is to be taken as a prophetic perfect is difficult to say. If the meaning of this passage is exhausted in the Holy Spirit as a dove descending upon our Lord at the time of His baptism, it would seem that the verb is to be taken as a prophetic perfect. On the other hand, if this is a general declaration of the fact that God prepares the servant for his difficult mission by the enduement of His Spirit, then it is not necessary so to construe the verb.

In 61:1 the servant himself speaks: "The Spirit of the Lord is upon me." The enduement has taken place, for God has anointed him to preach good tidings. In 48:16 the Lord sends the servant and the Spirit. In the light of these passages it is probably preferable to regard the declaration of the Lord as a general statement of the fact that He has fully equipped the servant for his mission.

---

[4] I incline to regard נפשׁי as more forceful than merely a substitute for the pronoun, but cf. *HS*, p. 32.

[5] The combination of *spirit* and *upon him* is found elsewhere only in 11:2-4. This is clearly a Messianic characteristic.

In the present verse the mission is stated simply, and there is no implication that in its performance there will be unusual obstacles. The simple words, *he shall cause judgment to go out to the nations*, declare that the servant will accomplish his end.[6] Does the phrase *he shall cause to go out* refer to preaching or prophetical activity, or does it suggest that the servant will himself establish judgment in the world? Does the servant proclaim justice or does he establish it?

The Gospel of Matthew would seem to support the former of these alternatives: "And he will announce judgment to the nations" (Matt. 12:18b). Matthew's usage does not necessarily decide the question, nor does it rule out the other interpretation of the Hebrew of Isaiah. First of all, the verb does not mean "to call" or "to proclaim," but "to cause to go out." Secondly, the enduement with the Spirit seems to point to the difficulty of the task. Thirdly, the language of verse 4 (*till he have set judgment in the earth*) shows that something more than proclamation is here intended.

The servant by virtue of the Spirit causes judgment to go out (probably from Zion) throughout the world. The thought is basically the same as that of 2:2ff. The word translated *judgment* comes from a root meaning "to judge." It is therefore that which a judge has decided, *a judgment*, which stands in accord with a standard or norm.

The legal decisions are those pronounced by God Himself, and embrace the entirety of revealed religion.[7] Religion is here conceived of in its judicial aspect, for it has to do with the conduct of men, and its decisions either condemn or justify a man. This judgment the servant will bring to the Gentiles, who know not Israel's God. His work, therefore, is missionary. "Christ," says Calvin, "was sent in order to bring the whole world under the authority of God and under obedience to him."

2 This verse consists of three negative verbs, which describe the unostentatious and unobtrusive working of the servant. He stands in sharp contrast to the loud worldly conqueror who proclaims to all his deeds. In ancient times when a new religion was presented to a people it was introduced by their conqueror, who

---

[6] The concepts *law, judge,* and *nations* are found elsewhere only in 2:3, 4. Cf. also 51:4, *law, judgment, peoples.*

[7] *Justice* is too restricted in meaning. Appeal is often made to Ar. *din*, used in the same sense.

forced it upon them. The servant does not act like such a conqueror, nor does he seek to force upon anyone a particular program. It is simply because of his own great confidence in God and his quiet manner of working that he succeeds in the most difficult of all missions.

With what is the contrast actually intended? Some think that a definite contrast with Cyrus is in view;[8] others that the contrast is with the type of prophet who engaged in frenzied behavior and ecstasy. It has also been held that the contrast is with the great preaching prophets who proclaimed judgment and thundered forth the wrath of God upon an evil nation, or with wandering preachers and prophets like medicine men and the Cynics.[9]

Perhaps these questions cannot receive a definite answer. Indeed, the quiet manner of the servant sets him forth in contrast to all who call attention to themselves. His demeanor is different from that of ordinary men. He will not cry out, either against oppression, as some of the prophets had done, or for revenge. Nor is his cry for help or of lament. Possibly the verb suggests the cry of one ready to proclaim a message, for the Gospel of Matthew interprets, *he will not strive*. Our Lord fulfilled this prophecy in that He did not enter into a violent dispute with the Pharisees, and He furthermore charged the masses to keep silence. In the bringing out of judgment to the nations, the servant will not cry out in strife, but he will proclaim his words of truth softly.

The second verb may be rendered, *he will not lift up*, and indicates a lifting up or raising of the voice.[10] It has been suggested by some who apply the passage to Cyrus that the reference is to a constant rebuke to the subject population. Others have applied the verb to the calling up of levies for military service in the subject provinces. Such interpretations, however, read a great deal into the text; and there is no warrant for departing from the simple meaning of the verb. It serves as a parallel expression to the first verb, and simply declares that the servant will not raise his

---

8 E.g. *PIAI*, p. 123.

9 Cf. Volz, *in loc.*

10 When it is clearly understood what the object is, that object is often left unexpressed; cf. 3:7; 1 Sam. 20:16; Jer. 3:5, etc. Such a use of נשׂא is not found elsewhere apart from 3:7. Cf. also Num. 4:1; Job 21:12; Isa. 42:11. Ellison (*The Servant of Jehovah*, p. 18) has well pointed out the sharp contrast between the quiet acting of the servant and the noise of armies, toppling idols, etc., in chap. 41. Cf. also Fry, *in loc.*

voice. He will speak with calmness and quiet, for he has no need to raise his voice in strife or argument.

Lastly, *he will not cause his voice to be heard in the street.* Grotius offered the strange suggestion that this simply meant that the servant would not raise his voice so high in the house that it would also be heard in the street. But this verb is really parallel in thought to the first two, and simply means that while he is in the street, he will not raise his voice. Those who gather about him to hear his teaching will discover that he spoke as never man spoke. His teaching was not accomplished through loud proclamation but by quiet instruction.

Alexander suggests that these verses do not describe Christ's human virtues but simply set forth the nature of His kingdom. But must such a sharp contrast be made? Surely this verse does set forth the nature of Christ's kingdom, but is it entirely silent with respect to Christ's human virtues? Does it not rather declare in cogent manner how Christ entered upon His earthly ministry?

3 The description is continued, pointing out how the servant acts with respect to the weak and oppressed. His mission is to bring blessing and not to destroy. The figures employed are themselves easy to understand, but it is not clear precisely what they signify.[11] The reed grows in the marsh or on the river bank. In itself it is weak, but it has in addition been bruised or broken, probably by the wind.

Likewise, the smoking flax is simply the wick that is burning and is practically extinguished. Obviously, however, these figures are to be taken as symbolical. They are objects and are placed for emphasis' sake before the verbs; hence they are evidently regarded as important. Furthermore, this position of the objects contrasts with the word order of the preceding verse.

Tertullian referred the reed to the faith of Israel and the flax to the momentary zeal of the Gentiles. Hahn takes the reed as the heathen in their ethical depravity, in which, not standing in the truth of God, they are blown by the spirit of error, and not standing in the life of God, they are blown by the power of sin. Possibly one should not seek so specific an application. The reed would seem to refer to men who are weak, whatever their nationality may be. Furthermore, these men are bruised, a word that seems to refer

11 Begrich suggests that these words may refer to legal practices (*SZD*, p. 163). Cf. *ILCH*, p. 55. Note also R. Marcus in *HTR*, Vol. 30, 1937, pp. 249-259.

to oppression (cf. the pl. *r*e*tzutzim* = *oppressed*). Just as the bruised reed cannot withstand any force that might soon break it, so weak men, broken in power and strength because of oppression they are suffering, will collapse under violent force. The servant does not destroy such weak men. Rather, he takes pity upon their low estate. His actions are in strong contrast to those of earthly conquerors.

Likewise, the smoking flax does not necessarily refer to the Jews or the Gentiles, nor does it point to the Egyptians.[12] It is a phrase parallel in force to *broken reed*, and so refers to broken men, whose hope is extinguished because of outward oppression and perhaps also because of inward disillusionment with the life of this world. The New Testament refers to such in the Beatitudes. They will not be destroyed by the servant; he will not quench them so that they no longer live.

Rather, in accordance with the demands of the truth he will bring forth judgment. This phrase strengthens the contrast with the false way of oppression and violence that characterizes human conquerors. If judgment is brought forth in accordance with the truth, it is therefore brought forth in a true manner. And it is well to note that the repetition of the phrase, *judgment he will bring forth*,[13] again emphasizes the fact that the servant will be successful in his mission. Furthermore it will be seen from this verse that violence and oppression are not justifiable means of accomplishing an end. It is the truth that conquers, and the servant acts only in accordance with the dictates of truth. What Isaiah writes is in agreement with what he had earlier penned concerning the Messiah in 11:3, 4, a commentary upon these verses.

4 In verses 2 and 3 five negative verbs described the manner of the servant's work. Two more negative verbs now continue that description. A certain gradation is discernible. In verse 2 there were three negative verbs and no mention of the completion of the servant's work. In verse 3 there are two negative verbs and a statement of the successful outcome of the servant's task. The present verse also contains two negative verbs and a statement of the completion of the servant's work, together with an additional

---

12 Cf. the discussion in *COT*, *in loc.*

13 Matt. 12:20 reads ἕως ἂν ἐκβάλῃ εἰς νῖκος τὴν κρίσιν, which is probably merely a free translation.

statement expressing the expectancy of the isles for the teaching of the servant.

The first two verbs obviously reflect upon the similar roots employed in the preceding verse, and this reflection is presented in chiastic fashion. Thus:

v. 3 *Bruised reed (ratzutz)*   *smoking (kehah)*
v. 4 *He will not grow dim (yikheh)*   *he will not be crushed (yarutz).*

The precise significance of the first verb is difficult to determine. Whether it means that the servant will not grow dim and thus weaken in his task, or that he will not faint, is of little moment. The important thing is that it expresses the magnitude of the work that lies before him as not adversely affecting him.

As in the first verb there is reflection upon the *kehah (smoking)* of verse 3, so also in the second there is a reflection upon the *ratzutz (bruised)* reed. We may probably translate, *he will not be crushed*; and this would perhaps be similar to our saying, "he will not go to pieces," until the successful completion of his mission.[14]

Implicit in both the verbs is the thought of difficulty. There is a possibility of the servant's growing weak so that he cannot fulfill his task, and also of his being broken by outside forces so that he will fail. Nevertheless, he will successfully carry through his task to its completion, namely, *he will place judgment in the earth.*[15] In this connection *earth* is not limited to Palestine, but refers to the whole earth, and thus points up the universality of the servant's work. Furthermore, the servant will actually place judgment in the earth. When he completes his work, judgment will be found in all the earth. The conversion of the heathen is not the result of one mighty, eschatological act, but of the gradual, tireless work of the servant. Hence, it may also be said that inasmuch as the servant works through his servants, they too are included here in the mysterious figure of which the chapter speaks. Twice Isaiah has used the verb *yotzi' (he will bring out)*, but now he strengthens it with *yasim (he will place).*[16]

14 There are some *Ayin-Ayin* verbs that have *u* in the imp.; cf. also *yārûn*, Prov. 29:6; *tittum*, Ezek. 24:11; and *tārutz*, Eccl. 12:6. The verb may be pointed *yĕrôtz*, although in light of the examples just given this is not necessary.

15 The future is here used of an event prior to another event in the future; cf. also Gen. 11:6; 15:4; Isa. 7:23; 53:10.

16 Even though Matt. 12:18b renders ἀπαγγελεῖ, we are not to follow Sellin, "he will announce" (*soll er kundtun*). To bring out truth is a work not applicable to any mere human being.

The last clause is construed by some as dependent upon 'ad (until), so that the force is, "until he place judgment in the earth and until the isles await his law."[17] It is better, however, to take the last clause as an additional independent statement, in which the emphasis falls upon the first word, *law*. This law refers to the servant's teaching or doctrine which the servant will give to the world. The content of this teaching is simply the Gospel itself.

For this law the isles await with yearning expectation. Probably the last verb is to be translated by the present rather than the future, and so expresses a condition existing at the time when the servant engages in his work. In His strange providence God brought it about that at the time of Christ there was present an expectation coupled with a dissatisfaction with the religion of the ancient pagan world. And yet this is not simply a waiting for something better but an actual waiting for the truth itself.[18] As an example of what is meant we may refer to the God-fearers of the book of Acts and also to Isaiah 2:1-4.

Cyrus' kingdom was to be limited in extent, and Moses' law was directed to the Israelites; the servant's law and his kingdom know no barriers of nationality and race. He places judgment in *the earth*.

5 Thus saith the God, the LORD, Creator of the heavens and the one who stretches them out, the spreader-out of the earth and its issue; the giver of breath to the people upon it and spirit to those that walk in it.

6 I the LORD have called thee in righteousness, and I hold thee fast by thy hand; and I kept thee and I give thee for a covenant of the people, for a light of the nations.

7 To open the eyes of the blind; to bring out from the prison the prisoner, from the prison house the dwellers in darkness.

8 I am the LORD, that is my name; and my glory to another I will not give, and my praise to idols.

9 The first things, behold! they have come; and new things I cause to make known, before they spring forth, I cause you to hear them.

5 The magnitude of the message is now strengthened and

[17] Thus Schmidt had commented, "*donec parat in terra iudicium et donec in lege eius exspectabant insulae.*" So also Penna; *contra*: Feldmann, Volz.

[18] Reichel, writing in 1755, mentions as an example "poor, heathen America" (*das arme heidnische Amerika*). As Alexander points out, the hope upon which the Gentiles depend for salvation is objective.

confirmed by an appeal to God the Creator.[19] One who was to place judgment in the earth must be supported by God the Creator. He who has spoken and now speaks through the prophet is *'el*, the absolutely Mighty One; God, in distinction from man.[20] He is also the Lord, Israel's covenant God. The participles are best rendered by the past, for they refer to the creation which once for all has taken place. In general the order of Genesis is followed. *Bara'* is here used only of the heavens and *raqa'* of the earth. God has created the heavens and, having created them, has stretched them out. This latter word sets things forth from the standpoint of an earth dweller. To one living upon this globe the heavens, reaching from one end of the horizon to the other, appear to be stretched out.[21] The two participles taken together simply state that the heavens owe their existence and present condition to the God who is their Creator. At the same time, the participles express not only the original act of creation but also the creative power of God as exercised in the continued existence of His works.

God also has stretched out the earth and all of its issue. The participle, based upon the same root as the word translated *expanse* or *firmament* in Genesis 1, suggests that the earth is a flat surface, spread out by God.[22] The word is poetic, and merely pictures the earth as it appears to the human eye. The word *issue* comes from the same root as *yatza'* ("to go forth"), used in the first chapter of Genesis. There it was said that the earth "caused to go forth" grass, and so here, the issue (*tze'etza'eyha*) is probably the grass that grows upon the ground.[23] The picture is that of the wide expanse of the earth covered with the greenness of grass. Like a tapestry, verdure covers the wide earth. Possibly the prophet was thinking of Palestine during the winter time, when the bare hills are covered with green.

Isaiah had remarked in 2:22 that man's breath was in his nos-

---

[19] It is important to note the close connection of vv. 1-4 with what follows, for Duhm maintained that only partly did the servant passages have a relationship with their context. Lindblom held that vv. 1-4 do go with vv. 5ff. but are divorced from their context; cf. *The Servant Songs*, p. 20.

[20] Note the perf. אמר. God's words were earlier than the prophecy that announces them.

[21] In the participle the final radical, although quiescent, is restored: *nôṭēyhem*.

[22] The root רקע means *to beat out thin*; the form is probably construct with *Pataḥ*.

[23] The conjunction *waw*, like Russian c, has the force *together with*.

trils. Now he affirms that it is from God that the peoples receive their breath, the vital principle of life without which men cannot live. The word *spirit* is more or less synonymous, and it would not be pertinent to seek any particular distinction. The word *people* points to the unity of the human race, whereas the participle *going* pictures these people pursuing their appointed courses of life.

The two prepositions are not essentially different in meaning. The people are said to be *upon* the earth and also to walk *in* it. Perhaps the latter preposition brings to emphasis the fact that the people live in the sphere of the world, and the other simply indicates that they are upon the earth's surface.

6 The speaker now identifies Himself, and places the pronoun *I* in the position of emphasis. He who speaks is the God of Israel's covenant, who, when presenting His covenant to Israel at Sinai, made known to the people the significance of His glorious Name (Ex. 3:15; 6:3). He in whose hands lies the origin, formation, and sovereign dispensation of the covenant has also called the servant through whom the bestowal of the gracious provisions of the covenant will be administered and in whom the covenant will realize its full and true embodiment.

The calling involved a selection, designation, and providential preparation for the task of being a servant.[24] A genuine selection was involved, for God rejected all others that He might designate this particular one as His servant. In the nature of the case, vocation involves election. In similar manner God had also called Cyrus (41:9).

Not arbitrarily, however, did God call the servant, but in righteousness. In the act of calling God exercised His own righteousness, and the calling was *in the sphere of righteousness*. Thus the servant's mission is rooted and grounded in God's righteousness.

What, however, is this righteousness? The root suggests conformity to a fixed norm or standard. A weight, for example, is said to be righteous (*tzedeq*) because it conforms to the standard (cf. Deut. 25:15). To act in righteousness, therefore, is to act in accordance with what is right, that is, with absolute justice. Not that there is some abstract standard of absolute justice independent of God, to which He must conform, but in and of Himself God is

---

[24] The perf. gives the general fact of the calling, the separate particulars of which are given distinctness by the following imps. each introduced by weak *waw*.

absolute justice. He acts in accordance with His will, and His will is just. The act of calling was in accord with strict righteousness, but so also are the servant's preparation and mission. In the carrying out of His mission this righteousness will manifest itself in love and salvation to those of His good pleasure, and in wrath and eternal punishment, however, to those who perish. In both instances the calling and mission are in accord with perfect righteousness.

and I hold by thine hand — i.e., "I will hold thy hand,"[25] a beautiful and tender expression which stresses the fact that the mission of the servant is one in which God will sustain him. Volz really deprives the clause of its force when he says that hand in hand with God the servant may enter his task. Rather this clause is similar in meaning to *I will hold him fast* in verse 1. Luther went to the heart of the matter when he said that God would hold the servant by the hand, "namely, for this reason, that Satan and the world with all their might and wisdom will resist thy work." The clause calls attention to the fact that the servant's task is difficult and that great obstacles will stand in the way.

and I kept thee — The Hebrew text is difficult, and possibly this is the best translation. If so, the verb refers to God's protecting the servant so that he may best be able to perform his task.[26]

and I have given thee for a covenant of the people — If the preceding phrase refers to the divine preparation, this one refers to the purpose for which the servant was appointed. To "give a person" means to "set" or "appoint" him, and the purpose for which the appointing occurs is stated in the words *a covenant of the people*. The force of the phrase is *a covenant belonging to the people*, i.e. "a covenant to (for) the people."

Who are the people? Two principal views are held. It is claimed that *people* may have the same sense as in verse 5, where it clearly is not restricted to Israel.[27] Furthermore, it is held, when *people*

---

25 Note the substitution of *Tzere* for *Ḥireq*; cf. also Ex. 19:3; Num. 22:19; 1 Sam. 14:36; 1 Kings 8:1 and 2 Chron. 5:2. The reference is to an inner, tender, personal, enduring relationship. Hattusilis uses the somewhat similar language of Ishtar: *GAŠAN-YA ḫu-u-ma-an-da-za-be šU-za ḫar-ta am-mu-uk-ma-za* (*Apology*, line 46).

26 The form ואצרך may be derived either from יצר (cf. Jer. 1:5) or from נצר. The sequence of thought would support a rendering *and I have kept thee*. B has ἐνισχύσω; 1Q *w'tzwrkh*. I understand the form as *weʾetztzorkā*.

27 Lindblom, *PIAI*, p. 400, takes the phrase *berit ʿam* to mean a confederation of peoples, holding that Israel and the converted Gentiles will form a spiritual unity. Israel will thus mediate welfare and salvation to the pagan nations.

refers to Israel alone, it is generally accompanied by the definite article; and instead of there being an antithesis between *people* and *nations*, the two words may just as well be correlative, the latter being epexegetical of the former. Between *covenant* and *light*, it is argued, there is no antithesis, for the two are practical synonyms and not mutually exclusive. Those who receive the covenant at the same time receive light, and those to whom the light comes have thereby participated in the blessings of the covenant.

On the other hand, it is claimed, and rightly, there may indeed be an antithesis between *people* and *Gentiles*.[28] In the full sense only Israel can be called a people, for it alone possesses an internal unity. The Gentiles are not regarded in the Old Testament as a people, it is argued (cf. Deut. 32:21), because they lack the real bond of unity. Furthermore, the covenant can belong only to that people "of whom are the covenants" (Rom. 9:4). Scripture knows nothing of covenants with the Gentiles. Perhaps the strongest argument in finding an antithesis between *people* and *Gentiles* is the usage the apostle Paul makes of this passage in Acts 26:17, 18. This antithesis can be present even though the words *covenant* and *light* are practically synonymous. Isaiah is not saying that the servant is to be a covenant to the Jews but a light to the Gentiles; rather, he is *covenant* and *light* both to the Jews and to the Gentiles.

The language is striking, for the servant is actually identified as a covenant. A covenant, however, in this instance is not a pact or agreement between two equal parties. From the parallel word *light* (i.e. *salvation*), we learn that it is actually a divine bestowal of grace. God sovereignly dispenses to man His blessings of salvation, and it is this sovereign dispensation that is called a covenant.

That the servant is identified with the covenant of course involves the idea of his being the one through whom the covenant is mediated, but the expression implies more. In form it is similar to our Lord's, "I am the resurrection and the life," or the phrase in 49:6, "to be my salvation."[29] To say that the servant is a covenant is to say that all the blessings of the covenant are embodied in, have their root and origin in, and are dispensed by him. At the

---

[28] Cf. *COT, in loc.*

[29] Other examples of this idiomatic usage are Ps. 45:7; 109:4; 120:7; 119:172, and possibly Num. 12:6. Cf. *MSTP*, pp. 48, 49.

same time he is himself at the center of all these blessings, and to receive them is to receive him, for without him there can be no blessings. Such language could not apply to Israel, but only to One who may truly be designated a covenant. There is thus gradation in the description of the servant. Moses was a mediator of the covenant, but the servant *is* the covenant. In New Testament terms, this means that they to whom God sovereignly bestows the grace of salvation receive the Servant Himself.

Parallel to the expression *covenant of the people* is the phrase *light of the Gentiles*. Not merely does the servant bring light or lead into light, but he is himself the light. Light is a figurative designation of salvation (49:6). The Gentiles are as yet in darkness, i.e. the bondage that sin places upon men, and from this darkness there is no deliverance until the Light of the world shines upon them.

7 This verse sets forth the purpose of the servant's appearance upon earth and indicates how the covenant will be administered.[30] The reference is not to the return from exile, but to the salvation of Jews and Gentiles, who so desperately were in need of the covenant and of the light. Here is prophesied the shining of the Light of the world upon those who walked in darkness. Here is seen the administration of the covenant of grace to those who lie in bondage. This deliverance is set forth in figurative terms.

To open the eyes of the blind[31] — The reference is not to those who are physically blind, nor even to the spiritually blind, but to the condition of blindness that is the result of sin. All sinners are blind in that they cannot see reality as it is. What they need is an opening of the eyes. Christ also spoke of Himself as the Light of the world, i.e. the bringer of light to those who are blind.

In the light of Paul's usage of this passage in Acts 26:17, 18 it would seem that the reference is universal and not to be restricted to either the Jews or the Gentiles. Christ is the Light of the *world*.

to bring out from the prison the prisoner — The need of the world is described as deliverance from prison. Man's "normal" condition is not really normal. Because of sin he is bound and not

---

[30] Grammatically, the subject of the infinitive might be God, but the context shows that it must be the servant. Apparently there is a conscious contrast with the work of Cyrus, a factor supporting the Messianic interpretation. It is the contrast of a real person with a real person.

[31] עינים is not construct, but absolute before a genitive.

free. Freedom comes only when the servant sets men free.

from the house of prison the dweller in darkness — Those who are in prison are regarded as dwelling in darkness. Light and freedom are found only when men are delivered. This is a work that they cannot of themselves perform; it must be wrought for them by the servant.

8 Again the declaration *I am the Lord,* which follows naturally after verse 7. The phrase *that is my name* means simply that God's Name is Yahweh. The certainty, expressed in verse 7, that the servant will not leave God's people in darkness, lies in the fact that God's Name is LORD. This does not mean that the Name of God is simply the vocable Yahweh, but rather that what is expressed by the word Yahweh is God's Name. In the Semitic languages the name expresses the nature of a person.[32] God is Yahweh, and when we understand what is signified by that word, we know what is the Name of God. There is obvious reflection upon the revelation of the name at Sinai. Until the time of the exodus God was known to His people as El Shaddai. At the time of the exodus, however, He gave to them a further revelation of His nature, which found expression in the word Yahweh. From a reading of Exodus 3 we learn that this word has to do with the eternity or aseity of God, and that it reveals this eternal God as the One who sovereignly chooses His people and performs for them an act of redemption.[33] This covenant name is Yahweh, who has chosen the servant. Therefore, because God is the eternal One who has entered into covenant with His people, the truth stands unchangeable that the servant in whom the Lord delights will come to bring salvation to this people and to deliver them from their bondage. Inasmuch as the Name of the Lord is Yahweh, He will not give His glory to another. The reference here is to His essential glory,

32 This point has recently been discussed by Pedersen, *Israel, Its Life and Culture,* pp. 245-259.

33 The significance of the word Yahweh is to be derived, not from etymology, but from the context of Ex. 3. The word expresses God's independence, aseity, and self-determination (this is supported by the New Testament—I AM). In the choice of Israel, God is sovereign and not determined by causes outside Himself. The form *yahweh* I cannot explain. That the *w* is due to dissimilation (Noth) is questionable. Cf. Young, "The Call of Moses," *WThJ*, May 1967. Holwerda's idea (*Dictaten I; historica revelationis Veteris Testamenti,* Part 2, Kampen, 1961, pp. 240-250), *Ik ben, ik de handelend optretende God,* is only partly correct.

which He possesses in and of Himself. Were God to give His glory to another, He would be denying Himself, negating His own nature.

Calvin adopts a slightly different view of the word *glory*. This word, he thinks, refers to the fulfillment of what God has promised. On this view, God is simply asserting that He will not turn over to another the carrying out of His promises. This is true, but it does not appear to do justice to the context. It is God who is speaking, and He will not deny Himself by refusing to do what He has promised.

The expression is striking. There is no hint that another could take the glory from the Lord; if there is to be any transfer of that glory, He will take the initiative. The situation lies entirely in His hands. Parallel is the assertion that He will not give His praise to idols. The praise belongs to Him, just as the glory is His. He alone has rightful claim upon them, and He is jealous for them. Inasmuch, however, as He is jealous, there is the assurance that He will see to it that the servant faithfully carries out His work.

Volz remarks that this verse sounds more warlike than any other in the poem. His observation is perhaps correct, for the work of the servant, carried out in quiet and love, is nevertheless one of conquest. He is to deliver those who are in bondage and dwell in darkness, the prisoners of an enemy.

SPECIAL NOTE

In this verse divine jealousy and exclusiveness are revealed. Idolatry may be tolerant of other religions, but the religion of the LORD is not tolerant. Worship and praise must be given to the LORD alone; it cannot be shared with idols. True religion possesses a divine exclusiveness. Yet, because glory and praise belong to God, He is able to carry through His work with the servant; were He to forfeit that which is His due alone, He would be as impotent as the graven images.

9 It is difficult to tell whether the speaker is the prophet or the Lord. At any rate, the reference to the former and new things is evidence that God is carrying out His purposes of deliverance with the servant. Isaiah places the phrase *The former things* first and thus gives it emphasis. These former things are probably prophecies already uttered.[34]

---

[34] Some refer it to the first victories of Cyrus, which would have taken place before the downfall of Babylon. Probably, however, if we can find any reference

If then in *The former things* there is reference to earlier prophecies, in the *new things* there is reference to the work of the servant. The new things are those which man has not yet experienced and of which he knows nothing. The prophet (for probably he is the speaker, rather than the Lord) declares these new things. They are compared to plants whose seed is still in the earth and has not yet appeared above ground. Even before the first trace of these world events could be discerned in world history, Isaiah caused his readers to hear them. Alexander is on good ground when he writes:

> The strong and beautiful expression in the last clause can only mean that the events about to be predicted were beyond the reach of human foresight, and is therefore destructive of the modern notion, that these prophecies were written after Cyrus had appeared, and at a time when the further events of his history could be foreseen by an observer of unusual sagacity. Such a prognosticator, unless he was also a deliberate deceiver could not have said of what he foresaw, that he announced it before it had begun to germinate, i.e., while the seed was in the earth, and before any outward indications of the plant could be perceived. As this embraces all the writer's prophecies, it throws the date of composition back to a period before the rise of Cyrus, and thereby helps to invalidate the arguments in favour of regarding it as contemporaneous with the Babylonish exile.

10   Sing to the LORD a new song, his praise from the end of the earth, ye who go down to the sea and its fullness, ye isles and their dwellers.

11   The desert and its cities will lift up (the voice), the courts wherein Kedar dwells; the dwellers in the Rock will shout, from the top of mountains they will cry aloud.

12   They will place to the LORD glory, and his praise among the islands they cause to make known.

---

at all it would be to the fall of Babylon and to the return to Palestine. When Isaiah composed these lines, he, living in the 8th century or in the very early 7th century, was looking ahead through the Spirit of prophecy to behold the deliverance of his people from exile. In announcing the coming of the servant he characterizes the whole future deliverance as the things to come. Now, he declares, the former things (i.e. in keeping with our interpretation of the phrase in chap. 41, the first parts of those things to come) are occurring. Thus, in dim vision the prophet sees the first approach of God to His people to set them free from captivity through Cyrus. Actually, therefore, when Isaiah declares that the former things come, they have not yet taken place; he merely sees them as taking place and so declares to his hearers. Inasmuch as these former things are taking place, he can also declare that the new things (the great salvation through the servant) will also come to pass.

13 The LORD as a mighty one goeth out, as a man of wars he stirs up zeal; he crieth, yea, he shouteth, over his enemies he prevaileth.

10 The announcement that Isaiah is declaring the coming new things even before any sign of them has appeared is warrant sufficient for the people to sing a new song. Those who hear or read these prophecies are the recipients of the command. The song is to be addressed to the LORD, who alone, in distinction from the helpless idols, can bring to pass all that He has promised. The song is new, for it is to celebrate the new things God will accomplish. A wholly new manifestation of God's power and goodness calls forth new, fitting songs. The word *new* does not necessarily indicate excellence and beauty in distinction from common and ordinary songs; and yet, because these are songs of the new economy they are songs of excellence.

What were the old songs with which the new are to be contrasted? Were they the songs of the old dispensation, which now must give place to new songs, more fitting to accompany the age of grace about to be ushered in? Not necessarily so. Were these new songs in contrast to the old songs that had been sung for idols? Again, not necessarily; there is no evidence that songs were sung to the idols. Rather, these are songs such as have never been heard upon earth; songs that are fitting to celebrate the wonders of the new age when the Servant of the Lord performs his matchless work of redemption. They are the songs of the redeemed, the songs of Zion, the songs of those who have been washed in the blood of the Lamb.

These are God-glorifying songs, and their content is found in the words *his praise,* which is the heart of worship. The phrase *from the end of the earth* means, "from one end of the earth to another." The work of the servant will affect the entire earth; a universalism will follow such as human empires could not produce and such as the world had never seen.

Those addressed are *those who go down to the sea,* by which is meant those who sail the sea. The sea is conceived as lower than the land, so those who sail the sea, in order to reach it, must descend to it.

Probably the words *and its fullness* are also ruled by the phrase *they who go down.* The thought is that men go down to the sea and also to its fullness. Their life has to do with the sea in its

125

entirety. Probably the reference is to the water of the sea and to the creatures that live therein. All of the sea with all that it contains is subject to those who sail it, and these are commanded to sing a new song to the Lord. They who sail from one land to another and thus cover the entire earth will learn that the blessings of the servant are universal and so will be in a knowing position to sing God's praise.

Lastly, the isles, places distant from Palestine, and their inhabitants, are also commanded to sing. The verse simply commands all men, everywhere, to sing the praise that belongs to the wondrous God of Israel.

11 The command continues, identifying the various classes who are to sing God's praise. Now, for the first time in all its history, the entire earth has an occasion to sing God's praise. The spread of the human ecumenical empire was no time for singing praise to God, but the servant's redemption was such a true occasion.

The wilderness and its cities are commanded to lift up the voice. As in verse 2 the object is missing, so also here.[35] The servant would not lift up his voice, but those who praise him are commanded to do so. No particular desert is intended; rather, wherever there is desert, it and its cities are to lift up the voice in praise to God. The command also includes the villages, places of no particular importance, which Kedar inhabits. Kedar is probably mentioned as representing the Bedawin, and there is no need to discover any typical meaning in it, as though it referred, for example, to the heathen world in its ethical depravity.[36]

Isaiah selects his examples from Arabia, and so appeals to those who dwell in Sela, the Rock, i.e. Petra. Possibly this is an example of one of the cities of the desert that the prophet has in mind. As befits the message they are celebrating, they are to cry aloud from the top of the mountains.[37]

---

[35] There is no need to insert קולם as Marti suggests.

[36] Hahn refers the desert to the heathen world, Kedar (*black*) to the entire heathen world and its ethical depravity, which darkens the image of God, and Sela to the hard, fruitless ground of heathendom. Reichel comments that such dwellers of the cliffs are today the inhabitants of Greenland and other wilds in America.

[37] Note that the medial *waw*, a weak letter, remains and gains strength because of the final *Ḥeth, yitz-wā-ḥû.*

12 God would not give His glory to another nor His praise to idols. Hence, those who sing His praise are to give glory to Him and make His praise known in the islands. The sentence is arranged chiastically, beginning and concluding with a verb. The verse has somewhat of a resumptive character, and brings to a conclusion the command to sing. Marti does not understand how the desert and inhabitants of the rock can praise God in the islands, hence he regards the verse as a gloss. But the summons to praise is general, and not restricted as in verse 11. Even if the subject were the desert inhabitants, there is no difficulty, for the purpose is simply to show that men are to make the praise of God known to all the creation. In placing glory to the Lord the worshippers are acknowledging that He is the true God, who alone should possess glory, and are at the same time declaring that His praise belongs to Him alone and not to idols.

13 From the effect of God's action, the prophet turns to the efficient cause. We have here the reason for the command to praise God, together with the explanation that the Lord's glory will be revealed in the redemption of God's people from judgment. Emphasis falls upon the first word, *The Lord*. As a hero or mighty one He comes forth, probably from heaven, in order to perform His work. The verb "to go forth" (*yetze'*) is probably a technical term for going forth to war (cf. 2 Sam. 11:1; Amos 5:3).

Now at last the Seed of the Woman will bruise the serpent's head; now the great battle of the ages is to take place; the times of this ignorance have passed and the fullness of time has come. God will send forth His servant to do His will in delivering His people, and this action is here represented by the prophet as a coming forth to battle. God the Warrior challenges the Evil One, and fights the fight that will save His own; and this He does through the work of the servant.[38] The language is reminiscent of 40:10, "the Lord God as a Strong One will come."

Parallel to the first clause is the second, *as a man of wars he stirs up zeal,* i.e. a jealousy for God's own honor and for the welfare of His people; as though this jealousy had long been asleep, the Lord now arouses it, by crying and shouting. The reference is not to the

---

[38] The reference is not to the victories of Cyrus, nor are the enemies merely the Babylonians. Near Eastern texts offer formal parallels to the concept of going forth to war.

proclamation of the Gospel (so Reichel), but to a cry to a holy battle. The outcome is stated clearly, for God prevails over His enemies. There is an interesting word play. The Lord comes forth as a hero *(gibbor)* and prevails *(yithgabbar)* over His enemies.[39]

14 I have long been still, (saying,) I will hold my peace, I will restrain myself. Like the travailing one I will groan, I will pant and gasp together.

15 I will lay waste mountains and hills, and all their herbage will I dry up; and I will turn streams to islands, and pools will I dry up.

16 And I shall cause the blind to walk in a way they do not know, paths they do not know will I cause them to tread; I will place darkness before them as light, and rough places for straight; these are the things that I have done, and I have not left them.

17 They are turned back, they shall be ashamed with shame, those trusting in graven images; those saying to the molten image, Ye are our gods.

14 The Lord begins His own discourse with a reveille to war. He declares that He has long been silent. The word *'olam* (eternity) does not refer to the beginning of the exile but to the whole period previous to God's sending of the servant. God has watched man form a kingdom of his own, which would include the theocracy and relegate Yahweh to a position equal with that of the idols. From the beginning God has kept silent; but the time has now arrived when He will hold His peace no longer but will declare war on faithless mankind, which has set itself in opposition to Him.

The two phrases *I will hold my peace* and *I will restrain myself* are to be introduced by the word *saying*, understood. God's keeping silence was not due to indifference, for He had expressed His intention so to do until the time for speaking arrived.[40] Thus, the two imperfects are circumstantial and not coordinate with the phrase *I have kept silence.*[41]

---

[39] Cf. S. D. Goitein in *VT*, Vol. 6, 1956, pp. 4ff. Morgenstern (*To Do and to Teach*, essays in honor of Ch. L. Pyatt, Lexington, 1953) holds that vv. 10-13 are an inserted fragment of a psalm composed between 516-485 B.C.

[40] This is the answer to Dillmann's contention that the three verbs do not describe the actions of a warlike hero.

[41] Or, to use Driver's terminology, the verbs may be described as synchronous with the preceding. Note that all the verbs except the last are asyndetic.

Before the second line of the verse we should understand a phrase such as *But now.* From eternity God has been silent, but the time for silence has now passed. "I have long enough kept My peace and been silent, but now the time has come for Me to shriek." A strong figure introduces the second line and is placed first for emphasis. As the travailing woman shrieks in pain, so will God also do, for, as Calvin justly remarks, it is only by such figures of speech that God's ardent love toward us can be expressed. The implication is that it has been difficult for God to hold His peace when He beheld wicked men forming a kingdom with the express purpose of destroying His own kingdom and bringing His purposes to naught. His own loved ones were the objects of the enemies' wrath, and yet God must constrain Himself. Yet He longs to deliver His own, and now shrieks aloud, as though unable to endure longer. The time for action has arrived.

Two further verbs strengthen the picture. God will gasp and pant, and this at once. It is as though He can no longer wait for the moment when He is to step forth into action. "Some great thing," remarks Delitzsch picturesquely, "with which Jehovah has, as it were, long been pregnant, is now about to be born."

15 God announces what he intends to do, using as a figure the complete metamorphosis of nature. Both lines are arranged in chiastic fashion, each beginning and concluding with a verb. At the end of each line occurs the phrase *I will dry up*, an example of anaphora, so characteristic of Isaiah. To lay waste mountains and hills is so to devastate them that they are changed into their opposite. The tragedy of the change appears in that the herbage will be dried up. Rivers will become islands — a strange figure, but as Torrey remarks, the poet should be allowed to make his own picture.[42] Probably the thought is that as the rivers dry up, the islands rise and appear. The water is soon gone, and the islands stand out alone; a complete reversal of nature has occurred. The pools that had been a blessing to man are dried so that they entirely lack water. Thus, the radical nature of the change is portrayed by this figure taken from nature. What must be noted is the emphasis upon the divine activity. The work to be performed is of God, not of man.

---

[42] The expression וְשַׂמְתִּי followed by לְ occurs in 28:17; 42:15; 49:11 and nowhere else (cf. Mic. 4:7, which uses the definite article before the object).

16 The picture of total, radical, all-embracing change is continued, expressed by different figures. The reference is not to a return from exile in Babylon, but, as in the preceding verse, to the majestic change that will occur when the Lord acts. It is not specifically to Israel, nor even to those who are spiritually blind. Rather, the change God will bring to pass is so entirely radical that even blind people will go on a way that they do not know.

The same thought is expressed in parallel fashion, and the first line of this verse, like the two of the preceding one, is arranged chiastically. That the blind are thus able to act contrary to their condition is due to the sovereign work of God: *I shall cause to go* and *I shall guide them.*

Those who journey are blind, and the way is dark. Hence there is a double difficulty, one both subjective and objective.[43] Nevertheless, they journey even on an unknown way, and this with unfailing certainty.[44] God has removed the darkness so that it is light, and the rough places have been smoothed out so that they are level.

In abrupt fashion the Lord declares that these are the things that He is to do, and then states simply, *I have done them,* and *I have not abandoned them.* The magnitude of what is to be accomplished is almost unbelievable, for it is a work impossible to man. So great is the work of redemption that it is represented by the figure of a complete change in nature. Yet the Lord says simply, "These are the things. I have done them and I have not given them up."[45]

17 God's work is twofold: judgment for idolaters and salvation for His own people. Verse 17 speaks of this work of judgment as already accomplished, and mentions the results of the judgment before mentioning those who are judged. *They are turned back, they are ashamed with shame.*[46] The effect of the destruction is in a backward direction, which suggests the total, utter desolation of the idolaters. Furthermore, judgment brings with it the sense of shame as men realize the folly of sin. The idolaters are described as

---

[43] In an attributive clause when it is the direct object, there may be an ellipsis of the relative.

[44] The exodus from Egypt probably serves as the background of this description. The way home from Babylon was certainly well known.

[45] B translates these verbs as futures.

[46] Note that an intransitive verb governs a cognate accusative.

those who trust in graven images and who ascribe deity to the molten images. Possibly there is reflection upon the action of Aaron in declaring that the golden calf had brought the Israelites from Egypt (Ex. 32:4).

18 Ye deaf, hear! and ye blind, look to see!
19 Who is blind but my servant? and deaf as my messenger whom I shall send? Who is blind as the one in a covenant of peace, and blind as the servant of the LORD?
20 Thou hast seen many things and wilt not hearken. To open ears, and he will not hear.
21 The LORD is willing for the sake of his righteousness; he will magnify the law and make it honorable.
22 And it is a people spoiled and plundered, ensnared in holes all of them, and in houses of confinement they are hidden. They have become a spoil; and there is none delivering; a prey, and there is none saying, Restore.

18 Isaiah now addresses the people.[47] After declaring the marvelous works of the Lord, and in particular after setting forth the effect of judgment, he now commands the people to repent. The figure of deafness applies to those who have not heard the voice of God.[48] At Sinai the nation had listened to His voice, but now it is deaf. Possibly this blindness is the result of deafness, for the Law of God, as Hahn points out, enlightens the eyes. More likely, however, both figures simply describe the lost condition of the people. Isaiah therefore addresses them as deaf and blind, and commands them to do what they are unable to do. If Israel would turn from her deafness and hear and open her eyes and see, she would be spared the judgment. Yet Israel does not have the ability to do this. If there is to be deliverance, it must be by sovereign grace alone. The infinitive with which the verse closes expresses purpose; we may render, *look for the sake of seeing.* More than a mere

---

[47] החרשׁים — the noun preceding the imperative has the value of a full clause. With the article it has the force of a vocative. Note the unusual pointing of the article in העורים.

[48] Muilenburg seeks to find a difference between this passage and Isaiah's vision in that there deafness and blindness are the judgment upon Israel, whereas here blindness is Israel's sin, and the blind are commanded to see. All men are blind and deaf; some see and hear; others do not and are punished with deeper blindness and deafness. The use of these words to express spiritual blindness is characteristic of Isaiah. Cf. *TII*, pp. 57-60. A distinction must be made between the blind and deaf and the speaker.

opening of the eyes is needed; there must be a looking to see what is to be seen.

19 Yet Israel is blind. If other peoples are blind, how much more so is Israel. The questions point out that Israel is blind above all others, and because of the intensity of her blindness will not hear the word of the Lord. By means of rhetorical questions Isaiah points out that none are as blind and deaf as that nation whom God had chosen to bring light to the Gentiles. The servant in this chapter is the Messiah as head of His body. Here, where reproach predominates, the reference is to the body. Israel cannot call the Gentiles to see if she herself is blind, nor being deaf can she cause them to hear. Furthermore, in her blindness Israel is incomparable. The first question is not, "Who is as blind as Israel?" but, *Who is blind but Israel?* The answer expected is, "No one but Israel is blind."[49] The other three questions, however, contain contrasts, such as, *and deaf as the messenger whom I send?*[50] Hence, we may assume that the purpose of the four questions is to show that Israel is more blind and deaf than any other. When compared with the blindness and deafness of God's servant, that of other nations is as nothing. The first question, however, is particularly emphatic. In comparison to Israel's blindness, no one is blind.

Unto Israel the oracles of God had been committed; she had been blessed as no other nation in that God had chosen her to be His servant. He still acknowledges the nation as *my servant*. But the people see not and so cannot perform the task of the servant. Not only do these remarkable questions clearly bring out the contrast between Israel's great mission and her inability to perform that mission, but they also show that if the task set forth in verse 1 is to be accomplished it cannot be done by Israel but only by One who truly fulfills the ideals and requirements embodied in the word "servant." The servant cannot be blind and deaf, if he is to bring judgment to the Gentiles.

The second question brings out the fact that the servant is also a messenger (cf. 44:26). The relative pronoun is omitted in Hebrew but we should translate, *my messenger whom I send.* The Hebrew

---

[49] After a question requiring a negative answer, *ki 'im* has a restrictive sense.
[50] The concepts of servant and messenger appear again in 44:26. The word *messenger* points to the servant's task. There is a strong contrast between the glorious task and the condition of the servant. Cf. also 48:1-11 and 65:1ff.

imperfect may be rendered by either the present or the future. In either case it would imply that the servant's mission has not yet been completed as it was described in 42:1-4.

The third question involves difficulty, revolving around the meaning of the word *meshullam*, which we may render *a perfected one*.[51] This word is indefinite, whereas each of the other three designations of the servant is defined. The word is used elsewhere in the Old Testament as a proper name, but that usage does not here fit the context well. We should expect an epithet similar to those found in the other three questions. It is dangerous, however, to insist upon a precise English equivalent, inasmuch as we do not really know the word's precise meaning.

Lastly, as though to revert to the first question, Isaiah again speaks of the servant's blindness. The Servant of the Lord should not be blind; Israel is blind, and therefore does not fulfill the requirements necessary for being the Lord's servant.

20 The verse alternates between *thou* and *he*, and the first question is probably addressed to Israel, the latter question likely being a general address to those beholding Israel.[52] There is thus an emphatic repetition of the thought of verse 19. Although Israel

---

[51] The form מֻשְׁלָם is a *Pual* part. singular. It is absolute, not construct, and so is to be rendered by the indefinite article. If the word is derived from the denominative שָׁלֹם it means, *one in a covenant of peace* with Yahweh. If it is derived from שָׁלֵם *to be sound, complete*, it means, *one repaid* or *requited* or *one perfected*. B reads οἱ κυριεύοντες αὐτῶν, i.e. כִּמְשְׁלִיהֶם, S ο τελειος, T ο απεσχηκως, Vulg. *nisi qui venumdatus est*. The Targum does not help. Torrey aptly calls attention to the usage of the *Pa'al* passive part. in Syr. used in the sense of the perfect. He points also to the Palestinian Syr. *me-shal-lam*, and Matt. 19:21; John 17:23, and to the Heb. Job 8:7, *šillam*. Possibly Heb. 5:9 τελειωθείς reflects upon Isa. 42:19.

The derivation from *muslim, one devoted (to Allah)*, cannot be correct, inasmuch as *muslim* is a causative participle, active, IV stem, which should be rendered in Heb. by the *Hiphil*, not the *Pual*. Vitringa: *consummatus*; Rosenmüller: *persolutus*, i.e. *pro quo persolutum est pretium emptionis*. Saadia has translated "servant of punishment" (*'abd 'aqûbah*); Luzzatto: *uomo pio*. J. L. Palache (*The Ebed-Jahweh Enigma in Pseudo-Isaiah*, Amsterdam, 1934) identified the servant with Meshullam, the elder son of Zerubbabel (1 Chron. 3:19).

[52] רָאִית — as pointed the form is evidently intended as an inf. absolute. 1Q has ראיתה, and the form should probably be pointed 2 m. s. perf.; but cf. Jouon, § 79. The verse recalls 6:9; cf. also Jer. 5:21; Ezek. 12:2 and Deut. 29:1; Matt. 13:14; John 12:40; Acts 7:51; 28:25. The language presupposes in Israel full, conscious responsibility (Penna).

133

has seen many manifestations of the power, love, and glory of her wondrous Jehovah, she does not keep these before her so as ever to be reminded of them.[53] The verse may be construed either as a statement or as a question. In either case, the meaning is essentially the same. To keep the things Israel has seen would involve preserving them in her mind so that she would observe and obey them.

Israel's ears were open, but she did not hear. What she was to hear was the high calling God had set before her. He had called Israel to be His servant and had proclaimed to her His will. She, however, did not hear; her open ears were insensitive to the voice of God.

21 Here is the conclusion to verses 18-20. God will bring His law into force and magnify it by threatening judgment over the blind and deaf people.[54] Let Israel be blind and deaf as she will, the Lord (the word is emphatic by position) intends to act. For the sake of His righteousness God will be pleased to magnify the law. The righteousness here spoken of bestows mercy according to God's good purpose.[55] Isaiah uses a direct expression, "He is pleased for the sake of His righteousness; He will magnify the law." Magnifying the law is the manifestation of the Lord's pleasure in His righteousness.

Israel's present condition stands in glaring contrast to the riches, beauty, and purity of the law of God. The word *law* should not be restricted to the Sinaitic legislation, but should include as well the teaching that God had given through the prophets. Israel's sinful and rebellious condition had despised the law, but it is God's intention to carry out His purposes. He will magnify and make honorable His law that all the world may see the honor and majesty of His truth and authority. The magnifying of the law would also and primarily consist in its being carried out and

---

[53] The manner of life of a covenant member is *keeping* the Lord's commandments. Israel does not act as a covenant nation. There had been so many experiences, so many revelations from God, but no *keeping* on Israel's part. She is unfit to be a servant.

[54] The complementary verbal idea in Heb. is subordinated to the principal verb. *The Lord was pleased that He should make the law great and glorious,* or *was pleased to make great, etc.*

[55] The word may denote here faithfulness to God's promises, which is one phase of the divine righteousness, or generally, His righteousness manifested in the putting away of sin.

obeyed. The law is not to go by default, but will be shown by God Himself to be glorious and honorable.

22 The prophet contrasts the actual condition of Israel with what God intends to do for His people. He pictures the people as plundered, like a caravan travelling across a desert place attacked by bandits. The introductory *But it* introduces the contrast and the consequences of what is stated in verse 21. Isaiah does not name the agent of the plundering, nor is the reference only to one particular action or one particular condition. The figures seem to refer to an outward condition, yet the people may be despoiled inwardly and outwardly, totally undone. Whereas the picture does fit the Babylonian exile, there is no reason to limit it to such a reference.

All of the young men have been ensnared without exception. The people have also been imprisoned or hid in houses of prison.[56] The verb lays stress upon being hidden in darkness, a symbol of the greater darkness of sin and ignorance.

From this captivity there is no one to deliver or to command the restoration of what had been seized from the people. The statements are absolute, and point out that among the people there is no deliverer.[57] Deliverance can be the work of God alone.

23 Who among you will give ear to this, will hearken and hear for the time to come?

24 Who has given Jacob for booty, and Israel to spoilers? Has not the LORD against whom we have sinned, and they were not willing to walk in his ways, and did not hearken to his law?

25 And he poured upon him wrath, his anger and the strength of war; and it set him on fire round about, and he knew not; and it burned him, and he will not lay it to heart.

23 The prophet tears aside the covering of outer misery to reveal the deep corruption underneath. His language is either a question or a wish, "O that one would!" (cf. 2 Sam. 15:4; 23:15). What he wants the nation to hear is the entire message, and not merely the content of verse 22. "Is there no one among you who will give ear to this message that I am proclaiming?" The two final

---

56 Note that both nouns in the genitival relationship are in the plural.

57 הָשֵׁב — note the *Patah* in pause for *Tzere*. The form is *hāšēḇ*, a *Hiphil* imperative.

verbs are synonyms of the first. "Who will give ear and who will hear, with the sense of paying attention to and obeying what is being said?"[58] The final word of the verse seems to point to the time that is yet to come.

24 Again the prophet employs a question to cause the nation to consider its condition. There might be wrong answers. Possibly some might have said that the gods of Babylon gave Israel to the plunderers and robbers.[59] What the people suffer, however, and what they have suffered, have been brought upon them by their own God against whom they have sinned.[60]

God is in control of all things. Upon His people He can bring times of blessing and refreshment, but also suffering and punishment. If He hands them over to the robbers, there is none that can deliver but He Himself. In this action His justice is shown. When the Canaanites had so sinned that it was better for the world for them to be removed from Palestine, God gave the land to the Israelites. Likewise, when the theocracy had become so worthless that it really no longer was a theocracy, God removed it from the land of promise. Thus He gave the people over to the robbers and spoilers. This was for the good of Israel, that through the form of a servant she might learn that God had a purpose for her in the world, and that the only deliverance she could hope for could come not from herself but from God. Through the humiliation of the outpoured wrath of God, when Israel lay in the hands of the robbers and plunderers, she must learn to cease from man and turn to God, who through His own servant would rescue Israel from her dark distress.

In the confession Isaiah unites himself with his people. He describes the transgression of the nation as sin, as refusing to walk in God's ways and not hearkening with obedience to His law.[61] It was long and persistent rebellion against the teaching of God through the written law and the instructions of the prophets.

25 Isaiah now continues and concludes the description of God's judgments and Israel's insensibility. He expresses here the thought

---

[58] The order *give ear, attend,* and *hear* is found elsewhere only in 28:23.

[59] מְשׁוּסָה, 1Q מְשׁיסה, B εἰς διαπαργήν.

[60] The demonstrative *zû* has the force of a relative, and suffers no change of gender or number — 1Q זו.

[61] *to walk* — the inf. absolute is the direct object of the verb. Note its position at the end of the clause, the phrase *in his ways* preceding. Cf. Deut. 28:56.

of verse 24a in different language. The manner of giving over to the robbers is a pouring out of God's wrath, and that wrath is further described as *his anger*.[62] The words *his anger* thus set forth more precisely the nature of the burning heat or wrath God has poured out.

Here is the true explanation of the exile. It is erroneous to assert that the Babylonians, being more powerful than Judah, were finally able to destroy Jerusalem and to take the people captive. In their own strength the Babylonians could have accomplished nothing. The time had come, however, when God must punish His elect nation. Therefore, He poured out wrath upon it, which came to concrete expression in the strength of war.

As a result of the outpoured wrath, the anger burned Israel on all sides; but Israel was unable rightly to interpret the meaning of the calamities that had come upon her. These calamities did not come by chance or accident. They were manifestations of the burning anger of the God of the covenant. The reason why Israel does not know the truth of what is happening is that she does not set her heart to consider the meaning of these events. Her thoughts are far from God and she does not look unto Him as the One who dispenses all providence. In manifold ways God had pointed out the nation's iniquity and the nature of the coming judgment, but Israel hearkened not. Now that the punishment has come, Israel does not consider it nor understand it. This chapter thus contains a mighty contrast. It begins with the servant, who will successfully discharge his work, and concludes with the nation in the condition of servitude not yet having learned its lesson. The servant obeys and carries out His task; Israel the servant hearkens not, and knows not the meaning of the day of her humiliation.

---

[62] The verb governs two nouns in apposition. The second noun is explanatory of the aspect under which the first is viewed, so defining it as to prevent any possible misunderstanding; *and he poured out upon it fury,* (namely) *his anger.*

CHAPTER FORTY-THREE

1 And now, thus saith the LORD, thy creator, O Jacob, and thy former, O Israel; Fear not, for I have redeemed thee, I have called thee by thy name; thou art mine.

2 When thou dost pass through the waters, I am with thee, and through the rivers, they will not overflow thee; when thou walkest through the fire, thou shalt not be burned, and the flame shall not kindle upon thee.

3 For I am the LORD thy God, the Holy One of Israel thy Savior. I gave Egypt as thy ransom, Cush and Seba instead of thee.

4 Since thou wast precious in my eyes, thou hast been honored, and I have loved thee; and I have given a man instead of thee, and nations instead of thy soul.

1 The introductory words *And now* form a logical rather than a temporal connection with the preceding. They present a contrast between the dismal present condition of the people and the glorious redemption they are to enjoy in their God.[1] In their deep distress their own God speaks to them, and identifies Himself as their Creator and Former. The participle *creator* suggests creation out of nothing.[2] Yahweh chose the nation at Sinai, created it out of nothing, and made of it the theocracy. When He approached Israel in covenant, it was a slave people in Egypt, not even an independent nation able to stand on its own. What Israel has become, therefore, is due to the pure grace of God alone.[3]

[1] *and now* — adversative, but cf. H. E. von Waldow (*Denn ich erlöse dich,* Neukirchen, 1960), who holds that the words indicate the change from the complaint to an answering oracle, and not a connection with the preceding.

[2] בראך — *Qal* active part. with suffix. *Aleph* retains its consonantal value; *Patah* under *Resh* is due to the following compound *Shewa*. Thus: *borē'>bore'ak̄ā>bora'ak̄ā.*

[3] Hence, I cannot agree with Penna, "*che con la schiavitu ha espiato le sue colpe.*" The exile is in no sense to be regarded as an expiation upon Israel's part.

Indeed, the participle poses a problem that cries for solution. How is one to explain the ancient nation of Israel? It did not grow of itself, and attempts so to account for it are doomed to failure. Nor did it become a theocracy merely because it thought that Yahweh had chosen it. The only explanation that satisfies is that Israel's God, who is the true God, created Israel out of nothing. Its coming into existence is so remarkable that Isaiah can employ a word used of the original creation. The word points to the complete distinctiveness of the theocracy. Israel and Jacob are the creation of God in a sense that is true of no other people. In their creation, sovereign, efficacious grace was at work.

Moreover, the nation was also formed of God, and here the prophet takes a word from the creation of man (Gen. 2:7). All the care and thought that went into the formation of the original man was also expended in bringing Israel to be a nation. Possibly the first word has more particular reference to the actual beginnings, when God called Abraham from Ur of the Chaldees,[4] and the word "formed" refers to the actual forming of the people into a nation at Sinai. Yet, despite the differing nuances of the two verbs, they may simply refer to the fact that God created Israel to be His peculiar nation. They are words of comfort, and set forth the deepest reason why the people of God cannot be destroyed.

Two names designate the people who inherit God's blessings, Jacob and Israel. Thirteen times within the compass of chapters 40–49 Isaiah uses this double designation, and with one exception (41:8), in this order. Jacob was the deceiver and had to become an Israel. Hence in this order of the names there may be a hint that the Jacob character of the nation had to be abandoned. Implied also may be the thought that in *Israel* is expressed the true destiny of the people. They are to become an Israel, and as such the heirs of the promises that had once been made to their ancestor Israel. Despite the use of the two names, however, the people are addressed in tender fashion in the singular.

Fear not.[5] Upon another occasion God had spoken the same word to His people in the person of their king, Ahaz. At that time, when, according to human understanding, salvation was im-

---

4 "God created and formed Israel, in that he chose her in Abraham (41:8)" (Dillmann).

5 North thinks that we should instead expect a command to rejoice. But the people have not yet learned that the promises will be fulfilled; they are still fearful. At the proper time they will be told to rejoice.

possible, God said, "Fear not." Isaiah now sees the people in bondage, and again God says, through him, *Fear not*. The implication is that there is nothing that should cause God's people to fear. The redemption will certainly come. At the same time, this command does not mean that the people will suffer no harm whatever. They will not be immune from suffering. But they are not to fear that things have somehow gotten out of God's control.

There is a reason for not fearing: God has redeemed His people. The expression points back to the redemption from Egypt, but its meaning is not exhausted in that event. Nor is it exhausted in the deliverance from exile. The verb implies that the people are in bondage from which by their own efforts they are not able to free themselves. That they may be set free, a price of redemption must be paid, and that by God Himself. We have adopted the position that Isaiah, toward the close of his active ministry in the latter days of the reign of Hezekiah, looked forward in the Spirit of prophecy to the time when his people, disobedient to God in that through Ahaz their representative they had rejected the promises of the Messiah and had willfully chosen the help of the power that was eventually to destroy them, would go away into physical captivity to Babylon. This physical captivity, however, from which they must be delivered if the redemptive promises of God were to be fulfilled, was but typical or expressive of the deeper captivity in which the nation found itself, a captivity not physical but spiritual. This deep bondage, manifested in the physical conditions of the exile, was no cause for fear, however, for God had paid the price to redeem and set free the people. As a sign of that deliverance there was to be the return to Palestine from exile, but the return was only a sign. The real redemption would be accomplished at a later time, when God Himself would offer up His only begotten Son. Reichel goes to the heart of the matter when he writes:

> We cannot comprehend what an inexhaustible depth this word *gealtika* (I have redeemed thee) contains within itself. . . . Redemption, redemption, redemption, that should be our creed, our theology, our distinctive character, our daily song of praise, our secret wisdom, our pearl of great price, our invaluable jewel, our one and all. . . . May we know nothing but the wounds which have redeemed us; may we look at nothing, but the blood which has saved us. May I think of nothing else, see nothing, feel, hear, love, honor nothing else than thy love and thee.[6]

[6] *Com. ad loc.*

The verb is in the perfect and yet does not refer to a past act. The redemption is yet to be accomplished. We must therefore construe the word as a perfect of certainty or a prophetic perfect. Only if the heart of this word is found in the blood of Jesus Christ can there be any meaning to the command *fear not*. If the reference be only to the exodus from Egypt or only to the deliverance from exile, there is no ground for the command not to fear. The situation in Babylon, considered merely from the physical standpoint, was not particularly oppressive. We may remember, for example, the success of the Murashû Brothers,[7] and the fact that many of the exiles preferred to remain in Babylon rather than return to Palestine. Among them even was Daniel. The later schools of Sura and Pumbeditha attest the fact that life in Babylon was not necessarily oppressive. The thought that the nation was fearing because it was in exile seems more to exist in the minds of certain critics than to be in accord with actual fact. The reason for fear was not merely that the nation was in exile but that the ancient promises made to the fathers might not be fulfilled. Hence, God reminds the nation that He has redeemed it, and as an attestation thereof makes it possible for His people to return to their own land. The heart of the word, however, is in the cross of Christ; and the exile was the first step in the restoration and the period of expectation and preparation.

I have called thee by thy name — This expression seems first to indicate the actual calling of a person by pronouncing his name. "I have called with the name Bezalel" (Ex. 31:2; 35:30). Thus, by using the names *Jacob* and *Israel*, God calls or summons the nation to be His and to serve Him. Despite König, this does yield a good sense. God has called Israel to be what the true Israel should be.[8] In 48:12 the nation is designated "my called." Thus, in this expression the idea of Israel's election is prominent.

thou art mine — The consequence of the redemption and the calling. It is pedantic to attempt to compel the two verbs (both perfects in Hebrew) to refer to actions of God that must be contemporaneous. The verb *qara'thi* (*I have called*) is to be understood as a simple perfect referring to a past event, the

---

[7] The cuneiform tablets published by Albert T. Clayle (*Business Documents of Murashû Sons of Nippur*, Philadelphia, 1898, Vols. IX, X), derive from the period 424-404 B.C. and yet are relevant to the point.

[8] Volz correctly asserts that this word designates Yahweh's whole, personal interest in His people.

manifestation of the eternal purpose of God in the election of His own people to be His peculiar possession. On the other hand, although *ga'alti* (*I have redeemed*)[9] is also a perfect, in the nature of the case it must be interpreted as above. In point of fact, God had called His people before He had redeemed them. *Ga'alti* is first mentioned because it is the one basic reason why God's people need not fear. And the redemption is sure, for those redeemed have also been called by their name. They belong to the Lord and to no other.

2 Yet the redeemed must pass through fiery trials. Addressing His people as an individual and hence using the second person singular, God assures them that they have nothing to fear. Water and fire, taken together, form a picture of every danger that could come, and include above all the water and fire of judgment (cf. Ps. 32:6; 42:7; 124:4ff.). In the days of Noah the waters overflowed the earth and God promised that never again would the earth be subjected to such a judgment. Yet the judgment to come will be as in the days of Noah when the Son of Man comes again to earth (cf. Luke 17:26). In water and fire this world will come to an end, but those whom God has redeemed will pass through such judgment in safety. At the same time, it does not seem legitimate to restrict the reference to the field of eschatology. Indeed, the introductory particle *ki* may be rendered *Whenever*,[10] and hence the verse enunciates a general truth that whenever God's redeemed must pass through the waters of sorrow and the fires of affliction they will not be harmed.

This is a general truth, and yet it may be applied to the individual believer by accommodation, for they are individual members of the entire body of the redeemed. Isaiah uses short utterances, and in two words states his message of comfort, *with thee am I*. There is chiasm in the first sentence, and a contrast between the people and God: "*thou* passest, with thee am I." In their affliction they are not alone; God is with them.

When the Egyptians were in the rivers they were overwhelmed; not so the redeemed. The rivers will not overwhelm them. Nor

---

[9] By this action of redemption the Lord renews acquisition of what was rightfully His on the basis of covenant relationship.

[10] The hypothetical particle *ki* extends its force to include the protasis of the second clause also.

142

will they be burned by the fire of judgment. Not even a flame will singe the people of God.

What is stated here is the same truth as that found in the eighth chapter of Romans. Afflictions must come and the redeemed must pass through them. They will not, however, be harmed by them, for God is present with them.

3 Isaiah carries out the thought of verse 2. There are three epithets attached to the word *I*, "For I, Yahweh thy God, the holy One of Israel, thy Savior, have given, etc." Israel's God is Yahweh, who entered into covenant with them at Sinai and delivered them from Egypt. He is again acting on their behalf. Furthermore, that they may not forget, it is again stated that the Lord is the Holy One of Israel. Finally, the Lord is the Savior of Israel. Duhm does not wish to read Christian conceptions into what he thinks is a concept derived from the Hellenistic world. The concept, however, goes back to the deliverance from Egypt. As in those days God had delivered His people, so again, from the present woes that have and will encompass them, He is the One who saves.

The word rendered *ransom* has the literal significance of *covering*. God has set Egypt as the covering for His own people. By means of substituting the nations in their stead, God procured Israel as His own. Under the Mosaic law the Israelite redeemed his own by the payment of a price, the offering of a substitute. The thought here is that instead of Israel's having been given up, three nations have been offered in its place. They are its substitutes. Quite likely the three are mentioned as representative of the heathen nations at large. The judgment that resulted in destruction fell not upon Israel but upon these nations. They became the vicarious compensation for Israel.[11]

4 The introductory words are not to be understood as "From the time when," but rather "Due to the fact that." This verse gives the reason why God has redeemed Israel. In His eyes Israel has been precious. God has placed upon that nation an esteem He did

---

[11] Perhaps the general thought is simply that in choosing Israel God passed by other nations and thus they were sacrificed (i.e. were the ransom price) in its place. To suggest that there is a reference to Cambyses' conquest of these lands (cf. Herodotus iii.15; Xenophon *Cyropaedia* viii.6.20) is to miss the point. Torrey's strong language is justified. He adduces interesting parallels from the Arabian poets.

not show to other peoples. Love involves choice and exclusion. In regarding Israel as valuable and precious, God singled them out for particular attention; and inasmuch as He so regarded them, He redeemed them. They were honored, not through works of their own or because of their own deserving, but because God so regarded them.

The last verb (*I have loved thee*) in the first line does not express the consequences of Israel's being honored but a thought correlative with the two other thoughts expressed in this half of the verse. Israel is precious in God's eyes, they are honored, and God loves them.

Hence He has given men for their ransom.[12] Whether the reference is to the three countries mentioned in the preceding verse, or whether it is a general statement of the truth that men were given for Israel's ransom, is difficult to determine. That Israel might be ransomed, and its very soul preserved alive, other nations were given up to destruction and judgment.

> 5 Fear not, for with thee am I; from the east I shall bring thy seed, and from the west will I gather thee.
> 6 I will say to the north, Give, and to the south, Withhold not; bring my sons from afar, and my daughters from the end of the earth.
> 7 Every one called by my name, and for my glory I have created him; I have formed him, yea, I have made him.

5 So great are the difficulties in which God's people are found and so unbelievably wondrous is the redemption God will perform that again He consoles and encourages them with the command, *Fear not.* The regathering of His people is a certain event, for He has sworn of an oath and will perform it. The four cardinal points are mentioned in this and the following verse to show the totality of the dispersion. The actual exile was a symbol of the separation of His people from Himself, and the first step toward the fulfillment of the promise was in the return from exile. That, however, was only a first step, and the prophecy is by no means to be restricted to this return. In a far deeper sense it is addressed to all those who are afar off, who can be brought to the true Mount Zion only by the gracious working of the Lord. Hence, there is no point

---

12 Note imp. with weak *waw*, which introduces the apodosis; the protasis consists of the three correlative thoughts.

in discussing questions such as whether Palestine is able to support all those who are regathered.[13] The reference is to the spiritual gathering of lost sinners in Jesus Christ. All God's people, scattered throughout the world, will one day be brought together, just as the historical Israel was brought back from Babylon and other lands of dispersion to Palestine.

The seed refers to the descendants, and this in itself shows that the reference is to something more than the Israel of that time. What is of supreme significance is that the gathering of God's people unto Him is His own work.[14]

6 The first word is to be read as an imperfect and not as a participle, and so to be translated, *I say,* or *I shall say.* The verse continues the description of verse 5, but amplifies it in poetic fashion. Instead of saying, "I shall bring from the north," the prophet changes his mode of expression, *I shall say to the north, Give.* It is interesting to note that the word translated "say" practically has the force of "command" which it has regularly in Arabic and other Semitic languages. In parallel fashion God commands the south, *Do not hold back.*

The imperatives are feminine, for both the four quarters and the four winds are of that gender. Some believe that the word *wind* should be understood, but that is not necessary. The commands call to mind the exodus, when as God once commanded the Pharaoh who unjustly restrained His people, so again He enjoins the four quarters, i.e. the entirety of the earth, to yield up what it cannot rightfully claim to be its own.

In the second line, as Alexander has pointed out, the imperative practically has the force of *suffer to come,* an emphasis supported by the contrast with *Keep not back.* God identifies His people here not merely as sons (as He does so often in Isaiah) but as both sons and daughters. That the reference is to more than the return from the exile is shown by the phrase *from the ends of the earth.* Both this phrase and the words *from afar* point to the great distance that has separated the people from their God.

To be noted also is the fact that according to this verse, God can command the entirety of His creation. The world in all its extent is His and must do His bidding.

[13] Cf. North, com. *in loc.*
[14] *Dagesh forte* when it appears in a final consonant is generally in a word in pause.

7 The sons and daughters are further identified as those who are called by God's Name. Underlying this expression is the thought that such have been conquered by God and belong to Him as His subjects. It is a clear identification of the ones whom He shall bring back to Himself, and it is furthermore an indication of the fact that not all who bore the name of Israelite also bore the Name of God.

The second half of the verse states the reason why God created Israel. It is for His own glory, and this phrase *for my glory* is placed first to receive the emphasis that is its due. This stands in relation to the first word of the verse, *All*, which also has the position of emphasis. Thus, two thoughts are made prominent. (1) ALL who are called by God's name will be delivered, and (2) FOR GOD'S GLORY He has brought His people into existence.[15] Three words describe the formation of the people, and inasmuch as these three words are taken from Genesis 1, it would seem that they point to an event of as great significance as the creation itself. As God once created, formed, and made the world, so now He will create, form, and make His new creation, the redeemed. Whether we are to discover a distinction in the connotation of the different words is a moot question. Delitzsch, for example, believes, and rightly, that the three synonyms bring out the might, freeness, and riches of grace; and he brings out the thought by using the Latin words, *creavi*, to produce a new thing, *formavi*, to shape what has been produced, and *perfeci*, to make perfect or complete. Isaiah is speaking of an utterly new and supernatural work, the creation from an Israel that was such in name only and hence no Israel, of an Israel that is one in deed and truth. To compare this work with the original work of creation is to stress its magnificence and importance. The verbs are in the first person singular. It is God alone who performs the wonder of a new creation, the redemption of His elect people.

> 8 Bring out a blind people and they have eyes, and deaf ones, and they have ears.
>
> 9 All the nations are gathered together, and the peoples are assembled. Who among them declares this, and causes us to hear the former things? Let them give their witnesses, that they may be justified, and let them hear and say, The truth.

[15] Lit., *and for my glory I have created him*, i.e. *whom I have created for my glory*. But cf. *Biblische Zeitschrift*, Vol. 8, 1964, No. 1, p. 106.

CHAPTER FORTY-THREE

10 Ye are my witnesses, saith the LORD, and my servant whom I
    have chosen; to the end that ye may know and that ye may
    believe me, and that ye may perceive that I am he, before me
    was not formed a god, and after me there shall not be.
11 I, I am the LORD, and there is no Savior besides me.
12 I have made known, and have saved, and have caused to hear,
    and there is no stranger among you; and ye are my witnesses,
    saith the LORD, and I am God.
13 Also from the day I am he, and there is none delivering from
    my hand; I do, and who causes it to return?

8 The first verb is treated by many writers, following the
Vulgate, as an imperative.[16] As Alexander points out, however,
the form is actually not an imperative but either a perfect or an
infinitive construct. He counts thirty-five occurrences of this form
as a perfect and thirty as an infinitive. The subject is then best
taken as the Lord, and we are to understand the verse as teaching
that the Lord has brought forth blind people that have eyes. This
fits in well with the general declaration of God's purpose of restoration made in the preceding two verses. The people mentioned
have been blind and deaf in that they have not seen the wondrous
working of God in the earth nor listened to the heavens declaring
His glory. To the truth they were blind and deaf. Now, however,
they have both eyes and ears,[17] for they now see and hear, and
willingly follow Him who has brought them forth out of the
darkness of bondage and ignorance. In the broadest sense this
passage is a prediction of the conversion of the Gentiles unto God.
The leading out, or causing to go out, is a reference to the place of
confinement in which the people had been and to the deliverance
from that place. It is the calling out of darkness into the marvelous
light of God Himself.

9 Emphasis now falls upon all the nations, that they may be
seen in contrast to what God has done. It is important to notice the
force of the first two verbs. The first verb is to be translated by the
past, not by the future and not as a jussive.[18] The verb expresses

---

16 If הוֹצִיא is an imperative (e.g., GKC, Delitzsch), the retention of the long
i is unusual, and is probably due to analogy with the perfect.

17 *and eyes* — may be a circumstantial concessive clause, *although they have
eyes.*

18 To construe this form as an imperative (Ewald, GKC) seems to me unwarrantable. Note the chiasm: subject, verb—verb, subject.

an action already accomplished, and stands in parallel to the perfect of the preceding verse, which speaks of the Lord's having brought out the people. The second verb, on the other hand, is an imperfect introduced by the weak conjunction and so is to be translated as expressing action about to take place. The first verb indicates that the nations, all of them, have been gathered together; and the second either suggests that the process of gathering is not complete or may simply strengthen the thought of the first, as though the prophet were to say, they have been gathered, indeed, they will be gathered.

Considering the entirety of the nations the prophet now asks the question, "Who among these nations will make this known, or who will cause us to hear the former things?" By the term *this* the prophet has reference, it would seem, to the gathering of the nations, i.e. to their conversion to the true God, and so to their inclusion in His Church. It is thus equivalent to the phrase *new things*, and like that phrase, stands in contrast to the concept *the former things*. "Not only can no one among them make this present gathering together of the nations known, but even events that have occurred before this they cannot cause us to hear." Both verbs are causative. Not only did no one among the nations know of these things himself but no one could cause others to hear about them.

The last line of the verse is capable of varying interpretations, but we may perhaps justifiably translate, "Let them give their witnesses that they may be justified, and let them hear and say, 'It is truth.'" The thought is that the nations are now given an opportunity to justify themselves in their past conduct. If they have any witnesses who can testify that they have declared the work of God and the former things, they may now present those witnesses, that they may be seen to be justified in their assertions. The nations in times past had ignored God and walked in the ways of their own devising. Yet the gods whom they served could not predict for them the future nor even explain to them the course of life of the nations in time past. Only the God who is now gathering the peoples together can do that. If the nations cannot produce their own witnesses, let them hear what God is saying and let them acknowledge that God's witness is true.

10 From the use of the third person the prophet turns to the second, and addresses the redeemed people. "Ye, Israel," we may paraphrase him as saying, "are my witnesses; and not only are ye my witnesses, ye are also my servants." That God has dealt graciously with the world is manifest by the history of Israel. That nation is a living testimony to the fact that the true God has sent salvation into the world, that He is strong and powerful to deliver and to save. God has chosen Israel that they might witness to Him and be His servant.

Actually, the historical Israel never fulfilled this high ideal. Never could she say, "Lo, I come to do thy will," as the true Servant, embodying all that Israel should have been, did say in truth. Note the plural *witnesses* and the singular *servant*, for the aspect of a servant actually comes to true expression in the Servant *par excellence*.

Isaiah states the purpose of the divine election in the three verbs following *that ye may*. It is best to construe these verbs with the expression *I have chosen*. The choice is to instruct Israel and give them the knowledge that their God is the true God. This is the purpose of Israel's election, and during the long centuries of their history they learned somewhat of this truth; but it was only in the work of the true Israel of God, the Servant of the Lord, that the nation came to know God as He is.

The knowledge of God is the possession only of those whom God chooses. It is a fruit of the divine election and so a gift of His free grace.

Not only is Israel to know but they are also to believe God as He has expressed Himself through the mouth of Isaiah and of other faithful prophets, and they are thus to perceive that He who speaks to them is the *I AM*, the one who is, the existing, true, actual God. The old gods of Israel's period of idolatry must go, and Israel must know that Yahweh of hosts alone is the true God. Before Him there was no true God formed, nor will there be any other after Him. The word "formed" may cast some reflection upon the fact that the idols are formed by molding. The God of Israel, however, is superior to them, for He has no beginning nor ending.[19] This profound truth is not the fruit of the speculative mind of a prophet, but is a revelation from the one eternal God. Perhaps there is some significance in the use of the word *'el* (god) instead of *'elohim*. The former refers to an actual God, and in Isaiah is

[19] In Enuma Elish the gods are created; "the gods were created within them" (1:9). Later gods replaced the earlier; Amon replaced Re, Marduk Bel, etc.

THE BOOK OF ISAIAH

used of the true God. What the prophet means to say is that no
god, no matter how great or powerful, nothing that might be
looked upon as a god, existed before the true God. "The sarcasm,"
remarks Alexander, "is rendered still more pungent by the use of
the divine name el, thus bringing into the most revolting contrast
the pretended divinity of idols and their impotence; as if he had
said, none of these almighty gods were made before I had a being."

11 As a triumphal conclusion to the truth expressed in the
preceding verse, the Lord now identifies Himself as the one true
saving God. The personal pronoun in its long form is repeated,
thus receiving stress. Attention is thus directed to God Himself as a
Person, one who identifies Himself by the personal pronoun. There
is question as to whether we should read "I, I the Lord," or "I, I
am the Lord."

At any rate, the covenant name is used with particular emphasis.
It calls to mind the eternity of God, the great I AM, who revealed
Himself to Moses at the burning bush. At the same time the
thought of salvation is immediately introduced, just as it was also
at Sinai. There the Name was revealed, but that Name, expressing
God's eternity, was connected with an act of powerful redemption
and deliverance.

The true God can explain the past and interpret the future, but
also He can manifest power in the deliverance of His people. Not
only could He predict salvation; He could also actually save.

12 Again this verse begins with the emphatic personal pronoun.
Our attention is kept upon Yahweh, the only Savior. In the preceding there has been emphasis both upon God's foreknowledge and
upon His power. Now the two concepts are combined. God has
made known; He has also saved, and He has caused the people to
hear concerning these truths.[20] When God did this there was no
strange god among the people. The word translated *stranger* refers
often to men, but here indicates that there was no strange or
foreign god present to announce or to perform the things Yahweh
has announced and performed. The word need not be taken as a
denial of the presence of idolatry, but is simply a strong way of
asserting that there is no god among the people who can do the
things their God has done.

In striking contrast to the *and I* of the first line is the *and ye*

20 The weak *waw* connects verbs that enumerate acts of like character.

introducing the second line. Israel is a witness not only to the utter impotence of the idols but also to the truthfulness of what their God has spoken. They are a witness belonging to the Lord, whom He can produce at His will.

The last words do not constitute the object of witness, as though the Lord had said, "Ye are my witnesses that I am the Lord." It is better, because more in keeping with the grammar, to render, *Ye are my witnesses, and therefore I am God.* The thought is that "ye who witness for me must witness to the truthfulness of what I have said and done, and thus, it is evident that I am God, the One who is absolutely Powerful." The word *'el* is here used to signify the almighty power of the Speaker.

13 An exegetical question revolves around the opening words. Do they mean that from this very moment God will show that He is the true God? Or, in accord with an ancient interpretation do they refer to the first day, when time began, i.e. "from when there was a day?"[21] In favor of this latter interpretation is its universality; "Over every object and in every age the power of Jehovah had been clearly proved to be supreme and absolute" (Alexander). The thought then is not that God will from this present time show Himself to be what He is, but that as long as time has existed He is God and has so manifested Himself. The latter view appears to have the most to commend it.

Two further statements are added, designed to exhibit God's power. From God's hand, none can deliver. If God takes someone in His power, then none can set him free. The second statement declares that if God does something His act cannot be frustrated. The apodosis is expressed by a question, "Who will turn it aside?" and thus redundancy of expression is avoided and force given to the statement of the argument. The obvious answer implied is that none can turn it aside.[22]

> 14 Thus saith the LORD, your Redeemer, the Holy One of Israel: For your sake I sent to Babylon and have brought down fugitives, all of them, even the Chaldeans in the ships of their shout.
> 15 I the LORD am your Holy One, the Creator of Israel, your King.
> 16 Thus saith the LORD, who giveth a way in the sea, and in mighty waters a path.

21 B ἀπ' ἀρχῆς, Vulg. *ab initio.*
22 Hebrew expresses the neuter concept by a feminine suffix.

151

17 Who bringeth out chariot and horse, force and power; together they will lie, they shall not rise; they are extinct, like a wick they are quenched.

18 Remember not former things, and the things of old do not consider.

19 Behold! I am about to make a new thing, now it will sprout, do ye not know it? Surely I shall place in the desert a way, in the wilderness streams.

20 The beast of the field will honor me, jackals and ostriches; for I have given waters in the wilderness and streams in the desert, to give drink to my people, my chosen.

21 A people that I have formed for myself, my praise they will tell.

14 This verse bristles with difficulties, particularly in the second part. It begins with an impressive introduction in which God is designated with two titles, *your Redeemer* and *the Holy One of Israel*.[23] Whereas the first appears only in the second part of the prophecy, the second characterizes the whole book, binding it together with the remembrance of the holiness of Him who called the prophet to his mission. This appearance of the titles is what might be expected, for the first part of the prophecy centers about the theme of Messiah's person, whereas in the second part His work of redemption receives prominence. *Your Redeemer* is therefore a fitting designation to appear in these chapters.[24] For this concept, however, preparation has been made; and as early as 35:9 the people are designated "the redeemed." Although a different word is used, the concept of redemption first appears in the introduction to the entire book (1:27).

The first title reflects upon the redemption from Egypt but is used here to show that God will perform the great work set forth in this verse in His character of Redeemer. Thus we come to the heart of the covenant.

That the Lord can be a redeemer and also holy is a remarkable truth, for His holiness demands the punishment of sin. When God revealed Himself to Isaiah at the inaugural call, the prophet's message was to be one of judgment. God is still the Holy One of Israel, yet He is also Israel's Redeemer. This can only be explained by the fact that in the work of the servant holiness and mercy meet

[23] These designations also serve to prevent *thus saith Yahweh* from becoming an empty formula. The combination *thus saith* plus *the Holy One of Israel* is found only in Isa. 30:12, 15; 43:14; 45:11; 48:17.

[24] In 41:14 these designations also occur side by side.

152

one another. Holiness is maintained and vindicated, yet mercy and redemption are revealed.

We shall translate the remainder of the verse literally, *For your sake I have sent to Babylon and I shall bring down the fugitives, all of them, even the Chaldeans in the ships of their shout.*[25] The verb, *I have sent*, is probably to be taken as a prophetic perfect, and if so describes an event that has not yet actually occurred. No object of the verb *send* is stated, but it is generally thought that the reference is to God's sending Cyrus to conquer the city. This reference is also possibly suggested by the phrase *for your sake*, inasmuch as in 45:4 the victories of Cyrus are said to be "for the sake of Jacob my servant." The emphasis, at any rate, is not upon Cyrus but upon the action of the Lord.

It is possible to render the next word as *fugitives*, thus construing it as a circumstantial accusative and taking *all of them* as the direct object. If the conjunction before *Chaldeans* be rendered *even*, then a positive identification of the fugitives is given. Whereas expositors differ, it does seem that the word *fugitives* is intended to designate the Babylonians themselves. Yet it is possible to take the word *fugitives* more generally, and support for this might be found in the command of 48:20. Underlying the passage is Exodus 14:5.

The last words, *in the ships of their shout*, have occasioned great difficulty. The construction is: *the ships in which they rejoiced* (the rejoicing being expressed by means of a ringing cry). These ships were the object of their exultant pride. Herodotus (i.194) describes the ships that discharge in Babylon. Evidently these were small ships that sailed the Euphrates and the Persian Gulf.[26]

15 The personal pronoun with which this verse begins takes up the thought of the preceding and shows that the One who sends and brings down is the Lord, Israel's covenant God. The shorter form of the pronoun appears, so that the emphasis is different from that in verse 11. Here it is not upon the personal pronoun, but upon the combination "I the Lord," in order that it may clearly appear that the Holy One who belongs to Israel is the Lord. Furthermore, He is Israel's Creator, and hence has the power to do

---

[25] 1Q follows M save for minor divergencies of orthography.
[26] Cf. *KAT*, p. 351, "He brought the gods, the protectors of his lands together, loaded them on ships, and set out toward the city Nagiti-Rakki." Cf. also Strabo 16.1, 9ff.

with Israel what He will. Israel therefore is not to worship idols or look to any other gods, or to be in bondage to another.[27]

16 Isaiah now points to an example of God's redemption in times past.[28] Although the participles taken by themselves may suggest continuous action, in the light of the subsequent verses it is clear that the reference is to a past deliverance. The way in the sea is the path of deliverance through the Red Sea, which this same Lord made for His people at the time of the exodus. The adjective *mighty* calls attention to the power of the waters that stood in the way of the deliverance of God's people. This deliverance forms the background for a consideration of the far greater deliverance God is to accomplish for His people through His servant. It is not a contrast between the redemption from Egypt and the deliverance from Babylon, but between the redemption from Egypt and the redemption that the servant will perform. Inasmuch as God had once done the seemingly impossible in making a path through the sea, so in the future He will deliver His people from the spiritual bondage in which they find themselves. The verse climaxes in the word *path*, which is the symbol of deliverance.

17 The first participle (lit., *He who causes to come out*) may be rendered *He who causes to perish*. The reference is to the Lord's causing the chariot and horses of Pharaoh to perish in the Red Sea. Are we, however, to render *a force and a strong one*, thus creating a parallel to *chariot and horse*, or should we render, *a strong force*, taking the word *'izzuz* in the sense of an adjective? It is difficult to determine this question, but it does not materially affect the meaning. All four words refer to the Egyptian army, which was drowned in the Red Sea. The word *together* points to the completeness of the destruction the Lord caused.

The second line describes the result of this action of the Lord's. All of these lie down and will not arise. Their lying down is permanent and from it there is no arising; it is the sleep of death. The description is strengthened by two more statements; *they are extinct*, for they have passed from the scene of human history and will appear no more, and *like flax they are quenched*. The refer-

---

[27] In view of the world situation at that time, the fact that Yahweh is Israel's King is significant. The royal functions of the covenant King in His warfare against His enemies are judgment and redemption.

[28] Verses 16-21 expand *for your sake* of v. 14.

ence is to the ease with which smoking flax is quenched. The second line begins with an imperfect but concludes with a perfect, the imperfect expressing an enduring condition, *they lie down*, and the perfect pointing to the finality of what has transpired, *they are extinct* and *they are quenched.*[29] A striking contrast also appears between the words *force* and *flax*.

18 Great indeed was the deliverance at the time of the exodus. Nevertheless, this was but a foretaste of a deliverance far greater. Therefore, the people are not to remember the exodus and to consider it as the full object of their attention. Not that they are to give no thought at all to what God has already done, but what He is about to do is so much greater that they should turn all their thought to what is yet to come.

The prophet strengthens his command by the chiastic arrangement of the verse: imperative, object; object, imperative. *First things* and *former things* are really synonyms and refer to the things that took place long ago when the people were first formed into a nation. The negatives are not expressed by *lô'*, as though to give a strict prohibition, but by the milder *'al*; hence, *Ye should not remember, etc.* Thus the prophet prepares the people's hearts and minds for a consideration of the wondrous deliverance to come. To this new thing their entire undivided attention and thought must be given.

19 By means of the introductory particle *Behold!* the Lord calls attention to Himself and what He is about to do. The wonder of the coming deliverance is that God acts. Following the introductory particle is a participle suggesting action in the future, *Behold, I am about to do, etc.* The object of the participle is the noun, *a new thing*.

In this verse the new thing is something God is about to perform, although it is described as now springing forth. In 42:9 Isaiah had made a contrast between former things and new things, and had declared that the new things had not yet sprouted forth. This verse probably represents a step in advance, in that here the new thing is already incipient. The word *now* seems to suggest that even as the Lord speaks, this new thing is coming into being.

Alexander takes the word *now* in an adversative sense, *it is yet to*

---

[29] Gesenius adduces an Ar. parallel: *he extinguished their fire.*

sprout; but it is better to take it as indicating that even now this new thing is sprouting up. The work of planting has already taken place, and now the time has come in which it is sending forth shoots. To strengthen the statement a question is asked, directing the attention of Israel to God's work.

In order properly to understand the nature of the new thing we must contrast it with the former things that God had done for His people. These former things were performed at a time when Israel was in bondage and needed deliverance. They were acts of wonder in that through them God set His people free. As the former things were pervaded with the wonderful and the miraculous so also will be the new. Yet, wondrous and filled with miracle as were the former things, they are nevertheless to be forgotten in order that the glory of the new may stand out alone. So far superior is the new to the old that the old is to be put out of mind. What then is the new thing the Lord is about to perform?

In the nature of the case, it is a work of redemption. If Isaiah in the Spirit of prophecy is speaking to the people in Babylonian bondage, it would seem that the first beginnings of the mighty redemption were taking place when the people were permitted to return to their home. In itself, however, this is not the deliverance intended, for it is not far superior to the deliverance from Egypt. In that redemption the mighty power of Yahweh over the gods of Egypt was manifested, but it is difficult to see how the return from Babylon is such a display, for the exiles returned home through the permission of Cyrus. At the same time the return from exile brought the nation into its land, where in time the promised Messiah would be born. Insofar as the return from exile marked a cessation of the period of bondage and disgrace, it may perhaps be regarded as the beginning or first stages of the new thing God would do for His people. The new thing in itself, however, is the wondrous new redemption that was wrought for His people when the promised Messiah died upon the Cross of Golgotha.

In the second line, by means of beautiful figurative language, in which he depicts a radical change in the order of nature, the prophet indicates the revolutionary character of the new thing. In the wilderness, where now men are easily lost, because there is no way of travel, God will place a way, and in the desert rivers.[30]

---

[30] With the article, *yešîmôn* refers to some part of the Judean wilderness, bordering on the Dead Sea from Pisgah, Num. 21:20; by Peor, 23:28; cf. also 1 Sam. 23:19, 24; 26:1, 3 and Num. 33:49. The word refers to a Judean, not

The wilderness will thus no longer be a wilderness, but a place easily traversed; and the desert will no longer be a desert but a fertile land of rivers.

20 The revolutionary change is all-embracing, so that the entire world is affected. This is brought out by a further contrast with the deliverance from Egypt. The miracles performed by God through the hand of Moses and Aaron resulted in death for the fish of the Nile, and in suffering and death for the beasts of the land. The new wonder, however, results in the fact that the animals give honor to God. Perhaps there is reflection upon the first chapter of Genesis, in that Isaiah mentions the beast of the field. This is a general statement, which then becomes specific in the mention of jackals and ostriches (lit., "daughters of howling").

Delitzsch points out that the redeemed are the center of humanity and humanity the center of creation. Deliverance for the redeemed brings blessing (though not redemptive nor saving blessing) to the remainder of humanity, and the sighs of all creation are turned into praise.

The animals that honor God are inhabitants of a desert region, the jackal and ostrich.[31] The desert and wilderness were symbols of the obstacles standing in the way of deliverance. They were the regions of darkness, and creatures who occupied them, subject as it were to the demonic power of darkness, now praise and honor the God of Jacob. God has performed a miracle of transformation. The land of death has become the land of life; desert and wilderness are now habitable and filled with water that gives life. Those commentators are correct who see here a sensitivity of feeling for the lower creation.

The purpose of this act of wonder is to give water to God's people, His elect.[32] In the land of death the people of God will

---

a Mesopotamian desert. 1Q reads נתיבים; cf. Orlinsky in *BASOR*, Vol. 123, 1951, pp. 33-35. B has ποταμούς, which, being the more difficult reading, is to be preferred.

[31] The mention of these animals shows that the reference is not to a literal return across a literal desert. Knobel, however, apparently thinks that literal animals are praising God in a literal desert filled with water for Israel's sake. Duhm remarks that the poet does not consider that ostriches would run out of this transformed desert as quickly as they could.

[32] In apposition the suffix may be repeated: *my people, my chosen one.*

be supplied with life, for the giving of drink is a symbol of the giving of life.

21 More than the beasts of the wilderness, Israel itself will praise God's Name. Israel is the people God formed for Himself that it might declare His praise. In the second half of the verse *my praise* occupies the position of emphasis. Israel is to recount not its own merit, but God's praises. It is His grace and love they are to declare, not their own works and achievements. Herein is stated the purpose of Israel's election; they are to be a people that will praise their God. No better commentary upon this verse can be found than that given in 1 Peter 2:9: "But ye are a chosen generation, a royal priesthood, an holy nation, a peculiar people; that ye should show forth the praises of him who hath called you out of darkness into his marvellous light."

22 And not me hast thou called, O Jacob: that thou shouldst have been weary of me, O Israel!
23 Thou hast not brought to me the sheep of thy burnt offering, and with thy sacrifices thou hast not honored me. I have not made thee serve with oblation, and I have not wearied thee with incense.
24 Thou hast not brought me sweet cane with silver, and with the fat of thy sacrifices thou hast not drenched me; thou hast only made me serve with thy sins and wearied me with thine iniquities.
25 I, even I, am he that blotteth out thy transgressions for mine own sake, and will not remember thy sins.
26 Cause me to remember; let us plead together: state (thy case) that thou mayest be justified.
27 Thy first father sinned, and thy interpreters rebelled against me.
28 And I will profane thy holy chiefs, and will give up Jacob to the curse and Israel to reproaches.

22 Seven times in verses 22-24 Isaiah employs the negative *not,* and two of these are with the conjunction, *and not.* A climactic negative follows in verse 25, "and thy sins I will not remember." The most emphatic thought of these verses is negative, and thus by pointing out what the truth is not, the prophet enables one the more clearly to discern what it is.

After the first negative occurs the emphatic word *me.* It is what Israel has not done to the Lord that forms the action expressed by the first verb. Two principal interpretations are advanced. Gener ally it is assumed that the verb *qara'* in this verse refers to prayer or invocation of God's Name. The thought is then that Israel has not looked to God in prayer but to other gods. Penna, for example, asserts that the nation has shown signs of disgust for prayer. On this interpretation the action of the verb is one of worship, and in particular that of prayer. According to Delitzsch the law did not permit the bringing of sacrifices outside the holy land. This implies that the nation was actually in Babylon, and hence should have called upon God in prayer at least, even though not permitted to offer sacrifices.

Another view is also possible, which in the light of the context yields an excellent sense. This interpretation takes up the thought just expressed in the last words of verse 21 (*my chosen*) and refers the verb *qara'* to the fact of calling or election. The thought then is that Israel did not call God, but rather the reverse, God called Israel. This removes every vestige of boasting in which the nation might trust. Her very existence is due to God's sovereign choice, and not to her own will. The same thought is later expressed by Christ, "Ye have not chosen me, but I have chosen you, etc." (John 15:16a).

The second member of the verse is explanatory of the first, "It is not that thou, O Jacob, didst call me, for so far art thou from having called me that instead, thou wert wearied with me." The same view of the second member would obtain even if the first view mentioned above should be adopted. To paraphrase, "Thou hast not called me in prayer, for thou hast instead wearied of me." Between the two positions above presented it is difficult to make a positive choice, although perhaps the second view, because of the context, has more in its favor. Inasmuch as we have rendered the conjunction *ki* by *for*, it is necessary to take the verb *yaga'* in the sense either of *labor* or *toil*, and not merely *to seek for*. Each member of the verse concludes with an address to the nation, designated both as Jacob and Israel.

23 This verse continues the thought expressed in verse 22, either, "You have not called My Name in prayer, nor have you brought to Me the sacrifices you should have brought," or, if the second interpretation suggested be adopted, "You have not called Me, but I have called you; neither have you honored me with the sacrifices you have brought."

The passage does not teach that Yahweh had never commanded

sacrifices, or that they were of priestly and not of divine origin.
Hence, to reason as Volz does here, that the people could sacrifice
all they wished, yet they would not be honoring the Lord, for He
had not commanded the sacrifices, is to go beyond the text. The
true meaning, rather, is that the people did not honor God in the
manner in which they brought their sacrifices. Although the nation
did bring sacrifice (compare what Isaiah earlier says on this question, 1:10ff.) it did so in such a way as not to honor Yahweh, its
God. In reality, therefore, it did not bring sacrifice to God.

The first verb, *Thou hast not brought to me*, is not a categorical
denial that sacrifices were brought, but in the light of the other
verbs must mean that there was no true bringing of the sheep of
burnt offerings to the Lord. "What you brought," we may paraphrase, "was a sham offering and not the real thing. The sheep of
your burnt offering, which should have been devoted to me with a
whole and pure heart, you did not bring."[33] Parallel to the first
verb, *Thou didst not bring*, is the second, *thou didst not honor
me*,[34] which expresses the fact that in the worship of Israel God
received no honor. The phrase *I have not made thee to serve*[35]
does not mean that God had not required sacrifice, but simply that
God had not imposed sacrifice as a wearisome burden of no profit.
Lastly, *I have not caused to weary thee* brings out the same truth,
that God has not wearied or exhausted the nation with His requirements for offerings. Thus, the entirety of the sacrificial system
was not intended to be a burden of no profit, but rather a joyful
offering of sacrifices in which the offerer would approach the Lord
with a willing heart. Such, however, was not the service that Israel
rendered.

There is nothing in the language that would point to one
particular period alone as the time of fulfillment. The verse does
not well fit in with the time of the exile. Rather, it is a general

33 By the mention of some of the principal offerings the whole Mosaic
ritual is represented. עולה — general offering for expiation; זבחים — animal
sacrifices generally; מנחה — meal offering; also a general term for offering;
לבונה — an offering of aroma. שׂה — includes goats and sheep. The word is
construct and so must represent *say*; cf. Ar. *šā'ah*; Akk. *šu-'u*; Egy. *sau*; Ug.
š, a head of small cattle — a sheep or goat.

34 *thy offerings* — I do not take this as a double acc. (cf. *HS*, § 94b) but as
an acc. of specification.

35 Note the pointing of this same verb in Jer. 17:4. The shift from
Ḥaṭeph-Segol to Ḥaṭeph-Pataḥ often occurs in the *Hiphil* perf. with *waw*
consecutive. The shift may be due to the throwing forward of the accent.

statement of Israel's history. There is nothing in the way they approached their God in worship that would lead to any claim of merit upon their part.

The construction of the verse is noteworthy. In the first line there is a chiastic arrangement: negative, verb, object; object, negative, verb. In the second line there are two negative verbs in the *Hiphil* stem, with a suffix of the second masculine singular followed by a prepositional phrase. These two constructions are parallel one to another and form a striking contrast to the chiastic arrangement of the first line.

24 A further example of what should have been brought is mentioned, namely, sweet cane, used in the preparation of incense. There is a play upon the words *sweet cane (qaneh)* and the verb, *Thou hast not brought (qanitha)*.[36] Commentators mention the remark of Jarchi to the effect that this sweet cane was a common product of Palestine and hence did not have to be bought. Others, however, such as Kimchi, think that the cane was exotic. The mention of this particular item in the sacrifice, as is really also the case with the other items previously mentioned, shows that such things had been required by God. What would be the point in complaining that the people had not brought the sweet cane, if the incense or ointment in whose preparation it was required had not been enjoined by the Lord?

Furthermore, the fat pieces that came upon the altar in the peace offerings had not *drenched* the Lord. This strange expression simply means that the nation had not brought cheer to the Lord by means of the abundance of its offerings.

In the last line the prophet presents the true state of the case. God has not burdened Israel with demands for sacrifice; on the other hand Israel has burdened the Lord with their iniquity. The great contrast is introduced by the important particle *'ak* (surely). Israel's sins have made Yahweh to serve, by imposing upon Him a heavy burden. Their iniquities have wearied him. Thus the position is reversed. It is not Israel who has been burdened, but Yahweh, Israel's God. Hence, Israel has been a burden to Him (cf. 1:14).

---

36 קנה — *acorus calamus*, an aromatic plant of India and Arabia. Cf. Pliny *Natural History* xii.104-106. Cf. Jer. 6:20; Ex. 30:23. Gesenius identifies it with Ar. *ḏarîrah*. B οὐδὲ ἐκτήσω μοι ἀργυρίου θυμίαμα, Aq T S κάλαμον.

25 If the people, instead of calling God and worshipping Him as they should, have rather wearied Him with their false worship, and He then shows mercy, it must be of His unmerited grace alone. The only possible conclusion to which one can come is that the deliverance is the work of God and in no sense that of the people themselves. Hence, the prophet again introduces the Lord as speaking, with the repetition of the first person pronoun. This double occurrence of the pronoun is further strengthened by the third person pronoun, so that the emphasis is upon God alone as the One who blots out transgressions.

The debt man's transgressions incur is written down in God's book, and must be punished. God, however, blots out or wipes out what is written down, so that it can no longer be seen and no longer is present to accuse the transgressor. Whereas this present verse does not state the method God employs in blotting out transgressions, the context makes clear by its condemnation of the nation's sins that this blotting out was not done at the expense of justice and honor. The debt those transgressions incurred has been fully paid, and God's blotting out is an act of justice and mercy. It is mercy, for He does it of His own good pleasure; and it is just, for the debt has been paid. From later revelation we learn that this debt was paid by the Servant of the Lord, whose vicarious sacrifice rendered satisfaction to God's justice upon the basis of which He might pardon our transgressions.

There is strong emphasis in the phrase *for my own sake*, which excludes all reliance upon human merit.[37] There is a vivid contrast between *thy* transgressions, and for *my* own sake.

The verse concludes with an additional statement, *and as for thy sins, I will not remember them.*[38] As the transgressions have been blotted out, so they can no longer be seen. It may be that the word *sins* includes both the rebellious act itself and the punishment thereof, but at least it is primarily the rebellious act that is in view. "The things that you have done contrary to My law, I will not call to mind."

26 Taking up the last word of verse 25, the Lord uses it again as an imperative. "I will not remember" (*lo' 'ezkor*) becomes *Cause to remember* (*hazkireni*). The command is uttered in a tone of irony, and Israel is thus given the opportunity of bringing

37 Cf. Ps. 115:1, 2; Dan. 9:17.
38 Cf. Pedersen, *Israel*, I/II, 106ff.

before the Lord any works of merit they may possess. "If," so the thought goes, "there is any merit upon your part which I have forgotten and overlooked, cause Me now to remember it. Bring it before Me and refute the charge which I am about to make (v. 17), or which I have already made (vv. 22-24)."

If they can cause God to remember any merit upon their part, they are to judge with Him, i.e. submit to a trial in which the case may be considered. The last verb does not mean that they might be justified before God as righteous, but that they may be justified in the claim they make for themselves and in their attitude and actions. The challenge is a strong way of emphasizing that the Israelites are without merit and have no justification for their conduct. It would then seem to be implied that if the Israelites cannot justify themselves they should submit to the righteousness of God so freely offered to them when He blots out their transgressions.

27 Israel cannot meet the challenge God throws down to them. Even this command of His they will disobey; for they dare not stand before Him in judgment. They have no merit whatever; instead, from the very first they have been a sinning and transgressing nation. The phrase *Thy first father* points to the one who is the father of the nation, from whom the nation is descended. Who this first father is, however, is difficult to determine. Depending upon how we construe the concept of first father, the individual might be Adam or Abraham or Jacob. The reference may be to Abraham, who was a friend of God and loved of Him, and yet also was a sinner. It may truly be said that the people were descended from him.

The important point is that the first father of the present nation was a sinful man and hence not one who could justify himself before God. This was also the case with those who followed him, the interpreters who acted as intermediaries between God and the nation. The word evidently refers to all such mediators, namely, prophets, priests, and kings, all who would in some way bring the message of God to the people and instruct it in the way it should go. Like the first father, these also had transgressed against God. The entire nation was rebellious and so had no claim whatever to merit that it might plead before Him.

28 The interpreters[39] are now called holy princes,[40] and these God will profane,[41] rendering them the opposite of what they are; no longer will they be officers of the theocracy but secular individuals incapable of performing the tasks of the theocracy. Hence the calamities that are to come upon the nation.

As for Israel it is to be given to the ban, devoted to destruction. It will no longer be the people of God, the light of the world, but a nation set aside for destruction. Jacob will simply become reproaches, which explains the strokes to fall upon the people. If Israel is the elect nation, why do such calamities befall it? The answer is that Israel acted as a nonelect people. Hence, the nation must perish. Nevertheless, there would be deliverance and salvation; but these would be of God's grace alone and in no sense of Israel's merit, for they had none. They were wholly abandoned to depravity.

[39] The singular probably rules out a collectivistic interpretation. *thy interpreters* — intermediaries between God and man; cf. Job 33:23; 2 Chron. 32:21 and Gen. 43:23; B οἱ ἄρχοντες; Vulg. *interpretes tui*.

[40] *princes* — indicates the high position of the officers.

[41] *and I shall profane* — as it stands the form is imp. with weak *waw*; the reference therefore is to the future or possibly the present.

CHAPTER FORTY-FOUR

1 And now, hear! O Jacob, my servant, and Israel whom I have chosen.

2 Thus saith the LORD, thy Maker, and the One who formed thee from the womb, He will help thee; Fear not, my servant Jacob and Jeshurun whom I have chosen.

3 For I shall pour waters upon the thirsty and flowing (waters) upon the dry ground, I shall pour my Spirit upon thy seed and my blessing upon thy issue.

4 And they shall spring up in the midst of the grass, as willows upon the streams of waters.

5 This one shall say, "To the LORD I belong," and this will call by the name of Jacob; and this will write his hand, To the LORD, and with the name of Israel will he entitle.

1 The introductory *And now* brings to the fore the sharp contrast between the threats of the preceding verse and the promises to follow in verses 3-5. The connection, therefore, is logical and not temporal. Even though punishment must come, Israel is to hear the message God proclaims. The designations Jacob, Israel, servant, and elect have already occurred; but this in no sense detracts from the profundity and beauty of their significance. Israel is God's servant, and Jacob has been chosen to be a servant. The reference is not to eternal election of individuals but rather to the choice of God's people to be separate from the world and to become His servant.

2 This verse presents the other side of the transition. The Lord utters a message in which the true nature and destiny of Israel will be set forth. On the whole the verse is similar to 43:1, but the addition of the phrase *from the womb* carries us a step further. Jeremiah (1:5) evidently reflected upon this verse. Yahweh Himself, the God of Israel, is here set forth in terms that portray His almighty power. There is no question but that He is the God of creation. In speaking of Him as the Creator of Israel, Isaiah refers not to creation as such but to the act whereby God brought a band of slaves from Egyptian bondage into the wilderness and made of them His own peculiar people. In this act there is also the tenderness of a mother, for Yahweh formed the nation from the womb. The two words are participles, *thy maker* and *thy former from the womb*. *From the womb* is to be construed with what precedes and not with what follows, as is clearly indicated by the Masoretic accentuation.

It would seem that the reference is to the prenatal period (cf. Job 3:11; Jer. 20:17). Even before Israel was born, God was forming her. Translated into history, this would refer to all the period before the actual constitution of Israel as a nation. It would include the time of bondage in Egypt and also the period of the patriarchs.

The two participles are followed by a verb in the imperfect, which is to be translated by the future. Hence we are to render, "Thy Maker, thy Former — He will help thee."[1] That He is the Creator is the guarantee that He will preserve His work and continue it in life.

There is good reason then why Israel is not to fear. The reference is not specific, as though it were a command not to fear the dangers on the march home from Babylon. Rather, the prohibition is general. No matter what the obstacles in the path of Israel, she is God's servant and therefore is not to fear.

The latter clause of the second line is similar in construction to the latter clause of verse 1, save that in place of Israel the word Jeshurun is used. This form occurs only here and in Deuteronomy 32:15; 33:5, 26. It is difficult to know precisely its significance, but it may quite well be an honorific title, designed to suggest that Israel is right or straight in contrast to the root on which the word Jacob is built, which means overreacher or deceiver. The fact that Yahweh has chosen Israel is sufficient ground for the exhortation, *Fear not*.

3 The Lord gives a further reason why His people should not fear, namely, He will change the situation in which they find themselves. By means of the figure of water in a waste and dry land He indicates the spiritual blessings to come. Stress falls upon the divine activity. Salvation by grace stands out in this verse. The

---

1 Note the pausal suffix with *Dagesh forte*.

word *thirsty* is masculine, and probably refers to an individual rather than to a thirsty land. Upon dry land (the article is omitted) God will pour out flowing waters (lit., *descenders*). Marti's view that the figures denote the exile is without warrant. They simply designate the spiritual blessings that God intends to bring to His people.

This is substantiated by means of a gradation. From pouring out water, the text goes on to speak of the pouring out of the Spirit, by which is meant the divine power that creates and gives life. The seed of Jacob, languishing in its condition of spiritual bondage, will come to life because of God's action in the pouring out of His Spirit.

Parallel to the *Spirit* is the *blessing*, which God will pour out upon the issue of Jacob and Israel. Hence the cry, "Fear not."

These verses contain some definite Isaianic traits. The expression Creator[2] used of God as the Creator of His people is found only in Isaiah, as also the parallels *Maker* and *Former*.[3] Likewise the word *offspring* is characteristic of Isaiah,[4] as is also the usage of the word *thirsty* as a noun and not an adjective.[5]

4 As a result of the divine effusion mentioned in verse 3, a rich and luxuriant blessing, figuratively pictured as an abundant growth of grass and trees, will come upon the people. The introductory verb may express result, although justice is done to it if it is rendered as a simple future. It then adequately expresses the effect of the divine outpouring just mentioned.

If the following words are taken as they stand they are to be translated, *in the midst of the grass*. This is certainly preferable to the emendations proposed, and should not be summarily rejected. Possibly, however, the word *ben* designates a particular type of tree, perhaps a species of the moringa, distinguished by the greenness of its leaves.[6] This furnishes a suitable parallel with the mention of the willows in the second half of the verse, although it involves other difficulties. If this interpretation is correct, the word

---

2 I.e. יצר.

3 Cf. 22:11; 27:11; 44:2. In each case the word has a suffix.

4 Cf. 22:24; 34:1; 42:5; 44:3; 48·19; 61:9; 65:23.

5 Cf. 21:14; 29:8; 32:6; 44:3; 55:1. For its use as an adjective cf. 2 Sam. 17:29; Prov. 25:21.

6 Possibly the *populus euphratica*, although not necessarily so. Cf. *ZAW*, Vol. 63, 1951, pp. 154-56, and Vol. 64, 1952, pp. 249-251.

hatzir (*grass*) must serve as an adjective. The tree of grass would then be a verdant tree.

In the second half of the verse the reference is probably to a kind of poplar, which is pictured as growing abundantly and luxuriously because planted along the channels of water. All circumstances seem to preclude the growth of plants, so that when they do grow they are like a "root out of a dry ground"; but when the tree is planted along a course of water it springs up richly. When in inexhaustible fullness the grace of God flows continually to His people, they will grow powerfully in the uninterrupted enjoyment of that grace.

5 When once again God's people flourish prosperously, men one by one will proclaim that they belong to the Lord. The threefold use of *zeh* (*this*) brings to the fore the fact that the reference here is to individuals and not to a mass confession of the Lord. It would seem that the prophet is speaking of the heathen, and if so, the passage teaches that as a result of the renewal of the Israelites even the heathen, one by one, will begin to align themselves with the Lord.

In the statement, *"To the Lord am I,"* Lord is placed in a position of emphasis. It is a true confession in that it brings to the fore the Lord and not the confessor. The second statement may be rendered either, *this will call on the name,* or *this will call by the name.* One will call using the name of Jacob and so engage in the praise of the God of Jacob. As Delitzsch remarks, he makes "Jacob the medium and object of solemn exclamation." Thus to identify oneself with Jacob is to identify oneself with Jacob's God.

We may translate the third sentence literally, *and this will write his hand to the Lord.* It has been suggested that the reference is to tattooing or to the inscribing upon the hand of some sign or mark. In ancient times slaves, soldiers, and other dependents were marked with the name of their owner. Such a practice, however, would seem to be precluded by Leviticus 19:28; and in the light of this prohibition it would indeed be strange if the prophet were to mention such a forbidden practice as a characteristic of the age of blessing to come. Nor would it seem likely that this phrase refers to the binding of written passages upon the hand. Usually the language is taken to mean to write with the hand, but as North asks, With what else would one write? Nor does the meaning *to write upon the hand* satisfy. Possibly the literal force of the words should be retained, *to write the hand,* that is, *to write.* North cites a parallel in the phrase, *witness the hand,* and so the whole is simply a way of saying *to write.* By words of mouth and also by writing men confess that they belong to the Lord. To write the phrase, "To the Lord," is to write a sign of ownership, just as to say, "To the Lord am I." Thus, by all modes of expression, men will assert that they are the Lord's.[7]

With the last clause also there is difficulty. The root of the verb (*kanah*) is related to the Arabic root that comes to expression in the noun *kunya,* a word referring to the surname whereby a man, after the birth of his son, designates himself. Thus, Abu-Bekr, i.e. the Father of Bekr. Whether the Hebrew root actually has this force or not is questionable, but it may mean that a man will use the name Israel as a title of honor. To entitle oneself an Israelite will be to give oneself a title of honor, for the Israelite is the one who knows the Lord.

> 6 Thus saith the LORD, the King of Israel, and his Redeemer, the LORD of hosts, I am the first and I am the last, and apart from me there is no God.
> 7 And who like me will call and make it known and will state it to me, since my placing the ancient people, and coming things and those which will come they will make known to them?
> 8 Tremble not and fear not, have I not since then let thee hear and told thee, and are ye not my witnesses? Is there a God without me? And there is no Rock, I know none.

6 This verse serves the double purpose of identifying the God whom the individuals acknowledge and of preparing the way for the challenge to the idols. In his inaugural vision the prophet had spoken of Yahweh as *the* King as though to suggest that king Uzziah was not the real king of Israel. And Gideon had made it plain that the Lord was to rule over the people (cf. also 1 Sam. 8:7 and 1 Kings 22:19). The theocratic ruler was merely a representative or vicegerent of the true *King of Israel,* the Lord of hosts. The Lord is not only King but also Israel's *Redeemer,* and by His acts of redemption has shown that He alone is deserving of being King. Redemption probably refers to the general fact that Yahweh is a

---

7 Penna appeals to Hammurabi, Laws 226, 227. Cf. Paul's expression in Gal. 6:17; Seneca *De ira* ii.3.6; Quintilian *Institutio oratoria* vii.4.14. I am grateful to Penna for these examples.

redeemer, but it would seem that there was particular emphasis upon the great act of redemption when this same God brought His people out of the bondage of Egypt. He is also the *Lord of hosts*, and in this connection the expression would seem to point to His divine essence. The word "hosts" includes all within the sphere of creation, and Yahweh is the Lord of all. Whatever there be in heaven and earth He is its creator and He its ruler, and to Him it must do service. Thus God's omnipotence, eternity, and unity are proclaimed.[8]

He is the first in that He is before all creation as well as in the beginning of human history, but He is also the last in that He is above human history. The two expressions are designed to show His eternity and His complete independence of the creation. Before human history began He is, and when it shall finish, He is, the unending, eternal, and true God. All the gods of the nations are but idols, those that are called gods (1 Cor. 8:5); but these possess no independent existence.

7 To show that the Lord alone is God, the gods are challenged to stand in contest with Him. The introductory words, *And who like me will call?* are equivalent to saying, "If there is anyone like me, let him call, etc." The verb *yiqra'* (*will call*) refers to the announcement or proclamation of the prophecy. Others may proclaim, but they cannot prophesy with respect to the future nor can they tell the course of history. Nor can they "make known," in the sense of explaining in advance or setting forth in advance the course of things to come. Nor can they prepare and arrange their case so as to set it forth. The root *'arak* is really forensic, and refers to the setting forth or exposition of a case.[9] The gods cannot present their case in order before the true God.

We should construe *from my placing* with *like me* and thus obtain the sense, "Who like me can call as I have done since I have placed, etc." The people of eternity are people of very ancient times. The prophet takes us back to their first beginnings. The proclamations of the Lord and His remarkable prophecies reach back to Paradise, when the first man existed.

The *coming things* point to the future, possibly, as Delitzsch suggests, to the absolute future; and *those which will come* may

---

[8] 1Q inserts שמו.

[9] The verb possibly suggests the legal emphasis Isaiah often uses in his contest with the idols. Note the simple in place of compound *Shewa*.

refer to things soon to come to pass. If the gods can tell both the near and the remote future, let them make it known to Yahweh, the true God. This is the challenge.

8 Inasmuch as God is the first and the last and there is no God beside Him, the people are enjoined not to fear.[10] The prohibition is plural and the explanation in the singular. This interchange of number, however, shows that Israel is treated as a singular individual. The object of fear is not stated, but it would seem to be whatever obstacles might arise to destroy the nation's confidence in its God.

By means of a question the truth is borne home that since that time (probably the time of the founding of the people) God has caused it to hear that He is the only God. Perhaps there is little distinction in meaning between the two verbs, one referring to the fact of God's causing the people to hear and the other pointing out that he has caused to tell them the truth. They have heard the truth so that they know it. Both verbs stress the divine activity.[11]

On their part the people are God's witnesses. In all their life and thought they constitute a witness that beside the God of Israel, Yahweh, there is no other God. By another question Israel is caused to discern that to which they are to witness. The last clause is not to be taken as a relative but as an independent statement, *I know not any*. The God of Israel is a Rock, and this forceful figure emphasizes that Yahweh is the unchangeable support and refuge of His own.[12]

> 9 The formers of images, all of them are unreality and their delights do not profit; and their witnesses themselves will not see and will not know that they may be ashamed.

10 *tirehû* — as it stands the form is from *rhh*, occurring only here. 1Q reads *tyr'w*, which is probably correct, and seems to be supported by the *Hireq* (a defectively written naturally long vowel?) in a distant open syllable.

11 The weak *waw* before the preterite introduces an equivalent expression. Cf. *Biblische Zeitschrift*, Vol. 8, No. 1, 1964, p. 105, for *we'ên*.

12 North aptly points out that *tzûr* as a designation of God occurs often with *sela'* (crag) or *miśgāb* (inaccessible height) or *metzûdāh* (fastness), features of Palestine but not of Mesopotamia. Hence, North thinks that the epithet did not originate with "Second" Isaiah. But does not this epithet here point to Palestine rather than Mesopotamia as the place of composition of these chapters? הַמֵּה — M has marked this word with the *punctum extraordinarium*, possibly to explain that it forms dittography with the preceding. In 1Q it is written in small letters above the line. If it be retained, it is emphatic.

10 Who hath formed a god and cast an image, that it does not profit?

11 Lo! all his comrades will be ashamed, and the workers themselves are of men; they shall assemble all of them, they shall stand, they shall tremble, they shall be ashamed together.

9 As further evidence that there is but one God and that there is no reason to fear, the prophet calls attention to the folly of idolatry. Those who have apostatized from God have sought to pull Him down to the level of the creature and to honor Him by means of images their own hands have fashioned. They are *tohu*, a word used in Genesis 1:2 to describe the waste and uninhabitable earth. Here the word stands as a parallel to *they do not profit*, and suggests an absence of all life and power. Like the idols their hands make, they themselves are vain and void, filled with nothingness.

The desired or favorite things are the unprofitable idols themselves. Like their makers, they too are nothingness. The God of Israel is a Rock who abides and in whom His followers may find refuge and safety. The idols, on the other hand, have nothing to offer their worshippers, for they themselves are nothing.

As for the witnesses of the idols, the idolaters, they do *not see* and they do *not know* so that they may be ashamed. The object of the two verbs is not expressed, but it would seem to be the fact that the idols are not profitable. This obvious fact is not perceived by the idolaters, so steeped are they in folly and the darkness of misunderstanding. Their will is perverse, and they engage in blindness in order *that they may be ashamed*. This last clause shows that the sinners are not innocent. The worshippers of idols are not free of guilt, but they purposely follow idolatry with a depraved will; and they are permitted to remain in the darkness of ignorance that their shame may be seen.

10 Some commentators interpret the introductory word *Who* as an indefinite pronoun, *Whoever*, or *Whosoever*. On this construction we must connect the thought with the preceding and assume that the verse is a development of 9a. "Those who make images produce that which is of no profit (v. 9a), ... whosoever forms a god, etc." It is probably better, however, to construe the word in its normal sense as an interrogative pronoun and to find in the subsequent verses the answer to the question raised in this verse.

"Who forms a god?" the prophet asks, choosing a word that sets forth the distinction between God and man, and thus engaging in forceful sarcasm. Perhaps there is reflection upon the language of Genesis in which it is said that God formed man, dust from the ground. The very asking of the question points to its utter folly. "A man form God?" — the conception is ridiculous, and yet in these words there is the heart of idolatry. In the second question Isaiah points out how man must form a god, namely, by the pouring out of an image. It is an act involving time and labor and forms quite a contrast to the ease with which the Lord God formed man, dust from the ground.

The prophet concludes with a strange statement, for he seems to suggest that the purpose of making idols was that they might be of no use. The language expresses purpose or intent, as though the result described had actually been the intention of the idolater. Idols cannot deliver from the punitive wrath of the true God that will be poured out upon the people and the makers of images.

11 Isaiah now points out what result there will be from the fact that idol manufacture is of no profit.[13] *Companions* would be those who are in one way or another associated with the idol, but in what sense is this to be understood?[14] Some seem to find the reference in the associates of the maker of the idol. Conceivably these might be members of a guild or class that made idols, but if they are so to be understood they are associates of the idol and not of its maker. It has been well pointed out that if the phrase is to be taken in the sense of associates of the idol's maker, then the maker himself is not mentioned in the coming condemnation. Hence it is more natural to understand the associates of the idol as those who follow it or worship it. The phrase is thus set in contrast to the *workmen* mentioned immediately afterward. These associates will be ashamed because they will find that the idols are of no profit to them in the time of need.

Furthermore, the workmen themselves who have constructed the idols are *of mankind*, i.e. they are mere men and so unable to make anything that is greater than man. The true God can create that which is lesser than Himself, but the creature that partakes of flesh and blood cannot produce what is divine. The idols, being under men and inferior to them, cannot help men.

13 *Behold!* (*hēn*) serves to introduce the condemnation.
14 *his companions, fellows* — Volz correctly points out that the word has a religious sense. Does it ultimately prepare the way for Mohammed's strong condemnation of making fellows for Allah?

In the last part of the verse the verbs may be construed as jussives or as simple futures.[15] Perhaps it is better to take them as futures, to show how the idols will condemn one another and all together will come into great confusion. All of them will gather together in an assembly and will stand in order to speak. This will simply result in their fearing and being ashamed. The subject of the verbs is the associates and workmen of the first half of the verse. They will come together but they will receive no assistance from the work of their hands, and so confusion and shame will be the result.

12 He has carved iron with an axe and he has wrought in the coals, and with the hammers he will shape it, and then work it with his arm of strength. Also he is hungry and has no strength, he has not drunk water and is faint.

13 He has carved wood, he has stretched a line, he will mark it with the awl, he will form it with the chisels, and with the compass he will mark it; and then he will make it like the structure of a man, like the beauty of mankind to dwell in a house.

12 Isaiah now proceeds to point out how the idols are made, the very description constituting a mockery of idolatry. Although the general sense is clear, there are difficulties with respect to the details. The first word may be rendered as a verb and is best translated by the past tense, for it expresses the initial act of the carver. The substance of which the idol is manufactured is iron, and the tool used is the axe. The word rendered *axe* seems to refer to a pointed tool, perhaps one that could be used in cutting. On the Gezer calendar the root (*'tzd*) occurs in the expression, "in the month of the cutting of the flax." On this construction the *ma'ªtzad*, whatever be its precise nature, is the instrument with which one works the iron. It has been objected that an iron worker would not employ the tool of a woodworker, but we do not understand sufficiently the precise significance of the word to say this with surety.[16]

With this tool the worker beats out the iron upon the anvil and

[15] The asyndetical verbs in the imp. vividly bring out the particulars in the enumeration.

[16] Cf. also Ar. *mi'ḍad*. A wall painting in Egypt from the time of Amenhotep II at Thebes shows different craftsmen at work on the preparation of a sphinx. Cf. *VBW*, Vol. III, p. 72.

174

he also works with red hot coals. The direct object after the verb *works* is not expressed, although it is clearly understood to be the iron. By means of hammers the workman forms the iron into the desired shape and produces the form of the image with his strong arms. This clause is rendered literally, *and he makes it with the arm of his strength,* i.e. with his strong arm. Attention may be called to the expression of Vergil (*Georgics* iv.170-175):

> *And as the Cyclops forge in haste bolts from the tough ore,*
> *Some with bellows of ox-hide make the blasts come and go,*
> *Others touch the hissing brass into the lake; Aetna groans*
> *under the anvils imposed upon her;*
> *They, among themselves, with great force raise the arms*
> *in a cadence measured, and with gripping tongs turn the iron.*[17]

Nevertheless, despite the mighty strength that the smith must have in order to perform his work and produce the idol, he himself is but a man. If he hungers, he no longer has strength; and if he does not drink refreshing water he becomes weary. He is himself but a mortal and subject to human infirmities, and the god he has constructed is unable to give him relief. Yet he bends his energies to the completion of his task.

13 Some interpreters assume that the subject matter is changed, and that the prophet is speaking in this verse of the construction of an idol of wood. In the process the worker has cut wood and stretched out a line for measurement. His work is careful and precise. The workman marks the idol out with red chalk, shapes it with chisels, or tools for scraping, and marks it with a compass.[18]

Lastly, the idol is formed according to the model or shape of a man and after his beauty, and the idol is to dwell in a house. The description clearly brings out the fact that the idol is constructed in the image of man its maker. Whatever form and beauty there is in mankind is to be found in the idol as well.

---

17 E.T. in Loeb Library Edition.
18 *yeṭā'ᵃrēhû* — to trace out, draw in outline. GKC § 64 i suggests that an imp. *Poel* was intended by the Masora with an irregular shortening of *ó* to *ō*. The second occurrence is *yeṭo'ᵒrēhû,* which I cannot explain satisfactorily; the first is *Piel. śereḏ* — a stylus, or marking tool for wood, Aq παραγραφίς. North takes it as *red chalk. maqtzŭ'ôṯ* — scraping tools, used in fashioning idols. *meḥûḡāh* — *compass, circle-instrument.* For an illustration cf. *VBW,* Vol. III, p. 73.

It is difficult to ascertain positively whether Isaiah here is speaking of the construction of two different kinds of idols, one of iron in verse 12 and one of wood in verse 13, or whether he is simply speaking in great detail of the construction of one idol. If the first view be correct, there would seem to be an imperceptible change of subject at the beginning of verse 13, the prophet simply speaking of one carving wood, without indicating that this is a different subject from that of verse 12. On this view the subject is not expressly mentioned, but must be assumed. In both verses it is represented by the English word *he*. Then, in verse 13, without indicating that there is a change of subject, Isaiah simply says, *he cuts wood*, etc.

It is also possible that verse 13 simply continues the description introduced in verse 12, referring to the wood that constitutes the body of the idol and its form, whereas verse 12 refers to the iron used in the idol's construction. In either case, the fact stands out how completely dependent the image is upon the weak man who has made it, the man who suffers in its construction and whose suffering it is in no wise able to relieve.

14 To cut for himself cedars; and now he has taken a cypress and an oak, and has strengthened it for himself among the trees of the forest—he has planted a laurel and the rain will increase it.

15 And it shall be to man for a burning, and he has taken from them and warmed himself; yea, he will kindle and bake bread; yea, he will form a god and worship; he has made it a graven image and bowed down to them.

16 Half of it he hath burned in the fire, on half of it he will eat flesh, he will roast and be filled; yea, he will warm himself and say, Aha! I am warm, I have seen fire.

17 And the rest of it he has made into a god, into his graven image; he will bow down to it, and will worship, and will pray to it, and say, Deliver me, for thou art my god.

14 That he may point out how completely foolish idolatry is, Isaiah now goes back to the place from which the wood for the idol originates, the trees of the forest. The subject of the infinitive *To cut* is impersonal, and we may render *One cuts, etc.* This infinitive may be taken as a finite verb, or as a gerundive, *They must be cut*; but it is more naturally taken in its ordinary sense, *To cut for himself cedars*, and then a verb of going is possibly to be understood.[19] The words *for him* are an ethical dative of advantage. The cutter cuts the wood for his own purposes, thinking that the god he is about to construct will bring him profit. The cedars were well known, particularly the cedars of Lebanon; but they were not particularly characteristic of Mesopotamia. If the reference were to Mesopotamian idolatry, it is strange that the idolaters would use the cedars.

At this point the prophet interrupts his syntax, and goes back to the act of cultivating the tree. The point seems to be that somehow the man is regarded as the controller of the wood. He produces that which he later worships. And to do this he takes trees that have been planted by the eternal God. If God had not provided the material of the creation, man the creature would be at a loss to know what to use in constructing his idols. There is a question as to the precise identification of the tirzah and oren[20] trees, although the cedar and oak are well known.

If the ordinary sense is allowed to the verb, it means that the planter causes the tree to become strong by taking care of it; thus he causes it to grow. His choice among all the trees of the forest falls upon this one. It is the object of his special delight and attention, and as a result of his care it stands out as a strong tree ready for the purposes he has designed.

Having done his part, the devotee waits for the rain from God to water the tree. The whole picture shows that the tree grows naturally, dependent upon the forces of nature for its strength, yet subject to the devoted care of the one who has chosen it.

15 This verse continues the description of the preparation of idols, each phase of which brings to .the fore the folly involved. Muilenburg thinks that the prophet does not have a true understanding of the pagan mind. "He does not sense the numinous quality in the idol, the thing that evoked wonder and awe and reverence and fear before it" (*IB*, p. 515). But, as North has pointed out, even the heathen poets have shown themselves caustic on the subject. Calvin seems to have been the first to quote Horace, but almost all commentators have quoted the poet's well-known words, "Once I was a trunk of a fig tree, a useless piece of wood,

---

[19] לכרת — may this be an imp. introduced by *Lamed*? M is supported by 1Q.
[20] The *'ōren* is often identified with the laurel; cf. Syr. *'ro'*, Ar. *ghār*. Some trees were sacred to certain deities in Babylonia (Muilenburg), but this was also true of Palestine.

when a carpenter, uncertain whether to make a bench or a Priapus, preferred that I should be a god; and so I became a god."[21]

The fact that Isaiah does not allude to the fear sometimes found in the worshippers of idols does not mean that he was not aware of it. By bringing out into the open the utter folly of idolatry he is able also to destroy whatever fear may attach to the worship of an idol. One is not likely to be impressed with the numen that inhabits a stick of wood if one's own hands have used that stick of wood, partly for worship and partly for ordinary trivial needs of everyday life.

A literal rendering of the first clause is, *And it becomes for mankind for a burning.*[22] This rendering brings out the fact that the wood is for the service of mankind, for the word *'adam* is here best taken as referring not to a particular individual but to mankind generally. In burning the wood he has cultivated, man is using it for fuel.

The words *from them* would seem to refer either to the trees mentioned in verse 14, or to the sticks that come from these trees. A man takes for himself a part of these sticks and with them warms himself.[23] He also lights another part of the wood and with the fire it provides he bakes bread.

From the part of the wood not used for burning the man makes a god; the word *'el* here is almost sarcastic. This god is made in the form of an image, and to it the worshipper does obeisance. This is a strange outcome; actually the god should be thankful to the devotee in that the stick of wood from which he was made was not chosen for fire to bake bread or to warm the man. Instead, and wholly by chance, the worshipper has chosen the piece of wood from which he has made the idol, and then bows down to it in gratitude and devotion.[24]

16 Isaiah reverts to the thought of 15a and carries it out further. The principal question of interpretation has to do with

---

21 "*Olim truncus eram ficulnus, inutile lignum, Cum faber, incertus, scamnum faceretne Priapum, Maluit esse deum*" (*Satires* i.8).

22 An Isaianic expression; cf. also 5:5; 6:13. 1Q, however, reads *whgh*.

23 *and he has become warm* — cf. Ug. ḥm, Akk. *emmu*, Egy. *šmm. yaśśiq* is *Hiphil* imp. of *šlq, to burn, kindle*, with frequentative force, and is followed by the perf. with *waw* consecutive, with similar force, *kindles and bakes*; cf. 5:12; 27:10. למו — the suffix here is probably to be construed as singular.

24 עשׂהו — the preterite denotes an act contemporaneous with that expressed by the preceding imp., *yip̄'al*; the writer now looks back upon the act as accomplished, whereas in *yip̄'al* he regarded it as future expectation.

the words *half of it*. This phrase is repeated, and in the following verse occur the words "its remainder." How can the prophet speak of the two halves and also of the remainder? It has been suggested that in a satirical work we should not expect arithmetical precision. It has also been held that the second *half of it* should be emended to read, "and its coals."[25] But there is not sufficient textual evidence to support this proposal, nor, for that matter, is it necessary. A common solution of the difficulty is to assume that the words "the remainder of it" in verse 17 mean the same thing as the second occurrence of *half of it*. This is a possible interpretation; it is also possible to take both occurrences of *half of it* in verse 16 as referring to the same half. On this interpretation we may paraphrase, "He burns half of it in the fire, and on (the same) half of it he will eat flesh."

The words *half of it* are emphatic, to show that not all the wood is used either for the construction of the idol or for purposes of everyday life, but that the uses to which the wood is put are diverse. With the fire kindled by the burning of half of the wood, the worshipper prepares food to eat. This preparation is done by means of roasting, and it brings satisfaction to the eater.

In addition to eating, the man warms himself with the fire. Of interest in this and the preceding verse is the frequent use of the particle *'aph*, which may be rendered, *nay more, moreover*. It is a characteristic word of these verses. The satisfaction the fire brings to the man is expressed by his statement, *Aha, I have seen the fire and I am warm*.[26] There is no need of taking the word "see" in any other than its ordinary sense. Luther brought out the true meaning when he said that man has a desire to look into the fire. He sees and feels the fire and expresses his joy and satisfaction in its possession. In becoming fuel for fire, the wood truly serves man; in becoming an idol it does not serve him, but becomes an occasion for his stumbling.

17 Isaiah now reverts to the thought of 15b and carries it out further. The remainder is the half that has not been used for fuel and heat. With this half the worshipper makes a god in the form of an idol. To this he prostrates himself and looks for deliverance.

[25] So 1Q. Duhm. *VBW*, Vol. III, p. 74, reproduces a stone Egyptian statue (middle 3rd millennium B.C.) of a woman sitting beside an oven. With one hand she tends the ashes, with the other she holds her temple as if to feel the heat.

[26] *ḥammôti* — the accent is *Milra*.

The last phrase, *my god art thou*, makes the words *my god* emphatic; but *thou* is also stressed, as though to say, "My god art thou and thou alone." Half of the wood is thrown into the fire in order that man may be warmed thereby and may cook his food; the other half becomes an idol to which he cries out, "Thou alone canst save me." Indeed, the cry is a command, "Deliver me."

In both this and the preceding verse the use of the verbs must be noted. In each verse the first verb is a perfect and should be rendered by the past tense; the subsequent verbs are imperfects to be rendered by the present. Thus, the point of view of the prophet is that of one who is beholding the process while it is in the course of being carried out.

18 They have not known, and they will not understand; for he hath smeared their eyes from seeing, and their hearts from doing wisely.

19 And he will not cause it to return unto his heart, and there is not understanding to say, Half of it I have burned in the fire, and have also baked bread on its coals; I will roast flesh and eat, and the rest of it I will make an abomination, to the trunk of a tree I will bow down.

20 Feeding on ashes, his heart is deceived, it has led him astray, and he cannot deliver himself, and he will not say, Is there not a lie in my right hand?

18 Those who have formed an idol lack understanding with respect to their own true nature.[27] They do not see the folly of using temporal material for forming gods, which do not owe their origin to themselves, but to the most high true God, who created the material from which the gods are made, and partly to men, who instead of employing the material for other purposes used it for making gods.

Some commentators have regarded this verse as out of place. Volz and Condamin consider it a later gloss, and Kissane places it after verse 11. These positions, however, are not supported by manuscript evidence. It is best to take the verb rendered *smeared* as a perfect in the singular with "Yahweh" as the subject.[28] The reference is not to a literal smearing but to spiritual blindness; hence the language is also applicable to the heart. Israel, as God's servant, should have dealt wisely; and He who is the true Servant

27 The preterite is used either with the sense of the future or to express a general truth.

28 Note that the pointing is with *Patah,* but cf. Lev. 14:42.

will deal wisely (52:13); but the empirical Israel was in a condition of such blindness that it could not act wisely. To act wisely is
to reject idolatry and to serve the one true God in accordance with
His will.

19 This verse carries on the description. Not only does the
worshipper not know and perceive but he also *does not cause to
return unto his heart, etc.* The phrase is stronger and more forceful than the ordinary "to place upon the heart"; it suggests that
the one who meditates has control of his thought. If he did
actually permit himself to know what he was doing and to perceive
its true significance he would realize his folly and abandon it. Were
the worshipper to state what he has done, he would bring the
details in all their petty significance before his mind and so clearly
recognize what folly it was to worship what he himself had created.
Isaiah purposely uses the same words over and over again in order
to press home the truth of his message.

Why, however, does the worshipper call the idol an abomination? Probably the prophet simply wishes to show what the devotee
would say if he saw his idolatry as it really was. In his spiritual
blindness he says, "My god art thou"; did he recognize the true
nature of the case he would say, "An abomination art thou."[29] In
the last clause the unusual word *bul* refers not to what the tree
itself produces but to what man brings forth from the tree.[30]

20 Actually the worshipper cannot see that the idol is an
abomination because he has deceived himself by nourishing himself with ashes. As his pasture he deliberately chooses what cannot
profit and is satisfied that it should be his portion. Perhaps the
figure is suggested by flocks feeding in a pastureless, barren, rocky
waste. Penna asks whether the prophet is engaging in sarcasm or
whether his words exhibit a true compassion for the pitiable condition of the people. Perhaps there is an admixture of both, but it
does seem that the heart of the prophet is filled over the condition
of those about whom he is speaking. The second clause states the
result; *Feeding on ashes, his heart is deceived.*[31] Thus, two independent statements are made concerning the one who pastures on
ashes. The result of being led astray is that he does not (cannot)

---

[29] Cf. Rom. 1:18-22.
[30] Lit., *dry wood*; cf. Akk. *bulu.*
[31] הותל — *Hophal* preterite of חלל; lit., *a heart, it is deceived.*

deliver his soul, i.e. himself, from the judgment that comes.[32] Nor does he even acknowledge that in his hand there is a lie. The service of idolatry is deceptive; it permits the idolater to remain ignorant of his true state and deludes him into believing that he is doing wisely. He refuses to believe that what he holds in his right hand, i.e. in his close possession, is a lie. It is a lie, for it gives the impression of being what it is not and so deceives the hopes of the one who trusts in it.

21 Remember these, O Jacob, and Israel, for thou art my servant: I have formed thee, a servant unto me art thou; Israel, thou shalt not be forgotten by me.

22 I have blotted out as a thick cloud thy transgressions, and as a cloud thy sins; return to me, for I have redeemed thee.

23 Sing, O barren, for the LORD hath done it; shout, ye lower parts of the earth; break forth, ye mountains, into song, the forest and every tree in it; for the LORD hath redeemed Jacob, and in Israel he will glorify himself.

21 According to many interpreters *these things* refers to what has preceded; and Israel, on this interpretation, is to remember the fact that idolatry is a lie. Quite possibly, however, they may also refer to what follows, and thus are a command to Israel to remember that she is the servant of Yahweh. At any rate, *ki* may be understood as introducing a reason, and so the fact that Israel is God's servant is the reason why she is to remember. If she keeps in mind that she belongs to Yahweh as His servant, she will forget the deceptiveness of idolatry.

The nation is apostrophized with its double name, *Jacob, Israel* (cf. 40:27). Perhaps there is reflection upon the ancestor as well as upon the nation itself as his descendant. This nation is Yahweh's servant, which in all things should be ready to do His will and hence not be forgetful of its solemn position in the world.

The first clause of the second line states the purpose of Israel's existence. Her God, Yahweh, formed her that she might be His servant. We are, therefore, not to regard Israel merely as an ethically gifted or a spiritually attuned nation that on her own brought deep religious insights into the world. Rather we must see her as a servant, existing in the world simply for the purpose of obeying her God in the performance of what He had commanded. For this end

[32] 1Q has *ywkyl,* and omits the interrogative particle before the negative.

He formed her. Emphasis falls upon *to me*, a dative expressing advantage. Israel exists not primarily for the benefit of other nations nor for the general welfare of mankind, but to be a servant to her God. Contrast is brought to the fore between *to me* and *thou*. Whereas the last words are difficult, they are probably best translated, *thou shalt not be forgotten of me*.[33] God has formed Israel, she is His servant; hence, He will not forget her.

22 As a proof that Israel will not be forgotten of the Lord the fact is announced that He has blotted out her transgressions, hence there remains no obstacle to Israel's returning to Yahweh. Differences of opinion exist as to the precise significance of the words *I have blotted out*. Some would connect this with the blotting out of a stain, as in Psalm 51:3, 11; others with the idea of blotting out a writing or an entry in a book, e.g. Exodus 32:32. And Colossians 2:14, which may reflect upon this passage, reads, "blotting out the handwriting of ordinances that was against us, which was contrary to us, ... (he) took it out of the way, nailing it to his cross." Others refer the act of blotting to the removal of the clouds. Perhaps each detail of the figure may not be clear, but to the present writer the following seems to be the basic thought.

God will blot out from His book Israel's transgressions and sins just as the wind removes completely from sight the clouds in the sky. The reference is to the ease with which the clouds are removed. This seems particularly to be true in the Near East. In Egypt one August day the sky filled with clouds in the early morning, yet long before mid-morning was entirely devoid of clouds. It is the transitoriness of the cloud that is in view. To blot out the transgressions is no more difficult for God than to remove the clouds. The first word (*'av*) denotes a heavy cloud, and the second is the ordinary word for cloud. Whatever kind of cloud there may be will be blown away easily. The clouds intervene between heaven and earth just as sin and transgressions intervene between God and His people (cf. 59:2).

If transgressions and sins are blotted out they are regarded as no longer existing and are not imputed to the people. It is a radical and real removal, accomplished only by divine grace; and the

---

[33] *ṭinnāšēnî* — as it stands, the form is *Niphal* with a verbal suffix that may have an agentive force, as is the case with the Hurrian verb and the *śdm.n.f* form in Egyptian. Cf. *tzamtunî* in Zech. 7:5, *ye fasted for me.* 1Q reads *Hiphil, tś'ny.*

blotting out of the transgressions makes possible the command, *return unto me*. Thus, even in conversion the initiative is on the part of God.[34] God addresses the nation tenderly in the singular, *return thou indeed unto me*.[35] The emphatic form of the imperative is not to be overlooked. To return involves turning from the direction in which one had been facing to another direction. In this case it is a turning from the place where sins and transgressions had led the people and a turning unto God. A complete change is required. "Turn thou us unto thee, O Lord, and we shall be turned; renew our days as of old" (Lam. 5:21).

The last statement gives the reason for the imperative, *I have redeemed thee*. This verb is not to be eviscerated of its meaning. As in Jeremiah 31:18, 34, it refers to redemption from sin and guilt, and implies more than the forgiveness of sins; it implies that a price has been paid in order that the people may be bought back from their sins and upon the basis of which God may forgive those sins. A command to repent is given, because God Himself has paid a price to purchase His people. It is that concept that lies at the heart of the matter. Although the verb is in the perfect, nevertheless, as Volz points out, it is the perfect of certainty. The reference is not to the return from exile, for that act could not really be designated a redemption paid by God; the reference is to a ransom paid for deliverance from sin and guilt, and the price God paid for that deliverance was His own Son, in whom we have redemption through His blood, the forgiveness of sins.

23 This verse contains an emphatic repetition of the promise of verse 22, pointing out that the glorious redemption of Israel is cause for all creation to rejoice. All nature is bound up with the history of mankind; as the curse affects it so that it groans and travails in pain, so also is it affected by the redemption of the human race (cf. 1:2; 11:6ff.; 35:1; 41:18; 43:20; Deut. 32:1ff.; Rom. 8:19-22). The prophet therefore bursts out into exultant command, and the heavens are enjoined to sing. Exultation is to characterize all parts of the universe, whether in the height or in the depth.

A reason is given, namely that Yahweh has done it, i.e. has

---

[34] So Penna, rightly: "*In fondo anche nella conversione l'initziativa è sempre dalla parte di Dio.*"

[35] Note the position of the accent, apparently because the following guttural requires greater energy of voice for distinctness in pronunciation.

redeemed His people.[36] That which to human understanding would seem to transcend the bounds of the possible has been done by the all-powerful God of Israel. In contrast to the heavens, the lower parts of the earth are to shout. This would include Sheol, the place of the departed, as in Psalm 139:15; but it would include also the caves, pits, and deep abysses within the earth. All that is comprised by the term *lower parts* is included. Thus, height and depth, the entirety of what God has created, are to burst forth into exultation, shouting and singing because of the great triumph their Creator has wrought.

By means of parallelism the same thought is again expressed, only this time the objects addressed are the mountains and the forests. The mountains, which rise up from earth and point toward heaven and in which men so often have found their pride and delight, are to burst forth into singing; and the forests, together with all the individual trees, which cover the earth with beauty and lift their tops toward their Creator on high, are to do likewise. Mountains are not places for the practice of idolatry, nor are trees to be used for the manufacture of idols; but both are to sing in exultation, because He who made them has brought redemption to the earth.

The last line gives the reason for the rejoicing, namely that Yahweh has redeemed Jacob and will glorify Himself in Israel. Israel is the occasion through which or by means of which God will get glory for Himself. Whereas the mountains and trees of the forest manifest in wondrous fashion the glory of God their Creator, the redemption of Israel is an act in which the saving and redeeming glory of God will be displayed. Even more wonderful than the creation is the new creation, the redeemed humanity that Yahweh, the God of Israel and the Creator of heaven and earth, has brought into existence.

24 Thus saith the LORD, thy Redeemer, and the One who formed thee from the womb, I am the LORD who doeth all, who stretcheth out heavens alone, who spreadeth out the earth, and who was with me?

25 Who frustrateth the signs of boasters, and enchanters he brings into confusion; who causeth to turn the wise men backwards, and their knowledge he maketh foolish.

36 The verb has absolute meaning; cf. 41:4. The perf. indicates certain promise; Isaiah is so sure of the redemption that he commands the choir of creation to sing in praise.

185

26 Causing to stand the word of his servant, and the counsel of his messengers he will fulfill; who saith to Jerusalem, Thou shalt be inhabited, and to the cities of Judah, Ye shall be built, and her ruins I will raise.

27 Who saith to the deep, Be dry, and thy rivers I shall make dry.

28 Who saith to Cyrus, My shepherd, and all my desire he will perform; and saying to Jerusalem, Thou shalt be built, and the temple shall be founded.

INTRODUCTORY NOTE

Verse 24 contains an introductory phrase, "Thus saith the LORD, thy Redeemer and thy Former from the womb." Then occurs the statement, "I am the LORD," and this is followed by nine participles. The verses are further divided into three strophes or sections. In the first section (24b) there are three lines, each beginning with a participle.

The second section (vv. 25, 26a) consists also of three lines, each beginning with a participle and concluding with a verb in the imperfect. Each line also consists of two parts, arranged in chiastic fashion. Thus, for example, "Who frustrates the signs of babblers, and the diviners he maddens."

In the third section there are three lines (vv. 26c-28a) each commencing with the participle and the definite article and concluding with a verb in the imperfect. The first line consists of three parts, whereas the other two lines have two parts each. In the first and second line the verb is in the first person imperfect, whereas in the third line it is in the third person. Finally, the last line of v. 28 begins with the infinitive construct of the verb *say* (which verb had been used in the participles introducing each line of the third section), and this line also consists of two parts and concludes with a verb in the imperfect.

24 With these words the prophet introduces a new stage in the development of his theme. From 44:24—48:22 he speaks of Cyrus the anointed and of the deliverance he is to bring. At the same time Cyrus serves as a preparation for the understanding of the work of the unique Servant who will bring a spiritual deliverance to the people of God. Although a new section is here introduced, it would be a mistake to find too sharp a division between this section and what has preceded. The words *Thus saith the Lord* flow naturally from the truth stated in verse 23. Indeed, that verse was a preparation for verse 24.

Emphasis is given to the solemnity of the message by means of the introductory words, *Thus saith the Lord.* With two participles the prophet sums up Israel's history. He speaks first, however, not of the forming of the nation, but of its redemption, for that is the great theme of these passages. Furthermore, the root "redeem" connects with what has just been said in the preceding verse. Even more important than the fact that Yahweh has formed the nation is the fact that He has redeemed it. And He who redeemed it is He who has formed it in the womb (cf. comments on 44:2). Throughout its entire history, from its formation until its redemption, Israel has stood in peculiar relationship to its God. He, the God of its history, can therefore speak concerning its future as no one else can do.

The first statement, "who maketh all," refers to the fact that Yahweh is the Creator. Here Isaiah stresses clearly the divine monergism. There is nothing that does not trace its origin to Him as the Creator. The second line limits the effect of this divine monergism to the heavens and adds the word "alone" (lit., *to my separation*), thus denying that there was any helper or co-worker with God. He alone stretched out the heavens. Finally, in the third line a participle is used that reflects the word *expanse (raqia')* of Genesis 1, and teaches that God alone spread out the earth. To show that He alone is the Creator, the question is asked, "Who was with me?"[37]

> In the third line, which speaks with still greater definiteness of *"the earth"* (הארץ) the monergism is declared in the form of an almost contemptuous challenge "who was with me?" (מי אתי) a challenge to man to deny that God alone created this earth in which he lives, to deny that God alone is great. In the increasing stress laid on the monergism of Jehovah the theme of the strophe shows a decided climax, together with, and the importance of this feature will appear more clearly later, an element of increasing definiteness (all, heavens, *the* earth).[38]

The question implies a negative answer, No one was with me.

For the word *all* no qualifier is needed. If God made all, obviously there was no helper. For *heavens,* vast as they are, He worked

---

37 Read with the *Ketiv, mi 'itti.* So 1Q, B; Vulg. *nullus mecum.*
38 Oswald T. Allis, "The Transcendence of Jehovah God of Israel," *Biblical and Theological Studies,* New York, 1912, p. 605. I am deeply indebted to this article for help in the study of this section.

alone; for *the earth* (note the definite article) no one was present. The variety of expression is particularly striking. This verse stresses the work of Yahweh as Creator, and refers to events lying in the far distant past, as far back as man can go in his thought, to the creation of all things. It brings us to the point mentioned in Genesis 1:1, and indeed serves as a reminder of and offers comment upon that verse.

25 As the first strophe (v. 24) refers to the remote past, so the second (25, 26a) refers to the present. It deals with the attitude of God toward "the longings, the efforts and the pretentions of mankind to discern the future, to know 'The times or the seasons which the Father put in his own power.' The answer is unequivocal — the future belongs to God. He baffles every attempt to enter his domain and covers the intruder with confusion. But just because it belongs to him, he only can and does reveal its secrets and also bring to pass all that he has revealed."[39] Thus, there appears a sharp contrast between the uncertainty of human methods of discerning the future and the certainty of divine revelation.

The *baddim* are praters, or chatterers, who babble about what they do not understand. Hence, there is implied the thought that they are also speakers of falsehoods and lies. The reference is to prophets who speak what is not the truth.[40] The signs are those wonders that these false prophets perform in order to prove that they are messengers from the god. Many commentators refer the word "signs" to the omens that the prophets use, but in the light of Deuteronomy 13:1-5 it may be that the reference is to the signs themselves, the apparent wonders that are performed. These are powerful signs, but the God who is in control of all history is able to thwart them so that they make their performers appear to be foolish.

The word rendered *diviners* is a general term. Underlying is the conception of one who obtains an oracle by means of the drawing of lots. In the Old Testament the root has a fairly wide use; it is employed, for example, of Balaam (Josh. 13:22), of the witch of Endor (1 Sam. 28:8), and of the false prophets (Jer. 27:9; 29:8; Mic.

[39] *Ibid.*, p. 602.

[40] It is questionable whether there is any particular relationship with the *baru* priests of Babylonia, as suggested by J. W. Behr, *The Writings of Deutero-Isaiah and the Neo-Babylonian Royal Inscriptions,* Pretoria, 1937, p. 28. Cf. also Volz.

3:7), as well as of Philistine soothsayers (1 Sam. 6:2). These people God renders mad so that they are as fools. They are representative of the religious class; they believe in the supernatural in a certain sense; at least they believe that there is a power greater than themselves, and they seek on their own and by means of their own devising to employ this power in order to obtain information concerning the future.

The wise men mentioned in the second line do not manifest the same open hostility or opposition to God as do those mentioned in the first line, and hence are not dealt with so harshly or severely.

> Yet in another sense there is a slight advance corresponding to the slight advance in metrical form. For while the 'Wicked' of the first line seem to recognize supernatural power and agencies although enemies of Jehovah, the 'wise men' of the second line ignore him. 'Like the fool', they have said in their heart, 'there is no God': like the modern Positivist they have gotten beyond the religious stage, an attitude which in some respects at least is even more culpable than open opposition.[41]

The wise men regard themselves as wise in their own wisdom, for they have not received wisdom from above. They are representatives of the wisdom of this world, which perishes. We do not know in what particular form this wisdom manifested itself, although Penna may be correct in saying that these were men who thought themselves gifted with a particular perspicacity and ability in giving practical counsels (cf. 29:14).

David had prayed that God would turn the counsel of Ahithophel into foolishness (the same verb is used as here), and so God turns the wise men backwards; that is, He brings them into defeat, failure, and disappointment. Before His mighty power their wisdom appears the very opposite, namely folly. What they proclaim and exhibit as knowledge He turns into folly and thus brings them into shame.

26 The first line of verse 26 constitutes the third line of the second strophe and stands in contrast to the first two lines, forming an antithetic parallelism. Not only does the Lord establish the word of His servant, but also He accomplishes His purposes. The signs the praters offer will be confounded and all the wisdom of this

---

41 Allis, *op. cit.*, p. 606.

world turned into foolishness, but the word that the Servant of the Lord speaks will be confirmed. Earlier (40:8) Isaiah had stated that the word of God would stand forever; and now, employing the same verb, he points out that God causes His servant's word to stand. Emphasis falls here upon propositional revelation. In contrast to the devious and esoteric means of the soothsayers and diviners, who represent human wisdom apart from God, God Himself speaks by means of words. He has given to man a verbal revelation and this revelation He causes to stand. He can affect the revelations of worldly wisdom, but His own revelation cannot be affected; it will stand. It would be out of order to emend the text so as to read the plural "servants," for the reference is to the one who is uttering this particular prophecy, namely Isaiah himself. In contrast to the superstitions that tell the future apart from God, the prophet is now delivering this one true prophecy of Israel's salvation. This word is established, and it alone will stand.

In the latter part of the second member of the line the reference is to the prophets as such, of whom Isaiah is one. These prophets are sent from Jehovah to bear His counsel, His own wise plan of salvation. This plan is the manifestation in history of the divine counsel and planning. It is a plan that must be revealed to man and declared to the nation by the Lord's messengers, not by messengers that set themselves up upon their own authority and are not truly His. This counsel He will bring to fulfillment and completion. Thus, history unfolds itself according to a plan predetermined by the God of Israel, and it will continue so to unfold itself until the entire divine plan is complete. The signs of babblers, therefore, are frustrated and come to naught. They are meaningless and accomplish nothing. On the other hand, the word of Yahweh's servant will stand in that it will surely come to pass, and the divine wisdom expressed in the plan of deliverance will come to fruition.

With the second line of verse 26 the third strophe begins. This line, like the two that follow it, is introduced by the present participle of *'amar* and the definite article. In English we may render *who says*, the reference in each case being to the Lord. As the first strophe had dealt with the past and the second with the present, so this one speaks of the future. Furthermore, as the first strophe had spoken of the very remote past, so this one, we may legitimately assume, looks to the far distant future. It is therefore incorrect to say that the prophet speaks here as a contemporary of Cyrus or as one who expects the Persian king to appear shortly upon the horizon. From the standpoint of the prophet the appearance of Cyrus is in the distant future.

God speaks to Jerusalem as a city that has long been abandoned and robbed of her inhabitants. The long period of the indignation will come to an end, and once again Jerusalem will be full of people. Likewise, the cities of Judah, which have long lain in ruins and desolation, will be built up. This is to be accomplished through the work of the Lord Himself. The restoration of Jerusalem is the work of the God of Israel.[42] Thus, the exile is not a permanent condition but a period of wrath, which, because of their sins, had come upon the chosen people.

27 Verse 27 consists of one line, which is the second line of the third strophe. Like the first line of this section it is introduced by "Who says" and the object of address is *the deep*. Expositors have differed as to the significance of *the deep*; the Targum, for example, takes the words as a metaphorical description of the wealth of Babylon. It would seem that the word signifies the obstacles that stand in the way of God's restoring His people to Jerusalem, and in the light of Jeremiah 23:7, 8 we may probably say that there is reflection upon the miracle at the Red Sea. Just as at the first exodus the power of God was exhibited in the safe passage of the nation through the Red Sea waters, so now, in the deliverance from the world power, represented by Babylon, that power will again be seen, and whatever may stand in the way will be completely removed.[43]

At the same time, the allusion to the crossing of the Red Sea does not exhaust the reference; and there would seem to be some allusion also to Babylon as the enemy of God's people. This does not mean that we can accept the older interpretation, which saw in these words a reference to the diverting of the Euphrates by Cyrus from its natural channel to make the capture of Babylon possible, for cuneiform records have shown that Herodotus' account is at this point untenable. At the same time, that which prevented the furtherance of the kingdom of God and the coming of Christ was Babylon, the heart of man's worldwide empire. Like a great deep, this Babylon must be removed; yet even Babylon is no match for

---

42 Here the prophet reverts to the 1st person, to prepare for the address to Cyrus.
43 Cf. Allis, *op. cit.*, p. 607.

the Lord of all creation, who can issue a mere command with the result that the deep will be dry.[44]

Perhaps the phrase *thy rivers* is simply another designation for the deep. Elsewhere the word is used of the ocean (cf. Ps. 24:2; Jon. 2:4). The suffix *thy* would seem to refer to the deep itself; thus the rivers belong to the deep. Evidently the whole is intended to give a picture of completeness. All nature must obey the commands of Israel's God. Variety is obtained by making the first verb an imperative and the second an imperfect. Thus there is a connection between God's word and His power. He speaks and He acts. Not to be overlooked also is the relation between *Be dry* (*ḥᵒravi*) in this verse and *wastes* (*ḥorvotheyha*) in the preceding.

28 The prophet now becomes more definite. Whereas the first line of this section speaks of the restoration of Jerusalem and Judah with no mention of the release, and the second line mentions the release and deliverance, this third line names the one who is to accomplish both restoration and deliverance. "The reference to Cyrus is consequently the climactic element in this line. It is the mention of his name and the declaring that he is the deliverer which is significant and which forms the climax of the line, of the strophe and of the poem."[45] Thus there is introduced a contrast between the Lord (cf. "I am the Lord," v. 24) and Cyrus. In contrast to Yahweh, Cyrus is as nothing, for he is a mere instrument in the Lord's hands. The great and wonderful works of Israel's God have been set forth in the early lines of the poem, and in contrast with these Cyrus in himself can accomplish nothing. At the same time Cyrus is exalted, for he is said to be the shepherd of the Lord who accomplishes all His pleasure. His task is remarkable and unusual. It is this mention of Cyrus that forms the climax of the section. If his name be deleted, the force of this passage is greatly minimized if not destroyed. And, inasmuch as the reference to Cyrus occurs in the last section, we may assume that he is here pictured as one who is to come in the yet distant future. Of himself Isaiah of course could not have known his name, but as a true prophet, inspired by the Holy Spirit, he could have spoken the name of Cyrus in this definite manner.

Cyrus is said to be the Lord's *shepherd*, who will pasture His

[44] The root *'mr* may here possibly have the sense of command (as in Ar.). Gesenius thought that the reference was to Cyrus' drying up the Euphrates (Herodotus i.185, 190).

[45] Allis, *op. cit.*, p. 609.

people who are now languishing in the barren wilderness and who
will shepherd their return to their homeland. This term *shepherd*
has a wide variety of use. It is applied to God Himself (Isa.
40:11), and to the Christ (Ezek. 34:23; Matt. 25:32; John 10:1-14;
1 Pet. 2:25). It is used also of kings as the heads of their
people (2 Sam. 5:2; Jer. 3:15).[46] The word shows the close relationship between Jehovah and Cyrus in that Cyrus is permitted to
perform this important function of shepherd over God's own people. At this particular point in the history of redemption a Persian
king is given the task of gathering the lost sheep of the house of
Israel. By the use of this designation Cyrus is greatly honored, for
to shepherd God's people is the task of the Messiah, and Cyrus
here stands as a type of the Lord's Servant, the true Messiah and
Shepherd of His people who gives His life for the sheep.

In the capacity of shepherd, Cyrus will complete all the pleasure
of God. The phrase is naturally limited, not referring to the whole
counsel of God but only to the deliverance and restoration of the
Jews from exile. All that Yahweh has decreed concerning the
restoration of His people, Cyrus, God's shepherd over these people,
will bring to fulfillment.

An exegetical question arises as to the proper interpretation of
the difficult phrase *and saying.* Luther takes it indefinitely, "that
one may say." Others refer it to the Lord. Possibly it is best to refer
it to Cyrus. "He will do all my pleasure in that he will say to
Jerusalem, etc."[47] The last words are then to be taken as a direct
address to Jerusalem and the Temple, and translated by the second
person.

The Temple is the end toward which the work of Cyrus as
shepherd is directed. If the Temple is to be founded the city must
also be built, and it is Cyrus who makes this possible. This is not
the end of God's purposes with His nation, but it is the necessary
step that must be taken in order that they may be reestablished in
their land, that from the line of David the Messiah may finally be
born in Bethlehem.

---

46 The epithet occurs frequently in the literature of the ancient Near East,
e.g. Amarna, text 288, "I am a shepherd of the king"; *Iliad* ii. 243, ποιμὴν λαῶν;
and see Behr, *op. cit.*, p. 22, for further examples. The usage here proves
nothing (contra Behr) respecting the date of the passage. Cf. Wm. W. Hallo,
"New Hymns to the Kings of Isin," *Bibliotheca Orientalis*, Vol. 23, No. 5/6, 1967,
pp. 239-247. On the inscriptions are such expressions as "the hero, the righteous
shepherd" and "the true shepherd" (2100-1800 B.C.).

47 The inf. construct with *waw* continues the previous finite verb.

1 Thus saith the LORD to his anointed, to Cyrus, whose right hand
   I have held fast, to tread down before him nations, and the
   loins of kings I will loose; to open before him double doors,
   and gates shall not be shut.
2 I will go before thee, and uneven places I will make level;
   doors of brass I will break, and bars of iron I will cut.
3 And I will give thee treasures of darkness and hidden riches of
   secret places, in order that thou mayest know that I the LORD,
   the One calling thee by name, am the God of Israel.
4 For the sake of my servant Jacob and Israel my chosen;
   therefore will I call thee by thy name, I will give thee a title
   and thou hast not known me.
5 I am the LORD and there is no other; except me there is no
   God: I will gird thee, and thou hast not known me.
6 To the end that they may know from the rising of the sun,
   and from the west, that there is none; I am the LORD, and there
   is none else.
7 Who formeth light and createth darkness, who maketh peace
   and createth evil; I am the LORD, who doeth these things.

1 The introductory words call attention to the dignity of the
message. Although they constitute a certain break which directs
particular attention to what is to be announced, they do not
necessarily indicate an entirely new beginning. What follows has
been prepared for by the immediately preceding. It is well then to
consider what follows as the actual words of the Lord and thus to
receive the divine assurance that this is the message of the God of
Israel to Cyrus.

Anointed continues the thought of the close personal relationship in which Cyrus stands to the Lord, a thought introduced by
"my shepherd" in the preceding verse. In the Old Testament the
term "anointed" is used rather broadly. 2 Samuel 1:21 probably
speaks of a shield as anointed; Psalm 105:15 mentions the prophets

as anointed ones (cf. the parallel in 1 Chron. 16:22), and numerous passages speak of kings and priests as anointed of the Lord. The term is also used (despite assertions to the contrary) of the Messianic Redeemer King in Psalm 2:7 and Daniel 9:25ff.

The form *mashiªḥ* (*anointed*) is stronger than the passive participle, *mashuªḥ*. It denotes in the first place the fact that an anointing has taken place. Secondly, not only has the act been performed upon a person, but from that time on he is regarded as an anointed one. The permanent now attaches to him; he perpetually bears the character of an anointed one. Lastly, what is imparted is the Spirit of the Lord, so that the anointed one is one upon whom that Spirit rests.

The results that accrue to the anointed one are not necessarily the same in each case. Thus, the Redeemer is an anointed One in a sense far deeper than was Cyrus. That Cyrus has been anointed suggests that God has placed His Spirit upon Cyrus so that he may accomplish a specific task. It does not necessarily imply that Cyrus becomes a true worshipper of the God of Israel. Nor does the anointing imply, as many commentators have suggested, that he is sanctified, and inducted into office as king. The term rather suggests that there is a specific task that he is to accomplish and that for this he has been anointed by the sovereign God of Israel, who has imparted to him His Spirit to equip him for the performance of this task. In this sense Cyrus is a type of the Messianic Servant of the Lord, upon whom the Spirit came in greater measure, that He might be equipped for the task, infinitely greater than that of Cyrus, of setting His people free from the spiritual bondage of sin and guilt.

The remainder of the verse constitutes a description of the Lord's relationship to Cyrus, the actual address to the king beginning in the next verse. The act of clasping the king by the hand suggests that he is under Yahweh's control. He has been raised up by the Lord, who holds him that he will not fail, nor will any be able to thwart him.[1] His life is in the hand of Israel's God. What his right hand decides to do, it does only because it is directed by God. Cyrus is not the master of his fate, even though he may think that such is the case.

The following clauses state the purposes of Cyrus' reign. God

---

[1] Lit., *which I have strengthened* (i.e. *sustained, supported*) *with his right hand.*

will *tread down nations before him*.[2] Cyrus will see himself a conqueror before whom nations one after another will fall. Furthermore, God will *loosen the loins of kings*, i.e. He will remove or undo the binding girdle, so that they will be unable to fight. The mighty conquests of Cyrus could not have occurred were the king left to his own resources. It is the hand of God that makes the enemy kingdoms weak so that they cannot stand before the Persian monarch.

In the mention of *doors* we are probably to see a specific reference to Babylon itself. Perhaps Herodotus exaggerated when he wrote of Babylon, "There are a hundred gates in the circuit of the wall, all of bronze with bronze uprights and lintels" (i.179). When the doors of the city are opened the conqueror may enter and take possession. Furthermore, the *gates* of the city will not stand in the way, for they *will not be closed*.[3] Free access is given to Cyrus, who is in the Lord's hand.

2 With this verse the direct address to Cyrus begins. It is the language of redemption, although it does not refer to the actual redemption itself but only to the preparation for it. The stage must be set, and the proper conditions established for the Deliverer to appear. To bring about this condition there must first be a setting free from bondage in Babylon, and it was Cyrus who accomplished this. The introductory words call to mind Exodus 23:20ff. Emphasis falls upon the personal pronoun. If Yahweh goes before Cyrus, a successful outcome is assured. A contrast appears between *I* and *thee*. The word h^adurim is difficult, for its precise connotation is not known. The context, however, shows that it refers to the difficulties that would stand in the Persian king's way.[4] God will smooth out these difficulties, so that the way is plain and level. The gates of bronze cannot restrain Cyrus, for God will break them; and if there be bars of iron He will cut them down. The two figures suggest serious obstacles, but they will easily disappear before the Lord. In all probability there is an allusion to the actual

---

2 רד is a contracted form, with *Pataḥ*.

3 Cf. Neh. 3:3, 13-15. North holds that the gate (*ša'ar*) comprised doors d^elāṯayim), bolts, and bars. *yissāḡērû* − frequentative imp., separated from *waw* by the negative, and following the inf., possibly for variety's sake.

4 h^adûrîm − *swelling places; swells of land;* B ὄρη; 1Q hrrym. Cf. Ovid *Amores* ii.16, "At vos, qua veniet, timidi subsidite montes, Et faciles curvis vallibus este viae."

gates of the city of Babylon, this being, as Alexander says, "one of those minute coincidences with history."[5]

The victorious march of the Persian king is not to be attributed to his own wisdom and power, but to the working of the Lord. God causes all the events of daily life so to work that the way of the king will be easy and the difficulties removed.[6] To the world it would seem that Cyrus was a mighty conqueror, wise in the ways of warfare; but whereas this may have been the case, the ultimate reason for his victories was that God was carrying out His purposes of redemption. It was His will that His people should return from Babylon to Palestine and that there the Christ should be born.

3 Not only will Cyrus find easy access to the cities that lie in his way but he will also take possession of their treasures. The words *treasures of darkness*, in light of the parallel clause, would seem to refer to treasures that are hidden away from men, namely the treasures of the cities Cyrus will conquer. The *hidden things of secret places* are the treasures, such as jewels, that belonged to the city in which they were hidden.[7] All these will be taken by Cyrus, but not in his own strength. It is the God of Israel who will give them to him.

The first reason for God's action is introduced by *lᵉmaʿan (to the end that)*. Cyrus is to know that the God of Israel, who calls Cyrus by his name (see comments on 43:1), is the Lord.[8] Duhm thinks that access to the treasures of Babylon is no ground for knowledge of the fact that the one who has given victory to Cyrus is Yahweh. This hardly does justice to the situation. The climax of Cyrus' actions is the freeing of the Jews and permitting them to return to Jerusalem (Ezra 1:1-4). Through all his successes, climaxing in this act, he is to come to the knowledge that the One who has directed his ways is the God of the Jews. The language does not necessarily suggest a true conversion upon Cyrus' part, but simply that he will be able to identify the One who has used him in his accomplishments. There is an interesting statement in Josephus to the effect that the prophecy of Isaiah did actually have

---

[5] Cf. *Iliad* ix.383.

[6] אושר — 1Q *y'wsr*. I incline to regard the *Ketiv* as original.

[7] Cf. Xenophon *Cyropaedia* v.2, 8; vii.2, 11; Pliny *Natural History* xxxiii.15, passages that reflect upon the wealth of Babylon. Cf. also Herodotus i.178-183; Aeschylus *Persians* 52f. Gesenius appeals to Brerewood, who estimates that there were in all about 126,224,000 pounds sterling of gold and silver.

[8] Cf. Cyrus' Cylinder, *ANET*, pp. 315f.

an influence upon the king.[9] That such was the case is not as impossible as some would have us believe. Cyrus was a man interested in various religions, and in his proclamation of emancipation for the Jews he does attribute the deliverance to Yahweh, the God of Israel. Inasmuch as he was interested in the different religions, he may very well have wished to see the sacred writings of the Hebrews, and were that the case, would have read this present prophecy. When one strips away all the presuppositions that must accompany the position that there was a "Second Isaiah" it is quite probable that Josephus' report is correct.

4 This verse contains a second reason why God is using Cyrus. It is for the sake of His servant Jacob and Israel His chosen one. What Cyrus does he does not for his own sake but for the people of God. The conjunction *waw* (*and*) before the imperfect (*I shall call*) is best rendered in English by *therefore*. It resumes what has been introduced in 4a, and gives emphasis to the previous words.

It is for Israel's sake that God has called Cyrus by his name, distinguishing him from other rulers and giving to him titles of honor such as *anointed* and *shepherd*. This God did even though Cyrus had not known Him. The latter clause probably refers to the time before birth, just as the Lord says to Jeremiah, "Before I formed thee in the womb, I knew thee" (Jer. 1:5). The reference, however, may be to a time when Cyrus was yet steeped in idolatry, long before he could have known the name of the God of Israel.[10]

5 If Cyrus ever read these words he did not heed them, for although in his proclamation in Ezra 1:1-4 he acknowledged the

---

9 "Cyrus knew these things since he had read (ἀναγινώσκων) the book of his prophecy which Isaiah had left behind (κατέλιπεν) two hundred and ten years earlier" (*Antiquities* xi.1.2f.) . Some have sought to show that Scripture at this point has been influenced by Babylonian court style. Cf. R. Kittel, *Geschichte des Volkes Israels*, Vol. III, 1927; Ernst Sellin, *Studien zur Entstehungsgeschichte des jüdischen Gemeinde nach dem babylonischen Exil*, Leipzig, 1901; and above all Behr, *The Writings of Deutero-Isaiah and the Babylonian Royal Inscriptions*.

10 Note the chiasm in 4a; *my servant Jacob and Israel my chosen.* וָאֶקְרָא — imp. with *waw* consecutive following a statement of cause, introduced by *lᵉma'an*, which may be regarded as a protasis. *'ăkannekā* — imp. employed in prophetical style to express an event that is nascent (γιγνόμενον). This lends vividness to the picture. וְלֹא — *but thou*; the clause is circumstantial; i.e. *under the condition that thou, etc.*

sovereignty of Israel's God, nevertheless, in his proclamation to the Babylonians he also acknowledged the existence of Marduk. These words therefore stress the fact that the one who has raised up Cyrus and brought about his significant career is Yahweh, the only God.

Yahweh also girds Cyrus, strengthening him personally and investing him with royal dignity so that for Israel's sake he will be victorious.

6 A third reason for the work of Cyrus is that all men may know that there is no god beside Yahweh. The expressions *from the rising of the sun* and the *place of its setting*[11] include the entire inhabited earth. All flesh is to possess this knowledge, and not merely Cyrus. In what sense, however, did the release of the Jews from Babylon cause all flesh to know that Yahweh alone is the true God? Obviously the return from exile did not accomplish this end. Nevertheless, this is the end for which Cyrus was raised up. We need not necessarily assume that this purpose would be immediately accomplished. Cyrus was raised up that the Jews might return to Palestine and that Christ might then be born in Bethlehem, and that when redemption had been accomplished and its message proclaimed there might be a universal acknowledgment that the God of Israel is the true God. The prophecy would find fulfillment in the conversion of mankind, and more particularly at that time when every knee should bow and every tongue confess that Jesus is the Lord to the glory of God the Father. As verse 5 began with this remarkable utterance, so the present verse concludes, *I am the Lord and there is none else*.

7 Within the present context (namely vv. 5-7) there appears to be a double reference. Thus, when the prophet speaks of doors of brass, etc. he is evidently alluding to something specific, such as the doors of Babylon, yet at the same time is referring to obstacles generally that will stand in the way of Cyrus' approach. In now speaking of light and darkness he may be alluding to the dualistic religions of the time of Cyrus,[12] and yet he is employing the words also in a far more profound sense to combat the basic dualism that is found everywhere in the heart of fallen man. To

---

11 The f. suffix has *Raphe* instead of *Mappiq*.

12 Muilenburg (*IB*) notes that the view that there is here a polemic against Zoroastrian dualism has been generally and properly discarded. Isaiah is combatting not one, but all false religions.

the objection that this might have given offense to Cyrus it can only be replied that the prophet Isaiah was writing in opposition to error, and his clear statement of the truth in which the God of Israel is magnified would serve to point out to all who read it that the dualism that lies so deep in the human consciousness is an evil thing.

At the same time it is not doing justice to the text to see in it merely a reference to calamities and well-being. The light is formed by God Himself, and is a figure for salvation and truth, which come from God alone. Likewise, He creates the darkness, the opposite of light. The verb *bara'* implies the ease with which God by the Word of His power brings darkness into existence. The reference is not to the black of night, but to the opposite of light. As light involves truth and salvation, so darkness must be dispelled if there is to be light.

Instead of saying that Yahweh forms peace, the prophet asserts that He makes peace. The word includes wholeness and well-being. The Qumran Scroll reads *good* in place of *peace*, and this is the opposite of *evil*. With the word *evil* the same verb *bara'* is employed. There is no reason why the word is not to be taken in an all-inclusive sense. The absence of light and peace is darkness and evil. In the very context, then, we are compelled to admit that the word includes all evil, moral as well as calamities.

Does not this passage, therefore, teach that God is the author of sin? Delitzsch speaks of a *decretum absolutum*, which, he thinks, would deny creaturely freedom. In our approach to this difficult subject we must be guided alone by what Scripture says, and at this point the significance of systematic theology becomes very clear. The Bible teaches that there is a *decretum absolutum*, that God has foreordained whatsoever comes to pass.[13] Likewise, the Bible also teaches the responsibility of the creature. Both are scriptural truths and both are to be accepted. To stress the first aspect of the truth at the expense of the second is to fall into the error of fatalism or hyper-Calvinism. To stress the second at the expense of the first is to fall into the error of Arminianism. There is a third position, namely to accept both aspects even though one cannot harmonize nor reconcile them. They can, however, be reconciled by God. Hence, even though we say that God has foreordained

13 E.g. Ps. 33:11; Isa. 14:24; 46:9, 10; Dan. 4:35; Acts 2:23; Rom. 11:33-36; Eph. 1:4; 3:9, 11; 2 Tim. 1:9; 1 Pet. 1:20, 21; Rev. 17:17.

whatsoever comes to pass, we are not thereby denying the responsibility of the creature.

But this is not to assert that God is the author of sin. The statements of the present verse must be explained in the light of the whole Bible. Scripture is its own interpreter, and Scripture makes clear that God is not evil and not the source of evil. God has included evil in His plan, and has foreordained its existence; and yet He Himself is not evil nor is He its author. Again, we have a line of teaching that we as creatures are unable to harmonize or reconcile; we must be believers. We gain nothing by seeking to minimize the force of the present verse. "O the depth of the riches both of the wisdom and knowledge of God! How unsearchable are his judgments, and his ways past finding out! For who hath known the mind of the Lord? or who hath been his counsellor? Or who hath first given to him, and it shall be recompensed unto him again? For of him, and through him, and to him, are all things: to whom be glory for ever. Amen" (Rom. 11:33-36).

> 8 Drop, ye heavens, from above, and let the clouds pour out righteousness: let the earth open, and let salvation and righteousness grow, let her bring them forth together, I the LORD have created it.

Verses 8-10 constitute a unit, each verse beginning with the Hebrew letter, *He*; v. 8 serves as a statement of the truth and the two following verses point out the folly of disbelief in the truth. Whether v. 8 also serves as a conclusion to vv. 1-7 or whether it is actually independent, constituting a new section of the prophecy, is difficult to determine. Certainly the verse advances to new heights, and yet at the same time is also a beautiful conclusion to the earlier verses.

8 By means of a command to the heavens and the clouds Isaiah gives a prediction of future events. The first verb is rare and means "to drop down, to fall down in great drops."[14] This command does not mean, as Volz suggests, that heaven and earth are themselves bringing and mediating our salvation. Rather, the picture merely indicates the abundance of righteousness. Heaven itself is not conceived as the source or origin of the salvation. The verb is causative, however, and so the heavens above are pictured as obeying the command of God and causing the rain to drop down.

14 Cf. Ar. *ra-'a-fa*, "to flow (of blood) ," "to bleed"; 1Q *hry'w*.

Parallel is the command to the clouds to pour out righteousness.[15] Here the verb is best taken as a jussive, *let them pour out.* By many, *righteousness* is regarded as a synonym for victory or prosperity. In the light of the context, however, this definition proves unsatisfactory. The word is closely related to *salvation*, and the two words often occur together. Indeed, *righteousness* points to a manifestation in which God is seen to be righteous in all His works and ways, and in which there is a righteousness among men whereby they are right with Him and also faithful in their dealings. In the broadest sense the term is a practical equivalent of *salvation.*

The earth beneath is also addressed. Perhaps the verb should be taken as a jussive, *and the earth* (in distinction to the heavens) *let it open* (its bosom) *in order that they may be fruitful.* Although no object is expressed, the verb is transitive and the object is understood. The following verb, *be fruitful,* causes difficulty; and perhaps the best way of rendering the entire line is: *And let the earth open that they* (i.e. heaven and earth) *may be fruitful with respect to salvation.* The entirety of nature must together bring forth the blessings commanded. If the earth does not open her bosom to receive the rain, then heaven and earth have not been successful in bringing forth salvation. The construction is difficult, and as Pieper says, this is an old *crux interpretum*; but the meaning is clear.

In the last line we may either render, *and let righteousness cause to grow,* or, *and let it cause to grow with respect to righteousness.* Between the two words *tzedeq* and *tzᵉdaqah* there is no essential difference of meaning. The water that comes from under the earth will water righteousness as a plant, so that it will grow. Thus, the earth, together with the heavens, causes the growth of righteousness in which the divine justice is realized in the promises made to Israel.

In the last verb the suffix is best understood in a neuter sense, as in Amos 1:3.[16] All the picture of blessing that this verse sets forth is a creation of God. Although the verb is perfect, it nevertheless expresses the future as a certainty.

That which is brought into being through God's agency is new and is described as creation. The sovereign power that brought

15 *šeḥāqîm* — *dust clouds, fine clouds.* 1Q enlarges the text and substitutes *wyiprh.*

16 The m. suffix refers to the general proposition previously stated.

heaven and earth into existence now is employed in bringing about the abundance of righteousness and salvation.

> 9 Woe to him who striveth with his Maker, a potsherd with potsherds of earth. Shall clay say to its former, What doest thou? and the work, He has no hands?
> 10 Woe to him who saith to a father, What wilt thou beget? and to a woman, What wilt thou bring forth?

9 These verses are probably to be taken in a general sense to point up the folly of any complaint against the supernatural work God will create.[17] The interjection may best be rendered *Woe,* for it is a cry of lament over any who would disbelieve in the certainty of the promised salvation. Such are to be pitied and are also the objects of displeasure. Although the subject of the participle is not mentioned, we may take it in an indefinite sense, *Woe to anyone who strives.* The language is terse, but the sense clear. "He who strives (in argument) with the One who formed him is an object of displeasure." To strive with God is to contend with Him in argument with the purpose of showing that what He has promised will not come to pass.

The second half of the line is explanatory of the first, and the word *potsherd* is epenthetic to the indefinite subject *anyone.* One who strives with his former is but a potsherd among the potsherds of the earth. The preposition *'eth* cannot have precisely the same connotation that it does in the first half of the line. This is no objection against the rendering adopted, for parallelism need not be complete in every respect. A potsherd from the potsherds of earth is simply an ordinary piece of pottery which has been made of clay.

In order to make clearer the absurdity of the creature's complaining against the Creator, Isaiah now speaks of the clay from which the sherd is made. "Shall the mere clay say to the former, i.e. the potter, etc." The double occurrence of *its former* is striking, first used in its general etymological sense of "former" and then in the sense of "potter." The verbs are imperfects, and hence are to be rendered by either the present or the future. Probably the first question may be translated, *What art thou doing?* i.e. What is the purpose of Thy action?

17 Volz would assume that the prophet's contemporaries were complaining about a heathen king being a *māšiah.*

203

Is the last question a continuation of the first, *and as for thy work, it has no hands?* or is there a second question, *and thy work, shall it say, He* (i.e. God) *has no hands?*[18] The latter construction better preserves the parallelism and is more in keeping with the Masoretic accents. Thus, *the clay* and *his work* are parallel, except that there is a certain amount of gradation in the expression *his work*. The very thing the potter has made asserts that the potter has no hands and cannot make anything, a statement whose absurdity is obvious.

The difficulty in finding a second question in the last line is the presence of the suffix *thy*. The question must then be understood as addressed either to God or to the potter. If this latter be correct, we may render, "and does thy work speak to thee, O man! He has no hands?"

10 The same thought is now expressed under a different figure; but the ethical viewpoint is stronger than in the preceding verse, and as Alexander says, "in a form still more emphatic and revolting." Whereas there are many parallels to the figure of a potter and the clay there apparently are none to the figure herein employed. There is no suffix with the word *father*, which would suggest the disrespect of the speaker. Likewise, the word *woman* instead of *his mother* probably points to the same thing, unless the word is to be rendered *wife*. The two verbs are futures. It is of course objected that the passage then makes no sense. How can a son that is not yet born complain to its father about what the father will bring forth or to its mother about her bearing?[19] Obviously the thought is an absurdity, but that is the very point of the passage: it is just as absurd for Israel to complain about what God will do in the future.

One who thus contests God's promises engages in the baldest kind of rationalism. The omnipotent and omniscient Creator in grace announces that He will bring to this earth an abundance of righteousness and salvation. The creature, however, declares that such a promise is not possible. In making such a judgment he has ruled God out of his thoughts and based his assertion merely upon the dictates of his own mind. He allows the mind of man to set up the bounds of what is and what is not possible. Well may Isaiah begin this verse with the terrible word "Woe!"

[18] The phrase may also be understood, *thy work* is that of a man *who has no hands.*

[19] תחילין — the termination corresponds to Ar. *-ina*, and bears the accent.

11 Thus saith the Lord, the Holy One of Israel and its former,
    Ask me of the things to come, concerning my sons and con-
    cerning the work of my hands ye may command me.
12 I have made the earth, and man upon it I created; I—my
    hands stretched out the heavens and all their host I com-
    manded.
13 I raised him up in righteousness, and all his ways will I make
    straight; it is he that will build my city, and my captivity he
    will send home, not for reward, and not for hire, saith the
    Lord of hosts.

11 With this verse the Lord begins His reply. The language is
appropriately stately and majestic. The nation is reminded that the
Speaker is the Holy One in Israel and also Israel's Former; hence
they are in no position to complain about what He does. God does
not wish to keep Israel in the dark respecting the things to come,
but commands the nation to ask Him concerning these things, for
He alone can give information about them. He not merely grants
Israel permission to ask but commands them so to do. Emphasis
falls upon *the coming things,* inasmuch as these words are first in
the clause. The imperative may either take two accusatives, *Ask me
the future things,* or the first word may be taken as expressing
specification, *With respect to the coming things ask me.*[20]

The second verb is probably best construed as a jussive, *ye may
command me.* The expressions *my sons* and *the work of my hands*
are parallel in meaning, both referring to Israel itself as the
creation of God.

12 Israel should give full trust to God's promises, for God has
created all things and has the power to carry out anything that He
has promised. The personal pronoun at the beginning of each line
of the verse calls attention to God Himself, the Speaker. It sets
forth God in contrast to Israel and to all that is not God. The first
line is chiastic, containing verb and object, then object and verb. *I
have made* calls to mind the question of verse 9, "What dost thou
make?" In mentioning man upon the earth the prophet uses the
verb *bara'* (create), and the language calls to mind Genesis 1:27.
The verse also reminds of the phrase "the people upon it" (42:5).

In the second line an alternative form of the personal pronoun

20 *še'ālûnî* — the ordinary imperative is *ša'alûnî,* singular, *še'al.* In pause,
however, the *a* vowel reappears with *Aleph* as *Qametz,* which is normal.

205

appears, which, like that in the first line, calls attention to God as the only Creator. The construction is, *I—my hands have stretched the heavens,* i.e. "my very hands." *My hands* calls to mind verse 11. With respect to the last clause the word *host* is best understood as referring to all that the heavens contain, and the verb practically has the force of *called into being.* In favor of this view, as over against that which would render *all the host of heaven I commanded,* is the parallelism.

13 This verse forms a conclusion to the thought just expressed. Through His power as the almighty Creator, God will give victory to Israel through Cyrus. The creation of all things had afforded a sufficient proof of the divine power, but now Isaiah exhibits the particular exercise of that power in the raising up of Cyrus, although he does not mention the latter by name. In translation the past should be retained, for the verb shows that the appearance of Cyrus upon the scene of human history is the work of God. That Cyrus had not actually appeared at the time when the prophet wrote is shown by the entire representation, which places him in the future. Cyrus' appearance is not by chance nor an event of questionable meaning for the Israelites, for he has been raised up in righteousness. In his appearance the righteousness of God has been manifested, which shows itself in His dealings with His people and in His faithfulness to the promises made to the fathers. Cyrus' appearance, therefore, should be a sign of hope to the Israelites, for it reveals God's righteousness.

It is Yahweh who will make smooth the ways upon which the king must travel (the expression is similar in force to 40:3). Cyrus' work is stated very succinctly: the building of Jerusalem, which God identifies as His city, and the sending forth (from bondage) of God's captivity. Emphasis falls upon the personal pronoun as though to stress, "it is he who will build, etc." When Cyrus gave permission to the Jews to return from Babylon (Ezra 1:1-4) he was indirectly responsible for the rebuilding of Jerusalem. In accomplishing this purpose Cyrus receives no reward of money or payment.

14 Thus saith the LORD, The toil of Egypt and the gain of Ethiopia, and the Sabeans, men of stature unto thee will pass and to thee they shall belong; after thee they shall go, in chains will they pass over; and unto thee will they bow

themselves, and to thee will they pray. Only in thee is God, and there is none beside, no other God.

15 Surely thou art a God hiding thyself, O God of Israel, the Savior.

16 They are ashamed and also confounded, all of them together, they are gone into confusion, the carvers of images.

17 Israel is saved in the LORD, with an everlasting salvation; ye shall not be ashamed, and ye shall not be confounded for ever.

14 Isaiah reverts to the thought of verses 6 and 7. With the appearance of Cyrus a change takes place in the history of the chosen people. Israel is to be exalted and the heathen nations are to come over voluntarily to her. It does not follow, however, that what is here described is to occur immediately after the liberation Cyrus procures; nor does it follow that the nations herein mentioned, Egypt, Ethiopia and the Sabeans, are precisely the nations in existence during Isaiah's day. Throughout history Egypt and Ethiopia served to represent a double people. At one time Egypt occupies the position of prominence; at another Ethiopia. Egypt was Israel's early persecutor and oppressor, and after the deliverance remained as an enemy of Israel until the rise of Assyria. In the conquest of Egypt and Assyria, Israel's exaltation is seen to be that much more significant and grand; and these conquered nations themselves are not left unrewarded for any good that may have come to Israel through their hand. The heathen nations are mentioned not so much for themselves but as representatives of the heathen world. Their conquest is spiritual in nature; they come to Israel in Jesus Christ.

The *toil of Egypt* signifies what Egypt has acquired by labor, and the *commerce of Cush* is that obtained by Cush (Ethiopia) through trade. Through the regular overflowing of its banks by the Nile, the land was rendered rich and fertile; and what Egypt toiled to produce grew in this fertile soil. Herodotus (iii.97, 114) mentions the articles of commerce in which Ethiopia dealt. The word *Sabeans* is probably best taken as an independent noun and not dependent upon *commerce*. It seems to refer to those who dwell in "Upper Egypt" between Egypt proper and the Lower Sudan. These are described as *men of measure*, i.e. of some stature. These countries with their wealth willingly pass over unto Israel. Emphasis is given by placing *unto thee* before the verb. The first preposition is a practical equivalent of 'el- (*unto*) and indicates direction, whereas the second (*to thee*) signifies possession. Having voluntarily passed over to Israel, the nations now belong to her. Instead of striving any longer for the gain that their own countries could provide, they will come over to Israel, where true gain is to be found. Indeed, as slaves they will go after Israel wherever it may lead. This phrase *after thee* explains *they shall be to thee*. They will come voluntarily and in chains. This phrase *in chains* does not mean that Israel has physically conquered them, nor that they have voluntarily placed physical bonds upon themselves, but is simply descriptive of the fact that they come to Israel as bondslaves.

Isaiah sets forth their attitude in the vigorous words, *and unto thee they shall bow down*. He does not mean that they will worship Israel, but that in bowing down they are acknowledging that only in Israel is the true God to be found. Likewise the prayer to Israel is not worship but the confession that in Israel God is truly present. The relationship between Israel and God is similar to that of Christ and His Church (cf. 1 Cor. 12:12). Paul evidently reflects upon this language when he says, "and declare that God of a truth is in you" (1 Cor. 14:25). The last clause is particularly forceful; *and there is none else; no deity at all*, i.e., "There is no God beside thee; absolutely none." There has been a whole-souled turning from idols to serve the one living and true God.

15 Who speaks these words? Some have thought that it is those who turn to God, and who are here speaking to their own idols and accusing them of being hidden gods, in that they cannot reveal the future nor display themselves as capable of bringing deliverance. However, this demands a change of subject in the second half of the verse, and such a change is quite abrupt and unnatural.

Far more likely the first half of the verse is addressed to the true God, and the language is that of Isaiah himself, an apostrophe, as it were; overcome with the strange wonder of the grand message that he has uttered he breaks forth into comment about God Himself. On this construction we may interpret, "If these things concerning the deliverance of Israel and the conversion of the heathen nations are to come to pass, then, indeed, Thou who art the Savior of Thy people art a God who hides Himself." The participle is reflexive, and suggests that God keeps hidden under the clouds of the contemporary situation the purposes of mercy He is about to reveal.

The profound truth is that God cannot be known by man apart

from revelation, and His ways are hidden from the eyes of man until He Himself makes them clear. If one were to examine the situation at the close of Isaiah's lifetime he would not know that the nation was to pass through a period of indignation when it would cease to exist as the theocracy. The distinction between *'el* and *'elohim* is significant. Isaiah addresses God as *'el,* and thus preserves the full distinction between God and man. When, however, he speaks of Israel's God he uses the common word *'elohim,* giving to Him what is almost an epithet, *Savior.* Thus, the wondrous hidden mystery of God and His purposes of salvation go hand in hand.[21]

16 This verse sets forth the great contrast between God's people and the makers of idols, which will become manifest when God exalts Israel. It carries out the thought of 15a. Although the verbs are perfects, they refer to the time when the prophecy will be fulfilled and bring out the certainty of what they express. Their subject is the last two words, *the carvers of images.*[22]

The idol makers are ashamed, for their idols are of no profit. Moreover, they are confounded. The shame is perplexing and embarrassing. This applies not to some idol makers but to all of them. Together they have gone into confusion, the end that awaits them.

17 In contrast to the idol makers, however, Israel will be saved with an everlasting salvation. This fact also suggests that the shame and confusion mentioned in verse 16 are not temporary, but the shame and ignominy of everlasting punishment, the opposite of what Israel receives.

Israel is emphatic, and forms a striking contrast to the last two words of the preceding verse, *carvers of images.* This juxtaposition of the two expressions is interesting, for it also throws some light upon the usage of the word *Israel* in verse 17. Many of these carvers of images were Israelites, and hence Israel here is not necessarily coextensive with the empirical entity, the historical nation. It is the spiritual Israel and not Israel after the flesh that is in view. This Israel will be saved in the Lord, i.e. its salvation will

---

[21] The verse attains a remarkable climax in the word *Savior.* Cf. *ANET,* pp. 368ff., for a formally similar hymn to Amon.

[22] *tzirim — images, forms.* Cf. Ar. *ṣûrāh.*

be spiritual.[23] The contrast is not therefore between those Israelites who were delivered from Babylon and those who remained behind.

It is important to note the preposition. Israel is saved "not merely through the Lord, but in him, i.e. by virtue of an intimate and vital union with him, as genuine and living members of his body" (Alexander). Hence, to render the preposition *by* does not do it full justice. The Lord is more than the agent through whom the salvation is obtained; He is Himself that salvation and in Him Israel finds deliverance. This is supported by the additional statement, *a salvation of eternities,* which in this particular context points out that the salvation is not a temporary deliverance but one that will endure for all time.

Furthermore, those who are the recipients of this salvation will not be *ashamed* nor *in confusion,* even for worlds of eternity. Whereas such shame and confusion may come upon those who worship idols, it will never come to those who receive eternal salvation of the Lord. The last three words, each beginning with the consonant *Ayin,* create a telling effect in stressing the eternity of the Lord's salvation.

18 For thus saith the LORD, creator of the heavens, he is the God, Former of the earth and its Maker; he established it, not a desolation did he create it, for dwelling he formed it. I am the LORD, and there is none else.

19 Not in secret have I spoken, in a dark place of the earth, I have not said to the seed of Jacob, In vain seek ye me. I am the LORD, speaking truth, declaring right things.

20 Gather yourselves and come, draw near together, ye escaped of the nations. They know not, those carrying the wood, their graven image and praying to a god who does not save.

21 Make known and bring near! Yea, let them consult together. Who has caused this to be heard of old, since then has declared it? Have not I, the LORD? and there is no other God besides me; a righteous and a saving God, there is none beside me.

18 The introductory *For* gives the reason for the statement just made. The idol makers will fall into confusion, but Israel will go

---

23 Isaiah here goes to the heart of the matter. God used Cyrus to bring to an end the period of wrath and to permit the exiles to return home. This, however, was but a preliminary, preparatory step toward the coming redemption which the Lord Himself would accomplish.

into everlasting salvation, because the Lord is the Creator of heaven and earth, who created them for a specific purpose and will see that that purpose is carried out. The descriptive phrase *creator of the heavens* is not to be construed with *Lord* but rather with what follows, thus: "The Creator of the heavens He is THE God." The personal pronoun is emphatic; it takes up the thought expressed in *creator of the heavens* and also serves as predicate to *THE God.* That the Lord is the Creator is made clear by the entire context and by the explicit statement, *I am the Lord, and there is none else.*

What is taught in this language is that the true God (note the force of the definite article with *'elohim*) is identified by the fact that He has created the heavens. Emphasis also falls upon the phrase *creator of the heavens,* for this sets forth the distinguishing mark of the true God.

The second line is to be construed in similar fashion, the emphatic clause coming first; *the Former of the earth and the One who made it; He has established it.* The two participles may serve as a hendiadys, *he who made the earth by forming it;* and the last verb is best taken in its ordinary sense of *establishing.*

A statement of the purpose of creation follows in the verse's third line, namely that God created the earth to be inhabited. Isaiah uses a word that appeared in Genesis 1:2; but Duhm comments that the prophet's language has nothing to do with Genesis 1:2, for if it did the prophet would have been able to see that in the beginning the earth was a *tohu (desolation)*. This, however, is a misunderstanding of the language. Isaiah does not deny that the earth was once a *tohu;* his point is that the Lord did not create the earth to be a *tohu,* for an earth of *tohu* is one that cannot be inhabited, and has not fulfilled the purpose for which it was created. The purpose rather was that the earth might be inhabited. Those commentators who see herein a reflection upon the Holy Land are probably correct. Isaiah's meaning apparently is that the world, including the Holy Land itself, was to be inhabited and not desolate. We must, however, note the deeper significance. Sin destroyed the human race in that it separated the race from God. God's purposes of salvation were not to deliver a few isolated individuals from the fallen race, but rather to save the world; and the redeemed world will be inhabited by those who sing God's praise.

He who utters this stupendous pronouncement is Yahweh, the

God of Israel, who is thus identified as the one true God beside whom there is no other. The negative exclusive statement is essential, for it accentuates the positive *I am the Lord* and in the clearest possible manner rejects any form of polytheism.

19 As in the creation of the world the Lord has shown Himself to be the one true and living God, so He continually shows Himself in His clear revelations to Israel His people. The first clause, *Not in secret have I spoken,* is usually interpreted to mean that the act of God's speaking has not been in secret, but openly, through His prophets. This is of course true, but it may be that the adverbial clause *not in secret* is better understood with the subject, rather than with the act of speaking. Thus, "I in secret have not spoken." On this construction the emphasis falls upon the fact that God has not been in secret when He has spoken; rather, He has been open and has spoken revealingly. The distinction is a fine one, and whichever of the two options we adopt we must note that the stress falls upon the fact that God's revelation is a spoken one.

The second clause by its number of constructs adds to the indefiniteness of the phrase, *in the place of the land of darkness.* It is likely, as Torrey suggests, that this may mean nothing more than "some spot in some dark land." The basic thought is that the revelations of God are open and accessible to those who would receive them. God does not render Himself obscure so that those who seek Him must resort to the devious practices of magic and superstition that characterized seekers after false gods. There is not necessarily any reference to Sheol here nor to the darkness of Genesis 1:2. Rather, the point appears to be to contrast God's method of revelation with the dark practices of the heathen soothsayers.

In the preceding verse the word *tohu* had the sense of desolation, as in Genesis 1:2. In this verse, however, it seems to have the sense of *in vain.* Yet, despite this slight modification of connotation, it is correct to say that as God's creation was not for the purpose of being a *tohu,* so also His revelation is not a *tohu* but fulfills its purpose. The difference in connotation is not as great as at first sight appears. If the original creation was *desolation* man could not live upon it, and hence as far as fulfilling the purposes for which it had been created it was in vain. So when God commands His worshippers to seek His face, they are not to come in some way that will not bring them near unto Him, for such would be to come in vain. The imperative *seek*, as used here, is possibly a cultic term.

God characterizes Himself as One who speaks righteousness and effects the proclamation of *right things*. The two words may have slightly different connotations, but the context would require that both be understood in the sense of *truth*. The things God declares are right things for they are true. In contrast to the dark and mysterious practices of magic and sorcery to which the heathen world resorted, God proclaimed His word far and wide in tones that all might hear and understand. The culmination of this method of revelation is found in the revelation of a Son who in the days of His flesh declared: "I spake openly to the world; I ever taught in the synagogue, and in the temple, whither the Jews always resort; and in secret have I said nothing" (John 18:20).

20 As a conclusion the Lord commands the escaped of the nations to assemble together,[24] that He may declare that He is the only Savior and that He may command them to turn unto Him. The two imperatives that introduce the verse are to be construed together, almost as a hendiadys (cf. 49:18 and 60:4; note also 41:21 and 43:9). The nations are to come gathered together. Although this is an invitation it is nevertheless couched in the imperative, for it is the voice of absolute authority. Parallel in thought is the third imperative; the assembly is not to take place at a distance but the escaped of the nations are to draw near that they may hear what the God of Israel has to say. The address is made to the escaped ones of the Gentiles, i.e. those of the Gentile nations that have escaped the judgment of God. In the redemption and deliverance of Israel judgment will also fall upon the Gentiles. The reference is not to any particular victory of Cyrus, but to the great victory when the "prince of this world is cast out." It is a remnant of the heathen that constitutes the fullness of the Gentiles, and it is this escaped remnant that is commanded to come together.

Included would be any that yet trusted in idols. The folly of their belief is shown in that whereas the idols should bear and support them in time of need, they themselves actually carry the wood of their idols. It seems best to supply an object, rather than to take the verb intransitively, *they do not know*. In the last clause

[24] 1Q reads *w'tyw*, i.e. *and come!*

the word *'el* seems to be chosen to show that the idol is supposed to be a true god distinct from man.

21 The first two imperatives have no objects. Most expositors, therefore, assume something like "your arguments" or "Declare what will take place in the future." The imperative is thought to be a command to the escaped to set forth their cause if that were possible. The first imperative refers to the act of proclaiming or declaring, whereas the second has in mind that of bringing near the cause. There is then a transition from the second person to the third, and the verb is to be construed as a jussive. The introductory particle *'aph* permits the rendering, *Let them indeed confer together*. It is possible, as Alexander suggests, that the change of person indicates that "they are unable or unwilling to accept the challenge, or at least in doubt and hesitation with respect to it. They are therefore invited to deliberate together, or, as some understand it, to take counsel of those wiser than themselves." The word *together* suggests that if individually the heathen cannot recognize and foretell the future, they possibly can do it together.

The Lord does not wait for the heathen but immediately presents His own cause, by means of a question that shows that He alone has the power of foretelling what would come to pass. *This* would refer to the judgment and deliverance spoken of in the preceding verses. Perhaps it is correct to say that its immediate manifestation was seen in the fall of Babylon, although there is no reason for so restricting it. No one but the God of Israel has caused this fact to be heard (i.e. through proclamation) from ancient times. The Lord foretold the exile and the deliverance as well as the ultimate salvation before these things had taken place. Parallel is the expression *me'az* (lit., *from then*). The language might include that which was quite recent; nevertheless, in this context it would seem to suggest that these prophecies were ancient ones, uttered some time before the events predicted. Possibly the reference is to prophecies concerning the downfall of Babylon, such as those found in chapters thirteen and twenty-one. The answer intended by the double question is that no one has caused this to be heard and no one has declared it from before. It is a challenge Yahweh, the God of Israel, alone is able to make.

In the last sentence the parenthetical clause, *and there is no other God beside me*, may be rendered freely, *beside whom there is no other God*. The only One who has been able to predict beforehand the judgment and deliverance is the God of Israel, Yahweh, who is the only God in existence, and who has shown Himself to be just in that He has acted both in judgment and in salvation in accordance with the strictest demands of His holiness. He is also a Savior, whose salvation is not proffered at the expense of justice, but is accomplished to its satisfaction.[25]

A helper just He comes to thee, His chariot is humility,
His kingly crown is holiness, His sceptre pity in distress.
The end of all our woe He brings: Wherefore the earth
*   is glad and sings*
We praise thee, Saviour, now; mighty in deed art thou.

22   Turn unto me and be ye saved, all ye ends of the earth, for I am God, and there is none else.

23   By myself have I sworn; the word has gone out of a mouth of righteousness, and will not return, that unto me every knee shall bow, every tongue shall swear.

24   Only in the LORD have I, he says, righteousness and strength; unto him shall he come, and all that were incensed at him shall be ashamed.

25   In the LORD they shall be justified and boast themselves all the seed of Israel.

22 As far as form is concerned, this verse with its imperative preceded by a declarative statement is similar to the saying of Jesus, "Come unto me all ye that labor." Before uttering that command our Lord had made a stupendous declaration concerning Himself and His intimate relationship with the Father. Here too, the Lord has asserted that He is both just and a Savior and that He alone has been able to foretell the judgment and salvation. It might seem then that for the heathen there remained nothing but destruction. Such is not the case, for an invitation of mercy is extended to them. They are not to continue in their former ways but are to turn from them. The verb suggests a turning away from something and a turning to something; a true conversion. Conversion is similarily presented in the New Testament (cf. 1 Thess. 1:9; Acts 14:15; 15:19).

Although the verb is plural, and although the subject is found in the expression *ends of the earth,* the reference is to men individu-

---

[25] Despite some commentators the verse teaches that God is both righteous and a Savior.

ally. If the ends of the earth turn unto God, it is only because the individual men who make up the ends of the earth have themselves turned. There is a stress upon individual conversion.

The invitation to turn, like the invitation of Christ, is couched in the imperative, and thus the responsibility of the individual is set forth. Duhm, however, is somewhat incautious when he says that it is "the affair of the individual, whether he wants to allow himself to be saved in the kingdom of God or not." Although God here commands men to turn to Him, it does not follow that He gives to all who hear the command the power and ability to obey. Augustine's *"da quod iubes et iube quod vis"* is perfectly scriptural. It is God who commands; and man, the creature, has the responsibility of obeying.

The phrase *the ends of the earth* (lit., *the farthest ends of the earth*) includes all who dwell upon the earth. Penna beautifully stresses the close relationship between true conversion and the universality of the Gospel message. The two imperatives belong together; the first, as has often been pointed out, is hortatory, and the second promising. The thought is, "turn to Me and ye will surely be saved."[26] Lastly, the reason for these things is found in the fact that Yahweh is the true God.

Monotheism, true conversion, and universalism go together. Out of true monotheism, the doctrine that Yahweh, the God of Israel, is the only true God, Creator of heaven and earth, flows the fact that there may be a true conversion. Men have rebelled against God, and can only find salvation when, having turned from the vain idols of abomination, they turn to the God who has made them. Furthermore, inasmuch as all men have rebelled, the invitation is open to all men to turn. In the Gospel alone is true universalism to be found.

23 That men will turn to Him and bow the knee before Him will so surely occur that the Lord has sworn by Himself, for there is no greater by whom He may swear. The form of the oath is in the words, "As I live," and Paul retains this in his use of the verse. The second line is not the content of the oath, as though God had said, "By myself have I sworn that the word has gone out, etc." but is really a parallel to the first. *By myself* (and the position of the words renders them emphatic) *have I sworn; the word has gone*

---

[26] The second imperative gives the result of the action expressed by the first.

out, etc. To speak of a word going out is to speak of God's uttering or speaking a word (cf. Dan. 9:23, 25). It is best to construe *mouth* with *righteousness* and to translate, *there has gone out from the mouth of righteousness a word, and it will not return.* The mouth of righteousness is God's mouth, the mouth that speaks only righteousness. Stress here falls upon a verbal revelation. The word of promise comes from a mouth of righteousness. This word is efficacious and will accomplish its purpose, not returning unfulfilled to the mouth that spoke it.

The content of the promise is that *every knee will bow* and *every tongue will swear.* Perhaps the two verbs do allude to cultic acts, but in this particular context the thought is that of complete submission to the Lord God of Israel. To kneel and to swear involve full and complete recognition of the sovereignty and power of the One to whom such homage is rendered (cf. 1 Kings 19:18). The imperfects contain the thought of compulsion; this clause tells what will surely be, and is stronger therefore than a promise. In his usage of the passage in Philippians 2:10, Paul adds that every tongue should confess "that Jesus Christ is Lord, to the glory of God the Father" (cf. also Rom. 14:11). It does not follow, however, that this is a picture of universal salvation. The submission herein pictured would seem to be both voluntary and involuntary. Even though not all men turn to the Lord in true repentance, nevertheless, every knee will bow and every tongue will swear, for God is sovereign and all creation must so acknowledge Him.

24 The primary sense of *'ak* is affirmative (*surely*), and out of this grows its restrictive force, "Surely in Yahweh, and indeed, in the company of no other God but He." Differences of opinion exist as to the proper interpretation of the parenthetical words, *to me he says.* The phrase is usually rendered, *one says to me,* or *men say of me;* but this is not clear. Possibly the thought is that men say to God that salvation is found only in Him, or men assert concerning God that only in Him is salvation. It is, however, also possible to take *'amar* (one says) as parenthetical, and to connect *to me* with *righteousness.* On this construction the meaning is, "Only in the Lord, say men, is there salvation for me," or "Only in the Lord, men declare, do I have salvation." On either construction the sense is essentially the same, and what is to be noted is the emphasis placed upon *the Lord* as the source of salvation.

The plural of *righteousness* is probably intensive to indicate the

217

abundance of righteousness found in the Lord. So Paul says that "grace did more abound" (Rom. 5:15). Although *tzᵉdaqah* is capable of varying connotations, there is no good reason for not giving to it here its common meaning of righteousness. Together with the richness of righteousness is strength, which man needs to live in this world. Delitzsch therefore is essentially correct when he speaks of "the strength of sanctification, and of the conquest of the world."

The second line begins with an emphatic *unto Him*, i.e. unto Yahweh; and this is followed by a verb in the singular. The subject is *he who bows the knee to the Lord*. He is the one who comes in repentance unto Yahweh. On the other hand those who are incensed at Yahweh will be ashamed. The two verbs stand in juxtaposition the one to the other, and thus yield an effective contrast which is rendered more striking by the alliteration of the first two letters of each verb in the Hebrew (*yb*). The enemies of Yahweh are inflamed; their attitude is not one of neutrality or passivity; they are active in their indignation against the God of Israel, and their end is shame.

25 This verse constitutes a concluding declaration of the salvation of the true Israel taken from the whole human race. Again the emphasis falls upon the *Lord*, in that the word is placed first. The two verbs do not constitute a hendiadys; rather, the first states the fact that Israel will be justified, and the second that, as a consequence of their justification, they will sing praise to God. The concept *justify* is here about equivalent to *salvation*, as is often the case in these particular chapters of Isaiah. At the same time it is not a precise equivalent, for it also stresses righteousness. In saving Israel God has shown Himself to be just. As a result of such salvation all the seed of (i.e. those descended from) Israel will boast themselves or praise God.

The reference is not to the historical entity Israel, for not all of the historical Israel repented. Indeed, there were those who belonged to the historical Israel who opposed our Lord and cried out for His death while He was here upon earth. The reference rather is to the Israel of God, the true believers in Israel whose company was increased in multitude by the addition of those from the Gentiles who turned from idols to serve the living and true God.

CHAPTER FORTY-SIX

1 Bel crouches, Nebo is stooping, their images are for the beasts and the cattle. Your burdens are packed up as a load to the weary.
2 They are stooped, they are crouched together, they are not able to escape the burden; even themselves are gone into captivity.

1 In the preceding chapter Isaiah has shown what awaits redeemed Israel, and now he proceeds to point out what will happen to Babylon. Even the greatest of Babylon's gods will be destroyed. The prophet begins with a perfect to express the certainty of what he will describe; then, for the sake of liveliness and variety he continues with a participle. The first verb suggests a crouching or sinking down upon one's knees (cf. Judg. 5:27; 2 Kings 9:24; Ps. 20:8). Bel is sinking down, for he has been struck by the destroying blow of Yahweh in the judgment that comes over the heathen empire of man. The second verb is found only here and in the following verse. It seems to be related to *qeres* (*hook*) and possibly suggests a bending over.[1]

Bel and Nebo were the two most prominent deities in the Babylonian pantheon. Bel (compare the Canaanitish Baal) here probably signifies Marduk. In fact the idol is sometimes designated Bel-Marduk, and it may be, as Pieper suggests, that the two names bear about the same relationship one to another as Yahweh and Elohim in Hebrew. Nebo (*Nabu*) was the son of Bel-Marduk and was worshipped chiefly at Borsippa (Birs Nimaud), about three hours south of Babylon. Here a temple was dedicated to him and

[1] Ugaritic offers parallels to the thought, e.g.,
   There collapses Yam, he falls down
   To the ground; there quivers his face and crumble his features.
(Cf. *Baal*, text on p. 82 of *CMAL*.) Different verbs, however, are here employed. Cf. also p. 78, where the verb is *t'gly*.

with it a tower (*e-ur-imin-an-ki*). He was the god of writing and divine interpretation and seems to have been an object of devotion on the part of the intellectual world. In the New Year's Festival both these gods were together. They are probably mentioned as representative of the religion of Babylonia; when they fall the religion itself is destroyed.[2]

It was believed in the ancient world that the fortunes of a nation were bound up with its gods. Hence, if the gods were destroyed the nation itself perished; and likewise, if the nation had been defeated in war the gods themselves were done for. The carrying of the gods in a procession would signify the defeat or carrying away of the conquered nation itself.[3]

The suffix in the phrase *their images* is best referred to the idols themselves to distinguish between the gods and their representations in images. The images are now for the beasts and the cattle to bear.

Isaiah addresses the people and speaks of *your burdens*, i.e. the things that are carried by them. The reference is to the statues of the idols, Bel and Nebo. These burdens have been loaded on the weary animals. They should bear the people throughout their life; instead, they themselves must be borne.

The prophet does not state why the idol images are borne. If it be in a procession, why are the animals spoken of as tired? Possibly the statues are placed upon beasts that were handy in order to carry them away, and thus there might be symbolized the destruction of the enemy itself. Volz also suggests that the images were valuable in themselves. If this is correct it points to a gross humiliation for the idols. Once they were borne in proud procession; now they are carried away on tired beasts.[4]

How can what is related here be harmonized with Cyrus' actions at the downfall of Babylon? Cyrus did not destroy the idol religions, but granted a freedom of religion to the conquered people.

---

2 A boundary stone of the Kassite period (12th cent. B.C.) shows the crowned Marduk with a horned mythical animal at his feet. At Calah a statue of Nebo from the time of Adad-nirari III (810-782 B.C.) was excavated, bearing the inscription: "Trust in Nebo; do not trust in any other god." See *VBW* for illustrations.

3 Cf. *KAT*, pp. 272f.

4 Volz suggests that *tired* is a fine and ingenious (*geistreich*) touch in the description. The gods give no power, but weary even the creatures that must be associated with them. That there is reflection upon the Akitu festival is questionable.

This passage, however, is not to be understood as a description of the fall of Babylon but as a figurative statement of the truth that the religion of the kingdom of man will come to a final end. Bel and Nebo were the chief representatives of that religion; and when, like Dagon in the temple at the time of Samuel, they had fallen down, that religion of hostility to God was also done away. The picture is that of the carting away of these images so that they will no longer be honored or seen.

2 Isaiah takes up the thought of verse 1a, using the same verbs but in inverted order. They have stooped and crouched together, i.e. have crumbled to pieces entirely, in that they are either completely destroyed, or the two have fallen side by side. The verbs appear asyndetically, and this lends vividness to the expressions.

Inasmuch as the gods have completely crumbled they are not able to deliver the beasts from the burden their images have made. Isaiah makes a distinction between the lifeless statues themselves and the numina or divinities, which are supposed to be distinguished from the actual statues. As Delitzsch remarks, they are beingless beings whose personality "consists of nothing more than the wood and metal of which their images are composed." The subject therefore of *are able* is Bel and Nebo. If the great gods cannot save their burdens, how much less can the minor deities do so.

The prophet uses a reflexive pronoun, placing it first in the clause and so emphasizing it. He speaks of *their soul,* which here refers to the inmost being or essential nature of the idol. The word distinguishes the idols from the statues representing them. Inasmuch as they did not have any existence apart from the wooden and metal statues, the whole seems to have a tone of sarcasm. Alexander brings out the force, "The whole god, soul and body, all that there was of him, was gone into captivity."

In the last clause each word is significant; first *their soul;* then the phrase *into captivity,* which, coming before the verb, is emphatic; and finally the verb, consisting, inasmuch as it is in pause, of three tone-long vowels, which as North indicates suggests utter weariness.[5]

> **3** Hearken unto me, O house of Jacob, and all the remnant of the house of Israel, those who are born from the belly, who are carried from the womb.

[5] *hā-lā́-ḵāh* — it has gone; 1Q *hlkw.*

4 Even unto old age I am He, and unto gray hair I will bear
you; I have done it and I will carry, and I will bear and I
will save.

5 To whom will ye liken me and make me equal, and compare
me that we may be equal?

3 Isaiah now introduces the Lord as commanding the nation to
hearken unto Him. The *house* of Jacob includes all the descendants of Jacob alive at that time. In Isaiah's day the exile had not
yet occurred; but the prophet, looking into the future in the Spirit
of prophecy, sees his people in captivity. The terms *house* and
remnant are therefore equivalent. At the same time, inasmuch as
the address is to those alive in Isaiah's day and the northern tribes
have already gone into captivity, we are probably correct in assuming that the address is to Judah itself. The prophet describes
these people by using the masculine forms of the participles he had
employed in the feminine in verse 1. The idols have been carried
on beasts of burden, but the house of Jacob has been carried by its
God from the beginning of its existence. The words *belly* and
womb point to this beginning. It is perhaps difficult to tell precisely what is intended as far as the actual history of Judah is concerned, whether it be the call of Abraham or the events of the
exodus. The point is that God has been with Judah throughou
the entirety of her existence, even carrying her before she wa
born. When man carries his god, the end is destruction; when the
true God carries man, the end is salvation. The gods of Babylor
are so lifeless that they must be borne on weary beasts in flight; th
God of Israel, on the other hand, has carried His own peopl
through the entire course and history of their existence.

4 A mother carries her child and watches over it while it :
young. As it advances in life, it must go out on its own. For Israe
however, the protecting care of God extended not merely throug'
out the beginning but even to the end of life. Up to and eve
including the period of old age, I am He, that is, I am the sam
the absolute God who powerfully bears His people and watch
over them. In the second part of the line the parallel expressic
reads, *and up to old age I shall bear you.* The word *seybah* impli
hoary old age: *to the very end.* The verb is used of the bearing of
heavy burden.

To be noted is the fivefold use of the first person pronoun, *I.* It

222

Yahweh alone who is prominent. *I have done* means that God has acted in the past, bearing the people, and so will continue to do. Hence, as He has already done, so He will carry (lit., *lift*), and He will bear and will finally save. With this last verb there is again a contrast with the idols. They are unable to deliver their statues; but the God of Israel, having borne the nation throughout its history, will ultimately deliver it. The personal pronoun is omitted before the last verb. With each of the other verbs this pronoun has appeared, calling attention to the fact that Yahweh has acted and will act in Israel's history. The final work of deliverance, mighty and wondrous as it is, is simply stated, *I will deliver.*

5 This verse gives the logical conclusion of the preceding. Inasmuch as the idols are dead and lifeless and must be borne about, unable in any sense to save themselves, let alone to save others, and inasmuch as the eternal God has borne Israel throughout its long life, it follows that this God cannot in any sense be compared with His creation. Least of all may He be compared with idols. The verse is similar in thought to 40:18, 25, save that here the verbs of comparison are heaped together. There is a greater urgency in the language, which arises from the constant use of the first person pronoun in the preceding verse. The One who has done the things mentioned in verse 4 is One who is incomparable.

The introductory *To whom* possibly suggests the idols. God is not to be compared with any of the numina to which the heathen bow down. The first verb suggests a likening[6] and the second a making equal. In the third verb the causative force should be noted. The threefold expression is similar to 41:10, 20 and 43:7, and the conjunctions are not *waw* consecutive but merely correlative. With respect to the last verb, Hahn would make it depend upon *To whom* so as to obtain the sense, "To whom shall we be like?" It is better, however, to take the conjunction as expressing purpose and to render *that we may be like.* The thought then is that there is no one in the creation with whom God may be compared in order that they (God and the idol) may be like. By means of this question the utter folly and impossibility of comparing the incomparable eternal God with the created finite creature is brought out into the open.

---

6 *will ye liken me?* — note retention of final *yod* in imp., supported by 1Q.

6 The lavish ones weigh gold from the purse, and silver with
the rod of the balance they weigh; they hire a gilder and make
it a god; they bow down, yea they do obeisance.

7 They carry him; upon the shoulder they bear him, and they
cause him to rest in his place, and he stands, from his place
he will not move; one even cries unto him and he does not
answer; from his affliction he does not save one.

6 Verse 5 is transitional; it concludes what has preceded and
also introduces what follows. We may take the participles as subjects of *they will weigh*. The first participle refers to those who
pour or throw out gold. The *kis* (bag) seems to refer to the
container where specimens of gold were weighed, whereas the
qaneh is actually the beam used for the balance itself. The thought
of the first line is: "Those who pour out gold from the bag will
weigh silver with a balance"; literally, *They who pour out gold
from a bag, even silver with a balance they will weigh*. The reason
for this activity is not necessarily to pay the worker, but to provide
the metal necessary for the idol. Idols, useless and helpless as they
are, cost gold, hence the stress here upon gold.

Once the metal has been provided, the next step is the hiring of
a goldsmith who will fashion it into a god. This he will do by
overlaying the wood so that dead gold and silver now become a
living god. The worshippers themselves cannot make the metal
into a god; they can but hire a smith at their own expense, and in
return for this hire he fashions gold and silver that they have
provided for him into a god.

When the work is completed and the dead gold that came from
mines under the ground is made into a god, the worshippers
engage in the act of supreme folly in that they bow down to what
has just been created at their own expense. This is the fourth time
that the making of idols is described (cf. also 40:19; 41:7 and
44:9ff.).

7 Once the gold has been made into a god it is still as dead and
lifeless as before, even though its worshippers bow down to it. It
cannot move about and so those who worship it must themselves
carry it. The phrase *upon the shoulder* is to be construed with the
following verb, and the entire phrase is then explanatory of the
first verb. The purpose in lifting up the idol is to carry it to its
permanent place. Moving the large and heavy god from one place to

another is wearisome and involves toil and trouble.[7] Finally they cause the idol to rest in its position (lit., *under it*). There is assonance in the repeated sound of the suffix *-uhu* which concludes the three verbs.

When the worshippers have placed their god in its place it stands there firm and immovable (cf. Ps. 115:7). Nor can it answer prayer. It is an immovable god which is also deaf and dumb. The verb is in the singular, suggesting that it is an individual who calls for help. It is foolish to cry to the idol, however, for it cannot save one from the affliction and straits in which he may find himself.

8 Remember this and show yourselves men; bring it home, ye apostates, to your heart.

9 Remember the former things from eternity, for I am God, and there is no God besides, and there is none beside me.

10 Who maketh known from the former things the latter, and from ancient time the things that are not yet done, saying, My counsel shall stand, and all my pleasure I shall do.

11 Calling from the east a bird of prey, from a land of distance the man of his counsel; I have both said and will bring it to pass, I have formed and will also do it.

8 A command is given to the Israelites to remember the impotence of the idols. As a result of remembering these things, the worshippers are to take courage and stand firm. The second verb is one whose precise meaning is not known, but possibly we may render, *put yourselves on a firm foundation*. At any rate, the verb stresses the result of the first imperative. If the worshippers will consider both the impotence of the idols and the constant providence of their own God, they can strengthen themselves in their faith and in devotion to their God.

In the last part of the verse, the worshippers are addressed as *transgressors*, for they have broken God's commands in the worship of false gods. These are commanded to cause to return (the causative force should be noted) upon the heart what had long been away from the heart. The expression is stronger than *to place upon the heart* and implies a serious meditation upon and consideration of the fact that the gods whom they worship are vanity,

---

[7] A relief found in the palace of Tiglath-pileser III at Calah (modern Nimrud) shows the Assyrian troops carrying four statues of gods. A representation is given in *VBW*. Cf. Amos 5:26.

whereas their own God, Yahweh, is the eternal, ever living, sustaining God of His people.

9 The command *Remember* takes up the similar "Remember" of the preceding verse. Not only are the transgressors to remember and call to mind the facts just declared but they are also to remember the former course of their own history. The former things would seem to refer not to earlier prophecies, but to early events in Israel's history, such as the exodus and conquest. To indicate the antiquity of the former things the prophet adds the phrase, *from eternity* or *from olden time*. Inasmuch as the people are commanded to remember these things, they must have taken place in time; hence it is better to translate in this context, *from olden time*.

Many commentators take *ki* in the sense of *that*, and then regard it as introducing the object, as though the thought were, "Remember the former things, namely, that I am God, etc." It is better, however, to take the word as a causal conjunction, *because*, thus giving the reason for remembering. If God had nothing to do with these former events, as the idols had nothing to do with them, there is no reason for calling them to mind. From these former happenings, however, the fact of God's omnipotence is to be seen. Israel, therefore, is to call them to mind, because He is their God and in them they may see His hand at work directing their own history.

The Lord makes two statements concerning Himself, and to each of these there is appended an explanatory clause. First, *I am God;* *'el* points out that He is the true God in distinction from man the creature. The explanatory clause asserts that there is none else, and the phrase *and there is not* is emphatic. Secondly, as a predicate to *'anoki (I)* is *'elohim* (God), to show that He is true divinity, "the Being who united in Himself all divine majesty by which reverence was evoked" (Delitzsch). To this predicate there is added a phrase, *and there is none like me*. Again the emphatic declaration *there is none* is placed first, and the final words, *like me,* provide a sufficient answer to the question raised in verse 5.

10 The participles are probably to be construed with *me* in *like me,* so that the force of the whole is, "And there is none like me who makes known, etc." The participles pass over into the imperfect. The verse merely points out that in one respect God is incomparable and unique, namely His ability to foretell the future.

226

The first participle, *causing to declare*, refers to the announcing in words of the outcome of events. From the beginning or first part of these events the Lord can make known what their latter part or eventuation will be. Even though they have not yet fully run their course, God can tell how they will climax, merely from the first part or beginning of them.[8]

Parallel is the word *qedem*, which here means *long before* or *from of old*. From these God can tell what things will take place even before they have been done, and this He does through the medium of prophecy. Predictive prophecy is a proof of the divine omniscience, and far from being condemned is to be regarded as praiseworthy. This is the essential nature of prophecy, its predictive character. In the Old Testament the prophecies are teleological in that they point forward to events of salvation that have not yet been accomplished, and the fact that Yahweh is able to tell of these events is an evidence that He is the omniscient God.[9]

He can thus predict the future, for the future is the unfolding of what He has Himself already determined. It is His plan, which is not yet revealed, designated here *My counsel*. The counsel originates with Him; He has not obtained it in consultation with the creature; it is the product of His mind alone. This counsel will stand and not be changed, for He Himself has decreed it. The verb is absolute, and means that the counsel will stand and continue to stand.

The parallel expression, *my pleasure*, means *that which I have determined upon, that which I have been pleased to do*. Nothing can prevent God from doing all that is His pleasure, i.e. His counsel; and inasmuch as He will perform it, it will stand.

11 The language continues with a participle and passes over from the general declarations of God's providential workings and their fulfillment to a specific example of the same, namely the calling of Cyrus. The participle *Calling* suggests not merely that God has summoned Cyrus to appear upon the scene of history but also that He has brought it about that Cyrus actually has appeared. By *east* is to be understood Persia.

---

[8] Note absence of the article in a familiar expression.

[9] Penna correctly states that the greater the time between the utterance of the prophecy and its fulfillment, the more efficacious the proof of the divine transcendence will be.

Cyrus is designated an *'ayiṭ*, lit., *a screamer*. The word is probably onomatopoetic. As to what bird of prey is intended it is difficult if not impossible to decide. North gives the interesting suggestion that it is a falcon. The word is often rendered *eagle*, and sometimes there is thought to be a relationship with the Greek word *aetos* (eagle).[10] Whatever bird may be intended, it is one that is known as rapacious and also fierce. Cyrus came rapidly from the east in conquest, and wherever he went seized much booty and made himself master. In the parallel expression *east* is explained as *from a land of distance*. The language makes a light transition from the first to the third person and designates Cyrus, as a parallel to *bird of prey*, as *the man of his counsel*. What is meant is not a man who gives counsel to God, but one who carries out the counsel God has already determined upon. The Lord is in need of no counsel from men.

In the second line there is a threefold usage of *'aph* (surely). As used here it has the force of *not only. . .but also.* "Not only have I spoken but I will also bring it to pass." The speaking refers to the declaration of the divine counsel through the mouth of the prophets. The suffix of the imperfect is feminine but refers to what the Lord has spoken. It is important to note the tenses.

Corresponding to *I have spoken* is *I have formed*, which would refer to the conception and establishment of the purpose in the mind of God and the bringing of the plan to fruition in history. It is the counsel that He has devised. Perhaps the third occurrence of *'aph* may be rendered *surely*. There are four verbs; the first refers to the initiation or declaration of the plan, the second and third refer to the placing of that plan in motion, and the fourth to its completion.

> 12 Hearken unto me, ye mighty of heart, who are far from righteousness.
> 13 I have brought near my righteousness, it shall not be far off; and my salvation, it shall not tarry; and I will give in Zion my salvation, in Israel my glory.

12 After the imperative of verse 3, with which the address to Israel began, the prophet passed to "Remember" and now returns to the command with which he began, *Hearken*. Those addressed

10 Cyrus' ensign was a golden eagle. For the rapidity of Cyrus' conquests cf. Xenophon *Cyropaedia* vii.1.4. Cf. Dan. 8:5.

are the *stout of heart,* a phrase that has occasioned much difficulty. It reminds of the "strong of heart" of Ezekiel 2:4. In itself the word simply means *mighty* or *stout,* but in this context the *strong of heart* may be those who exercised this strength in hardening their heart against the grace of God. This does not mean, as Hahn suggests, that they could not be conquered through either the love or the wrath of God, but simply that they made their hearts to be strong in resisting the overtures of God.

The meaning of the phrase is seen in the further designation, *those who are far from righteousness.* There is much discussion as to the meaning of *righteousness,* but it would seem that in this verse it is to be used in the same sense as in the subsequent verse, where it is a synonym for salvation. Here it refers to those who have no righteousness before God, who themselves are not righteous. Those who are far from righteousness are those who are far from being right with God, and so are deep in their own sin and depravity.

13 The glorious news those who are far from righteousness are to hear is that God has brought His own righteousness near. What must be noted is the divine action. Man is not commanded to obtain salvation or righteousness or to approach them. Rather, the emphasis falls upon what God has done; salvation is a gift from Him alone. Emphasis lies upon the nominal suffix. "The righteousness is *My* righteousness, for it finds its origin in Me and comes from Me." God manifests His righteousness in the salvation of His people, and also in the fact that in this salvation His people receive His own perfect righteousness. It is also true that in the salvation of sinners the destruction of the wicked is to be seen. The stout of heart are far from righteousness; nevertheless, the righteousness of God will not be far away, for God will bring it nigh.

The effect of the approach of righteousness is salvation, and the conjunction may therefore be rendered *even.* What God brings to His people is righteousness, even salvation. It is this that man receives; it will not delay, for God will bring it near. This salvation is to be historically mediated, in that God will place it in Zion, the city from which the word of the Lord will go forth. Hence it could be said that "salvation is of the Jews." This action is for the sake of Israel, for if God does not act, Israel cannot be saved. The glory Israel possesses, it possesses not in and of itself but receives from its Lord as a gift.

Of itself Israel is stout-hearted and far from righteousness. The nation will be the glory of the Lord, when His righteousness is brought near to them and they have received of His salvation. Then will it appear to all the world that the God of Israel is a God of grace who saves the stout of heart and those far from righteousness. Through the saved Israel, the glory of the Lord, will be seen the Lord of glory, the Savior of His people.

CHAPTER FORTY-SEVEN

> 1 Come down, sit on the dust, virgin daughter of Babylon, sit
> on the earth, there is no throne, daughter of the Chaldeans;
> for thou shalt not add to be called tender and delicate.
> 2 Take millstones and grind flour; uncover thy veil, take off thy
> skirt, uncover the leg, cross streams.
> 3 Let thy nakedness be uncovered, likewise let thy shame be seen.
> I will take vengeance, I will not meet a man.
> 4 Our Redeemer, the LORD of hosts is his name, the Holy One of
> Israel.

1 Isaiah continues the proclamation of judgment, advancing
from Babylon's idols to the city itself, which he mentions as the
representative or focal point of the whole nation in its opposition
to God.[1] Babylon is directly addressed and commanded to do that
which will show its humiliation. The command is issued by the
Lord in heaven. It consists of two imperatives, which provide an
interesting assonance. Involved in the first *Go down* or *Get down* is
the idea of humiliation, the descent from a height to a lower place.
By the second imperative, *sit*, the language has reference not to
mourning but to the degradation and humiliation involved in
dethronement.[2]

Babylon is addressed as *virgin daughter Babylon*. The first two
words are in the construct, *the virgin of the daughter of Babylon*.
The reference, however, is not to the people but to the city itself.
Babylon can yet be designated a virgin, a term that in this context
would seem to suggest that for a long time the city has been

---

[1] A striking Ug. parallel to the thought is found in the Baal and Anat
cycle, *UH*, p. 149.

> *Thereupon Ltpn the god*
> *descends from (1) the throne; he sits*
> *upon the footstool and from (1) the footstool he sits*
> *upon (1) the earth.*

[2] The two imperatives imply, *she shall surely come down and sit.*

immune from the attacks of foreign invaders. The alliteration in this phrase is striking.

In the second line the imperative is repeated, *sit with respect to the earth*, i.e. *on the earth* (cf. 3:26). Earth and dust are parallel and show the lowly condition to which the once queen of empires had been brought. This condition is emphasized by the explanatory phrase, *there is no throne*, i.e. *without a throne*.[3] From sitting upon the world throne Babylon comes down to sit in the dust. It is also possible to connect this phrase with the preceding, *sit upon the earth since you have no throne*. Whether the word *dust* bears the connotation *grave*, signifying the full death of the once haughty Babylon, is difficult to say. Parallel to *daughter of Babylon* is *daughter of the Chaldeans*. The genitive is to be construed as appositional, *daughter Chaldeans*. Like Babylon, the Chaldeans are regarded as a woman, the term being employed to designate the country itself.

In the last line a reason is given for the command. Isaiah begins with a statement in the second person feminine singular, *for thou shalt not add*.[4] Abruptly, however, he changes the person, *they will call to thee*. The abrupt change is vivid but natural if we allow life to the language, and the meaning is obvious. The two words *tender* and *delicate* seem to point to the kind of life that a queen would live.[5] Luxury alone had at one time characterized Babylon's life, but all that is now gone.

2 This verse continues the argument with six feminine imperatives. *Sitting in the dust* is more than mere humiliation; it involves the work of the slave handmaiden. Engaging in the task of the lowest menial slaves, Babylon was to take *millstones*, the two stones that formed the hand mill (cf. Ex. 11:5; Matt. 24:41), and was to grind meal.[6] Furthermore, Babylon is to *uncover* (lit.,

---

3 This is a circumstantial clause expressing the secondary predicate.

4 תוסיפי — *Milra*. To this verb another in the imperfect is subordinated, without intervening auxiliary words such as "to," "in order that"; lit., *thou shalt not add that they call thee*, i.e. *thou shalt no longer be called*. Compare *quid vis faciam* and *volo hoc oratori contingat*.

5 *'anuggāh* — *delicate, dainty*. For the luxury of Babylon cf. Herodotus i.195, 199; Quintus Curtius v.1.

6 Not to sit upon a chair was regarded in Babylon as a sign of degradation (cf. Jer. 13:18). A relief from Nineveh (see *VBW*, Vol. II, p. 78) shows Assyrians carrying away Elamite captives, who at a halt in the march are seated on stones eating food their wives have prepared for them. *The reḵeḇ* (upper

reveal) her *veil*, and thus subject herself to deep degradation. The word *tzammah* probably means *hair*, and the command seems to have reference to the exposing or uncovering of the tresses. There is question as to the precise connotation of the fourth command; *shovel* refers to a flowing garment such as a train, and possibly the rendering *lift up thy skirt* is satisfactory.[7] The fifth command, *reveal the leg*, serves to point out that the woman was about to cross the streams, not rivers to be crossed as one goes into exile, but streams that must be crossed daily as by a working person.

3 This verse continues the description of Babylon's humiliation, carrying it out, as Alexander says, "to a revolting extreme." Instead of the feminine imperatives, however, the verse continues with jussives and passes over to imperfects in the first person. *Let thy nakedness be revealed* is not to be understood literally, but simply means that Babylon will be seen for what she truly is. Outwardly she may have appeared to the world as a mighty and powerful kingdom; now, however, her true inward condition, which is nakedness, will be made manifest. Her reproach is the shame that had been seen in her acting. Whether or not the language reflects the disgrace that comes to a woman when the object of her shame (the pudenda) is seen may be difficult to decide.

Babylon meets One that is far stronger than herself, who will act and take vengeance for her evil conduct. The final words, *I shall not meet a man*, have been the cause of much disagreement on the part of interpreters.[8] Perhaps it is best simply to take them in the ordinary sense that no man will be able to withstand or resist God.

4 In response to the Lord's declaration in verses 1-3, the people of God break forth in acknowledgment of the power and might of their true Redeemer. Judgment has been threatened against Babylon that redemption might be brought to Israel. He who possesses

---

millstone) was moved with grinding motion over the *shekeb* (lower millstone). For illustrations cf. *VBW*, Vol. I, pp. 138, 209, 281. Cf. also *Odyssey* xx.105-108; vii.103, 104; Terence *Phormio* ii.1.19. Gesenius remarks that waterwheels were a discovery of the age of Augustus.

7 *ḥeśpî* — 1Q *ḥśwpy*; lit., *strip off*. The *Dagesh* is unusual, making the penult a closed syllable; cf. also Jer. 10:17, *'ispî*. The normal imperative is with vocal *Shᵉwa*; the *Sᵉgol* before *Dagesh* is strange; one would expect *Ḥireq*.

8 אפגע — B παραδῶ; S ἀντιστήσεται; Vulg. *non resistet mihi homo*. Some commentators render, *I will spare no man*.

the sovereign power to destroy the world empire also has the power and will to redeem His people. The words *Our Redeemer* stand first and so are emphasized. Israel knows who its Redeemer is, the Lord of hosts. Involved in the phrase as it appears here is reflection upon the covenant relationship of Israel and also upon the absolute power of their God. Whether there is also some definite opposition to the star worship of Babylonia is difficult to determine. All hosts, wherever they may be, belong to the God of Israel and are subject to His control.

Furthermore, in the redemption holiness is displayed, such holiness, indeed, as belongs alone to Israel's God. Thus the redemption is spiritual, and in no sense to be restricted to the return from Babylonian captivity. Three attributes are given to the Lord, a characteristic Isaianic touch. He is the *Redeemer*, and so has the power to do what His people need; He is the *Lord of hosts*, who wills to redeem them; and He is their *Holy One*, who in perfect righteousness and holiness accomplishes their redemption.

> 5 Dwell in silence, and go into darkness, daughter of the Chaldeans, for thou shalt no longer be called mistress of kingdoms.
> 6 I was wroth against my people, I profaned my heritage, and I gave them into thy hand: thou didst not show to them mercy; on the aged thou didst make heavy thy yoke exceedingly.

5 The Lord again utters commands to Babylon, which take up the commands of verse 1. The language seems to refer to the absolute dejection that comes over someone whose shame has been exposed.[9] Yet there is gradation in the stages of degradation. Babylon is to go into darkness, a word suggestive of grief and anguish. Whether it actually means prison is difficult to tell. Alexander thinks that darkness as a metaphor for prison does not here suit the context. The word does, however, connote the deepest obscurity. Babylon had ruled with a high hand, confident that her power and might over the kingdoms would endure forever. She was at the center of attention, with the light focused upon her. Now, however, the daughter of the Chaldeans is to be so abased that she will be covered over with darkness and no longer seen.

Repeating the change of person and number used in verse 1, the

---

9 *dūmām — silent*, considered to be a participle, formed like *šôbāb*, *'ôlāl*, etc., standing for an original *dômām*. It is m., following a f. imperative, and serves as a Ḥal accusative of state. I am not convinced that it is a participle.

prophet explains that no longer will Babylon (i.e. the Babylonian empire) be regarded as the queen of nations.

6 The prophet now gives the reason for God's judgment. The verbs are in the perfect, and in translation it is best to retain the past. God simply is stating in general terms the course of His relations to Israel. If it be insisted that the nation is in exile, the imperatives of verse 1 show that Babylon has already been humbled, and verse 4 presents Israel as acknowledging their Redeemer. The prophecy, then, would have to be uttered after the downfall of Babylon.

Israel's entire history has been one of rebellion and transgression, and for this reason God is angry at the nation. This divine anger manifested itself in God's regarding His people as profane. He describes them as His inheritance, which suggests that they are perpetually His. The literal force of the word is not to be pressed; God does not "inherit" anything in the manner of human inheritors. To profane God's inheritance means no longer to regard it as holy. Only a holy people could be the Lord's; in His profaning them He has rejected them.

This fact is manifested in that He gives them (and He alone has the power to do with them as He will), the people of God, the once holy nation, into the hand of the secular, profane nation of the world. Babylon was unaware of the purposes of the sovereign God and believed that she was in control of her actions. She misused her privilege and opportunity and exhibited cruelty in her dealings, and so she must be humbled. Unawares, Babylon was carrying out the designs and intents of God, yet her own motives were sinful and corrupt. The cruelty of Babylon is presented in the general sentence, *thou didst not place mercy upon them* (i.e. thou didst not show mercy to them), and also in a specific application, namely that Babylon had caused her yoke to be heavy upon the elderly. The *old one* here mentioned is not the nation itself, but the elderly individuals in the nation. These were made in one way or another to feel the heavy yoke of Babylon just as were other members of the profaned people.

> 7 And thou didst say, Forever I shall be mistress; till thou didst not place these things upon thy heart, thou didst not remember its latter end.

7 The *And* introducing this verse has the sense, *in addition.*

Not only had Babylon dealt harshly with God's inheritance, which He had placed in her hands, but in addition she had spoken as though she would be a mistress of peoples in her own strength. She had no understanding of the fact that her time would soon run out and that the God of the people whom she oppressed was about to introduce a change in the condition of world affairs. In her credo, *Forever I shall be mistress*, the word *Forever* received the emphasis, bringing to the fore the idea that the head of the kingdom of man attributed to itself the attributes of deity in claiming eternity as its own prerogative.[10] Inasmuch as the language contains an obvious allusion to the thought of verse 5, it would seem that Alexander is correct in regarding the rendering *queen* as weak. Babylon is more than a queen; she is an actual mistress of kingdoms. Furthermore, contrary to Duhm, the Masoretic accentuation is to be observed, and the word *queen* is not to be construed with the following *of eternity* but to be taken as an absolute.

The word *'ad* may be taken in the sense of *'ad 'asher* and rendered, *till that*, i.e., "Thou didst speak thus about thyself until thou didst not place, etc." Babylon assured herself of her own eternity till she could see no need for any other thought, and so did not consider that God was in control of her destiny. She had persisted in this evil self-delusion until it blinded her eyes to the truth; and she did not, as a consequence, look unto God. The idea of result is not entirely lacking. The evil course of Babylon's thinking brought about the result mentioned.

To "place upon the heart" involves giving thought to something and acting in accordance with that thought. Babylon did not consider these, namely, the judgment of destruction and her deposition from her throne. The heart is conceived as a receptacle upon which the thoughts of man are to be placed. These thoughts in particular should have been placed upon Babylon's heart, but she did not place them there and so was derelict in her duty. Her own assertions of vain power precluded her doing what she should have done.

Furthermore, Babylon should have remembered (i.e. been mindful of) the latter part of the events that were transpiring. Babylon

---

10 As the text is pointed, עַד should be construed with לֹא, being joined thereto with *Munaḥ*. Thus: *Forever I shall be a mistress // till thou*, etc. *gᵉḇāreṯ* is a construct in pause, the normal absolute being *gᵉḇîrāh*. *BH* would take the word out of pause, to construe it with *'aḏ*, which gives the verse a much weaker sense.

would have a future to which she should have given thought. That future would be destruction. She would be deposed from her throne, whereas the captive daughter of Zion would once more be exalted and the period of her salvation would dawn. Babylon's *latter end* is the prelude to Israel's dawn when the Dayspring from on high will visit the earth.

> 8 And now! hear this, O voluptuous one, the one sitting in security, the one saying in her heart, I am, and none else; I shall not sit as a widow, and I shall not know the loss of children.
> 9 And they shall come to thee, these two, suddenly in one day, loss of children and widowhood; in their perfection they have come upon thee, despite the multitude of thy enchantments, in the abundance of thy charms exceedingly.
> 10 And thou didst trust in thy wickedness; thou hast said, There is none seeing me; thy wisdom and thy knowledge, it has seduced thee; and thou saidst in thy heart, I am, and there is no one else.
> 11 And there cometh upon thee evil, thou shalt not know from whence it riseth; and mischief shall fall upon thee, thou shalt not be able to avert it; and desolation shall come upon thee suddenly, which thou shalt not know.

8 Isaiah continues with one of his favorite expressions, *And now,* as though to say, "Inasmuch as what has just been said is true, pay attention to what follows." A feminine imperative places before Babylon what Yahweh of hosts requires.

Babylon is addressed as *voluptuous one,* with evident reference to her wealth and prosperity, from which she is about to be separated. She is further described as *sitting* in security. The word *beṭaḥ* seems to imply a spiritual security and is apparently chosen to form a contrast with the same root in verse 10.

Because she is voluptuous and filled with wealth, Babylon speaks of herself in the most exalted of terms. As the true God, the Lord of hosts, had spoken of Himself, "I am the Lord, and beside Me there is none else," so Babylon adopted similar language, frivolously deifying herself. Here is the pinnacle of Babylon's pride; here is the self-confidence of the kingdom that sought to oppose itself to and exalt itself above the kingdom of God.

Sure of herself and of her position, Babylon had spoken in defiant terms, giving assertion to her conviction that she would not suffer the two greatest calamities to come upon a married woman. The figure of a virgin is changed for that of a married woman, for what is important is not the sign itself but rather what is signified. To sit as a widow simply means to be a widow. In what sense may Babylon be said to have become a widow? The term would imply the loss of what was essential to her position as mistress of the nations. Whether it be the idols or the nations is difficult to determine. She who sits secure as mistress of the nations, and is confident in her boasting, will be so degraded and fall so far that she may be compared to the married woman who has lost her husband and must live as a widow.

Furthermore, Babylon has boastfully asserted that she will not know by experience what it is to be deprived of children, which may be an allusion to the loss of the citizens of the country.

9 The introductory conjunction may be rendered *And yet*: "Thou hast said such and such, and yet, the two things that thou hast asserted would not come upon thee are not far off and will come." From these two things Babylon had thought herself forever immune. Yet, both of them will come to her suddenly, in an instant and in the same day.[11] She will not have the one without the other; it will be a double calamity.

In the second line both of these calamities are mentioned, and both stand in the position of emphasis, as though to say, "the very things from which Babylon thought she was secure will come upon her." There is, however, a chiastic arrangement, loss of children being mentioned before widowhood. Following these two nouns comes the expression *according to their completeness*, i.e. *all unawares*, or *as complete as possible*. The language is martial, as though the calamities were enemies on the march.

That Babylon had a multitude of magical practices is well known, and that she engaged in enchantments is also well known. These were for protection, to avert danger and calamity. The word *'otzmah (abundance)* refers not to the supposed inherent power of the spells as much as to their numerical strength. The adverb *exceedingly* is to be construed with the verb *they will come*.

The certainty of the coming calamities cannot be denied. Though there is an abundance (possibly referring to inherent

---

[11] *in one day* — this phrase at the end of a clause is Isaianic; cf. 9:13; 10:17; 66:8 and Zech. 3:9, the only non-Isaianic occurrence.

strength) of magic and a vast array of spells, these cannot help, for
the coming will be strong.

10 Isaiah takes up again the thought of verse 8 and in particular reflects upon the phrase *in security,* declaring that Babylon has
been secure in her wickedness.[12] The verb is often rendered *And
thou hast trusted;* yet, as Alexander points out, it is difficult to
conceive of wickedness as an object of trust. The sentence is an
expression of Babylon's attitude. She considered herself secure, and
so continued in her wickedness with no thought of abandoning it
and with no thought that because of her wickedness calamity might
befall her. By wickedness we are probably to understand the whole
course and manner of Babylon's life.[13] The fear of God was not
before her eyes, and her life was manifested in acts of cruelty and
tyranny; she did not recognize the people of God for what they
were, for she did not know their God.

No one is seeing me. Babylon did not speak these words aloud,
but thought them in her heart.[14] They were the expression of her
godless attitude. The language does not mean that no one has seen
how Babylon acts. The Israelites knew only too well what Babylon
did. What is meant is that there is no one who sees and is able to
punish and to restrain. This is tantamount to declaring that there
is no God who directs the affairs of men and who can intervene to
dispense judgment and punishment as He desires.

Stress falls upon the words *thy wisdom and thy knowledge,*
which are said to have betrayed Babylon. No doubt the words
include the wisdom that comes to expression in the arts of astrono-
my and exorcism and the knowledge of these practices. Possibly
also they may refer to political wisdom and sagacity, but it is not
necessary thus to confine the reference. Nor is the language necessarily ironical. What is intended is the wisdom and knowledge that
enabled the country to exist as it did and to carry on its policies as
it was doing. Included in this of course were the practices of the
magicians and astrologers as well as the political insight that had
permitted and enabled Babylon to become what she was. Wisdom
and knowledge are to be included as a single emphatic concept, for
the relative is singular, and we must translate *it has seduced*

12 The imp. with *waw* consecutive follows *berōḇ* of v. 9.
13 1Q reads *bd'tk, through thy knowledge.*
14 *rō'ānî* — 1Q *rw'ny;* a participle. The *Qametz* is unusual, but may be due
to pause. The suffix denotes the object.

*thee.*¹⁵ The verb means *to turn aside* and here refers to the turning aside from one way to another, the leading into a wrong path.

This wrong path was one of self-deception, so that as a result Babylon asserted her sole existence. The language is that of arrogant self-confidence as Babylon declares her uniqueness. It is as though she had declared, "I am what I am and there is no one else like me." Wisdom and knowledge should lead one to confess that the Lord is God and that there is none else; instead Babylon's wisdom and knowledge (which flowed from an unregenerate heart) assert that no one else is what Babylon herself is.

11 The actual course of historical events did not coincide with the beliefs of Babylon. This contrast is brought out by the introductory conjunction, which is probably not *waw* consecutive. In the light of the context it may be best to render by the past, so that the contrast between what Babylon had boasted about and the actual course of history may stand out in bolder relief. The language has martial overtones and suggests that evil has come against Babylon in the capacity of an enemy. *Evil* forms a striking contrast to the *evil* in which the city rested secure, "so as to suggest an antithesis between natural and moral evil, sin and suffering, evil done and evil experienced" (Alexander). In return for Babylon's evil she herself will receive evil, such as she will not be able to cope with;¹⁶ her magic arts will be of no avail and she will not be able to charm the evil away.¹⁷

Parallel to the first verb is the second, *and there will fall,* which suggests that certain calamities will come down upon Babylon from above. The three words expressing these calamities form a vivid assonance, *ra'ah, howah, sho'ah.* Probably they also constitute a gradation, and the threefold sound may express certainty. That they are represented as demons to be frightened away is a conjecture without warrant. *Howah* is misfortune or disaster. As Babylon did not possess the knowledge requisite for charming evil away neither does she have the power to appease disaster. The verb

¹⁵ 3 f.s. perf., and so accented *Milel.* Note that the suffix is *-ek* and not *-āk* as elsewhere. Cf. also Ruth 4:15. הִיא reinforces the subject, lending emphasis.

¹⁶ Note that a m. verb percedes a f. subject. לֹא twice introduces a negative circumstantial clause.

¹⁷ שַׁחְרָה — lit., *her dawn,* i.e. *its origin.* The word may, however, signify *to enchant* (cf. Ar. *saḥar*), although this is questionable.

kaphar in this present context seems to imply that Babylon cannot pay the price necessary for the relieving of disaster. The prophet varies somewhat his manner of statement in describing the coming of the third woe. After the verb and the phrase *against thee* he inserts the word *suddenly*. In the second half of the line he varies the order, giving the subject first and thus emphasizing it, and then including a relative verbal clause, *which thou dost not know*. It may be, however, that this last clause is independent, *thou dost not know it*. Babylon has never known by experience a crash such as this one. In the root there is a play upon "thy knowledge" of verse 10. The threefold occurrence of *against thee* characterizes the verse and stresses the sureness of Babylon's doom. Taken with the preceding verb in each case, this threefold occurrence shows that the calamities come from without, thus belying Babylon's claim that she was unique. There is One far greater than Babylon whom she has not known, and she has now become the object against which He sends the calamities.

12 Stand now in thy spells and in the abundance of thy charms in which thou hast wearied thyself from thy youth; perhaps thou wilt be able to profit, perhaps thou wilt terrify.
13 Thou art wearied in the multitude of thy counsel; let them now stand and save thee, the astrologers, the star gazers making known at the new moons, from these things that shall come upon thee.
14 Behold! they are as stubble, a fire has burned them; they cannot deliver themselves from the hand of the flame; it is not a coal for warming oneself, a fire to sit before.
15 Thus are they to thee, with respect to whom thou hast labored; thy merchants from thy youth; each to his own side they have wandered, there is no one saving thee.

12 If, having heard the declaration of oncoming disaster and her own inability to meet that disaster, Babylon will still stand relying upon her enchantments, she is enjoined to do so. The particle *na'*, as Alexander remarks, gives a kind of concession to the people. The command is not necessarily sarcastic, but is designed rather to convince Babylon of the impossibility of relying upon enchantments. Despite their multitude, they are of no help.

Since the beginning of the nation, when it might be regarded as in youth, it has toiled and labored in these enchantments. The suggestion is made that perhaps Babylon can find profit in so standing, but the implication obviously is that she will not do so. Perhaps also she will be able to terrify the enemy of calamity so that she can stand; but again, this is not to be. This last verb is a specific application of the idea of succeeding. If Babylon can do what is suggested by this last verb, she will have derived profit from her enchantments.

13 Babylon has become wearied in the multitude of her counsels.[18] The preposition involves more than an expression of the cause; it suggests that being involved in them she has become wearied. The counsels are probably all the plans and devices of Babylon for the management of her government and for self-defense. These were many in number, indeed, so many and of such overpowering effect that they simply brought weariness.

In a short, independent sentence, a challenge is thrown out, *Let all these counsels stand now.* The sense of the verb is the same as in verse 12. If they stand when judgment is threatening, the counsels will show themselves to be true. If they fall, they will of course have proved themselves to be false.

Continuing, the prophet suggests that the *dividers of the heavens* (i.e. the *astrologers*) should save Babylon.[19] These were men whose business was to divide the heavens into constellations and signs of the zodiac, and from these deduce the course of events on earth. The things that happened on earth were determined, according to the Babylonian belief, by the motions of the heavenly bodies. The Lord, who created both the earth and the heavenly bodies, now challenges these dividers of the heavens to save Babylon. An explanatory clause states their work. They look at the stars, and as a result of their observations they are supposedly able to tell what months will bring good fortune and what bad.

The last clause is difficult to understand because of its relation to the remainder of the sentence. Is it to be construed with *let them save thee?* If so, the sense is, "let them save thee from that which is coming against thee." This yields a good sense; but there are quite a number of intervening words, hence this construction is unnatu-

---

18 *counsels* — The noun is s. with a pl. suffix, probably to give the noun a collective force.

19 *hoḇerēy* — lit., *dividers* (of the heavens) . 1Q *hwbry*. Cf. Ar. *ḥabara*, to cut in pieces; here, distinguishing some astrological division of the sky. But cf. Ug. *hbr*, to bow down. Hence, the phrase may designate those who bow down to the heavens. Aq S T *caelos observantes* (see Ziegler) .

ral. On the other hand, it may be that these words are to be connected with the participle, *who cause to know*. The connection would then be, "who cause to know with respect to the months (new moons) from those things that are coming against thee." If this construction is adopted, the *min (from)* is given a partitive sense. This is possible. It is probably best to adopt the first position. The assertion is then made that certain things are coming against Babylon, and the astrologers should now save the country from them. The impossibility of the exhortation is obvious.

14 The true nature of the astrologer is introduced by the particle *hinneh (Behold!)*. Their destruction is now something that can be seen. The interjection brings it before the eyes of men who are to turn their attention to it. The verbs may be rendered by either the past or the present. *They were as stubble,* "whose end is to be burned" (Heb. 6:8b). The combination of stubble and fire is interesting (cf. also Isa 5:24; Obad. 18; Mal. 4:1 and Nah. 1:10). The second clause is more vivid if taken independently, *fire has burned them.* The comparison with stubble is not merely to show how worthless stubble is, but how quickly and easily it is burned. The astrologers were mighty in their prognostications; their true nature appears in that before the punitive hand of the almighty Lord they disappear as rapidly as stubble is devoured by fire. They do not even have the enduring power of wood in the fire, for they are consumed instantly, and are not able to save themselves from the flame that devours them. If they cannot save themselves it is foolish to look to them to save Babylon. This fire is consuming and devouring, not the pleasant fire before which one may sit to warm himself. *There is not a coal for warming, a fire for sitting before it.*[20] This independent utterance boldly states the fact that this fire does not bring comfort to man; it is a fire of destruction. The figure of fire for judgment is a favorite one of Isaiah (cf. 34:9ff.; 50:11; 66:16, 24).

15 *Thus* sums up the destruction of Babylon's astrologers. The outcome that overtook the astrologers was not one of benefit to Babylon but the opposite.[21] The relative *ᵃsher (which)* refers to

---

20 לחמם — a triliteral inf. of the *Ayin-Ayin* verb *ḥmm, for warming.* The form may also mean *their bread.* The more usual writing is *laḥᵃmām.*
21 *to thee* — ethical dative of disadvantage.

the subject implied in the plural verb, *with respect to whom thou hast toiled*. The body of astrologers and of all their company was toil for the Babylonians, yet despite all their toil the astrologers were unprofitable to them. The words *thy traders* may be construed as explanatory of the implied subject of the verb *they were*. In English we may render, *even thy traders*. Those who from the youth of Babylon (i.e. from her beginnings) were her traders proved to be of no profit to her. It is also possible that the pointing of the Masoretes has set forth the correct arrangement of the words, so that there are actually two classes of people. On this construction we should read *thy merchants from thy youth, each one to his side do they wander, there is no one helping thee*. Why does Isaiah use the term *thy merchants*? By a slight emendation some would obtain the reading *thy sorcerers*, but this is not warranted. It is true that the word introduces a new element; but as North points out, it is one that is found in denunciations of rich and decadent world powers. He appeals to Nahum 3:16; Isaiah 23:1-8 and Ezekiel 27:12-36. And of particular significance is Revelation 17, which clearly reflects the present passage. Babylon's merchants have had no genuine concern for her but have dealt with her merely for their own advantage. In the time of crisis they flee for safety, unconcerned about the fate of the city.

At the time of judgment, when the hand of the God of Israel falls upon the kingdom of man, that kingdom goes down to destruction. All upon which she had relied and with which she had toiled now forsakes her, leaving her desolate. Each of the merchants wanders to his own side or place, in order, were it possible, to find a refuge. There is no concern for Babylon; none at all are saving her.

CHAPTER FORTY-EIGHT

> 1 Hear this, O house of Jacob, who are called by the name of
> Israel, and from the waters of Judah they have gone out; who
> swear by the name of the LORD, and by the God of Israel they
> make mention, but not in truth and not in righteousness.
> 2 For from the holy city they are called, and upon the God of
> Israel they lean; the LORD of hosts is his Name.

1 Like chapter forty-nine, which introduces the second portion of
40–66, this chapter, the last in the first section, begins with a
command to *Hear*. What is to be heard is indicated by the word
this, and refers not merely to what immediately follows or precedes
but to the entirety of the argument of the Lord. The purpose is to
bring home to the people their sinful and unworthy condition.
Emphasis is placed upon hearing, the root *šm'* (*to hear*) occurring eleven times, and the practical synonym *qšb* (*to hearken*)
once (v. 18). The message of God was delivered by word of the
prophet's mouth. An obedient nation is a hearing nation, and a
disobedient nation one that does not hear.

The address is made to the Israelites, descended from *Jacob*.[1]
There may be implied the suggestion that although the people
were called Israel, their conduct had removed them from being an
Israel so that they were in fact only Jacob. Pieper views this as a
cold and external address. God does not call the people Israel but
Jacob. They themselves use Israel, the covenant name.

The prophecy soon passes over to the third person; Isaiah ceases,
as it were, to address the people directly and instead describes them
to those who might be listening. He characterizes them as having
gone out (i.e. *descended*) *from the waters of Judah*, which seems
to imply that Judah is a source from which the nation has sprung.
In passages like Deuteronomy 33:28 and Psalm 68:26, *fountain* is

---

[1] Twice in this verse a part. with the definite article having relative force
introduces a clause concluded by a relative clause with a verb.

used. The thought is simply that Judah is the headwater from which the people are descended. This is in keeping with the preeminence given to Judah throughout the Old Testament history.

Although the people were only nominally Israelites they nevertheless swore by the Name of Yahweh. This was an outward manifestation of a recognition that God exists and that He demands respect and adoration from men (cf. 19:18). By such an act the people solemnly made known that they belonged to this God. In addition they also made mention or called to remembrance the God of Israel by acts of worship performed in the religious service, by which the people distinguished themselves from those who worshipped other gods.[2]

The cultic or worship acts, however, were not performed out of loyalty to the covenant, nor in sincerity or rectitude. Isaiah gives us here a general description of hypocritical worship, which may apply any time of Israel's history. The nation outwardly in its religious profession was orthodox. As a matter of actual fact it was not orthodox, but exhibited a kind of dead orthodoxism, possessing the form of godliness but denying the power thereof. Although the forms of true worship were followed and the Name of the true God invoked, the hearts of the people were far from God and they did not call upon him in spirit and in truth (cf. John 4:24). The faith of the patriarchs from whom they were descended was completely lacking. Calvin has gone to the heart of the matter: "But here he attacks hypocrites who with open mouth, loudly boasted of the name of God, and frequently mentioned his name, and yet in their hearts were greatly opposed to him" (*Com. in loc.*).

2 The introductory *ki* has puzzled commentators, but it seems best to take it in its ordinary sense, *For*, as thus continuing the description. Isaiah is speaking of the people of God, whose hypocritical hearts are far from Him. The thought is not so much that an unholy people wishes to be called after a holy city, for that would localize the description in what seems to be an unwarranted manner. Where God's dwelling is, there is a holy place. Yet, as His dwelling is at Jerusalem, in that sense the city is intended. Isaiah had earlier spoken of the remnant in Jerusalem as holy (4:3), and

2 It does not necessarily follow that these words were spoken during a cultic act (Volz).

the designation of Jerusalem as the holy city is one that gained currency in Israel's history, particularly during the time of the exile and later. Even today the Arabs designate it *el-quds* (*the holy*). Because the dwelling place of Yahweh on earth is holy, the people who worship Yahweh are therefore called holy. Upon this One they lean for support and sustenance, and recognize and confess that He is the eternal, true God.

3 The former things from time past I have declared, and from my mouth they went out, and I caused them to be heard; suddenly I do them, and they come to pass.

4 From my knowing that thou art hard; and an iron sinew is thy neck, and thy forehead brass.

5 Therefore I made known to thee from time past, before it came to pass, I caused thee to hear it: lest thou shouldst say, My idol hath done them, and my image and my molten image have commanded them.

3 That Israel may understand the reason for the judgments, she must know that God has foreknowledge of all things. He has made known *from then* (i.e. from olden times) the *former things*. There are two basic interpretations. Hahn thinks that the *former things* has reference to those things that have not yet occurred but are yet to take place. Of these future things, the former things are the first to happen. It is as though Isaiah is saying "From of old I have made known to you the first parts of those things that are yet to come." The actual reference would then be to the liberation under Cyrus and the deliverance from Babylon with the return to Palestine.

Another interpretation is to see in the phrase a reference to things that have already transpired. The first things, on this interpretation, are things that God has already accomplished. This might refer to the exodus from Egypt, the downfall of Jerusalem, and other predicted events of Israel's history. Inasmuch as the word *ri'shon* actually means *first*, we cannot on the basis of the word alone decide between these two interpretations; but the context would seem to support the second view.[3]

These things have gone out from God's mouth, a clear picture of propositional revelation and of the divine origin and authority of

[3] Cf. also C. R. North in *Studies in Old Testament Prophecy*, ed. H. H. Rowley, pp. 123ff.

the commands of God. The revelation is not in vain, for God causes men to hear it.[4] This hearing is not a mere listening, but a hearing leading to obedience.

Before men realize it, God acts suddenly and performs what He has announced. The fulfillment can be wrought only by God's power. His predictions are not in vain like the empty utterance of the soothsayers, but are spoken in connection with His all-wise plan of salvation. In His own good time He will bring about the fulfillment of all that has gone forth out of His mouth.

4 This verse probably gives the explanation of "suddenly" in the preceding. God acted suddenly because He knew what kind of nation Israel was. *From my knowing*—This could be taken in a temporal sense, *Since I knew*, but it is then difficult to understand how the words can be connected with the third verse. Hence, it seems better to render *because I know*, giving the reason why God acted suddenly.

What God knows is that Israel is hard. The adjective is probably to be considered as an ellipsis for the expressions *hard of neck* or *hard of heart*. The hardness is exemplified by the two expressions that follow, *a sinew of iron is thy neck*,[5] which stresses the perversity of Israel and her unbending, unyielding character, and *thy forehead is bronze*, which points to that shamelessness that persists in sin and opposition to truth. With bold effrontery Israel continues its refusal to acknowledge the truth.

5 The introductory conjunction connects with the preceding verse, and may best be rendered *Therefore*. The connection then is: "Because I knew thee that thou art hard, etc., therefore I made known, etc."[6] This proclamation was made *from then*, i.e. from that time long ago. The revelation was made by God long before the fulfillment of the prophecy, that Israel might not attribute the fulfillment to its idols. Furthermore, the revelation was made specifically *to thee*, that Israel might have no excuse for not obeying.

Had God's earlier revelations not been delivered, Israel might attribute the downfall of Jerusalem to Marduk or to any of the

---

4 The imps. following a preterite denote an act that, although past at the time of speaking, is subsequent to the event described by the preterite.
5 *gíd* — *sinew*; cf. Akk. *gídu* and Ug. *gd*.
6 The imp. with *waw* consecutive follows *midda'tí* in v. 4.

other idols. Three words designate the idols. The first contains the thought of toil and grief, and also of an image. The idol is a pain or misery; thus the prophet puts into the mouth of the Israelite a true characterization. "This idol of mine, this misery that I worship has done them," i.e. has brought to pass the fulfillment of the events predicted. *My molten image* and *my graven image* have reference to the form of the idol as an object of devotion, and both also imply that the idol is something formed and poured out by the hand of man. Taken together, the three words point to idolatry as a rather foolish and profitless institution. Note Jeremiah 44:18, "But since we left off to burn incense to the queen of heaven, and to pour out drink offerings unto her, we have wanted all things, and have been consumed by the sword and by the famine." The phrase *they have commanded them* is used as in 45:12, "to command them to come into being." The events prophesied have eventuated, and Israel was not to say that its idols had commanded them to come into existence.

6 Thou hast heard, see all of it. And ye will not declare: I have made thee to hear new things from now, and things kept, and thou hast not known them.

7 Now they are created, and not in time past, and before today, and thou hast not heard them, lest thou shouldst say, Behold! I knew them.

8 Neither didst thou hear, also thou didst not know, also of old thine ear did not open; for I know thou wilt surely deal treacherously, a transgressor from the womb thou wast called.

6 Israel has heard the prediction of what would come to pass. Now, the nation is commanded to behold the fulfillments in their entirety. By this command Israel is forced to contemplate all that had been predicted; they could not then well escape acknowledging that God had fulfilled His predicted Word. Following this abrupt address there is a question directed to the nation, designed to bring before them the necessity of confessing that what God has been declaring is true. There is a change from singular to plural, possibly to portray the individuals as comprising the body of the nation. Now that Israel has heard and seen, must they not also declare that God is a God of truth and power? On this interpretation the words *will ye not declare* have a different connotation from that which they bore in the preceding, being practically equivalent to *will ye not grant that it is so?* This seems more

satisfactory than to interpret, *will ye not also predict?* God is bringing to bear argument upon Israel that they may realize that they must acknowledge the folly of idolatry and believe that He, their sovereign God, has spoken the truth concerning the events that have come upon them.

The second line of verse 6 takes up the thought of the preceding verse. *From now* means *from this time, when I am speaking.* The object of God's proclamation is described as *new things* and *kept things.* If the words *first things* in verse 3 refer to things already predicted, as seems to be the case, then the *new things* stand in contrast and have not yet been predicted. The first verb, therefore, should probably be rendered by the present. The object of proclamation is also characterized as *kept things*, which would suggest that they have been kept in reserve by God and as a result Israel has not known them. It would, in other words, be impossible for Israel to know these events from past predictions, because they are new and kept by God, unknown to the nation.

7 This verse continues a description of the new and kept things, by asserting that they are created *Now*, at the time the prophecy is uttered. This is emphasized by the phrase *and not from then*, i.e. not from a long time ago. The words *they were created* call for comment. The root employed is the same as in Genesis 1:1, where it denotes a *creatio ex nihilo.* Here it indicates the startlingly new character of the *new things*, which have been kept by God until now. At the same time, the verb need not necessarily refer to the actual fulfillment of prophecy in history, nor even to the appearance in history of the new things. The creation of the *new things* could refer to their first announcement in prophecy, or simply indicate that now at the time when the prophet is speaking these new things are being created, and that in God's time they will appear in human history.

Parallel to the phrase *from then* is *before a day.* Evidently both of these mean something like *from a former time*, or *from long ago.* Some would take *day* as signifying *today* and so render, *before today*; but this is questionable. Possibly the preposition is employed in the sense *together with* (as in Ps. 72:5), so that *together with a day* would mean *just today.* These new and kept things are those which Israel has not yet heard.

The reason why God is forming these things now is that Israel not attribute to herself some knowledge and say, *Behold! I have known them.* This verse is used by some defenders of a supposed "Deutero-Isaiah" to show that the prophecy could not have come from the eighth-century Isaiah. If the *new things* were not to take place for two centuries (i.e. in the sixth century B.C.), it is argued, how could Isaiah in the eighth century assert that *they are created now?* Furthermore, if Isaiah had uttered these prophecies, how could it be said that those who lived in the sixth century (two hundred years later) had never heard of them? Delitzsch quotes Ruetschi to the effect that if "the older Isaiah had predicted this, he would have acted in direct opposition to Jehovah's design." But the difficulty is not as great as might at first sight appear, for the new things are not to be restricted to the Babylonian captivity or to the deliverance therefrom, but are events that have to do with God's work of deliverance for Israel from their sins. These events are new in that they qualitatively differ from the events of old. As such they were unknown to Israel, and the announcement concerning them could just as well have been made by Isaiah as by anyone living during the exile. The reason why the "critics" find a difficulty here is that they insist upon referring the *new things* to the work of Cyrus.

8 The reason why Israel had not heard these things before was that God knew their true wicked nature; He knew they would pervert the truth and ascribe the fulfillment of the predictions to idols and not to God Himself. Alexander, perhaps more than any other commentator, has gone to the heart of the matter and given the true explanation of the apparent contradiction. He says:

> Having given the perverseness of the people as a reason why they knew so much by previous revelation, he now assigns it as a reason why they knew so little. These, although at first sight inconsistent statements, are but varied aspects of the same thing. God had told them so much beforehand, lest they should ascribe the event to other causes. He had told them no more, because he knew that they would wickedly abuse his favour. In a certain sense and to a certain extent, it was true that they had heard and known these things beforehand. In another sense, and beyond that extent, it was equally true that they had neither heard nor known them. . . . It is true that they had heard, but it was also true that they had not heard.

The prophet employs three verbs to indicate that the Israelites had not known the revelation of God. The first two (*hear* and *know*) have already been used, but the third (*to open the ear*) gives added force to the utterance. To say that Israel's ear has not been opened is to say that the truth has not been revealed to them (cf. 50:5).

The second line gives the reason why these prophecies had not been revealed to Israel. It is because God knows that they would deal treacherously.[7] The infinitive absolute lends strength to the expression, and the imperfect is to be understood as potential, *dealing treacherously thou wouldst deal treacherously*. The infinitive absolute suggests both certainty and intensity, particularly the latter. If there is anything sure, it is that Israel would act treacherously. This treachery would manifest itself against the truth, for Israel, the sinful nation, would attribute its deliverances to idols and not to the true God.

That Israel would so act lies in the fact that the nation is a transgressor. Indeed, this is the designation that has been given to them from the very beginning of their existence. Coming first in the clause, the word *transgressor* receives the stress. By *womb* we are probably to understand the very beginning, without any particular reference to specific events in Israel's history. Transgression and dealing treacherously were inveterate faults of the people, and not merely occasional sins. To say that Israel was thus called means of course that this was Israel's true nature. In accordance with Hebrew idiom the verb *to call* is used to indicate the true nature or character of a person.

> 9 For my name's sake I will prolong my anger, and as to my praise
>   I will restrain it toward thee, so as not to cut thee off.
> 10 Behold! I have refined thee, and not with silver; I have chosen
>   thee in the furnace of affliction.
> 11 For my sake, for my sake I shall do it, for how will it be pro-
>   faned; and my glory to another I will not give.

9 This verse apparently has reference to the new and the first things, insofar as it shows that the wrath of God poured out upon Israel is not to consume them utterly. In order that the Name of God may be recognized by men as honorable and true, God will prolong His anger, that is, He will defer its outpouring or cause it to tarry and delay. This anger will not pour out in full force upon

---

[7] *I know* — the *verbum sentiendi* is followed by indirect discourse, here an independent verbal clause.

the wicked and apostate nation, but will tarry. Nevertheless, God is angered at His people, and they deserve to feel its full force. Furthermore, with respect to Israel (dative of respect) God will restrain His praise. Emphasis falls upon *my praise*, the praise offered to God, and is really a parallel to *my name*, also dependent upon *for the sake of*. North suggests the meaning *renown*, which would bring out the essential idea. By restraining or taming with respect to Israel, God will not cut the nation off so that it is destroyed. The language calls to mind the phrase, *to cut off from the congregation of Israel*, and in this context seems to indicate a cutting off from life. Were Israel to be cut off, it would be completely destroyed. Were that to happen, then the promise of salvation uttered by God to the patriarchs would be seen to be null and void, and the praise of God could not be sounded by His people, nor would His Name be the Name of One that is true to His promises. If, then, Israel perishes, God's promises are seen to be of no effect. The purpose of God, however, was to bring into this world a Redeemer; and nothing must stand in the way of bringing to fruition that promise. Hence, God patiently holds back or delays the punishment.

10 It has been God's purpose to try His people, that through their redemption His glory might be seen. The judgment is not for the purpose of destruction but for transformation. The first verb is commonly used of the refining of metals, and may be rendered, *I have melted thee*. The following explanatory words may literally be rendered, *and not with silver*. It has been suggested that the preposition expresses price, as though the Lord had said, "I have melted thee, but not for silver." Others have taken the preposition in the sense of *as* and rendered, *I have melted thee but not as silver*. Again, some have interpreted, *I have melted thee but not with* (i.e. not in accompaniment with) *silver*. Another possibility is to take the words in the literal sense, *and not with silver*, implying that the result of the process of melting is not silver. On this interpretation the thought is that the melting does not result in pure silver as would be the case were the nation pure. The nation cannot then be compared with pure silver. As far as grammatical considerations are concerned, each of the above is a possibility, but perhaps the last mentioned is to be preferred, for it fits in well with the context. No merit belongs to Israel, and when God tries them they are not like silver.

Parallel with the first verb is the second, *I have chosen thee.* By assuming an Aramaic influence, many interpreters believe that this verb in this particular context is practically equivalent to the Hebrew word *bohan* (to prove) and hence would render *I have proved.* Nevertheless, there actually is no evidence to support such a rendering here, and it is best to retain the verb's normal and well-attested meaning. The furnace of affliction is the place in which Israel was when God chose it. If there is a reference to some historical situation, it would probably be to Egypt, which is often designated an iron furnace. That Israel was in a furnace of affliction would seem to suggest that they were chosen when they were in dire need. Their election is entirely of God's good grace and not of their own deserving.

11 This verse concludes the proclamation and sums up its content. It begins with a repetition similar to that found in 40:1, and in this repetition we are given the reason why God will carry out His purposes. That His Name and His honor may be upheld, He will not utterly destroy the nation. *I will do,* He says, and in this verb sums up the three verbs of the preceding verse. If God should destroy the people and thus show Himself untrue to His covenant, His Name would be profaned. Were Israel to perish in the judgment the heathen would assume that Israel's God was powerless to save.

The question *how shall it be profaned?* implies that God will not allow His Name to be profaned. The honor that is His He will not give to another as He would be doing if His purposes should fail.

12 Hearken unto me, Jacob, and Israel my called; I am he, I am the first, also I am the last.
13 Also my hand hath founded the earth, and my right hand spread out the heavens. I am calling unto them; let them stand together.
14 Be gathered together all of you and hearken, who among them hath made known these things. The Lord loves him, he will do his pleasure in Babylon, and his arm (will be upon) the Chaldeans.
15 I, I have spoken, surely I have called him; I have brought him, he causes to prosper his way.
16 Draw near unto me, hear this; not from the beginning in secret have I spoken, from the time it appeared there am I; and now, the Lord God hath sent me and his Spirit.

12 Verses 12-16 sum up the principal thoughts of chapters 40–48. A tender, friendly tone appears as God commands His people to hear Him. The imperative is followed by the vocative, then another vocative; but in place of a concluding imperative the people are designated *my called one*. The word occurs only here, and is probably more pregnant than the clause *I have called thee by thy name* (cf. 43:1). It either refers to the call to be a people or may be a substitute for "who is called by My Name."

Due attention must be paid to the preposition and suffix (*unto me*), for Israel has all along been hearkening to the idols and to the false prophets. Israel is to hearken unto its God, who alone has the words of life and truth and who alone can deliver.

The reason is stated in the threefold assertion, *I am He; I am the first; also I am the last*. The words *I am He* mean more than "I am the God of whom we are speaking." They mean, "I am the One who is, the actual, living, true God." The words *first* and *last* suggest that God is the beginning and ending of all things, and explain the statement *I am He*. Before all things He is; and after all things He is. Unlike man and the creation, which are temporal and change, God is eternal and changes not. There is a certain gradation introduced by the particle *'aph*. "I am the first, and more than that, I am also the last." Thus, the absolute independence of God over His creation is given the emphasis. To such a God Israel is commanded to hearken.

13 Continuing the gradation introduced by the particle *'aph* in verse 12, this verse is introduced by the same particle. God is the first; more than that, He is also the last; more than that, He has created the world. Thus the particle practically introduces another reason why the Israelites should hearken unto God. He is the Absolute and Eternal One and in addition He is the Creator. *My hand* means *my power*. To found the earth means to bring it into existence and to establish it so that man can dwell upon it.

Parallel to *my hand* is *my right hand*. We may render the verb *ṭippᵉḥah* by *spread out*, or *spanned*. As in 51:13, the founding of the earth is connected with the spreading out of the heavens. Earth is mentioned before heaven. Penna says that this is the accustomed description of the creation according to the cosmological ideas of the ancient Hebrew mentality. We prefer rather to consider this as a description of what actually took place.[8]

[8] Creation is an act that took place once for all (contra Muilenburg). We must distinguish between God's works of creation and His works of providence.

In the second line the participle is to be translated as a present, *Calling*[9] *am I unto them; they shall stand,* or, *let them stand together.* The reference is not to the original creation, but rather shows that God the Creator possesses absolute authority over the work of His hands. When He calls them, they stand ready to obey and to serve Him. The language thus joins together the two ideas of creation and service to God. "Thou hast established the earth, and it abideth. They continue this day according to thine ordinances; for all are thy servants" (Ps. 119:90, 91). There is purpose in the creation. God did not create a dead mass, which would have no reason for existence. He brought all things into existence that they might be His servants and do His bidding. The verb *they shall stand* means that they shall stand at attention or in readiness to obey God. For references to creation in Isaiah note 40:12ff., 22, 26, 28; 42:5; 44:24; 45:12, 18.

14 It would seem, because of the change of person, that those here addressed are different from the ones indicated by the suffix of the preposition. The reference then would be either to the heathen nations or to Israel itself. If the reference is to the heathen, they are commanded to gather themselves together to hear God's challenge. Yet, inasmuch as Israel is God's people, they must be made to see that their God is all-powerful and the idols of the nations are nothing; hence it may well be that the command is addressed to Israel.

All who are addressed, without exception, are to gather themselves together (the *Niphal* here has reflexive force) to hear the challenge God gives. The phrase *among them* refers to the idols. By *these things* we are probably to understand what is stated in 14b. All that God is accomplishing could have been foretold only by Himself. No one of the idols has made known or told these things.

In line two there is a significant exegetical question, namely, whether the object of Yahweh's love is Israel or Cyrus. We may render, "Yahweh loves (or has loved) him, i.e. Israel, and will do His pleasure against Babylon and His arm (against) the Chaldees." We may also render, "Yahweh loves him, i.e. Cyrus; he (Cyrus) will do His pleasure against Babylon and His arm (i.e. manifest His power) (against) the Chaldees." Without question the majority

9 The participle precedes the pronoun, thus lending it emphasis.

of interpreters refer the passage to Cyrus. Those who thus refer it often translate in the following unwarrantable manner: "He whom Yahweh loves will do His pleasure, etc." If the reference is to Cyrus, we are told that he is the object of God's love; but such love is not necessarily saving love; it merely indicates a choice of Cyrus for a specific purpose (cf. 41:2; 44:28; 45:1, 13; 46:11). God has singled out Cyrus to be the object of His affection and to serve Him in the conquest of Babylon.

The last words, *and his arm*, are probably to be taken as a subject rather than an object. God's arm, the seat of active power and strength, is said to act against the Chaldeans. Whereas Cyrus would take Babylon, the ultimate explanation of the action is that the power of the Creator God has been directed against the Chaldeans. A mighty world city can be overthrown by Almighty power, and such power is manifest in the approach of Cyrus.

15 To give, as it were, an attestation of what has just been said, God declares that He has spoken. The personal pronoun is repeated, although the shorter form is employed. Thus attention is drawn to the speaker. Isaiah uses three verbs, and introduces the second with the particle *'aph*, thus giving it a particular emphasis. The first verb, *I have spoken*, indicates that God has spoken in advance concerning the coming of Cyrus and the deliverance. He has also called Cyrus. As He calls heaven and earth and they do His bidding, so also He has called Cyrus, who will carry out His purpose. Lastly, He has brought Cyrus, which means that He has caused him to appear upon the scene of history, ready to perform God's purposes. If the suffixes of the verbs refer to Cyrus, then the teaching of the verse is that the whole course of Cyrus' life and activity was in the hands of Israel's God.

We may render the last words *and he will prosper his way*. The reference is to the subject indicated by the suffixes of the previous verbs, either Cyrus or Israel. Quite probably the language does refer to Cyrus, for taken in connection with the thought of accomplishing God's will against Babylon, Cyrus seems best to fit the context. Cyrus was a great conqueror, not because of his own might and wisdom, but because he was an instrument in the hands of Israel's God.

16 The principal difficulty in this verse revolves around the change of persons. If the speaker in 16a is the Lord, obviously a different speaker is present in 16b. Inasmuch as in both the preceding and following contexts the Lord is the speaker and inasmuch as similar language is employed of Him in 45:19, the Lord is probably the Speaker also in 16a. The command involves tenderness, for the message is of a particularly intimate nature. *This* refers to what follows.

Not from the head (i.e. the beginning) *in secret have I spoken.* The thought is the same as in 45:19, that from the beginning God has not spoken to His people in secret. That the negative is placed before *from the beginning* and not before *in secret* seems strange, but the prophet may wish to emphasize the fact that even from the very beginning God has not spoken in secret. *Beginning* refers to the time when God first began to give prophetic revelations. From the moment that God first spoke to man through the prophets He did not speak in secret but openly and clearly.

In the words *in secret* there may be a reflection upon the esoteric nature of heathen soothsaying. Israelitish prophecy was not involved in dark, esoteric hidden mysteries, made known gradually only to the initiates. Rather, the Old Testament prophet appeared in the nation as a forthright speaker on behalf of the God of Israel. In biblical prophetism the delivery and proclamation of the message was the principal thing, for the biblical religion was practical and aimed at the instruction of the hearer that he might worship his God aright.

Isaiah is not denying the teaching of Numbers 12:1-6 that the revelations God gave to the true prophets of Israel were received in dreams and visions. He is not denying the mystery involved in prophetic revelation but is asserting that from the very beginning the will of God was clearly made known. God's faithfulness in communicating His Word to His own was abundantly manifested, so that the people in not heeding it were utterly without excuse.

In the parallel clause, *from the time of its being there was I,* the principal exegetical question has to do with the reference of the suffix *its*. Possibly the language refers to the events connected with Cyrus; if so, what the prophet means to say is that from the very beginning of these events God was present. They are not new to Him nor unforeseen by Him. Emphasis falls upon the word *there,* which stresses how closely God was connected with these events.

Who is the speaker in the third clause? Obviously it cannot be the Lord, for a distinction is made between the speaker and the Lord. *And now* sets forth a significant contrast. As so often employed in the prophecy, these words present the contrast between the old dispensation and the new. It is in looking forward to the new dispensation that they are here employed. A contrast is to be introduced between the prophets of the Old Testament economy and the Son of the New (Heb. 1:1, 2). This is substantiated by the words *the Lord God*, which prepare for the somewhat similar usage in 50:5, 7, 9. The speaker is the Servant *par excellence*, already introduced in 42:1ff., and about to be brought more prominently into the picture in chapters forty-nine, fifty, and fifty-three. Here he declares that God had sent him, for he is the true instrument who will accomplish the great redemption that alone can bring well-being and peace. The work of Cyrus was but a preparation for his coming; it was the first step in the great turning. The people were not to languish in the bondage of a heathen nation with the promises of salvation going by the board. There was a change, wrought by God; and the instrument whom He used to introduce this change was Cyrus. Cyrus permitted the people to return to Palestine, but he gave them no spiritual victory and no true peace. With chapter forty-nine we pass on to a new phase of Isaiah's message. The fullness of time is coming, and eternal life will appear upon earth. The people of God will experience the heavenly, and in their hearts will be a new song. For God will send forth His Son, and through Him will accomplish a redemption with which the work of Cyrus cannot for an instant be compared.

The King James Version renders, *the Lord God, and his Spirit, hath sent me.* Are the words *and his Spirit* part of the subject, or are they to be construed as an object?[10] If the Spirit is subject, the teaching is that the Lord together with His Spirit has sent the servant. If, on the other hand, the words are object, then the verse teaches that the Lord has sent the servant and also has sent His Spirit. We incline toward this latter position, for the subject is made emphatic by being placed before the verb. The work of the servant is in the hands of the Lord God, and hence it would seem best to regard the Lord God as the only subject. The words *and his Spirit* in any case are in a somewhat subordinate position. If taken as an object, then the conjunction would probably have the force *together with*, and the teaching would be that the servant did not come alone but that his entire ministry was in the power of the Spirit, a definite Messianic concept.

10 Numerous emendations have been proposed. M is supported by 1Q.

17 Thus saith the LORD, thy Redeemer, the Holy One of Israel: I
am the LORD thy God, who teacheth thee to profit, causing thee
to tread in the way thou shalt go.
18 Oh! that thou hadst hearkened to my commandments; then
had thy peace been as a river, and thy righteousness as the
waves of the sea.
19 Then should thy seed have been like the sand, and the issues of
thy bowels like its loins; not will be cut off and not will be
destroyed his name from before him.

17 It is particularly appropriate that in this context Yahweh be
designated *thy Redeemer*,[11] for the prophecy is about to turn to a
consideration of the redemptive work of the servant (cf. also 41:14
and 43:14). God introduces Himself as Israel's God, who teaches
them what is for their profit and causes them to step in the way
they are to go. Duhm makes a strange remark to the effect that
religion is conceived from the eudaemonistic side as an arrangement for man's blessedness; with this eudaemonism there regularly
goes hand in hand, so he tells us, a kind of rationalism, for which
religion is doctrine. But true religion must be founded upon instruction. Israel is unable to walk in the proper way unless they
first know how to do so. To learn this they must be taught what is
profitable. The reference is not merely to the giving of the law at
Sinai but to all the instruction God has given and does give His
people through the ministry of the prophets.

18 Difficult as is the language of this verse, it would seem that
there is only one correct rendering, namely, *Oh!*[12] *that thou hadst
hearkened to my commandments; then had thy peace been like a
river, etc.* Despite what is sometimes said to the contrary this
translation fits the time of Isaiah very well. The prophet looks
back over the history of his people and laments that that history
has been a sinful one, filled with apostasy and rebellion against the
Lord. Because of this sinfulness, punishment is to come instead of
rich peace and righteousness. Penna aptly calls attention to the
similar expressions of our Lord as He wept over Jerusalem (Luke
19:42). The punishment that will come upon Israel in the exile

---

11 *gō'alkā* — The form seems to have undergone the following development:
gō-'ēl > *gō-'a-le-kā* > *gō-'al-kā*.
12 לוֹא with the perf. serves to express a wish that has not been realized,
when there is no apodosis. The following imp. also has hypothetical force: *and
so*, i.e. *then*.

and the cessati n of the theocracy are in no sense due to a lack of
faithfulness u on God's part. He has constantly warned about the
sin of the n tion. The nation itself is responsible for what has
come. Throughout chapters 40–48 Isaiah has been pointing out the
faithlessness of the nation, and now laments that such faithlessness
is an actual fact.

God's revelation is authoritative, expressed in commandments. It
requires that man assume the position of recipient and listener. To
hearken to these commandments means to give obedience to them.

Had Israel been obedient they would have enjoyed *peace* that
might be compared with *a river*. Just as a stream is full and
overflowing, so also would Israel's peace be. The language does not
necessarily presuppose a Palestinian for its author, as Duhm suggests; indeed, from this language alone it would not be possible to
discover the abode of the writer. Just as the river flows on without
cessation, rich and full, so is the peace of Israel. Here the word
peace seems to have its original sense of abundance of well-being,
and this includes salvation. There can be no true well-being upon
earth unless God Himself gives peace, in which is included the
thought that the Israelites would be right with God and would
enjoy all the spiritual blessings that flow from that state.

Israel's *righteousness,* probably a comprehensive term for salvation, is compared to *the waves of the sea.* As the waves, with
mighty force, follow one after another in continuous succession, so
the righteousness of God will roll in upon the people. For them
there would be never-ending blessing. Richness and abundance
characterize the gifts of God; they are never exhausted nor do they
ever fail.

19 Verse 19 continues the apodosis. The language reflects upon
the promise made to Abraham (Gen. 22:17; 32:12). Certain emphasis falls upon *the sand,* an expression that indicates that the
seed of Israel would be innumerable. The suffix in *me'otaw (thy
bowels)* apparently refers to *sand.* As to the interpretation of this
word it may be remarked that some would make it a practical
equivalent of *me'eyka (thy bowels),* which immediately precedes,
so that the suffix refers to the sea, and the reference is to the beings
that fill the heart of the sea.[13] Another possibility is to take the
word as signifying grains of sand. This interpretation has fewer

13 Omitted in 1Q. B ὡς ὁ χοῦς τῆς γῆς; Aq S T ως αι κεγχροι αυτης. The word
is a pl. of *mā-'āh* with a m. suffix.

261

difficulties than the other; and inasmuch as it fits the parallelism well, we have adopted it here.

The implication of the apodosis is that Jacob's seed has not become as the sand, whereas the promise to Abraham was that his seed would be as the sand upon the seashore. Some seek to explain the difficulty by the assumption that the promises of God are all conditional, and that inasmuch as the descendants of Abraham were a rebellious people they forfeited the right to receive the fulfillment of the promise. But this is a promise of salvation, involving the descendants of Abraham, all the people of God, and as such is given to mankind as a covenant. In 2 Samuel 17:11 there is mentioned a partial fulfillment. What is stated in the present verse is that there would have been a greater fulfillment up to this time. The final fulfillment, however, is yet to come, and does come in the preaching of the Gospel and the gathering unto God of all those who are His. In the last great day there will be a multitude, like the sand of the sea for number, that has been delivered from the bondage of guilt and sin through the blood of Jesus Christ.

The second line of the verse offers difficulties. *Name* is used in the sense of *memory,* and to speak of the name as being cut off is equivalent to saying that the memory of the people would be effaced. The last phrase, *from before him,* has reference to God.

It seems best to construe this second line as a clause explanatory of the apodosis, "and thy seed would have been as the sand, without thy name being cut off, etc." Isaiah is bringing to the fore the climax of Israel's long course of apostasy. Had there been hearkening and obedience upon their part, they would be as the sand of the sea, a great multitude. Instead of that, their very name is to be cut off from before God; not that Israel as a nation will no longer exist, but that Israel as the theocracy, the people of God, will no longer continue.[14] Their very name, "holy nation," will be completely destroyed. The glorious theocracy, with all its wondrous prerogatives, is to go into oblivion and to be thought of no more before God; and Israel will continue a dull existence as a nation until the fullness of time comes, when the age of shadow and type shall pass away and the great King of Kings appear upon earth to gather together His people.

> 20 Go out from Babylon, flee from the Chaldeans, with the voice of a cry, declare it, cause this to be heard, bring it out unto

14 Cf. 55:13; 56:5; Ruth 4:10.

the end of the earth; say, The LORD hath redeemed his servant Jacob.

21 And they thirsted not when he caused them to go through the deserts, water from a rock he made to flow from them; and he clave the rock, and waters gushed out.

22 There is no peace, saith the LORD, to the wicked.

20 Even though the name of Israel's seed be cut off before God, there is to be deliverance from the oppressing enemy that would destroy Jerusalem, the capital city of the theocracy. The prediction of deliverance, however, is clothed in the form of a command. It is not a command to return in the near future (Kittel). Emphasis rather falls upon the absolute break the people of God are to make with Babylon. Whether the second verb be rendered *flee* or *make haste,* there is something of the urgency expressed by *to flee* in the verb. There is no contradiction with the words of 52:12, *ye shall not go out with haste, nor go by flight,* for in the present verse the emphasis falls upon an ethical admonition, the need for complete separation from Babylon, whereas in 52:12 a description of the actual departure is given.

The separation from Babylon is the first step in the new order of things, which will culminate in the advent of the Messiah; hence, with the sound of a shout the Israelites are to make known and cause this to be heard. *This* refers to the fact that the Lord has redeemed His people. The verb *cause to go out* has the same force as in 42:1. By means of proclamation the truth of redemption is to be made known. This proclamation is to be worldwide, extending even to the earth's very ends, and not limited to those who were in actual physical bondage in Babylon. The true meaning is brought out by the book of Revelation, ". . . Come out of her, my people, that ye be not partakers of her sins, and that ye receive not of her plagues. For her sins have reached unto heaven, and God hath remembered her iniquities" (Rev. 18:4, 5).

Jacob is identified as God's servant, for he is here viewed in his true light as the people whom God chose to serve Him. Here the emphasis falls upon *Go out from Babylon,* in 40:2 upon *her warfare is accomplished.* In both places imperatives are employed. The conclusion to this first section of chapters 40–66 sets the seal upon the introduction.

21 The new redemption is described in terms of the exodus from Egypt. Hence, the verbs describe the condition of the people after the event of redemption, and are to be translated by the past, *And not did they thirst in the deserts* (through which) *he led them*. As in the first exodus so in the new, God provided for the people's needs in that He made water to flow for them from a rock. The following clause is explicative. He did this by cleaving the rock, and waters gushed out. The subject of the verbs is not Moses but the Lord.

It is perhaps best to understand the language as spoken by those who have been delivered. Obviously there is reflection upon the actual events of the wilderness. Again, there is a wondrous deliverance in which the Lord intervened in order to bring rich blessing to His own. Kimchi expressed surprise that the book of Ezra did not recount these wonders on the return from Babylon if they had actually happened. But the prophet is not describing a literal return from Babylon, as most modern commentators, as well as Kimchi, appear to believe. What he is describing is something infinitely greater, the deliverance the Lord Himself accomplishes from the bondage of sin. The language is figurative, the picture of the exodus furnishing a fitting symbol of the new exodus in Christ.

22 In sharp contrast to the blessedness that God will bring to the righteous is the end of *the wicked*. There will be redemption, not because of any merit upon the people's part, but only because of God's grace. The righteous will suffer for their sins, but they will not utterly be destroyed. The wicked among the people, however, will not receive the *peace* God has reserved for those that love Him.[15]

The *wicked* are those among the Israelites who would live without law. Of them Paul writes: "But unto them that are defiled and unbelieving is nothing pure; but even their mind and conscience is defiled. They profess that they know God; but in works they deny him, being abominable, and disobedient, and unto every good work reprobate" (Titus 1:15, 16). Delitzsch appeals to the primary meaning of the root and characterizes the wicked as loose men, "those whose inward moral character is loosened, without firm hold, and therefore in a state of chaotic condition, because they are without God."

These wicked receive and possess no peace. In this passage the word has a slightly different connotation from what it has in

[15] The relative is omitted when it is an indirect object.

verse 18. Here the stress falls upon peace with God, which God alone gives, wherein God shows Himself to be peaceably disposed toward man. This perfect peace is not the possession of the wicked. In the midst of the declaration of salvation we are reminded that not all will be saved. This is not merely Isaiah's thought, but the Lord's revelation, for it is reinforced by the words *saith the Lord.*

C. JERUSALEM'S INIQUITY IS PARDONED (49:1–57:21)

CHAPTER FORTY-NINE

1 Hearken, O isles, unto me, and hearken, O people from afar;
the Lord from the womb hath called me, from the loins of my
mother he hath caused my name to be remembered.

2 And he hath set my mouth as a sharp sword, in the shadow of
his hand he hath hidden me; and he hath set me as a polished
arrow, in his quiver he hath concealed me.

3 And he said to me, My servant art thou; Israel, in whom I am
glorified.

4 And I said, For nothingness have I toiled, for emptiness and
vanity I have consumed my strength; surely my judgment is
with the Lord, and my work with my God.

5 And now, saith the Lord, who formed me from the womb to
be a servant to him, to return Jacob unto him, but Israel will
not be gathered unto him; and I shall be honored in the eyes
of the Lord, and my God is my strength.

6 And he said, It is a light thing that thou shouldst be my
servant, to raise up the tribes of Jacob, and the preserved of
Israel to restore; and I have given thee as a light to the Gentiles
to be my salvation unto the end of the earth.

1 The passage begins in the imperative with an address to the
isles and the nations similar to 41:1, where Yahweh is the speaker.
The audience is as wide or even wider than the one to whom
Yahweh speaks. This consideration in itself is not without significance, for the servant speaks with absolute authority, commanding
the world to listen. What they are to hear is not merely the
following declaration, which is a vindication of the servant's right
to speak, but they are to listen to him generally.

The words *unto me* serve as a proper introduction to this section
(49:1–57:21). In the previous section (40:1–48:22) Cyrus was prominent, for he was God's instrument to make it possible for Israel to

leave Babylon and return to its homeland. In him the world power was concentrated and made subservient to the kingdom of God. Although Medo-Persia was a part of the colossus of Daniel 2 and thus a member of the anti-God world power, nevertheless its king Cyrus was chosen by God to take the first steps in breaking the power that had destroyed the theocracy.

In the present section Cyrus is not mentioned, for the prophet now concentrates upon the delivery from sin to be brought about by a Deliverer infinitely greater than Cyrus, the Servant of the Lord. He who speaks with such compelling authority is the Messiah, as Head of His people, "and as forming with them one complex person" (Alexander). As the isles are to hearken unto Him, so our attention is to be directed unto Him throughout this section.

In 48:20 the people had been commanded to declare that God had redeemed His servant Jacob. Thus there is preparation for the worldwide proclamation of the present section. Not merely is the message addressed to Israel but to the whole world. The isles indicate not merely actual islands, but the coasts of the Mediterranean Sea; and the nations are the Gentiles. Thus the address includes the entire heathen world. It is probably best to construe *from afar* with *nations*, thus emphasizing that the nations are far away. The second verb, *give ear*, is stronger than the first. The heathen world is not merely to hearken; it is attentively to give ear to what the servant proclaims.

The servant emphasizes the word *Lord*. He has not abruptly come forth upon his own, but as one whom the Lord has prepared. When the world power first began its rise and threatened the kingdom of God, its first king, Tiglath-pileser III, was a usurper. Not so the one who will establish an eternal kingdom. He comes to do his Father's will.

The expression *from the womb* supports the fact that the servant is an individual. In itself it does not necessarily exclude the collectivistic interpretation, but it does indicate personal election and specific appointment to office, which at the most could only apply to a personified Israel. The phrase is used also of Jeremiah's call (Jer. 1:5). In itself the phrase merely indicates a divine call to a particular work.

In *from the loins of my mother* there is more than a parallel. The expression *my mother* precludes regarding the speaker as a personified group. The words can be used only by an individual speaking of his own mother. Penna thinks that to discover a precise prophecy in the verse is to sin by exaggerated literalism. But has Hahn gone too far when he speaks of a human mother on earth, and declares that she is none other than the virgin of 7:14? Or has Delitzsch really overstated the case when he says, "We call to mind here ... above all the name Immanuel, which is given by anticipation to the Coming One in ch. vii. 14"? We think not. It is this reference to *my mother* that makes it clear that the speaker is the Messiah.

The final words may be literally rendered, *he caused my name to be remembered.* The thought is not so much that of naming a person as of designating a person by name. Thus the name denotes the servant's office and vocation.

Paul reflects upon both Jeremiah's call and the present passage when he refers to his own call: "But when it pleased God who separated me from my mother's womb" (Gal. 1:15). To be compared also are Luke 1:41; 2:21 and Matthew 1:21.

When Assyria was coming to prominence Isaiah predicted the coming of the King, the virgin's Son. Now that the world power is exercising its might and will take God's people captive, Isaiah announces the Servant of the Lord as the true Deliverer. Thus the two epochs point us to the Messiah, first to His Person and then to His work.

2 The introductory *And* indicates more than a mere continuation of the discourse; it serves rather to set forth the more detailed preparation of the servant for his public ministry. There may be implied a contrast with the calling and preparation of Cyrus, who came with armies of war as his weapons (cf. 41:2ff., 25; 45:1ff.). There is parallelism between 2a and 2c and also between 2b and 2d. Both 2a and 2c refer to the preparation of the servant, whereas 2b and 2d refer to his relationship to God. Both 2b and 2d point to the source from which emanates that which is stated in 2a and 2c. Whether they actually give the reasons for what is there stated is difficult to determine.

And he set my mouth is equivalent to *And he made my mouth to be.* From the mouth the word comes forth, hence *mouth* is used by metonymy for discourse, words, or speech, for the words of the servant cut like a sword. His is an office of the mouth, his task a declaration of the Truth; for he is a prophet *par excellence,* and his word is the Gospel, which to the one is a savor of death unto death, and to the other the savor of life unto life (cf. Heb. 4:12; also Rev. 1:16; Jer. 23:29). In order that He may bring to naught all the opponents of God's Holy Name, the Lord will send His servant to earth. Likewise, through the servant's mouth the truth of redemption will be proclaimed to the poor and needy. These two concepts should not be separated; for what is set forth here is the servant as prophet, and the word of that prophet brings life and judgment.[1]

It is interesting that the words *mouth* and *sword* are brought together, for they call to mind the expression "mouth of the sword," i.e. the sword's sharp edge. In Isaiah 1:20 *sword* and *mouth of the Lord* occur together. This suggests the piercing incisiveness of the word that proceeds from the servant's mouth.

The *shadow of his hand* is probably the shadow produced when an object is held in the hand and so concealed, rather than the shading a hand may cause when placed between a certain object and the sun. Whether the reference is to protection or to concealment is difficult to determine, and it may be that both are intended. In the nature of the case, the object is concealed, held ready for use like a sword in its scabbard (cf. 51:16).

The comparison with a polished arrow suggests that the servant is equipped to destroy even the enemies of God that are far away as well as those near by.[2] The thought of piercing, penetrating power is present (cf. Ps. 45:5). Alexander suggests that there may be an additional allusion to directness of aim and swiftness of flight. This arrow hits the mark with penetrating deadly accuracy. As yet, however, the arrow lies concealed in the quiver. This second line is parallel in thought to the first. To be noted is the causative force of the two final verbs in each line. The Lord causes His servant to be hidden until he appears upon earth ready to exercise his ministry.

3 The words *And he said* continue the detailed description begun in verse 2. Emphasis falls upon *my servant* (cf. Ps. 2:7). God acknowledges to the servant that the servant is His, a declaration of consolation and strength which will sustain the servant in the task that lies ahead of him.

---

1 Gesenius adduces classical parallels: Diodorus Siculus xii.40; Pindar *Olympian Odes* ii.159, 160; ix.17.

2 *ḥēṭz* — *arrow*; cf. Akk. *uṣṣu*; Ug. *ḥẓ. bārûr* — *polished*; cf. *burru, purified*.

As the Hebrew text stands it must be rendered, *Thou art my servant, Israel, in thee I shall be glorified*, i.e., "Thou, Israel, art my servant in whom I shall be glorified." The verse is similar in construction to Genesis 45:4 and Numbers 22:30. The suffix, *thee*, may correspond to the subject of the principal clause, *thou*, even though the relative, *whom*, refers more directly to the antecedent in the third person, *Israel*. Thus the servant is directly identified as Israel.

In what sense, however, is the word *Israel* to be understood? In the light of the fact that the servant is the speaker himself and his address to God is so individualistic in nature, it is clear that the reference is not to the nation. The people of Israel, personified, are not the speaker. This appears also from the close connection between *servant* and *I shall glorify myself*. It is the servant character of Israel that brings glory to God. To be God's servant is the highest privilege, and it is in performing the work of servant that God is glorified. This could hardly apply to the recalcitrant, sinful nation, for this nation was unable to be the true Israel. All that the prophet writes concerning Israel makes clear that they could not be what the Servant of the Lord should be. When the servant accomplishes his task, God is glorified; the empirical Israel could not accomplish that task; hence, whatever be the force of *Israel* here, it is not merely a designation of the nation.

It has been pointed out that *Israel* is not a vocative nor a mere apposition to *servant*, but a name that is predicated and hence may be a name of honor.[3] It is not merely a reference to the nation's ancestor, Jacob, nor necessarily to a second Israel, as Nägelsbach suggests. The emphasis rather is upon Israel as Israel should be. There is ample preparation for this idea. Thus, "Truly God is good to Israel, to such as are of a clean heart" (Ps. 73:1). Hengstenberg well says, "All those declarations of the Old Testament, in which the name of Jacob or Israel is used to designate the *election*, to the exclusion of the false seed, the true Israelites in whom there is no guile,—all those passages prepare the way for, and come near to the one before us."

Israel then is a designation of the true people of God, the whole body of the redeemed as members under the Head, the Messiah. After mentioning the human body Paul says, "So also is Christ" (1

3 So E. Burrows, *The Gospel of the Infancy and Other Biblical Essays*, 1941, p. 63.

Cor. 12:12). Israel, therefore, is the Messiah conceived as the Head of His body, the true Church, although the emphasis at this point falls upon the members of the body. Calvin says, "In a word, the Lord honours by this name the Church, which is the spouse of Christ, just as the wife is honoured by bearing the name and title of her husband."

There is no reason for abandoning the ordinary meaning of the verb "to get glory for oneself." It ties in with what is said elsewhere about the successful completion of the servant's work. In the performance of the work that only the servant can perform, the God of Israel is glorified.

4 The servant continues his soliloquy. In striking contrast to what God had said, he states what he himself had said. The personal pronoun is emphatic. "But I—in contrast—said." It is not necessary to assume that the servant interrupts the Lord's speech.[4] What God has said is complete in itself (v. 3), a statement embodying full confidence in the servant. As the servant surveys his work, however, he gives expression to disappointment, as did the Owner of the vineyard in Isaiah 5. There is no need to take the verb "to say" in the sense of "to think." The verb may often be so used, but here (and also in v. 3) the verbs seem to point to stronger action. It seems best, therefore, to consider this language as a direct reply to God rather than as a mere expression of the servant's work.

In 42:4 there had been a preparation for this expression of disappointment. The words *in vain* (lit., *in respect to vanity*, i.e. without result, to no purpose), are placed first for emphasis. (Note also 65:23, where the same words appear.) The basic meaning of the verb *yaga'* is "to grow weary." In combination with *riq* it means "to grow tired laboring in vain" (lit., *I have grown weary with respect to vanity*). The implication is that the servant has toiled, but his wearying toil has been to no purpose.

This is supported by the parallel *with respect to desolation and vanity my strength I have exhausted.* The word *tohu* (desolation) is a favorite of Isaiah's, and in this context simply points out that the toil of the servant was fruitless.[5] A further Isaianic touch

---

4 So, e.g., de Leeuw, *op. cit.*, p. 191.
5 The word occurs in 24:10; 29:21; 34:11; 40:17, 23; 41:29; 44:9; 45:18, 19; 49:4; 59:4.

(found only here and in 30:7 and nowhere else in the Old Testament) is the appearance of *hevel* (*breath, vapor*) in close connection with *riq* (*vanity*). The servant, as it were, has poured out his strength to accomplish the work God had given him, but the result is to no purpose; it is desolation and a vapor.

The perfect is not to be emphasized, as though Isaiah were describing an event that occurred in the past. Rather, in somewhat mysterious fashion and without any particular chronological emphasis, the prophet presents a soliloquy of the servant, the purpose of which is to point out the task that the servant must accomplish. The expression of discouragement is no thought of unbelief, but simply of a genuine modesty borne from a consciousness of one's own weakness. It is, we believe, Jesus Christ in His humiliation of whom the prophet speaks.[6] Although He is God's eternal Son and one with the Father, yet for our redemption He humbled Himself, "being born, and that in a low condition, made under the law, undergoing the miseries of this life, the wrath of God, and the cursed death of the cross. . . ."[7] As man He was weak and tempted in all points as we, but without sin. In Gethsemane He suffered the deep anguish of grief, trembling, and fear. He sought the companionship of His disciples; He prayed; He sweat great drops of blood. In the days of His flesh He offered up prayers and supplications to Him who was able to save Him from death, and He was heard for His godly fear (Heb. 5:7). The prophet's language points forward to the humiliation of our Lord: true man yet sinless; true man yet very God. Before the sublime mystery of the Person of our Lord we can but bow in reverent wonder. The psychological problem we cannot answer.

Passing from an expression of despondency to one of sure confidence, the servant sets forth his firm assurance that God is with him. The particle is to be rendered *surely,* for it is asseverative. *Judgment* here does not refer to lawsuit or to a case at law, but to the judgment of justification that God will pronounce upon the servant. *My judgment*[8] is the decision God utters concerning the servant and that decision will declare (and has already declared;

---

[6] This position may of course be held only if the Bible is a special revelation of the one triune God.

[7] Question 27, The Westminster Shorter Catechism.

[8] Cf. Ps. 9:4; Mic. 7:9. That the common *rib* pattern may underlie this language is possible, but we do not wish thus to straitjacket the profundity of Isaiah's thought.

cf. 42:1, etc.) that his work is successful. This judgment is not man's to make, but lies with the Lord.

The parallel expression means *my doing, my work*, i.e. the fruit or result of his labor. The outcome of the servant's toil lies in God's hands. In the expression *my God* appears the servant's confidence that God has not forsaken him.

5 This verse forms the true contrast to 4a, in that it gives the Lord's answer to the servant's disappointment. This contrast appears in the conjunction *and* before *now*, in contrast to *and* before *I* in the previous verse. The purpose is to confirm what has been uttered before and to show what the consequence is. "And now," we may paraphrase, "it is much more the case that, etc." Thus, the phrase *and now* need not necessarily introduce a new beginning.

The actual speech of the Lord, however, does not appear until verse 6, where it is again introduced with "And he said." Apparently the words *And now* are the Lord's; but before reporting the Lord's speech further, the servant gives a long statement concerning the Lord and his own relationship to the Lord.

The servant is conscious that God has prepared him for his mission, even knowing that God had formed him from the womb (cf. Jer. 1:5; Gal. 1:15; possibly Rom. 1:1; also Ps. 139:13-16). The servant was born to accomplish a specific mission. The language emphasizes the fact that the servant is God's and serves Him. Hence, the Lord did not separate the servant in vain from his mother's womb. Even though similar language is used of the nation (44:2, 24) in this passage, it seems to point to an individual as the speaker, and perhaps contains also a hint of royalty. The expression occurs on some of the neo-Babylonian inscriptions with reference both to Nabonidus and to Nebuchadnezzar II.[9] The purpose of the servant's being formed, however, is not primarily to be a king, but to be a servant.

A twofold task is ascribed to the servant. The infinitive "to bring back" is factitive and has the servant, not Yahweh, as its subject.[10] The reference is not to a return from Babylon, but a

---

[9] Cf. Behr, *The Writings of Deutero-Isaiah and the Neo-Babylonian Royal Inscriptions*, pp. 21, 22.

[10] Cf. A. Goetze, "The So-Called Intensive of the Semitic Languages," *JAOS*, Vol. 62, No. 1, March 1962, pp. 1-8. To avoid the supposed difficulty of Israel the servant restoring Israel the nation, some have construed Yahweh as subject of the inf.: *Yahweh has said . . . that He would restore Jacob, etc.*

spiritual return to God.[11] Those who identify the servant with the nation Israel assert that just as one might say that the Church has a mission to the Church, so also Israel the servant has the task of returning Israel the nation to God. Such a conception, however, is out of harmony with those passages that teach that spiritual salvation is the work of an individual (Isa. 53).[12]

In the following clause the negative appears to conflict with what has just been said. It is possible to retain the negative and to render, *and Israel will not be swept away.* This, however, is not satisfactory, for it merely brings in an additional clause with almost irrelevant meaning. It is perhaps best to render, *and Israel will be gathered to him.*[13] Thus there is a striking parallelism and an interesting chiastic arrangement. Sin divides and disperses, but the servant unites. Only in God is a true union to be found, hence the servant brings Israel back to God.

Finally, the servant again utters his assurance that he will be vindicated. To insert this line after verse 4 is not warranted, for such parentheses are characteristic of this section of the prophecy. It is true that this language constitutes a consequence of what has just been stated, but it probably also gives a second purpose for the servant's having been formed, namely, that he should be glorified.[14] To be honored in the eyes of God is to be honored before God in His sight.

The last clause, *and my God is my strength,* is explanatory, being a new expression of confidence. It is perhaps best to retain the sense *strength* for *'oz.* The strength or power that the servant possesses to accomplish his work is found in God.

6 After the parenthesis of verse 5, the Lord's language is continued, *And he said* taking up *saith the Lord* of verse 5. The purpose is to show that the restoration of Israel is not a sufficiently great task for the servant; he is also to be a light to the Gentiles and God's salvation to the ends of the earth.

11 This is supported by *'ēlāyw, unto him.*

12 There is a distinction in Israel, but the wicked will be cast out, not returned to the Lord. Only the true Israel, the elect, will be brought unto the Lord, and this by the work of the servant.

13 1Q has *lw, to him;* so also Aq T and 9 Heb. MSS. B has προς αυτον; Vulg. *non congregabitur.*

14 Note the weak *waw.* De Leeuw would (erroneously, I believe) point as *waw* consecutive. But cf. J. Lindblom, *The Servant Songs in Deutero-Isaiah,* Lund, 1951, p. 26.

The verse is difficult, but there is no need to form a question, for the language may be rendered as a simple indication, *It is too light a thing that thou shouldst be my servant*.[15] The verse thus consists of a protasis and an apodosis, the latter beginning with *so I have set thee*. By *light* we are probably to understand "small" or "insignificant" rather than "trifling" (BDB). To restore Jacob is a great task, but it is not great enough for *my servant* (emphasis falls upon *my*). He has a greater task.

In the protasis there are two purpose clauses each introduced by an infinitive. The first means *to raise up* and is used of God's establishing the various institutions in Israel (cf., e.g., Amos 9:11). Here the reference is to the raising of Jacob's tribes to the position of dignity they do not now enjoy. They are fallen tribes, and the servant's task is to raise them up again, restoring their position as true tribes of Jacob.

To restore the tribes is not necessarily a political task, but is to be understood in the same sense here as in verse 5. The coming salvation is one in which the dispersed and fallen people are again raised and united. In chiastic fashion (not necessarily an Aramaic construction) Isaiah repeats the thought, *and the preserved of Israel to restore*. The word *preserved* refers to those who have been saved from calamity.[16] In this verse a different form is used for *restore* from that found in verse 5, but between the two there is no essential difference. The raising up and restoring of the people is essentially the same work as becoming a light and salvation. It is in his being a light and salvation to Israel (apart from the fact that he is also that to the Gentiles) that the servant raises up and restores Israel. The first step in the work of restoration was the return from exile, to which the language of this verse may allude. But, as Pieper says, this restoration only served to make possible the spiritual restoration of Israel accomplished by Christ. That the reference is to the spiritual Israel or the elect is clear from the whole context. Nowhere does the Bible teach that the entire physical Israel will be saved.

Yet the servant's work is greater than the redemption of Israel. The greater task, however, does not exclude the lesser. That the

---

15 נָקֵל — *Niphal* perf. of קלל. The stative verb here expresses a quality of being; lit., *it is a light thing from thy being to me a servant*; B μεγα σοι εστι. The *mem* expresses comparison.

16 וּנְצִירֵי — attested also by 1Q. Note position of the inf. at the end of the clause.

work is of supreme significance appears in the introductory *I have set thee*. God has appointed the servant to this work and determined that he should carry it out. *Light* is intimately connected with salvation. The Gentiles are conceived as being in spiritual darkness, and when light comes to them they are delivered from their darkness. This *light* is the servant, just as Jesus in the days of His flesh declared, "I am the light of the world" (John 8:12).

The last clause might be rendered, *that my salvation should be to the end of the earth*; but this is somewhat unnatural, inasmuch as the preposition *to* should be taken in the same sense as in the preceding clause. Hence, we may better bring out the force by translating, *that thou mightest be my salvation*. The servant is both light and salvation.

Just as in the first part of the verse the reference is to the spiritual Israel, so here it is to the elect among the Gentiles and not to all Gentiles indiscriminately. For this reason the view that identifies the servant with Israel fails. Israel alone never was the instrument of the world's redemption. Paul's use of this verse (Acts 13:47) supports the identification of the servant as the Messiah and His people. When His people labor in His Name as Paul and Barnabas were doing, He works through them.

OBSERVATIONS

(1) The Gentiles are in darkness and need light. They are not already redeemed but are lost in the darkness of sin and ignorance. Hence the need for vigorous missionary work. One religion is not as good as another. Christ alone is the Light of this dark world.

(2) Israel is the first-born in the household of faith. Therefore, we Gentiles who have been brought in from without must love Israel and must bend every effort to bring the Gospel to the Jews.

(3) True unity is found in Jesus Christ alone in whom both Jew and Gentile have become one.

7 Thus saith the LORD, the Redeemer of Israel, his Holy One, to the heartily despised, to the nation exciting abhorrence, to a servant of rulers; kings shall see and rise up, princes, and they shall bow themselves, for the sake of the LORD who is faithful, the Holy One of Israel, and he hath chosen thee.

8 Thus saith the LORD: In an acceptable time I have answered thee, and in a day of salvation I have helped thee; and I will keep thee and I will give thee for a covenant of the people to raise up the earth, to cause to inherit the desolate heritages.

7 What follows is a response on the Lord's part to the utterance of the servant. The servant has appeared speaking without particular introduction; but the language of the Lord is introduced with *Thus saith the Lord*, and He is described as the Redeemer of Israel and its Holy One. In this context the term Redeemer is particularly applicable, for the great work of the servant just described is redemption. Furthermore, in the accomplishment of this redemption God has maintained His holiness.

In the following clause the prophet sums up what has been said about the servant. Hence, we should best render the preposition *with respect to*; thus we may translate, *with respect to the one despised of soul*,[17] an apt description of the servant.

The following words complement what has just been stated of the servant. *To him that causes to excite the abhorrence of the nation* is a possible rendering.[18] This is but another way of saying that he was abhorred of the nation. Here, it would seem, the emphasis is upon the contrast between the servant as an individual and the mass of people who abhor him. It is in this same sense that the next words also are to be understood. The servant is a slave and the rulers are evil rulers. Not only did the masses despise the servant, but also the kings. He who is the Servant of the Lord is also the slave of tyrants. This despised one is to receive the homage of which the remainder of the verse speaks.

The true dignity of the servant breaks through and men see him for what he actually is. For the sake of completeness the word *princes* is added, and we are to understand the verb *will see*. Thus, the rulers as a whole are included. And when the princes see, they will do obeisance, for the servant is deserving of their deepest adoration. The thought anticipates the statements of Isaiah 52:15.

This obeisance is for the sake of the Lord, for the kings realize that He has brought the servant into glory,[19] and they themselves would through their action glorify him.

8 *Thus saith the Lord* resumes the introduction, and strengthens or confirms what is to follow. The meaning of *time of favor* is determined or at least influenced by the parallel *day of salvation*.

---

17 *liḇzōh* — inf. construct. But 1Q reads *lbzwh*, a passive participle. The thought is *deeply despised*. B τὸν φαυλίζοντα τὴν ψυχὴν αὐτοῦ.
18 *meṯaʿēḇ* — a Piel participle. Many would point as Pual, *meṯōʿāḇ*.
19 The imp. with *waw* consecutive continues the preterite contained in *who is faithful*, namely, *who hath chosen thee*.

The thought is based upon the year of Jubilee, described in Leviticus 25:8ff. It is that time when God shows favor to His people, namely, the period when Christ was upon earth, the fullness of the times (Gal. 4:4). It lies not in the past but in the future.[20] Paul agrees with Codex Vaticanus in rendering *an accepted time* (2 Cor. 6:2).

Inasmuch as the favorable time is in the future the two preterites must be construed as prophetic futures: *I will answer thee,* and not, *I have answered thee.* The verb is probably to be understood as a response to the complaint of the servant. He had believed that he had labored in vain; now in the time of favor God will answer him in that He will come to his help (cf. Ps. 22:19-21). The meaning of the first verb is established by that of the second.

The day of salvation is the day when God will accomplish salvation for His people. *Day* here is not to be taken literally, but is equivalent to *time. Salvation* expresses the same thought as *time of favor,* but more exactly. The time of favor is one in which the salvation of God will be seen. At that time God will help the servant. This and the preceding parallel verb refer to continuous action rather than to an act performed once for all. They give a hint of what is to follow in chapter fifty-three, namely, that at the time when God accomplishes His salvation, the servant will be in need of help.

The words *time* and *day* are significant, for they make clear that God does not act capriciously or haphazardly. At the time determined He performs His work. Our Lord expressed the same thought when at the wedding feast at Cana He remarked, "My hour is not yet come."

For an explanation of the following words see 42:6. That the servant should be a covenant is the grand and central point of the passage, for it expresses the end God had in mind in forming him. This is followed by a statement of the purpose for which the servant is made a covenant of the people. As far as syntax is concerned, the subject of the infinitives may be either the servant or God. In the light of the context, with its strong emphasis upon the preparation of the servant, it would seem best to construe as subject the servant.

Under the imagery of the restoration of a devastated land, the

---

20 L. Itkonen (*Deuterojesaja* [40–55] *metrisch untersucht,* Helsinki, 1916, p. 66) ties in this day with the death of Sargon.

gift of salvation is described. The description reflects upon the division of the land under Joshua, and leans upon the expressions used in verse 6. *To raise up the land* has primary reference to the land of Palestine, and the parallel expression *desolate inheritances*[21] reflects upon the desolation that has come upon the land of promise. These inheritances had been distributed by lot under Joshua (cf. Josh. 13ff.). The reference is not merely to the southern kingdom but to the entire land. The picture refers primarily not to the return from the exile, but to the reestablishment of the Davidic kingdom under the Messiah, when all the true seed of Abraham will receive their promised inheritance.

9 Saying to the prisoners, Go out, to those who are in darkness, Be ye revealed; upon ways they will pasture, and in all bare hills is their place of pasture.

10 They will not hunger and they will not thirst, nor will there smite them the burning and the sun; for he who has mercy upon them will lead them, even by springs of water will he lead them.

11 And I shall place all my mountains for the way, and my paths shall be high.

12 Behold! these from afar shall come, and behold these from the north and from the sea and these from the land of Sinim.

13 Shout, O heavens, and rejoice, O earth, let the moutains break forth into shouting; for the LORD has comforted his people, and his afflicted ones he will have mercy upon.

9 *Saying* is a correlative of the infinitives in the preceding verse, "to raise up the land, and to apportion the desolate inheritances, and to say to the prisoners, etc." The language is taken from the exile, but the release is greater; it is a release accomplished by the Gospel. Isaiah varies his method of expression by using imperatives. The prisoners, bound in sin, are commanded to go out. Obviously they are unable to do this, for they are imprisoned; but the command is similar to all commands to repent and believe the Gospel. Christ commanded, "Come unto me," but no one can come unto Him unless the Heavenly Father draw him. The second command does not mean "come to the light," but *be ye revealed* or possibly *show yourselves*. Those who are in darkness are to come out of that darkness so that they will be seen of men.

---

21 *šōmēmōṯ* — note retention of *Tzere*, probably because of the pause accent.

Beginning with the second line of the verse the servant recedes into the background to come forth later more prominently, and the prophet describes the blessedness of the life of the prisoners and those who had been in darkness. They are pictured as a flock that will pasture on ways that had formerly been without pasture.[22] Now there is a complete change, and along the ways as they go the flock will find pasture. Likewise the bare hills where nothing grew now prove to be the pastures for the flock.[23] Thus, the flock need not even turn aside far to find pasture, and where one would least expect it, it is present. In fact, the most unlikely places are the places of pasture.

10 The prophet continues the figures of a flock. As a result of the rich pasturage they will neither hunger nor thirst. The second half of the line states that the flock will be protected from the burning sun of the desert. The translation of *sharav* as "mirage" is questionable.[24] Elsewhere the word appears only in 35:7 (see discussion of that verse). Here it apparently means something like *burning*, for it stands before *sun*. As the sun will not smite, so the *sharav* will not smite. The verb *smite* is opposed to the rendering "mirage." That the sun by its heat should smite is a biblical conception (cf. Ps. 121:6). Possibly therefore the two words are to be taken as a hendiadys, *heat of the sun* or *burning of the sun*.

Isaiah is apparently reflecting upon the exodus, for as Calvin well says, ". . . It is customary with the prophets to mention the departure of the people out of Egypt whenever they intend to demonstrate the kindness of God, either publicly towards all, or privately towards any individual." In the second line of the verse the reason is given for what is stated in the first. In fact, the last sentence gives the reason for what is stated in the five preceding sentences, although the reference to springs of waters actually refers only to what has just been asserted in the first line of the verse.

The people will not wander through the desert aimlessly, nor will their leader be unconcerned about them; but He will show them mercy. The participle expresses tenderness and comfort. He

---

22 1Q כול חרים עַל; B, however, has ταῖς ὁδοῖς.

23 *šepāyim* is pl. of *šepi*, *bare place, height*; B ἐν πάσαις ταῖς τρίβοις.

24 Cf. Akk. *šarrabu*, a demon of fever. Koran 24:29, *Ka-sa-rā-b bi-qī-'ah*, "like a mirage in the desert."

who leads His people through desolate places is concerned to show them mercy. Isaiah employs the beautiful figure of springs of water to express the truth that God provides for all the needs of His people and blesses them abundantly.[25] They find not merely a small stream, but flowing, abundant springs of water, even in desolate places.

11 The prophet continues his description of God's gracious work, changing the figure to that of a marching people. In the way of their march there will be obstacles of all kinds, but God will remove these. These obstacles are pictured as *mountains*. The reference is probably to all mountains; these belong to God, and He has sovereignty in disposing of them as He will. Inasmuch as He is their Creator, He is able to lower them so that they become the way itself. Thus, a complete reversal of the situation occurs. To deny any reference to a return from the exile is as wrong as to insist that the only reference is to such a return. But the main emphasis of the prophet is upon a spiritual return from the bondage of sin unto the one living and true God. The thought is similar to that expressed in 40:4.

In the last clause there is a feminine subject and masculine verb. This enallage of the gender is strange, but not necessarily to be rejected, for the sense is clear. The ways of God are those artificially raised up so that an army or a group of people can march upon them. The verb would seem to suggest a special raising of the ways. On the other hand, it may be that the language merely intends to suggest that the way over which the people are to travel is specially raised up, so that their way will be clear to them, preventing them from going astray and protecting them from the ravages of any wild beasts.

12 The prophet now points out the extent of the dispersion in that he indicates the places from which the redeemed will come. The dispersion was worldwide; here there is no talk of a return from Babylonian exile. It is rather a regathering of the children of God that were scattered to the four corners of the earth (cf. 43:5ff.). At the same time only two technical terms are used to indicate the directions, *north* and *sea*. The first points to the

---

25 *mabbúʻēy* — cf. Akk. *nambaʻu*, Ar. *man-baʻ*, Syr. *mab-búʻ*, and Isa. 35:7; Eccl. 12:6.

regions north of Palestine and the second to the isles of the Mediterranean Sea.

The other two directions (if the reference really is to them) are indicated by more general terms. If the first term *from afar* refers to the far east, then the strange word *Sinim* would appear to refer to the south; but this cannot be pressed. Possibly the words *from afar* are merely intended to indicate a great distance, without any stress upon the particular direction involved. If this is the case, it may be that the phrase *land of Sinim* is intended to express the same thing. Thus, both the first and the last members of the verse express the thought of great distance, whereas the two middle members point to specific directions. In any attempt to identify the land of Sinim we must look for a place far from Palestine. An ancient interpretation would identify it with China, and this, despite alleged difficulties, is a possibility (see SPECIAL NOTE: "The Land of Sinim"). It need not be maintained that each of these words represents a place where the Jews had actually been in exile. The language is universal; at the destruction of the theocracy the concentration of God's people in a nation had been destroyed and they were cast out in the earth to live among other peoples. Now, however, when the day of favor has come, they return unto the Lord from all the earth. The earth gives back what belongs to the Lord.

13 Commensurate with the magnitude of the salvation is the command that all nature rejoice. Isaiah is nothing if not grand in his commands. By thus commanding all nature to rejoice he is foretelling the joyful change that the day of favor will bring. As in 1:2 so here also, both heaven and earth are used without the definite article. The first two verbs are imperatives, *Shout* and *rejoice*. The heaven and earth are to shout for joy at the marvelous redemption the God of Israel has accomplished. They that proclaim the glory of God (Ps. 19:1) are now to break forth into joyful shouting (cf. 42:10-12; 44:23; 52:9 and 55:12ff.).

The third verb is a jussive, *let the mountains break forth*, i.e. *let them open their mouths in jubilation.*

Finally a reason is given why nature should thus rejoice, and this reason is presented by means of two verbs. The first is a preterite, which is to be construed as a prophetic future, but which yet expresses a once-for-all act. The word is generally rendered *comfort*, although Pieper may be correct in indicating that the Niphal has a further connotation, namely, that of reestablishing. The thought is that God has shown comfort to His people in that He has once more established them as such. The phrase *his people* refers not merely to those who were Israelites after the flesh but to all whom He has chosen unto life eternal.

Parallel is a verb in the imperfect, which expresses a continuous work, namely, that of showing mercy. The objects of this mercy are the afflicted ones who belong to the Lord. The noun is parallel to *his people* in the first clause. The word reflects upon the previous condition of the people and also upon the fact that the One who shows them mercy is their true Protector. The chiastic arrangement of the verse yields a striking effect.

14 Yet Zion said, The LORD hath forsaken me, and the Sovereign One hath forgotten me.

15 Will a woman forget her suckling, so as not to have mercy on the son of her womb? Even these will forget, but I will not forget thee.

16 Behold! on my palms I have engraven thee; thy walls are before me continually.

17 There hasten thy sons; thy destroyers and thy wasters from thee go out.

18 Lift up round about thine eyes and see; all of them will be gathered together, they shall come to thee; As I live, saith the LORD, (I swear) that all of them as an ornament thou shalt wear, and thou shalt bind them like a bride.

19 For thy ruins and thy waste places and the land of thy desolation; for now thou shalt be too constricted for an inhabitant, and thy devourers are far distant.

20 Still do they say in thy ears, the sons of thy childlessness: Too narrow for me is the place, draw near to me that I may dwell.

21 And thou shalt say in thy heart, Who hath borne for me these, since I was bereaved and barren; exiled and turned aside, and these, who has brought them up; behold! I was left alone; these where are they?

22 Thus saith the Sovereign One, the LORD, Behold! I shall lift up to the nations my hand, and to the peoples shall I lift up my banner, and they will bring thy sons in the bosom, and thy daughters on the shoulder will be borne.

23 And kings will be thy nursing fathers and their queens thy nursing mothers; faces to the ground they will do obeisance to thee, and the dust of thy feet will they lick, and thou shalt know that I am the LORD, whose trusters will not be put to shame.

283

14 The redemption just pictured was contrary to Zion's expectations. Not only had Zion not wrought that redemption herself, she even believed that her God had forsaken and forgotten. The first verb is best rendered as a past, for it expresses the attitude of Zion before the deliverance was accomplished. Isaiah obviously is not addressing exiles in Babylon, nor is he speaking of the city of Jerusalem, which remained desolate after the exiles were taken to Babylon. Were this latter the case, it would be difficult to understand the long discourse that follows. *Zion* rather designates the chosen people, whose great city is Zion, the capital and center of the true religion.

Zion's despair is expressed in a chiastic manner. The first verb suggests an outward abandoning, whereas the second suggests an inner forsaking. Zion believed that she was completely forgotten of her God. That cry is one of unbelief and doubt, for God had promised that the Messiah would come, and that there would never be wanting a man to sit upon the throne of David. *The Sovereign One* (*ᵃdonay*) is a designation of Israel's God the Lord. The word seems to indicate the depth of Zion's doubt; even the Sovereign One has forgotten Zion. Thus when the people of God, the true Zion, are plunged into the darkness of despair and doubt, the glorious light of the day of favor appears to them.

15 The Lord takes up the thought with which the previous verse closed and sets it in its true light. He asks a question to which a negative answer would be expected. How great is the love of the mother for the little child that she suckles; surely she will not forget it, for it is the son that has come forth from her own womb. There is a certain refinement in the choice of language. The prophet employs *woman* rather than *mother*, for the idea of motherhood is brought out sufficiently in the words *her suckling*. The verb contains the implication of ability, and hence may rightly be rendered, "Can she forget?" How can a mother forget her suckling? Night and day it demands her attention and affection. For this reason the Lord speaks of the mother rather than the father. That a mother should forget her child is unthinkable. For this reason too the word *suckling* is chosen rather than *son* or *child*. It is the one who is wholly dependent upon the mother that is thus brought before our eyes.

There is a certain advance or climax in the thought. In the first clause it is implied by the question that it is impossible for a mother to forget her suckling. Now such an implied impossibility is shown to be a reality. It is a rare reality, but nevertheless happens. A mother may forget her child.[26]

Commentators differ as to the rendering of the first clause of the second line, but there is no reason for departing from the ordinary sense of the words. They bluntly state a fact; *Even these will forget.*[27] It is a tragic truth, but a truth nevertheless, which deeply stirs the emotions of the heart. Mothers do forget their sucklings, for mothers are sinful and their love is sometimes overcome by baseness. Even the greatest of human love may fail.

On the other hand, God's love, in distinction from even the highest of human love, will never fail. Isaiah introduces the pronoun with emphasis, *but I;* and these words not only form a contrast with *Even these,* but they also bring the Lord before our eyes. Not merely will God not forget, He cannot forget. This is one of the strongest, if not the strongest expression of God's love in the Old Testament, and is often compared with Jeremiah 31:20. Volz asserts that the reference here is to God's love of a nation and a city rather than to His love of individuals. The nation, however, consists of the individual members. What is a nation apart from its members but an abstraction? Hence, when we are told that God will not forget Zion, we are to understand that He will not forget the individuals who go to make up Zion. "In a word," says Calvin, "the Prophet here describes to us the inconceivable carefulness with which God unceasingly watches over our salvation, that we may be fully convinced that he will never forsake us, though we may be afflicted with great and numerous calamities."

16 As an evidence of His unforgettable love and also by means of another comparison, the Lord states that He has engraven Zion upon His palms so that He will not forget her. The meaning is not that God has designated Zion with His hands, nor are they the hands of Israel; but God has engraven Zion upon His own palms. The verb, which is used by Ezekiel to describe the portrayal of Jerusalem upon a brick (Ezek. 4:1), means "to cut into" or "to engrave." Not that the Lord engraves a plan or map of Jerusalem upon His hands, but the name of Zion is engraved upon God's

---

[26] According to Gesenius, Bar Hebraeus says in his description of the slaughter at Edessa, "The mother forgot to show mercy to her child."

[27] The sense is not essentially modified if *gam* be taken as introducing a concessive clause: *yea, though these, etc.*

hands. Nor are the various references to tattooing necessarily relevant. The practice of tattooing is strongly condemned in Scripture (e.g. Lev. 19:28).[28]

As the name of Zion is engraved upon both His hands, so the walls of Zion stand ever before Him as a memorial. Even though the forces of infidelity and unbelief, of indifference and ignorance, may attempt to overthrow the Church, yet God is with her, for she is ever before His eyes.

17 That God has not forsaken His Zion is shown in that Zion's sons are hastening to her. The verb implies that the action has begun and is continuing. By a slight change of the pointing some would read *thy builders* instead of *thy sons*.[29] This seems to fit in better with the parallel, *thy destroyers* and *thy wasters*. At the same time the Masoretic text, *thy sons,* fits in better with what follows, particularly in verse 22.

Isaiah has arranged the sentence in chiastic order. Those who will hasten are sons, but those who will depart are destroyers. Whatever may be the precise significance of *thy destroyers* (whether internal enemies or foreign oppressors), they are in opposition to the God of Israel, and instead of building up His city are in one way or another destroying it. The enemies of the kingdom will depart and the true citizens will take their rightful place therein. They come not slowly but in haste, for they would help the distressed Zion.

18 Zion the mother is commanded to behold her sons returning to her (cf. 60:4). She is first to *Lift up* her *eyes round about* (for she had been dejected), looking in all directions, because her sons are coming to her, not merely from the east but from the entire world. *All of them,* i.e. all her sons, are *gathered together* or have gathered themselves together. The second verb is to be translated by the perfect, *they have come to thee.* Both verbs either express action already completed or are prophetic perfects. The language is more forceful on the first construction. Zion lifts up her eyes and sees that her lost sons are already gathered together and have come to her.

That there may be no doubt as to the truthfulness of what has

28 Pieper remarks that forbidding the practice does not prohibit use of the figure.

29 1Q *bwnyk*; B οἰκοδομηθήσῃ; Aq T οικοδομουντες; S οι υιοι σου.

just been stated, the Lord engages in an oath. The oath formula is a common one, and means, "So true as it is that I[30] live, saith the Lord, etc." Still addressing Zion, God declares that she will wear all her sons as an ornament. The true beauty of the Church is found in the work of grace in the hearts of believers. "But the true dignity of the Church is internal, so far as it consists of the gifts of the Holy Spirit, and of progressive faith and piety" (Calvin).

Zion will *bind* her children on herself as a bride binds ornaments. If it be objected, as it has been, that a bride does not have children, it may be replied that the point of the comparison lies in the idea of decoration. As a bride binds ornaments upon herself for decoration, so Zion will bind her children on herself.

19 The thought of this verse is clear, but the construction of the words is not. The desolation now present will pass, and the time will come when Zion will be too narrow to contain all her inhabitants. Each line of the verse is introduced by *for* (*ki*); and probably each of these is to be construed as following the oath of the preceding verse, just as the *for* (*ki*) of that verse follows the oath. Nevertheless, the first line is incomplete and is probably an anacoluthon. The conclusion is probably *I shall restore*, but of this one cannot be certain. Indeed, the language is more forceful without a conclusion expressed. The second line would then follow, *that thou shalt be too constrained from (possessing) inhabitants, etc.*[31] The last line contains a promise, backed up by God's oath, that Zion will one day be so filled with inhabitants that she will be too narrow to contain them. In addition, those who now swallow up the city will be removed far away so that there will be nothing remaining to fear from them.

20 Perhaps the introductory word '*od* (*Yet, Still*) should be taken in the sense *Furthermore*.[32] It is frequently employed to introduce future declarations of promise (e.g. Jer. 31:3, 4, 22; 32:15; 33:10; Zech. 1:17; 8:4). Thus, "and thy swallowers will be removed far away; furthermore the sons will say, etc." The verb may also express frequentative action, *They will continually say*.

The speech of the children is not a soft whisper, but one that

---

[30] '*ānî* — note the pausal form with a conjunctive accent.

[31] *tētzerî* — *thou shalt be cramped*; the first three subjects are taken up in *thou*, the subject of the verb.

[32] Alexander would take it as either *moreover* or *again*.

will be repeated in the ear of the mother, so that she can clearly hear it. Zion is conceived as a woman who has been violently deprived of her children (Lam. 1:5).[33] Basic to this thought is the fact that during the exile Jerusalem was left alone, her sons having been deported to Babylonia and elsewhere. *Sons of thy bereavement* are sons born while the mother is bereaved, or else, as Jarchi explains it, *the sons of whom thou wast bereft.* The former explanation seems satisfactory. Even during the exile the tide was turning. God was raising up Cyrus, who would make it possible for the exiles to return to their home. In this return there is seen the first fulfillment of this promise, but in the deeper sense the fulfillment takes place in the distant future when the Gentiles are brought into the Church of Christ. Zion is bereaved, but she has children, so many that there is no room for them.

The language of the sons reflects upon the third clause of verse 19. They are speaking not to their mother but to one another. The place where the sons are to dwell, where Zion is, they assert is too narrow for them, which implies that they are very numerous. The following clause means *draw near for me,* or *with respect to me.* Jarchi renders, *draw near to one side for me.* Actually, the direction intended is not stated. The command is given so that there will be more room and the person who speaks may find a place in which to dwell.

Zion regarded herself as a widow; as a matter of fact, her Husband, the Lord, had not forsaken nor forgotten her. The children who will one day crowd to her are legitimate children, begotten through a lively faith.

21 The Lord continues His address to Zion, reporting what her reaction was to the presence of her children. Her words are not a response to the children's words, for this is not a conversation between Zion and her sons but an utterance of surprise and astonishment that she has children. Where, however, have these children come from? *Who has begotten these for me?* The verb is masculine and refers to the father, yet Zion does not regard herself as the mother. In fact, the question is general and somewhat indefinite. The thought is not, "What man or what woman has borne these for me?" but simply, "Whence have they come? I am barren; how could they have been begotten?" Zion's thought had been on her

---

33 The form *šikkul* possibly adds a shade of intensity to the conception.

barrenness and bereavement, and not on the fact that the promises of God would come to fulfillment.

That there should be so many sons is particularly strange and difficult for Zion to grasp inasmuch as she recognizes that she is both bereaved of children and also barren.[34] The Hebrew introduces her explanation with the coordinating conjunction *and*, which we may render *inasmuch as*. Two further words are used to describe Zion's tragic condition, *banished* and *forsaken on the way*.[35] Yet the sons speak in her hearing, and hence she asks, *Who brought these up?* As God had once brought Israel up (lit., *made great*; 1:2), so Zion asks concerning the upbringing of these sons.

Zion appears more and more astounded inasmuch as she complains that she had been left alone, i.e. without a husband. Where then were these whom she now sees before her eyes? To the eye of mankind she seemed to have lost her former glory and power so that she had, as it were, practically disappeared from the earth. The basic reason for this was her own sin, and the corresponding removal from her midst of the true teaching of God. Furthermore, she apparently believed that God had forsaken her, and hence expressed surprise that she should have children. The Church is forsaken when her members turn to sin and forsake the doctrine of the Lord. When, therefore, He brings showers of refreshment upon the Church, she is surprised and wonders from whence they have come.

22 In response to the doubt and surprise of Zion, the Lord speaks with firmness, stating what He intends to do. Whether these words are an explanation of the reason why Zion now beholds so many children, or whether they are simply an additional statement of God's action, is difficult to determine. God is the Sovereign One and the covenant God—a fitting combination, for in the mighty work of redemption the covenant God is acting, and yet this work requires sovereign power.

Behold! calls attention to what the Lord will do. The language reflects upon 13:2, which also speaks of lifting a banner and

---

[34] *galmûḏāh* — *barren, sterile, incapable of begetting.* Cf. Ar. *jal-mad, hard stone;* B χηρα.

[35] *gōlāh* — *one taken into exile, Qal* f. participle. *sûrāh* — a *Qutal* form, possibly a passive part., but cf. GKC §72.

shaking the hand. Indeed, this combination of the expressions *raising, ensign, lifting up,* and *hand* is found elsewhere only in Isaiah 13:2 and nowhere else in the Old Testament.[36] The lifting up of the hand is for the benefit of those nearby, whereas the raising of an ensign is for those far away. No essential distinction need be made between *nations* and *peoples*; both words refer to the heathen nations; the two actions are intended to embrace all who are without the covenant nation.

Stress falls upon the divine activity, for apart from God neither can the people of themselves come to Zion nor could the heathen nations bring them. The lifted up ensign is a rallying point and a summons for action. What is new in this description is the fact that God's action causes the heathen nations to bring the sons of Zion to her.

The nations' response is loving and joyful, for they tenderly bring back Zion's sons. The precise connotation of *hotzen* (*bosom?*) is not known, but the word may signify the space between the bosom and the shoulder, and so suggest that the sons are carried in the arms of the nations. Zion's daughters will be borne upon the shoulders, a tender and loving action. In the preceding verse the children appear for the first time and hence surprise Zion. Now it is stated that the nations will bring these sons. We are not to look for a literal fulfillment of this promise. It rather refers to a conversion of the Gentiles, who as converted bring to Zion the converted sons of Israel. To restrict the reference to the return from Babylonian exile does justice neither to the consideration that the sons appear before Zion for the first time, nor to the fact that nations and peoples (not just Cyrus and Babylon) are mentioned. Pieper is correct in regarding this passage as supporting his statement, "The mission to the Jews is an enduring task for the church taken from the nations, even to the last day."

23 The description is continued, although different figures are employed. In place of the nations and peoples, kings and princesses are mentioned; and in place of the sons and daughters Zion herself is substituted. There is an almost imperceptible substitution of Zion as the object of the love and affection of others. Yet the meaning is essentially the same, for Zion and her sons and daughters are one and not to be distinguished. For this reason it is

36 Isaiah uses *nēs* in 5:26; 11:10, 12; 13:2; 18:3; 30:17; 62:10.

incorrect at this point to identify Zion with the historical Jerusalem abandoned at the time of the exile. The *foster fathers* (lit., *supporters*) are said to be *kings*, and those who give suck to her are princesses (i.e. women of royal station, *queens*). Thus the language advances. Even the highest and most powerful rulers of the heathen nations will reverence the Church and devote to her all their wealth and power. Like the two verbs in the preceding verse, *foster fathers* and *those who give thee suck* express the tender love with which the nations cherish Zion and her sons.

This love rises to such an extent that these royal persons bow down to Zion and touch the ground. The expression *nostrils-earth*, as Alexander points out, is a kind of compound somewhat like *arm-in-arm* or *sword-in-hand*, and shows that there is reference to an actual prostration.[37] These kings and queens were accustomed to have their own subjects bow down to them; now they in turn do the same thing to Zion, thus expressing their recognition that Zion is royal. It is an action of complete resignation and submission. There have been times when it has been fulfilled literally. Pieper remarks: "Every prayer of a Saxon elector or of a Gustavus Adolphus, every song of an Emilie Juliane or Ludamilie Elisabeth is a literal fulfillment of this prophecy." But the prophet's point is simply that the royalty of this earth will do obeisance to Zion the royal bride of Christ.

The expression *and the dust of thy feet they will lick* indicates complete and absolute submission to Zion. Zion rules, or rather, God rules through her; and those who belong to her have been wholly taken captive by Him.

A further consequence of God's acting is stated in the last clause. Zion will then know, fully and repeatedly (for the perfect expresses continuous action) that God is the Lord. Those who hope in God (i.e. *my hopers*) will not be ashamed. Those who have throughout relied upon His Word, even in times of great doubt, will see that their trust is well placed.

24 Will there be taken from the mighty one the prey? and shall the captivity of the righteous be delivered?

25 For thus saith the LORD, Even the captivity of the mighty one will be taken, and the prey of the terrible shall be delivered;

37 Ancient Oriental literature is filled with such allusions, e.g., "Thus says thy servant Abdiheba: At thy feet, my lord, I bow down seven times and seven times" (Amarna letter 287).

and those who strive with thee I will strive with, and thy sons I shall save.

26 And I shall cause thy oppressors to eat their own flesh, and as with new wine, with their blood shall they be drunken; and all flesh shall know that I the LORD am thy Savior, and thy Redeemer the Mighty One of Jacob.

24 An objection arises, namely, can such a deliverance take place? The objection appears in the form of a question, to which the Lord responds in the following verse. The question is thrown in, as it were, and we are not told who asks it. Its design is to show that even the difficulties raised can easily be overcome by the God of Israel. In the first part of the question there is a play on the words *will be taken* (*yuqqah*) and *prey* (*malqo^ah*). He who is in possession of the prey is the strong, mighty warrior. Who then is able to take it away from him?

The second part of the question is intended to express essentially the same thought in slightly different words. (The combination of captivity and prey occurs also in Numbers 31:11, 12, 27 and 32.) Although the noun is an abstract, *captivity*, it stands for the concrete, *captives*. In what sense, however, can *righteous* be taken as a synonym of *warrior*? The first Qumran Scroll has a reading that has long been proposed as a substitute for *righteous*, namely *despot*.[38] This would seem to remove the difficulty and is probably supported by the presence of the same word in the following verse. If correct, the enemy who holds God's people is described as both a mighty one and a tyrant.

But is there sufficient textual warrant to support such a reading? Inasmuch as *tyrant* (*'aritz*) is so clearly the easier reading, we may question its validity. To render *captivity of righteous men*, as Delitzsch and others have done, seems without warrant, for among other things this destroys the chiastic arrangement of the parallelism (*captivity-prey*; *righteous-warrior*; *will escape-will be taken*). Actually, the two questions of the verse are essentially one. Hence, some interpret *righteous* (*tzaddiq*) as a synonym of *warrior* (*gibbor*), and render with words such as "giant," "powerful one," "unconquerable." But this is questionable. If the word be retained, the only possible construction is, *and shall the captivity of the righteous be delivered*? If the captives of a righteous conqueror will not be delivered, how much less those taken by a warrior? The

---

38 1Q has *'rytz;* B ἀδίκως; Vulg. *a robusto;* Aq S T δικαιον.

second question is introduced by the interrogative particle used when a negative answer is anticipated. Difficult as are the details, the general sense is clear, namely that captives taken by an unjust oppressor will not be delivered.

25 This verse gives the Lord's answer to the preceding questions. In order properly to understand the connection between the two verses we must note that an intermediate thought is to be supplied. In answer to the question posed in verse 24, the prey and captivity shall indeed be delivered, for the Lord has spoken. The introductory particle *For* (*ki*) is therefore to receive its usual sense, and not to be rendered by a simple affirmative. Hence, the words of the Lord constitute the ground for belief that the captivity of the oppressor will be taken. The words of the preceding verse, with the exception of *righteous* (*tzaddiq*), are repeated, but not in the same order. The statement constitutes a positive, strong, affirmative answer to a question that expects a negative response. The two verbs are the same as in the preceding verse, and lend strength to the affirmation. No matter how powerful or tyrannical the captor may be, the Lord will deliver from his hand.

Furthermore, against those who have quarrelled with Zion, God Himself (note the emphatic use of the personal pronoun, *I*) will quarrel. The language calls to mind the idea of a lawsuit. God will plead for His people. The outcome need not be stated; it is sure. When God takes up the cause of His own, they are sure of vindication.

In the final clause God sums up the entire situation. *As for thy sons,* He says, *I* (again the pronoun is emphatic) *will save them.* The deliverance is not by man, for no man could deliver the prey from the oppressor; it is wholly of grace.

26 As is often the case in Isaiah, the conclusion consists of a short statement of the opposite of what has just been in the foreground. Instead of it being impossible for prey to be taken from the oppressor, God will cause Zion's oppressors to eat their own flesh. In 9:20 we read of men in rage eating human flesh, and possibly that is the meaning here. If so, the enemy is reduced to such straits that individuals in desperation and rage and bereft of their senses eat their own flesh. On the other hand, the word *flesh* may denote near kin (cf. 58:7); and if this is the sense, then the enemy oppressor is pictured as having fallen into cannibalism.

The *'asis* (*new wine*) is the freshly pressed-out juice of the grape, which was considered better than that squeezed out by the press. So great is the desperation of the enemy that it drinks its own blood, and is as drunken therewith as though that blood were a heady wine. The chiastic arrangement of the first line is not to be overlooked.

Again Isaiah uses the term *flesh,* but this time to refer to mankind generally. The result of the tragic condition just described is that all flesh will know that He who speaks is the Lord who delivers Zion. The designation *Mighty One of Jacob* is similar to Isaiah's earlier *Mighty One of Israel.* Thus God is set forth as the Redeemer, Deliverer and Defender of His people, who is willing to be known as the Mighty One of Jacob. All flesh is to know that God is Zion's Deliverer and that her Redeemer is the Mighty One of Jacob. Israel has learned this truth through the experience of salvation; the enemies have learned it through the experience of judgment.

SPECIAL NOTE: THE LAND OF SINIM

In 49:12 the phrase *behold these!* occurs twice, and *these* alone appears once. This calls attention to the wide dispersal of God's people. In contrast to the north and the sea (*yam*) the land of Sinim is mentioned, and the context indicates that a very distant place is intended. B renders ἐκ γῆς Περσῶν, which is a translation, as far as we know, without objective support. Vulg. has *et isti de terra australi* (southern). This tradition is also supported by the Targum מארע דרומה (from the land of the south).

Some have sought to identify the word with the Sinites of Gen. 10:17 and 1 Chron. 1:15. Appeal has also been made (Jerome) to the Wilderness of Sin. J. H. Michaelis (1775) suggested emending the text to *sewenim* and finding the reference in Sin or Peleusium (Aswan) in southern Egypt (*swn* on Elephantine papyri). Cf. Ezek. 29:10; 30:6. This seems to be supported by 1Q, which gives the consonants *swnyym,* possibly to be read *se-wā-niy-yim.* Why, however, is the district identified by the name of one of its cities and that not a particularly well-known city? More important, this forms no suitable contrast to the north and sea of the preceding. It is a place too near at hand.

Quite possibly, therefore, the reference is to a district to the east, so far away that it stands for a quarter of the earth. China may be that reference. The Arabic *tsin* may favor this. One cannot, however, be dogmatic. What is important is that a faraway district, a quarter of the earth, is intended, for the return to God in Christ will be worldwide.

1 Thus saith the LORD, Where is the writing of divorcement of your mother, whom I have sent away, or which of my creditors is it to whom I have sold you? Lo! for your iniquities ye have been sold, and for your transgressions your mother has been sent away.

2 Why did I come, and there is no man? Why did I call, and there was no one answering? Is my hand shortened, shortened from redemption? and is there with me no power to deliver? Behold! by my rebuke I will dry up the sea, I will make streams a wilderness; let their fish stink for want of water and die of thirst.

3 I will clothe the heavens in blackness, and sackcloth I will make their covering.

1 Isaiah now takes up the thought introduced in 49:14, of God's having forsaken His people, and points out that Israel's separation from God is the result of their own sin and not because God has forsaken them. The introductory words, *Thus saith the Lord*, indicate a new beginning, although there is no essential break with what has gone before. Likewise, these verses fit in well with the subsequent text, and are simply to be regarded as a particular part of a continuous discussion.

The prophet addresses the children in distinction from the mother; at the same time the children and mother are to be conceived as one whole entity, the chosen of God. Both children and mother are Israel according to the Spirit. Yet by addressing the nation as sons, the prophet enables them to look more objectively at Zion and to ponder the reasons for her sad condition.

To the first question a negative answer is expected. Zion has no writing of divorcement and hence cannot produce one, for God has never sent her away. The interrogative pronoun is literally to be rendered *Which?* or *What?* but inasmuch as it often is followed by a noun of place, we may translate *Where? Writing* or *book of divorcement* has reference to the law in Deuteronomy according to which a man who had divorced his wife could never remarry her if she had married a second man, even after her second husband died (cf. Deut. 24:1-4).[1] The same form of expression is maintained in the New Testament (cf. Matt. 19:7; Mark 10:4 and note Matt. 5:31). This writing of divorcement was the legal instrument by means of which the husband declared that his wife was divorced from him.

The relative clause may be translated *whom I sent away*, in which case the relative pronoun refers to *your mother*, or it may refer to the writing, *with which I have sent her away*. In favor of the first rendering is the fact that the relative is similarly used in the following line. "Send away" is a technical term for divorce.

Not only has God not divorced Zion but He has also not sold her children to creditors. If a man was unable to pay a debt, his creditor might take either the debtor in payment or his wife and children (2 Kings 4:1; Neh. 5:1-5; Matt. 18:25). God, of course, has no creditors, nor does He owe anything to anyone. The figure of the marriage relationship is thus maintained. Zion is separated from the Lord, her true Husband. This has not come about, however, through any writing of divorcement that He has given her, nor has He sold any of her children to creditors.

Isaiah introduces the reason for the separation with *hen* (*Lo!*), which, as North indicates, may call attention to some fact upon which action is taken or upon which a conclusion is based. Isaiah first addresses the sons and then the mother, whereas in the first two lines of the verse he had spoken first of the mother and then of the sons (*you*). We might have expected *her* transgressions; but Isaiah is speaking directly to the people, showing that the tragic situation is the result of their own doings.

2 The separation of Israel can in no wise be attributed to a lack of loving concern upon God's part. He came to His own, but they received Him not; He called to them, but no one answered. The Targum applied the language to the coming of God in the prophets, and this view has been widely adopted. In particular God comes to His own through Isaiah, and in this very message is so coming to them. Volz thinks that God comes to them through Second Isaiah, but the entire conception of a Second Isaiah and all

---

[1] Compare the laws of Hammurabi's Code, §§ 141ff.

that it involves is mere fancy (but see Appendix: "The Authorship of Isaiah"). Delitzsch offers a beautiful interpretation in which he applies the words to the coming of the servant and remarks how his coming is connected with the period of the captivity. Israel's punishment, Delitzsch tells us, terminates with the end of the captivity; and on the border of the captivity the final glory of Israel and the salvation of mankind appear. This is true, but God's coming embraces all His appearances to mankind. Time and time again He came, but there was no man present to receive Him, until in the fullness of time He came unto His own and they received Him not. Whenever He called to His people, no one responded. Blind and deaf they wandered on their own way into transgression, not heeding the divine presence and warnings.

That the Lord has the power to redeem is brought out by means of questions.[2] Emphasis is given by the infinitive absolute, *Is it that shortened, my hand is shortened from redemption?* Shortness of hand is a common figure for weakness or lack of power. Parallel to this question is the second, *is there in me no strength to deliver?* Merely to ask these questions is to reveal the folly of neglecting the all-powerful Lord of Israel.

To illustrate His great power, Isaiah uses a favorite expression, *by my rebuke* (cf. 17:13; 30:17; 51:20; 54:9; 66:15), which indicates God's control over the elements of nature. It may be that these words contain a reflection upon the drying of the Red Sea, but this thought is not necessarily prominent. This ability to change the course of nature also appears in God's power to change streams into a mere wilderness. The result of such an action is that the fish, no longer having water, will stink[3] and die.

3 The prophet continues his description of the display of the Lord's power; what is stated here is carried out by God's rebuke. The word *blackness* is probably to be taken as a sign of mourning (cf. Jer. 4:28). Whether there is a specific allusion to the phenomena of the exodus is questionable. If there is any reflection upon the exodus, it is only as a specific example of God's providential power.

The latter part of the line is stronger than the first, and there is a

2 *why?* — the interrogative pronoun governs two coordinate clauses.
3 *tib'aš* — the voluntative without *waw* indicates that the divine will shall be fulfilled. To discover in this verse allusion to a mythological background seems unwarranted.

question whether Isaiah means to say *I shall place sackcloth as its covering* or *I shall place its covering as sackcloth.* How God performs these works, we are not told. What stands out prominently is the fact that He is able to control the heavens as He will.

> 4 The Lord GOD hath given to me the tongue of those who are taught, to know to help the weary with a word; he will arouse in the morning, in the morning he will awaken for me the ear to hear like those who are taught.
> 5 The Lord GOD hath opened my ear, and I did not resist; I did not draw backward.

4 As in chapters forty-nine and sixty-one, the Servant of the Lord, unintroduced, begins speaking. It is difficult to establish a logical connection with what precedes. At the same time, this "servant" passage is in an appropriate place. Having shown the omnipotence of God with respect to nature and hence the sureness of His promises, the prophet introduces the servant soliloquizing over his suffering and so prepares for the great account of deliverance in chapter fifty-three.

The servant here (but nowhere else) uses the designation *The Lord God (ᵃdonay YHWH)*, which occurs four times in this passage and always at the beginning of a verse (vv. 4, 5, 6, 9). This combined name lends a tone of majesty and impressiveness to the servant's words. What the servant speaks is truth because of the covenant God who has all power over the creation. This God who can clothe heavens with blackness has equipped the servant for his task, and has given a ready tongue to him (lit., *a tongue of the learned ones*). The phrase designates a tongue such as learned or skilled men have, and hence a ready, expert tongue. The learned are instructed by the Lord; the tongue belongs to one taught of God, and so it is the tongue of a person instructed and illumined by His Spirit.

The servant is speaking of his prophetical ministry, and states that the purpose of the divine gift is that he may *know to help the weary with a word.*[4] The word that he speaks is to be timely or fitting so that it will be of true blessing. The weary are the bruised reed and smoking flax (cf. Matt. 11:28).

---

4 לָעוּת — of uncertain meaning, yet attested by 1Q. B ἡνίκα δεῖ εἰπεῖν λόγον; Aq ὑποστηρίσαι; Vulg. *sustentare.* Targ. *leʾallāp̄āʾ, to teach.*

Each morning God awakens the servant's ear so that he may obediently hear as do the learned ones. The reference is not to the manner of the prophetic revelation but to the servant's preparation for complete obedience. The repetition as well as the imperfect form of the verb point to a constant action upon God's part, and also suggest that without reserve the servant submits to the divine word. Obedience characterizes his whole mission, for his object is to bless and help the suffering and afflicted.

5 This verse, again beginning with *The Lord God*, continues the thought of the preceding and expresses assurance that God has equipped the servant for his task. *To open the ear for me* means to open it so that he will be able to hear. It is but another way of indicating the servant's preparation, having essentially the same force as the phrases preceding. Thus the servant was prepared that he might know the divine will and obey it.

With the second line Isaiah introduces a new thought. The introductory *and I* stands in definite contrast to *Lord God* of the preceding line. To this preparation the servant did not show himself rebellious or disobedient. The word refers to an inner attitude or disposition. Whatever hindrances there were toward accomplishing the work that God had set before him, they came from without and not from within the mind or disposition of the servant. Moses had objected, and also Jeremiah. Jonah had even sought to flee from the presence of the Lord (cf. Ex. 4:10ff.; Jer. 20:7ff.; 17:16; Jon. 1:3). These were sinful human messengers who could not escape God's commands, for when God spoke, the prophet had to prophesy (Amos 3:8). No suggestion of rebellion, however, was found in the servant.

Neither was there any outward manifestation of hesitancy in obedience to God's preparation. The servant did not turn back as a faithless one would have done (cf. Jer. 38:22). By placing the word first in the phrase, Isaiah gives to it a certain emphasis: *Back I did not turn*. No rebellion, no apostasy, no treacherous faithlessness is found in the servant.

6 My back I gave to the smiters and my cheeks to those that pluck out the hair; my face I did not turn from shame and spitting.

7 And the Lord GOD will help me, therefore I have not been put to shame; therefore I have set my face as a flint, and I know that I shall not be ashamed.

8 Near is he that justifies me; who will dispute with me? let us stand together; who is the master of my judgment? let him draw nigh unto me.

9 Behold! the Lord GOD will help me; who is he (that) will harm me? behold! all of them as a garment wax old; a moth devours them.

6 The servant now presents details to show how he was not rebellious. The striking language calls to mind immediately the physical sufferings of our Lord (cf. Matt. 26:67ff.; 27:26ff.; John 19:1ff.). The description makes clear how completely and fully obedient the servant was. There is majesty in the description, as though the servant were in full control of the situation. He sets himself forth as one who acts. Instead of saying that men beat him, he declares that he himself gave his back to those who struck him. He either voluntarily yielded himself to flogging, or he offered himself thereto. The *strikers* or *smiters* would be those who have the public duty of beating a criminal. Beating on the back would seem also to be the custom in the punishment of evil men (cf. Prov. 10:13; 19:29; 26:3 and cf. Ps. 129:3).

In addition the servant gave his cheeks to those who pluck out the hair. The reference is to those who deliberately give the most heinous and degrading of insults. The Oriental regarded the beard as a sign of freedom and respect, and to pluck out the hair of the beard (for *cheek* in effect would refer to a beard) is to show utter contempt.

The servant faced the greatest of insults without turning his face from them. The reproaches were probably verbal insults and taunts, accompanied by that most insulting and degrading of contemptible gestures, spitting. The language speaks much about the servant, but it also speaks much about those who were responsible for these vicious cruelties. Men who are entrusted with the carrying out of punishment degrade themselves when they act in a merciless and insulting spirit. One may well wonder whether human nature, fallen as it is, ever becomes lower than when it turns in cruel contempt upon those who are under its power. The brutal practices of dictators, such as took place in the concentration camps of a Dachau or a Mauthausen, reveal the viciousness of depraved humanity. But if these words manifest the detestable nature of the persecutors, they also speak volumes as to the nature of the sufferer. There is perhaps a certain gradation in the enumeration of the acts of shame, yet through all of these the sufferer maintains a spirit of meekness and lack of revenge. It would be impossible for any sinful human being, no matter how fine a person he was, to undergo the sufferings herein described without a spirit of rebellion welling up within him. And if a spirit of revenge took hold of him, we might well understand. Even Jeremiah complained at the way he was being used (cf. Jer. 20:9, 14ff., and note Job 3). Only one who was entirely without sin could undergo such suffering without a rebellious spirit. For this reason, as Pieper has so accurately pointed out, if the prophet is here describing the nation Israel, even the best part thereof, he is giving a picture that is untrue and false. The only One who can so patiently suffer is the One without sin, the Christ of God. At this point I find myself unable to agree with those who see here a reference to the body, the Church, as well as to the Head.

7 The introductory conjunction *And* serves to bring to the fore the inward thought and conviction of the servant even in the midst of his severe sufferings. Throughout it all, when men ruthlessly rose up against him, the thought filled his mind that the Lord God was helping him. *Therefore* introduces the conclusion of the thought introduced by *And*. Inasmuch as the Lord God was helping him, the servant was not confounded. He was the object of reproach (*kᵉlimmah*) but he was not confounded (*niklamti*).

For this reason also he is determined to face the suffering that lies before him. No temptation will deflect him from his God-appointed course. Obedience to God's will looms paramount in his determination. He has set his face like a hard rock[5] so that it cannot be turned to one side or the other. So it is written of Christ that He set His face to go to Jerusalem (Luke 9:51). The conviction is sure with the servant that he will not come into shame. The word is not as strong as *I have not been confounded*. Inasmuch as God is with him to help him, he has not been confounded, nor will his sufferings lead to shame. The shame and reproach heaped upon him will lead only to greater glory and honor for him.

8 In an exclamation of triumph the servant declares that God will help him. Placing all the stress upon the first word, he asserts, *Near is the one who justifies me*, i.e. the justifier is at hand, ready

---

5 *ḥallāmîš* — flint, cf. Akk. *elmēšu, diamond.*

to pronounce him just. *He who justifies me* is used in a strictly forensic sense, as is δικαιόω in the New Testament, and means "to declare to be just" or "to pronounce one just." As in the New Testament so here also there is the legal background. The one who pronounces the servant just is a Judge, even God Himself. God is at hand to declare that the servant is innocent, and stands in a right relationship with the law, being free of iniquity. In this case the declaration agrees with the actual state of the servant, for the righteousness the servant possesses is his own. The claims he has made for himself as to his person and work are thus declared by the sovereign Lord to be true and just. Thus the pronouncement of the divine Judge fully vindicates the servant. Enemies had thought he was being punished for his own sins, but the divine vindication shows how wrong they were.

Being assured that God is at hand to vindicate him, the servant throws out a bold challenge, *who will contend with me?* The language refers to a controversy at law, and the one who contends is considered a legal opponent. If there is anyone bold enough to enter a legal suit against the servant to show that he is not what he claims to be, *let us stand together* in such a legal contest! The boldness and eagerness with which the servant speaks point clearly to his innocence of wrongdoing as well as to his confidence that he will be legally vindicated.

In a second question he singles out in more specific terms the opponent at law, designating him as *the master of my judgment.*[6] The phrase apparently was widespread in the ancient world, the Romans speaking of the *dominus litis* as the prosecutor and the cuneiform languages using the same expression *bel dini.* Thus, *the master of my judgment* is the one who possesses a judgment against him. There is a certain gradation in the expressions of this verse.

9 This verse gives the summary and conclusion of what has preceded. By means of an introductory *Behold!* the prophet directs attention once more to the Lord God, from whom the servant's help will come. The following question is stronger than the one in verse 8, and is about equivalent to saying, "Who is it then that will condemn me?"[7] The verb *condemn* is the antithesis of *justify,* and

---

6 B ὁ κρινόμενός μοι.
7 הוא serves as an enclitic to emphasize the interrogative. GKC § 136 c compares *nam* in *quisnam.* The relative pronoun is omitted before the finite verb.

refers to the pronouncement of a sentence of condemnation. No one is able to pronounce such a sentence upon the servant, for the Lord God will help him and vindicate him.

That the enemies of the servant were not imaginary is shown by the statement about their outcome. They will grow old or worn out as garments do. Scripture uses this figure to express gradual decay (e.g. Hos. 5:12). As old clothes are devoured by the moth, so the enemies and accusers of the servant will pass away and come to naught. When they stand in court to bring accusations against the servant, they will be put to shame as easily as a moth devours the worn-out clothes.

> 10 Who among you is a fearer of the LORD, who hearkens to the voice of his servant, who has walked in darkness and there is no light to him, let him trust in the name of the LORD and lean upon him.
>
> 11 Behold! all of you are kindlers of fire, girders of sparks; go in the light of your fire, and in the sparks that ye have kindled. From my hand was this to you; at the place of torment ye shall lie down.

10 The prophet gives a fitting conclusion and even summary of the preceding verses. He addresses those among the people who fear the Lord and who walk in darkness. Such are to follow the example of the servant and to place their entire confidence in God. By using the term *servant*, Isaiah now makes clear that the One who has just been speaking is the Servant of the Lord, the same person who has appeared in chapter forty-nine. Fearing the Lord and hearkening to the voice of His servant go hand in hand. If one hears in obedience the voice of the servant, that one is a fearer of the Lord. In the light of this strong statement, it is difficult to understand how the servant can be the nation Israel or the best part thereof; but there is no difficulty if the servant is that unique individual who stands in an unparalleled relationship to God, the Head of the Church, the suffering Savior.

If the first word be taken as a mere interrogative pronoun, *Who?* there is difficulty in determining the conclusion of the question. There are three possibilities, namely: (1) with *the Lord*, (2) with *his servant*, or (3) at the end of the verse. It seems best to take the word as indefinite, *Whoever*. It then connects three attributes or characteristics of the one who fears the Lord. The first two are expressed by participles (the first participle being in the construct state) ; the third attribute is introduced by means of the relative pronoun, *who*, and is modified by a circumstantial clause, *who walks in darkness, and there is no light to him*. The fearer of the Lord is not one in abject terror, but one who reverently and in awe fears before the Lord. Such godly fear manifests itself in obedience to God's commands.

If one fears the Lord he will also hearken to the voice of God's true Servant, believing what the Servant proclaims about Himself and His mission (cf. John 5:23). The Servant's word is God's word, for God has set the Servant's mouth as a sharp sword (cf. 49:2). "This is my beloved Son, hear him!"

The third attribute shows the condition in which such God-fearing ones were. The darkness was spiritual so that no light could shine into it. Thus the circumstantial clause strengthens the expression. The verb (*walk*) is not to be expressed by the past but by the present, for it sets forth a condition actually in existence.

The two concluding verbs may be construed as jussives. To *trust in the name of the Lord* is to trust in the Lord as He has revealed Himself to His people. The parallel *to lean upon* brings out the essential idea of faith, namely, confidence reposed in a person; it is stronger than the preceding.

Thus, those who do fear the Lord and obey the voice of His true Servant may nevertheless be in darkness. Like the Servant Himself, they too must be subject to afflictions and follow their Lord through affliction, death, and hell that they may come to the celestial city. In this world they will have tribulation; but the Servant has overcome this world, and they have but one recourse, to trust in the Lord who has revealed Himself to them in His ways and works, and to lean for support upon their God, who will never fail them.

11 As the previous verse had been addressed to believers among the people, so this is directed to those who do not believe in the servant but remain unrepentant in the hardness of their hearts. The introductory particle *hen* has an affirmative sense.

It would seem that the figures refer to a fire that men have kindled for the sake of the light that it gives. They walk in darkness and seek to escape the darkness by means of a fire of their own kindling. What is meant by the phrase *girding with sparks* is difficult to ascertain.[8] It may be that the thought is simply that of equipping or preparing oneself with fiery darts to be used in time of attack or battle.

To those that kindle a fire, a command is given to go in their fire, i.e. to continue to profit from the fire that they have lighted. It is possible, as Calvin suggests, that this command contains a touch of irony, as though the prophet had said, "You have rejected the Lord and kindled your own fire to escape the darkness; well, go now and take your course of life in that very fire. See how it will become not your salvation but your destruction!" Emphasis is placed upon the fact that the fire belongs to those who have kindled it (*your fire*) and the sparks are those which they have burned (*ye have burned*).

The outcome is decreed of God. It comes from His hand, i.e. from His power. Probably the word *this* refers primarily to what follows, the final punishment of the wicked. The prophet's writing is forceful. With respect to the place of torment, *ye shall lie down*. The accent falls upon the last syllable of this final word, giving, as Delitzsch suggests, a dictatorial conclusion. "It has a terrible sound, but still more terrible (apart from the future state) is the histori- cal fulfillment that presents itself to the eye" (Delitzsch).

8 מאזרי — 1Q supports M. *ziqôṯ* — *sparks, missiles*. Cf. Syr. *zîqeṯô'*, *shooting star*, and Akk. *zaqātu, to be pointed.*

CHAPTER FIFTY-ONE

1 Hearken unto me, ye pursuers of righteousness, ye seekers of the LORD; look unto the rock from whence ye were hewn, and unto the hole of the pit from which ye have been digged.

2 Look unto Abraham, your father, and unto Sarah that bare you; for as one I have called him and I blessed him and I caused him to increase.

3 For the LORD hath comforted Zion, he hath comforted all her waste places, and he hath placed her wilderness as Eden, and her desert like the garden of the LORD; joy and gladness will be found in her, thanksgiving and the voice of song.

4 Hearken unto me, my people, and my nation, unto me give ear; for the law goes forth from me and my judgment for a light of the people I cause to rest.

5 Near is my righteousness, my salvation has gone forth, and my arms will judge peoples; unto me the isles wait, and unto my arm they will hope.

6 Lift up to the heavens your eyes, and look unto the earth from beneath, for the heavens like smoke will be dissolved, and the earth like a garment will grow old, and its inhabitants likewise will die; but my salvation shall be forever and my righteousness shall not be broken.

1 Turning from the godless, the Lord addresses the godly among the nation. The chapter divides itself into two principal divisions, verses 1-11 and verses 12-23, and each of these again falls into two smaller divisions, verses 1-6, 7-11 and 12-16, 17-23. By the introductory command, *Hearken unto me*, the speaker would turn the minds of the hearers unto Himself. It is, as Alexander points out, a common formula, when the writer or speaker turns away from one subject to another. At the same time it is an imperative, and places a solemn responsibility upon those addressed.

These are characterized as *pursuers after righteousness* (cf. Deut. 16:20). This implies an active, vigorous seeking after righteousness, a hungering and thirsting thereafter, which results in action. By many commentators *righteousness* is taken to denote a quality, a conformity to the law of God. This ethical emphasis is supported by the parallel clause, *who seek the Lord*. On the other hand, some apply the word to the concept salvation, giving it an eschatological connotation. A sharp distinction between the two is really not possible. Those who pursue righteousness are dissatisfied with their sin and long for a life that conforms to God's requirements. To them evil in all forms is abhorrent, and they would be like the Lord, whom they love. At the same time such a longing would more and more make clear that such righteousness is impossible as a result of human efforts. Man would then look to the Lord as the only source of righteousness. It is quite possible that both concepts are bound up in the one word. Those who seek after the Lord are those who long for Him, yet who realize that if He hides His face they cannot attain Him. The gift of Himself is a gift of His grace.

To convince the godly of the truth of what He is declaring, the Lord commands them to *look to* (i.e. to *think upon* or *consider*) *the rock* from which they have been hewn. Isaiah is employing metaphors, the explanation of which he gives in the second verse. The Lord simply commands the people to consider their origin. They are like a rock hewn out of a greater piece of rock, or like earth taken out of a pit. In itself the rock is not Abraham, and to argue that Abraham is called a rock because of the steadfastness of his faith, or that Sarah is called a pit, is to misunderstand the metaphors. Both metaphors express the general idea of a descent, a more precise explanation of which is given in the second verse.[1]

2 The few who seek the Lord are to *Look unto Abraham,* who is their *father* (i.e. their ancestor), and *unto Sarah who bore* them. This is one of the few references in the Old Testament apart from Genesis to Sarah. Actually in the birth of Isaac the Israelitish nation was born, for he was the seed of promise. That Isaac was born manifests the fact that the power of God overcame the forces that would withstand the fulfillment of the promise of salvation.[2] In Genesis 15:5 God commands Abram to look to the heavens and

---

[1] Both metaphors also symbolize Israel's solidarity and common origin.

[2] תחוללכם — *Polel* imp. of חול, *whirl, dance, writhe.* The imp. thus standing alone is to be translated by the past, presenting the action with particular vividness.

promises him a seed as numerous as the stars of heaven. Now, the believing few are commanded to look to Abraham. As he had acted in faith so are they to act.

The thought turns now to Abraham alone, for when he was *one*, i.e. *alone, one individual, a solitary person*, in distinction from the great nation that his descendants were destined to be, God called him (cf. Ezek. 33:24, which brings out the antithesis between the lone Abraham and the many descendants). As a solitary person God called Abraham from a pagan background that He might make of him a mighty nation.

The last two verbs reflect the language of Genesis 12:1-3. As pointed they are probably to be rendered by the past.[3] Thus, they add to the force of the promise made in Genesis. God had called Abraham with the understanding that He would bless him. This He has indeed done, in that the nation of Israel has sprung from Abraham; but the epitome of blessing and increase is yet to come. Thus, comfort and encouragement are given to those despairing ones who hear the words of the promise. The ancient promise looks forward to its most glorious fulfillment: God will bless Abraham and multiply him in bringing blessing and increase to his descendants.

3 As God once made a great nation from the one man Abraham, so will He bring the small group of faithful to the point where they too will see a great increase. The connection between this and the preceding verse is clear: "I have called, etc., for the Lord will comfort Zion, etc." Although the tense of the verbs is preterite, in order to bring out the idea of certainty they are to be rendered by the future. They do not describe an action already accomplished, but one yet to occur in the future.

How can God comfort the waste places of Zion? The answer is shown in the following clauses. As the barren Sarah was given an innumerable seed, so Zion with her waste places will see a great multitude of believers in God's promises.

Zion's wilderness will be as Eden and her desert like the garden of the Lord. The thought is not that there will be a return to Paradise, or that *Endzeit* will be *Urzeit*. Rather, the coming salva-

---

3 Cf. GKC § 107 b N. The imp. with weak *waw* vividly represents the past as though it were now occurring or were on the point of occurring. It also expresses purpose. 1Q substitutes *w'prhw* for the first verb.

tion will be like the original state before the fall. Comparison
rather than identity is intended. The present desolate condition of
Zion will one day be like the garden of Eden; hence there will be
available for all who are there joy and gladness,[4] with thanksgiving and the sound of song. It is a strong contrast: on the one hand,
waste, desert, and desolate places; on the other, joy, gladness,
thanksgiving, and the voice of melody.

4 With this verse a new strophe begins, similar to the preceding
in that it consists of two imperatives. The people and the nation
are addressed, and thus there appears a slight shift in the subject
from the preceding verses. The people are addressed as God's, a
common designation in Isaiah. Emphasis falls upon the first person
suffix; *Hearken unto ME, MY people, and MY nation, unto ME
give ear.* "What is here demanded, is attention," says Calvin, "to
sustain our hearts by patience, till the season of grace be fully
come."

A reason is given for hearkening unto God, namely that from
God there goes forth law. This is not the Mosaic law in distinction
from the Gospel, but the expression of God's will which constitutes
man's rule of duty. In particular it is the law of faith, given "by
the commandment of the everlasting God, made known to all
nations for the obedience of faith" (Rom. 16:26). It is that authoritative expression of the will of God that sets before man what God
requires of him. The form of expression is thoroughly Isaianic, the
word *torah* (*law*) receiving the stress. Stress is also found in the
combination *from with me*, as though to emphasize the fact that
law goes out from the very presence of God.

Parallel to the statement concerning law is the last clause of the
verse. *My judgment* is that which serves as the rule of right in
God's kingdom, and so is a synonym for true religion, or for
salvation; the just pronouncements of the Lord having to do with
the conduct of men are unknown to the nations who walk in the
darkness of ignorance and sin. These God will cause to return as a
light for the benefit of the Gentiles. In their fullest sense, law and
judgment refer to the dispensation of the Gospel; they are the
grace and truth introduced by Jesus Christ. *I shall cause to return*
(*to rest*) means simply *I shall establish*. Note the emphasis upon
divine activity.

4 The s. verb has a pl. subject; 1Q reads *ymtz'w*.

309

5 Stress falls upon the first word *Near*, for it brings out the most important point concerning the Lord's righteousness. Balaam said of the Messiah, "I behold him, but not near" (Num. 24:17), by which he meant that the approach of the Messiah would not be for a long time to come. Here, too, the temporal sense of *near* seems to predominate. Actually it was many years before salvation was manifested. Deliverance from Babylonian captivity was only a forerunner or first taste of the promised salvation.

As the righteousness is near, so also has the salvation gone forth from God who is in heaven. *Has gone forth* and the adjective *near* express the same thought. The righteousness and salvation are near at hand, having come from God. Here the two terms, righteousness and salvation, are practically synonyms. The salvation is spiritual, characterized by righteousness. When the salvation comes there is a manifestation of God's righteousness. This righteousness appears in the fact that God righteously keeps His promises and satisfies His justice, but in a righteousness that sinful men may receive. Those who pursue righteousness find it only in the righteousness God provides in His salvation.

In the treatment of sinful people also, the justice of God appears. His *arms*, and the seat of His power, *will judge peoples*. In contrast to the manifestation of the righteous salvation, this is a judgment that results in condemnation. It is a significant emphasis of Isaiah's that salvation and judgment go hand in hand.

Judgment will reach the nations, but among them also are those who will wait for the appearance of God. The *isles*, which abide in darkness, wait until the light of God's judgment is established (cf. v. 4) and His *arm* revealed. For the meaning of *isles* see the comments on 41:1. When God's mighty power is revealed (note the singular) the isles will be enlightened and saved, for until they hear of the way of salvation they are in the darkness of ignorance. To dispel this darkness the power of God is needed. The Gospel is a revelation of God's mighty strength.

6 In Luke 21:33 Jesus Christ sets forth the essential truth of this verse, "Heaven and earth will pass away, but my words will not pass away." Those who are longing for the coming salvation should lift up their eyes and behold the created universe (cf. the beginning of 40:26).

As for the *heavens, like smoke* they will be *dissolved away*. The *earth* for its part *will wear out,*[5] *and its inhabitants likewise*[6] *will die.* The created universe, i.e. heaven and earth, is temporal; as it had a beginning, so does it have an end. The heavens and earth, which seem to endure forever, will one day come to an end and be no more. That there will be a new heaven and earth, while true, is not stated in this particular verse, the purpose of which is to contrast sharply the temporality of the created universe with the eternity of the Lord's salvation and righteousness.

In contrast to the transitory character of creation, God's *salvation will be* (i.e. *will endure*) *forever.* Likewise, His *righteousness will not be broken* (i.e. will never cease to be what it is). These will not endure in the abstract but will manifest themselves in men who have received the righteous salvation and who will be in the new heavens and earth wherein dwells righteousness (cf. 2 Pet. 3:13).

7 Hearken unto me, ye knowers of righteousness, a people in whose heart is my law; fear not the reproach of mankind, and from their rebukes be not afraid.

8 For like a garment the moth devoureth them, and like wool will the worm devour them; but my righteousness shall be forever, and my salvation from generation to generation.

9 Awake, awake, clothe thyself with strength, O arm of the LORD; awake, as the days of old, the ages of eternities. Art not thou the same that hewed Rahab in pieces, that wounded the serpent?

10 Art thou not she who drieth up the sea, the waters of the great abyss; who placed the deep places of the sea a way for the crossing of the redeemed ones?

11 And the ransomed of the LORD will return and will come to Zion with singing, and the joy of eternity upon their head; rejoicing and joy will overtake them, sorrow and sighing will flee away.

7 The second minor division of the chapter begins similarly to the first. A command to hearken unto God introduces the section, and those addressed, the same as those designated *pursuers of*

---

5 מַתְחַת — followed in 1Q by *wr'w my br' 't 'lh* and continued with *wywsbyh,* omitting the two intervening clauses which appear in M. *nimlāḥû — will be dissipated, dispersed in fragments.*

6 *kēn* — may mean *gnat,* which is more forceful. But B ὥσπερ ταῦτα. Cf. *ZAW,* Vol. 53, 1935, pp. 270f.

THE BOOK OF ISAIAH

righteousness and *seekers after the Lord* in verse 1, are here
denoted the *knowers of righteousness* and *those in whose heart is
the law.* In the ethnic Israel they are the true Israel, the kernel in
the mass, to use Delitzsch's language, the people of God. The
knowledge is not merely intellectual but implies also an experience
of righteousness, an inner seizing and grasping thereof. Yet the
intellectual element must not be depreciated; there is a true recognition and understanding of righteousness. A whole-souled embracing of righteousness is what is implied.

It is significant that those who know righteousness are described
as the people in whose heart is God's law. Not merely have they
heard the law but they have eagerly embraced and apprehended it
and look to it as their rule of life. It follows, therefore, that this
law is something outside of the people, objective to them, and must
consist of divine law given either in oral or in written form. The
law must have been presented in an available form, so that the
people might intelligently embrace it. This phrase well corresponds to the *seekers of the Lord* in verse 1.

The Lord commands His true people not to fear the *reproach*
(the word is not as strong as the following *gidduph, rebuke*) of
man. The word *man* derives from a root that would indicate that
man is weak and frail. Mere man is not sufficient reason for fear on
the part of the people of God.

The profundity of this teaching is not to be overlooked. Men are
afraid of many things, mostly of what man can do to them. There
is but one way in which such fear can be overcome, and that is to
know righteousness and to possess the law in one's heart. This way,
despised by men, is nevertheless the only way to true security; and
those who possess it need not fear the rebukes and reproaches that
an unbelieving world and church may heap upon them.

8 As the enemies of the Servant of the Lord will easily perish
(cf. 50:9), so also will those who revile God's people; but whereas
they will perish, the righteousness and salvation of God will abide
forever. Two figures are employed to stress the transitoriness of the
enemies. As a garment is eaten by moths and as worms devour
wool, so will the enemies be destroyed. The figures imply that the
garment and the wool are already moth- and worm-eaten. The
seeds of their own destruction they bear within themselves. The
figures correspond to the use of *'enosh (frail man)* in the preceding
verse to denote man.

312

"*Salvation* is in God, that by it he may preserve, not himself but us; *righteousness* is in God, that he may display it for our defence and preservation" (Calvin). When the reproaches and revilings of the world strike us, we are often in suffering and turmoil of mind and heart. Such reproaches, however, are but for a moment; and the blessedness of the Lord's salvation, which brings to us His own perfect righteousness, will never pass away.[7]

9 The prophet now varies his mode of expression, and instead of setting forth the comfort just declared by means of further argumentation, addresses the *arm of the Lord,* the seat of the Lord's strength. In characteristic fashion the prophet commands the arm of the Lord twice, *Awake, awake!*[8] which implies that the arm has been lying asleep and inactive. The arm is physically conceived, for it is charged to *clothe* itself *with strength*, i.e. so to gird itself with strength that it will be able to accomplish the task set before it. The figures set forth the idea of preparation for battle.

A third time the command *awake!* appears, this time to introduce a comparison with former awakenings. In particular there is reflection upon the supreme, incomparable act of deliverance at the time of the exodus. Inasmuch as the mighty arm of the Lord has already once delivered the people in a miraculous fashion, so it will be able to do it again. For emphasis and variety's sake the prophet introduces a question addressed to the Lord's arm, and in this question portrays the defeat of Egypt. As in Psalm 87:4; Isaiah 27:1; 30:7; Ezekiel 29:3 and 32:2, the terms *Rahab* and *Tannin* (crocodile?) are symbols for Egypt. It may be that these figures originally signified the power of chaos at the creation, but such mythological connotations are here completely lost.[9] As God once delivered His people from the mighty power of Pharaoh, so now will He again deliver them from whatever powers stand in the way of their salvation.

10 Continuing with a question the prophet emphasizes that the

---

[7] *generations of ages* — the plural of both nouns expresses the plural idea.

[8] *'úrî* — *awake!* accent *Milra*, whereas in the third occurrence it is *Milel*. The *Milra* accents are probably intentional variations for rhythmical effect.

[9] Cf. O. Eissfeldt, *Baal Zaphon, Zeus Kasios und der Durchzug der Israeliten durchs Meer*, Halle, 1932; Wm. F. Albright, *Archaeology and the Religion of Israel*, 1942, pp. 148-150; Young, *Studies In Genesis One*, 1964.

Lord brought the Israelites from Egypt in a miraculous way through the Red Sea. The designation *tᵉhom* (*abyss*), which usually signifies the primeval ocean, need not possess that connotation here. It serves simply to point out that the sea is a great deep of water, a formidable and (to man) impossible obstacle to cross. What to man was a *tᵉhom*, the arm of the Lord made to be dry.

This interpretation seems to be borne out by the subsequent clause, *who placed*[10] *the depths of the sea as a way for the passing over of the redeemed.* The contrast between *depths of the sea* and *way* is striking. If the depths of the sea can be made passable then truly the arm of the Lord is powerful. The reference of course is to the miraculous crossing of the Red Sea. A God who can deliver from such an obstacle is a God who can deliver at any time, no matter what the obstacles may be.

11 This verse forms a fitting conclusion to the section. It is taken almost letter for letter from Isaiah 35:10, which likewise forms a conclusion. (For the detailed exposition see comments on 35:10.)[11] In this context, although *ransomed ones* had been mentioned, the fact of redemption and deliverance is now brought out plainly. Isaiah does not hesitate to employ the same thoughts and language that he had earlier used in a similar context; yet, in accordance with Semitic custom, he does not give a slavish imitation of his previous usage.

12 I, I am he that comforteth you; who art thou, that thou fearest from man, who will die, and of the son of man who like grass will be given?

13 But thou hast forgotten the LORD thy maker, who stretcheth out the heavens, and foundeth the earth, and has trembled continually all the day, from before the wrath of the oppressor as he made ready to destroy. And where is the wrath of the oppressor?

14 He hastens bowing to be loosed; and he will not die in the pit, and his bread will not fail.

15 And I am the LORD thy God, rousing the sea, and its waves roar; the LORD of hosts is his name.

16 And I have placed my words in thy mouth and in the shadow

10 *haśśāmmāh* — *Milel*, and hence the perf. is intended.

11 *yaśśîgûn* — *overtake*. The imp. is followed by the perf. without *waw* consecutive, which describes the future and brings to focus a particular aspect of the description.

of my hand have I covered thee; to plant the heavens and to found the earth, and saying to Zion, My people art thou.

12 The prophet continues with the same theme, the salvation and glorification of Zion, but treats it differently. By repeating the personal pronoun the Lord draws attention to Himself as the only sure source of comfort. This fact is also strengthened by the third person pronoun. Using the same root as appears in 40:1, the Lord declares that He comforts the people. This is in reality the basic theme of the entire prophecy. The first section (1–39) pictured the nation as foolishly turning from the Lord's promises and trusting in Assyria and Egypt. In place of the royal Messiah to come, the people looked to a human ruler. The result was that calamity came upon the nation, manifesting itself primarily in the cessation of the theocracy and the carrying away into captivity. Thus there was need for the message that true comfort (consisting of deliverance from sin and its consequences) would come from the Lord, Israel's God.[12] It is this theme that Isaiah develops and propounds from chapter forty on, and in this verse the theme finds a classic expression.

Inasmuch as God is the Comforter of the people, who is Israel that it should fear men?[13] To fear implies presumption on the one hand and a disbelief in God on the other. God has commanded, "Fear not"; to violate this command is to be presumptuous, to assume that God's command is without meaning. Furthermore, it is to attribute to man a power and ability that he does not possess. Calvin accurately describes the nature of fear: "The consequence is, that when dangers arise, they are terrified and confounded, and attribute far more to the power of mortal man in attacking than to the power of God in defending."

The language brings out the position of Israel, *who art thou, and thou hast been afraid?* The thought is, "Thou art nothing, yet thou hast feared from man, who is *'enosh*, weak and frail, and who dies."[14] In the parallel expression it is said of the son of

---

12 Pieper takes the participle in the sense of *renew*, and renders, *who creates new things for you.*

13 Inasmuch as the imp. with *waw* consecutive follows a phrase suggestive of present time, it must itself be rendered as a present. It may be concessive, *and yet thou fearest.*

14 יָמוּת — the imp. attached to the substantive has practically the force of an adjective; *a man, he will die,* i.e. *a mortal man.*

man, *like the grass he is given.* The thought seems to be that man will become as weak and as easily destructible as grass.

13 In fearing man the people have forgotten God and His power. It is interesting to note the change in gender: in verse 12b the feminine, for there Zion is the object; and here the masculine, for Israel is in view. The people have forgotten God as Creator; it seems to be implied that they consequently doubt that God is their Creator. *Making thee* probably refers to the forming of Israel to be a nation.

Such forgetting of God leads to abject fear. The cause of this fear is the wrath of the oppressor, who was setting about to slay; but such fear was folly, for this wrath has disappeared. This latter fact Isaiah brings out by means of a rhetorical question. The oppressor is pictured as preparing his bow and adjusting the arrow to shoot at the people. He is a ready, active enemy, bent upon the destruction of the nation; but God is their Comforter; and the enemy's wrath, where is it? The very question implies that it is gone, never to reappear.

14 The warning of the preceding verse changes to a promise, in which Israel is depicted as a prisoner to whom the doors of the prison have suddenly been opened. We should construe the first verb adverbially, *In haste is the tzo'eh freed;* literally, *The tzo'eh hastens to be set free.* The thought probably is that the deliverance is at hand, rather than that the *tzo'eh* is hastening excessively, manifesting an impatient desire for deliverance.

There is question as to the precise connotation of *tzo'eh.*[15] By means of a minor change in the pointing the word can be rendered *marching*; this is questionable, although supported by numerous commentators. The root meaning is *to stoop,* and the participial form here therefore means, *one stooping, bending,* as though under a burden. Possibly therefore it refers to those who sit in prison bent over, and so may be rendered in English by *prisoners.* Although the Hebrew is anarthrous (for this is poetic language), in English we may render, *The prisoner hastens to be delivered.*

This interpretation seems to be supported by what follows, *and he will not die with respect to the pit.* The promise of blessing is that there will be a genuine deliverance and the prisoner will not

---

15 1Q *tzrh.*

316

die in the prison. Such a death would probably be due to hunger, as the following clause implies. It is possible that *shahath* refers to Sheol, but this is not certain. Whether it is to be taken as a general term for the grave or prison may be difficult to determine. The thought is that the captive will not perish in his captivity. The food that he needs to sustain life will always be present.

15 As a pledge of the truthfulness of the promise just made, the Lord directs attention to His almighty power and to Himself. Again we have a verse beginning with the emphatic personal pronoun. The Masoretes rightly pointed the pronoun with the disjunctive *Pashta*, and so we must render, *And I—am the Lord thy God.* As North points out, the Semitic languages employ the conjunction *and (waw)* lavishly. Here we may render *For,* inasmuch as this verse presents a ground for confidence in the promise just uttered. The fact that He is the covenant God of Israel is in itself cause for trust and assurance.

The following clauses illustrate the power of God. He rouses up the sea with the result that *its waves roar.*[16] To the Israelites, who were not primarily a seafaring people, God's power over the sea was evidence that He was omnipotent. The reference is general, indicating that "the winds and the waves obey Thy will."

The Name of the One who possesses this omnipotence is *the Lord of hosts.* This phrase has appeared a number of times in Isaiah. In its very nature it has a military connotation, for the hosts contend for and do combat for the Lord who possesses them. In the broadest sense the phrase may simply designate all of creation, the thought then being that the Lord is Lord of all creation, which does combat for Him against all that is contrary to His will. If all hosts are the Lord's, no mortal enemy can possibly keep His people in bondage.

16 Having stated that God the omnipotent One will bring deliverance, the text now points out the means employed, namely the revelation of God. The introductory words, reminiscent of Deuteronomy 18:18, suggest a prophetical work, the declaration of a message to Zion. Hence, some refer the passage to the prophets as those in whose mouth God places His words. On this construction, the words describe the reception of the prophetic revelation and

---

[16] Here *waw* consecutive denotes result; cf. note 13.

the preparation of the prophets for their ministry. Yet the second half of the verse seems to suggest that the work therein described is to be carried out by those in whose mouth God has placed His words. They are to plant the heavens and found the earth. God places His words in their mouth that thereby the heavens and earth may be founded.

The nature of the work described in the second half of the verse, however, is not such as Isaiah himself or the prophets generally accomplished. May the reference then be to Israel? This is possible if we take it in the sense that it is Israel as represented or culminating in the servant. Yet in light of the nature of the work to be accomplished, it seems best to regard the One in whose mouth God places His words as the Messiah Himself, the One who is to plant the heavens and found the earth and bring a message of comfort to Zion.

The *words* to be spoken find their origin in divine revelation. Here is a propositional revelation, which God places in the mouth of His servant. The message does not originate with the messenger but with God, and it is this message that the servant delivers. Furthermore, as in 49:2 God protects the servant in preparation for his work.

To plant the heavens is a strange expression, and probably is to be interpreted in the light of the parallel, *and to found the earth.* Inasmuch as the heavens and earth are already founded, it would seem that the reference is to the new heavens and earth, wherein dwells righteousness. This mighty work, as mighty as that of the original creation, is to be accomplished by the words God has placed in the mouth of His servant. To inhabit this heaven and earth there must be a people; and these are Zion, to whom the servant is to declare, "My people art thou." "The outward economy," as Alexander so well puts it, "should all be new, and yet the identity of the chosen people should remain unbroken."

17 Arouse thyself, arouse thyself; arise, Jerusalem, who hast drunk from the hand of the LORD the cup of his wrath; the bowl of the cup of reeling thou hast drunk, thou hast wrung it out.

18 There is none leading her of all the sons she has brought forth, and no one grasping her hand of all the sons she has brought up.

19 Both these are about to befall thee: who will mourn for thee? Wasting and ruin, famine and sword: who but I will comfort thee?

20 Thy sons were faint; they lie at the head of all the streets, like a wild bull in a net; filled with the wrath of the LORD, the rebuke of thy God.

21 Therefore, hear now this, thou suffering one; and drunken, but not from wine.

22 Thus saith thy Lord, the LORD, and thy God, he will strive for his people. Behold! I have taken from thy hand the cup of reeling, the bowl of the cup of my fury; thou shalt not add to drink it anymore.

23 And I shall put it in the hands of those that afflicted thee, and said to thy soul, Bow down that we may pass over; and thou didst lay thy back as the ground, and as the street for those who pass over.

17 This verse is similar to verse 9, although the double imperative here is stronger. As there the arm of the Lord was conceived as inactive, so here Jerusalem is a woman lying in the sleep of faintness and stupor on the ground. Probably the command is given by God Himself, who has just spoken, so that in reality this verse is a continuation of the preceding. The double imperative serves to recall Jerusalem to consciousness. Perhaps the reflexive force of the *Hithpael* stem should not be overlooked. By the imperative *qumi* (*arise*) attention is directed to the remaining bodily strength of Jerusalem. She is not merely to awaken but to stand up, erect, as she should be.

What Jerusalem has drunk is *from the hand of the Lord*, and this phrase recalls 40:2. The *cup of his wrath* is the cup that contains His wrath. When it refers to the elect, *cup* indicates the moderation of the divine judgment. It is only a cup of wrath, not an oceanful.

In the second line *the bowl of the cup of reeling* is the cup that brings about the reeling of drunkenness to those who drink from it. The word *kos* (*cup*) possibly refers specifically to the interior, and *qubba'* to the convex surface. It is possible that the construction is pleonastic, and that we should render *goblet-cup*, a poetic amplification of *kos*.[17] We have here a case of *continens pro contento*, the cup standing for the wrath within. God has brought this cup to Jerusalem and she has been compelled to drink the entirety of it,

---

17 This same combination occurs in Ug.: *ks . bdy . qb't . bymny (.t)q.*, "Take the cup from my hand, the goblet from my right hand" (Aqht i.4.54-56). Cf. also Akk. *qabu'ātu, goblets*.

even to the last drop. The two final verbs are very effective, *thou hast drunken, thou hast drained it dry* (cf. Ezek. 23:32-34). Delitzsch speaks of the plaintive falling of the tone in these two verbs. Furthermore, their asyndetic position beside each other is most striking.

18 The speaker now changes the person, mentioning Jerusalem in the third person and then again in the subsequent verse reverting to the second person. "With respect to her (this is the force of the preposition *Lamed*) there is no one leading from among all the sons she has borne."[18] Emphasis falls upon the miserable condition of Jerusalem rather than upon the particular details of that condition. Hence, it is not necessary to conceive of her as a widow (although this thought is found in Lamentations, e.g. 1:1), nor need we assume that she is stumbling about as still drunken and in need of someone to guide her. Emphasis falls upon the inability of anyone to help Jerusalem.

Her children are those who have gone forth from her. Her own inhabitants, be they ever so strong and willing, nevertheless cannot lead the city at this time when the wrath of God has been drunk by her. Nor can they seize her by the hand to help. The close relationship of the sons to the mother is expressed by the poignant phrases, *from all the sons she has borne . . . from all the sons she has raised*; and Delitzsch rightly speaks of the elegiac music to be found in these phrases.

The poignancy of the situation lies in the fact that man cannot help himself from his condition of sin. Pieper is to the point when he says: "O the miserable, sick humanistic babblers, who would redeem from the wretchednes of this life mankind that lies under the wrath of God, that has corrupted itself in sin, through any kind of philosophy, through a moral gospel or through social measures, through human culture in man."

19 The first words of this verse may be rendered, *These are the two things that meet thee.*[19] Jerusalem is now addressed in the second person. What is intended by the *two things*? In the following line four things are mentioned, and this is thought by some to

---

[18] Cf. Aqht ii.1.30ff., which speaks of a son who "takes his hand in drunkenness, steadies him when he is sated with wine." Cf. *DOTT*, p. 125.

[19] 1Q ·*hmh*. The predicate stands first, the pronoun occurring before the subject. The pronoun has the force of *those, illa*.

be in conflict with the two things first mentioned. Some combine the four words of the second line so as to obtain *wasting and famine, ruin and sword,* and so two classes of calamity. Another possibility is to interpret *wasting and ruin such as are produced by famine and sword.* There is difficulty in any case, and it may not be possible to give a sure interpretation.

The first words, *These two are they that meet thee,* stand in formal parallel relationship to the four nouns of the second line. Each is followed by a question introduced by *mi (who?).* Hence, it may be that the two things are those just mentioned in the preceding verse, namely, the not being led by the children whom she has borne and the not being seized by the hand by the children whom she has brought up. We set this interpretation forth with some hesitation, merely acknowledging it as a possibility, one that appears to involve less difficulty than to find an equation of meaning between the first words of the verse and the four nouns in the second line.

The first question may be literally rendered, *who will nod* (the head) *for you?*[20] to express sympathetic grief as was done by Job's friends (cf. Job 2:11; 42:11).

In the second line each of the nouns possesses the definite article, for they are the well-known calamities that will come upon Jerusalem. The first two have particular reference to the city; the second two affect its inhabitants.

The last question is also an expression of mourning. The interrogative *mi (who?)* may be taken as an adverb, *how shall I comfort thee?*[21] It is also permissible to render, *who am I that I should comfort thee?* or, *who but I may comfort thee?* No human comforter could render solace, only the Lord Himself.

20 The prophet now gives the reason why Jerusalem's sons, i.e. inhabitants, could not help her. Their senses have become so dulled that they have fainted away. As a result they are lying down *at the head of all the streets,* where they would be conspicuous and in full view. What the head of the streets was cannot be determined. What is significant is that a conspicuous place is intended. Thus Jerusalem sees her streets filled with her own inhabitants, who cannot aid her.

20 ינוד — *will show grief* (by shaking or nodding the head).
21 1Q has the 3rd person as also B Vulg. Syr. Targ. But cf. Isa. 10:12. For the adverbial interrogative cf. Ethiopic *mi?* Cf. *Biblica,* Vol. 38, Fasc. 1, p. 70.

A comparison describes the condition of the fallen ones. They are said to be like an oryx of the net,[22] an oryx that has been caught in the net and so cannot escape. Penna suggests that the animal has probably become caught in a noose, possibly in a ditch, so that there would be no chance of escape.

The reason why they thus lie is that they are *filled with the wrath of the Lord*. They have drunk exhaustively of the cup of His wrath, and being filled with this wrath they are unable to deliver themselves. This wrath is identified as the rebuke of Israel's God, and *rebuke* here has a strong sense, almost approaching the force of *curse*.

21 Inasmuch as Zion has drunk to the dregs the cup of God's wrath, she is assured that the Lord will bring His mercy and will contend for her. The introductory *therefore* marks the transition between the ground for the promise and the promise itself. Zion has endured the full measure of wrath; now let her hear the announcement of blessing. Note the mild form of the imperative. *This* refers to what follows.

Babylon had been addressed as *voluptuous*; Zion is addressed as *suffering one*.[23] The reference is to the fact that Zion has drunk the cup of wrath and is in misery. The same thought is expressed by the following phrase.[24] Note that the preposition *min* (*from*) expresses cause. The conjunction before *drunken* may be rendered *even*.

22 This verse contains the address of the Lord to Zion. Elsewhere in Isaiah the plural *'adonim* (*lords*) applies only to human masters. Here it is used of the Lord, evidently because Zion is conceived of as His bride. The word points out that the Lord is the Head or Master of Zion. To stress the solemnity of the address two further designations are employed, namely *the Lord* and *thy God*.

To take the phrase *he contends for his people* without a relative gives a certain amount of strength. This verb is employed of the law court (cf. 45:9; 49:25; 50:8). Here the controversy is not with

22 תוא — construct of *te'ô*, antelope. B σευτλίον; Aq S T ορυξ. *mikmār* — net, snare (bring an animal to its fall). Cf. Akk. *kamâru, overthrow* and *kamâru, net.*

23 There may be an intentional play between *'adināh* (47:8) and *'aniyyāh.*

24 *šekurat* — *drunken*. The feminine ending -*ath* may be intentional to avoid the hiatus -*āh* *we.*

God's people but for them. On their behalf He contends and pleads, hence there can be no question as to the outcome. In the latter part of the verse God's sovereignty stands out clearly. As He had given to Zion the cup of wrath to drink, so now He of His own volition removes that cup. He alone decides when it is to be offered and when removed. The perfect is prophetic, *I have taken*, i.e. *I shall take*. The cup of reeling (i.e. the cup that causes reeling) is conceived as yet in Zion's hand, and from this goblet-cup Zion is no more to drink. The original is forceful: *thou shalt not add to drink it again.*

The absoluteness of this last statement suggests that the cup of wrath poured out reflected one particular manifestation of God's anger. The exile is known as the period of indignation, and it is this period that lies at the basis of the thoughts of this chapter. This does not, however, mean that the exile had yet begun to run its course. In looking forward Isaiah sees his people as the objects of wrath, and announces that the period of indignation such as Israel must suffer will never again be repeated.

23 The introductory conjunction (*waw*) in this context has an adversative sense. Zion will no longer drink from the cup but God will place it in the hands of her oppressors. Isaiah uses a root also found in Lamentations 1:12, and the reading is confirmed by the Qumran Scroll.[25]

To thy soul is not a mere synonym for *to thyself*, for were that the case it would not be necessary; it would then have been sufficient to say, *to thee*. By means of speaking to Zion the oppressors have greatly distressed her.

We are to understand the language of the oppressors, uttered as a command, in a figurative sense, although there are examples of such cruel treatment literally carried out (cf. Josh. 10:24; Zech. 10:5; Judg. 1:7). The Assyrian monuments show how the victor trampled on the conquered who were lying on the ground.[26] Zion

25 In the *Hiphil*, *yāgāh* means *to cause grief* or *sorrow*. 1Q also adds *wm'nyk, and thy afflictors* (cf. 49:26).
26 Cf. the rock carving of Anu-banini in *AOTB*, Table VIII, No. 254. Lactantius relates that the Persian Sapor stepped upon the prisoners taken from Valerian when mounting his chariot (see Gesenius). Volz remarks that he personally knows that the Palestinian, when he would excuse himself and express shame, remarks, "My face is under your shoe." Gesenius gives further examples, e.g. the Arabic proverb, "To the one who has been gracious to me, I will be earth to him" (*Kun-tu la-hu 'ar-dan*).

was compelled to comply with the demands of her cruel oppressor. Quite possibly the thought is that the Babylonians, because of their haughtiness, will themselves be compelled to drink the cup of God's wrath. Calvin, however, goes to the deeper meaning when he asserts that "the Lord will not only deliver the Church from those heavy distresses, but will also lay upon her enemies the calamities with which she is afflicted."

1 Awake! awake, put on thy strength, O Zion; put on thy beautiful garments, O Jerusalem, the holy city, for henceforth there shall no more come into thee the uncircumcised and the unclean.

2 Shake thyself from the dust, arise, sit, O Jerusalem! loose the bands of thy neck, O captive, daughter of Zion.

3 For thus saith the LORD, For naught were ye sold; and not for silver will ye be redeemed.

4 For thus saith the Lord GOD, To Egypt did my people go down at the first to sojourn there; and Assyria oppressed them for nothing.

5 And now, what is it to me here, saith the LORD, that my people have been taken in vain; its rulers howl, saith the LORD, and continually, all the day, my name is blasphemed.

6 Therefore, my people will know my name; therefore in that day, for I am he who speaketh, behold me!

1 Using the same command as was employed toward the arm of the Lord (51:9), Isaiah now commands Zion to awake from the stupor of mourning and drunkenness. He speaks as God's messenger, commanding Zion to clothe herself with strength. The command is shorter than that of 51:17, for Zion apparently is in sufficient command of her faculties to respond instantly to the command.

Zion puts on her beautiful garments when her people long to be clothed with holiness. Jerusalem in the eyes of her Lord is *the holy city*, and will again be seen by men to be such.

A reason is given for Zion to put on strength, namely that never again will an uncircumcised person enter her.[1] Zion had been

---

[1] *yôsíp* — *add*, followed by a verb in the imp. in which the complementary verbal idea is subordinated; cf. Isa. 47:1, 5.

desecrated, for unclean persons had come into her midst, corrupted the pure worship of God, and, as Calvin says, afflicted consciences by tyranny.

Zion is commanded to do what in her own strength she is unable to do. In obeying her Lord, Zion sees God Himself act. He brings her out of despondency into strength and from stupor to her beautiful garments, and encourages her with the promise that henceforth the unclean will no more enter her.

2 The command continues, addressed to Jerusalem. The first imperative is reflexive, *Shake thyself from the dust.* Probably this is the dust in which she has been sitting, although it may have been the dust of mourning sprinkled upon her head (cf. Job 2:12). Attention should be directed to the contrast with 47:1, where similar commands are given to Babylon. Jerusalem, however, unlike Babylon, is to arise and sit. This does not mean to stand up and then to sit down again, but to arise from the prostrate position in which she found herself and to sit upon a chair from which she may act as the true Jerusalem. It may not be amiss to render, *sit upon thy throne.* As a prisoner, Jerusalem had no seat to sit upon; now she may sit as one that is free.

Jerusalem must also *loose the bands* about her *neck.* When the fetters that kept her a prisoner are loosed she will be an honored and respected person. From her degrading slavery[2] she is to be restored to a position of honor and dignity. The language symbolizes the deliverance of God's people from tyranny and oppression.

3 As the command to awake in verse 1 is grounded upon the fact that there will never again enter an unclean one into Zion, so here, the declaration that Zion will be redeemed is grounded in the assertion of the Lord Himself. With a formal and solemn introduction the assertion is presented. Inasmuch as the people have not been sold in vain they will not be redeemed for a price. The thought is not new, the latter part at least having already been presented in 45:13. Under the figure of a legitimate transaction, Isaiah makes clear that God is the sovereign Owner of His people. They were sold for nothing; and inasmuch as no money had been paid for them, they still belonged to the Lord. For this reason, they

---

2 Lit., *O captive* (who art) *daughter of Zion.* Šebiyyāh is a noun, not an adjective.

would not be redeemed with silver or with anything else, for the Lord owed nothing to anyone for them. Compare 50:1, where the same verb, *ye were sold,* occurs.

The verb *to redeem* teaches that the people who had been estranged from God have been brought back to Him legitimately. Those who had possession of the people must give them back. God neither receives nor gives a recompense for His people. The relationship of the two clauses is that of protasis and apodosis; "As ye were sold for nothing, so will ye also not be redeemed for silver."

4 In an introduction stronger than that of the previous verse, Isaiah states the history of affliction that Israel has endured and thus prepares the way for the declaration of the following verse. He uses the strong term *the Lord God,* which, as Pieper suggests, shows that *'ᵃdonay* can and Yahweh will carry through the word that is spoken.

As an accusative of direction (*toward Egypt*), *Egypt* is placed first, in the position of emphasis. God's people went down willingly, indeed, at the invitation of Pharaoh (cf. Gen. 45:18ff.; 47:5, 6) ; and their purpose was simply to sojourn and to enjoy the privileges of sojourners. The words *at the first* evidently refer to the beginning of Israelitish history. What must not be overlooked is the stress upon *my people.* It is the whole nation that God so designates that is said to have gone down into Egypt. This conflicts with the idea that only a part of the tribes were in Egypt.

Isaiah's manner of speaking is elliptical and the conclusion of the first assertion is omitted. We are probably to assume a thought such as, "and the Egyptians ill treated them" (cf. Deut. 26:5, 6).

Chronologically, the next affliction that came upon Israel was by Assyria. As Egypt stood first in the clause so also does Assyria. Different interpretations of *bᵉ'ephes* have been given, but the word may simply mean, *without reason* or *right.* Assyria afflicted Israel, but had no right to do so. Their oppression was an unjust one, for they arrogated to themselves a prerogative that was not theirs. Both Egypt and Assyria are dealt with very briefly, for the attention of the prophet is to fall upon the affliction the people are suffering in the bondage of the Babylonian exile.

5 By means of the introductory words *And now,* the prophet introduces the contrast between the affliction of Egypt and Assyria and that of the present situation. The words *what to me here?* probably signify, "What is it that I must do here?" *Here* either refers to the captivity of Israel or to the present situation. What is to be done in the situation at hand? To these questions the expected answer is, "I must deliver the people. Their bondage is no longer to continue, for the time of deliverance has come."

There then follows a recital of the tragic condition that has come upon the people. The captivity is pictured as at hand, the actual act of exile is described by a verb in the perfect and the actions of the rulers by verbs in the present. The *people have been taken* and the *rulers are howling.*[3] It is difficult to know precisely in what sense this verb is intended. It refers to an action of the enemy rulers, and may indicate their harsh cries as they deal with the captives.

Coupled with this howling, however, went a constant blaspheming of the Lord's Name.[4] The language that indicates the continuity is striking, *always, all the day.* As long as the people are in bondage the name of God is blasphemed, for the rulers do not respect the God of Israel but despise Him as they do the gods of other nations.

6 With this verse Isaiah introduces the conclusion. Because God's Name is so continually blasphemed among the heathen, His own people will know His Name. There is a certain artistic force in the juxtaposition of the two words *'ammi (my people)* and *sh^emi (my name).* The knowledge referred to is not merely intellectual, but comprises an experience of the manifestation of God's self-revelation, insofar as He shows Himself to be the true Deliverer and Redeemer of Israel. *Therefore (laken)* is repeated, having resumptive force. The phrase *in that day* tells when the people will know, namely, in the day when God manifests His power.

It is difficult to determine whether the clause introduced by *ki* should be rendered *that I am he that speaketh* or *for I am he that speaketh.* In either case the meaning is essentially the same. In the one case the object of the people's knowing is that God is the

---

3 *yehēylîlû* — they howl. Note retention of ה. 1Q *whwllw.*
4 *minnō'ātz* — blasphemed. The form is *Hithpoel,* the *t* being assimilated, for *mitnō'ātz.* The *Holem* appears in a near open syllable, inasmuch as the *Aleph* does not take *Dagesh.*

One who speaks; in the other, they are assured that they will know, for God Himself has given the assurance. The final ejaculation is equivalent to *here I am*. This is not a mere reiteration but contains a new thought, calling attention to God's presence.

7 How beautiful upon the mountains are the feet of him that bringeth good tidings, that publisheth peace, that bringeth good tidings of good, that publisheth salvation; that saith unto Zion, Thy God reigneth!

8 The voice of thy watchmen, they raise the voice, together will they shout; for eye to eye will they see when the LORD returneth to Zion.

9 Break forth, shout together, ye waste places of Jerusalem; for the LORD hath comforted his people, he hath redeemed Jerusalem.

10 The LORD hath laid bare his holy arm to the eyes of all the nations; and all the ends of the earth shall see the salvation of our God.

11 Turn ye, turn ye, go out from there, touch not the unclean; go out from her midst, be ye clean, ye bearers of the vessels of the LORD.

12 For not in haste will ye go out, and in flight ye shall not go; for going before you is the LORD, and your rear guard is the God of Israel.

7 No formal connection with the preceding section exists, but there is an inner connection of thought. What in the previous section had been promised is here represented as fulfilled. As Pieper remarks: "The Lord has made true His *hinneni* (*Here I am!*) ." By means of speeding messengers Zion receives the announcement of her deliverance. The word *na'wu* may originally signify something like *timely* or *seasonable*, like ὡραῖος.[5] At the time needed, the messengers have appeared with their tidings of good. From the connotation *timely*, it is not far to that of *beauty*. In speaking of the *feet* the writer is employing *pars pro toto;* what he means is that the appearance of the messengers upon the mountains is beautiful. The mountains are evidently those about Jerusalem, but there is no reason to assume that the announcement has to do with the return of exiles from Babylon. It is rather a general proclamation of

---

[5] *Piel* perf. of *nā'āh*, for *nā'ʾwú*. Cf. Song of Sol. 1:10. The perf. expresses a fact that was long before accomplished, whose effects remain in the present. *They have been and so are now beautiful.*

salvation and deliverance, and Paul so interprets it of the preaching of the Gospel (Rom. 10:15). The participle refers to the proclamation of a message of good tidings.

Three participial phrases explain the nature of this proclamation of good tidings.[6] First, the messenger causes *peace* to be heard; i.e. the message that he delivers has peace as its grand subject. We are not to conceive of three different messages, for each statement is an aspect of the same blessed theme of salvation. We shall understand the word *peace* not through etymology, but through its usage in the prophecy. It is one of Isaiah's favorite words, and refers not merely to the ceasing of hostilities among warring nations, but to a peace that the Lord gives to His people. There is peace to be proclaimed, for the Lord no longer stands in a hostile relation to His own.

Secondly, the messenger proclaims *good*, a word that characterizes the content of the message. This message originates with God, and refers to the blessing that alone is good, the salvation of sinful mankind. Finally the messenger causes *salvation* to be heard. The word calls to mind the very name of the prophet. It is a salvation that finds its origin in God and comes from Him. He dispenses this salvation, for it is a salvation from all those things that bring God's wrath upon men. It is far more than a mere delivery from the captivity in Babylon; it is a spiritual salvation, characterized also as good and peace.

The content of the message is the fact that Zion's God reigns. Should we interpret *Thy God reigneth* or *Thy God has become king?* The thought is essentially the same as that announced in the New Testament, that the kingdom of God is at hand. There is no thought that God has abdicated the throne during the period of the exile, although to Israel it may at times have seemed that such was the case. What the messenger declares is that Israel's God will now manifest the fact that He is upon the throne.

If we take the verb as inchoative, the thought would simply be that God is now making it clear to Israel that He is reigning, although to Israel it might appear that He was beginning to reign. In any case, we must avoid the modern interpretation of this verse,

6 Nah. 2:1 (Heb.) reflects upon this verse. For the relation of Isaiah to later prophecies cf. my article, "Isaiah 34 and Its Position in the Prophecy," *WThJ*, Vol. 27, No. 2, 1964, pp. 93-114.

which would see here a reflection upon an annual ascent of the throne (cf. APPENDIX II, "Thy God Reigneth").

8 The language begins with a poetic apostrophe or exclamation, as though to say, "Hark! I hear a voice" (cf. Song of Sol. 2:8 for an example of this well-known construction). It is the *voice* of Zion's *watchmen*, who are not the prophets but the watchmen upon Zion's walls. There is no need to assume that at this time the walls were not standing, and that the prophet idealizes or imagines the walls as rebuilt for the occasion (North). When the approaching messengers stand upon the mountains with their announcement of peace, then Jerusalem's watchmen lift up their voice, and shout in unison. If we press the verbal forms—and there would seem to be no reason for not so doing—they teach that the watchmen have already raised the voice, and now together break into shouting. Perhaps this shouting is simply a glad reaction to the approach of the messengers; more likely the watchmen themselves take up the good tidings and repeat them to the inhabitants of Jerusalem.

The phrase *eye to eye* does not mean the same as the common English expression, to agree upon something, but rather, as in Numbers 14:14, describes two people as being so close that they can look into one another's eyes. Their seeing is immediate and clear.

Before the infinitive construct the preposition *Beth* is to be construed temporally, and the infinitive itself is to be taken intransitively, *when the Lord returns to Zion.* The glorious appearance of God, which all flesh shall see, is to be clearly seen by the watchers of Zion. Yahweh, whom Israel regarded as having abandoned Zion, will now return to His holy city, there to reign in peace and good and salvation.

9 Occasionally Isaiah appeals to an inanimate object, here the waste places of Jerusalem (cf. 44:23; 49:13; 55:12). Instead of the usual imperative and noun, however (namely, "Burst forth into shouting"; cf. 14:7; 44:23; 49:13; 54:1 and 55:12), the prophet employs two asyndetical imperatives for the sake of greater emphasis, *Burst forth, shout* (cf. also Ps. 98:4, where the same construction occurs). The ruined places are to break forth together, i.e. all at once; with united voice they are to break forth into shouting.

A reason is given, namely that the promise of comfort has now become fact. The word, Delitzsch suggests, has become act. We are probably to understand the verb in the same sense as in 40:1. God has comforted Jerusalem in that He has redeemed her. *Waste places of Jerusalem* does not necessarily conflict with the mention of watchmen. Isaiah in the Spirit looks forward to the time when the city will be forsaken and pictures her thus. Hence, he can speak of her watchmen and also speak of her as though she were a desolate city.

10 There is every reason for shouting in exultation, for Yahweh the God of Israel has won a great victory. His holy right arm He has brought forth, and removed from it whatever would hinder it in the exercise of its power. The arm is conceived of as in the breastplate. From this it has now been brought forth and exposed. It is a *holy arm*, and the connection between holiness and strength points to the nature of the deliverance. This laying bare has been performed before *all the nations*, that they might learn that the God of Jacob is the only true God, whereas their own gods are nothing.

As a result of the laying bare of God's holy arm, *all the ends of the earth will see* the salvation that the God of Israel has accomplished.[7] *The salvation of our God* is the salvation our God has wrought. When the nation had fallen into the darkness of the exile and the theocracy was no more, the first glimmers of deliverance were seen when Cyrus permitted a return from bondage. Through this act it already appeared that the first kingdom of the great colossus, the Mesopotamian power, was temporal and local. Israel in one sense or another would still be under the power of man's great empire, but when that empire was at its height the spiritual Israel would receive a deliverance of which Cyrus' act was but the forerunner. When Rome was in power God delivered His people in the work of His Son, Jesus Christ. This is the heart of the message that Isaiah is here proclaiming.

11 Having proclaimed the Gospel, Isaiah now commands the people to believe and to manifest their trust in departing from Babylon. The words *from there* would seem to refer to Babylon,

---

7 *and they will see* — the perf. with *waw* consecutive after a prophetic perf. expresses the future.

and it would appear also that this command is addressed by someone who himself is not in Babylon.[8] Begrich argues that this need not follow, that the prophet may be in some other part of Babylonia than the city herself, and that preaching from his own locality he commands the Jews to go out from the city of Babylon.[9] This is strange and unlikely. It was not the city of Babylon that was the oppressor, but the country itself. The command is to go out of the land of exile and to return to the land of promise. We may render the first imperative *Turn aside*, but we should also note the force of Gesenius' translation as an adverb, *away*. The imperative is repeated. The third imperative signifies a going out or departure from the place in which the people were. It is a command to depart from all sin. This departure, however, is not to be one in which men acquire for themselves material possessions as they had done at the exodus from Egypt. Rather, in leaving the spot where they are, they are to touch no unclean thing. Those things that belong to the world are unclean and are not to enrich the people of God who depart from the world.

Not only are they not to touch unclean things, but they are to purify themselves (an imperative with the same force as those in 1:16, 17), for they carry the armor of the Lord. The reference is probably to the utensils employed in the service of the Lord. Those who bore these did so that again they might worship the Lord in the place of His choosing. They who would serve Him are themselves to be pure and not to enrich themselves with the unclean possessions of the heathen. Quite possibly the departure from Babylon lies at the base of this prophecy, and in a certain sense the fulfillment is found in the fact that Cyrus directed that the golden and silver vessels be returned to the exiles (cf. Ezra 1:7-11). At the same time the prophecy is not exhausted in such a reference. In the wider and deeper sense it is a prediction of the departure of God's people from the bondage of sin. Calvin suggests that the address is basically to the priests and Levites who officiate in the divine services, and that they stand by way of eminence for the whole people. This may be correct; it is certainly the people considered in the aspect of worshipping God officially that is in view here.

8 This is really supported by Muilenburg's assertion that the prophet places himself imaginatively in Jerusalem.

9 *SZD*, p. 96: ". . . So ist durchaus vorstellbar, dass der Prophet von einem anderen Ort Babyloniens aus dieses Wort gesprochen hat."

12 The introductory *For* probably refers to the entire thought of the preceding verse, rather than to one particular aspect thereof. Thus, "In your departure you are not to touch any unclean thing, but rather to purify yourselves, for. . . ." The reason for the departure and the manner thereof is that this new exodus is wholly different from that from Egypt. In that departure the people ate the passover *in haste* (lit., *in trembling, anxious fear*; cf. Ex. 12:11 and Deut. 16:3). At that time there was fear and trepidation, but such are not present in this new departure. The prophet probably introduces a gradation with the word *flight,* which again (although a different root is employed) calls to mind the exodus from Egypt ("When the king of Egypt was told that the people had fled . . ." Ex. 14:5). In contrast to the haste and flight of the first exodus, this one will be quiet and with dignity. Considerable effectiveness is achieved by the variety with which Isaiah uses the negatives: *NOT in haste . . . and in flight ye shall NOT go out.*

As the first part of the verse begins with *for,* so does the second; and the second part gives a reason for the statements of the first. The participle has a military connotation as does also *your rear guard* (cf. Num. 10:25 and Josh. 6:9, 13). Again there is a reminiscence of the exodus, when the ark of the covenant went before the people (Num. 10:33-36) and the Lord Himself preceded them in a pillar of cloud and fire (cf. Ex. 13:21; 14:19, 20, etc.).

Your rear guard serves to show, when taken together with *goeth,* that in the departure the people would have their God before them and behind them. No enemy could possibly touch them, for the presence of God was all about them. The presence of God is prominent; if the people go out without Him they will not go out at all.

13 Behold! my servant will deal prudently; he shall rise and be exalted and be high exceedingly.
14 Even as many were astonished at thee, so disfigured from man was his appearance, and his form from the sons of men.
15 So shall he sprinkle many nations, at him kings shall shut their mouths, for that which had not been told to them have they seen, and that which they had not heard have they perceived.

13 In language of unspeakable force and beauty the prophet has portrayed the great deliverance of the Church. The grace of God has brought the people out of the bondage of sin. It is now fitting that the prophet should also portray the exaltation of the One who accomplished the deliverance and should point out the vicarious suffering He had to undergo to deliver His people. Verses 13-15 form an introduction to the fourth passage concerning the Servant of the Lord, and in reality belong with chapter fifty-three, which should begin with 52:13.[10]

By means of an introductory *Behold!* a favorite beginning of Isaiah, the prophet directs attention to the figure of God's servant. The verb is capable of several connotations, but at its heart is the thought of prudent and wise dealing. He who deals wisely will obtain success; the servant uses the best means to obtain the highest ends. The translation *will prosper* is not sufficiently accurate, for the verb probably includes the thought of both intelligent and effective action.[11] Success does not result from lack of effort but from effective action. In accomplishing his mission upon earth, the servant will be successful. This thought is introduced even before the servant is mentioned, and it is not brought in again until the tenth verse of the following chapter. At the outset it is necessary to stress the servant's wise dealing, for in the subsequent verses the servant appears as one whom men regard as punished for his own sins.

It is God who introduces and identifies the servant, who belongs to God and serves Him. In 42:1-4 Isaiah had already presented him as one with a mission to perform who would successfully complete that mission. In 49:1-7 he had again been presented, but this time there are great difficulties in the execution of his work. In 50:4-9 the servant himself had spoken, mentioning the suffering that he was to face. Yet no reason was given for this suffering, for it is reserved for the present passage to tell why the servant must undergo severe suffering and degradation.

The three verbs of the second half of the verse set forth the consequences of the servant's wise dealing.[12] With the third verb

---

10 At the same time these verses do build upon vv. 1-12.

11 The verb is used of leaders (Josh. 1:7, 8; 1 Sam. 18:5, 30) and kings (1 Kings 2:3).

12 The combination of *rûm* (to exalt) and *nāśā'* (to lift up), intransitive and referring to the same subject, is found in Isa. 33:10 but nowhere else in the prophets. Cf. the combination of these roots in 6:1. North (*The Suffering Servant in Deutero-Isaiah*, London, 1956, pp. 165-69) lists the words that are peculiar to this passage (52:13–53:12), but maintains that on the grounds of vocabulary alone it is hazardous to deny its authorship to the author of Isa. 40–55. The subject matter explains the use of this particular vocabulary.

note the stative force and also the modifying adverb setting forth the final point of exaltation. He will rise in that he will not remain in his condition of humiliation; he will stand out in that he raises himself, and he will be in an exalted condition towering high above all else. It is impossible to read these words without being reminded of the exaltation of Christ depicted in Philippians 2:9-11 and Acts 2:33; note also Acts 3:13, 26.

Some commentators see in these three verbs a hint of the stages in the exaltation of our Lord, His resurrection, ascension, and session at the right hand of the Father.[13] Yet the prophet's purpose seems not so much to present the actual details of our Lord's life as to set forth a picture of the suffering servant as such. Whereas man's kingdom perishes and its idols fall, Bel sinking down and Nebo bending over, the servant, ruler of redeemed mankind, receives the highest exaltation. A complete and utter exaltation will come to the servant. In seeking to identify the servant, therefore, we must take this factor into account. One may very legitimately ask whether Israel or the prophets or anyone other than Jesus Christ was ever conceived of in the Old Testament as dealing so wisely that the result would be an unparalleled exaltation.[14] Only One who will Himself be gloriously exalted can bring about the deliverance of the people just depicted.

14 Having stated the supreme exaltation of the servant the prophet now introduces a contrast, addressing the servant himself in an objective tone. The construction of the following clauses is difficult, but it seems best to construe them as follows:

Protasis: Even as many were astonished at thee
　　　　　　Parenthesis: (so was his appearance disfigurement
　　　　　　from men, and his form from the sons of
　　　　　　men)

13 So, e.g., Stier.
14 Quite probably the verb does reflect upon David; cf. 1 Sam. 18:14, 15; 1 Kings 2:3; Ps. 101:2; 2 Kings 18:2-7 (Hezekiah). The Messiah, like his ancestor David, will wisely administer His kingdom. Cf. Jer. 23:5, where this root stands as a parallel to *mālaḵ*, a passage that may reflect upon the present one. The servant will deal wisely, for he is God's servant, and God, the source and fountain of wisdom, supplies the blessings that accompany the servant's wise deeds. *He shall cause to prosper* (53:10) is related to the servant's doings.

CHAPTER FIFTY-TWO

Second Parenthesis: (so shall he sprinkle many nations)
Apodosis: kings shall shut their mouths at him, etc.

Thus the contrast appears between the action of the many with respect to the servant and that of the kings; the many are astonished, the kings close their mouths.

The prophet delights in contrasts. From the statement of the servant's exaltation he plunges at once to a contemplation of his deep degradation. Indeed, for this reason Isaiah has mentioned the exaltation. As his exaltation and glorification were of the highest, so his degradation will be of the deepest. Our contemplation of the servant's sufferings might easily lead us to conclude that they would destroy the servant and that he was justly suffering for his sins. To prevent us from this error the prophet stresses at the outset the exaltation that will surely come to the servant.

The verb *astonished* suggests a disconcertment brought about by a disturbing and paralyzing astonishment. Those who beheld the terrible disfigurement of the servant were appalled and struck by awe, for they regarded the disfigurement as a punishment for the servant's own sins.[15] So men, according to Ezekiel 27:35, would react when they saw the ruined city of Tyre. They would be struck with awe, for they would realize that God's punishing hand has visited the city.

There is a quantitative contrast between the *many* and *thee*,[16] which often characterizes Messianic prophecies. By this contrast the servant as an individual stands out over against the many on whose behalf he acts, who have so persistently misunderstood his sufferings and their purpose and nature.

In the first parenthetical clause the prophet gives the reason for the misunderstanding of the many, expressed in the words, *disfigurement from men is his appearance*. This does not mean that he appears to be more disfigured than other men, but that his disfigurement was so great that he no longer appeared as a man. What might be seen of him, i.e. his appearance, was disfigurement. Parallel to this thought is the second, namely that his form was away

15 מִשְׁחַת — construct; abstract for concrete; *disfigurement*. 1Q reads *mšḥty*; cf. *BASOR*, No. 134, 1954, pp. 27, 28.
16 So 1Q; not to be emended to the 3rd person. The change to the 3rd person in v. 15 is occasioned by the prophet's parenthesis, in which the servant must be described in the 3rd person.

from the sons of man, i.e. that his form was so disfigured that he no longer resembled a man. This is an extremely strong way of saying how great his sufferings were.

Of interest is the chiastic arrangement of the last line, and also the two words for man. He is more disfigured than an *'ish* (the better class of men) and his form[17] more than the *sons of men* (ordinary men).

15 By means of a second parenthetical clause the prophet explains why he was disfigured. *So*, i.e. in this condition of disfigurement, *he will sprinkle many nations.*[18] As one who is disfigured, the servant does something for others, in that he performs a purifying rite. His disfigurement, therefore, was mistakenly regarded as a punishment for his own sins, whereas it was rather the condition in which he would himself bring cleansing to the nations.

The verb *he shall sprinkle* is a technical word, found in the Mosaic law for the sprinkling of oil, water, or blood as a cleansing or purifying rite. Thus, "And he shall sprinkle upon him that is to be cleansed from the leprosy seven times" (Lev. 14:7a) ; "And the priest shall dip his finger in the blood, and sprinkle of the blood seven times before the LORD, before the veil of the sanctuary" (Lev. 4:6); "And he sprinkled thereof upon the altar seven times, and anointed the altar and all his vessels, both the laver and his foot, to sanctify them" (Lev. 8:11).

The purpose of the sprinkling was not decontamination, but to obtain ritual purity; hence the one who does the sprinkling must himself be pure and innocent.[19] It is the work of a priest that is here set forth, and the purpose of this work is to bring purification and cleansing to others. Men regarded the servant as himself

---

17 *weṭo'arô — and his form.* We should expect *to-'o-rô* as in 1 Sam. 28:14.

18 1Q *yzh.* I have discussed the reasons for this rendering in *SII*, pp. 199-206. Cf. T. C. Vriezen, *OTS*, Vol. 7, 1950, p. 204.

19 But cf. North, *in loc.* The outward, material purification, however, often denotes an inward, spiritual cleansing, e.g., Ps. 51:9; Ezek. 36:25. What is done to outward impurity is done to sin, and thus the sprinkling has reference to cleansing from sin. Cf. the N.T. allusions, 1 Pet. 1:2; Heb. 10:22; 12:24; and also 9:13, 14. Both sprinkling with oil and that with water have as their basis sprinkling with blood. Note Ex. 29:21 (oil) and the fact that only that water was sprinkled which contained ashes from the sin offering of the red heifer. Heb. 9:13, 14 includes both. What in the typical sacrifices was separated is united in the antitypical.

unclean and in need of purification, whereas he himself as a priest will sprinkle water and blood and so purify many nations. He does this as a sufferer, whose sufferings are for the sake of an expiatory purification and produce a profound change in the attitude of those who behold him. This is the work that he will prudently perform, and because of which he will be so greatly exalted.

In the concluding clauses the prophet states the successful results of the servant's work, placing the words *at him* first to emphasize them. Closing the mouth signifies speechless astonishment, a being struck dumb. The speechlessness is to be understood as a sign of awe and honor. These kings will stand in silent awe before the servant, just as the many had once despised and rejected him. By mentioning kings the prophet introduces an intentional contrast. The many, including men of ordinary rank, despised the servant; but as a result of his saving work even the most exalted of men will stand in awe before him. They who were astonished were, at least outwardly, members of the covenant; they who are reverent, however, are Gentiles.

Isaiah gives a reason for this attitude, namely the utter novelty of the future salvation. "And from eternity have they not heard, they have not given ear, eye hath not seen, a God apart from thee, who will do for him that waiteth for him" (Isa. 64:4). The novelty appears in the fact that the kings have come to experience the truth that the servant has died in their stead and has come to life again, thus bringing life to all his seed.[20] This message has never been told to them nor have they ever heard it, but now they have both seen and perceived it. In former prophecies of the Messiah the message of salvation has been presented in veiled form, but now for the first time it is set forth with glorious clarity. It is a message that could not possibly have had its origin in the sinful heart of man, for all religions of human origin find in man himself the answer to all problems, but this message points to the Servant of the Lord as their only Hope.

---

[20] On the basis of B, some would translate, "They to whom it has not been told see, and they who have not heard have understood."

1 Who hath believed our report; and the arm of the LORD, upon whom hath it been revealed?

2 And he came up as a suckling before him, and as a root from a dry ground; there is no form to him nor splendor, and we see him, and there is no appearance that we should desire him.

3 Despised, and rejected of men, a man of sorrows and acquainted with grief; and as a hiding of faces from him—despised, and we did not esteem him.

1 The body of the fourth servant passage begins with a rhetorical question, which, as Pieper correctly observes, is more an exclamation than a question. It does not demand a negative answer, but is designed simply to call attention to the paucity of true believers in the world and especially among the Jews. We cannot agree with those who find the Gentiles to be the speakers, for such a position entails too many difficulties. It is better to understand the prophet as the representative of his people, speaking and expressing dismay that so few believe. The plural does not demand that the Gentiles be the speakers (Edelkoort), for it applies well to the prophet as speaking for his people.

An exegetical question revolves around the interpretation of *our report*. In itself the word means simply, *the thing heard*. Is this a message we ourselves have heard[1] or a message that we proclaim? Adopting this latter position, Luther rendered *our preaching*. This is the position of the New Testament (cf. John 12:38 and Rom. 10:16), and it also fits in better with the context. What caused the

[1] This interpretation has been well defended by Hengstenberg, in *COT*. It has recently been held that the chapter has its roots in ancient mythology, being an imitation of the dying and rising savior-god; hence *our report* means, "the tradition that we have received." Cf. H. S. Nyberg, "Smärtornas man. En studie till Jes. 52,13–53,12," *Svensk Exegetisk Årsbok*, Vol. 7, 1942, pp. 5-82; Ivan Engnell, "Till frågan om Ebed.Jahve-sångerna och den lidande Messias hos 'Deuterojesaja'," *Svensk Exegetisk Årsbok*, Vol. 10, 1945, pp. 31-65; E.T. in *Bulletin of the John Rylands Library*, Vol. 31, Jan. 1948.

kings to shut their mouths was what they had not heard (shame‘u), and it is what we cause to be heard (sh‘emu‘athenu) that is ignored by the many.

The parallel expression also supports this interpretation. The *arm of the Lord* is used by metonymy for the Lord's strength. The revelation of the Lord's strength and believing what we have proclaimed are two aspects of the same thing. The revelation of God's arm upon a person is one of power (cf. Jer. 17:5), and hence to believe the report proclaimed is evidence that the Lord's power has been manifested. It is the arm of the Lord that brought the nation out of Egypt (cf. 51:9-10; 63:12), and this arm of power enables a man to believe. The passage clearly teaches that faith is a gift of God and not a work of man's unaided power. It also teaches that unless God manifests His power, men will not be converted. We must ever depend upon God to work that His kingdom may be extended.

2 Having expressed surprise at the paucity of believers, the prophet now sets forth the course of the servant's life. The introductory conjunction (*waw*) may be rendered *And* or *For*. It introduces a verb in the past (*waw* consecutive), and the entire description given in the body of the passage is in the past. This is to be understood as a prophetic perfect. To the mind of the speaker, what he depicts is so vivid and sure of occurrence that he sets it forth as already having taken place. What is sure is that the prophet is not speaking of someone who has already lived upon earth before the prophet's own time.

The first verb, *And he came up*, refers to the appearance of the servant upon earth and the course of his life, and the phrase *before him* is best taken as referring to God. The servant lived the entire course of his earthly life in the presence of God (cf. 1 Pet. 2:4). The phrase is essential to show that the servant's life was kept in the power of God and lived before Him.

To men, however, the servant appeared as a suckling, a tender twig that grows on the trunk or branch of a tree and draws its life and strength therefrom.[2] Men cut off the sucklings, because they

---

[2] The part. means lit., *a sucking one*; cf. Job 14:7; Ezek. 17:22. B παιδίον; also Peshitta. Engnell, *op. cit.*, E.T., p. 31, thinks that we are in a Tammuz ideological context. North (*in loc.*) effectively points out the irrelevancy of this view. A good discussion is found in V. de Leeuw, *op. cit.* The root (שׁרשׁ) denotes its product, that whereby it becomes visible, its sprout.

take the life from the tree and in men's sight are to be cast out.

A second comparison sets forth the servant as a root that has come up in a dry, unpromising ground or soil. Here there is quite likely a reflection upon Isaiah's earlier prophecy: "And there shall come forth a shoot out of the stock of Jesse, and a branch out of his roots shall bear fruit" (11:1). *Dry ground* refers to the lowly conditions and background in which the servant was to appear. It suggests the miserable nature of the conditions in the midst of which the servant's life was lived. To refer it to Bethlehem or to the Virgin Mary is without warrant.[3] A root in a dry parched ground must struggle to preserve life; so men regarded the servant, comparing him not with the tall cedars, but with the lowly root. David was a man of form, by which is meant that he was a comely person (1 Sam. 16:18). The servant, however, has neither form nor glory. Those things that in the eyes of many are requisite for leadership were not found in him. Yet the reference should not be restricted to outward qualities and appearance. The two nouns, used elsewhere also in combination (cf. Gen. 29:17), denote the entirety of the servant's humiliation. When we see the servant we find no beauty that we should desire him.[4] Our judgment, in other words, is according to the outward appearance and is not just and true. It is a sad picture. The servant dwelt in the midst of his own people, and behind his physical form the eye of faith should have seen the true glory; but looking upon his outward appearance, Israel found nothing of beauty to delight its eye.

This verse does not describe the physical appearance of Christ. On that subject the entire Bible is silent. Rather, the purpose is to show that the appearance of the servant was such that man, judging from a wrong perspective, would completely misjudge him.[5]

3 From the general statement of humiliation given in verse 2, the prophet passes on to a more detailed description. The verse con-

---

3 Ernst Sellin (*Serubbabel*, Leipzig, 1898, pp. 153, 154) refers the dry ground to Babylon.

4 The weak *waw* and jussive constitute a consecutive clause, *that we should desire him*. Isaiah uses the present, *we see him*, for he views the sight as present before his eyes. That construction, advocated, e.g., by S, which interprets "no glory that we should see him, etc." (i.e. see him with favor), imputes to *rā'āh* a sense that it has only when construed with the preposition *b*.

5 Calvin applies this description not merely to the Head, but also to the body, the Church.

sists of a series of predicates, the subject not being expressed. In translation we may represent the thought as follows:

(He is)   *despised,*
          rejected of men,
          a man of sorrows, etc.

The first predicate represents a gradation of thought over "we esteemed him not" in verse 2.[6] That expression was negative but this is positive. The general concept is clear; Esau, for example, despised his birthright (Gen. 25:34); Saul was despised as king (1 Sam. 10:27); Michal despised David (2 Sam. 6:16), as also did Goliath (1 Sam. 17:42); Jeremiah 22:28 and Daniel 11:21 speak of kings that were despised. The word is of frequent occurrence, and simply signifies that men have rejected the servant and thus despised him. The word is introduced again, this being a characteristic of Isaiah's style; and it sets the sad note for the entire verse.

The Hebrew word rendered *rejected* is actually an adjective, *ceasing* or *lacking*, the verbal form appearing in Job 19:14. We should render not by the active, *ceasing from men* (i.e. in the sense of avoiding them), but by the passive; hence the common rendering, *rejected of men,* is satisfactory. The one who fails of men or who is lacking of men is one whom men have rejected. It is of significance to note that *'ishim* (*men*) is not a synonym of sons of men (*b*e*ney 'adam*) but rather designates the better class of men.[7]

The juxtaposition of *'ish* (*man*) with *'ishim* (*men*) is important. Although the best of men reject him, he is himself a man, yet one whose characteristic is found in griefs.[8] The entire life of the servant was filled with griefs; these involved bodily suffering, but they were also spiritual.

The English translation *acquainted with sickness* is accurate, for

---

6 Thus, even though there may not be a grammatical connection with the preceding (e.g. V. de Leeuw), there is a connection in thought.

7 De Leeuw holds that the unusual plural has no particular significance ("*geeft elders niets bijzonders aan*"). Muilenburg beautifully brings out the tragedy of loneliness, appealing, e.g., to Lam. 1:1-3; 3:7, 14, 17; Job 19:13-19. The designation does not necessarily denote leprosy, although lepers were separated from men; cf. 2 Kings 15:5; 2 Chron. 26:21; Ps. 88:5.

8 Lit., *pains*; Vulg. *virum dolorum.* De Leeuw gives a good discussion of the supposed relationship of this passage to the Tammuz mysteries.

the passive participial construction is thus retained.[9] The thought is that the servant himself has been made to know sicknesses. Again, the picture is not that of one whose body is weakened by physical sickness, for the word *sickness* here stands for sin. Isaiah is using the same figure that he had earlier employed (1:5b, 6).

The following predicate is capable of two interpretations, either *and as a hiding of faces from us,* or *and as a hiding of faces from him.*[10] On the first construction the thought is that he hid his face from us; on the second, we hid our faces from him. The second is to be preferred, for the context pictures the reaction of men to the servant, and not that of the servant toward men. We found him so revolting to look upon, because of the griefs and sicknesses that characterized him, that we turned our faces away from him as though he were sticken with some repulsive disease.

As the verse began so it concludes; hence Isaiah again employs the word *despised,* and adds to it the tragic statement, *and we esteemed him not.*[11] Perhaps the purpose is to make even sharper the strong contrast in the following verse.

The unbelief that Isaiah here depicts is the same unbelief found all about us today. Men say pleasant and complimentary things about the Lord of Glory. They will praise His ethics, His teaching, declare that He was a good man and a great prophet, the only one who has answers to the social problems that today confront the world. They will not, however, acknowledge that they are sinners, deserving of everlasting punishment, and that the death of Christ was a vicarious sacrifice, designed to satisfy the justice of God and to reconcile an offended God to the sinner. Men will not receive what God says concerning His Son. Today also, the Servant is despised and rejected of men, and men do not esteem Him.

4   Surely our griefs he hath borne, and our sorrows he carried

---

[9] It may be that ידע is here a cognate of Ar. *wadu'a (wd')*, *humiliated*. This has been argued by D. Winton Thomas in *Record and Revelation*, 1938, pp. 393ff., and *JTS*, Vol. 38, 1937, pp. 404-405. Cf. also G. R. Driver in *JTS*, Vol. 38, 1937, pp. 48, 49. This is possible but questionable. Cf. also J. Reider, *JBL*, Vol. 66, 1947, p. 317. The word *sickness* is not merely figurative, for *heḥeli* in v. 10 seems to reflect upon the word *ḥoli* found here. Sickness comprehends the pain that comes from wounds; cf. 1 Kings 22:34; Jer. 6:7; 10:19. Sorrow may bring disease with it, for an afflicted heart may be accompanied by a weary and bruised body.

[10] Lit., *hiding, act of hiding.* The word is a noun, but cf. 1Q, *mstyr.*

[11] The *waw* may express result, *so that we esteemed him not.*

them; but we esteemed him stricken, smitten of God and afflicted.

5 But he was pierced because of our transgressions, bruised because of our iniquities; the chastisement of our peace was upon him, and with his stripes we are healed.

6 All of us like a flock have gone astray, each to his own way we have turned; and the Lord has caused to meet in him the iniquity of us all.

4 With this verse the prophet sets forth the true state of the case. The servant is indeed characterized by griefs and sorrows, but they were not his own. Hence the verse begins with an affirmative particle, Surely,[12] and thus a certain grandeur is introduced. The chiastic order is of interest; in contrast to the order of the previous verse (griefs, sicknesses), we now have sicknesses, then griefs. To be noted also is the juxtaposition of us and he. We may render: The sicknesses of us he bore. This contrast brings to the fore the idea of substitution, which characterizes this section of the chapter. It points to the fact that the contrast between the one and the many is not merely quantitative but also qualitative. The One is righteous; the many have sicknesses and griefs.

The reference in Matthew 8:17 is appropriate, for although the figure of sicknesses here used refers to sin itself, the verse also includes the thought of the removal of the consequences of sin.[13] Disease is the inseparable companion of sin.

Emphasis falls upon the pronoun he. The verb naśa' (to bear) means more than to take away. The thought rather is of a lifting up and carrying.[14] This is shown by the parallel with the following verb and by the general context, as well as by the usages of the verb. The servant takes the sicknesses that belong to us and lifts them upon himself, thus carrying them. The second verb perhaps does exhibit a gradation, for it definitely refers to the carrying upon oneself of sicknesses and griefs. In applying this verse to

12 Omitted in B. At times the particle is adversative, and it is true that it here introduces a contrast.

13 Hence, Hengstenberg correctly states that the servant bears sin in its consequences, and among these sicknesses and pains occupy a prominent place. Cf. Jer. 10:19. It should be noted that Matthew deliberately deviates from B, which reads τὰς ἁμαρτίας ἡμῶν, to stress the fact that Christ actually bore our sicknesses.

14 Cf. Lev. 5:1, 17; 10:17; Num. 14:34; Ezek. 18:20. Cf. the striking usage in the Code of Hammurabi, the guilt of that judgment he shall bear (a-ra-an di-nim šu-a-ti it-ta-na-aš-ši), Law 4 (vi.3-5). Cf. also Law 13 (viii.23, 24).

Christ, Peter has rightly brought out the meaning, "Our sins he himself has borne in his body upon the tree" (I Pet. 2:24). It should be noted that the consequences of sin and not sin itself are mentioned. Nevertheless, when it is said that he bore our sicknesses, what is meant is not that he became a fellow sufferer with us, but that he bore the sin that is the cause of the evil consequences, and thus became our substitute.

In the last line the prophet gives emphasis to *we*, for instead of understanding the true reason for his suffering, we regarded him as one punished by God with a loathsome and hateful disease. Actually, the reverse should have been the case. We should have been horror-struck at ourselves, the guilty ones, and filled with loving admiration for him, the innocent sinbearer. *Naguᵃᶜ* (*stricken*) has been interpreted by many to refer to smiting with leprosy. In 2 Kings 15:5 we read, "And the Lord afflicted the king, and he became leprous." Among the Jews there was a tradition that the Messiah should be a leper,[15] and this thought is also expressed in some of the ancient Greek versions.[16] Duhm also maintained that the servant was a leper who died from that disease. But it is probably going too far to insist that the Hebrew word necessarily indicates leprosy. Certainly it does suggest the infliction of a hateful disease, as for example in Genesis 12:17a, "And the Lord afflicted Pharaoh with great afflictions." The precise character of the sickness is not mentioned, but we are probably on safe ground in saying that it was a loathsome, disgraceful disease, which resulted from the striking.

By means of a minor change in the pointing the next two words (*smitten of God*) may be made to read *a smitten God*. This, however, is without objective textual support, and certainly contrary to the context.[17] Those who regarded the servant[18] did not consider him[19] a God, but rather one severely punished by God. The final word gives the climax of the false opinion that men

---

15 Cf. Sanhedrin xi (Soncino Edition, p. 664). Cf. Ps. 73:14. Hengstenberg asserts that in Lev. 13 נגע is a *nomen proprium* for leprosy.

16 Aq ἀφήμενον; S ἐν ἀφῇ ὄντα; T μεμαστιγωμένον; Vulg. *quasi leprosum*.

17 Some Heb. mss. do read *Segol* in place of *Tzere*.

18 *but we* — the personal pronoun forms the subject of the circumstantial clause, which here has concessive force, *although we*.

19 *we esteemed him* — as is generally true of verbs that express the preparation, forming into, or making of something, *ḥāšaḇ* takes a double accusative, the first being the proper object and the second an accusative of the product.

had of the servant. It suggests a humbling and oppressing, and is probably to be taken as a general term including the two preceding ones.

5 It is difficult to bring out the connection between this and the preceding verse. We may render the introductory conjunction *But*, and thus emphasize the contrast between the erroneous opinion of those who regarded the servant and the real reason for his suffering. Another emphasis is found in that the pronoun *he* is placed first, thus to show that in contrast to those who really had deserved the punishment, he bore the sins of the guilty.

The predicate is not to be rendered *wounded*, but rather *pierced through*, and there accompanies this thought usually that of a piercing through unto death.[20] Perhaps there is also included the idea of a violent death. The thought is that because we had transgressed, he was pierced through unto the death.

The parallel expression, *crushed because of our iniquities*,[21] means that because we had done iniquitously he was crushed or bruised. The participle suggests the complete destruction of the person involved. Both the expressions in the first part of this verse are to be taken with the statements concerning the servant in verse 4. The transgressions and iniquities, whatever may be the original sense of those words, here refer not to the transgression of human laws but of the law of God. If the iniquities are merely unfortunate errors that we have made, and so in the light of human standards we are not all that we might be, that is one thing. It is then very difficult to understand why our failure to live up to or to obey human laws should result in the death of the servant as our substitute. If, on the other hand, the prophet is talking about something far more serious, namely iniquities and transgressions that God regards as such, then the profundity of the passage immediately becomes clear.

The sins we had committed were borne by the servant. Inasmuch as sin, however, is something immaterial, how can one be said to bear it? The answer is that sin involves not merely an inward

---

20 *meḥōlāl* — *pierced*; cf. Ar. *ḥalla, perforate, transfix*. Cf. Isa. 51:9; Job 26:13. The part. expresses a fact that has become completely accomplished. The servant has died, and not merely fallen into suffering; and his death was violent and painful. Cf. Zech. 12:10.

21 מדכא — *crushed, broken in pieces, shattered*. Cf. Isa. 19:10; Job 22:9; Jer. 44:10.

corruption of the heart but also guilt before God. In saying that the servant bore our sins, therefore, Isaiah is in reality declaring that he bore the guilt of our sins. Yet even guilt is intangible; but guilt involves liability both to censure and to punishment, and with this we meet the heart of the matter. When the servant bore the guilt of our sins, we are saying that he bore the punishment that was due to us because of those sins, and that is to say that he was our substitute. His punishment was vicarious.[22] Because we had transgressed, he was pierced to death; and being pierced and crushed was the punishment that he bore in our stead. It may be that in the violence of the figures used there is a secondary reference to the actual death of the crucifixion, but the main thrust is that as our substitute he bore the penalty that was rightfully ours. If, however, the language is to have meaning, the servant must be one who was himself utterly free of transgression and iniquity, else his vicarious suffering could be of no avail. If one who himself was iniquitous bore the sins of another, then there is a travesty upon justice, for the sinbearer in this case would have need that his own sins be borne by another. Inasmuch as the vicarious suffering is for those who had transgressed God's holy law, and inasmuch as the vicarious punishment of the servant actually sets us free in the sight of a holy God, we may say with assurance that there is only One of whom these words may be spoken, namely Jesus the Christ.

The statement is next made that *the chastisement*[23] *of our peace* (i.e. that procured our peace) *was upon him* (i.e. the servant) like a pressing burden. *Musar is correction, discipline,* or *chastisement,* and does not refer to retributive punishment but often contains the thought of remedy or correction. Perhaps the rendering *chastisement* is most satisfactory. If peace is to be procured, there must be chastisement; and that chastisement fell upon the servant. By the word *shalom* (peace) we are to understand the peace that God maintains toward men.[24] The word involves more

22 At the same time, if we merely say that the servant bore the punishment of our sins, we have not done justice to the scriptural teaching. We must insist that in their fullness he bore our sins. Cf. J. Hein, *Sünde und Erlösung, nach biblischer und babylonischer Anschauung,* Leipzig, 1930.

23 מוּסָר does not mean *instruction* in this context. It is rather a chastisement in which an evil was inflicted upon the servant, and as a result of which he has procured God's peace for us. ". . . As He enters into our guilt, so we now enter into His reward" (Hengstenberg) .

24 "Peace," says Hengstenberg, "stands as an individualizing designation of salvation; in the world of contentions, peace is one of the highest blessings."

than a sense of well-being or weal. Because of our sins, so the thought may be paraphrased, God was not at peace with us. If He was to be at peace with us, there must be chastisement. We deserved that chastisement, but it fell not upon us, but upon the servant. In our place he was punished; and inasmuch as he was punished, God was at peace with us. One is not reading into the text if he asserts that the chastisement that fell upon the servant was for the purpose of propitiation. Because of the servant's chastisement, our deep need of peace was fulfilled. If *peace* refers only to well-being or to material prosperity it is difficult to perceive why the death of the servant was necessary to procure that peace. Rather, this peace is the peace of God that passeth understanding.

Finally, Isaiah declares that for us there is healing, and this healing is procured by his stripes. For us there is now a complete freedom from all those things that caused the servant to die. Actually the verb is impersonal, and we may best render, *and by his stripes there is healing to us,* or *healing was imparted to us.*

6 With this verse the prophet injects a new factor into the picture, namely the reason why the servant had to suffer. *Like a flock* of sheep that has lost its shepherd, *all of us have gone astray.*[25] The verse begins with *kullanu* (*All of us*), and concludes with the same word. Hengstenberg brings out the thought, ". . . We walked through life solitary, forsaken, miserable, separated from God and the good Shepherd, and deprived of His pastoral care." It is best to render the verb by the pluperfect, *we had turned astray.*

The first half of the verse sets forth the reason for the servant's suffering, and the second asserts that the Lord Himself made the servant suffer by placing on him the iniquity that belonged to us all. The verb describing the latter act is in the causative stem and

---

Those things that once stood as barriers between God and ourselves have been removed, and we are now in a right relationship with Him.

25 The reference is not to be restricted to idolatry, nor is there particular reflection upon the state of exile; but it is a designation of being destitute from salvation; cf. Ps. 119:176. In ourselves we are scattered; cf. 1 Kings 22:17; Num. 27:17; Ezek. 34:4-6; Matt. 9:36. Perhaps the emphasis here falls more upon the misery of the scattered people than upon their sin itself. *Flock* suggests the solidarity of the people. The emphasis is not upon individual sheep, but upon a flock that, following one who leads it from the right path, has gone astray. Jer. 50:6 teaches that false shepherds led the people astray; cf. John 10:8.

means *to hit* or *strike violently*. The iniquity of which we are guilty does not come back to us to meet and strike us as we might rightly expect, but rather strikes him in our stead. The Lord caused our guilt to strike him not merely in the soul but in the whole person. The thought of violence is not entirely lacking. The guilt that belonged to us God caused to strike him, i.e. he as our substitute bore the punishment that the guilt of our sins required. Consequently, we are no longer without a shepherd, for the shepherd has given his life for the sheep. Those for whom he served as substitute are designated *all of us*.[26] In this phrase the prophet includes himself and all for whom he speaks. It is not warranted to draw from these words a doctrine of universal atonement.

> 7 He was oppressed, and he suffered himself to be afflicted, and he does not open his mouth, as a lamb to the slaughter he is led, and as an ewe before her shearers is dumb; and he does not open his mouth.
> 8 From prison and from judgment he was taken, and among his generation, who takes thought that he was cut off from the land of the living; for the transgression of my people he was smitten.
> 9 And he gave with the wicked his grave, and with the rich in his death; since he had done no violence, and there was no deceit in his mouth.

7 Although the Lord was the ultimate cause of the servant's suffering, the servant endured that suffering with patience. Inasmuch as the suffering was vicarious and voluntary, it was spontaneous; hence the servant bore it patiently. The words *he was afflicted*[27] form the main sentence, and the two following clauses are circumstantial, expressing the conditions under which the servant was afflicted (cf. Ex. 3:7; 1 Sam. 13:6; 14:24). The Egyptians in afflicting Israel caused them to suffer griefs and to cry out. Similarly the servant has been afflicted as though by a cruel taskmaster. He, however, does not cry out. The following circumstantial clause may be rendered, *and he suffered himself to be afflicted*. In being afflicted he was voluntarily suffering. The same thought is also expressed by the second circumstantial clause, *and he opens not his mouth*. Israel cried out by reason of her bondage, but not the

---

26 Members of the covenant community are conceived as partaking in the general human destiny and not necessarily in opposition to the remainder of mankind.
27 These words sum up the content of v. 6.

servant. No self-defense or protest issued from his mouth. One cannot read the prophecy without thinking of the fulfillment, when before the judgment seat of Pilate the true Servant answered not a word. "When he was reviled, He reviled not again" (1 Pet. 2:23).

Isaiah enlarges upon the words *he opens not his mouth* by comparing the servant with a lamb. Men bring the sheep to slaughter to sacrifice it, and as men shear the lamb it stands dumb. Isaiah repeats the clause not needlessly but to emphasize the wondrous and strange conduct of the servant in his affliction. Possibly the mention of a lamb reflects upon the sacrificial lamb of Exodus 12:3; and John the Baptist, in designating our Lord the Lamb of God, based his language upon this present verse (cf. also 1 Pet. 1:18, 19; Acts 8:32-35). It is the patience of the lamb that is here stressed, and so the female sheep, the ewe, is mentioned as silent before her shearers. The last clause, however, refers not to the lamb but to the servant (cf. Matt. 27:12-14; Mark 15:5; Luke 23:9; John 19:9).

8 Having stressed the patience of the servant in his suffering, the prophet now enters upon a more detailed description of that suffering. The preposition is best rendered in a separative sense, *From prison*.[28] The precise force of the word *'otzer (oppression?)* is not clear, but it may suggest arrest or confinement.[29] In connection with judgment, it indicates a judgment involved in confinement or oppression, one that is unjust. As in the actual fulfillment with respect to Jesus Christ, the hatred of the servant's enemies worked within the sphere and limits of judicial procedure. But the human judgment in itself had no real power over the servant, for behind it was the judgment of God, which punished the servant as he suffered for his people (cf. Jer. 1:16; Ezek. 5:8; Ps. 143:2). God does carry out His judgments in the midst of His people, and the supreme manifestation of His judgment was that which fell upon the servant. It is best to understand *he was taken* as referring to a being taken away by death from the unjust trial.

---

28 H. H. Rowley takes the preposition in different senses, *by oppression and without justice was he taken* (*The Biblical Doctrine of Election*, Naperville, Ill., 1950, p. 116). The preposition may express separation, *from* coercion; or reason, *by reason of* coercion; or lack, *without* coercion, etc., i.e. without a legal trial, etc. The verb *hiqqāh* suggests snatching away, *abreptus est*; cf. 52:5; Ezek. 33:4.

This is supported by the parallel *he was cut off*[30] *out of the land of the living* (cf. Prov. 24:11). From the midst of his suffering he was taken away by death.

Differing interpretations of the following words have been given, but we may take the particle *'eth* as a preposition and render *with* or *among*:[31] *among the contemporaries of the servant, who considered, etc.*[32] The verb implies meditation or giving serious thought to something. That the servant was cut off from the land of the living did not form the object of meditation upon the part of his contemporaries. They should have considered, but did not.

The final words may be rendered, *for the transgression of my people there was a stroke to him.*[33] It is God who speaks. The stroke fell not on behalf of all men but on behalf of *my people*. Again, when speaking of his death, Isaiah must give the reason for that death, namely its substitutionary, propitiatory character.

9 As verse 8 spoke of the servant's death, so verse 9 speaks of his burial. The first verb may either have the Lord understood as subject, or be taken impersonally and rendered in English by the passive. This latter construction is preferable, for actually there is a double subject. What was to be given to the servant by men was dishonor and disgrace; what God would give him was honor in his burial. The sense is *to appoint*, and possibly the verb has a modalistic shade, *one wanted to appoint. The wicked* are criminals who have done wickedly. Men assigned the grave of the servant with the

---

29 The noun *'ōtzer* occurs four times: Judg. 18:7; Ps. 107:39; Prov. 30:16 and Isa. 53:8. In each instance the rendering *restraint* or *coercion* seems suitable. The verb occurs frequently, *to restrain, shut up, keep from*. In 2 Kings 17:4 and Jer. 33:1; 39:15, *imprison* is a suitable rendering.

30 נָגַז is always used of a violent death.

31 The word את may indicate a new beginning (GKC, § 117 i-m), and is an adverbial accusative (specification). On the other hand, the KJV rendering is permissible.

32 The construction of this verse is extremely difficult, and we have set forth the position that seems to be most free of difficulty. V. de Leeuw insists that the particle be construed as *nota accusativi*, and gives to *dôr* the sense that it has in Isa. 38:12, *life: and who is there that still thinks about his life?* B reads, τὴν γενεὰν αὐτοῦ τίς διηγήσεται; and this is followed by Hengstenberg. It is, I think, a legitimate rendering. Note that M places the *Atnah* with *yeśôḥēaḥ*.

33 In the light of Ps. 11:7 and Job 22:2 we are warranted in saying that the suffix is singular. Cf. Gen. 9:26, 27; Deut. 33:2; Isa. 44:15.

criminals.[34] After he had died a painful death, however, he was with a rich man. The two words *grave* and *death* are to be taken together; in his death and burial the servant was with the rich and with the wicked. At the same time his exaltation and glorification, in a certain sense, may be said to commence with his death,[35] for the death was honorable, and not that which wicked men intended. In the second half of the verse Isaiah gives the reason for the turn in the servant's fortunes. The servant was given an honorable burial after his dishonorable death because of his perfect innocence.[36] Inasmuch, therefore, as he had not acted like his criminal enemies, he would not receive disgraceful burial with them, but honorable burial with the rich.

10 And the LORD was pleased to bruise him, he hath made him sick; when his soul shall place an offering for sin, he will see a seed, he will prolong days; and the pleasure of the LORD will prosper in his hand.

11 From the travail of his soul he will see, he will be satisfied; by his knowledge will my servant as a righteous one justify many; and their iniquity he will bear.

12 Therefore I shall divide to him among the many and with the powerful he will divide the spoil, because he poured out to death his soul, and with the transgressors he suffered himself to be numbered; and he the sin of many did bear and for the transgressors he makes intercession.

10 Despite the innocence of the servant, the Lord took pleasure

---

[34] There is no need to assume that עָשִׁיר necessarily connotes rich men who are evil, although that is sometimes the case (Prov. 11:28; Mic. 6:12) ; and there is no reason for textual emendation. Why may not the text mean what it says? The designation of Joseph of Arimathea (Matt. 27:57) as a rich man seems to be a deliberate reflection upon this passage. The singular probably indicates an ideal person, the representative of the group of rich. Among the Jews, criminals received an ignominious burial. The preposition *'eth* must receive its full force. There was a close association in death, which would seem to imply that the rich man belonged to or was on the side of the servant as over against the criminals.

[35] *death* — the Heb. is an intensive plural; "in the condition of death," in contrast with "in life."

[36] עַל is sometimes taken in a concessive sense, *although*; but such a usage is, at best, rare (cf. Job 10:7; 34:6) . B has the causal sense, ὅτι ἀνομίαν οὐκ ἐποίησεν. Cf. 1 Kings 16:7; Ps. 44:22; 69:7; Jer. 15:5; Job 34:36. In reference to the fulfillment, cf. 1 Pet. 2:22. For *violence* Peter substitutes *sin* (ἀμαρτίαν) .

in bruising him. His death was not in the hands of wicked men but in the Lord's hands. This does not absolve from responsibility those who put him to death, but they were not in control of the situation. They were doing only what the Lord permitted them to do. Emphasis falls upon *Lord*, for inasmuch as the end to be attained, peace, is founded upon the divine nature, the means by which it is to be attained must also be in accordance with the divine character and of divine appointment. The pleasure of the Lord had in view the accomplishing of the divine will. Hence, all attempts of sinful man to produce a Utopia upon this earth are not only wicked, they are foolish.

In the Lord's pleasure there was no caprice, nor does the language mean that the Lord took pleasure in the servant's being bruised on the part of others, but rather that it was the Lord's pleasure Himself to bruise the servant. The following verb may be rendered, *he has made him sick*.[37] It is a terse designation of the general degradation that has come upon the servant, and with this verb the description of the servant's humiliation and suffering comes to an end. The following words begin the description of his exaltation.

If we permit the Hebrew text to stand as it is, the words *his soul* are to be construed as the subject of the verb *will place*. Some would take the verb as the second person masculine and render *thou shalt place*. The objection to this, however, is that God is not addressed in this passage but rather is spoken of in the third person both before and after this verb. Furthermore, sacrifices were offered up not by God but to Him. Although the Lord does bring about the death of the servant, He is not the Offerer. In verse 12 the servant receives the reward for his work, which proves that it is he himself who offers the sacrifice. *His soul* is not a mere substitution for *himself*, but shows that the very life is to be the oblation. The prophet speaks of the soul as performing what in reality is done upon it,[38] yet actually it is the spirit that is offered (cf. Heb. 9:14). This oblation is designated by the word *'asham*, which basically refers to an offense or trespass, and then to a trespass

---

[37] *Hiphil* perf. for *heḥeli'*. 1Q reads *wyḥllhw, that he might pierce him*; cf. note 20. In the *Hiphil* the root means *to make painful*; cf. Mic. 6:13. It may be construed as a hendiadys with the preceding, *he has bruised him painfully.*

[38] Cf. John 10:11, 18; 15:13. Note also Lev. 17:11.

offering.[39] In this passage the precise nature of the *'asham* is not primarily in view, but the word stands generically for expiatory sacrifice. The thought of the protasis is that the very life of the servant will be made an expiatory sacrifice. So in the New Testament Christ is said to be our Passover. The verb *śim* (*to place*), which in Job 17:3 is used of the giving of a pledge, further strengthens the idea that the sacrifice is expiatory.

Thus it may be seen that the results described occur only because the servant himself brings an expiatory sacrifice. The first of these results is that he will see a seed, i.e. his own seed, those whom he by his vicarious suffering and expiatory sacrifice has redeemed from the guilt and the power of their sins, a great multitude that no man can number. These are the ones for whom he offers his soul as an oblation, the many nations that he sprinkles, the many (v. 11) whom he justifies, whose sins he bears (v. 5), who are assigned to him and for whom he makes intercession. The term *seed* is obviously used in a spiritual sense, such as *sons of God* in Genesis 6:2; Proverbs 4:20; 19:27 and Ecclesiastes 12:12. Note also Matthew 9:2; John 13:33; 1 Corinthians 4:17; 1 Timothy 1:2; 1 Peter 5:13.

Hengstenberg suggests that in the death of the servant there will be an animating power and thereby he will found his Church. The introductory particle of the protasis, *'im* (*when*), shows that if there is to be a seed, i.e. the redeemed, the expiatory sacrifice of the servant must take place. Without the vicarious atonement there can be no redeemed people, no Church. Hence, all attempts to increase and to propagate the Church apart from the cross of Christ are in vain and doomed to failure. On the other hand, where the doctrine of Christ's satisfaction is proclaimed in its biblical fullness, there the true Church progresses.

It is of importance also to note that the servant himself will see the seed. If he were to die and remain dead, this would be impossible. Hence, this verb makes clear that death will not hold the servant, but rather, after his death he will again come to life and as a living one will see his seed.

---

39 Cf. Matt. 20:28. λύτρον clearly points to the *'āšām* of this passage. Cf. Num. 5:5ff. for the essential idea of the *'āšām*. It is the idea of incurred debt that is prominent, for sin is a robbing of God. Cf. Lev. 5:14-16; 7:17; 14:14-31; 19:20-22. For a thorough discussion cf. Hengstenberg, *Dissertations on the Genuineness of the Pentateuch*, Vol. II, pp. 174-179.

To *prolong days* is to live long years.[40] He will prolong days so that they stretch out into many years. The phrase shows that the servant will live eternally, for it evidently refers to the promise God gave to David and his seed (cf. Ps. 21:5; 2 Sam. 7:13, 16; Ps. 89:4 and 132:12). "It is," as Hengstenberg rightly points out, "the life of the Servant of God in communion with His seed, in carrying out the will of God," and not a life in isolation.

In a concluding clause Isaiah sums up the interpretation of the work of the servant. Through the hand of the servant, i.e. through his mediation, the thing that the Lord had pleasure in, namely the purpose that sinners should be redeemed and justified, *will prosper*. It is the servant who carries out and will carry out to its fullest extent what God has determined to accomplish. The word *hand* may denote ministry, as for example "by the hand of Moses" in Numbers 36:13.

Thus, the suffering of the servant is the will of God, and not in vain. Furthermore, through this death the blessings of redemption and the fulfillment of the pleasure of God are brought to pass.

11 The introductory preposition is causative and denotes the efficient or procuring cause of the exaltation. It thus expresses the same thought as verse 10. Because the servant has suffered such great anguish of soul, he shall have abundant satisfaction. Perhaps the two following verbs are to be taken as a hendiadys; *he shall see with abundant satisfaction*. No object is supplied, but we are probably to understand as the object all the fruits and rewards of his Messianic suffering.[41] This sight will be satisfied. As at the creation God exhibited satisfaction in His handiwork, so the servant sees the results of his ignominious death and is abundantly satisfied. The expiatory suffering has been successful. His people are redeemed and justified. Note the similarity of sound between *yir'eh zera'* (v. 10) and *yir'eh yisba'* (v. 11). In the light of 49:4, how glorious is this declaration!

According to the Masoretic accentuation the following phrase, *beda'to* (*through his knowledge*), is to be construed with what

---

40 This may be a reflection upon the royalty of the servant; cf. Deut. 17:20; 1 Kings 3:14.

41 1Q supplies *'wr* as object; likewise B δεῖξαι αὐτῷ φῶς. If this be correct, it would mean that the servant sees light, i.e. life, in the sense that he lives again. The reference cannot be to the light of salvation, for whereas the servant dies to procure that light for others, he himself is in no need thereof.

follows and not with what precedes.[42] Is the suffix, however, to be taken as subjective or objective? Is Isaiah speaking of the knowledge that the servant himself possesses or of knowledge of the servant on the part of others? Both of these positions have had their capable defenders.[43] If the suffix is subjective, then we are taught that the servant performs his work of justification through his own knowledge. The Spirit of wisdom and knowledge had rested upon him (Isa. 11:2), and so he judges the poor with righteousness (11:4b). On the other hand, if the suffix is objective, the phrase is speaking of a practical knowledge of the servant upon the part of others, a knowledge that approximates faith. Thus, Alexander has said, "The only satisfactory construction is the passive one which makes the phrase mean *by the knowledge of him* upon the part of others; and this is determined by the whole connexion to mean practical experimental knowledge, involving faith and a self-appropriation of the Messiah's righteousness, the effect of which is then expressed in the following words."[44] In this context the servant appears, not as a teacher, but as a savior. Not by his knowledge does he justify men, but by bearing their iniquities.

We may render the following clause: *my servant as a righteous one will justify.*[45] The verb has reference to forensic justification and not to the condition of the person justified. It does not refer to a *iustitia infusa.*[46] The qualitative distinction between the one and the many stands out sharply. The one possesses righteousness; the many, iniquities. Nevertheless, there is a glorious interchange, and it is this fact that determines the connotation of the verb *yatzdiq* (*he will justify*). The servant bears the iniquities of the many that he may expiate them, and they in turn receive his

---

[42] North, however, translates, *and have fullness of knowledge.*

[43] The best recent defense of the position that the genitive is subjective is given by John Murray, *The Epistle to the Romans*, Vol. I, Grand Rapids, 1959, pp. 375-383. Cf. also the discussion given by Delitzsch.

[44] Cf. *the love of God*, Luke 11:42. What justifies the many is not the knowledge of the servant but his bearing their iniquities. In any case, the interpretation *by his humiliation* (cf. note 9) is not satisfactory.

[45] It is true that the appositional relation of adjective and noun is not of frequent occurrence, but such a construction here yields a good sense. Actually *tzaddiq* stands substantively; cf. Jer. 3:7, 10. By this position of *tzaddiq* the righteousness of the servant and his work of justification stand side by side.

[46] At this point Delitzsch reads too much into the text. The emphasis is upon bearing iniquities.

righteousness. He pronounces them to be just. If the verb is not taken as forensic and if it is held that it refers to *iustitia infusa*, it would follow that the servant, in bearing the iniquities of the many, is himself infused with these iniquities and himself becomes sinful.

When the servant bears the iniquities of the many and has been punished for the guilt of these iniquities, the act of bearing the iniquities in itself has not changed the character of those whose iniquities are borne.[47] When the iniquities are borne, i.e. when the guilt those iniquities involve has been punished, the servant may declare that the many stand in right relationship with God. Their iniquities will no longer be able to rise up and accuse them, for the guilt of those iniquities has been punished. Thus, they are justified. They are declared to be righteous, for they have received the righteousness of the servant and they are received and accepted by God Himself. Of them God says that they no longer have iniquities, but they do have the righteousness of the servant. This can only be a forensic justification.

12 The introductory *Therefore* calls to mind the "Therefore" of Philippians 2:9. Inasmuch as the servant has so willingly suffered, therefore the Lord will act.[48] Some would take *the many* as object of the verb *he will divide*, but it is questionable whether this accurately expresses the original. Due recognition must be given to the preposition.[49] The thought is that the servant will be as successful and triumphant in his mission as other victors were in theirs. There are many who are victors and they will receive the spoils of their victory. Among them is the servant. Perhaps it is true that *many* here signifies *great ones*, or *mighty*, but of this one cannot be certain.[50] The speaker is God.

The following preposition is to be rendered *with*. The servant

---

47 We must maintain the distinction between justification and sanctification.

48 Some would connect *therefore* with the cause of v. 12c rather than as introducing an apodosis to v. 11. This is possible.

49 אחלק with ב signifies *to give a portion in, to divide among*, as in Job 39:17. B διὰ τοῦτο αὐτὸς κληρονομήσει πολλούς is incorrect, as is Vulg. *ideo dispertiam ei plurimos.*

50 Hengstenberg opposes this; Delitzsch favors it as being supported by the parallelism. To have a portion in something is to have a portion among the great. But a comparison with *rabbîm* in v. 11 and in 12c refutes this view. De Leeuw, however, remarks, "*Samen met machtigen duidt het op overwinnars in de strijd.*"

appears as the primary agent who divides the spiritual victories and fruits (i.e. the spoil) with the mighty (cf. Prov. 16:19). Those who are here spoken of as *the many* and *the strong* are the spiritual seed mentioned in verse 10. His people participate in the enjoyment of the spoils of his victory.

The chapter closes with a recapitulation of the reasons why the servant is so gloriously exalted. He exposed his soul unto death; he voluntarily laid it bare even to death. No man took his life from him, but he laid it down of himself. In the second clause the verb may have a reflexive sense *(he permitted himself to be numbered)*. In our Lord's being crucified between thieves we see one fulfillment of this prophecy, although the passage is not exhausted therein.[51]

Although he permitted himself to be numbered with the transgressors, nevertheless, he bore the sin of many.[52] These transgressors are not mere evildoers, but are criminals. Thus the New Testament interprets the passage (cf. Luke 22:37; Matt. 26:54, 56; Mark 15:28). This is a clear-cut declaration of the work of the servant in his suffering. Finally, the servant will make intercession for the transgressors. The conjunction suggests a gradation; in addition to having borne the sins of many, the servant will also make intercession for the transgressors.[53] Here again there is reflection upon a priestly work of the servant, who pleads before God the merit and virtue of his atoning work as the only ground of acceptance of the transgressors for whom he dies. The basis of the intercession is the substitutionary expiation of the servant. "Worthy is the Lamb that was slain to receive power, and riches, and wisdom, and strength, and honour, and glory, and blessing" (Rev. 5:12).

[51] These were not merely sinners, but actual criminals. Thus our Lord understood these words (Luke 22:37; cf. also Mark 15:28).

[52] והוא — *yet he*; the conjunction and pronoun show that the following words are not grammatically dependent upon *taḥat 'ašer*.

[53] Intercession and bearing sin are here brought intimately together. The intercession refers not merely to prayer but includes the bearing of sin. Cf. Rom. 8:34; Heb. 9:24; 1 John 2:1.

1 Sing, O barren, that did not bear; break forth into a cry and cry aloud, she that did not writhe: for more are the children of the desolate than the children of the married woman, saith the LORD.

2 Widen the place of thy tent, and the curtains of thy dwellings, let them stretch out, hinder it not; lengthen thy cords and strengthen thy stakes.

3 For right and left shalt thou break forth; and thy seed shall possess nations, and cause to inhabit desolated cities.

4 Fear not, for thou shalt not be ashamed, and be not abashed, for thou shalt not display shame; for the shame of thy youth thou shalt forget, and the reproach of thy widowhood thou shalt not remember anymore.

5 For thy husband is thy Maker, the LORD of hosts is his name; and thy Redeemer is the Holy One of Israel, the God of all the earth shall he be called.

1 In chapter fifty-two redemption and deliverance had been promised to the people of God, addressed as Zion and Jerusalem. (*Zion* occurs four times; *Jerusalem* four; *my people* three; *his people* once). In chapter fifty-three the work of redemption is described as spiritual. In the present chapter, therefore, the prophet turns to the redeemed ones, the Church, and speaks of its glorious exaltation. From this point on through chapter fifty-seven, i.e. to the conclusion of the second part of this larger section of the prophecy (40–66), the people are no longer addressed as Zion or Jerusalem. The names of the city, which figuratively had represented the Church, are now removed; and the prophet speaks of the spiritual glory that awaits God's people. By coming to the Church, Isaiah causes us to understand more deeply the value and efficacy of the servant's atoning work. The sufferings of the servant were for the Church, his body, and not for himself.

The Church is addressed as the barren one[1] that has not borne. Thus a double description, first positive and then negative, emphasizes Zion's barrenness.[2] She is commanded to *Shout* or *Sing*, i.e. to act as a barren person would not act. Instead of the mourning and lamentation of a childless one, the people are to exult in singing. Two further verbs strengthen the idea, *to break forth* into joyous cries and *to neigh,* which latter verb probably means that she is to utter a shrill cry of joy. Zion is addressed as *she who did not writhe,* the Hebrew using the third person, whereas in English we would employ the second.[3] The phrase *she who did not writhe* forms a parallel to *thou who didst not bear,* but it should be noted that there is no parallel to the vocative, *barren one.* The people are thus designated because through their sins desolation had come to Zion. As long as the Church groaned under her wretched bondage, and as long as she was impure within, no children could be expected from her. Until the Lord redeemed her, she could not prosper.

Now, however, there has been a glorious change. The servant has overcome death, redeemed his people, and breathed new life into his body, the Church. The Church has been in desolation (cf. 2 Sam. 13:20 and Isa. 6:13), but nevertheless she will have more sons than when she was the married wife of the Lord. As the one abandoned to desolation[4] she will have sons, even more than before. Throughout the long years of the theocracy the Lord visited His people, and there was a spiritual seed; but with the bondage a cessation appeared; Zion became a widow. The three imperatives (which probably represent a gradation) show that a new period of blessing has begun. The whole is strengthened by the words *saith the Lord.*

2 To prepare for the great increase in her sons, the Church is to enlarge the place of her habitation. Isaiah uses the figure of a tent, for Zion is conceived as a woman who dwells in her own tent (cf.

---

1 עקרה — the vocative without the article may signify indefiniteness.

2 Sarah's barrenness had also been emphasized; compare too the barrenness of Hannah. Such barrenness was a reproach.

3 Following a vocative the language of address may continue in the 3rd person; cf. Num. 16:6; 1 Kings 22:28; Job 17:10; 18:4; Isa. 10:5; 22:16; 48:1.

4 Note retention of *Tzere* in שוממה׳, which seems to be an exceptional form. The phraseology of this verse has affinities with Isa. 12:6; 14:7; 44:23; 49:13; 23:4; 56:7, 8; 26:18.

Gen. 24:67; 31:34) and is responsible to enlarge that tent. The figure may be intended to suggest that the Church has no permanent abode in this world but is like a nomad, travelling from place to place until she come to her final and enduring abode, the heavenly city.

The work of the tent, as is the case in Arabia today, was largely done by the women.[5] The *place* of the tent may either be the space within the tent or, more likely, the place upon which the tent is erected. The *curtains* are the cloth that is stretched from pole to pole to form the tent itself. These were generally woven from goat hair (cf. Ex. 26:7), and formed the *dwellings* (note the plural). The verb is masculine, and hence is perhaps to be taken impersonally: *let them stretch* (cf. 2 Sam. 16:22 for usage).[6] The *cords* are the ropes that tied the tent to the *stakes* or *pegs* driven into the ground.

The imperatives are striking. First the Church is to enlarge the place where her tents were located. Those who stretch the curtains are to make the curtains longer so that the tent itself will be larger. The Church is to spare no labor in obedience to these commands. She need not retrench but must make room for a great posterity. The cords she is to make longer than at present, and she is to make the pegs more firm in the soil so that they can hold the lengthened cords. Too much cannot be done to enlarge the tents, so gracious is the Lord in the promise of a large increase.

3 The prophet now gives the reason why the place of the Church's dwelling must be enlarged, namely that she, the Church, is going to burst forth on all sides; her seed will inherit the nations and repopulate desolate cities. If *right* and *left* indicate south and north, the Church then is conceived as facing the east. This is possible but not necessary, and it would seem that the intended meaning is *on all sides, on all hands.* The breaking forth calls to mind Genesis 28:14 and may suggest, as Penna points out, a peaceful penetration (cf. also Ex. 1:12). *Right* and *left* possess adverbial force, and indicate that the penetration will be worldwide. The

---

[5] Cf. Jer. 10:20, where the figure has a different application.

[6] The verb is used of the pitching of a tent, and there does not seem to be any instance where it simply means *to extend.* Nevertheless, the context demands such a usage here. Cf. North, *in loc.,* for discussion. The usage of *tent* and *stakes* together in the description of Zion is found elsewhere only in Isa. 33:20.

Church is outgoing, vigorous in its missionary endeavor. To refer the words to local countries, such as the lands of the Moabites and Ammonites in the east and the Philistines in the west, is to ignore the fact that Isaiah is using the figures of the Old Testament to portray or symbolize the great spiritual conquest of the nations through the worldwide preaching of the Gospel. The seed that the servant has obtained will inherit nations (cf. Deut. 2:12; 9:1; 11:23). It will conquer these nations and possess them, so that they too become the seed, adopted into the household of faith. The subject of the third verb (a masculine plural) is unexpressed and is probably the children to be born. The figures are taken from the exile, when cities were depopulated. Now, however, these desolate cities will be repopulated by the seed of the Church. When North, in discussing this passage, uses terms such as revanchism and irredentism, one can agree only if it be understood that the conquest herein depicted is spiritual and not physical. Perhaps there is an indirect reference to the repeopling of Judah's cities after the exile, but the thrust of the prophecy is far more glorious. At the Apostolic Council James brought out the true meaning, when he interpreted Amos 9:12 as speaking of "all the Gentiles, upon whom my name is called" (Acts 15:17).

4 Inasmuch as redemption has been accomplished, the Church is no longer to fear. She will not be disconcerted nor abashed. North points out that the rendering *be not ashamed* is not quite satisfactory; *be not abashed* in the sense of disconcerted with sudden shame is better. The shame is not merely because of disappointed hope, but also, as Alexander maintains, because of previous misconduct. Parallel to *fear not* is *be not humiliated*, i.e. confounded, dishonored; and the reason given is that *thou shalt not be embarrassed*. This last verb means to exhibit shame. North is correct in asserting that all three words display a feeling of inferiority.

It is difficult to determine whether *ki (for)* is causative or merely affirmative. Pieper takes it in the latter sense, and renders by *sondern, ja, vielmehr*; but the causative sense is equally admissible and possibly preferable. If so, the latter line gives a reason for the commands of the first line. The Church will forget the shame of her youth and will no longer remember the reproach of her widowhood. Many commentators refer the period of youth to the Egyptian bondage, when the people of God were yet an *'almah*, i.e.

unmarried, and God had not yet betrothed them to Himself as His bride. Likewise, they refer the reproach of widowhood to the exile, when the Church seemed to be abandoned by her husband and hence had to bear reproach. On this interpretation the figure of widowhood is simply a strong manner of stating that the people appeared to be abandoned, not that the husband had actually died. It is difficult to determine which interpretation is correct. What is clear is that the former sins of the nation from its youth on, which had brought it into the state of widowhood, would be forgotten, and the shame of that former time removed.

5 The prophet now gives the reason why the Church need not fear, namely, her husband is also her Maker. The first two words provide a striking assonance. The first word is a plural participle, and is probably (like *thy Maker*) a plural of majesty.[7] He who is indeed the husband of the Church also made the Church. The reference is probably to the constituting of Israel as the people of God. Parallel to these first two words is: *thy redeemer is the Holy One of Israel,* and each of these expressions points out the relationship God sustains to His people. Israel possesses a husband and a redeemer, although she had apparently forgotten this fact. She must remember that this husband and redeemer is all-powerful and is able to carry out what He has promised. He is the Lord of hosts and the Holy One of Israel. Here again these two ideas, which were made prominent at Isaiah's inaugural vision, occur together. As the *Lord of hosts* is His Name, so also the time will come when men will recognize that He is the God of all the earth and will so designate Him. The two expressions *Lord of hosts* and *God of all the earth,* although standing in a parallel construction in the verse, are nevertheless not mere synonyms.

Unlike Hosea and Jeremiah, Isaiah does not use the figure of the marriage relationship frequently; he rather stresses the holiness of God. Before a holy God the people are guilty; hence Isaiah stresses separateness rather than the closeness that the marriage bond would entail. Here, however, where he does introduce the concept of the marriage bond, he nevertheless maintains that the husband of the Church is the Holy One of Israel. The Church is His bride,

---

7 *bō'ᵃlayiḵ* — The word is evidently formed after analogy with *'ōśayiḵ,* which is plural probably because it expresses an attribute of God.

yet He is the Holy One, and the Church must abandon her impurity and be holy as He is holy.

6 For as a wife forsaken and grieved in spirit has the LORD called thee; and as a wife of youth, for she shall be rejected, said thy God.

7 In a little moment I forsook thee, and in great mercies I shall gather thee.

8 In an overflow of wrath I hid my face for a moment from thee, and in everlasting kindness I have had mercy on thee, saith thy Redeemer, the LORD.

9 For the waters of Noah is this to me, what I sware from the waters of Noah passing again over the earth; so have I sworn from being angry against thee, and from rebuking thee.

10 For the mountains will move, and the hills will shake; but my favor will not move from thee, and my covenant of peace will not shake, saith the one who showeth mercy, the LORD.

6 The prophet continues with the metaphor of matrimony. Zion is set forth as a woman that in her youth had been espoused, and then because of her sins cast off, and later again called back to be the wife. Emphasis falls upon the introductory words, *as a woman forsaken, etc.* The woman is *forsaken* and *grieved in spirit* (lit., *grieved of spirit*). Whereas there is probably a paronomasia between *'azuvah* (*forsaken*) and *'atzuvath* (*grieved of*), nevertheless, the phrase *grieved of spirit* is a parallel to *woman.* The call is a recall into the once existing relationship between God and the people. It is, however, possible to understand it as a call of God long ago to be His bride. Volz goes too far in rendering *He regards thee,* for the verb appears to designate a definite act of God.

We should understand *as* before *woman* in the second line, and render, *and as a wife of youth.* The phrase does not refer to a wife young of age but to one whom the husband married in youth. As a husband recalls the wife of his youth, so now the Lord recalls His rejected people.

The clause *for she shall be forsaken* is difficult. The thought may be paraphrased: "I have called thee, says the Lord, as a wife of youth, for she will be rejected." Implied is the thought that the woman who married in youth will be rejected, but nevertheless the Lord has called her. The verb is imperfect, and expresses what may happen momentarily but what does not become a finished, accomplished, and permanent condition. The phrase *saith the Lord* has asseverative force.

7 God's love, which once had been interrupted, will be interrupted no more. The phrase *In a little moment* may be an accusative of duration,[8] and serves to show that the forsaking was short-lived. God did forsake the nation Israel but not His Church; He had not abandoned His purpose of bringing salvation to the earth. Calvin has brought out the true meaning: "What the Prophet says in this passage must therefore refer to our feelings and to outward appearance, because we seem to be rejected by God when we do not perceive His presence and protection." Because of the sin of the people God withdrew His presence, and their sins hid Him so that they regarded themselves as abandoned and forsaken.

The rejection, however, is but for a moment, for God will regather the nation in great mercy. His tender and merciful love will endure forever. The plural suggests the rich abundance of mercy with which God will gather His people.

In this verse the God of Israel is set forth as the sovereign dispenser of the destinies of peoples, who holds their fortunes in His hands. If He will He can cast them aside and remove the light of His presence from them, but also, if He will, He can receive them to Himself again.

8 Isaiah now expresses the same thought more fully. The first two words constitute an interesting paronomasia, are emphatic in position, and modify the verb adverbially. God hid His face by means of an overflowing anger, which poured out upon the people as an all-devouring flood.[9] Nevertheless, it was a flood of short duration, for in a moment it was past. To those who suffer the removal of God's face, His wrath may seem to be long drawn out; but if they will look upon "the eternal weight of glory," they will see that actually His wrath endures but for a moment.

The loving-kindness that God will show, however, is eternal; and it is God, Israel's Redeemer, who thus speaks. The designation *Redeemer* suggests that mercy has indeed been shown. Isaiah repeats the promise, for during the period of God's indignation (i.e. the exile) it was difficult to perceive God's presence in favor, and the exiles needed the encouragement of this promise. The lesson, however, is true for each time when because of our sins the Lord removes His presence from us.

---

[8] As thus used to indicate a short period of evil the expression is Isaianic; cf. 26:20.

[9] שֶׁצֶף — *flood*, found only here. The reading is supported by 1Q.

9 This verse guarantees the truth of the preceding; "there can be no more outpouring of my wrath any more than there can be a repetition of the deluge of Noah." The particle *ki* (*For*) sets forth the identity of the outpouring of wrath and the flood. "This is the waters of Noah," i.e. "This outpouring of My wrath is regarded by Me (this is to Me) as Noah's deluge; hence, I shall regard my oath in the one case as surely as in the other."

We may render the relative *as*, or *in that*, and the entire sentence may then be translated, "In that I sware that the waters of Noah should not again pass over the earth, so have I sworn, etc." Just as God had sworn that the flood of Noah would never recur, so also has He sworn that He would never again be angry nor rebuke[10] His people as He had done. Neither of the events mentioned can ever be repeated, a truth secured by divine oath. The rebuke is one not merely of words but of deed, the outpouring of God's wrath.

This is not a promise that the Church of God shall never again suffer affliction or the removal of God's favor. It is, however, a promise that a visitation such as was the period of His indignation will never again come to the Church. The tragedy of the exile was that it brought the theocracy to an end, and so it seemed that the Davidic dynasty had perished and the promises of God were cast aside. Whereas other and terrible calamities would come upon the Church, never again would she have to experience anything like this.

10 The stability and immutability of God's promise of grace is now shown by a comparison with the mountains and hills. In the eyes of men, nothing seemed more permanent (cf. Gen. 49:26; Deut. 33:15; Hab. 3:6; Ps. 90:2). It is not necessary to translate the particle *ki* as concessive, *Although,* inasmuch as the normal rendering *For* yields a good sense. The language then becomes a prophecy, like that of our Lord, "Heaven and earth shall pass away, but my words shall not pass away" (Matt. 24:35). The first verb signifies a departing or removing, and the second a shaking or slipping. Sooner would the mountains move from their place and slip away than that God's mercy should depart.

---

10 *migge'or* — *from rebuking.* The form is *Qal* inf. construct, and the *u* vowel is written as *Qametz-Ḥatuph* in a closed, unaccented syllable.

The prophet emphasizes *ḥasdi* (*my mercy, steadfast love, covenant faithfulness*), and the conjunction is adversative, *but*. In distinction from the mountains and hills, God's mercy will not cease being with His people,[11] nor will His covenant of peace slip away. This is a covenant that brings peace to man, and is an equivalent expression for *my mercy*. The reference is to the covenant of grace, wherein God freely offers life and salvation to sinners. The choice of the word *peace* to express the blessings of God is typically Isaianic. Here the thought is that God has entered into covenant with man, and this covenant is of such a nature that it brings peace to man. This truth is confirmed by the utterance of *thy pitier*, i.e. the One who shows pity or mercy to the people, Yahweh Himself.

11 Wretched, storm-tossed, comfortless! Behold! I am about to lay thy stones in antimony, and I will found thee upon sapphires.

12 And I shall place thy battlements ruby, and thy gates, sparkling gems; and all thy border, stones of delight.

13 And all thy sons, disciples of the LORD; and great will be the peace of thy children.

14 In righteousness shalt thou be established: be far from oppression, for thou shalt not fear, and from destruction, for it shall not come near to thee.

15 Lo, they shall surely gather, not at my sign. Who has gathered against thee? He shall fall away to thee.

16 Behold! I have created the smith, blowing into the fire of coal, and bringing out a weapon for his work: and I have created the waster to destroy.

17 Every instrument that is formed against thee will not prosper, and every tongue that shall rise with thee in judgment thou shalt condemn. This is the inheritance of the servants of the LORD, and their righteousness from me, saith the LORD.

11 By means of a threefold address that reveals the depth of woe that has come to the people, the Lord speaks to Jerusalem. It is thus an address well suited to soothe the grief of believers, for, as Calvin remarks, "Whenever therefore we shall see her violently shaken by tempests, and weighed down by a load of distresses, and deprived of all consolation, let us remember that these are the very circumstances which induce God to give assistance." We may ren-

---

11 Note pointing of the suffix, *'it-tēk*, in place of the normal *'it-tāk*.

der *Thou afflicted one,* or *Thou miserable one, thou storm-tossed one,* and *thou who hast received no mercy;* hence, *Afflicted, storm-tossed,* and *without mercy.* These three words of address set forth the condition of the people.

The introductory *Behold!* draws attention to the Lord Himself, who declares that He is about to cause the stones of the city to lie down in *puk.*[12] This word is difficult to render; it refers to a black mineral powder, which was used as an eye pigment (cf. 2 Kings 9:30). North thinks that it may have been similar to the *al-kohl* that Arab women use, and that it would be mixed with a liquid to make a cement or paste. In this context the Lord is pictured as the Builder who will restore the city. Obviously, a builder would not cement stones with *puk,* and so we must understand the whole as a figurative description of restoring the people of God, His bride, to a condition of beauty and glory. Pieper is correct when he says that the reference is not merely to the stones of the city walls, but to every stone of the city; yet he goes too far in asserting that every stone will appear like the decorated eye of a woman.

Nor are we to understand a literal restoring of the city in lapis lazuli. The description is figurative and sets forth the beauty of the restored Zion. Delitzsch may be correct in asserting that the blue of sapphire is the color of heaven, of revelation, and of the covenant. The beauty the renewed Zion receives is given to her from God. She will not be established in her own beauty but in that heavenly beauty her God alone can give.

12 Isaiah now continues and brings to completion the beautiful description begun in the preceding verse. The precise significance of some of the words employed is not known, but the whole serves to give a picture of sparkling brilliancy (Alexander). The phrase *I shall place* simply means *I shall make,* or *I shall bring it about that,* i.e., "I shall make as ruby[13] thy pinnacles[14] and thy gates for stones of sparkling (fire stones, carbuncles?)." Perhaps this stone is to be regarded as not only attractive and beautiful for

---

12 פוך — *antimony, stibium* (of dark cement setting off precious stones). B ἄνθρακα; Aq S T εν στιμει.

13 כדכד — I cannot understand the orthography of *BH*; there should be a *Dagesh* in the second *Kaph, kadkōd,* not *kādekōd.* The word designates a precious stone; cf. Ar. *kad-ka-dah, bright, redness.* B ιασπιν.

14 Lit., *thy suns,* i.e. battlements, pinnacles.

God's people but also frightening for the enemy. *Border* is probably a poetical expression for *walls*. Thus Zion is to be surrounded
with *stones of delight*, i.e. stones whose appearance brings delight.
Delitzsch speaks of the "self-unfolding process of the divine glory
itself, which is reflected typologically in the several gradations of
the manifold play of colours and the transparency of the precious
stones." (Compare Revelation 21.)

13 Corresponding to the outward glory of Zion is the inner
glory of her sons, who belong to Zion because they have been
brought up and nourished by her. These sons are to be *taught of*
(lit., *disciples of*) *the Lord*. In John 6:45 our Lord refers to this
passage, "It is written in the prophets, And they shall all be taught
of God. Everyone who has heard from the Father and has learned
comes to me." The reason for the beauty of the inhabitants is that
the source of the teaching is God Himself, not by a secret divine
revelation to each believer but through the preaching of the truth.
Nevertheless, the proclamation of the truth in itself is not sufficient, for many who hear the truth reject it. In addition there must
be the internal work of the Spirit. Unless the Spirit of God makes
one willing and able to believe, he will not believe. We become
living and precious stones for building the Temple of God, says
Calvin, "when the Lord has formed and polished us by his Spirit,
and has added to the external preaching of the word the internal
efficacy of the Spirit."

As a result Zion's sons will possess an abundance of peace (Phil.
4:7; cf. Col. 3:15), such as comes only to those who know the Lord
and are His disciples.

14 Isaiah now sets forth another aspect of the truth, and so by
variety of presentation makes more emphatic the truth of the
future salvation. He emphasizes *righteousness* by placing it first.
Included in the compass of the word's meaning is the righteousness
of God, manifested in the salvation of the people and accompanied
by a display of inward righteousness upon their part, expressed in
their faithful obedience to Him. The verb may be rendered *founded*; thus, Zion's foundation is righteousness.

As a consequence Zion is to make herself far away from oppression; i.e. inasmuch as she will be founded in righteousness, she will
be far removed from the oppression of the enemy. Zion herself
cannot accomplish this end, but God accomplishes it by a mere

command.[15] The following clause gives the reason for the command, namely, there is no cause to fear. Between the term *destruction* and the preceding *oppression* there is a gradation. Not only will oppression not come near God's people, but even destruction cannot approach them.

15 If enemies should assemble against Zion it will not be by God's command, and even they will come over to Zion. The first word may be rendered *Behold!* It is not necessary and may even be questionable to render "If." Vividness and strength are lent to the verb by the infinitive absolute. The nuance of the verb is usually thought to be similar to that of its occurrence in Psalms 56:6 and 59:4, where it seems to have the sense of *gather*. Hence, it is thought here to refer to a gathering together with hostile intent. In this context it may also have the sense of *quarrel with*. We may render either *they will surely gather* or *they will surely quarrel*. Such gathering or quarreling, however, will not be at God's instigation (lit., *not from me*).[16] This is not to deny that God has foreordained whatsoever comes to pass, but simply to point out that God Himself does not instigate the gathering of enemies against His people.

To point out the truthfulness of this assertion, the writer asks a question, *Who has gathered against thee?* The last two words apparently form an idiom; *He will fall to thee,* i.e. he will desert to thee, come over to thy side. It is a graphic manner of stating that the enemies will be completely overcome (cf. 1 Sam. 29:3; 2 Kings 7:4; Jer. 21:9; 37:13, 14). Pieper points out that here is an addition to what was stated in 41:11ff.

16 That God's promise is true is shown by the fact that He is omnipotent. Not only does He make the weapons of war employed against His people but He also makes those who create such weapons. Because of the solemnity of the message the word *Behold!* is employed. The personal pronoun is emphatic; "It is I and not another." This repetition of the pronoun, as well as the repetition of *I have created,* lends an impression of majesty and striking effect. This verb *bara'* (*create*) is used not only of the original

---

[15] Lit., *be far from anxiety*; the imperative occurring in the midst of a series of verbs describing the future serves to express a definite assurance.
[16] The words may also be rendered, *not by my sign.*

creation and of the new heavens and earth but also of contemporary events. At the same time the thought may be that God has brought the very art of making weapons into existence. The artificer is one who blows into the fire of coals (in distinction from a fire of wood). The qualifying clause points out in what respect the man is an artificer. *Bringing out* refers to bringing out from the fire the weapon designed for its work of destruction. Note the distinction between *blowing into the fire* and *bringing out* therefrom the finished weapon.

Not only has the Lord created the workman but He has also created the one who uses the weapon for destruction, the warrior. The warrior does not act independently of God, even though he may think that he does. This verse is very instructive for the study of divine providence. It teaches that nothing occurs, not even the destroying acts of the enemies of God's people, apart from God Himself. At the same time we are not to blame Him for the evil that men do (cf. the express statement of the previous verse), but in His secret providence God governs the efforts and actions of men and employs them as the instruments of His anger.

17 Inasmuch as God has created the one who makes the weapon as well as the one who uses it, no weapon can possibly succeed in attacking Zion. The Hebrew says: *Every weapon formed against thee will not prosper,* which we render in English, *No weapon formed against thee will prosper.* The phrase *formed against thee* occurs for the express purpose of showing that weapons would be formed to oppose and destroy Zion. To say that these weapons will not prosper simply means that they will not succeed in their design or purpose.

Furthermore, every tongue that will stand with Zion in respect to judgment, Zion will be able to condemn as false. The reference is to a formal accusation brought in a court rather than to irresponsible gossip. The tongue represents the accuser. The phrase *with thee* is probably best taken in the sense *against thee.* When the accusations are brought, Zion herself will be able to declare that they are false. In both these forms of opposition the Church of God will be victorious.

In the second half of the verse *this* refers to the preceding, indicating that security is the inheritance of the servants of the Lord, and that their righteousness comes to them from God. The servants of the Lord are not the entire nation but the true people of God, of whom the blessings mentioned can truly be predicated. In this context it would seem that righteousness is equivalent to salvation, for this righteousness is that condition wherein the people will be secure from the attacks of weapon and tongue. In contrast to the gathering of enemies, which is not from God (v. 15), this inheritance and righteousness are from Him. The final *saith the Lord* is a strong affirmation, an Amen, to the truth of this assertion. The servants of the Lord receive the wondrous salvation herein depicted as the free gift of God's grace, only because the Servant of the Lord suffered vicariously in their stead, and made an offering for sin so that He might see a seed. These servants of the Lord are that seed.

1 Alas! every one that thirsteth, come to the waters, and he who has no money; come, buy and eat without money and without price wine and milk.

2 Why do ye spend money for that which is not bread, and your labor for that which is not satisfying? Hearken, hearken unto me, and eat that which is good, and your soul shall enjoy itself in fatness.

3 Incline your ear and come unto me, hear and let your soul live; and let me make with you an eternal covenant, the faithful mercies of David.

4 Lo! a witness of peoples I have given him, a prince and commander of peoples.

5 Lo! a nation thou knowest not thou shalt call, and a nation, they know not thee, unto thee they shall run; for the sake of the LORD thy God, and for the Holy One of Israel, for he hath glorified thee.

1 Redemption has been accomplished. Both in the introduction and in the conclusion of the fourth servant passage it was predicted that the heathen would belong to the servant. The blessings the servant has obtained for his people have been set forth abundantly (chap. 54) , and now the invitation is extended to all that are in need to come and to partake of the salvation the Lord offers. The introductory particle (*hoi*) is mainly an attention-getting device, but it expresses a slight tone of pity. The prophet is an evangelist with a concern for the souls of men and a realization of their desperate condition without the blessings that the servant has obtained. Those addressed are described by a figure taken from everyday life. In Oriental countries where water is scarce, water is sold by a vendor, who calls out attracting attention to his ware. It is not physical water, however, of which Isaiah speaks; but like

374

milk and wine, water is a figure of spiritual blessing, the water in particular signifying the spiritual refreshment that is offered.[1]

Although the subject is singular, *he that thirsteth*,[2] the imperative is plural, perhaps with universalistic intent. The command is essentially the same in meaning as our Lord's, "Come unto me, and I will give you rest" (Matt. 11:28ff.). Not only is the one addressed thirsty, but he is also unable to satisfy that thirst. In theological language we may say that he is totally depraved and totally unable to remove that depravity.

Five imperatives follow: *come, buy and eat, even come, buy*. The first implies that the needy one is not at the place of relief and must come to that place. The word for *buy* is used in particular of the purchase of food (cf. Gen. 41:57; 42:2, 5; Prov. 11:26). But how can one buy without money? The language is evidently designed to point out that the water, wine, and milk are obtained not by human purchase but by divine grace, the free gifts of God. Nevertheless, it may be that the form of expression chosen is also for the purpose of emphasizing the legitimacy of the transaction. Indeed, there was a price paid that man might have water, wine, and milk; and that price consisted in the fact that the chastisement of our peace was upon the Servant of the Lord. As a result of that transaction one may eat and his soul will be filled.

For the third time the imperative *come* is employed, and again emphasis falls upon the fact that the purchase is without silver and without price. As water signified the refreshment offered, so wine points to exhilaration and enjoyment, and milk to nourishment. This verse is equivalent to the divine imperative of the Gospel message, whereby men who are lost are commanded to come to Christ and in Him to find the blessings that they so desperately need and that He alone can give. To restrict this invitation to the exiles in Babylonia as hungry and thirsty is seriously to miss its deep spiritual import.

2 By means of a question the prophet, or rather God through the prophet, causes men to see the vanity of rejecting the free gift of salvation and seeking to labor to obtain it by their own efforts.

---

[1] Deut. 8:3; Ps. 42:2; 63:1; Prov. 9:5, 6; John 4:10ff.; Rev. 22:17. Cf. *JTS*, Vol. 36, 1935, p. 404.

[2] The use of *tzāmēʾ* as a noun seems to be characteristic of Isaiah; cf. also 21:14; 29:8; 32:6; 44:3.

The difficulty of such futile attempts is expressed by the verb *ye weigh*, which reflects upon the counting out and weighing of the price paid. In seeking to purchase bread they are deceived, for what they obtain is *not bread*.[3] The reference is not to excessive preoccupation devoted to obtaining material benisons in the land of exile. Rather, the reference is general, addressed to all in the servitude of sin. Nor are those addressed simply seeking to obtain the necessities of life; rather their entire endeavor is to procure the fullness of life that cannot be obtained by the efforts of sinful men.

Your toil is probably also to be understood as the object of *ye weigh*. Hence, the words refer to the result or product of the toil, what has been acquired through toil, perhaps *your wealth* (cf. Jer. 20:5; Hos. 12:8). Those addressed are weighing out what they have earned by toil for things that bring no satisfaction (lit., *for what is not for satiety*). The double occurrence of the root may be rendered, *Hear indeed* (lit., *Hear in hearing*). Alexander seeks to bring out the force, *Hearken! hearken!* which has the merit of preserving the double occurrence of the root. The words *unto me* are prominent. Hitherto the people had been hearkening unto everyone but the Lord. To hearken to God, however, means to shut out all other voices and to listen in obedience. *Eat good* is immediately connected with the preceding by the conjunction. If the people hearkened and also ate, their soul might *delight itself in fatness*. *Fatness* stands for the best of luxuriant food, in contrast to the leanness and nothingness of what the people were striving after, just as *good* in contrast to *not bread* signifies what is genuinely good. That *nephesh* (*soul*) should here be rendered by "taste" or "appetite" seems questionable. It appears to stand for *self*. "If you hear and eat, you will delight yourselves in fatness."

3 In slightly different language Isaiah repeats the thoughts of the preceding verse. To *Stretch* or *Incline* the ears is to set them so that they hear only what is being spoken by the One who utters the command. The singular *ear* is collective. The parallel manner of expression in the first part of the verse should not be overlooked:

> *Incline your ear . . . and come unto me*
> *Hear . . . and your soul will live.*

---

[3] The negative forms a negative compound, *the not-bread*.

Obviously *nephesh (soul)* cannot be rendered by "appetite" here, although North thinks that there may be an implied contrast between this usage and that of the preceding verse, for he says that here there is no emphasis on the soul as distinct from the body. This is true enough; but even though *nephesh* may here serve to indicate the person or self, it is possible that there is reflection upon the soul. While the whole person lives, the choice of this particular word may suggest the spiritual life. Note that the apocopated form may have the force of a future or possibly even of an imperative.

In the concluding half of the verse the Lord announces His gracious intention to make a covenant.[4] *For you* or *with you* is to be construed as an ethical dative of advantage, *for your benefit.* Note the divine initiative; it is God who approaches man in covenant. The word *'olam* may at times be rendered *lasting,* but the context here precludes it. The salvation is universal and spiritual; it is inconceivable that it is only to endure for a time. The covenant is an everlasting one, and hence is unlike that made at Sinai. *The faithful mercies of David* stands in opposition to *covenant.* *Ḥesed* designates the steadfast faithfulness that should characterize those who belong to the covenant. In the present context, which reflects upon 2 Samuel 7, the word calls attention to the faithfulness of God in giving the promises to David. *Mercies* may not be entirely inappropriate as a rendering, if we remember that the essence of the covenant is mercy shown to man and that this mercy is constant. These *mercies* are *faithful,* i.e. sure and constant, never failing.

4 The fundamental exegetical question in this verse revolves around the object of the verb *I have given.* Penna renders, *I have given thee,* and applies the object to Israel. This is without textual support. Others take the suffix, *him,* as referring to the historical David just mentioned. Thus Delitzsch holds that David was a witness by the power of his word, "the conquering might of his Psalms, the attractive force of his typical life." There are severe difficulties in such an interpretation. For one thing, the introductory *hen (Behold!)* usually refers to the future. More important, however, is the fact that a reference to what God did once for the

---

[4] The weak *waw* with the imp. with cohortative ending expresses determination.

actual David seems strange at a point where the thought has to do
with the introduction of the spiritual kingdom of the seed of
David. Nor does the description seem accurately to apply to the
historical David.

Perhaps the answer is suggested by the phrase in verse 3, *the sure
mercies of David*. These are the mercies that were promised to
David, namely that his seed should ever be upon his throne. In
Acts 13:34, the phrase is directly applied to Christ (cf. Isa. 9:6 and
Luke 1:32, 33). The suffix in the verb *I will give him* refers, it
would seem, to the seed of David, who is brought to the fore in the
phrase *the sure mercies of David*. The context requires that in this
verse the suffix refer to the seed of David, the Messiah. In the
following verse it is the seed of David who acts and calls the
unknown heathen into his kingdom. The subject in both verses is
the same.

Emphasis falls upon the position of the one whom God appoints.
He is a witness, not in the sense of a witness in court, but as one
who through his life and words proclaims the truth to the nations.
He will be a witness both against sinners (Mal. 3:5) and on behalf
of the truth (John 18:37). To the nations the truth was not known
as it was to Israel, and hence it is to them that the Messiah is a
witness. The repetition of *nations* is characteristically Isaianic, and
shows the importance that they occupy in this verse. They are the
ones to whom the truth is to be preached. They must learn of the
sure mercies of David. Two other functions are also mentioned;
the Messiah is to be a *nagid* (i.e. *prince, leader,* first among
equals). In Daniel 9:25 this designation is applied to the Messiah
(cf. the New Testament usage in Acts 3:15; Heb. 2:10; Rev. 1:5).
The third designation, *commander*, is essentially the same as *nagid*.
Perhaps *nagid* designates the person according to position and
authority and *m^etzawweh* (*commander*) according to work. In
these three designations there appears the work of prophet and
king, two of the principal functions of the Messiah.

5 As in verse 4, the introductory *hen (Behold!)* is asseverative,
and here apparently points to the future. The reference is not to
the nation Israel alone, but to the seed of David of the preceding
verse. Whether in its first occurrence *goi (nation)* is a singular or a
collective (*nations*) is difficult to determine. The modifying verb is
singular, whereas with the second occurrence it is plural. *To call*
here signifies "to call effectively," to bring by a call into the

kingdom. The Messiah is addressed, and his work is to call a nation he does not know so that that nation becomes his people, brought into the household of faith. The expression *thou knowest not* does not mean that the Messiah was unaware of the existence of this nation, but that he had not hitherto known it as his own. Herein lies the wonder of the work. Not only does the seed of David redeem his people whom he had known and over whom he rules on David's throne, but he also calls unknown nations to himself as members of his worldwide kingdom and rules over them.

In the second instance *goi (nation)* must be collective, for it is used with plural verbs. Nations that did not know the Messiah, when they hear his efficacious witness (for he is witness and prince) will run unto him. The verb *run* indicates the efficacy of the call. When unknown nations hear this call from David's seed, they come in all haste to him.

The concluding section of the verse gives the reason for these actions; they are for the sake of Israel's God. The two prepositions *for the sake of (lᵉmaʿan)* and *for (lᵉ)* are practically equivalent in meaning here. The Lord is the God of the Messiah, who abides with him throughout his entire ministry of reconciliation. He is also the Holy One of Israel, who is now to include others in his kingdom of righteousness. He has glorified the Messiah (cf. also John 17:1, 5; Acts 3:13). This God has done in making the Son of David the King over this universal and eternal kingdom of blessing in which both Jews and Gentiles are included.

6　Seek ye the LORD while he may be found, call upon him while he is near.

7　Let the wicked forsake his way, and the man of iniquity his thoughts; and let him return unto the LORD, that he may have mercy upon him, and unto our God, for he will multiply to pardon.

8　For my thoughts are not your thoughts, and not are your ways my ways, saith the LORD.

9　For as heaven is higher than earth, so are my ways higher than your ways and my thoughts than your thoughts.

10　For as the rain comes down and the snow from heaven and returneth not thither, but watereth the earth and causeth it to bring forth and to sprout, and giveth seed to the sower and bread to the eater.

11　So will be my word, which goes out from my mouth, it will not return unto me void; but it will do that which I please and it will prosper in respect to that which I have sent it.

12 For in joy ye shall go out and in peace ye shall be led; the mountains and the hills will break forth before you in a ringing cry, and all the trees of the field will clap the hand.

13 Instead of the thorn bush will come up the cypress, instead of the brier will come up the myrtle; and it shall be to the Lord for a name, for an eternal sign which will not be cut off.

6 After the glorious declarations of salvation just uttered, the prophet commands all men to seek the Lord. There is no reason to restrict this invitation to one particular period in Jewish history nor to the Jews generally; rather, it would seem, in the light of the fact that the Gentiles are to be included in the household of faith (vv. 4, 5), that the invitation is universal, addressed to all who are wicked and men of iniquity. *Seek* is not to be restricted to sacrifice nor even to prayer, nor to a combination of both. The basic meaning is "to tread," and the action of seeking is probably the stepping to God, or simply the coming to Him. This is to take place, however, when God permits Himself to be found (such is the force of the *Niphal* stem). Sovereign grace is apparent in these words. God cannot be found at any time but only when He desires to be found. What is implied is that the present, when these commands are given, is the time of salvation. The thought is similar to that expressed in 2 Corinthians 6:2 and John 12:35.

Parallel to *seek* is *call him* (i.e. *call upon him*). The two expressions together signify the repentance of faith and obedience. They involve an abandonment of the old way of life, the way of the wicked and the man of iniquity, and a whole-souled turning unto the true God in humble repentance. And this must be done *while he is near*. The expression does not suggest that He is a local God who can move about from place to place at will, but rather is a forceful way of stating—similar to the parallel *while he may be found*—that now is the day of salvation.

7 The command to repentance continues, although the imperatives are now replaced by jussives.[5] Furthermore, whereas verse 6 was positive, here the commands are negative. Thus the command is full, demanding not merely a turning away from what was evil but a turning to God and a wholehearted embracing of His promises of salvation. The *wicked* man is the one who is guilty of sin

5 The jussive has the force of a command as in Deut. 15:3.

against God, and his *way* is the evil course of life which he follows and upon which he walks. He is to abandon this, no longer walking upon it, but instead is to turn unto the Lord. Likewise, *the man of iniquity*, i.e. the man whose life is iniquitous in that all goodness is absent from it, is to abandon the *thoughts*, i.e. the evil designs and purposes, that fill his heart.

The prophet, or more accurately, God through the prophet, is not addressing two classes of people; but the terms *wicked* and *man of iniquity* are practical synonyms, and the command demands a complete abandonment of all evil, both of outward life and disposition and of the heart within. For if one abandons overt ways that are evil and yet regards iniquity in the heart, he has not truly repented, nor fulfilled the requirements of this verse.

Having forsaken these evil ways, the man of iniquity is to return to the Lord. The verb implies that he has once been with the Lord but has departed from Him to walk upon a way of evil and to abandon himself to designs of wickedness. Hence the force of the verb, *return*, must be noted. *And he will have mercy* is probably to be understood as a consequent of *let him return*. The thought is not that one must first return in order that God may show mercy, for the very act of returning is a manifestation of the mercy of the Lord. Rather, man is to return, and having returned will discover that God will show mercy.

Several commentators think that the words *our God* are out of place in an address uttered by the Lord Himself. But God utters these words through His prophet, in whose mouth they are practically a technical term. The suffix *our* reminds the hearers that Yahweh is their own God, who stands in covenant relationship to them. Even the "nation that thou knowest not" would derive comfort and assurance from the tenderness this term expresses.

The mercy proffered is not given in niggardly fashion, but God is said to *multiply* or *increase* or *make great to pardon,* i.e. He will pardon abundantly; in his pardon there is an abundance of mercy shown; for "where sin did abound, grace did much more abound" (Rom. 5:20). Volz calls attention to an Egyptian psalm, "If the servant is ready to trespass, the Lord is ready to be gracious."[6] But how different this is from the promise of goodness proclaimed by Isaiah.

6 Volz, *Jesaia II*, p. 144.

8 A striking chiasm characterizes this and the preceding verse. There the prophet spoke of *ways* and *thoughts*, here of *thoughts* and *ways.* The purpose is to state that God possesses *thoughts* (i.e. purposes and designs) and *ways,* and that these are not to be identified with those of man. The emphatic negative before *my thoughts* and *your ways* constitutes a full and complete denial of any identity.[7] Not to be overlooked is the chiastic arrangement of the suffixes: MY thoughts, YOUR thoughts: YOUR ways, MY ways. Emphasis is given to the whole by the concluding statement, *utterance of the Lord.*

9 In what respect are God's thoughts and ways not to be identified with those of man? The present verse answers that question. In order the better to understand what we believe to be the correct view it will be well briefly to examine some alternate positions. It has been suggested that man would never think that the wicked could be pardoned, but God thinks differently. The point of difference on this position has to do with what God and man think about salvation. But as a matter of fact the Jews did look for a deliverer to come, and the promises of salvation were actually known to them. A more general statement of this position is that to man salvation would appear impossible, whereas with God it would not be impossible. This interpretation is thus an example of what our Lord uttered in Matthew 19:26. But why should the Jews think that salvation was impossible when God had uttered so many promises concerning it? Again, it has been held that the Jews were prejudiced against the calling of the Gentiles and this promise was intended to correct that prejudice. Surely, however, this is not the natural conclusion that comes to one's mind as he reads the verse.

There does appear to be a connection between the ways of the wicked, the thoughts of the unrighteous man of verse 7, and the expression *thoughts and ways* in verse 8. The sinner must forsake his own ways, because his ways are not those of God. Alexander, we think, is correct when he says that this at least affords the formal basis of the true interpretation. But in itself this does not do sufficient justice to the language of the present verse. God's ways and thoughts, unlike those of the wicked, are righteous; and for that reason the wicked must abandon his own ways and thoughts.

---

[7] B weakens the verse by inserting ὥσπερ.

God's mercy and grace are such also as could never have entered the heart of the wicked man apart from special revelation, hence the wicked is to leave his own thoughts. God's ways and thoughts are sovereignly efficacious, in that they accomplish all that they are designed to accomplish.

Such thoughts, however, in contrast to those of wicked men, are as high[8] above mankind as the heavens above the earth. Emphasis falls upon the concept of height, and the position of the verb at the beginning of each clause is striking. The implication is that just as the heavens are so high above the earth that by human standards their height cannot be measured, so also are God's ways and thoughts so above those of man that they cannot be grasped by man in their fullness. In other words, the ways and thoughts of God are incomprehensible to man. Even though God reveal them to man, he cannot fully understand them; to him they are incomprehensible. It is for this reason that God's ways are not to be identified with man's ways.

10 The mention of heaven and earth suggests another comparison, which the present verse introduces. The verse also forms a protasis and verse 11 an apodosis. The emphasis falls not so much upon the return of the elements as upon their being sent forth and accomplishing the purpose for which they were sent. The first two verbs are best rendered by the present, *comes down—returns*.[9] Note the chiastic arrangement of this first part of the sentence. The subsequent verbs, however, may be rendered by the past. That the rain and snow are effective is shown by the verbs, *has watered,* and *has caused it to bear,* and *has caused it to shoot forth,* and *has given.* The subject is the rain and snow. Instead of returning[10] to heaven without having accomplished their intended purposes, they fulfill the purpose for which God sends them. In the rain and snow, falling from heaven, we see the power of God bringing to completion His purposes in nature.

11 If in matters so transitory God's power is efficacious, what will it not be with respect to the word that proceeds from His mouth? The introductory *So* (*ken*) refers to what has just been

---

8 The perf. indicates a physical condition (stative).

9 The imp. expresses what is habitual or customary.

10 There is no reason to assume that the prophet was ignorant of the fact of evaporation.

stated. The *word* is whatever proceeds from the *mouth* of God, and does not refer merely to some specific prophecy or utterance. Actually the word of God which comes from His mouth is made known to man by means of the media of revelation. The thought is the same as in 2 Timothy 3:16, in which the Scriptures are said to be God-breathed (θεόπνευστος). The reference is to propositional revelation, and the origin of this propositional revelation (as also in 2 Tim. 3:16) is in God Himself. The word originates in the mind of God, goes out from His mouth, and comes to man either in spoken or written form through the divinely appointed media of revelation. There is no magical power in this word, nor is it charged with a power akin to mana. The reason why it unfailingly accomplishes the purpose for which it is sent forth is that it is divine. It is the very expression of the truth itself and hence cannot fail. It is "quick, and powerful, and sharper than any two-edged sword, piercing even to the dividing asunder of soul and spirit, and of the joints and marrow, and is a discerner of the thoughts and intents of the heart" (Heb. 4:12). The word is God's; it belongs to Him, and for this reason fulfills its task.

The word does not return to God in vain, but rather accomplishes what He has desired and succeeds in that for which He has sent it. What is stressed is the utter efficaciousness of God's word to accomplish the purpose for which He has sent it forth. In this particular context the element of blessing seems to predominate (cf. vv. 1-6); but the thought is not thus limited. Just as the word is efficacious for the salvation of believers, so also is it abundantly efficacious for condemning the wicked. "The word which I have spoken, that shall judge him at the last day" (John 12:48; cf. also Jer. 23:29ff.; Rom. 1:16).

The verse is placed in the future, for the word of God, which will bring about the establishment of God's eschatological kingdom and the accompanying salvation and judgment, has not yet in Isaiah's day gone forth from God's mouth. The final three words are to be rendered, *and it will succeed in respect to that for which I have sent it*. The verb actually takes two accusatives.[11]

12 The introductory *ki* (*For*) is not causal but merely affirms what the Lord has said. Emphasis falls upon the two nouns *joy* and

---

[11] The instrument of an action is here regarded as a secondary object; lit., *which I have sent it*, i.e. *for which I have sent it*.

peace, which when used with the preposition have adverbial force, describing the manner in which the people will go forth. *Joy* or *rejoicing* points out that there will be an absence of fear and a rejoicing in the fact that deliverance has come. Thus Machen, reflecting upon the language of *Pilgrim's Progress*, writes of his hope for the conversion of men, "that at that sight the burden of the guilt of sin, which no human hand could remove, may fall from their back into a sepulchre beside the way, and that then, with wondrous lightness and freedom and joy, they may walk the Christian path."[12] *Peace* here sets forth the condition of being undisturbed by enemies as well as a full trust, confidence, and satisfaction in the One who leads the people along. The two verbs are striking; *ye shall go out* perhaps has its roots in a reflection upon the exodus from Egypt, and signifies the departure of God's people from the bondage of sin in which they had been held captive. If there is any reflection upon an exodus from Babylon, such a departure is only one example of the deliverance intended. The second verb, *ye shall be led*, may possibly reflect upon a processional march (cf. Ps. 45:14ff.). Duhm is correct in speaking of this word as festive. It contributes its share to indicating that the exodus is a glorious one.

Not only will there be no obstacles in the way, but the very mountains and hills, which normally are obstacles to be crossed, themselves break out into a ringing cry of joy and thus participate in the glory of the return of God's people, for redemption is the redemption of all creation. Here is the opposite of the picture given by Paul, that "the whole creation groaneth and travaileth in pain" because of man's sin (Rom. 8:22). The hands of the trees are their branches, but it is obvious that these figures are not to be understood literally.

13 The glorious condition is further described by a change in nature herself. The *thorn bush* (camel thorn?) is mentioned only here and in Isaiah 7:19. In its place the *juniper* will come up. The *sirpad* (nettle? the word appears only here) will give place to the *myrtle*. Thus noble trees take the place of useless and offensive plants, and North may be right in suggesting that the verb *will come up* hints at rapid growth.

The subject of *it shall be* is the glorious change itself. The

---

12 J. G. Machen, *What Is Faith?* New York, 1933, p. 142.

preposition before *Lord* may be rendered either *for* or *to*; possibly the latter is preferable. The prophet is stating, now that he has dropped his figurative language, that the change will exist for the glory of its author. It will be a *name* or *memorial* in that it will ever call to mind and exalt the Name of its author. It will be also *for a sign of eternity*, which will ever testify that God is the Redeemer. The eternity is stressed by the statement that the sign *will not be cut off*, i.e. *destroyed*.[13] The language may have royal overtones. Human kings and conquerors erect memorials to testify of their mighty deeds. The King of Kings also has a memorial, the redemption of the creation. The inscriptions of human kings are often destroyed, or their letters become blurred like the inscription at the mouth of the Dog River in Syria. No later king, however, will ever undo the deeds of Israel's King, nor will any later conqueror ever erase His words. He has redeemed His people, brought them out of the servitude and bondage of sin unto Himself, established them in the heavenly life, and brought about a new heaven and a new earth. His sign will never be cut off.

---

13 לֹא יִכָּרֵת — i.e. indestructible. The imp. may be attached to a substantive, with omission of the relative, to denote a general attribute belonging to it. It thus has practically the force of an adjective. Cf. also 40:20; 51:12.

CHAPTER FIFTY-SIX

SPECIAL NOTE

According to Bernhard Duhm, chaps. 56–66 are the work of Trito-Isaiah, a man who lived after the exile in Palestine at a time when the land was inhabited and the city built. Yet the time was tragic, and there was no human agent, such as Cyrus, to improve conditions. In addition there were enemies, such as the false brethren who desired to construct a rival temple. When the day of revenge came, however, then Jerusalem's walls would be rebuilt.

Duhm held that Trito-Isaiah fell below Deutero-Isaiah in matters of style. His tasks were unlike those of Deutero-Isaiah, in that he believed it his duty to bring before the people their sins, announce the coming day of vengeance, and declare the Gospel to the poor.

In chap. 56 we find a condition, Duhm holds, in which the leaders of the people do nothing, the rich oppress the poor, and the truly pious ones are dying out. 56:1-8 is doctrine (*Thora*) relating to the admission into the cult of eunuchs and foreigners, and whereas it has a superficial connection with Deutero-Isaiah it has no connection with what follows.

Whereas Duhm maintained that chaps. 56–66 were the work of one man, others have held that they are the work of several men. In our exposition we shall seek to point out the relationship of these chapters to the remainder of Isaiah. At the close of the chapter is a list of works that treat particularly of the character of these chapters.

1 Thus saith the LORD, Keep judgment and do righteousness; for near is my salvation to come and my righteousness to be revealed.

2 Blessed is the man who doeth this, and the son of man who will hold fast to it; who keepeth the sabbath from profaning it, and keeps his hand from doing all evil.

3 And let not the foreigner say, who has joined himself unto the LORD, saying, The LORD will surely separate me from his people; and let not the eunuch say, Lo, I am a dry tree.

4 For thus saith the LORD to the eunuchs that keep my sabbaths,

and choose that in which I have delighted; and take hold of my covenant.

5 That I shall give to them in my house and in my walls a hand and a name, better than sons and than daughters; an eternal name will I give to him, which will not be cut off.

6 And the foreigners who join themselves to the LORD to serve him, and to love the name of the LORD to become his servants; everyone keeping the sabbath from profaning it and holding fast to my covenant.

7 Then I shall bring them unto the mount of my holiness and I shall make them rejoice in the house of my prayer; their burnt offerings and their sacrifices are for acceptance upon my altar: for my house shall be called a house of prayer for all people.

8 Saith the Lord GOD who gathereth the dispersed ones of Israel, Yet will I gather upon him for his gathered ones.

1 Those who have received mighty blessings from the Lord have an obligation faithfully to do His will, and in the Old Testament dispensation this would be accomplished by keeping the law and observing the sabbath. As Smart points out, there is in this verse an inversion of style. Instead of saying, "My salvation is near, therefore give ear," the prophet declares, "Keep judgment, for my salvation is near." Emphasis falls upon man's responsibility. The introductory phrase occurs only five times in chapters 56–66 but at least fourteen times (with variations) in chapters 40–55 and several times in 1–39. Likewise the linking together of *judgment* and *righteousness* is characteristic of the entire prophecy of Isaiah.[1]

The prophet is resuming the thought of 55:6ff., and Penna is correct in his assumption that 56:1, 2 may be considered a comment or enlargement upon that passage. Men are to seek the Lord by keeping judgment and seeking righteousness. In chapter fifty-five they were to seek the Lord while He is near, and now the declaration is made that His salvation is indeed near.

Judgment is practically an equivalent of *torah (law)*, as in 51:4. He who keeps judgment seeks to obey God's revealed will (cf. Jer. 5:1). To assert, as does Duhm, that the *righteousness* of this verse is a works-righteousness is to miss the point. Smart also maintains that this verse moves in the direction of the later Judaism, in which God's coming salvation is made to depend upon the nation's keeping of the law. That, however, is not what this verse teaches.

---

1 Cf. 1:27; 5:7, 16; 28:17; 32:16; 58:2; 59:14.

Men are to do righteousness, not in order that God's salvation may come, but because it is already near. Inasmuch as the salvation is near, they are to seek the Lord. Peter expressed the same thought to Cornelius: "Of a truth I perceive that God is no respecter of persons, but in every nation he that fears him and works righteousness is accepted of him" (Acts 10:34, 35). In exercising righteousness the people will prepare themselves for God's righteousness.

The reason for this cry for repentance is given in the second half of the verse, and this reason is stated in words similar to those found in 51:5. *Near* is emphasized by its position at the beginning. This is the Old Testament proclamation of "Repent, for the kingdom of heaven is at hand." The salvation of God[2] has not yet appeared but is near at hand, i.e. will shortly come; and His righteousness will soon be revealed. The righteousness will be revealed in the salvation, just as Paul says, "For therein is the righteousness of God revealed" (Rom. 1:18). When the salvation of God comes, His righteousness is also revealed. Both terms refer to the Messianic deliverance. It is a righteous salvation. Quite possibly the prophet anticipates Paul, and the righteousness of which he speaks originates with God and comes to man from Him, and in it man may stand before Him.

2 By an exclamation expressing the blessedness of those who repent, the prophet actually urges men to come to the Lord. The introductory *Oh! the blessednesses* (*'ashrey*) is found in 30:18 and 32:20, and the combination *'enosh* (*man*) and *ben 'adam* (*son of man*) is used here as in 51:12. The word *'enosh* points to man as weak and frail,[3] and *this* probably points to what follows. *Son of man* is merely equivalent to *man*, and the phrase *holding fast in it* means "persevering in it." The man who does the things that follow and persists in them is the one who is happy.

First of these duties is the keeping of the sabbath so as not to profane it. The expression of the true religion is therein manifest, for this observance constituted a regular remembrance and recognition of the truth as well as a constant profession of the faith. The

---

[2] The phrase *my salvation* is definitely Isaianic; cf. 12:2; 49:6; 56:1 and cf. 51:6, 8.

[3] A common designation of mankind in Isaiah; cf. 8:1; 13:7, 12; 24:6; 33:8; 51:7, 12; 56:2; also Jer. 20:10. The word is found in no other prophetical book. The combination *'enôš* and *'ādām* (13:12; 51:12; 56:2) appears in no other prophet.

weekly observance of the sabbath was tantamount to an acknowledgment that the God of Israel was indeed the Creator of heaven and earth,[4] and that He had delivered His people from the bondage of Egypt and had set them apart unto Himself as a peculiar nation. He who in sincerity and truth observed the sabbath was truly devoted to the religion of Israel, for next to circumcision, the sabbath was the central sign of the covenant (cf. Ex. 31:13ff.; Ezek. 20:12ff.). The sabbath was made for man, and its observance would bring delight and rest to him. At the same time, Calvin is probably correct in holding that the sabbath is used as synecdoche and stands for observance of all that God has prescribed. As a weekly recurrence, however, it would call to mind all that God had done for His people and all that was involved in their relationship to Him.

From the last clause of the verse it is apparent that a mere form of religious service was not sufficient. Man must keep the sabbath positively and not profane it; negatively, he must keep his hand from all evil.[5] Duhm may call this a paltry ideal, but who among the sons of men has ever been able to fulfill it? What God here demands is absolute perfection; note the expression *all evil*.

3 The variety the prophet employs in carrying out his theme is striking. Instead of an affirmative declaration that external disabilities will not exclude a foreigner from the kingdom, the prophet issues a mild command. The foreigner (lit., *the son of foreignness*) is not to say[6] that God has separated Himself[7] from him, for the foreigner has associated himself with the Lord.[8] This foreigner is to be distinguished from the sojourner (*ger*) in that he belongs to a foreign or strange country, and is probably a proselyte. In mentioning the foreigner the prophet is reverting to what he has already introduced in 44:5. Inasmuch as the Lord's salvation is

---

4 The sabbath rest is a creation ordinance. As in Genesis the sabbath follows the act of creation, so here it follows the declarations of the creation of new heavens and earth.

5 A parallel construction to this phrase is found elsewhere only in 33:15.

6 Cf. a somewhat similar construction in 33:24.

7 *yabdîlanî* — note the *-anî* suffix, and cf. *yakkirânû* in 63:16. This form may be a *yqtl* perfect. Cf. J. Friedrich, *Phönizisch-Punische Grammatik*, Rome, 1951, pp. 14, 53. There are, however, instances where *a* serves as a connecting vowel with the imperfect. Cf. Gen. 19:19; 29:32; Ex. 33:20, etc.

8 Note the article with *Niphal* perfect (with *Aleph* in 1Q). Cf. Josh. 10:24; Judg. 13:8; 1 Chron. 26:28; 29:17; 2 Chron. 1:4; Gen. 21:3; 18:21; 46:27, etc.

near, all personal and national distinctions and disabilities are to be abolished.

The eunuch also, who cannot produce seed, nevertheless is not to permit this fact to discourage him, for it will not exclude him from God's kingdom. According to Deuteronomy 23:1 eunuchs were excluded from God's assembly. Isaiah is not ignorant of this law nor is he endeavoring willfully to disqualify it. In pointing to the Messianic age, however, his prophecy transcends the restrictions that the civil law of the Israelites had imposed. The expressions *foreigner* and *eunuch* are intended to represent more particulars than they express. No personal disabilities will exclude one from God's kingdom.

4 This verse is a confirmation of the preceding, and also serves as a protasis, the conclusion or apodosis following in verse 5. The eunuch need not fear exclusion from God's kingdom and favor if he keeps God's *sabbaths*, i.e. the actual sabbath day occurring each week and all the sabbatical institutions that God has ordained; the primary emphasis, however, falls upon the observance of the sabbath day itself. Yet outward observance is not sufficient, for the eunuchs must choose those things in which God delights, namely the humble walking in obedience to His commands; and they must also be preservers of His *covenant*, i.e. they must carry out the responsibilities that devolve upon members of God's covenant people. What is required is the same thing that is required of all who would come to God, a heart of obedience. The variety of expression is striking; an imperfect followed by a perfect with *waw* consecutive and finally a participle.

5 The *house* and *walls* of God do not specifically refer to the Temple in Jerusalem, nor does this verse teach that the eunuch will possess a material monument in the Temple.[9] It is as representative of a particular class, namely the helpless and weak, who have no claim to righteousness, that the eunuch is mentioned. Even those who are so unworthy as to be "dry trees" (v. 3) will receive a blessing from God, for they will dwell in His house forever. Does the glorious salvation of the Lord and His coming

---

9 *and I shall give* — the perf. with *waw* consecutive is about equivalent to an apodosis following the protasis contained in the general statement of v. 4. Thus, *if the eunuchs will keep my sabbaths, etc., then I shall give.*

kingdom mean no more to the eunuch than that he should have a tablet erected to his memory in the Temple yard? What comfort would this be? Furthermore, what warrant would Isaiah have had for declaring that eunuchs could have memorials erected to them in the Temple precincts? This would indeed have been an innovation, and one wonders what led the prophet to think that he had the right to make any such promise. If this is all that the present prophecy means (and Duhm and Volz insist upon this interpretation), how barren it is!

The blessing to the eunuchs is of grace, given to them by God. The words *house* and *walls* have the same significance as *house* in Psalm 23:6, namely, they refer to the household or family of God. The *hand* and *name* are difficult to interpret. Quite possibly they do refer to a memorial (cf. 1 Sam. 15:12; 2 Sam. 18:18), but in view of the general context the language is to be understood figuratively as referring to the perpetuation of the name. This will be better than the honor that a long line of descendants would bring or even the comfort that comes from children. The thought is that what the eunuch receives from God is better than what sons and daughters could give. So great will this blessing be that the prophet likens it to the results that God's word produces; for as the word of God is a sign of eternity that will never be cut off (cf. 55:13), so also will the eunuch receive a name that will never be cut off. As J. D. Michaelis points out, the converted Ethiopian eunuch has a name in the Church that is far more honored "than it could have been by a long line of illustrious descendants" (Alexander).

6 The entire verse stands as a *casus pendens,* the fundamental assertion following in verse 7. As the preceding two verses had spoken of the eunuch, so this and the following mention the son of foreignness. Note the resulting chiasm: son of foreignness (v. 3) and eunuch (v. 3); eunuch (vv. 4, 5) and son of foreignness (vv. 6, 7). The joining oneself to the Lord is spiritual in nature, the "betrothing in mercy and faithfulness" of Hosea (2:19, 20). The stranger has joined himself to the Lord for the purpose of serving Him.[10] The word applies to the service of priest and Levite (cf. 61:6) and thus shows that the strangers will serve the Lord as do

---

10 After *servants,* 1Q adds additional words which may be translated, *and to bless the name of the Lord and they who keep the sabbath.*

His regularly appointed servants. To love[11] the Lord's Name means to love Him as one's own personal God as He has expressed Himself in all His works and ways. The strangers will be servants who serve in love. They are further identified as keeping the sabbath[12] and holding fast the covenant. Hypocrisy is excluded; those who serve must love God.

7 The first verb[13] suggests that the strangers are far away, not from the historical city of Jerusalem and its Temple, but from the household of faith; and that God Himself must bring them to His holy mountain and cause them to rejoice in His house of prayer. Quite possibly the historical Temple suggested the language; but the meaning is not, as Duhm states, that those of foreign birth who submit themselves to Judaism, including circumcision, may be permitted to pray in the Temple. Rather, God brings the strangers into the household of faith and there causes them to rejoice.

The worship of the eunuchs and strangers will be acceptable, for they will worship God as do His own from Israel. This worship is described in terms of the Old Testament dispensation, namely by the offering of sacrifices. *Burnt offerings and sacrifices* stand here to designate offering as such. All the legitimate sacrifice of Israel, that is, the prescribed worship of the Lord, will be acceptable as a delight upon God's altar.[14] The last sentence gives the reason, namely that God's *house of prayer* is *for all people*.[15]

The prophecy has to do with the future. At the time that Isaiah speaks, it is not yet a house of prayer for all people, but this is the condition that will obtain when God brings the eunuchs and strangers into His kingdom. In the old dispensation the Lord was worshipped by one nation in the Temple; when His glorious eschatological kingdom comes, however, the lines of demarcation will be broken down, and all peoples, nations, and tongues will serve Him. This truth is set forth under the ceremonies of the law, which were types of that which is to come. The emphasis upon

---

11 וְלַאֲהֲבָה — as shown by the accents and parallelism, the inf. is to be construed with *those who join themselves* rather than with *to serve him*.

12 *from profaning it* — the particle *min* (*from*) is used with the inf. in a negative sense.

13 *and I shall bring them* — the perf. with *waw* consecutive has the practical force of introducing an apodosis.

14 1Q inserts a verb, *y'lw* (*will come up*) , before *rātzón*.

15 Cf. Matt. 21:13; Mark 11:17; 1 Tim. 3:15 and Jer. 7:11.

prayer shows that the holiness of the Temple consists of prayers
continually being offered there. Here is the beauty of holiness; men
from all nations, brought to His household by sovereign grace, lift
up the sacrifice of prayer unto His holy Name, which they love,
and in His Name serve Him in His house.

8 Not only is there no reason for supposing that those Gentiles
who love the Lord will be excluded, but more than that, it is the
Lord's purpose to bring them into His kingdom. Hence, the
present verse is introduced by the solemn phrase, *Utterance of the
Lord God.* The solemnity appears in that this expression never
occurs at the beginning of a sentence except here.[16] It is used
instead of the ordinary "Thus saith the Lord." The thought has its
roots in 49:6. The Lord God who speaks is He who gathers the
dispersed ones of Israel.

We may render the last clause literally: *Yet will I gather upon
him* (i.e. in addition) *to his gathered ones.* The thought is either
that in addition to those of Israel already gathered God will gather
more Israelites, or else that in addition to the gathered ones of
Israel He will gather others. On this latter view there is a contrast
between regathering the outcasts of Israel and those of other nations.
Perhaps, in view of the prominence of Israel the nation in these
chapters and the similarity with 49:6, we should adopt this second
view. Hence, Isaiah is pointing forward to the truth that Christ later
enunciated: "Other sheep I have which are not of this fold: them
also I must bring, and they shall hear my voice; and there shall be
one fold and one Shepherd" (John 10:16). By the words *upon him*
Isaiah points to the vast accumulation that will occur; nor does the
Lord cease His work of gathering until the last of His elect will
have been brought into the fold.

> 9 All ye beasts of my fields: come to eat, every beast in the
> forest.
> 10 Its watchmen are blind, all of them, they do not know, all of
> them are dumb dogs, they are not able to bark; panting, lying
> down, lovers of slumber.
> 11 And the dogs are greedy, they do not know satiety, and they are
> shepherds, they do not know to understand; all of them have
> turned to their way, each to his own gain from his end.

---

16 In Zech. 12:1 it does begin an utterance after an introductory phrase.

CHAPTER FIFTY-SIX

12 Come ye, let me take wine, and we shall intoxicate ourselves
with strong drink; and like today will be tomorrow, great,
abundantly, exceedingly.

9 What is pictured here is essentially the same as that which is
set forth in Jeremiah 12:9 and Ezekiel 34:5, 8. The shepherds and
watchmen, who should guard the flock and be aware of dangers,
are asleep and unaware. Grievous wolves will enter the flock and
devour it (Acts 20), and it is this fact that is prophesied here
under the form of a command to the enemies of God's people.
These are designated *beasts of my fields* and *beasts in the forest*. As
the verse stands its arrangement is strange; twice the enemies are
designated, and between the two designations occurs a command[17] that relates to both the designations. Delitzsch prefers
another arrangement, namely, *All ye beasts of the field come near!
to devour, all ye beasts in the forest*. There is also the possibility of
making the last designation an object of the infinitive *to devour*, so
that the verse would read: *All ye beasts of the field, come to
devour all the beasts in the forest*. On this construction the beasts
of the field are the enemies, and the beasts of the forest Israel.
Why, however, should Israel be so designated? The construction of
the verse is difficult, but we prefer the first interpretation and
construction.

10 The reason why the enemies will enter the fold and destroy
the sheep is that Israel's watchmen are asleep and unaware of the
enemies' approach. The suffix *Its*, in *Its watchmen*, refers to Israel,
already mentioned in verse 8; and this shows that no new beginning is made here. Gesenius says that the writer merely pauses to
take his breath. What we have here, therefore, is connected with
what precedes. By the watchmen, we are to understand the prophets, who during the exile and subsequently were often unfaithful
(cf. Jer. 29:1-32; Ezek. 34:1-8 *et passim*). The result of the blindness is that the watchmen do not know; not that they know
nothing, but that they do not recognize the nature and approach of
the enemy, who always comes subtly. They do not understand the
nature of the danger. Isaiah speaks not of physical blindness but of
spiritual. The watchman was one who stood upon the tower or

17 Note that in אתיו the *yod* is retained. The form occurs in 21:12; 56:9, 12
and nowhere else in Scripture.

wall of the city to observe whether an enemy was approaching, or
if the word be applied to shepherds, one who kept watch to see
that wild beasts did not approach the flock. From this it is clear
that one portion of the prophetical work was to warn the nation of
its enemies, to tell of impending danger and disaster. A blind
prophet could not know the nature of the danger. The tragedy was
that this condition of blindness applied to *all* the prophets. Isaiah
employs the word *all* twice in this verse.

Changing the figure the prophet compares the prophets to dogs.
The sheepdog (Job 30:1) was kept to bark at the approach of wild
beasts, but Israel's prophets were like dumb dogs that could not
bark. When the enemy approached, they raised no voice of warning. The language is strong; not only did they not raise the voice,
they could not do so, for they were overcome with dumbness.

Isaiah gives a reason for this faithlessness in the following three
participles. *Dreaming*—possibly *raving*; instead of forthrightly proclaiming the revelations of God, the prophets spent their time
dreaming, concerned with their own visions. It may be, however,
that the thought is merely that of inactivity, a detachment from
active and vigorous life. *Lying down*—instead of actively carrying
on their proper work. *Loving to sleep*—concerned about their own
enjoyment and comfort and not about the condition of God's
people. The whole picture is one of devotion to self-enjoyment and
satisfaction and neglect of duty.

NOTE

In the text we have adopted the position that the reference in v. 10
is to the prophets. If this is too restricted, and the prophet has in
mind all the rulers and leaders of the nation, including the false
prophets, as Gesenius suggests, this does not materially affect the
thought. Certainly, the prophets in any case are prominently in view.

What is clearly taught here is the necessity for those whom God
has appointed to watch over His people to declare unto them the
approach of danger. Translated into modern terms this means that
the minister of the Gospel has a duty solemnly to warn his people of
the nature of the heresies and false theories that are ever about them.
He who keeps silent on these matters, under the guise of not wishing
to disturb the peace of the Church, is a faithless shepherd. It is true
that those who have warned Zion throughout the ages have been
accused of causing trouble, of upsetting the progress of the Church, of
destroying her program, etc.; but nevertheless God has built His
Church upon men who have warned that Church of the nature of

error, such as Athanasius, Augustine, Luther, Calvin, and in recent times Machen. When the minister does not warn the flock of false doctrine, he ceases to be a faithful undershepherd of the sheep, and instead becomes a dumb dog that cannot bark.

11 Using the figures of the preceding verse the prophet now gives them a new use. The dogs of which he has just spoken may not know how to bark but they are strong of *nephesh*, i.e. they are *greedy* and their throat can devour all that they seize.[18] Indeed, so strong is their appetite that they do not know satiety. They have never seized or devoured enough to satisfy themselves. Then the prophet adds ironically: *and they are shepherds.* As shepherds, however, they do not know how to perceive, i.e. to act in accordance with prudence. They do not possess the spiritual insight to act as shepherds should act, but rather they are brutish in understanding, and act like dogs. In language reminiscent of 53:6 the prophet points out the selfishness of Israel's shepherds. Their own way occupies their interest, and this is a way of gain for themselves. The last phase may literally be rendered *from its end,* i.e. to its end, to the extremity. The false shepherds sought for all the gain they could obtain. Volz is correct in his assertion that verse 10 pictured the lack of ability of the shepherds and this verse sets forth their character. From being watchdogs, he says, they became a common street dog that "in its voracious desire sticks its snout into everything." When greedy gain fills the hearts of ministers, disaster is sure to follow; their usefulness in God's service is at an end.

12 Not only is the indulgence of the shepherds avaricious, it is also voluptuous. Verse 12 forms a climax, for now one of the shepherds is introduced, without being identified, as speaking and inviting the other shepherds to intoxication and debauchery. This explains the alternation between the plural and the singular; *Come ye and I shall take,* etc. The third verb forms a climax, *we shall intoxicate ourselves with strong drink.*[19] The invitation is to utter debauchery, involving a complete blotting out of any concern or thought for the welfare of Israel. Furthermore, this debauchery is to continue. *And it shall be as this the day of tomorrow,* i.e.

---

18 עֲזֵי נֶפֶשׁ — lit., *strong of soul, life, appetite,* i.e. *voracious, insatiable.*

19 *wᵉnisbeʾāh* — to imbibe, drink largely. Cf. *sabû,* sesame wine. B omits v. 12, although it was apparently kept in Aq S T.

tomorrow's debauchery will be as extreme as that of today when we began to drink. The last three words are an adjective and two adverbs, *great, abundantly,* and *exceedingly.* Penna thinks that possibly we have here a poetic passage that was sung to incite to drink, and compares 23:16.

SPECIAL BIBLIOGRAPHY

Bernhard Duhm, *Jesaia,* 2nd ed., Göttingen, 1902, pp. 379-384.

Karl Elliger, *Die Einheit des Tritojesaia,* Stuttgart, 1929.

Edward J. Young, *Studies in Isaiah,* Grand Rapids, 1954, pp. 39-61; *WThJ,* Vol. 10, No. 1, Nov. 1947, pp. 23-45.

1 The righteous perisheth, and there is no man laying it upon his heart; and men of mercy are taken away, with none perceiving that from the presence of evil the righteous is taken away.

2 He will come in peace; they shall rest upon their couches—walking straight before him.

1 Verses 1 and 2 form a continuation of the thought of the previous chapter. That chapter concluded with a climax, pointing out the drunken debauchery of Israel's shepherds. But what about the righteous? Their end is mentioned in the present verse. *Righteous* stands first, forming a striking contrast with the preceding. In this context the righteous is to be conceived as the opposite of the faithless shepherds, hence, the man who is true to the covenant, righteous in his life and actions because he is himself right with his God. Inasmuch as he seeks not his own, as do the false leaders of the people, he walks in faithfulness to the promises of the covenant. He dies, however, possibly an untimely death (cf. Eccl. 7:15). The statement is succinct. No man places such a death upon his heart, i.e. he does not perceive that the righteous has died, nor does he consider what the meaning of such a death may be. The righteous dies unobserved.

Parallel to *righteous* is *men of steadfast love,* i.e. men of devotion to the arrangements and obligations of the covenant. The term *gathered* is used in the Old Testament of a man being gathered unto his fathers, i.e. dying (cf. Gen. 49:29), and here serves as a parallel to *perishes.* This is not ordinary natural death, but rather sudden death, a dying before one's time. Such deaths are not understood[1] by the godless, for they do not realize that God in His goodness often takes righteous men to Himself to deliver

---

[1] באין — the ב is probably to be rendered *from,* i.e. *from not (without) perceiving.*

them from some impending catastrophe. The *evil* mentioned is general; and from before it the righteous are gathered. Calvin illustrates this point by mentioning the death of Luther,

> . . . who was snatched from the world a short time before that terrible calamity befell Germany, which he had foretold many years before, when he exclaimed loudly against that contempt of the Gospel and that wickedness and licentiousness which everywhere prevailed. Frequently had he entreated the Lord to call him out of this life before he beheld that dreadful punishment, the anticipation of which filled him with trembling and horror. And he obtained it from the Lord. Soon after his death, lo, a sudden and unforeseen war sprang up, by which Germany was terribly afflicted, when nothing was farther from her thoughts than the dread of such a calamity.[2]

This verse begins and concludes with the words *the righteous.*

2 The prophet continues the description of the righteous. *Peace*[3] is a designation for departing this life. To the wicked there is no peace, but the end of the righteous is peace; and here the word has all the fullness that belongs to it. The *bed* is the deathbed, but it is a place of rest. The final clause is a further description of the righteous, *walking straight before him,* i.e. on the straight way he had set before him.

3 And ye draw nigh hither, ye sons of the soothsaying woman; seed of the adulteress and the harlot.
4 At whom do ye amuse yourselves? At whom do ye enlarge the mouth, prolong the tongue? Are ye not children of rebellion, a seed of falsehood?
5 Inflaming yourselves among the terebinths, under every green tree; slaughtering the children in the valleys, under the clefts of the rocks.
6 Among the smooth stones of the brook is thy portion; they, they, are thy lot; also to them hast thou poured out a drink offering, thou hast brought up a meal offering. Shall I for these things be consoled?
7 On a high and elevated mountain thou hast placed thy bed; even thither hast thou gone up to offer sacrifice.
8 And behind the door and the door post thou hast placed thy

2 Translation by William Pringle, Grand Rapids, 1956, p. 196.
3 A verb of motion may have as its object the place with which it is immediately concerned.

memorial; for away from me thou hast uncovered, and hast gone up, thou hast enlarged thy bed, and hast covenanted from them, thou hast loved their bed, thou hast provided a hand.

3 In contrast to the righteous the wicked are now addressed. Hence, *And ye* at the beginning of the sentence forms the opposite of *righteous* at the beginning of verse 1. It is God who speaks through His prophet, and who commands the wicked to approach, i.e. to the place where He is speaking. The command reminds of the judicial processes at law (cf. 41:1; 45:20; 48:14ff.). Two designations identify the wicked. They are *sons of the soothsaying woman*, a case of synecdoche, for soothsaying evidently stands for idolatry generally. It was surely a part of idolatry, although from the word itself the precise nature of this soothsaying is difficult if not impossible to determine. In any case the reference is to the mother of the wicked.

With respect to the second designation there is a difficulty of syntax. The first two words we may render *seed of an adulterer.* The last word is a verb, and we should render either *and thou thyself hast committed adultery* or *and of her that has committed adultery.*[4] Adultery and soothsaying are two designations for idolatry. Idolatry involves a seeking after information from the creature instead of the Creator and a consequent bowing down in worship to the creature; hence it is unfaithfulness to the only One to whom worship may be given. The terms *sons* and *seed* are to be understood spiritually.

4 To impress upon them more forcefully their wickedness the prophet asks some rhetorical questions. The first verb suggests the making of malicious sport over someone or making merry at someone else's expense. The objects of this mockery were the godly of verses 1 and 2. Enlarging the mouth and prolonging the tongue were signs of derision (cf. Ps. 22:8; 35:21; Lam. 2:16). Such actions show that those addressed were children of transgression. The pointing of *yildey* (*children*), occurring only here, is probably intended to be depreciatory. The wicked are not a true seed, but

---

[4] In this clause governed by a noun in the construct state the relative is omitted, and is connected with a preceding participle by *waw* consecutive, *seed of an adulterer and (of one who) played the harlot;* i.e. *seed of an adulterer and a harlot.* This construction of a noun in the construct followed by a finite verb is well attested in Ugaritic. Cf. Gordon, *Ugaritic Textbook,* 1965, § 8.16, p. 56.

one of falseness; here the word seems to suggest that they are not genuine.

5 By means of participles this verse continues the description of the wicked. The first participle is reflexive, *Inflaming themselves* (i.e. arousing sexual desire).[5] What is meant is the strong desire for the idolatrous practices that took place among the *terebinths* (cf. Deut. 12:2; 1 Kings 14:23; Jer. 2:20; 3:6, 13; 17:2; Hos. 4:13ff.; Ezek. 6:13). Among the green trees the terebinths played an important part in the idolatrous rites. These rites were not merely idolatrous but often immoral. The worst of these practices was that of child sacrifice, which was carried out in the valley of the sons of Hinnom (Gehenna; cf. Jer. 32:35; Ezek. 20:26-31). In Deuteronomy this practice is described as causing one's son to pass through the fire. *In the valleys* suggests the wadis of Palestine; the description is certainly not applicable to Mesopotamia. The same is true of the *clefts of the rocks,* an apt description for Palestine but not for Mesopotamia.[6] Possibly this phrase suggests that these rites were at times practiced in secret. Child sacrifice may have been for the purpose of appeasing the gods, just as the rites under the green trees were quite possibly fertility rites, engaged in for the sake of offspring. All of this was in the eyes of the holy God of Israel an abomination.

6 This verse continues the description of the depraved idolaters, which are represented by the feminine singular as a collective, possibly suggesting that Israel is a faithless woman. The verse, however, abounds with difficulties. Does the first word mean *portion* or *smooth things?*[7] Its root is the same as that of *thy portion*

---

5 הנחמים — *han-nē(ḥ)-ḥā-mîm*; the antepenult is opened *iḥ* > *ē*, and therefore cannot drop to *Shewa*; hence it is accompanied by *Meteg*. The form is a *Niphal* participle. B οἱ παρακαλοῦντες. The root appears in Ug., e.g. *ḥm lšrr, burned to rule* (*CMAL*, p. 82, line 33). A Babylonian document, while showing no moral antipathy to marriage with a prostitute or temple harlot or courtesan, nevertheless advises against it on practical grounds; cf. *DOTT*, p. 106.

6 This phrase is Isaianic, occurring elsewhere only in 2:21. Cf. Judg. 15:8, 11, where the language differs.

7 The *Dagesh* is separative, which apparently indicates more distinctly the vocal nature of the *Shewa*. On the basis of an appeal to Ug., W. H. Irwin ("The Smooth Stones of the Wady, Isaiah 57,6," *CBQ*, Vol. 21, No. 1, Jan. 1967, pp. 31-40) makes out a plausible case for identifying *ḥlq* with a root *ḥlq, to die, perish.* The reference then is to the dead of the wadi; those addressed are characterized as apostates, and the valley is the place of their

(*ḥelqek*), but the pointing shows that a different connotation is intended. Possibly the word is to be rendered *smooth things* and inasmuch as these *smooth things* belong to the valleys (i.e. *wadis*) they are generally thought to be the boulders which the water during the course of years has worn smooth. Possibly there is a figurative reference to the worship of Moloch, which occurred in the Hinnom valley. At any rate, instead of the Lord being the portion of His people, they found that portion in the smooth things of the valley. The play on words is significant. The repetition of the pronoun, *they, they*, is emphatic. The Psalmist (16:5b) could say, "thou holdest my lot"; but the lot[8] (i.e the destiny) of the wicked Israelites was in the smooth things (the dead?) of the valley.

Israel in her depravity poured out libations to the smooth things (Jer. 7:18; 19:13; 32:29; 44:17-19, 25). Likewise the people brought up to them (upon the altar) a meal offering. The introductory words *even to them* point out the folly of Israel's idolatry. In the light of such base abominations should God be comforted or should He not take vengeance? The thought expressed by the rhetorical question is whether in the light of Israel's idolatry God should be satisfied, show pity and take comfort, or whether He should not rather take vengeance.

7 In language reminiscent of 40:9 (cf. also 30:25), Isaiah describes the abominations practiced upon the high places of Palestine. The reference is to the sacrifice and worship of Baal and Astarte. Through contact with their Canaanitish neighbors the Israelites learned these practices. Perhaps the thought underlying such worship was that on the top of a high mountain one would be nearer to the divinity. At the same time Calvin may be correct in pointing out that such a place of worship indicated that the worshipper, like a harlot, was not ashamed but would boldly act in the open where he could be seen of all men. This is supported by the statement, *thou hast placed thy couch*, i.e. the couch of thy harlotry. Israel takes the initiative in all this idolatrous action. They have identified themselves with the worshippers of Canaan

---

destruction. The imagery is probably that of the Hinnom valley; and if so, this would support a Palestinian provenance for these chapters.

8 For the combination of *ḥlq* (*portion*) and *gôrāl* (*lot*) cf. also 17:14 and note 34:17.

and have themselves ascended the high mountains in order there to sacrifice.

8 Like the preceding, the present verse also bristles with difficulties. The first clause seems to refer to the act of putting something in an inconspicuous place. Do the *door* and *door post*[9] refer to a private house or to the temple wherein the abominations were practiced? Volz maintains that they belong to the public sanctuary. Perhaps this question cannot be answered apodictically, but we prefer the interpretation that refers the *door* and *door post* to the private home. According to Deuteronomy 6:9 the Israelite was to write the declaration that Yahweh is God upon the door posts of his house. Now, Israel has become so abandoned that they no longer place this memorial upon the door posts but behind them, so that they will not be reminded that Yahweh is their God. Also this gives more room for a memorial to the idol that the inhabitant worshipped. Such an interpretation, however, even though adopted by profound commentators, has difficulty. If the Israelites had become so abandoned, would they even bother to place the memorial behind the door? Would they not simply throw it away and destroy it altogether?

Possibly therefore the memorial was a reminder of the idol they now worshipped. That it is to be identified with *hand* in the latter part of the verse is not at all clear (cf. Penna). Possibly it was the image itself. The following expression, *for away from me thou hast uncovered*, does not demand that the memorial be a reminder of the true God. Contrariwise we may paraphrase: "The reason why thou hast placed a heathen memorial is that thou hast uncovered thyself away from me." Although no object is supplied to the verb *thou hast uncovered*, we are probably to understand something like *thy nakedness* (cf. Ezek. 16:26; 23:18). Idolatry is thus described as adulterous intercourse. It is not merely unchastity or fornication but actual adultery, for Israel is faithless to the One who has espoused her and has committed spiritual adultery with the gods of those nations that were in strong enmity with Israel's own God. To commit adultery with a friend of the husband is wicked; to do so with an enemy who would destroy the husband is the height of abandoned wickedness. Israel has uncovered herself, but her

9 *mezûzāh — door post,* from *zûz*; cf. *zâzu,* "move."

404

action reveals how far she is from her Lord. The two following verbs take *thy couch* for an object. Perhaps in the phrase *thou hast gone up* there is reference not merely to entering the couch but to ascending the high place. To "make broad the couch" means simply to prepare it for the act of adultery with the chosen partner. In all this Israel takes the initiative.

The purpose of the following clause is to point out the intimacy with which Israel identified herself with the heathenish worship. "And thou hast cut for thyself (i.e. for thine own advantage) from them."[10] The word "covenant" (*b^erith*) is probably to be understood, and the whole phrase shows not that an actual covenant had been made, but simply the close relationship between Israel and the idolatrous worship. Israel has been like an adulterous woman who has prepared her own couch for her lover, and has in turn loved the couch of these heathen lovers. Not only have they come to her, but she has gone willingly (*thou hast loved*) to them. Instead of the covenant of God's grace Israel has willfully chosen pacts with idolatrous lovers who could only bring destruction to the nation.

Probably the last clause is to be understood in the sense of 56:5; 1 Samuel 15:12; 2 Samuel 18:18, and as perhaps referring to the memorial mentioned earlier. Passages such as Ezekiel 16:26 and 23:20, as well as analogies from the Arabic, suggest that the word *hand* may indicate the *membrum virile*.[11] The verb, however, better supports the first view. It indicates a seeing, in the sense of providing for; and this would naturally apply to the providing for a memorial or idol.

9 And thou hast gone to the king in oil, and hast multiplied thine unguents; and hast sent thine ambassadors even afar and hast brought down even to hell.

10 In the greatness of thy way thou hast labored, thou hast not said, There is no hope; the life of thy hand thou hast found, wherefore thou hast not become weak.

11 And whom hast thou feared and been afraid of, that thou shouldest lie? and me thou hast not remembered, thou hast not

10 Inasmuch as no particular emphasis falls upon the gender, the m. verb is used. This may also be influenced by the proximity of *lāk*.
11 Cf. Gesenius' discussion. H. L. Ginsburg has called attention to a parallelism *ahbt* ‖ *yd* in Ugaritic. Cf. Gordon, *Ugaritic Textbook*, p. 253; *JBL*, Vol. 69, 1950, p. 59.

laid to heart. Is it not that I hold my peace, and that of old, yet me thou wilt not fear?

12 I will declare thy righteousness; and thy works, and they will not profit thee.

13 In thy crying, let thy heaps save thee! And yet all of them the wind will take up, and a breath will take away; and the one trusting in me shall inherit the land and possess my holy mountain.

9 The figure changes somewhat. Israel had exhibited an adulterous craving for the favor of idols, and now the people flirt with the world power of heathendom. We may render the first verb *And thou hast travelled*.[12] The reference is to something historical, and hence not a general description of present idolatrous practices. As an illustration we may remember the sending of Ahaz to Tiglath-pileser III, when he said, "I am thy servant and thy son" (2 Kings 16:7ff.). The oil here mentioned is apparently a gift, although Israel may have anointed herself with the oil the better to effect her coquetry. If this be correct it would mean that Israel went dripping in oil. *Thou didst multiply thy unguents* would then mean that Israel anointed herself in superabundance, rather than that she brought many unguents as gifts.

Whereas the first clauses of the verse express the thought in figurative language, this one speaks of the actuality. Israel has sent her ambassadors afar, as when Ahaz sent ambassadors to the Assyrian king Tiglath-pileser III. Distance was no obstacle to Israel's courting the favor of the heathen world. The nation even *caused to make low* (i.e. *descended*) to Sheol. This latter clause is not to be understood literally, as though Israel had descended to Sheol for the purpose of consulting its God, but simply indicates the extreme to which Israel was ready to go to accomplish its purpose.

10 *Thy way* is singular and is probably collective. It refers to all the efforts that Israel was making to accomplish its ends. It is the nation's full and complete devotion to idolatry. Whatever Israel could do in the service of the false gods and idols it was ready to do. Apparently no task or service was too great. Nothing seemed to weary Israel in its desire for idolatry. In all this endeavor Israel has

---

12 Accent *Milel. šûr* — *to travel, journey*; cf. Ar. *sāra*, and *siy-yâ-rah, caravan*. Irwin (*op. cit.*, p. 34) suggests a root *šwr*, to adorn, i.e. "become an object of pleasure." The remainder of 9a he renders, "you showered perfumes upon yourself."

never said, *It is of no use.* The verbal form is impersonal. In idolatry the people have found the *life* of their *hand,* i.e. their hand has come to life and so received strength. For this reason they have not become weak. What the prophet is saying is that idolatry proved to be vital and refreshing to the Israelites and for that reason they did not become weary nor weak therein.

It is often true that men whose hearts are far from God have found vitality and enthusiasm in a system of theology that is at variance with God's revealed Word. Being unwilling to submit themselves to the truth they find that error is exciting, and so, like Israel of old, deceive themselves.

11 By means of rhetorical questions the Lord causes Israel to see the nature of its actions. "Whom hast thou so feared that thou wouldst lie to Me?"[13] Israel had feared man and was seeking to obtain man's favor—for idolatry is after all merely the currying of the creature's favor—and the result was that the nation had been false in its dealings with the Lord. The first verb indicates an anxiety or concern, a preoccupation with something (cf. 1 Sam. 9:5; 10:2; Jer. 42:16), possibly becoming mere obsequiousness. The second verb indicates a reverential fear, which should have been devoted to the Lord Himself. Israel's whole concern was with the approval of men, and hence it showed itself false to God.

This false dealing toward the Lord appeared in that the people had not remembered God; He was not in their thoughts. The personal pronoun is placed first for emphasis. *ME thou hast not remembered.* Israel had not placed the thought of God upon her heart; she was indifferent to Him. It is a graphic picture of the life of the man without Christ. Anxious care and the fear of man fill his life, but he never thinks about God.

We may render the remainder of the verse: *Am not I* (emphatic) *the one keeping silence, and that from of old* (or, for a long time), *so that me* (again emphatic) *thou doth not fear?* The question shows why the Israelites had not feared God, namely for a long time He had been silent and they evidently regarded Him as dead. Had God intervened with wrath and anger they would have thought of Him. Because God was silent, Israel was faithless to Him and did not fear Him.

---

[13] Lit., *thou hast been afraid and thou hast feared,* i.e. *to wit, thou hast feared.*

12 God will not keep silence forever, but will make known what the righteousness of the nation is. The phrase *I shall make known* stands in contrast to "I am silent" in the previous verse; in both instances the personal pronoun is emphatic. In making known Israel's righteousness, God will show that it is a sham righteousness as is all righteousness that proceeds from the depraved human heart. God's words are not necessarily ironical. Rather He is speaking with earnestness, declaring that the time will come when He will make known what Israel's righteousness really is. Had Israel not been so steeped in its love for idolatry and faithlessness, it might have realized that its righteousness was nothing but filthy rags.

The verse consists of two parts, the second being introduced by the phrase *as for thy works*. These words are not the direct object of *I shall make known* but form a *casus pendens* which is completed by the words *they will not profit thee*. Note also the chiasm; *thy works* is explicative of *thy righteousness*. What Israel regarded as its righteousness consisted in the things the nation had done. These, however, were its practices of idolatry; and before the judgment of God they would be of no avail. The last clause may be rendered, *why they will not profit thee*.

13 When Israel sees that its works will be of no avail, it will cry out[14] in despair. When it does so cry out, then, let its gatherings deliver it. This is the thought of the introductory words; but what is meant by *thy gatherings?*[15] Because of the difficulty of the word—it occurs only here—some seek to emend the text, but the very rarity of the word is in favor of its authenticity. The root means *to gather* (cf. Prov. 28:8; 2 Chron. 24:5), and here would seem to depict the idolatrous objects that Israel has gathered and accumulated as a treasure. Gesenius may be correct in speaking of it as a pantheon, a collection of gods or idols. If these are to deliver Israel at the time of its crying, there obviously will be no deliverance. These collections are so dead and impotent that a wind will lift them up; even a breath will take them away.

---

14 בְּזַעְקֵךְ — *Qal* inf. construct. The *Holem* in the near open syllable *zᵉ-ʿō-qēk̠* drops to *Shewa*. Because of the guttural this *Shewa* is compound, and hence also points the preceding syllable with the vowel that is homogeneous to it, namely, *Pataḥ*. Cf. 30:19, the only other occurrence of this form with a suffix.

15 *qibbûtzayik̠* — *thy heaps*, 1Q *qwbtzyk*. B ἐξελέσθωσάν σε ἐν τῇ θλίψει σου. To emend to *šiqqûtzayik̠* as suggested e.g. in *BH* is not necessary. Torrey suggests that this word is a "massoretic creation based on" *šiqqûtz*.

The second half of the verse forms a contrast, depicting what happens to the one who trusts in the Lord. Not only will he be delivered but he will also inherit the land in accordance with God's ancient promise. Also he will possess God's holy mountain (cf. 49:8; 60:21; 65:9; Ps. 37:11; 69:35, 36; Matt. 5:5). This passage should be compared with 56:7, 8, for as Delitzsch suggests, what is here affirmed of the gatherings may stand in contrast with the words, "I will gather yet others to him besides those already gathered." Whereas the wind will carry away the vain idols in which the faithless had placed their trust, the one who waits upon the Lord in hope looks forward to the inheritance of the promises and the rich blessing of fullness of life with God.

14 And one will say, Cast up, cast up, clear the way; take up the stumbling block from the way of my people.
15 For thus saith the One high and lifted up, who dwelleth forever, and holy is his name, On high and holy will I dwell; and with the broken and humble of spirit, to revive the spirit of the humble and to revive the heart of the broken ones.
16 For not forever will I contend, and not to eternity will I be angry; for the spirit from before me will faint, and the souls that I have made.
17 For his covetous iniquity I am wroth and will smite him in hiding, and I will be wroth; for he has gone on turning away in the way of his heart.
18 His ways I have seen, and I will heal him; and I will lead him, and restore comforts unto him and to his mourners.
19 Creating the fruit of the lips; Peace: peace to those afar and those near, saith the LORD, and I heal him.
20 And the wicked are like the troubled sea; for it is unable to rest, and its waters cast up mire and dirt.
21 There is no peace, saith my God, to the wicked.

14 Delitzsch aptly observes that the previous verses constituting the first section of the prophecy are filled with threatening and conclude with a brief statement of promise. This and the following verses constitute the opposite, being filled with blessing and promise and closing with a brief statement of threatening (v. 21). The introductory *And one will say* is purposely vague and has an air of mystery, as in 40:6. In each of the three major sections of the second portion of the prophecy this same appeal is made (cf. 40:3, 4; 57:14 and 62:10). The subject is intentionally left obscure and undefined. The command given is to prepare the way for God's

people to return to Him. No objects of the command are mentioned, the thought being that now the time of restoration has come, and all obstacles are to be removed.

Note the repetition of the command. The first verb refers to the casting up or preparing of the way over which God's people are to travel. In 40:3 the noun occurs, *mᵉsillah (the highway)*. This is followed by *prepare the way*, which had also occurred in 40:3. The command to *lift up* calls to mind the same expression in the feminine singular in 40:9. *Mikshol* is an occasion of stumbling or a stumbling block, and here is figuratively employed to denote any obstacle standing in the way of God's people that might cause them to stumble and fall and so fail in their journey. To limit the reference to a return from Babylon does not fit in well with the preceding verses; the thought is general. In the great eschatological return, when God will gather together all His people that are dispersed (because of their sin), there will be no obstacles to the fulfillment of His purposes.

15 Isaiah now gives a reason why the promise just stated may be trusted. *Thus* refers to what follows. "You need not hesitate to trust the promise which is involved in this command, for the High and Holy One has made the following solemn declaration" (Alexander). Inasmuch as He who is high and exalted has spoken, the promise is sure and trustworthy. The language seems to reflect upon Isaiah's call. *Ram (high)* and *niśśa' (lifted up)* were used together of the throne in chapter six, and this combination is found nowhere else in Scripture (see comments on 6:2).

The following clause, *inhabiting eternity*, is probably to be understood in the sense of dwelling eternally, i.e., "one who eternally dwells." Compare "father of eternity" (9:6). Again, reflecting upon the inaugural call, Isaiah declares that God's Name is holy (cf. Vol. I, p. 242, note 19). The following word is to be taken adverbially, although it is a substantive, *On high*.[16] *Holy* is to be construed as modifying *height;* thus, "I inhabit a height and that a holy one." This connection of *to dwell* and *height (marom)* as referring to God is found also in 33:5 and nowhere else in Scripture. With the word *height* the actual speech of the Lord begins.

There is a noticeable contrast between the first and second halves of the verse. In the first part the epithets have stressed the

---

16 The *waw* is pleonastic.

exaltedness of God, whereas in the second half they emphasize the lowliness and weakness of man. It is also of interest to note, as Penna points out, that the characteristic designations of the poor are not used (i.e. *'evyonim, 'anawim, dallim*). The particle *'eth* introducing the second half of the verse is best rendered *with*. Hence the thought is: "a height even a holy one I shall dwell, and also with the crushed, etc." It is perhaps more effective to render *I shall dwell* than "I am dwelling," for even though God is with the crushed, etc., He will maintain His exalted position. The *crushed* are those oppressed by the burdens of sin and the weariness of life. The *low of spirit* are broken in heart (the seat of the affections) because of the calamities and tragedies of life (cf. Ps. 34:19; 51:17). With such God will dwell for the purpose of reviving their spirit. Note the effective chiasm: between *low of spirit* and *spirit of the low*, and also between *crushed* and *low of spirit* and *spirit of the low* and *heart of the crushed*. The artistic construction of this verse is masterful. When God dwells with them the heart of the crushed is renewed as though to come to life again. No greater blessing can come to the heart oppressed by sin than the presence of the living God.

16 The introductory *ki (For)* is not necessarily causal, but may be taken as affirmative or explicative, and simply serves to introduce an additional element in the revelation of God. Emphasis falls upon the negative, *not*. *Riv* here refers to outward manifestations of God's wrath, the presentation of His charges against Israel in formal, legal fashion. On the other hand *qatzaph* denotes the inner burning of anger. The second *ki (for)* is best taken as causative, for thus it yields a good sense, giving the reason why God will not forever be in anger, namely the frailty of the creature (cf. Ps. 78:38, 39). If God is angry forever, then the spirit (of man) will faint and also the souls He has made. *Neshamoth*, lit., *breaths*, is used as an equivalent to *soul* (cf. Prov. 20:27) and here serves as a parallel expression to *ruah (spirit)*. The reference is to the creation. Inasmuch as God is the Creator of human souls, He will have mercy upon them. In 43:1 the creation is also introduced in connection with God's showing mercy. *From before me*[17] points to the living presence of God before whom the spirit of man cannot stand.

---

[17] The *m*- enclitic may be used, in which case the text should read *ruah-m lepānay*.

17 Although God will not forever be angry, He must yet punish Israel's iniquity; and this verse gives the reason why, *Through the iniquity of his covetousness,* i.e. through his covetous iniquity. *Betza'* is unjust gain, or gain obtained by violence. Israel has committed the iniquity of gaining its acquisitions unjustly or through violence. Hence, God is angry and will smite it. The verbs are future, for the punishment has not yet occurred. The following infinitive absolute may be equivalent to a finite verb: *I shall hide myself and I shall be angry.* In the last clause Isaiah reverts to the past, giving a further reason why Israel must be punished. Israel went as an apostate or backturning one,[18] and this it did in the way of its heart, i.e. according to its own desire and inclination.

18 These ways in which Israel has wandered as an apostate are not unknown to God, for He declares that He has seen them. One who would walk in the ways of his heart is spiritually sick; hence the Lord declares that He will heal him, a figurative expression for the forgiveness of sins and the restoration to God's favor. Likewise the promise to guide is general, referring to God's providential governing and preserving of His people. In addition God will *restore comforts* to His people; the verb implies that these comforts had formerly been enjoyed but were taken away. Possibly the thought is also present that the comfort to be bestowed will make up for the period when comfort was absent. Perhaps the plural *comforts* implies a variety of comfort, or it may be intensive to indicate the fullness of comfort promised.

According to Volz and others, the addition of the words *and to his mourners* points to groups within the people, contrary to the unity expressed in verse 17. But this is the only word in the context of verses 17-19 that could suggest a division in the nation, and hence it is questionable whether such an interpretation is correct. Perhaps the easiest solution is to take the word as epexegetical and to render, *even to his mourners.* The mourning ones grieve over their sins and repent, longing for God's forgiveness.

19 This verse sets forth how God will heal the nation. *Creating*[19] *the fruit of lips* means causing lips to speak. The reference is to human lips, but whether the content of what these

---

18 *šôḇāḇ* is an adjective, *backturning* (apostate).

19 The part., modifying the subject as a secondary predicate, serves to introduce a circumstantial clause.

lips speak is found in the following *peace, peace,* or whether it is the speaking forth of praises generally, is difficult to decide. The word rendered *fruit* occurs only here and in Malachi 1:12.[20] It is of importance to note the absolute newness of what is created, for the word "create" suggests that God's power has been employed to bring about a startlingly new result.

This verse is difficult of construction, but it is possible to take the clause beginning with *Creating* as circumstantial, the main statement then following in *I shall heal him.* Thus: *I shall heal him in that I create the fruit of the lips.* If this construction is correct, then the fruit of the lips is the message *Peace,*[21] *peace to those that are afar and to those that are near.* Not only are the lips human, but they are the lips of God's messengers who have received from Him this divine message. The clause *saith the Lord* is parenthetical, the actual speech of the Lord including everything in this verse, or else simply introducing the following *I shall heal him.*

Those that are *near* may be those that belong in the covenant whereas those that are *far* are the Gentiles. The language anticipates the New Testament promises of Acts 10:36 and Ephesians 2:17, and probably includes Israel generally. The verse closes with the statement that God heals, calling to mind the first words of verse 18.

20 The promise just pronounced is not for all, for the wicked among the people will not partake thereof. These wicked are not the Gentiles but the godless among the nation, who refuse the promise and live according to their own way. The words *And the wicked* serve as a *casus pendens* and at the same time introduce a sharp contrast with the preceding. In each of the three major sections of 56:9–57:21 there is this common characteristic that the closing thought stands in sharp contrast to the message that formed the heart of the section. Thus, compare 57:1, 2 with the preceding 56:9-12; 57:13b with the preceding 57:3-13a; and 57:20, 21 with the preceding 57:14-19.

The wicked are said to be like the sea that is tossed (*nigrash*[22]

---

20 1Q reads *nyb.*
21 The word is followed by *Paseq,* which serves to separate two identical words.
22 Cf. Ug. *ygrš. ygrš. grš ym grš ym lks'h*; "Yagrush, Yagrush, chase away Ym, chase away Ym from his throne" (*CMAL,* p. 80) .

is the *Niphal* participle, singular, referring to *sea* and not to *wicked*). The point of the comparison lies in the following statements. Emphasis falls upon the infinitive absolute, *rest*.[23] Ever turbulent and restless are the waters of the sea, whose billows, Calvin remarks, even though not agitated by wind or tempest, carry on a mutual war and dash with terrible violence against one another. So are the wicked, whose consciences drive them to distraction. "They are terrified and alarmed by conscience, which is the most agonizing of all torments and the most cruel of all executioners" (Calvin). No more can the wicked still the motions of conscience than the waves of the sea can be still. Furthermore, the waters of the sea *cast up mire*[24] *and mud*. And so from the heart of the ungodly proceed thoughts, words, and works, unclean and ungodly, the mire and mud of a restless conscience.

21 As the waters of the troubled sea cannot be stilled and become peaceful, so the conscience of the wicked is agitated; and for the wicked *There is no peace*. Even membership in the covenant people is not a sufficient pledge of peace, for the *wicked* mentioned are those Israelites who have rejected the promises. Perhaps in the light of the preceding verse and also of the fact that it is *my God* who speaks, there is more of a pathetic tone to this utterance than was the case in 48:22. On this sad note the second section of the second main division of the book closes.

---

[23] The inf. absolute as direct object precedes the negative and the finite verb; cf. Jer. 49:23.

[24] *repeš* — cf. Ar. *rafaṭa*, "to talk or act obscenely."

D. JERUSALEM HAS RECEIVED OF THE LORD'S HAND DOUBLE FOR ALL HER INIQUITY (58:1–66:24)

CHAPTER FIFTY-EIGHT

1 Call with the throat, spare not, like the trumpet raise thy voice; and tell to my people their transgression and to the house of Jacob their sins.

2 And me day by day they will seek, and the knowledge of my ways they will desire, like a nation that has done righteousness and has not forsaken the judgment of its God; they will ask of me righteous judgments, the approach of God they will desire.

1 Although the present passage marks the beginning of the third part of the second main section of Isaiah's prophecy, it is also a continuation of the message just presented. The language calls to mind the early verses of chapter forty. Here the message is one of punishment, there of comfort. Here mention is made of the house of Jacob, there of Jerusalem. In both passages *call* is used and also *my people*. Then too, the command *lift up thy voice* is found in both places. It is God who speaks, but whether He is addressing the prophet or simply uttering a general command is difficult to determine.

To cry *with the throat* means to cry at the top of one's voice.[1] The prohibition is not absolute, but is used with the negative *'al* (*not*); and we may render, *you should not spare*. Here then is no whispering, no mere conversational tone, but a crying aloud with the full voice, that the hypocrisy of the people might clearly be revealed. To make the thought perfectly clear, the phrase is added *like the trumpet lift up thy voice*. *Trumpet* is emphatic.

In the second half of the verse the content of the message is

---

1 B rightly interprets ἐν ἰσχύι.

415

stated, and is introduced by a command, *tell to my people*. Parallel with the expression *my people* is *the house of Jacob*. The messenger is to be faithful in pointing out to the people of God what their sin is. And no messenger of God that fails to do this is faithful to the divine command.

2 The introductory *And* gives the reason why the cry is to be strong, namely, the people are daily seeking God as though they were a righteous nation. The conjunction may possibly be rendered *for*. The definite object *me* is emphatic. The worship is insulting, and the emphatic *me* makes clear that it is the holy God who is insulted. "Me from whom they have fallen away, they daily seek in worship." It is a constant seeking, *day, day,* i.e. *every day*. The word *seek* suggests a coming to God in devotion (cf. 55:6). Furthermore, men desire to know the ways of God. The verb *desire* is strong and perhaps suggests a delighting in.

These things Israel does like a nation that has done righteousness; hence the implication is that Israel itself is not such a nation. There are two principal interpretations of the verse. One, which is generally espoused today, maintains that the people are acting as they do to discover when God will act and how He will act. They are discontented with His slowness and want to know what He will do. Such desire on their part is more a concern for themselves than a true worship of God. Another interpretation is that the people are simply hypocritical in their approach to God. They act like a nation that actually has done righteousness and has not forsaken the judgment of its God, whereas as a matter of fact they themselves have not done righteousness and have forsaken His judgments. This latter interpretation is more natural. The final sentence is chiastically arranged, beginning and concluding with a verb. A nation that did righteousness might be expected to ask God for righteous judgments, and one that had not forsaken the judgment of its God might also be expected to take pleasure in His approach. Each of the verbs ends in the paragogic *Nun*, and the final syllable receives the stress. Delitzsch interestingly suggests that this answers the people's self-righteous presumption. An Isaianic trait appears in the repetition of *they will take pleasure*.

> 3 Why have we fasted and thou hast not seen, afflicted our soul and thou wilt not know? Behold! in the day of your fast ye will find pleasure, and all your toilers ye drive on.

4 Behold! for strife and contention ye will fast, and to smite with the fist of wickedness; ye will not fast today to make your voices heard on high.

5 Will it be like this, the fast that I shall choose, the day of a man humbling himself? Is it to bow his head like a bulrush and make sackcloth and ashes his bed? Wilt thou call this a fast, and a day of acceptance to the LORD?

3 In the first half of this verse we have the complaint of the hypocritical worshippers, and in the second God's reply. The construction of the question[2] is similar to that in 5:4 and 50:2. The meaning is: "Why is it that when we fasted thou didst not see it?" or "Why didst thou not see when we fasted?" Fasting[3] may have been prescribed for the Day of Atonement (cf. Lev. 16:29ff.; 23:17ff.; Num. 29:7). Later other fasts were observed (Zech. 7:3; 8:19). From these passages it will be seen that the following clause, *we have afflicted ourselves,* is probably a technical term for fasting (cf. also Ezra 9:5, where a different word is used). *Nephesh* in this context does not refer to man's soul, but probably to the entire person, inasmuch as the affliction mentioned, namely fasting, is of a corporeal nature. The people complain that God has neither seen nor does He know (the change in the tenses is significant) of their actions, and thus they accuse Him of indifference. Actually God has seen and does know their action; but He has not seen it with favor, nor does He know it in the sense of accepting it, inasmuch as their worship did not flow from a heart of devotion to Him, but was merely external. They were trusting in the outward merit of religious exercises and not in the living God. The question also reveals pride. "Why," they ask in effect, "should God not be pleased with our worship? Have we not done all that His law prescribes?" They murmur at God's providence and complain of His not accepting their worship; hence they are placing more confidence in that worship than in God Himself.

In the second half of the verse the Lord states why He has not seen nor known their worship. They have combined worship with their own pleasure. On the day of their fast, when the heart should be directed in meditation toward God, they have found a time for

---

2 The interrogative particle governs two coordinate questions, but is written only once.

3 Note separative *Dagesh forte* in *Tzade.*

their own *pleasure*. In addition they *drive on* their *toilers*.[4] The root of the verb[5] is found in the Amharic title of the king of Ethiopia, the Negus; and the root is used of the oppression of the Israelites in Egypt. These hypocritical worshippers regarded the day of fast as an ordinary day of work. The service of God was not going to interfere in any way with the service that they felt was due themselves. They could worship God and carry on their own pleasure and work at the same time (it is well to note that Isaiah mentions pleasure before work). To be noted also is the force of the verb, which suggests that these employers demanded from their workers all that they could get.

4 This verse probably sets forth the results rather than the purpose of the fasting, although the preposition *le* (*to, for*) does seem to suggest purpose. The tragic results of the fasting are introduced with *Behold!* as though to say, "This is what your fasting results in." The words *quarrel* and *strife* receive emphasis. The fasting of the hypocrites does not prepare their mind for prayer to God but produces contention and strife. Instead of the heart looking to God, the fasters became irritable and upset; and no doubt this was contagious. Indeed, this strife led to striking with the clenched fist, i.e. to fighting, lit., *with the fist of wickedness*. The chiastic arrangement is interesting. The reason for the fasting is stated negatively. The Israelites do not engage in this practice that their voice may be heard on high, for if they did so their entire approach to fasting would be different. While one cannot be dogmatic, it is quite likely that the phrase *on high* refers to heaven.

5 By means of rhetorical questions the Lord points out that the worshippers have not properly worshipped Him. The general sense of the verse is clear, although the details are difficult. The heart of the question is: "The fast that God has chosen as a day of humiliation and abasement, is it such as this one, merely an external fast alone?" *Is it like this* (i.e. what has just been described) *will be the fast I shall choose it?* i.e. "Will the fast that I shall choose be like this?" The question is paralleled by the expression, *the day of the afflicting of a man himself*, i.e. *the day in which a man afflicts himself*. This expression is a synonym for fasting.

4 ʻ*atztzeḇē* — The *Dagesh* in *Tzade* serves to indicate more distinctly the vocal character of the *Shewa*.
5 *tingōśú* — note that *Nun* is not assimilated.

418

The second question, introduced by the interrogative particle, points out that mock repentance is not acceptance with the Lord. *Is it for bending like a rush his head?* The straight rush is easily bent, and furnishes a suitable figure for the bent-over worshipper. Along with this mock humility the worshipper makes his couch *sackcloth and ashes.* An extreme of outward humiliation is pictured. It is true that sackcloth and ashes can be signs of repentance (cf. Jon. 3:5-9; 1 Kings 21:27-29), but unless they are accompanied by an inward repentance they avail nothing. We may render the last question: *Dost thou call this a fast, and a day of acceptance to the Lord?* If one regards this type of worship as acceptable to the Lord, he is grossly mistaken.

6 Is not this the fast that I will choose, to loosen bands of wickedness, to undo the fastenings of the yoke; and to send away the crushed free, and every yoke ye shall break?
7 Is it not to break unto the hungry thy bread, and the afflicted, the homeless, thou shalt bring home? For thou shalt see one naked and shalt clothe him, and from thine own flesh thou shalt not hide thyself.

6 There is, however, a fast that the Lord does choose, and that fast is now described negatively. The question demands an affirmative answer, and the mere mention of what God does approve makes clear that the opposite is not approved of Him. Even though *tzom (fast)* is without the definite article, the following verb with its relative force shows that we are to translate *the fast that I choose.*

That the character of the true fast is set forth by means of infinitives suggests the permanence of the divine requirements, and the imperfect that concludes the sentence lends variety and life to the mode of expression. *To loosen* (lit., *to open*) [6] *the fetters of wickedness* is to remove the wicked bonds or fetters that one has placed upon someone else. It is possible that this and the other phrases refer to the release of unjustly held slaves. According to the law, slaves of Israelitish descent were to be emancipated every three years. Jeremiah 34:8-22 presents an instance of a gross violation of this principle.

The second clause may be rendered, *to loosen* or *undo the bands*

---

[6] The inf. absolute is used as a finite verb; cf. 5:5. The combination of the roots *pth* and *ntq* is found elsewhere only in 5:27.

of the yoke bar; like the first clause it is a general figure of unjust oppression. Delitzsch points out that the *moṭah* was the cross wood that formed the chief part of the yoke. When these bands were loosed the yoke animal was free. The same thought is expressed in different language in the third clause, *to send the crushed ones free*. These crushed ones have been unjustly and even forcibly oppressed. As a concluding statement there is a phrase with an imperfect, *and the yoke bar they will snap*. The picture is one of complete destruction of the means of oppression.

Isaiah here depicts in figurative language the actions that will characterize those who truly fast. These cover the whole range of attitude toward those oppressed. If one has oppressed another in any way, he will remove that oppression and set free the one whom he has harmed. The reference may possibly be largely to the social sphere, but it is not confined to that. Furthermore, it must be remembered that the actions herein mentioned reflect the attitude of one whose heart delights in the Lord and who serves Him with unfeignedness. Indeed, unless there is a true love of God in the heart, there can in reality be no true service to those who are oppressed. One cannot even rightly diagnose the ills of mankind unless he has first learned their true nature from the Lord. The setting free of those whom we have wrongly oppressed only occurs when our own hearts are filled with God's love.

7 The description of the true day of fasting is continued, but in this verse the positive side of the picture is prominent. The infinitives still depend upon "This is the fast that I shall choose" in the previous verse.[7] The first clause signifies a sharing of one's own food with those that have nothing. Clothing is often associated with food as constituting the bare essentials of life. Here the two are connected by a beautiful chiasm, the first member of which is an infinitive absolute and the second an imperfect singular. The afflicted, even the wandering ones, are to be provided with the shelter of one's own home. The reference is evidently to those who because of oppression or victimization are homeless.

Likewise, when one sees another naked he is to provide covering for him. And he is not to hide himself from his own flesh, i.e. his own kindred (cf. Gen. 29:14; 37:27; 2 Sam. 5:1). It is also possible that *flesh* simply denotes mankind generally, for all men are flesh;

---

7 Cf. note 6 for use of the inf. absolute.

hence, to hide oneself from one's flesh is to refuse to act humanely toward any who are in need. Love toward all men is a hallmark of those who belong to the Lord, and this love will manifest itself in a true concern for their welfare.

8 Then shall break forth as the dawn thy light, and thy healing speedily shall spring up: then shall go up before thee thy righteousness, the glory of the LORD shall be thy rear guard.

9 Then thou wilt call, and the LORD will answer; thou wilt cry, and he will say, Behold me! if thou wilt put away from the midst of thee the yoke, the pointing of the finger, and the speaking of vanity.

8 The introductory *Then* is of tremendous significance, for it points to the time when the glorious change will have occurred and God's people will do those things just described.[8] In these first two clauses the emphasis falls upon speed. Elsewhere Isaiah uses the verb *break forth* of the hatching of eggs (59:5) and of water gushing forth (35:6). The word seems to suggest suddenness, swiftness, and novelty. In the Near East the light of day follows almost immediately upon the darkness of night. Hence, as the light suddenly breaks forth, replacing the night, so will break forth (the future is to be preferred to the conditional in translation) the people's *light*, i.e. their felicity of well-being, salvation (cf. 9:2; 60:1, 3).

The second member is introduced in chiastic order, the noun coming first and the verb concluding the clause. The word *'arukah* signifies the *healing* of a wound, or, if employed figuratively as here, the *restoration* of something. This healing is compared to a plant that quickly sprouts forth. In these two clauses the emphasis falls upon light and life and the rapidity of their appearance.

The second half of the verse also consists of two chiastically arranged clauses, in which a progression is suggested. *Righteousness* and *the glory of the Lord* are intended as parallel expressions, and therefore the significance of the first must be determined by the latter. The *righteousness* of the people is their Lord Himself, as Jeremiah says (cf. Jer. 23:6; 33:16 and also Isa. 54:17). The *glory of the Lord* is His declarative glory manifested in His works, or perhaps the Lord Himself in glorious manifestation. As in the

---

8 Cf. 35:6 for a similarly constructed verse.

wilderness He preceded His people in the pillar of cloud and fire, so now He brings up the rear of their march into newness of life. Thus the redeemed are surrounded by the divine protection. He in whom their righteousness is found precedes them, and His glory is their *rear guard*.

9 This verse appears to relate to the complaint uttered in verses 2 and 3. Continuing to address the people as an individual, the prophet indicates God's nearness by assuring that when the people cry out in prayer the Lord will give answer. The parallel verb means "to cry for help," and the expression *here I am* is used to declare that one is present, as at a roll call.[9]

The introductory *'az* (*Then*) points out that God only answers the call of His people after they have turned from their evil ways and repented. If God showered blessings upon us while we continued to sin, we should take His blessings for granted and cease to pray for them. It is after we have awakened from the deadness of our sin that in time of need we call out to God.

The second part of the verse speaks of the putting away of oppression, first in a summary fashion and then with two particulars. The *yoke* is a symbol of oppression generally. Sending (i.e. pointing) the finger was evidently a gesture of contempt,[10] and speaking of vanity is the speaking of falsehood (cf. Zech. 10:2), although there may be a particular allusion to the *strife* and *contention* of verse 4.

10 And if thou wilt let out thy soul to the hungry, and the afflicted soul wilt satisfy, then shall thy light arise in the darkness and thy gloom as the noon.
11 And the LORD will guide thee continually, and satisfy thy soul in scorched regions, and he will invigorate thy bones; and thou shalt be like a watered garden, and like a spring of water whose waters will not fail.
12 And they will build from thee the ruins of old, foundations of generation to generation thou shalt raise up; and it shall be called to thee Repairer of the breach, Restorer of paths for dwelling.

[9] The structure of 9a is interesting: imp. followed by an imp. preceded by Lord (emphatic); in the parallel, imp. followed by *waw* consecutive and the imperfect. This latter would seem to express the sureness of the action.
[10] Among the Arabs this gesture was a means of bringing misfortune upon others. Cf. König *in loc.*

13 If thou wilt turn away thy foot from the sabbath to do thy pleasure on my holy day: and wilt call the sabbath a delight. the holy day of the LORD, honorable, and wilt honor it by not doing thy own ways, by not finding thy pleasure and talking talk.

14 Then thou shalt be happy in the LORD, and I shall cause thee to ride upon the high places of the earth; and I shall cause thee to eat the heritage of Jacob, thy father, for the mouth of the LORD hath spoken it.

10 This verse continues the preceding thought, which began with the conditional particle in the midst of verse 9. In summary form the prophet brings together the heart of what he had stated in verse 7. *If thou wilt furnish for the hungry thyself*[11] sums up the manner in which one is to serve others. It is not a mere providing of material substances, but a giving of oneself to those in need, for "the gift without the giver is bare." One must provide for the needs of the destitute from a heart of love to them, and there can be no true love to them unless there is first the true love of God in the heart.

The juxtaposition of the two words *thyself* and *soul* is striking. Isaiah adds to the strength of the first two clauses by placing them in chiastic arrangement. *The afflicted soul* is parallel to the *hungry,* and probably designates those who have suffered an unjust oppression. It is the duty of God's people to satisfy such souls so that their needs are lovingly provided for.

Should God's people do these things their light will shine in the darkness, and the gloominess will be as the noon. These figures refer to the blessedness that comes after sorrow, the second word, *'aphelah (gloominess)*, perhaps being stronger than the first, *hoshek (darkness)*.

11 In clear language the prophet states what the nature of the future blessing will be, namely, that the Lord will always lead His people. More than that (there is a gradation), He will satisfy their soul in scorched regions.[12] In 57:18 God had already promised guidance, and now the fullness of that guidance is depicted. Here is a picture of the superabundant free grace of God. In regions

---

11 וחפק — *produce, furnish, Hiphil* jussive of פוק. So also 1Q. The protasis of a hypothetical condition is here expressed by a jussive and an imp., whereas the apodosis contains a perf. with *waw* consecutive.

12 *tzaḥtzāḥôṭ* — 1Q *tztzḥwt, scorched regions.*

where one can expect only to perish from lack of food, the soul is satisfied by God Himself. Such a blessing causes one to depend upon Him, for there is nowhere else to turn. A third statement indicates the rejuvenation and recuperation of strength that God will give His people in that He will *brace up* or *invigorate* their *bones.* Each statement of blessing proceeds a step beyond the preceding.

The result of God's action is that Israel will be *like a watered garden.* This water is a figure of blessing and richness; in the Near East water is not plentiful, and to discover a watered garden is to find a place of pleasant refreshment and delight. Isaiah often used the figure (cf. 30:25; 33:21; 35:6, 7; 41:17; 43:20; 44:4; 48:21; 49:10). In chapter one the prophet had set forth the obverse, *like a garden in which there was no water,* there depicting the spiritual desolation to come.

Furthermore, the people were to become like a spring of water (lit., *like the place of the going out of water*), and this spring is so rich and abundant (an unlikely feature in the scorched regions) that its waters will never fail nor disappoint. Thus, ever abounding continuous grace comes to man from the God of all bounty. It is only man's sin, as Calvin points out, that can stop its course. The boldness of the figure can only be appreciated by those who know the great dryness of the Near East. But then the grace of God is bold; what is impossible with man is possible with God, and the blessed fact, too good not to be true, is that the grace of God has appeared bringing salvation.

12 In this verse the prophet depicts salvation under the figure of the building up again of the broken-down walls of the city of Jerusalem. As the preceding verse began with a verb setting forth God's action, so this one commences with a verb stating the action of the people. But what is the subject of the verb? The difficulty appears because of the words *from thee.* Do they refer to that which goes forth from Israel into other lands and so to the conversion of the heathen? If so, we should paraphrase, "And they who go out from thee (as missionaries?) will build the ruins of antiquity." This is possible; but there is another possibility, namely that the words *from thee* refer to descendants. On this interpretation the reference is to those descended from the Israelites who will build again the ruined walls of Jerusalem. If this interpretation is correct, it does not fit in well with the idea of a "second" Isaiah addressing exiles who are soon to return to Palestine and themselves to have part in the rebuilding of Jerusalem's walls; but it does fit in very well with the times of the eighth-century Isaiah. The description of the ruins seems to suggest that they are well-known ruins, and so those of the city itself. If there is any actual reference to the physical rebuilding of Jerusalem's walls, this is only the first stage in the greater restoration introduced through Christ. The thought is the same as that found in Amos 9:11ff.

Ruins of antiquity are ruins that have existed for a long time, perhaps *ruins of perpetuity*; and *the foundations of generation and generation* are those which have existed through one generation after another. Both designations stress the great age of the foundations. The verb *(thou shalt raise up)* makes more vivid the fact that the foundations are in ruin.

Inasmuch as rebuilding is the central activity of those who have received the abundant grace of God, they will be called (the word is indefinite) repairers (lit., *one who builds a wall*) of breaches (the word has collective force). The final clause designates the people as restorers of paths for dwelling. The phrase *for dwelling* probably signifies that the paths will be restored so that the land may again be inhabited. The thought is that on these paths, now obliterated, men may one day walk in order that again they may inhabit the land.

NOTE ON VERSES 13-14

In vv. 13-14 Isaiah teaches that if the people obey the sabbath they will be happy in the Lord. Duhm, Elliger, and others insist that these verses must be very late in the period of Judaism, possibly the time of Nehemiah, for the sabbath was stressed at that time, which was supposedly a time when emphasis fell upon externals. Whenever, therefore, a passage is found in earlier books that exalts the sabbath, it is assumed to be late. If one grant the presupposition that the sabbath was stressed only late in Israel's history, then there may be some merit to denying the present passage to Isaiah (or to "second" Isaiah, or even "third" Isaiah, the willowy figures who are supposed to have had something to do with chapters 40–66). Smart, however, denies this passage to "second" Isaiah on the ground that it makes nonsense of the prophet's sermon to have him reject fasting as a substitute for works of love and mercy and then to insist that if only the people observe the sabbath, all will be well. Hence, he concludes that these verses come not from "second" Isaiah but from a later orthodox community which had an enthusiasm for the sabbath. With this introduction we may examine the text itself, and then seek to discover the reason why the sabbath is stressed at this particular point in the argument.

13 Isaiah evidently intends the first clause to be understood figuratively. To cause to turn one's foot from the sabbath[13] seems to imply that the sabbath is a place upon which one walks. Possibly the thought is that the sabbath is holy ground and therefore the unsanctified foot is not to walk upon it, which would be a figurative way of saying that one is not to profane the holy day. Or it may be that there is present the idea of treading down or suppressing the sabbath. The two ideas are not far removed, and the basic thought is that of refraining from desecrating the day, i.e. from *doing thine own pleasure*. *Thy pleasure* is that which pleases man instead of God. It is a gross misunderstanding to interpret as though the words meant "that which is pleasant" and to conclude from this that the prophet's only concern is that the sabbath be a day not of pleasure but of gloom. Rather, it is the pleasure of man in contrast to that of God that is brought to the fore, and in this fact we may see the beginning of an answer to the position of Smart mentioned above. Isaiah is not saying that fasting is no substitute for love and mercy whereas the sabbath is. Rather, he is inveighing against a false observance of the sabbath as well as against a neglect thereof. A proper observance of the sabbath is an exemplification of the fact that there is love and mercy. The reason for this command is that the day belongs to God and is holy. At the creation He set it apart and sanctified it, and therefore it is to be observed only in the manner pleasing to Him.

In the first part of the verse the stress was negative, but it now becomes positive. Instead of regarding the sabbath as a day for the doing of one's own pleasure, men are to call it (i.e. to regard it) a day of *delight* (lit., *exquisite delight, daintiness*). Instead of repeating the word *sabbath*, Isaiah uses an adjective as a parallel, *holy*, i.e. *holy day,* and this word is joined to *the Lord* again to emphasize the fact that this holy day is the Lord's. The designation that Israel is to give to the Lord's holy day is "To Be Honored." Israel is thus to regard the day as honorable and to be treated as honorable. Merely to acknowledge the sabbath as a delight and honorable, however, is not sufficient. The acknowledgment must be

---

13 Although the preposition *min* is written but once, it serves to govern two coordinate clauses.

translated into action, and the sabbath must receive the honor it deserves.

In three ways Isaiah points out how the sabbath is to be honored. The first of these, *not doing thy ways*, is parallel in thought to the earlier *doing thy pleasure*. There is no need to restrict these phrases to matters of business. The "way" is a course of conduct and refers to all courses and actions that men choose in preference to the commands of God. These courses and actions may be right and legitimate on other days, but when they obtrude in the place of that delight, which is to find expression in the observance of the sabbath, they are to be refrained from. Secondly, *not finding thy pleasure*[14] also refers to one's own pleasure in distinction from what pleases God; and the third expression, *speaking words* (the noun is best understood as collective), probably refers to idle and vain talk, in which God is forgotten or ignored. What is mentioned tends to draw the heart away from God to the consideration of one's own occupations. This is wrong conduct on the holy sabbath.

Why, however, is there mention of the sabbath at this point? Is it not that the sabbath was a unifying ordinance which at all times (and particularly in times of apostasy and the exile) would bind the people together as no other ordinance would do? For the sabbath was not merely a Mosaic ordinance; it was far more. It was instituted at the creation, and is a pattern of the heavenly sabbath rest which the redeemed are to enjoy in the presence of their eternal God. In the great calamity of the exile that was to come upon them, Isaiah stresses the sabbath as in a sense the heart of true devotion to God. He who keeps the sabbath as it is intended to be kept will be happy in the Lord of the sabbath.

14 "Then thou shalt take exquisite delight[15] not just in the sabbath itself, but in the Lord." Israel will enjoy God, for with a redeemed heart men will delight to do God's will; and His law, instead of being a burden, will become a delightful thing to them. To indicate the abundance and richness of the spiritual prosperity Israel will receive, the prophet uses a figure, *and I shall cause thee to ride upon the high places of the earth.* As triumphant conquerors the people ride forth. Possibly there is an allusion to the high places of Palestine, but this is questionable.

---

14 'ōneḡ occurs elsewhere only in 13:22. B τρυφερά.
15 tiṯ'annaḡ — from the same root as 'ōneg (v. 13; cf. previous note).

Lastly, the heritage promised to Jacob, the nation's father, now becomes the possession of the people; and they are to enjoy it in all the fullness and richness that it brings. By eating this heritage they will find their delight therein and also their subsistence. Upon this heritage they will truly live. But there must be repentance. The present love for idolatry and false repentance must give way to a true abhorrence of evil, and a true turning unto the God who alone can bring the blessing and can make of Israel the triumphal nation.

1 Lo! the hand of the LORD is not shortened from saving, and his ear is not heavy from hearing.

2 But your iniquities have been separating between you and your God, and your sins have caused to hide his face from you so as not to hear.

3 For your hands are defiled with blood, and your fingers with iniquity; your lips have spoken falsehood, your tongue will utter wickedness.

4 There is none calling with justice, and there is none contending with truth; they trust in vanity and speak falsehood, conceive mischief and bring forth iniquity.

1 The prophet speaks in a vein similar to the preceding. If it be asked why the promised deliverance has not come, the answer lies in the sinfulness of the people. Using a figure employed in 50:2 the prophet emphatically declares[1] that God has not lost His power to save. Isaiah calls attention to this fact (*hen*), pointing to it as though it were there before all to be seen. If a hand has been *shortened* it cannot reach the object after which it stretches; God's *hand* (i.e. *power*) has not thus been shortened so that it cannot save, nor have His ears become *heavy* so that they cannot hear when men cry unto Him. There must, therefore, be some other reason why salvation has not come to Israel.

2 There is indeed such a reason, and Isaiah presents it in this verse. Using the plural in place of the singular suffix he speaks of *your iniquities,* and characterizes them in language reminiscent of Genesis 1:6. In picturesque fashion Paul Volz says that the sins are like a firmament that separates between heaven and earth. Just as the expanse once was dividing the waters underneath from those above, so were the iniquities of the people *dividing* (past time and

---

1 B makes two questions of this verse, but Aq S T seem to follow M.

continuous action are represented by the participle) between the people and their God (note again the similarity with Gen. 1:6).

As at the head of the first line the prophet places the emphatic words *your iniquities,* so he puts in the place of emphasis at the head of the second line *your sins.* The following words, *they have covered a face from you from hearing,* mean that they have obscured God's face so that Israel no longer sees it. The language is not derived from the cult, as Volz suggests, but is expressive of the truth that God has a face. This is not to assert that God is physical, but the face of God suggests that God sees, hears, and knows all that man does. The word is anarthrous, but clearly refers to the face of God, and may be rendered *the face.* The expression is probably interchangeable for God's presence, for when our sins veil His face, it is as though there were a wall between Him and us and the light of His countenance is hidden from us.

3 In a characteristically Isaianic verse[2] the prophet illustrates the truthfulness of what he has said, and by pointing to the members of the body as the agents of iniquity removes from the people any escape. It is a bold message that Isaiah proclaims, and in proclaiming it he shows that he himself, although a sinner, is not guilty of the sins of which he accuses the people. He can speak boldly, without fear of an accusing finger being pointed in his direction. "We must be unlike those whom we reprove, if we do not wish to expose our doctrine to ridicule, and to be reckoned impudent; and, on the other hand, when we serve God with a pure conscience, our doctrine obtains weight and authority, and holds even adversaries to be more fully convicted" (Calvin).

The hands men stretched out to God in prayer were defiled[3] with blood. Here the thought is similar to 1:15. *Fingers* is a parallel expression to *hands,* to point out that iniquity and blood were involved in the actions of the people. Perhaps the definite article before *blood* and *iniquity* denotes these as well known. The entire being, inner and outer, was set for the commission of iniquity.

4 Here follows a further description of the nation's depravity. *There is none calling in righteousness* has been taken in a judicial

2 Cf. 1:15; 33:15.

3 $n^e\bar{g}\bar{o}'^a l\hat{u} = ni\bar{g}'^a l\hat{u}$ — not a *forma mixta* (GKC § 51f.) but a passive of the Ar. III stem, *'in-fâ-'i-la.*

sense, as though indicating that no one righteously summons another to trial. Luther equated it with proclaiming righteousness. The phrase may also be interpreted of praying (i.e. calling to God) in righteousness. The words *in righteousness* are to be construed with the participle adverbially as expressing the manner in which the calling is done.

In truth is to be construed adverbially, lit., *and it is not judged in truth.* The construction is impersonal, and in the light of 58:2, 3 would seem to refer to those who do not plead with God in truth but are hypocrites. The first two clauses, then, refer not to the relationship of men with one another but to their attitude toward God, for this verse forms a conclusion to what has preceded and is not an introduction to the following verses.

From the participles Isaiah turns to the use of infinitives absolute and thus introduces a variety in style that lends force and effectiveness. Instead of calling in righteousness, the people *trust* (the infinitive absolute is to be translated by a present expressing continuous action) *in desolation.* The word (*tohu*) is used in Genesis 1:2, where it expresses the fact that the earth was originally uninhabitable. Here it may be rendered *nothingness,* for the people's trust is in nothingness. It is useless and good for nothing. What they speak is *vanity,* for their fasts are not acceptable to God and their prayers are empty. Isaiah takes his language from Job 15:35, using what was probably a proverbial expression (occurring almost exactly in Ps. 7:14). The people are *pregnant with travail* or *trouble,* and they *bring forth iniquity.* The second noun is stronger than the first. They are laden with evil designs and plans toward others, and they themselves bring forth iniquity in their actions.

5   Eggs of the basilisk they have hatched, and webs of the spider they will weave; the one eating of their eggs will die, and the crushed egg will hatch out a viper.

6   Their webs will not become a garment, and they shall not cover themselves with their works; their works are works of iniquity, and the doing of violence is in their hands.

7   Their feet run to evil and are quick to shed innocent blood; their thoughts are thoughts of iniquity, wasting and ruin are in their paths.

8   The way of peace they do not know, and there is no judgment in their tracks; their paths they have made crooked for themselves, all who go in it do not know peace.

5 Not only have the people acted treacherously against the Lord but against others also. This truth is expressed by comparing them to a poisonous serpent and a spider. *They have hatched* is in the perfect, expressing what was once done and is now commonly done. The precise nature of the *tziph'oni (basilisk)* is not known; it is a poisonous snake,[4] and from its eggs more poisonous snakes will hatch. Furthermore, *they will weave* (note the future, which denotes what continues) spiders' webs (lit., *the threads of spiders*), a figure that suggests ensnaring. The eggs that have been hatched cannot be used for food; if one does eat them he *will die*. Anyone who takes part in the plans of the wicked will perish. The wicked affect not only themselves but also those with whom they come into contact. If one of these eggs is *crushed*,[5] it *will hatch out a viper*. The second word for "serpent" is specific,[6] whereas the first is general. Thus, men's evil works manifest their own corruption and produce no good fruit.

6 The general sense of the verse is clear, namely, the evil works of Israel will produce no blessing. Isaiah goes back to what he had said in the previous verse about spiders' webs. He interweaves the two figures of spiders' webs and clothing. As the spiders' webs cannot serve for clothing, neither can the works of evil men suffice for covering themselves, for they are futile and produce no good.

In the second part of the verse Isaiah gives the reason for the statements just made. The deeds are *deeds of iniquity*, and *the work of violence is in their hands*.

7 The *feet* are personified. Life is often depicted as a way along which one walks; but these men *run* (the verb shows the eagerness with which they anticipate participation in evil), and the purpose of their running is for evil, in particular that which harms others. Even the shedding of *innocent blood*, abhorrent as that is, is something toward which they hasten. There is no restraint in the doing of evil; it is their delight and they turn to it with all readiness. The *thoughts* (i.e. the intentions, plans, devices) are born in iniquity, lead to iniquity, and are themselves of iniquitous

---

4 Cf. 11:8. B ἀσπίδων.

5 *zûreh* — passive part. of *zûr, to press*. Cf. 1:4. The m. ending is used for the f., like *lāneh* for *lānāh* in Zech. 5:4; cf. *'āneh* in 1 Kings 2:36, 42.

6 Koehler and Baumgartner (*Lexicon in Veteris Testamenti Libros*, Grand Rapids, 1951, p. 78) identify it as *echis colorata*.

nature. Were one to walk upon *their paths* he would find only *wasting and ruin.*[7]

8 This description of evil men is employed by Paul in the third chapter of Romans to set forth the universal depravity of mankind. The *way* in which men walk (i.e. their course of life) is not one of peaceable conduct. In their hearts there is no *peace* of God; inasmuch as they are at enmity with God, and in reality with man also, they have no desire for peace. *They have not known* this way; they are utter strangers to it.

In their *tracks (entrenchments, ruts) there is no judgment.* This phrase is evidently to be considered as a parallel to the first; hence it may be that the judgment here is similar to the judgment of righteousness of 58:2. Inasmuch as the people do not have God's judgment, they themselves exhibit no right judgment in their dealings. More than that, *they have twisted* or *perverted their paths.* This they have done for themselves believing they would profit thereby, but actually the action has been to their own detriment. Moreover, whoever walks in it (i.e. *in this way;* the suffix is indefinite) does not know peace. In characteristic fashion Isaiah introduces the word *peace* again at the close of the verse.

> 9 Wherefore judgment has removed far from us, and righteousness will not overtake us; we wait for the light and behold! darkness, for brightnesses and in darknesses we walk.
> 10 We grope like the blind for the wall, like the eyeless we grope; we stumble at noonday as in twilight, among the stout like the dead.
> 11 We growl like bears, all of us, and like the doves moaning do we moan; we wait for justice, and there is none, for salvation, and it is far from us.

9 There must be evil results of such conduct, and indeed there are. As a result of what has just been described (*'al-ken*) the following evils have come. *Judgment* (i.e. righteous judgment such as God pronounces) has gone far away (and this state of things continues until the present). God has not come in judgment to save His people. Likewise *righteousness* (i.e. salvation) *will not overtake us* (this state of things, as the future shows, continues unchanged). Although the people *wait for the light* of salvation,

---

[7] Note the striking alliterations in the last line of this verse.

they receive only *darkness* (i.e. their present sinful, wicked condition continues without any relief). *Brightnesses* or *splendors* may be the people's expectation, but they continue to walk in deep *darknesses*. When men seek for salvation in any way other than that prescribed of the Lord, or when they continue in their sins, they will not find salvation.

For a proper understanding of this section we must note that *shalom* (*peace*) and *mishpaṭ* (*judgment*) in verse 8, as well as the words *'or* (*light*), *tzᵉdaqah* (*righteousness*), *nᵉgohoth* (*brightnesses*), and *yᵉshu'ah* (*salvation*), all refer to divine salvation, considered from different aspects.

10 In language of singular force Isaiah depicts the plight of the sinners, ever seeking an escape from their condition and only falling deeper therein[8] (cf. Rom. 7:14). The first line consists of a striking chiasm, beginning and concluding with the same word (*gashash*, found only here in the *Piel*), which differs only in that the second occurrence is pausal. The cohortative ending describes the efforts made to find the way, *We seek to feel.*[9] As blind men feel the wall with their hands seeking a way of escape from prison, so men in their sins grope about seeking for deliverance and never finding it. The phrase *and like those without eyes* (lit., *and like not eyes*) means those who are deprived of the use of their eyes.

"Although it is noon when the sun is high," we may paraphrase, "nevertheless, we stumble as though it were twilight. Although stout, in full strength,[10] we are as dead ones." Isaiah places these thoughts in the mouths of the people, not because the people actually said such things but to point out the hopelessness of the nation as long as it continued in its sin.

11 The description is continued by a change of the figures. Isaiah compares the frustration of the people to the growling of bears and the moaning of doves, figures classical writers have also

---

8 Pieper quotes Luther's hymn:
> *Ich fiel auch immer tiefer drein,*
> *es war nichts Gut am Leben mein,*
> *die Sünd' hatt' mich besessen.*

9 Perhaps even *we have to feel*; the cohortative ending may express that reluctant consent which is born of necessity.

10 The singular of *'ašmannim* (the stout?) may be an elative, like Ar. *'k-bar*, although if so, the doubled *Nun* is difficult to explain. RSV renders, "among those in full vigor we are like dead men."

used.[11] The structure of the first half of the verse is chiastic, but an infinitive absolute precedes the final verb. Both comparisons point to that sadness which is without hope.

"All their looking for righteousness and salvation turns out again and again to be nothing but self-deception, when the time for their coming seems close at hand" (Delitzsch). The judgment of God for which they wait is not forthcoming, and their hoped-for salvation (note that $y^eshu'ah$ is here used in place of tz^edaqah, an evidence that all these words refer to salvation) has departed far from them.

12 For our transgressions have increased before thee and our sins have answered against us; for our transgressions are with us and our iniquities we know them.

13 To transgress and lie against the LORD, and to turn back from behind our God; to speak oppression and revolt, to conceive and utter from the heart words of falsehood.

14 And judgment is driven back and righteousness stands afar off; for truth has stumbled in the street, and uprightness is not able to enter.

15 And truth was missed, and whoever turned aside from evil was plundered. Then the LORD saw, and it was evil in his eyes that there was no judgment.

12 It is difficult to explain the precise relationship of this verse to the preceding context. The complaints uttered do not appear to be sincere. Hence, it would seem that the prophet now speaks as a representative of his people and confesses before God their sins and their hopeless condition. In this confession he claims that the *transgressions,* i.e. the apostasy from the Lord and continual revolt against Him, *have multiplied*[12] (in number and possibly also in heinousness) before God. Over and over again the people transgress as though God were not present; but all is done before Him, for there is no escape from His all-seeing eye. Furthermore, the

---

11 Cf. Horace *Epodes* xvi.51, *nec vespertinus circumgemit ursus ovile*; Ovid *Metamorphoses* ii.485, *mens antiqua tamen facta quoque mansit in ursa*: *assiduoque suos gemitu testata dolores*; *Fasti* ii.186, *Et gemuit, gemitus verba parentis erant.* Cf. also similar expressions among the Babylonians, "I sigh like a dove night and day." Cf. Stummer, "Einige Keilschriftliche Parallelen zu Jes. 40–66," *JBL*, Vol. 45, 1926, p. 186; and Muilenburg, *com. in loc.*, for further references.

12 *rabbû* — accent *Milra*, whereas usually in *Ayin-Ayin* verbs it tends to be on the stem syllable, and always so in pause.

people's *sins have answered*[13] (in accusation) against them. This personification of the sins presents them as accusers against those who have brought them into being. The second half of the verse states that the *sins* and *iniquities*[14] (general expressions) are present with the people and that the people *know them*, i.e. they recognize them for what they are.

13 By means of infinitives absolute Isaiah enumerates the sins just confessed, and thus lends compactness and succinctness to his description. Going to the heart of the matter he lists *transgressing*[15] and *lying against the Lord*. The people in their worship professed to believe in the Lord, but in deed and thought they have fallen from Him; their worship gives an outward show of being directed to God but in reality is idolatry and hence falsehood. The acts of their worship are lies against the Holy One of Israel. The second clause also denotes apostasy, *to turn back from* (following) *after our God*; it brings into one expression the transgressing and lying against the Lord. *Speaking oppression and rebellion* means speaking in such a way as to bring about oppression and a turning aside from the Lord. In the last clause the depth of depravity is reached in that the people are pregnant with[16] and bring forth *words of falsehood*.

14 The first clause calls to mind the expression of the previous verse, "to turn back from after our God." *Judgment is thrust back* from the place it ought to occupy. Here *judgment* refers to justice or right judgment, which, because of the people's sin, is lacking. Likewise, *righteousness stands afar*, for while men continue in their iniquity there is no room for righteousness.

In language reminiscent of his third chapter Isaiah declares that *truth has stumbled in the street*. Truth can no longer come into the open, in public places, to be seen of men. In the marketplace, where judgment is pronounced, truth is not to be found, for there she has stumbled and fallen. If she is present, she simply wanders

---

13 '*ān*e*ṭāh* — s., since the preceding pl. is construed as a collective.

14 *and as for our iniquities* — a *casus pendens*.

15 *pāšōa'* — *transgressing*, the first of a series of six infinitives absolute governed by *we know them* of v. 12. Along with the second, it has as object *against the Lord*.

16 *hōrō* — *being pregnant with*; these forms are often regarded as absolute infinitives of the *Qal* passive. B renders each by the 1st plural.

about aimlessly, but is no longer in the heart of the nation. *Straightness*[17] (i.e. *uprightness, equity*), therefore, *is unable to enter*. It would appear that Judah took the lead in injustice. This would be strange if the people were constantly suffering injustice in the exile.

15 Truth has become[18] *left behind* (lit., *one left behind*), or *lacking*; and the one who has *turned aside from* (doing) *evil* has become one *despoiled*. Job is described as having turned aside from evil (Job 1:1), and Solomon describes the righteous man as one who departs from evil (Prov. 14:16). Calvin goes to the heart of the matter in declaring, "Whoever wishes to live among men must vie with them in wickedness." Unless one is as wicked as they he will suffer loss; thus widespread did the evil character of Judah become.

With the second half of the verse we enter a new section in the prophet's thought. The tragic condition was not unknown to God, who *saw* it; *and it was evil in his eyes* (i.e. He regarded it as something evil).

16 And he saw that there was no man, and he was astonished that there was no one interceding; and his own arm saved for him, and his own righteousness, it upheld him.

17 And he clothed himself with righteousness as body armor and a helmet of salvation on his head; and he clothed himself with garments of vengeance for clothing, and put on jealousy as a robe.

18 According to their dealings, accordingly will he repay, wrath to his enemies, their recompense to his foes; to the isles their recompense he will repay.

16 The close connection of this verse with the preceding is seen in the repetition of the words *And he saw*. God *saw that there was no man* whatever to stand for His truth and righteousness; He *was astonished that no one was interceding*. In all Israel there was no one who stepped into the breach that sin had made between God

---

17 For the remarkable structure of this verse cf. 32:16. Note also that only in these two verses do judgment (*mišpāṭ*) and righteousness (*tzᵉḏāqāh*) assume human qualities.

18 The imp. with *waw* consecutive serves as a kind of prophetic perf., "and it will be, truth is missed." The actual future begins with v. 18. Note the perf. in v. 17.

and man; no one intervened on behalf of the Lord. None defended
His cause or proclaimed His truth. In saying that God was astonished the prophet does not mean that God had been ignorant of
the situation until He saw it and then this sight brought astonishment to Him. Rather, the language speaks of a genuine astonishment, which would express itself in displeasure and yet in compassion for His own to such an extent that He Himself acts. "The
extraordinary character of this description, and the very violence
which it seems to offer to our ordinary notion of the divine nature,
unavoidably prepare the mind for something higher than the
restoration of the Jews from exile, or the destruction of Jerusalem
by the Romans" (Alexander).

Hence, God's *own arm* (i.e. His almighty power) *saved* the
people for Himself; and His *own righteousness sustained Him*[19]
(i.e. He relied on it alone). The power and righteousness of God
are here combined, as often when the work of salvation is described. Emphasis is lent to *righteousness* through the personal
pronoun *hi'* (*it*).

17 Isaiah now continues in detail the thought that the Lord
acted on Israel's behalf, and does so by means of figurative language. *Righteousness* refers to God's own righteousness, which He
has displayed on behalf of His people and also in judgment upon
the wicked. This righteousness is God's *body* or *breast armor*.[20]

As the first half of the verse commenced with *And he put on,* so
does the second. Both righteousness and salvation have to do with
the deliverance of God's people, but the second half of the verse
turns more to the thought of vengeance upon the enemies. For
raiment (*tilbosheth*) God put on *garments of vengeance* (i.e.
garments that would enable Him to execute vengeance). Finally,
as with a *robe* He enveloped Himself with *zeal,* a word that refers
to His intense concern for His people as well as His determination
that their enemies be destroyed. The armor mentioned is protec-
tive or defensive, which implies that there are several foes who
would attack the Lord and seek His destruction. All this figurative
language is a strong way of saying that God devoted Himself to the
salvation of His people.

19 Note the full m. suffix *-hú* with the 3 f. s. verb.

20 שִׁרְיֹן — cf. Akk. *širiyam,* Egy. *tu-ira-na,* Syr. *šer-yo-no'.* In Ug. (*CMAL,* p.
99; Baal ii. 6. 19, 21) *šryn* is a designation of the Anti-Lebanon. B θώρακα.

18 The general sense of this verse is clear, but there are difficulties of detail. The thought apparently is that God will recompense according to the dealings of men. To His foes He will repay wrath and to His enemies their recompense; to the isles He will recompense their just desert. The word g*emulah* may mean both *recompense* and *deed,* or *dealings;* here the latter sense is to be preferred. The second occurrence of the preposition *'al* (*upon*) is without an object, a phenomenon unparalleled in the Scriptures. We are rendering *accordingly* (lit., *like upon*), but we cannot be certain that this is correct. It is difficult to determine whether the *foes* and *enemies* are the wicked in Israel or the heathen. It is possible, in light of the preceding, that these two words do refer to those members of the chosen race who had steadfastly resisted the Lord and had shown themselves to be His enemies. If this is so, the final clause, with its mention of the *isles,* refers to the heathen, whose judgment is closely connected with that of the wicked in Israel (cf. Jer. 25:29; Ezek. 9:6; 1 Pet. 4:17).

The repetitions are characteristic of Isaiah. By this very succinctness the prophet makes clear how abundantly able God is to deliver and to judge.

19 And they shall fear from the west the name of the LORD, and from the rising of the sun his glory; for the enemy shall come like a stream, the spirit of the LORD raising a banner in it.

20 And the Redeemer shall come from Zion, and from the converts of transgression in Jacob, saith the LORD.

21 And as for me, this is my covenant with them, saith the LORD, my spirit which is upon thee and my words which I have placed in thy mouth; they shall not depart from thy mouth and from the mouth of thy seed, and from the mouth of thy seed's seed, saith the LORD, from now even for ever.

19 The verse commences with a general statement that men all over the world (such is the significance of the two directions given) will *fear* the Lord. This is a godly, reverent, childlike fear before Him in the acknowledgment of His wondrous *name* (i.e. Himself) and His *glory* (the two words are essentially the same in force; cf. 30:27; 35:2; 40:5; 42:12). Earth's remotest nations will worship the Lord.

In the second half of the verse the reason is given for this worldwide worship. It seems best to give the word *ki* (*for*) its natural significance; it then states the reason why there is universal worship of the Lord.

As is well known, the second half of this verse has been made the subject of many different constructions; and it is with some hesitation that one ventures to present his own view. With full realization of the difficulties involved, we believe that the reason for the universal worship of the Lord is that when an enemy would overwhelm the people, God is present in their midst, the result being that the enemy cannot prevent Him from delivering His people. We do not believe that there is warrant for departing from the Masoretic accentuation; hence we would separate *tzar* as the subject (no other subject is expressed), and render, *for there comes like a river the enemy.* It is perhaps correct to regard *nahar* as referring to the turbulent, rushing stream that flows down the narrow wadi bed, overwhelming everything before it.

If the phrase *ruᵃh yhwh* be understood as *a mighty wind,* one might take the verbal form as meaning *driving it on.* Although widely adopted, this is not entirely free from difficulty. It is also possible to translate, *the spirit of the Lord raises a standard in it* (i.e. in the river). In Isaiah the phrase *ruᵃh yhwh* refers to the Lord's Spirit, who endues the Messiah with the qualifications necessary to carry out His work (cf. 11:2ff.). A good case can still be made out for rendering *raises a standard.* The thought of the verse then is that whenever the enemy comes upon God's people, like a flood of all-engulfing water racing down a narrow wadi, the Lord in the very midst of the flood raises a standard, thus showing that He is in control of the situation. Hence, no enemy can conquer His people; He is ever present to subdue such an enemy and to show His sovereignty. For this reason, men from the east and from the setting of the sun worship Him.

20 *Redeemer* should here have its full force as the One who pays a price in order to set free His people. With the word *Zion* occurs a preposition that basically means *to* or *for.* It is not a preposition of motion, and the translation of the Septuagint, *for the sake of Zion,* is therefore quite appropriate. In Romans 11:26 Paul renders *from Zion,* which is correct grammatically, for the preposition may also have this force.[21] Alexander has brought out the basic point by saying that the phrase "strictly means

21 1Q '*l tzywn*. B ἕνεκεν Σιων; Rom. 11:26, ἐκ Σιων.

nothing more than that the advent of the great deliverer promised
has respect to Zion or the chosen people, without deciding what
particular respect, whether local, temporal, or of another nature
altogether." Perhaps, because of the parallel expression *for the
converts,* it is best to render *for Zion.*

The *converts of transgression* are those who have turned from
their transgressions (cf. 1 Thess. 1:10, "Ye turned to God from
idols, etc."). The words serve as an identification of Zion, for
Isaiah is not speaking of the physical city but of the coming of God
for His true people. These converts had once apostatized, but have
now turned from the transgression of apostasy. The reference,
therefore, is not to the nation as a whole, but to the seed according
to election, the true Israel. By the concluding words, *utterance of
the Lord,* the seal of approval is placed upon the promise.

21 With those who have turned from their transgressions the
Lord will make an everlasting covenant. The introductory words
And I make clear that the speaker is the Lord. They are also part
of the covenantal formula used in Genesis 9:9; note also Genesis
17:4. Thus, the very language calls attention to the grace that God
makes known in His covenantal dealings with Israel. *This* refers to
what follows, and the suffix *my* indicates that the covenant is
God's, finding its origin in Him and expressing His desires for
Israel. Here is the reason why God does not completely reject the
whole rebellious and apostate nation; within there was the true
Israel, the remnant of election according to the promise. Actually
this is not a new covenant, but a new administration of the
covenant once made with the fathers. That the language is particularly emphatic appears from the double usage of *saith the Lord.* It
is because the Lord once made this covenant with Abraham that
He will come for Zion.

The content of the promise is found in that the Spirit from on
high and the words placed in Israel's mouth will never depart from
them. In so speaking the Lord uses language similar to that with
which He spoke to Joshua (cf. Josh. 1:8). Thus the people are
reminded of their glorious heritage and emboldened to trust in this
particular declaration of the promise. The language *upon thee*
suggests that the Spirit has descended from above and now rests
upon Israel as a divine gift.

Parallel to the gift of the Spirit is the fact that God has placed
His *words* in Israel's *mouth.* Isaiah deliberately stresses the fact

that God has placed these words in the mouth of Israel to show that they are of divine origin; the Church likewise shall never forget that the Word is from God and not of human origin. The language is reminiscent of that of the prophetic inspiration (cf. Deut. 18:18; 30:14; Rom. 10:8). The gift of the Spirit (cf. John 16:13), who will instruct the Church in all truth and in the comforting, saving words that God has given her, will abide with her and with her seed forever. The Lord is declaring that His eternal truth, revealed to man in words, is the peculiar possession of His people. In the times of the Old Testament, this consisted of revelations made unto the fathers and the prophets. Today, the treasure of the Church is the Holy Scripture, the Word that cannot be broken, inerrant and infallible, the very truth of the eternal God. This Word and the Spirit will never depart from the Church, for the Church as the body of the Head is to declare the truth to all nations that the saving health of God may be seen by all. In language identical with that employed to depict the eternity of the Messiah's kingdom (9:7), Isaiah brings to a close this remarkable chapter. Despite the constant sin and apostasy of His people the Lord abides faithful; the promises will be fulfilled, and the Redeemer will come bringing rich gifts, even His Spirit and Word; and these will abide with His Church forever. To God alone be all the glory.

1 Arise, shine, for thy light is come; and the glory of the LORD
   is risen upon thee.
2 For behold! the darkness will cover the earth and gross darkness the people; and upon thee will the LORD arise, and his
   glory will be seen upon thee.
3 And nations shall walk in thy light, and kings in the brightness
   of thy rising.
4 Lift up round about thine eyes and see; all of them are
   gathered, they come to thee: thy sons from afar will come and
   thy daughters upon the side shall be borne.
5 Then shalt thou see, and shine, and thy heart shall be in awe
   and swell; when the abundance of the sea shall be turned upon
   thee, the strength of nations shall come unto thee.
6 A stream of camels will cover thee, young camels of Midian
   and Ephah, all of them shall come from Sheba; they shall bear
   gold and incense, and the praises of the LORD as good news.

1 This chapter continues the thought of the preceding; it
divides itself into two major divisions, verses 1-12 and verses 13-22.
Pieper calls attention to a chiastic arrangement, the first section
proceeding from internal to external exaltation, and the second
from external to internal. Isaiah begins with two effective imperatives, *Arise, give light.* He addresses Jerusalem or Zion, but it is
obvious that the physical city is not intended. Alexander points to
a similar usage of the word "Rome" to denote the Roman Catholic
Church. Zion is personified as a woman either sitting in dust and
ashes or prostrate because of her sins. Delitzsch rightly speaks of
the creative force in these two words. The command to arise is
accompanied by the strength to fulfill the order. Of herself
Jerusalem could not arise, for her sins had separated her from her
God. When Christ commands the leper, "Be clean," the leper does
not have the power to obey, but as Christ speaks the leper is

cleansed. So, when God through the prophet cries, *Arise*, He enables Jerusalem to arise. It is a word of power, as when Peter commanded Tabitha to arise (Acts 9:40). The second command is *be light* and forms a paronomasia with the following *thy light.* Having received from the Lord His own perfect, holy light, her true salvation, Zion is to radiate that light. As *Arise* refers to the outer man, so does *give light* to the inner. Were not the light of salvation in her heart, Zion could not arise.

The reason for the command is that Jerusalem's light has come to her. Isaiah uses the prophetic perfect; so sure is he of the fulfillment of this promise that he pictures it as already having occurred. Salvation is light, for it dispels the darkness of ignorance, sin, and evil. It is Zion's salvation, for in accordance with the covenant it has been promised to her.

Note the chiasm between *for there has come thy light* and *the glory of the Lord, upon thee it has arisen.* Like a blazing sun, so the glory of the Lord has risen upon Jerusalem, subjecting it to its full and glaring light.[1] This glory is displayed in the whole of the created universe, but was manifested in particular in the history of redemption, as in the Shekinah and the pillar of cloud and fire. It accompanies salvation, for salvation is a manifestation of the Lord's glory.

2 With this verse the prophet begins to amplify and to carry out in some detail the general statement just made. Thus, the introductory *For (ki)* serves to substantiate the utterance of verse 1. *Behold!* concentrates attention upon the significance of what is to be stated. Emphasis falls upon *darkness,* a symbol of ignorance, sin, sorrow, destruction, and perdition. Such darkness *will cover the earth* (not merely the land of Palestine), so that the earth is completely covered and no light shines through. Likewise heavy clouds, i.e. a thick, *heavy darkness,* will cover the peoples of earth. We have translated the verbs by the future inasmuch as the salvation is to come in the future, and this salvation imparted to Israel will draw nations out of darkness. However, the darkness that covers the world is not something to come in the future in accompaniment with salvation; it is already present. The thought is that even though darkness covers the earth, the Lord will arise as the sun upon Zion.

---

[1] It is possible that underlying this beautiful picture is the image of the early sun suddenly leaping upon the horizon from behind the hills of Moab.

The introductory *and* before *upon thee* is adversative. Upon Zion, however, instead of continuing darkness, light will shine. In the previous verse the Lord and His glory were combined as the subject of the verb; here *the Lord* is the subject, and *his glory* is created in a separate phrase. When Isaiah speaks the earth is still enshrouded in darkness, there being only the morning star of the divine promises; but when Christ came, the Sun arose and light broke forth. This light of salvation will draw the nations unto it, and therein lies the reason why Zion is glorious. Wherever the light of God does not arise there is darkness. But we have beheld His glory (John 1:14, 16; cf. also 1 John 1:2ff.) and majesty (cf. Matt. 17:2; 2 Pet. 1:16ff.). Zion becomes light for the nations, for she is the light of the world in that through her the true Light, even Jesus Christ, shines forth.

3 In language reminiscent of his first prophecy of salvation (2:3ff.) Isaiah declares that *nations will walk* with respect to Zion's *light*. The definite article is omitted from *nations*, for there is no false universalism presented here. Zion diffuses light as the moon reflects the light of the sun. It is not Zion's light in her own right, for her own light was darkness; but it is the light that her Lord gives her. The preposition has the idea of *with reference to,* and, as Alexander suggests, may be rendered *in.* As sailors, fearing shipwreck, are guided by the light that comes from the lighthouse, so nations will walk (i.e. carry on their life) in the light that comes from Zion.

Not only nations, but also *kings*, the heads of nations, will walk with respect to the *brightness* of Zion's *arising.* Isaiah probably mentions kings to show that not merely the common people but even those of high rank will come to the saving knowledge of the truth. Zion is conceived as rising, and in rising as shedding brightness. Calvin beautifully remarks: "He alludes to the dawn; for, as the morning-star begins the day in one quarter only of heaven, and immediately the sun enlightens the whole world, so the daybreak was first in Judea, from which the light arose and was afterwards diffused throughout the whole world; for there is no corner of the earth which the Lord has not enlightened by this light."

4 Continuing his command, Isaiah repeats verbatim in the first distich the language of 49:18, and the second distich reflects upon 49:22 (cf. also 43:5-7; 49:12; 57:14; 62:10; Deut. 28:64). *Saviv*

THE BOOK OF ISAIAH

(round about) should be construed with *śeʾi* (*lift up*).[2] *Kullam* (*all of them*) refers not to the kings but to the sons and daughters mentioned in the second distich; the masculine forms include both sons and daughters. Jerusalem is personified as a mother who looks about with love and tenderness as her children are gathered again unto her. The last clause is to be rendered, *and thy daughters upon the side will be borne*.[3] Evidently Isaiah is using the figure of carrying children upon the hips, although this cannot be dogmatically asserted; even the women are carried like children. The sons are pictured as walking, the daughters as being carried. Here the prophet refers not to apostate Israelites, but to the heathen who have been converted and are coming from afar in all directions. The picture is essentially the same as in 2:2-4. The heathen seek Zion, the dwelling place of the one living and eternal God.

5 The result of this great influx will be a wondrous and fearful rejoicing on Zion's part. We render the first two verbs, *thou shalt see and thou shalt be radiant*. This probably refers to the face's lighting up with joy, although it could refer to the heart's burning with happiness or gladness. Inasmuch as the following clause speaks of the heart, however, it probably refers to the radiance of the countenance. The heart will *throb* (lit., *tremble in fear*) and *swell* (lit., *grow broad*). Tremendous emotion will seize Zion as she sees the heathen coming to her in faith, her true sons and daughters.

In the second distich Isaiah gives the reason for Zion's emotion. The word *hᵃmon* is generally translated *abundance*, but whether this refers to the goods of the people or to their own persons is difficult to tell. Here *sea* stands for the nations, a figure taken over by Daniel (cf. Dan. 7:1ff.); and *the abundance of the sea* would be the fullness of what the sea possesses. All that at one time belonged to the heathen nations will now be turned over to Zion for the people and all that they have will be dedicated to Jerusalem. The final clause parallels the one just discussed by asserting that *the strength of the nations shall be brought* (the verb is impersonal) to Zion. Here the *strength* likely refers to the

2 The adverb occurring between the verb and the object is a characteristic of Isaiah; cf. 37:23; 40:26; 49:18; 51:6.

3 *teʾāmanāh* — *carried by a nurse*. In pause the *Dagesh* may be omitted from the *Nun*. The mention of *sons* and *daughters* expresses entirety; cf. 3:1; 16:6; 43:6; 49:22.

446

riches of the heathen, although the word often refers to military strength. It is no wonder that Zion is aroused, for she sees a blessing of which she had never dreamed. The nations and their wealth come to her, for "All things are yours," that they may be used for the glory of God.

6 Traders from distant nations will bring their treasures to the Lord. *An abundance* (Jerome picturesquely translates *inundatio, an inundation*) *of camels will cover* the land, in that they will be everywhere, just as though a flood had overflowed the land, covering all. The same verb is used in 11:9 of the waters covering the seas. The precise significance of *beker* is not known, but we may possibly translate it by *young dromedary*. These belonged to Midian and Ephah, words that probably indicate not the tribe but the tribal ancestor. According to Genesis 25:4, Ephah was the son of Midian and the nephew of Jokshan the father of Sheba. *All of these* (i.e. all the camels and dromedaries) *will come from Sheba,* a district in Arabia that may probably be identified with what is today known as Yemen. It is well to note the stress in this context upon the coming to Zion, in which fact there is revealed the attractive power of the Gospel.

The animals will not come empty but bearing burdens of precious gifts, *gold and incense,* substances that were highly prized among the ancients. At the birth of our Lord the wise men came bearing gifts of gold, frankincense, and myrrh (Matt. 2:11). Those who bring these gifts desire to offer the best unto their God. Here is the expression of a heartfelt devotion.

This devotion manifests itself in the praises of God which are proclaimed. The plural (*praises*) is perhaps for the sake of intensity. We may either construe *praises* as the object of the verb and render, *and the praises of the Lord they will proclaim,* or else render, *they will proclaim that others are praising the Lord.* On this latter rendering the meaning is that they are announcing as good news the fact that praises are being offered to the Lord. The subject must be the animals just mentioned, and it is possible that they proclaim the Lord's praises by their bearing of precious gifts to Zion.

> 7 All the flocks of Kedar shall be gathered for thee, the rams of Nebaioth shall minister to thee; they shall ascend acceptably my altar, and the house of my beauty I shall beautify.

8 Who are these that fly as a cloud, and as doves to their windows?

9 Because for me the isles are waiting, and the ships of Tarshish in the first place, to bring thy sons from far, their silver and their gold with them: for the name of the LORD their God, and for the Holy One of Israel, because he has glorified thee.

10 And strangers shall build thy walls, and their kings shall serve thee; for in my wrath I smote thee, and in my favor I have had mercy on thee.

11 And thy gates shall be open continually, day and night, they shall not be shut: to bring into thee the strength of nations and their kings led.

12 For the nation and the kingdom that will not serve thee shall perish, and the nations shall surely be wasted.

7 Nations will also bring their animals to serve the Lord in offerings. *All the flocks of Kedar* perhaps stands for all Kedar's wealth, and *the rams of Nebaioth* for the best that Nebaioth can offer. Kedar was the second son of Ishmael (Gen. 25:13), whose descendants lived in the desert between Syria and Mesopotamia. Nebaioth is mentioned only here and in Genesis 25:13; 28:9 and 1 Chronicles 1:29, and always in connection with Kedar or the descendants of Ishmael.[4] The reference is probably to the Nabateans, inhabitants of Arabia Petrea. Kedar's flocks *will be gathered* for the benefit of Zion, and Nabatea's rams *will serve* Zion.[5] The word suggests a free-will service as opposed to compulsory labor.

The second part of the verse points out how this service is performed, namely by ascending Yahweh's altar acceptably. Thus the Lord will beautify the house of His beauty, i.e. His beautiful house. This house of God, beautiful in its existence, will be further beautified through the offerings that the converted heathen bring.

In keeping with the general tenor of this context we interpret this verse as presenting, through the figures of the Old Testament dispensation, a worship that will be acceptable to God, because of the sacrifice of the Servant of the Lord. In other words, the prophet is presenting the New Testament truth in figures belonging to the Old Testament. It would be incorrect, then, to interpret this verse as teaching a revival or reinstitution of animal sacrifices.

4 Cf. "Ashurbanipal's Campaign Against the Arabs," *ANET*, pp. 298-300; and Pliny *Natural History* v. 12.

5 *yešāreṯûneḵ* — the suffix is appended to the imp. ending in -*ûn*, here with a connecting vowel; cf. 60:10.

To appeal to 3 John 7 to show that Christian ministers took nothing from the Gentiles is actually beside the point. The picture here given is that of Gentiles converted to Christ who bring all that they have and devote it to His service.

8 Variety is one of the distinguishing characteristics of Isaiah's style. To express the influx of the heathen he now asks a question. He looks out toward the sea (the Mediterranean), and sees there shadowy forms, which seem to be flying like a cloud. Does this looking toward the west suggest that the future of the Church lies in the west, and that from the west there will come those who are to enter the Church? Isaiah asks, *Who are these that fly like a cloud?*[6] Changing the figure he compares them to *doves* that fly unto their windows, i.e. to the place where their young are. The prophet probably addresses his question to Zion herself and prepares for the answer to be given in the following verse.

9 Alexander is correct in asserting that this verse contains a virtual if not a formal answer to the question just posed. Zion is not to wonder that the ships are approaching, for the whole world is awaiting God's command to bring Zion's sons to her. Hence it is best to translate *Because* or *For,* i.e. as giving the reason for the haste described in verse 8. In the hearts of those who hasten there is a lively faith; and Zion sees this hurrying, for the islands are waiting for God. The words *for me* are emphatic; *the islands* (i.e. the coastlands of the Mediterranean), with their *ships of Tarshish*[7] *in the first place,* are waiting to bring to Zion their sons who are far away. Indeed, they will also bring *their silver*[8] *and their gold* to the Name of the Lord. They realize to whom they are bringing Zion's sons, for they know His Name. He is both the Lord God of Zion and Israel's Holy One. Finally the reason for this action is given, namely that God has beautified Zion and so inspired the isles to wait for Him.

10 Continuing the description, Isaiah asserts that *sons of strangers* (i.e. *strangers*) will build Zion's walls. In 49:16 there is mention of these walls, and again in 62:6. The building is to be in

---

[6] The question *Who are these?* serves as a *casus pendens*; thus, *Who are these? — like a cloud they fly.*

[7] On Tarshish, cf. Vol. I, p. 128, note 52.

[8] *their silver* — introduces a circumstantial clause without *waw*.

the future. Likewise the kings of strangers will serve Jerusalem; for when God was angry with Zion He smote her, but when He had favor toward her He showed mercy to her. Thus, the second part of the verse gives the reason for what is stated in the first. Some have applied the fulfillment of the prophecy to the work of Cyrus, Darius, and Artaxerxes Longimanus; but their actions were only a prelude to the real fulfillment in Jesus Christ and the preaching of the Gospel unto the Gentiles (cf. Acts 15:14ff., where the rebuilding of David's booth is equated with the outcalling of the Gentiles). The prophecy is not speaking of the literal rebuilding of Jerusalem's walls, but of the building up of God's kingdom through the inclusion of Gentiles therein.

Calvin well remarks that when kings serve Zion they do not lose their status as kings, but on the contrary are then enabled to carry out their proper function so as to glorify God and to manifest righteousness in their reigns. Happy is that nation whose ruler looks not to man for the solution of his problems but walks in the light of the Lord.

The anger of God was brought about through the nation's sins, and hence He smote Zion. Her walls were not destroyed by the same strangers who now build them up, but the wickedness of the people themselves brought about God's wrath; and those who now build Zion's walls are willing, converted strangers. Because He is faithful to His promises of salvation God again showed favor to Zion, and had mercy upon her. This truth is stated lest the Jews think that the change in their fortunes was a matter of chance, common to the lot of the world. Although this prophecy is not to be restricted to the exile, nevertheless the first manifestation of mercy appeared in the return of the exiles to their homeland.

11 The action of the strangers is continuous, for Zion's gates will always stand open. The figure is not that of protection; the gates are open not because the enemy can no longer enter the city but in order that those who will may enter.

Isaiah gives the reason why this is so, namely, to bring unto Zion the strength[9] of the Gentiles. The kings of the Gentiles will also come, led as in a procession. The word suggests that they are escorted into the city, not against their will but freely and voluntarily, for they have been inwardly conquered and are true *douloi* of the Lord.

---

9 Cf. comments on v. 5 above.

450

John makes use of the language of this verse in speaking of the heavenly city: "The gates of it shall not be shut at all by day, for there shall be no night there" (Rev. 21:25). This usage is appropriate, even though it does not agree with the Masoretic accentuation; for Jesus Christ has brought His people into the heavenlies, and the eternal life in heaven is but a continuation of the heavenly existence His people now enjoy. Hence, the descriptions that characterize the Zion of salvation are admirably adapted also to express the characteristics of the heavenly Zion.

12 Zion's gates will always stand open, for many will enter them; but those who do not enter *will perish*. It is obvious that this prophecy does not fit the time of the restoration from exile. What nations at that time perished because they did not serve the empirical Zion? To lend intensity to his statement Isaiah uses the infinitive absolute. Sure desolation will be the lot of those who do not serve Jerusalem.

13   The glory of Lebanon shall come unto thee, the cypress, plane, and box together: to adorn the place of my sanctuary, and the place of my feet I will honor.

14   And they shall come unto thee bowing down, the sons of thy oppressors, then shall bow down to the soles of thy feet all thy despisers; and they shall call thee The City of the LORD, Zion of the Holy One of Israel.

15   Instead of thy being forsaken and hated and with none passing; and I will place thee for an exaltation of eternity, a joy of age and age.

16   And thou shalt suck the milk of nations, and the breast of kings shalt thou suck; and thou shalt know that I the LORD am thy Savior and thy Redeemer is the Mighty One of Jacob.

13 Zion is to be beautified with the glory that Lebanon[10] will bring. This glory, namely Lebanon's trees, will come unto Zion to be her perpetual possession. Three types of trees are mentioned, taken from 41:19 (see comments on that verse for a discussion of the nature of the trees). At one time (*together*) different kinds of trees will come for the sake of beautifying the place of God's sanctuary, i.e. the Temple. *The place of God's feet* is another designation for the Temple, which is often referred to as God's footstool (e.g. 1 Chron. 28:2). By such language, as Calvin points

---

10 *The glory of Lebanon* — found elsewhere only in 35:2.

out, God raises us from the feet to a consideration of the head. There is a double work of beauty. When Lebanon gives her glory, that will beautify the city; and God Himself will also honor Zion. Zion is beautified when those who are converted to the truth yield to the Lord all that they have. A heart that is deeply devoted to God and consecrates to Him all its possessions is a heart whose possessions beautify the place of worship.

14 Reflecting upon his earlier prophecy in 2:2-4, Isaiah declares that the former oppressors of Zion will come (flow?) unto her. Sons of oppressors are mentioned, which probably refers to the oppressors themselves, for in the parallel expression the despisers are set forth as acting in the same manner as the sons of the oppressors. The condition in which they come is *bowed down*,[11] i.e. humbled, as suppliants. The despisers bow down to the soles of Zion's feet, an expression indicating complete devotion and supplication. Such worship and adoration is not directed to Zion herself but to the Lord, who reigns in her midst. Thus is the grace of Israel's God able to change His enemies from being hostile toward His truth to eagerly embracing it.

That there has been a true conversion is seen in that those who come to Zion address her as *The City of Yahweh* (i.e. the city that belongs to Yahweh in a unique sense, for His presence is found there). A second appellation is *Zion of* (belonging to) *the Holy One of Israel*. This verse reflects upon 45:14 and 49:23.

15 We may render the first word either *Instead* or *Whereas*. The first rendering is intended to introduce a contrast: *Instead* of the former condition of forsakenness, there will be an eternity of blessing. The second is not essentially different: *Whereas* thou hast been forsaken, thou wilt be eternally blessed. Perhaps the first alternative is preferable. Instead of Zion's being a forsaken or abandoned one, such as she was at the exile and is whenever God withdraws His face, a new condition will appear. The word *hated* refers to the hatred men had for the Church; *and there is none passing* indicates that Zion is without inhabitants. This clause expresses a circumstance, which we may express, *abandoned and hated, while no one passed through*.

The apodosis is given in the first person, introduced by *waw*, a

---

11 *šᵉḥōaḥ* — an adverbial use of the inf. construct, denoting an external state, *bowed down*.

conjunction here difficult to translate. God *will place* the city *for an exaltation* and a *rejoicing*, i.e. He will make it such. Instead of being an object of despising, it will be an exaltation; and instead of being abandoned and hated, it will be an object of rejoicing.[12] This condition will endure eternally. In themselves the words are capable of referring to a long period of time, but here the context demands that God's work of salvation be an eternal salvation. The beauty of the last expression should not be overlooked. Throughout one generation after another the Church will be an object of rejoicing for all those whom God has made captive to Himself. Calvin remarks: " . . . The Prophet does not speak of a few years or a short period, but embraces the whole course of redemption, from the end of the captivity to the preaching of the Gospel, and finally, down to the end of the reign of Christ." And again, " . . . Under the Cross the glory of Christ shines forth, so that the name of God remains, and there is a people that calls upon him by faith."

16 Deriving a figure from Deuteronomy 33:19, Isaiah sets forth the great influx of wealth and power that will come to Zion from the converted Gentiles. As a mother gives the milk of her breasts to her child, so do the nations give of their own life and vital energy to the Church so that the Church is in possession of nourishing food for a healthful growth. To show the luxuriant quality and richness of the food that Zion receives, it is stated also that she will suck *the breast of kings*.

That the Church is exalted is manifested in that she possesses knowledge. She will come to know through experience of redemption that the One who has delivered her from her abandoned condition when she was hated and despised, and has raised her to eternal exaltation and rejoicing, is the Lord her Savior, and also her Redeemer, the Mighty One of Jacob (cf. comments on 1:24). Yet mere experience alone is not a sufficient teacher; there must be the accompanying word, by which means Zion will learn the meaning of the experiences through which she is to pass.

> 17 Instead of bronze I shall bring gold, and instead of iron I shall
> bring silver, and instead of wood bronze, and instead of stones
> iron; and I shall place thy government peace, and thy rulers
> righteousness.

12 The word *rejoicing, mesôs,* is a key word of Isaiah's; cf. 8:6; 24:8, 11; 32:13, 14; 62:5; 65:18; 66:10.

18 There shall no more be heard violence in thy land, desolation and ruin in thy borders; and thou shalt call thy walls salvation, and thy gates praise.

19 The sun shall no longer become light to thee by day, and for brightness the moon shall not shine to thee; but the LORD shall become to thee a light forever and thy God shall become thy beauty.

20 Thy sun shall set no more, and thy moon shall not be withdrawn: for the LORD shall become an eternal light, and the days of thy mourning shall be completed.

21 And thy people all of them shall be righteous; for ever shall they inherit the earth, the branch of my planting, the work of my hands, to glorify myself.

22 The small shall become a thousand, and the little one a powerful nation; I the LORD in its time will hasten it.

17 God declares in what manner He will beautify and stabilize Zion, namely by the replacement of good materials with better. Beginning with those materials that serve for Zion's beautifying, the list imperceptibly passes over to the mention of those which assure her security from attack. Everything that hitherto has been made of copper will from now on be made of gold. Emphasis falls upon the divine activity, in that the words *I will bring* occur twice. The outward beauty and stability will reflect an inner like condition. *Peace* is a predicate of *thy government,* for God will make peace to be Zion's government. Likewise, righteousness will be her rulers. This is not merely a strong way of saying that the government will be peaceful and the rulers righteous, but rather, peace herself is to be the government, and righteousness the rulers, as vicegerents of the Lord. No longer will human rulers be needed.

18 In the first distich Isaiah relates in negative terms what he has just stated positively. To say that *violence will no longer be heard* means that men will no longer know of violence, for there will be none. When God purposed to destroy the earth with a flood, the earth was full of violence; in the redeemed Zion, however, violence is unknown as well as its companions *desolation and ruin.* Zion is conceived as possessing a land and boundaries, and these will be completely free of those things that make impossible the presence of peace and righteousness. Instead Zion will see that her very walls are salvation (lit., *thou shalt call salvation thy walls,* i.e. *regard thy walls as salvation*) and that her gates are praise.

454

The walls, therefore, will afford salvation, for they will protect from the enemy; and the gates will be occasions of praise. When the Gentiles reflect upon Zion, that she is the city of the Holy One of Israel, her praise will be seen.

19 Isaiah returns to the thoughts with which he had begun this chapter, namely that Zion will be light, majestically unfolding this thought, and, as Delitzsch says, opening it up in all its eschatological depth. He sees the future salvation in its fullness, including both the New Testament age and the eternal state. With the first advent of Jesus Christ these prophecies received their fulfillment, but that fulfillment will not be realized to its greatest extent until sin is removed and eternity ushered in.

The introductory words, *There shall not be to thee,* call to mind the First Commandment, "There shall not be to thee other gods." Perhaps the resemblance is intentional, even suggesting a command, to show that any light other than the Lord is idolatry. *To thee* is the ethical dative of advantage, "for thy benefit and use." The passage does not actually state that the sun will be done away, but merely that it is no longer to give light to Zion by day. The chiasm should be noted. "Instead of the sun and moon there will be to thee (again dative of advantage) the Lord for light," i.e. the Lord will eternally be Zion's light. In Revelation 21:23 and 22:5 these figures are applied to the eternal city. The last clause should be rendered, *and thy God will become thy glory.* Darkness, the result of sin, is dispelled, and pure uncreated Light shines forth in Zion.

20 Zion will never again have a sun that sets nor a moon that disappears. Emphasis falls upon unbroken constancy, whereas in the previous verse it was more upon endless continuousness.[13] This constancy is due to the fact that the Lord will become an eternal light for Zion. As the previous verse concluded with the abrupt introduction of the phrase *and thy God for thy glory,* so this one closes with the words *and there will be complete the days of thy mourning.* This mourning was the period of sin and ignorance when the light of God's presence was not known. When His presence is near, sorrow and sighing flee away. For every member of Zion the period of mourning is at an end.

---

13 Note the chiasm in v. 20a; negative verb, subject: subject, negative verb.

21 Having spoken about Zion, the prophet now turns to her inhabitants, and begins with the declaration that all of her people *will be righteous*. The word is employed in the same full sense as *holy* in 4:3 (cf. also 35:8; 52:1 and Rev. 21:7, 27). It is the Church in its perfection that is in view, not as it is at any one particular moment, for in the Church there are hypocrites as well as the righteous. Daily Christ purifies His Church until finally the time of harvest comes. Psalm 73:1, "How good God is to Israel, to those who are of an upright heart," brings out the essential idea.

Those who are righteous *will inherit the land forever*, i.e. Palestine, which was promised to Abraham (Gen. 12:1, 7; 13:15; 15:18, etc.). In a sense the inheritance of Palestine is the inheriting of the earth (Rom. 4:13; cf. also Isa. 49:8). Obviously this language is not to be understood in a literal sense; are the righteous to live eternally in Palestine? Inheritance of the land is a symbol of the future spiritual blessings that come to man through Christ.

In the final half of the verse the people are characterized as the *shoot of my planting* and *the work of my hands*. The figure of a plant that God Himself has planted occurs often in Scripture (cf. Ps. 92:14; Matt. 15:13; John 15:1, 2; Isa. 5:1ff.). It expresses Zion's dependence upon God for the origin and sustaining of its spiritual life. The thought of the Church as God's workmanship is also found elsewhere (cf. Eph. 2:10; John 15:8). These phrases teach the profound and necessary truth that Zion the Church is the creation of God. It is not a human institution, and inasmuch as it is divine it must carry out its work in obedience to the commands of the One who formed it. Lastly, its purpose is that God be glorified. We may render either *for glorifying myself* or *to be glorified*. May we who are the people of Zion in no way hinder this purpose of the Lord!

22 The chapter concludes with a further statement of the increase of the Church. The *little one* refers to the individual in Israel; it may be rendered *the smallest*, although the superlative rendering is not necessary. Apparently the thought is that he who is now small will have a host of descendants so that he can be described as *a thousand*, and the little one will become *a powerful nation*. *In its time* (i.e. at the proper time determined by God, the fullness of time; cf. Gal. 4:4) God Himself *will hasten this*. The remarkable growth of Zion, a multitude that no man can number, from every kindred, tribe, and nation, is to be explained only

456

because God Himself brings it about. Although the work of God may seem slow to us, nevertheless, in His own time He hastens it (i.e. He suddenly acts when men are not expecting it) .[14]

Delitzsch points out that there is an ascending scale of addresses between 51:17-23 and the present chapter, which is the climax, and that the entire section forms a contrast with the address to the daughter of Babylon in chapter forty-eight.

[14] Cf. Vulg. *Ego Dominus, in tempore eius subito faciam istud.*

1 The Spirit of the Lord God is upon me; for the Lord hath anointed me to preach good tidings unto the afflicted, he hath sent me to bind up the broken-hearted, to proclaim liberty to the captives and the opening of the prison to them that are bound.

2 To proclaim the acceptable year of the Lord, and the day of vengeance of our God; to comfort all who mourn.

3 To place upon the mourners of Zion—to give them a crown instead of ashes, the oil of joy for mourning, a garment of praise for a weak spirit; and it shall be called to them the oaks of righteousness, the planting of the Lord to glorify Himself.

1 There is a close relation between this chapter and the preceding; having described the future blessing of Zion Isaiah goes on to introduce the One who is to bring that blessing. The introductory words suggest that the speaker is one called to and well endued for the prophetic office. The enduement of the Spirit implies not merely an anointing but also that in the anointing rich gifts were bestowed. *The Spirit of the Lord Yahweh* is the Spirit of the all-powerful God, who can accomplish the exaltation of Zion just described. Pieper correctly points out that this passage is a compound of 11:2; 42:1; 49:8 and 50:4, 5 in that what in those passages was promised now occurs. As in 49:1 and 50:4, the mysterious personage is introduced as speaking. Our Lord read this passage in the synagogue at Capernaum and remarked that "this day is this prophecy fulfilled in your ears" (Luke 4:21). Although Christ does not explicitly declare that He is the speaker, it is difficult to interpret otherwise, for the work described is such that only God can accomplish; it is Messianic. Hence, to limit the reference to Isaiah, or to the prophets generally, is not warranted. The speaker is the Messiah. On the other hand, Calvin is probably correct when he points out that the passage may apply to the prophets, in that

458

they were anointed of the Lord and spoke His words under His authority. Through their faithful proclamation Christ accomplishes the purposes set forth in this passage. At the same time the predominant emphasis is upon the servant himself. Never does the prophet put himself into the fore; he always keeps his own person in the background. What is said agrees admirably with what is said elsewhere of the work of the servant, and the previous "servant" passages prepare for this one.

We may render the particle *ya'an* by *for* or *because,* since it gives the reason for what has just been stated. To paraphrase: "Because the Lord has anointed me, the Spirit of the Lord is upon me." What was imparted to the speaker in the anointing was the Spirit of God (see comments on 11:1). Delitzsch is not amiss when he suggests that the choice of this word *(to anoint)* hints at the fact that the speaker and the Messiah are the same individual. There is a notable contrast between *Spirit* at the beginning of the first clause and *me* at the close of the second, and in each clause the Lord is mentioned. This is a Trinitarian shade that should not be overlooked. Not to be overlooked also is the emphasis upon *me,* which suggests that the speaker is a person of unusual significance. (For examples of anointing see 1 Kings 1:34; 19:16; Leviticus 8:12.) In 42:1 the Lord says, "I have put My Spirit upon him," and here the servant declares that the Spirit of the Lord is upon him. This anointing with the Spirit is essential and abiding so that the work described may be carried out.

What is pictured here reflects partly upon the exile but describes also New Testament and eternal relationships. It is the Messianic work, which no prophet in himself could carry out; hence the speaker not merely announces but also dispenses the great gifts of God. He preaches *good tidings to the afflicted,* i.e. he evangelizes them in that he declares to them deliverance from their bondage. He speaks, however, not of himself but as one sent from God. His purpose is *to bind up the broken of heart.* Their sins have weighed them down so that their heart is, as it were, broken, and there is no heart left in them. Healing is accomplished through the proclaiming of *liberty to the captives.* Isaiah employs a phrase used in the law of the year of jubilee, which occurred every fiftieth year after the seven sabbatical periods (cf. Lev. 25:10, 13; 27:24; Jer. 34:8-10; Ezek. 46:17). Whereas the phrase *broken of heart* characterized the inner condition of the *afflicted,* the words *captives* and *them that are bound* refer to their outward state. There may be a possible reflection upon the exile, but the captivity in which the true Israel of God lay was far deeper. The people were captives to sin and bound with the fetters of iniquity. For such there is to be a blessed release and an opening. Isaiah is not speaking of deliverance from a physical prison but from the spiritual darkness in which the people had been imprisoned. Deliverance from that spiritual darkness is an opening of the eyes, in contrast to the darkness in which the people were.

When Christ said that *this day is this prophecy fulfilled in your ears,* He did not mean that the prophecy was exhausted on that particular day, but rather that the time had now come of which Isaiah spoke, and that the prophecy would be fulfilled throughout the course of the Church upon earth. The passage brings to the fore the great work of redemption that the Messiah accomplished, and the proclamation of the Gospel that He and the disciples under His authority carry out.

2 The first clause may be rendered, *to proclaim a year of favor with respect to the Lord,* although some take the preposition as indicating the genitive, *of the Lord.* Isaiah uses *year,* it would seem, with reference to the year of jubilee upon which he has just reflected; thus the word is the practical equivalent of *day.* Some have suggested that the mercy is manifested in a year and the vengeance in a day. Isaiah elsewhere also uses these two words in parallel (cf. 34:8 and 63:4, and note 49:8). The reference is not to one particular year or day but to the time when God manifests His favor to His people and His *vengeance*[1] upon those who have persisted in their evil ways. As so often, Isaiah uses the words *Lord* and *our God* together. The passage goes back to 49:8, 9 (cf. 2 Cor. 6:2). The purpose of the proclamation is *to comfort all who mourn* (cf. 49:13; 57:18). This short clause forms the subject of the following verse.

3 The first infinitive in this context is best rendered *To put on,* for the prophet is speaking of placing a crown instead of ashes. The sentence is interrupted by a second infinitive, which also resumes the thought, a characteristic of Isaiah's writing. Isaiah does not correct himself, but simply adds to what he has just said. The first infinitive is suitable to express the thought of putting on a crown, but the second is necessary to show the abundance of good

---

[1] נקם — possibly *requital.*

gifts that God gives to those who mourn. By a change in the order of the consonants between *pe'er* and *'epher*, Isaiah contrasts *crown* with *ashes*. The mourners of Zion are either those who are mourning in Zion, or those who mourn for Zion. It is probably best, however, to combine the two concepts, inasmuch as both are involved. Only those in Zion mourn who grieve because of their own sins and the consequent hurt that their sins bring to Zion.

The phrase *oil of gladness* appears elsewhere only in Psalm 45:7. On occasions of joy, it would seem, men anointed themselves with oil (cf. Eccl. 9:8; Song of Sol. 4:10; 2 Sam. 12:20; 14:2; Ps. 23:5). From now on, all occasions will be joyful; and in place of the mourning of the present there will be the anointing with oil that accompanies gladness and rejoicing. *Garments of praise* are those which call forth admiration and praise on the part of those who behold them. The thought could also be that praise is the garment in which God's people will be clothed. In place of a faint spirit will be a vigorous bursting forth in bold praise of God. Such praise is the very opposite of a faint spirit; indeed, the praise of God is the best way to overcome a faint spirit.

Inasmuch as men see these signs of joy on the redeemed *they will call them* (or, *they will be called*) *the oaks of righteousness*. The oak (terebinth) is a sign of strength and durability, and the figure is applicable to the redeemed because through the righteousness of God they have been made strong and durable. They are trees that exhibit righteousness, which comes from God and is acceptable with Him, for they have been planted by Him for His own beauty (see comments on 60:21 for the meaning of this last phrase).

> 4 And they shall build up the ruins of antiquity, the desolations of the ancients they shall raise; and they shall make new the cities of ruin, the desolations of age and age.
>
> 5 And strangers shall stand and shepherd your flocks, and the children of the foreigner will be your ploughmen and your vinedressers.
>
> 6 And ye, priests of the LORD ye shall be called, the servants of our God it shall be said of you; the strength of nations ye shall eat, and in their glory ye shall substitute yourselves.

4 The subject of the verb *will build* is *they who mourn in Zion*. From the condition of grief and pining away men engage in strong activity, the building up of *the ruins of antiquity* (i.e. of ancient times) and *the desolations* that were present at the time of the ancients. The reference is not merely to the rebuilding of Jerusalem after the exile, for the language is hardly applicable to that, but to the building up of the Church from the ravages sin has made throughout the ages. (For the general thought of the verse, see the comments on 49:8; 54:3 and 58:12.) Note the chiasm in the first half of the verse. *Renew* is used in the sense of *repair* (cf. 2 Chron. 15:8 and 24:4). The cities are present but they are desolate, and these ruined cities must once more be built up so that they will again possess their former glory.

5 By means of beautiful Oriental symbolism Isaiah shows how the converted Gentiles will serve God's Church, the true Zion. The word *strangers* (*zarim*) often has the sense of enemy, but here all thought of hostility is lacking. It is difficult to determine the precise force of *shall stand*. It may have reference to service, but it may also be that it is only a description of the practice of Oriental shepherds. As to the agricultural side of Israel's life, *the sons of strangeness* (see comments on 60:10) will be her *husbandmen* (*ploughmen*) and *vinedressers*.

The verse does not teach that the Jews will be supplanted by the Gentiles; but rather in the Messianic kingdom all will work together, Jew and Gentile, for the distinction will then be broken down. The strangers are not Gentiles in opposition to Jews, but all who once were strangers to the commonwealth of Israel because of their sin. The terms *shepherds, husbandmen,* and *vinedressers* are figures to describe the work those who once were aliens will perform. They probably designate all the work necessary to maintain on this earth the Church of God.

6 There is a contrast between verse 5 and the present verse. Verse 5 stressed the work that the new converts will perform for Zion, and this verse in turn emphasizes what the people of Zion will do for these new converts. As they supply the temporal wants of Zion, so she in turn will supply their spiritual needs. Reflecting upon the promise in Exodus 19:6 the prophet announces that *as for you,* i.e. the inhabitants of Zion and members of the Church, *ye shall be called the priests of the Lord.*[2] The Church of the new

---

[2] "Not only as instructors and reclaimers of the unbelieving world do they enjoy this sacred dignity, but also as the only representatives of their Great High Priest, in him and through him possessing free access to the fountain of salvation and the throne of grace" (Heb. 4:4-16) (Alexander).

covenant possesses no outward priesthood, but every member is a priest before God and needs no human mediator other than the God-Man Jesus Christ. The offerings each priest brings are spiritual, for each is to present himself as a living sacrifice (cf. Rom. 12:1). The term *servants* (*mesharetey*) probably has reference to honorable and distinguished service. The first half of the verse begins with *you* and concludes with *to you*.

The last two phrases show that the Church will thrive on the goods of those who are converted to her. Alexander, in illustration of the contrast between this and the preceding verse, points to Romans 15:27 and notes that, inasmuch as the Israel of God is charged with the duty of communicating spiritual things to those who are without, so in turn is it entitled to become greater in strength through the goods of those who become part of it. For the significance of *heyl* (*strength*) see the comments on 60:5. Through eating this strength Zion will be nourished. The last clause is difficult to interpret because of the verb. If it comes from the root *yamar* (to exchange) it means that Zion will enter into the glory of the Gentiles by exchange, i.e. will substitute herself in the Gentiles' glory. On the other hand, if the root is *'amar* (to say) the verb used in the *Hithpael* would signify "to speak to oneself," i.e. "to boast." It is difficult to decide between the two, but in any case the thought is present that Zion will obtain the *glory* of the Gentiles, i.e. their wealth and possessions.

> 7 Instead of your shame, double, and instead of their confusion, they shall celebrate their portion; therefore in their land they shall inherit double, everlasting joy shall be to them.
>
> 8 For I the LORD love judgment, hating that which is taken away unjustly; and I will give their hire truly, and an everlasting covenant I make for them.
>
> 9 And there shall be known among the nations their seed, and their issue in the midst of the peoples. All seeing them shall acknowledge them that they are a seed the LORD has blessed.

7 Here is a further declaration of the glory to come in place of the present condition of desolation. Instead of the *shame* that now hangs over the people they will receive double honor or glory (cf. 40:2), and *instead of their confusion* (the change of person is quite frequent in Isaiah) they will give a ringing cry with respect to *their portion* (i.e. the portion of grace that they will receive from God). The preposition *tahath* (*instead of*) is omitted before the word *confusion,* for in exalted style the governing power of the preposition may at times be extended to the corresponding substantive found in the second member of a parallelism. This phenomenon, incidentally, occurs quite frequently in Isaiah (cf. 15:8; 28:6; 40:19; 42:22; 48:9, 14; 58:13; 61:7).

Therefore, i.e. inasmuch as this wondrous change will occur, *they will inherit double.* The phrase *in their land* refers to the land promised to them, namely Canaan, and is used as a figure of the blessings God has promised in the Messiah. For the sense of *double* see the comments of chapter forty, note 8. Lastly, to them there will be a *rejoicing of eternity,* i.e. *an eternal rejoicing.* The figures show how impossible a literal fulfillment would be. Are all the redeemed to live eternally in Palestine, having received a precise double honor for their former shame and possessing eternal joy? To ask the question is to answer it. God has something far greater for His elect than an eternal life in the earthly land of Palestine.

8 The introductory *ki* (*For*) seems to have reference not to the preceding but to verse 8b, and may be rendered *Because,* or *Inasmuch as.* The Lord loves and hates, but He loves *judgment* and hates the thing *taken away in injustice.* Hence, the absolute justice of God requires that He destroy His enemies and deliver His people. *Their hire* (i.e. the result of their work) God will give *in truth,* i.e. He will place it in security and safety. After God has placed His people in their possession as a recompense for their shame, they will forever enjoy this inheritance. They will never again, as at present, become a prey for unrighteousness; but the fruit of their work will be secured against unjust prey. The pledge of these blessings is that God voluntarily will establish an eternal covenant for His people. Although He owes them nothing, He is ever present, ready to aid and defend them.

9 This verse sets forth the result of God's saving work. The seed of God's people will be recognized *among the nations* as one that the Lord has richly blessed with salvation. Completing a partial chiasm, Isaiah states essentially the same thought, this time mentioning the issue or descendants. The picture is that of the true Israel and their children in the midst of heathen nations, who recognize that they are distinct. As Alexander states it, they are "recognized by clear distinctive marks as being God's peculiar people, just as the Jews took knowledge of Peter and John that they had been with Jesus (Acts 4:13)."

It will be so simple to identify the godly that everyone who sees them will recognize and acknowledge that God has blessed them. The verb translated *recognize* appears in the *Hiphil* stem and presents an intensive concept, which we may possibly bring out by rendering *recognize certainly*. Attention must be given to the suffix, *them*; and the force of the clause is best given by translating, *will recognize them that they are, etc.* The construction is the same as in Genesis 1:4. Thus, the object of *will recognize* is *them* and not *that they are, etc.* It is when men look upon the seed itself and its issue that they recognize the seed as blessed of God. This is far stronger, and the lesson it points up is one that every child of God must ever keep before him. When men see us, do they recognize that God has blessed us? We are living epistles, "known and read of all men" (2 Cor. 3:2).

10 I will greatly rejoice in the LORD, let my soul exult in my God, for he hath clothed me with garments of salvation, a mantle of righteousness has he put on me: as the bridegroom adjusts his priestly crown, and the bride arrays her jewels.

11 For as the earth puts forth its growth, and as the garden makes its plants to grow, so shall the Lord GOD make righteousness and praise to grow before all the nations.

10 The speaker in this verse cannot be the Messiah, for never in Scripture is the Messiah said to be clothed with the garments of salvation. The one who here praises God has received righteousness and salvation from the Lord. The Messiah on the other hand brings salvation; he does not receive it. Hence it is the Church of God, the elect, the true Israel, that here rejoices in the God of its salvation. This rejoicing is emphatically expressed through the infinitive absolute and the finite verb, *Rejoicing I will rejoice.*

My soul points out the inwardness of the joy. The source of the rejoicing[3] is *the Lord* and *my God*; and these words express the heartfelt devotion of the covenant-conscious person, who realizes what the great God of the covenant has done for him in clothing him with the garments of salvation. God's deed is presented chiastically. The *clothes of salvation* and the *garment of righteousness* are practically synonymous expressions. Salvation is righteousness, for

---

3 The jussive *tāḡēl* has the force of an imperative.

in the salvation of man the righteousness of God is revealed; salvation is a state of being right with God. In the cloak of this righteousness God has clothed the exultant believer.

The last half of the verse points out how God envelops the Church in salvation. The comparison is with a *bridegroom* who puts on a splendid turban such as the priests wore (lit., *who priests it with respect to a turban*). The term *pe'er* is used of the priestly mitre in Exodus 39:28 and Ezekiel 44:18. The comparison with fine dress is carried out in the last clause, for the ornaments with which the *bride* adorns herself point to the pride that she has in her bridal dress. So does the Church boast of its garment, its heavenly robe of righteousness which its Lord has placed upon it.

> *Jesus, thy blood and righteousness*
> *My beauty are, my glorious dress.*

11 As far as form is concerned this verse calls to mind 55:10. For the thought see also 45:8 and Psalm 85:11, 12. Isaiah's purpose is to attest the sureness of the coming salvation, and to do this he compares the sprouting forth of this salvation with that of growth from the earth. Note the suffixes in the first half of the verse: *its* growth, *its* plants; the growth and plants have been entrusted to the earth for the purpose of causing them to grow. Each of the first two clauses is introduced by a prepositional phrase, *like the earth, like a garden;* and the remainder of each of the two clauses is chiastically arranged, *causes to go out its growth . . . its plants it causes to sprout forth.* Isaiah reflects upon the account of creation in Genesis 1:11, 12 and also 2:9 and 8:22.

In the second half of the verse the comparison is completed. Possibly the introductory *so* reflects upon Genesis 1. Of significance also is the combined divine Name; it is the sovereign, all-powerful One who is the Lord, and He will *cause righteousness and praise to sprout forth.* The earth itself cannot cause these to sprout forth, nor can man, but only the Lord, who is omnipotent. *Praise* here probably signifies the response to *righteousness.* When men have received the heavenly righteousness, they break forth into praise, as in verse 10. And this will be before all the nations, for in the Gospel the righteousness of God is revealed, and the believing heart praises the God who has accomplished redemption. Isaiah speaks from the prophetic standpoint, for the blessings depicted have not yet actually occurred.

1 For Zion's sake I will not be still, and for Jerusalem's sake I will not rest; until her righteousness go forth as brightness, and her salvation as a lamp that burneth.

2 And nations shall see thy righteousness, and all kings thy glory; and a new name shall be called to thee, which the mouth of the LORD shall utter.

3 And thou shalt be a crown of beauty in the hand of the LORD, and a diadem of royalty in the palm of thy God.

4 Not will it be said to thee longer, Forsaken, and to thy land it will no longer be said, Desolate, but to thee it shall be called, My pleasure is in her, and to thy land, Married; for the LORD has had pleasure in thee, and thy land shall be married.

5 For as a youth marries a virgin, so shall thy sons marry thee; and with the joy of a bridegroom over a bride shall thy God rejoice over thee.

1 In this chapter Isaiah presents a situation that belongs before what was given in chapter sixty. What was there described as present is here set forth as in preparation. Most commentators think that the speaker is the prophet himself, but it may be that it is the Lord. The verbs of the first clauses are found in 18:4; 42:14 and 57:11 with God as the subject; but whereas this in itself is not sufficient to show that the Lord is the speaker, verse 6 seems to settle the issue. If the Lord is the speaker, then the persent verse teaches that He will not rest until He has accomplished what is here described. The second verb is stronger than the first. Not only will God not be still, He will not even rest. Emphasis falls upon Zion and Jerusalem. For their sake God will continue active until His salvation is accomplished. He has made covenantal promises to Zion; hence He will see those promises fulfilled. In this He sets the path for His ministers. All their labors must be for the Church, and no opposition or hindrance can stay them.

The language calls to mind the words about the Lord's servant in 42:4 (cf. also 42:14; 57:11 and 65:6). At the time of speaking Zion seems to be hidden or at least unnoticed, but her righteousness will go forth as the *brightness*. The word (*nogah*) sometimes is used of soft and mild light, as in 50:10 and 60:19. Perhaps it here forms a contrast with *lappid* (*lamp*), referring to the dawn, the first breaking forth of light. The last clause may literally be rendered *as a lamp it burns*, i.e. as a burning lamp. The imperfect is joined to the noun *lamp* without a relative, and so expresses a general attribute belonging to the noun. This construction appears several times in Isaiah.[1] Adding greatly to the effectiveness of the statement is its chiastic form.

2 When Zion's righteousness goes forth, then the nations will behold it. The verb implies not merely that they will see it but also that they will attentively note it. They will well know that Zion possesses righteousness and glory. Not merely are kings included, but *all* kings, for in the glory of Zion all other glory and kingship will pale into insignificance. As Calvin points out, kings do not willingly behold any rank other than their own; but so great will Zion's glory and righteousness be that all kings will be compelled to acknowledge it.

The *new name* is probably to be understood in the same sense as the *new song*, a designation of the change to be wrought when the New Testament age is founded. Heaven as it were will come to earth, and the old Zion must go to be replaced by the Zion of God in which the redeemed will dwell. As they sing a new song, so also will they bear a new name, *which the mouth of the Lord designates* (lit., *pierces*). God names His people in accordance with what they are, namely righteous and holy. Intimations of this change of name had already occurred when God gave new names to the patriarchs Abraham and Jacob.

3 In these words Isaiah describes the great beauty of Zion when she has been redeemed. *Crown of beauty* means *beautiful crown,* and *turban of the kingdom* means *royal turban.* These designations are intended to set forth the greatest beauty on earth, and so the Church is displayed as the masterwork of the Lord (cf. 51:6; 65:17), placed in the hand of the Lord that all the world may behold in wonder and amazement the work of God. Were this crown and

---

1 30:14; 40:20; 42:14; 51:12; 55:13; 61:10, 11.

turban described as resting upon the Lord's head and not in His hand and palm, the description would not be fitting, for this crown was wrought out in time and is a work of God to be seen by all of God's creation.[2] "The whole history of salvation," says Delitzsch, "is the history of the taking of the kingdom, and the perfecting of the kingdom by Jehovah; in other words, the history of the working out of this crown." Perhaps the symbolism also suggests that the Church is the Lord's bride, for "a good wife is the crown of her husband" (Prov. 12:4a). The figure is admirably adapted to express the object of love and affection. So Paul speaks of believers (cf. Phil. 4:1; 1 Thess. 2:19).

4 The prophet makes a distinction between the city and the land, pointing out that in the future they will be regarded in an entirely different light from what is now the case. Two of these designations were actually in use as proper names; Azubah was the mother of Jehoshaphat (1 Kings 22:42) and Hephzibah the mother of Manasseh (2 Kings 21:1). Zion will no more be called *ʿazuvah* (*forsaken*) and her land *shᵉmamah* (*desolate*), but (this appears to be the force of the particle *ki*) Zion will be called *hephtzi-vah* (*my delight is in her*) and her land *bᵉʿulah* (*married*). There appears to be a gradation between *will be said* and *will be called*, the latter being the stronger. It may be said that these are the new names to be given; at least they express the great change that God has wrought. There is also a certain emphasis in that *to thee* appears before the verb.

The change in the names, however, is not due to any merely human improvement in Zion's situation, but alone to the fact that God has shown favor. He has delighted in her, and her land will therefore be *married*, i.e. possessed, so that it will be cared for and protected and no longer abandoned. By the multitude of inhabitants the reproach of widowhood will be taken away.

5 By means of a comparison Isaiah confirms what has just been stated. The introductory *ki* is not the particle of comparison (which is omitted) but is to be translated *For*. Note the alliterations of the letter *b* in the first half of the verse; each root begins

---

2 Stummer (*JBL*, Vol. 45, 1926, p. 186) adduces a text, "Oh! Bel . . . . Borsippa is thy tiara (agûku) ." It is not necessary to assume that Isaiah was influenced by any such conception, for Zion as a crown does not beautify the Lord, whereas Borsippa as a tiara is conceived as beautifying Marduk.

with this consonant. Difficulty has been found in the thought of sons marrying a mother, but the difficulty is resolved if the connotation of *possess* be noted. As a young man marries a virgin, so the sons of Zion, through God's grace, will occupy and possess her. She will then no longer be desolate and forsaken but filled with her spiritual sons. As the bride of the Lord, Zion will also be recognized, and He will rejoice in her as an earthly bridegroom rejoices in his bride. The figure is designed to express the utmost of rejoicing. *Rejoicing* is an inner accusative; *and with the rejoicing of a bridegroom, etc.* When God receives the Church as His bride and rejoices at the multitude of her sons, then truly the Church is blessed.

6   On thy walls, O Jerusalem, I have set watchmen: all the day and all the night long they will not be silent. Ye who cause to remember the LORD, let there be no quiet to you.

7   And may you give no rest to him, until he establish and until he place Jerusalem a praise in the earth.

8   The LORD hath sworn by his right hand, and by the arm of his strength: Surely I will not give thy corn anymore as food to thine enemies, and the sons of the foreigner shall not drink thy new wine which thou hast labored in.

9   For those gathering it will eat it, and will praise the LORD; and those collecting it will drink it in the courts of my holiness.

6 Not only will God give to His redeemed Zion all that is necessary but in addition He will appoint watchmen upon her walls that she may receive the utmost in protection. It is God who speaks, for only He can accomplish what is herein stated. This passage cannot be made the basis for an appeal to an exilic date for the prophecy, inasmuch as the walls are already standing. It is upon these *walls* of Jersualem, which are in existence, that God will place the *watchmen*. Actually, of course, the fulfillment of the prophecy would not occur until Jerusalem was spiritually rebuilt, i.e. until what is predicted in verse 5 becomes a reality. The watchmen, therefore, are not prophets of the Old Testament dispensation, but faithful ministers of the Gospel, set for the defense of the faith. Whereas a minister has the task of preaching the Gospel to Zion and of comforting those that mourn in Zion through his pastoral counsel, he also has the solemn responsibility of protecting the flock, warning it against error and false doctrine. At every state of her existence the Church is in need of watchmen who will guard the flock from all that would destroy it. The ravenous wolves of heresy and false doctrine are ever ready to divide the Church and to destroy it, even when they appear as angels of light, as they often do at the present day.

Pieper may be correct in distinguishing these watchers from the door watchers (Neh. 3:29) and the watchers of the inner city (Song of Sol. 3:3; 5:7). The work of watching is continual, day and night. Their cry ever warns of approaching danger and encourages to faithfulness.

In the second half of the verse *hammazkirim* (*ye who remind*) is to be taken as a vocative. It is probably a designation of the watchers. The participle expresses the thought of calling something to God's attention, i.e. engaging in importunate prayer. The last clause may be rendered, *let there be no cessation* (or, *pause, quiet, rest*) *to you*. One of God's best gifts to His Church is faithful ministers who both warn the Church of error and constantly pray on her behalf. The work of defending the faith and the ministry of intercession go hand in hand in beautiful combination. Happy is the Church when she has such ministers!

7 Not only is there to be no cessation to the ones who pray fervently, but they also are not to give cessation to God, until He has made *Jerusalem a praise in the earth.* For the form of the last clause see the comments on 42:4. God will establish and set Jerusalem as a praise in the earth.

8 Further to confirm the truth of the promise, the prophet states that the Lord has *sworn by his right hand, and by the arm of his strength* (i.e. *by his strong arm*), both symbols of His power and strength. For the form of the oath, see the comments on 22:14.[3] The content of the oath refers to the work of God in His providence in which He had given Zion's *corn* into the hands of her enemies, i.e. He had permitted the enemies to rob and plunder Zion of what rightfully belonged to her. This manner of statement, however, is necessary in order to keep before one's eyes the fact that even the actions of nations lie in the hands of God and that they do not act apart from His will and permission.

---

3 אם אתן — lit., *if I give*; some such apodosis as "then I am not God" is expected. Hence we may translate, "Surely, I will not give." B renders literally, εἰ ἔτι δώσω.

9 Zion's products will henceforth be enjoyed only by those who have a right to them. The suffix *it* refers to the corn and new wine just mentioned, as is shown by the verbs *eat* and *drink*. The purpose of the verse is to show that those who have a right to the corn will eat it and those who have a right to the new wine will drink it. The language is figurative, carrying out the picture of life in ancient Israel. To assert that this verse teaches salvation by works would be to misunderstand the figure employed. The eating results in *praise* to the covenant God of Israel, and the drinking is to take place *in the courts of my holiness,* i.e. *in my holy courts.* According to the law the food was to be consumed before the Lord (i.e. in the sanctuary; cf. Deut. 14:22-27). This thought is evidently at the basis of the prophecy. What is meant by these types and symbols is that in the redeemed Zion men will enjoy abundantly the presence of the Lord and will serve and worship Him in accordance with His precepts.

> 10 Pass ye, pass ye through the gates, prepare ye the way of the people; cast up, cast up the highway, free it from stones, raise a banner over the nations.
> 11 Behold! the LORD has caused to hear unto the end of the earth, Say to the daughter of Zion, Behold! thy salvation cometh! behold! his reward is with him, and his work before him.
> 12 And they shall call them the people of holiness, the redeemed of the LORD; and to thee shall be called Sought, a city that has not been forsaken.

10 By means of rhetorical imperatives and emphatic repetition the prophet commands men to prepare for the exaltation of Zion and the manifestation of her salvation. The language reflects upon 40:3 and 57:14. The first command, *pass ye through the gates,* in itself leaves the direction unnamed; but inasmuch as this command precedes that to *prepare the way* it has been assumed that it refers to the passing through the gates of the cities of world heathendom and setting out on the way toward Jerusalem. This is possible, but the command may just as well refer to the entrance into Jerusalem and the passing through her gate. For the interpretation of the following commands see the comments on 40:3 and 57:14.

What is given is a command to all who are to enter Zion to prepare the way for such entrance. They are to clear the way of *stones* and to *raise a banner* high above the nations to enter **Zion** in triumph and victory. The reference is not to the earthly Jerusalem but to the Zion of God, and the picture is that of Zion's exaltation at the great influx of people. If there be any reflection upon a return from Babylonish captivity it is only as an example of this great return. The exiles and the nations come not merely from Babylon but from the far corners of the earth where they have been scattered. They come from a state of estrangement from God into the household of faith.

11 At the outset we are met with an exegetical question. What is the object of the verb *hishmi^{a‘} (has caused to be heard)*? Inasmuch as the following words appropriately fit, it is probable that they are to be understood as the object. They are the content, which the Lord has caused to be heard to the end of the earth. *Daughter of Zion* indicates the city itself, which is to hear the news that her salvation has come, i.e. has been realized.

The second half of the verse is parallel to 40:10 (cf. 40:10 for comment on the individual words). The suffix in *his reward* (*s^ekaro*), if these words are part of what God has caused to be heard, would probably refer to *thy salvation,* which might then be rendered *savior* as in some of the ancient versions. If, however, these words are not part of the quotation, then the suffix would refer to Yahweh. In either case, the meaning is not essentially different. The Lord has come to Zion, and with Him is a great multitude, the reward of His own labor through which the Church is greatly enlarged.

12 We must construe the first verb impersonally, and this may well be rendered in English by the passive, *And they will be called the people of holiness*. In Exodus 19:6 the people were intended to be a holy nation; and now that promise will find fulfillment, for the exaltation of Zion and the presence of her salvation is no human work but that of the Lord her God alone. When men look upon the Church as a secular institution and see her so involved with worldly matters that her Lord is crowded out of the picture, she is then no longer a holy people nor the redeemed of the Lord. Her solemn responsibility is that men should regard her not as a human institution but as a people of holiness.

From now on Zion will be *d^erushah (sought after)*, a passive participle which suggests that Zion is eagerly sought after by her

Lord in particular and also by men. The word is the opposite of *ᵃzuvah* (*forsaken*), a term that will no longer be applied to the holy city (cf. Jer. 30:14). In Isaiah 49:14 Zion had complained that God had forsaken her. That complaint will never again be raised.

1 Who is this who comes from Edom, bright as to his garments from Bozra, this one adorned in his apparel, bending in the abundance of his strength? I, speaking in righteousness, mighty to save.

2 Why is there redness to thy raiment, and thy garments like those of one treading in a wine press?

3 The press I have trodden by myself, and from the nations there was not a man with me; and I will tread them in my anger and trample them in my fury: and their juice will spurt upon my garments, and all my vesture I have stained.

4 For the day of vengeance is in my heart, and the year of my redeemed is come.

5 And I look, and there is none helping; and I was appalled, and there is none sustaining: and my own arm saves for me, and my fury it sustains me.

6 And I tread the nations in my anger, and I make them drunk in my wrath; and I bring down to the earth their juice.

1 Having described the exaltation of Zion and her enlargement through the influx of the Gentiles, the prophet turns to describe the destruction of Zion's enemies. Continuing his usage of imagery, he deals with the question of how Zion can safely endure as long as enemies as hostile and vicious as Edom are at hand, and pictures their destruction as a sanguinary triumph of the Lord. It is as though the prophet sees One in deep red garments and with proudly raised head coming from Edom and its chief city Bozra, and asks who He is, and permits the One from Edom to answer the question. In a second question (v. 2) he asks why the garments are so deep red, and receives the answer (vv. 3ff.) that this One, the Savior of Zion, has alone subdued and destroyed Zion's enemies.

The introductory question expresses wonderment; *Who then is this?* Isaiah omits a relative, *Who is this—he comes from Edom?* This omission lends vividness to the expression. It is as though the seer sees the mysterious Personage coming on the road from Edom to Zion. Even before stating the point of departure, the prophet describes the garments[1] and then adds that Bozra was the precise place from which this One had come. Again Isaiah uses the word *this,* as though to say, "this strange One, adorned in His clothing." By the phrase *bending[2] through the abundance of his strength,* the prophet wishes to show that the One who comes is completely victorious.

In answer the One who comes from Bozra introduces Himself with the word *I,* which calls to mind the numerous usages of this pronoun in chapters 40ff. *Speaking* is probably employed in a pregnant sense, *proclaiming, announcing.* The preposition *b* has here the significance *in the sphere of;* hence the speaker states that He proclaims in the sphere of righteousness. This righteousness is manifested in salvation, for He is mighty to save. John evidently reflects upon this passage: "And he was clothed with a vesture dipped in blood; and his name is called The Word of God" (Rev. 19:13). Note the relation between "Word of God" and *speaking.*

Bozra was the capital of ancient Edom. The Edomites were descended from Esau (Gen. 36:1, 8, 9) and were related to the Israelites. Throughout their history they displayed a vicious attitude toward Israel (cf. e.g. Amos 1:11-12). The Psalmist calls attention to their attitude (Ps. 137:7). Edom is mentioned as a representative of the powers that oppose God, and in its destruction we see their destruction. The reference is not to the destruction of the empirical nation of Edom, although that nation in course of time did pass away, but to the fact that all that would hinder the establishment of God's kingdom upon earth must pass away through judgment.

2 In the first verse the Victor was at a distance from the inquiring prophet. In this verse, however, He is so close that He can be addressed. Having heard the answer to his first question the prophet now raises a second. *What is the reason why there is redness to thy raiment, and thy garments (are) like (those of) one treading the wine press?* The question implies (particularly the presence of *Lamed* before *thy raiment*) that red was not the natural color of the garment. In fact, it is the unexpected presence of the redness

---

[1] חמוץ — *sharp, piercing, glowing;* "in garments of glowing colors."

[2] *tzŏ'eh* — one stooping; cf. 51:14.

that prompts the question. This redness is deep because it comes from blood. It reminds the questioner of the redness that comes upon the clothes of one who treads the grapes in the wine press, and whose clothing has become stained by the red wine (cf. comments on 5:2).

3 This verse gives the answer to the prophet's second question. A different word is used for *wine press*, occurring only here and in Haggai 2:16, and designating the place where the grapes were crushed or broken. The speaker had trodden the wine press alone, and from among the peoples there was no man with Him. The language is reminiscent of 44:24. In the work of creation, as in the work of salvation and judgment, God acts alone. There is no one with Him, for in these works none can help Him.

Commentators usually translate the next three verbs as though they were introduced by *waw* consecutive; it should be noted, however, that such is not the case. Rather, there is a series of imperfects introduced by weak *waw*, a phenomenon that appears several times in Isaiah (cf. 12:1; 27:5; 42:6; 51:2; 57:17). To translate these verbs as futures would suggest that the trampling of the wine press has not yet occurred, which would conflict with the express statement that it has already taken place. To preserve the future it might be assumed that there were two distinct tramplings, one of which had not yet occurred; inasmuch as none from the nations came to work with the speaker He would therefore trample them. This does not seem natural, for the picture of the approaching speaker suggests that His work of judgment is already completed. It seems best to take the verbs as descriptive of what has occurred, but as expressing that fact in the present.[3] Thus, *I trample them in my anger* is the speaker's description of the action He has already performed. The nations were the objects of the speaker's wrath, and in His anger He trod them like grapes in a wine vat. In His anger He stamped upon them and was determined utterly to crush them. The result was that their *juice* (the word is used figuratively of blood and gore) spurted upon His clothing and His vesture was stained.[4]

[3] This usage of the imp. to represent the past conceived as though it were occurring now, is characteristic of poetic and elevated style; cf. Isa. 51:2; Ps. 18:7; 78:15, 29, 45, etc.

[4] אֶגְאָלְתִּי is a form well attested in the Amarna letters and is not to be emended; cf. *WThJ*, Vol. 14, No. 1, 1951, p. 54.

That the picture here given is dramatic and vivid cannot be denied. The speaker comes to Jerusalem with the blood of the slain upon His garments, for He has executed His anger upon His enemies. This wrath is free of any malice or impurity whatsoever; it is God's just determination to punish the sinner for his sin. None of the blessings depicted in chapter sixty-two could be enjoyed were there not also a judgment.

4 The prophet here gives the reason why God has acted, namely that *the day of vengeance* (i.e. the time for taking vengeance) was in His heart (i.e. in His plans and purposes) and the year of His redeemed had come. Just as there was a year of favor for the Lord, so also is there a year of His redeemed (cf. 61:2); and inasmuch as this year had arrived, the Lord took vengeance upon the nations. The words *day* and *year* simply mean *time*.

5 This verse is evidently based on 59:16 (cf. 59:16 for discussion of individual words). The language continues with a verb in the imperfect introduced by weak *waw*. Possibly this interchange of tenses is due to the fact that the work of judgment is not complete, and the speaker looks forward to the final destruction of His enemies. At any rate the verse emphasizes the fact that the speaker must tread the press alone. He sees none to help, although He has looked for them; none sustains, although He is astonished; only His *arm* has saved for Him and His *wrath* has sustained Him.

6 The language continues with imperfects introduced by weak *waw*. *Trample*[5] is probably not as strong as the word used in verse 3 and yet stronger than *darak* in verse 3. The weak *waw* is probably best taken as descriptive, as in verse 3. Again the two words for *wrath* and *anger* ('*aph* and *ḥamah*) appear. Not to be overlooked is the gradation, *trample, make drunk,* and finally *bring down*. In His anger God makes the nations drunk so that they are filled therewith. To *bring down their juice to the ground* means to cause their blood to flow upon the ground and hence to *slay* them. Five words in this verse have *Aleph* as the initial consonant.

7   The lovingkindnesses of the Lᴏʀᴅ I shall cause to be remembered, the praises of the Lᴏʀᴅ according to all that the Lᴏʀᴅ hath done for us; and the abundance of goodness to the house

---

[5] *we'ābûs* — note the continued use of the imp. with weak *waw*.

478

of Israel which he has done for them, according to his compassions and according to the multitude of his lovingkindnesses.

8 And he said, Only they are my people, my children shall not deal falsely; and he became a Savior for them.

9 In all their affliction he was afflicted, and the angel of his face saved them, in his love and in his sparing mercy he redeemed them; and he took them up and carried them all the days of old.

10 But they rebelled and grieved the Spirit of his holiness; and he was turned from them into an enemy, he himself fought against them.

11 And he remembered the days of old, Moses and his people. Where is he that brought them up from the sea, the shepherd of his flock? Where is he that put within him the Spirit of his holiness?

12 Leading them by the right hand of Moses and his glorious arm, cleaving the waters from before them to make for him an everlasting name?

13 Causing them to walk in the depths, like the horse in the desert they shall not stumble?

14 As the cattle will go down into the valley, the Spirit of the LORD will cause him to rest. So didst thou lead thy people, to make for thyself a name of glory.

15 Look from heaven and see from thy dwelling place of holiness and beauty! Where is thy zeal and thy might? The sounding of thy bowels and thy mercies toward me have restrained themselves.

16 For thou art our father, for Abraham hath not known us, and Israel has not recognized us; thou, LORD, art our Father, our Redeemer, of old is thy name.

17 Why dost thou cause us to wander, O LORD, from thy ways; why wilt thou harden our heart from thy fear? Return, for the sake of thy servants, the tribes of thy inheritance.

The relationship of 63:7ff. to the preceding constitutes a serious exegetical question. While one cannot be dogmatic, we nevertheless suggest the following for consideration. In 61–63:6 Isaiah has brought to a conclusion the second section of his prophecy (40–60). Roughly speaking we may say that 61–62 correspond to 35 in that they present the exaltation of Zion. On the other hand 63:1-6 corresponds to 34 in that it speaks of the destruction of Zion's enemies, and in both instances Edom is brought forth as a representative of those enemies. Yet the judgment falls not only upon Edom but upon all nations. As the salvation is eschatological, so also is the judgment. Although the salvation and judgment appeared with the first advent of Christ, the full enjoyment and realization of salvation will not be until His second advent; and whereas at His first appearing the axe was laid at the root of the trees, the great day of judgment will not be until His second coming.

In 63:7–64:11 the prophet, as the representative of his people, prays to God, expressing thanksgiving and confession as well as beseeching God to be merciful to His people. Chapters 65 and 66 are in effect an answer to this prayer. The apostate Israel is to be rejected and only a devout remnant will be preserved.

7 On behalf of the Church, the redeemed of God, the prophet lifts his voice in prayer, immediately introducing his theme, *The mercies of the Lord.*[6] The word refers to God's acts of undeserved mercy, which in faithfulness to His covenant He has performed on behalf of His own. This word also closes the verse. If the reference is to men, the sense is that the prophet will celebrate these mercies; but, as Alexander points out, there is to be a prayer that God will renew His mercies, and so the action may refer to God. If so, the sense is that the prophet causes God to remember His mercies (the plural may suggest their abundance). These are *praises of the Lord* (i.e. matters for which the Lord is to be praised). This praise is to be offered in accordance with all that God has done for His people (for the construction cf. comments on 59:18), and the thought is that inasmuch as God has done so much for Israel His praise is truly great.

In the second half of the verse the prophet objectifies Israel, speaking of it in the third person plural. Perhaps the words *and the great goodness, etc.* are not to be construed as governed by *according to* but are introduced independently as a second reason for giving praise to God. *The greatness of the good* is another designation for *mercies* and *praises*. What has been done is in accord with God's compassion; inasmuch as He is compassionate, He has manifested mercy to His people.

8 With this verse we are taken back to the beginnings of Israel as a nation. The introductory particle is best rendered *only*, and although it immediately precedes *my people* it should be construed with *they* (which in Hebrew is legitimate). The sense then is that *only they* are God's people. This is a particular manifestation of the mercies of the Lord in that He acknowledges that Israel alone

---

[6] Note *Paseq* in M.

is His. As so often, Isaiah proceeds to designate Israel as *sons* who, inasmuch as they are sons, are not to deal falsely. The negative has the force of a strong prohibition, and we may render, *they shall not deal falsely*. The Lord is not uttering a vain hope that His chosen ones will not deal falsely, but is declaring that they are not to do so.

The final clause does not have a causal connection with what precedes, but simply adds another fact. Reflecting upon the language of Exodus 15:2, Isaiah (as in 12:2 also) declares that God became their *Savior*.

9 This is one of the most remarkable verses in the prophecy and one of the most disputed. It is necessary to make one slight change in the text and to adopt the reading of the $Q^e re$ rather than that of the $K^e tiv$.[7] We then obtain the rendering: *In all their affliction, there was affliction to him*. The meaning is beautiful, and filled with great comfort for God's people. Calvin says that in speaking this way God declares the incomparable love He has toward His people. "In order to move us more powerfully and draw us to himself, the Lord accommodates himself to the manner of men, by attributing to himself all the affection, love and compassion which a father can have." The language used points out forcefully that God bears our burdens and carries our sorrows. When affliction is directed against us and we must suffer for His sake, we may remember that He too is bearing that affliction and suffering. To support this interpretation appeal may be made to Judges 10:16 in comparison with 11:7. God feels the sufferings of His people as His own sufferings. The reference is not to any specific misfortune but to those misfortunes, afflictions, and sufferings that His people must bear in seeking to be what they should be.

So great was His love toward them that He sent *the angel of his face*, who *saved them* from all these afflictions and sufferings. This *angel* (the word means *messenger*) God had promised to send to His people (Ex. 23:20-23) and actually did send to them (Ex. 14:19; Num. 20:16). He is the Lord's angel (Ex. 33:14, 15) and is actually the Lord (Yahweh) Himself (Ex. 33:12). The angel of

---

[7] I.e. *lô* instead of the negative *lō'*, although 1Q retains the negative. B connects the words with what precedes, *and he became to them for salvation from all their affliction*. B renders *tzar* by πρέσβυς as though it were *tzû*. Muilenburg (*IB*) translates, "Neither envoy nor messenger—but his own Presence—saved them."

481

His face is the angel who is His face or in whom His face is made clear. In him the Lord is Himself present.[8]

In the following phrases, *in his love, etc.*, the suffix refers not to the angel but to God, and emphasis falls upon the personal pronoun; *He* redeemed them. This He did through His love and His forgiving gentleness. Possibly reflecting upon the language of Deuteronomy 32:11, Isaiah uses two verbs that show that the course of Israel's life was entirely in the hands of the Lord. They did not make of themselves a nation, but were borne and carried of Him as a mother carries[9] the child throughout life and so directs the course of its life.

10 In distinction from God's goodness the people were rebellious. Hence, the introductory *But they* is emphatic. Instead of gratitude and greater faithfulness on the people's part, ingratitude and rebellion followed the divine benefits. The two following verbs may possibly be understood as a hendiadys; *they rebelled and grieved*, i.e. *they rebelled in that they grieved*.

At the time of the exodus from Egypt the command had been given to the people, with respect to the angel who would go before them, "Beware before him and do not rebel against him, for he will not pardon with respect to your transgressions, for my name is in him" (Ex. 23:21). Yet, according to Exodus 17:1ff. and 32:1ff., the people rebelled from the very time of the exodus, and their entire history was one of rebellion. In itself, the phrase *the Spirit of his holiness* need not denote a personal being; but when the phrase appears in this particular context it is difficult to escape the conclusion that such is its significance. The fact that Israel grieved the Spirit shows that the Spirit is a Person; how can one grieve an impersonal spirit? Here the Spirit is set forth as the object of the people's action. Furthermore, as the Spirit is joined with the Lord here, so in the previous verse the angel was joined with Him (cf. Ps. 78:17, 40). Here, then, the Spirit of holiness is distinguished from the Lord in its personal existence, just as the angel is in the previous verse. The Spirit is here distinguished as a Person by the fact that He can be grieved and so feel grief. Upon the basis of this

---

[8] Cf. 2 Cor. 4:6. Muilenburg calls attention to the goddess Tanit as the "face of Baal"; cf. Cooke, *Text-Book of North-Semitic Inscriptions*, pp. 131-132. *DOTT*, p. 115, points out that the great gods sent a protecting genius to "go in front of" a man.

[9] 1Q reverses the order of the verbs.

passage Paul utters his remarkable statement: "Grieve not the Holy Spirit of God" (Eph. 4:30).[10] Thus, in these two verses there is a distinction of the three persons of the Triune God: He (Yahweh), the angel of His presence, and the Spirit of His holiness. In the history of the chosen people each Person of the Trinity was active.

The result of this rebellion was that God became what He was not before, *an enemy*. From One who was afflicted in all their affliction He was turned into an enemy and as such *fought against* the people. A strong contrast appears between the usage of *hu'* (*he*) in the last clause of this verse and *hu'* in the last clause of verse 9 (cf. also Matt. 12:31; Acts 7:51 and Heb. 10:29).

11 This verse bristles with difficulties. The first question revolves about the first verb: Is God the subject or are the people? Penna takes God as the subject, asserting that inasmuch as God is merciful and compassionate and does not forget the great personalities of Israel's past, He is moved to show mercy. In the second clause, however, the people obviously are speaking; hence it seems more consistent to regard the people as the subject of the first verb. Thus, in the first clause Isaiah describes the people's repentance, and in the second gives their own words in which they themselves contrast their present condition with the former status and blessing that were theirs.

It is not necessary to emend the first verb to the plural, for it may be taken impersonally, *one remembered*; and this is best rendered in English by the passive. Thus, *And the days of old were remembered, even Moses and his people*. The construction of *Moses, his people*[11] is difficult, but the words may be introduced by *namely* and the two words *Moses, his people* construed as in apposition to *the days of old*. It is necessary in English to insert a connective between *Moses* and *his people* and to construe the suffix *his* as referring to Moses. Thus, we get the thought that the people remember the days of old, even the days of Moses and of Moses' people. This construction is not without difficulty, but it is probably as free of objection as any.

Beginning with *Where?* we have the lament of the people who remembered the days of old. At the present time God seems to the

10 There is no warrant for the assumption that the Spirit here is not a hypostasis but merely a personification, and that to grieve the Lord's Spirit merely means to grieve the Lord.

11 Deleted in B, but retained in 1Q and in Aq S T.

people not to be as helpful and willing to save as He once was, and they want God to act now as He did formerly. The people's question is difficult to construe, but is probably, "Where is He that brought them[12] up from the sea, that brought up the shepherd of His flock?" On this construction the allusion is to the deliverance of the nation at the Red Sea. It is also possible to allow the particle *'eth* to stand and to construe the words *shepherd of his flock* as the subject. We then get the construction: "Where is the one that brought up the people from the sea, even the shepherd of his flock?" In either case the shepherd is Moses. On the one view it is God who delivered the people, and with them the shepherd of His flock; on the other it is Moses who as the shepherd brought the people up from the Red Sea. Although both constructions are grammatically possible the context seems to favor the first, for the lament of the people is that God, not Moses, is now not showing mercy to them. The last question also supports this interpretation, for it obviously refers to God.

The final blessing God once gave the nation was to place the Spirit of His holiness in its (the people's) midst. Thus the Spirit (here as in verse 10 a personal Spirit) was a gift to the nation whose blessings were manifested in that He was present in Moses, Aaron, Miriam, the Seventy, and the prophets also (cf. e.g. Num. 11:17, and note also Ex. 31:3 and 35:31). Alexander points out that the word *midst* is used as in 1 Kings 17:22. The Spirit with all the blessings that He brings was once within Israel itself.

12 By means of a participle without the definite article, the description is continued. The preposition before *right hand* indicates general relation and may be rendered *with respect to* (cf. Ps. 16:8); and, as Alexander here suggests, the specific sense of *by*, although not necessarily included, is suggested by the context. The word *yamin* means the *right hand* or *arm* of Moses, and is a symbol of the seat of strength. By many *the arm of his glory* is taken as the object and the whole rendered, *Who at the right hand of Moses causes the arm of his glory to go*. It is also possible to insert a conjunction *and* to introduce *the arm of his glory* as a correlative object of the preposition, thus, *causing them* (the people) *to go by the right hand of Moses* (*and by*) *his glorious arm*. Thus interpreted, the language refers to the wandering in the wilderness or

---

[12] The suffix is omitted in B and 1Q, both of which make *rō'ēy* the object of the participle.

the actual departure from Egypt, and lays stress upon both the work of Moses and that of the Lord who used Moses. Some see in the phrase *the right hand of Moses* not so much a general allusion to strength as a reference to the wielding of his rod. Some also refer the pronoun *his* to Moses, i.e. *the arm of his* (Moses') *glory*.

In the second half of the verse Isaiah definitely refers to the crossing of the Red Sea. The participle suggests the *cleaving* or *splitting* of the water (cf. Ex. 14:16, 21ff.; the theme is frequent in the festival Psalms, e.g. 77:16; 106:9; 114:3). This miracle God performed *before* the people (implying that previous obstacles that stood in their way were thus removed) so that His power would be clearly displayed to their eyes. In the statement of the purpose there is an exegetical question, whether the pronoun *him* refers to Moses or to God. In the one case the language states that the purpose was to honor Moses, and in the other to bring glory to God. The miracle of the Red Sea was memorable in that the people would ever remember what God had done and would honor His might and power (cf. 55:13; 56:5).

13 Continuing the description, the prophet employs a causative participle with a nominal suffix, which taken strictly should express possession, *Their one who caused to go,* i.e. God, who caused the people to go through the depths. In the light of Psalm 106:9 (possibly also 77:16) the reference seems to be to the crossing of the Red Sea. The progression of thought in the context, however, points to the crossing of the Jordan; and this position is adopted by several commentators. It is possible that we are not to press the order of statement; and it may be that the crossing of the Red Sea, the central miracle of deliverance, is what actually does receive the stress.

The desert is conceived as free of obstacles, so that the horse can march across it without stumbling; thus God caused His people to walk through the depths of the sea. The final clause is circumstantial and refers to the manner of the people walking, and not to the horse. It is grammatically to be construed with *Causing them to walk,* and may be rendered *without stumbling.* The comparison *like a horse* (the definite article in Hebrew is generic) *in the wilderness* is probably best taken as independent and not necessarily modifying grammatically the participle. Thus *Causing them to go—like a horse in the wilderness—they do not stumble.* God's

485

power enables His people to go in confidence and nobility, not being overcome or falling because of any obstacles in the way.

14 The first clause is to be rendered, *Like the cattle that will go down into the valley;* lit., *Like the cattle, into the valley, it will go down.* In both instances the article is generic. This beautiful figure illustrates the ease with which cattle descend into a wadi where there is abundant pasture, and so indicates a change from a previous location to one where the needs of the animals are abundantly supplied. In this manner *the Spirit of the Lord* (here again the context demands that the Spirit be understood as a Person) causes Israel (the pronominal suffix does not refer to the cattle) *to rest,*[13] bringing it to the *rest* of Canaan, the land flowing with milk and honey (Deut. 11:9; Ps. 95:11). In Canaan, the type of the heavenly Canaan, the people rested and were refreshed after the long desert march, just as the cattle descending to the valley find there their place of rest and refreshment. Thus, the work of bringing the nation into Canaan is represented as the work of God's Spirit (cf. Ps. 143:10).

With the last clause there is a change from the objective third person to a direct address of God in the second person. The introductory *ken (So)* sums up the entire course of God's bringing His people into the land of promise. As Alexander says, the prophet here resumes the tone of historical retrospection. Whereas the verb, *thou didst lead,* does sum up the whole, it also suggests the thought of a shepherd leading his flock. With the whole compare Psalms 78; 105; 106 and 107.

15 On the basis of the foregoing recital of God's grace to the nation of old, the prophet (perhaps as speaking for his people and representative of them) prays to God for new mercies. The two imperatives *Look* and *see* are verbs that in the Old Testament generally appear in this order. If any distinction in connotation is to be made, it is: *Look down* and, as a result, *see* our condition. It is as though the Lord had withdrawn into heaven and would know no more of His people. *The dwelling place of thy holiness and thy beauty* means *thy holy and beautiful dwelling place.* It is the presence of God that brings these attributes to His dwelling place,

---

[13] Vulg., however, *spiritus Domini ductor eius fuit,* as though the root were *nāḥāh.*

heaven. The word translated *dwelling place*[14] does not suggest a localized conception of God, but is used as Solomon had employed it in his prayer in 1 Kings 8:49.

By means of the question introduced by *Where?* the prophet does not deny the mercy of God, but simply asks where that once wondrous mercy is at present, implying that he would again have it shown to man. For *zeal,* see the comments on 9:7 and note also 59:17. The zeal once displayed in God's powerfully preserving and governing His people, what has become of it now? Accompanying that zeal were the deeds of might, a thought possibly suggested by the plural noun (cf. 1 Kings 15:23; 16:27; 22:45). God's zeal for His people was manifested in the mighty miracles and deeds of redemption that He performed in bringing them out of Egypt and into the land of promise.

By means of the final clause, the prophet gives the reason why he questions the presence of God's zeal and mighty deeds. *As for the noise of thy bowels and thy mercies, toward me they are restrained.* The first phrase, the *strepitus viscerum,* an expression shocking to our Western civilization, simply expressed deep love, concern, and sympathy (see comments on 16:11). The phrase *toward me* is probably to be construed with the final verb; and thus a statement of fact, rather than a question, is uttered. These mercies restrain themselves toward the prophet, and for this reason he asks the question that he does.

Several commentators call attention to Luther's remarkable translation: *"deine grosse herzliche Barmherzigkeit hält sich hart gegen mich"* ("Thy great compassionate lovingkindness deals harshly with me"). Not to be overlooked also is Calvin's profound observation that there is a difference between unbelievers and believers in that even when they perceive no tokens of God's kindness, believers acknowledge a powerful and kind God and call upon Him, for He always cares for His people (1 Pet. 5:7) and unceasingly governs every part of the world.

16 The introductory *Because* gives the reason why the prophet prays to God. To paraphrase the thought: "We beseech Thee to look down upon us with favor, for Thou art our Father." *Father* here signifies the One who brought the nation into existence (cf. Deut. 32:6). In love God founded the nation that was His creation,

---

14 זבל — *dominion;* cf. Ug. *zbl,* to rule? B ἐκ τοῦ οἴκου.

a people to bring light to the Gentiles and to make known His salvation unto the ends of the earth. In verse 8 Isaiah had spoken of the Israelites as sons (cf. also 64:8; Jer. 3:4; Mal. 1:6). In the Old Testament the designation *Father* for God is comparatively rare and possibly does not convey the wealth of meaning found in the New Testament *our Father*; nevertheless, it is a word of tender comfort, and shows that the theocracy was a work of God and not of man. If, then, the Father who has begotten the sons, Israel, withdraws His love and blessing, will not the sons perish? Hence the importunate petition of the prophet, speaking for the nation.

To emphasize the fact that God alone is Israel's Father, the explanatory statement is added that Abraham and Jacob cannot help, for they are not the fathers of a spiritual body. Both proper names are stressed; *for Abraham, he does not know us, and Israel, he has not recognized us.*[15] Both verbs are to be understood as implying a knowledge and recognition that carries with it the ability to be of aid (cf. Deut. 33:9 and Ruth 2:10, 19). Great and honorable as these two men were, they could not help the people. Perhaps the reason why Isaac is not here mentioned is that, although the promises were made to him, yet the fuller and more glorious declaration of those promises was given to the two mentioned. In this utterance there is no depreciation of the patriarchs, for only God could be the father of spiritual sons. Actually, this verse implies that the true Church of God and the outward nation of Israel in Old Testament times were not coextensive. It is the spiritual body that is here in view.

In the second half of the verse, the Lord is addressed directly as Israel's Father. The words of the final clause are to be construed, *our Redeemer from of old is thy name.* The Lord is known as the One who always has been Israel's Redeemer.

17 Isaiah becomes more emboldened in his prayer. Both verbs are strongly causative, a fact that appears particularly in that the second verb is a stronger expression than the ordinary verb for harden (*qashaḥ* instead of *qashah*), appearing elsewhere only in Job 39:16. The thought is that God causes the people to wander

---

15 *yakkirānû* — 1Q *hkyrnw.* B ἐπέγνω. This form has usually been regarded as an imp. with an *a* connecting vowel, due to the influence of the preceding *yᵉdā'ānî.* It is, however, a *Yaqṭil* causative, perf. as in Phoenician. In Heb. the form is a vestigial remain, although apparently normal in Phoenician. The *a* connecting vowel shows that the form is perf., and hence is not to be emended.

from His paths and to harden their hearts so that they will not fear Him. The prayer does not, however, absolve man of responsibility, for the people's lack of blessing is due to their own sinfulness. Thus, the prayer is a confession or acknowledgment that God has forsaken, but that the fault lies with the people themselves, so that God's vengeance and actions against them are righteous.[16] Says Calvin, ". . . Believers always look at the goodness of God, even when they acknowledge that they suffer justly on account of their sins." The fear of God is a term for true devotion and piety, and the force is, *from the fear of thee* (the suffix is an objective genitive). The verbs are probably to be construed so as to give the sense, " Why wilt Thou cause us to wander by hardening our heart?"

Implied in the imperative *turn* is the thought of a long absence. The returning will be accomplished when once more God manifests blessing to His people. By *servants* the prophet evidently intends a reference to the people, who are also identified as the tribes of God's inheritance, i.e. the tribes who are the inheritance of God. Inasmuch as the tribes are thus God's possession, the prophet prays that *for their sake*, i.e. for their benefit, God will return to them. This prayer does not lend support to the thought of praying in the name of or for the sake of the saints.

18 For a little thy holy people possessed, our enemies trod down thy sanctuary.
19 We have been of old, thou hast not ruled over them, thy name has not been called upon them. Oh! that thou wouldst rend the heavens and come down, that from before thee the mountains might flow down.

18 A number of exegetical difficulties appear in this verse. The first word may be rendered literally, *With respect to a little thing.* From the context it would seem that the reference is temporal; hence we may translate *For a little while.* A second question revolves around the point whether *people* is subject or object of the verb. Are we to render *they possessed the people of thy holiness* or *the people of thy holiness possessed?* The first construction would suggest that the enemies possessed God's holy people for a short time, the verb then being used as in Genesis 22:17; 24:60; Deuteronomy 9:1; 11:23, and the subject anticipating *our enemies*

16 Cf. the discussion of reprobation and human sin in Vol. I, pp. 259-261.

of the following clause. On the other hand, it is quite natural to take *people* as subject; and if this is done some object such as *the land* (Delitzsch) should be understood.

It is not necessary to introduce an adversative conjunction between the two members of the verse. The words *For a little time* may govern both parts. The thought then is, "For a little time the people possessed the land, for a little time our enemies trampled God's sanctuary." We are not to restrict the reference to the Babylonish exile, although that calamity may be included. In the light of eternity the events herein depicted would be a very little while.

19 There are different ways of construing these introductory words. The first words may be taken together, *We are from of old;* and thus they suggest that whereas God's people are of some antiquity, the enemies on the other hand are a comparatively new race. Over the enemies God has not ruled, as He had over His own people. The concepts of God as the King of Israel and of Israel as His property appear often (cf. 33:22; 41:21; 43:15; 44:6). It is not denied that God's providential rule extends over all peoples, but simply that the kingship that was manifested in the theocracy has been bestowed upon no other nation but Israel. When the Name of God is called upon a nation, it means that that nation has been spiritually conquered by God. No other nation but Israel has thus known God so as to be able to call upon His Name, nor has it been known by His Name (cf. 48:1). The complaint, however, shows that these blessings do not seem now to exist. Passionately, therefore, the prophet breaks out in an ardent appeal to God to come in blessing to His people as He had done in olden times.

The cry[17] may be rendered: *Oh! that thou hadst[18] now already rent the heavens.* It is for direct divine intervention that Isaiah prays. May there not be again a true theophany, such as once appeared at Mt. Sinai, for the purpose of destroying the enemies and again blessing the chosen people? May there not again be a sudden, powerful revelation of God's power, which now seems to be concealed in heaven? In verse 15 God is commanded to look down from the heaven; and now, the heavens apparently being conceived as an obstacle to His return, the wish is uttered that He had

17 63:19b is 64:1 in the English translations.
18 As in 48:18, *lû'* serves to introduce a wish that something expected in the future may already have taken place.

rent them and come down from them again to intervene in the affairs of His people.

Should God so come down, the mountains would quake at His presence, for in judgment He would cause the earth to tremble (cf. 2:19). Thus, in abandoned complaint the prophet, representing His people, beseeches God again to act.

Some think that this wish should form the first verse of the succeeding chapter, and it does indeed fit in well with what follows. It also fits in well with what precedes in that it grows naturally out of the prophet's complaint, and, as Alexander points out, is highly effective.

2 As fire kindles brush, fire boils water—to make known thy name to thine enemies; from before thee nations shall tremble.
3 In thy doing fearful things which we expect not, oh! that thou wouldst come down, and that the mountains might flow down from before thee.
4 And from eternity they have not heard, they have not given ear; eye hath not seen a God beside thee, he doeth to the one waiting for him.
5 Thou hast met with the one rejoicing and executing righteousness; in thy ways shall they remember thee: behold, thou hast been wroth, and we have sinned; in them is perpetuity, and we shall be saved.

2 As it stands, this verse is an unlikely beginning for a chapter, and we must understand it as bearing an intimate relationship with what has preceded. The comparative clause is parenthetical, and the final clause a continuation of 63:19. We may paraphrase the thought: "Oh! that thou wouldst have rent the heavens, that thou wouldst have come down, that the mountains might quake from before thee just as fire kindles brushwood and as fire boils water—that (thou wouldst come down) to make thy name known to thine enemies—that the nations should tremble before thee."

The Lord is to come down with the effect that fire has upon brushwood when it consumes it in flames and upon water when it causes the water to boil. We may render either *As the burning of a fire of brushwood* or *As fire burns brushwood*. The latter is preferable, not only because in the next clause fire is the subject, but because of the comparison, the point of which is to show that the Lord is effectual in what He will do as is the fire in the burning of brushwood. We may construe the second clause *as water which fire*

---

1 The numeration of the verses of this chapter follows the English versions; cf. note 17 to chap. 63.

492

boils, it being necessary to understand a preposition before *water* and a relative before the verb *boils.* In mentioning fire in connection with the judgment, Isaiah uses a common figure (cf. 1:31; 9:18; 10:17; 30:27, 30; 33:14; 65:5; 66:15). In this connection the figure of fire is apt, for God's coming is to cause His enemies to know His Name. In the coming down God will manifest Himself and His attributes to His enemies, and they will know that He is the God of sovereign power. The Name of God, the Holy One of Israel, will bring salvation to His people but judgment to His enemies. These enemies are not merely the Babylonians, but all who oppose Him.

The last clause seems to set forth the result that will be produced by the coming down of the Lord. The preposition governing the infinitive, *to cause to make known,* may also virtually govern the imperfect, *they shall tremble,* although this need not be insisted upon. As mountains had quaked at His presence, so will idolatrous nations who have refused to know Him; for all the power of man, manifested in atheistic human government, will fall to pieces at His presence.

3 It is difficult to construe this verse precisely. Perhaps it is least objectionable to regard the first half of the verse as an adverbial clause modifying the two purpose clauses of verse 1 (M 63:19b), and governed still by the particle *lu' (would that)* understood. The sense would then be: "Oh! that, when thou doest fearful things that we do not expect, etc." Isaiah then completes the sense with the second half of the verse: *thou wouldst come down, that the mountains might melt before thee* (cf. Luke 23:30; Rev. 6:16f.). Isaiah's wish is that when God performed these fearful deeds, He would come down.

The *fearful things* are acts performed by God when He comes down in judgment, and which produce fear in the hearts of the beholders. At the exodus from Egypt God performed fearful things, and possibly in the use of the word here there is a reflection upon that period. They are eschatological events ushering in the great judgment of God, events the mind of man has not conceived of nor expected.

Again the prophet introduces the thought of the mountains melting when God comes down in judgment. Such language must be understood figuratively of the cataclysmic changes that the approach of God in judgment will produce.

4 In this verse the prophet gives a reason for what was stated in verse 3. God can come down and perform fearful things, because there is no god like Him. No other god beside Israel's God has ever been seen or heard who has done to (acted for) those who wait for Him. This is the reason for the strong petition just uttered. To stress the uniqueness of God, the words *And from eternity* are placed first. What is to be related is completely new, never having been heard of before. It is not necessary to assume that the enemies are the subject of the verbs, for the verbs may be construed impersonally. *They have not heard* simply means that no one has heard. Note the combination of the two verbs for *hear,* which appeared at the outset of the prophecy (1:2). Not only has man not heard, but he has also not given ear, which seems to indicate activity upon the hearer's part.

With the phrase *eye has not seen,* a certain gradation appears. It is one thing to hear, but to see with the eye brings convincing proof. Yet, no eye has ever seen what the prophet here calls attention to. It is perhaps best to construe *'elohim* (God) as object rather than as vocative. The hearing and seeing refer to a knowledge of God obtained through His works. "Neither ear nor eye has known of any God apart from thee, Jehovah, who acts (inasmuch as the same root is employed as in the previous verse, "who does fearful things") on behalf of or for the benefit of those who wait for Him." This is a waiting in which hope, confidence, and patience are combined. The true God is thus distinguished from the idols, for none of the idols can perform nor have they ever performed fearful deeds on behalf of their devotees, whereas Yahweh, the God of Israel and the true God, can control all of creation and cause it to respond to His will when He comes down to earth to execute judgment.

In 1 Corinthians 2:9 (cf. also Matt. 13:17) Paul is not seeking to give an exact quotation of this verse, but rather is using the language and varying it as he will to express his own thoughts concerning the newness and uniqueness of the Gospel. "In that passage," says Calvin, "he [Paul] treats of the doctrine of the Gospel, which he demonstrates to surpass the capacity of the human understanding; for it contains knowledge that is widely different and far removed from the perception of our flesh, and, in short, is 'hidden wisdom,' so that Paul is justly led to view it with astonishment." And indeed, whether we contemplate what God does for His own in the bringing of benefits to them or the

494

performance of "fearful things," or whether we turn our thoughts to the excellencies of the Gospel, as Paul does, we cannot but be astonished at the wonder of God's works, for no mind can attain in itself to such loftiness.

5 "There is perhaps no sentence in Isaiah, or indeed in the Old Testament, which has more divided and perplexed interpreters, or on which the ingenuity and learning of the modern writers have thrown less light" (Alexander). Inasmuch as this is so, we shall briefly set forth what we believe the correct construction of the verse to be. The prayer of the preceding verse is continued. The first verb contains the idea of meeting for the sake of helping. Hence, the thought is that God has met with favor and aid everyone who rejoices to do righteousness. The doing of righteousness is the chief joy of those whom God aids. This first clause sets forth a contrast. Not all Israel received the blessing of God. Indeed, as a nation Israel was rejected; only those who rejoiced and did righteousness did God meet. The initiative is on the part of God.

In the second clause *thy ways* refers to God's dealings with mankind, and in particular His future ways. In these ways (i.e. when God works among men), those whom He has met in favor will remember Him. Such remembrance will find expression in acknowledgment of God's goodness.

In the third clause we have a reminder of the reason why God had been angry. This reason is introduced by the particle *hen* (*behold!*), thus directing attention to what is to be stated. The pronoun is also emphatic, for it is God Himself who had been angry. There was reason for God's anger, for the people had sinned.[2] Isaiah does not hesitate in these brief utterances to go to the heart of the matter and attribute the anger of God to human sin.

The final clause serves as a contrast; *in them* refers to the ways of God. The word *'olam* may be taken as a noun (*perpetuity*) and construed with *in them*; the thought then is that in the dealings of God with men there is perpetuity or eternity, and for that reason *we shall be saved*. That there is difficulty in this construction of the verse is not to be denied, but it seems to be more free of difficulty than any other.[3]

---

2 ונחטא — as in Gen. 43:9; *then we stand as sinners, as guilty persons.* The imp. expresses the practical consequence.
3 See SPECIAL NOTE: "The Text of Isaiah 64:4/5."

6 And we were like the unclean, all of us, and like a filthy
garment all our righteousnesses; and we faded like the leaf,
and our iniquities like the wind will take us up.

7 And there is no one calling on thy name, rousing himself to
lay hold on thee; for thou hast hid thy face from us, and hast
melted us because of our iniquities.

8 And now, O LORD, our Father art thou; we are the clay, and
thou art our former, and the work of thy hand are we all.

9 Be not angry, O LORD, to an extreme, and not to eternity
remember guilt; lo! look, we pray thee, we are all thy people.

10 The cities of thy holiness have been a wilderness; Zion was a
wilderness, Jerusalem a desolation.

11 The house of our holiness and beauty, in which our fathers
praised thee, has become a burning of fire; and all our desirable
places have become a desolation.

12 Is it upon these thou wilt restrain thyself, O LORD; wilt thou
keep silence and afflict us to an extreme?

6 After the expression of confidence just made, the people state
their true nature. The speaker is not the entire nation, for the
unbelieving portion of Israel would have no true knowledge of
itself. Beginning with a verb in the past, the confession concludes
with one in the future, for the purpose is to show what the true
nature of the people has been and what will happen to them if
there is no divine intervention. As in chapter fifty-three, emphasis
here falls upon *kullanu* (*all of us*), i.e. all who make this confession. The term *unclean* (*tame'*) is the technical word to indicate
a legal impurity (cf. Lev. 5:2; 7:19, etc.), and the people are
acknowledging that they were like those whom the law required to
cry out, "Unclean!" so that other men might not be contaminated
by them.

The second comparison, lit., *like a garment of times,* refers to
the menstrual periods of a woman. Both these comparisons are
intended to stress the character of sin as pollution and to point out
its disgusting nature. The righteous works that the people could
present before God were even in their own eyes as disgusting and
filthy as the menstrual cloths of women. Calvin objects to the use
of this verse to support the doctrine of total depravity, inasmuch as
he believes that it is primarily the utterance not of all the Jews but
only of those who, having experienced God's wrath, acknowledge
the true nature of their own righteousness. This is true, and yet the
comparison is an apt description of the true nature of all our

works of righteousness. When one loathes his own works, as did these Jews, there is hope that he will turn to the pure righteousness that God imputes to those who believe in Jesus.

Parallel in construction to the first clause is the third; together with the fourth clause, it points out what the result of the people's condition was and would be. To fade like a leaf simply means to lose all strength of life. In the last clause, *our iniquities* serves as a *casus pendens*; for the figures used and the form of the clause see Psalm 1:1 and Job 27:21.

7 Having described the condition into which the people had fallen, the prophet now continues that description, pointing out the desperate situation of the people because God had removed His face. Sin leads to forgetfulness of God; and no one was calling upon God's Name in prayer and intercession, invoking His aid and blessing. The lethargy of the people was so great that they would have to exert themselves strongly to *lay hold on* God importunately, not letting go of Him until again He blessed them. Yet there was no one that thus sought to arouse himself.

Inasmuch as God had hidden His face from the people, they could not come to Him. This thought is supported by the final clause, *thou hast melted us*;[4] the people became like wax, with no strength at all, a result God brought about through the instrumentality of the people's iniquities.

8 By means of the introductory *And now*, the prophet introduces a turn in the thought. It suggests that despite all, Yahweh is *our Father* (cf. 43:1). How can one expect God to show mercy to people who are unclean and as a filthy rag? Such detestable things should be cast out and destroyed; yet, although this is the confession that is made, and although God has melted the people through their sins, nevertheless they address Him as their Father. He is not a Father that finds satisfaction in the suppliants' condition, but in spite of that condition He will show mercy. Great as is the wickedness of the people, they know that Yahweh is their Father and they expect His grace.

In the following clauses, the sense of *Father* is brought out. Note the contrast between *thou* and *we*. Alexander correctly points out

---

4 *wattemûḡēnû* — an unusual contracted form for *wat-te-mō-ḡe-ḡē-nû*. 1Q *wtmgdnw*.

that in the original expression (lit., *the one who forms us*) there is more dignity than in the English word, *potter*. The figure has been previously used by Isaiah in 29:16 ("the unquestionable passage of Isaiah" [Delitzsch]) and in 45:9. Isaiah again takes up the thought of 63:16, yet he is speaking here not of the creation of man as such but rather of redemption, the formation of the Church in the old dispensation, the creation of the spiritual Israel. Clay, therefore, refers to what is mean and lowly; and God as potter has sovereign disposition over the clay; from this clay He has molded His people, who now confess that He is their Father. Note the concluding *all of us,* and the chiastic arrangement of the two final clauses. In looking to their origin, the suppliants do not find it in themselves but in God's mercy.

9 The people may and do pray to God, for prayer is the prerogative of those to whom the Lord is a Father. They entreat Him (*Be not thou angry*) that His anger be abated, that it not extend to an extremity or to the fullest measure (lit., *unto strength,* i.e. until it has reached its full strength). In the parallel clause the same thought is expressed in slightly different language, *and mayest thou not to eternity remember iniquity.* Note the relationship of these two clauses to one another and the partial chiastic arrangement. To remember iniquity is to visit it with the punishment that is its due. The prayer is that this remembrance will not be eternal (cf. 54:7, 8). The people are not rebuking God for punishing them nor are they praying wholly to be delivered from judgment; well do they recognize that the judgment is just, and they ask for an alleviation therefrom.

In calling attention to the reason for their prayer, the prophet uses the introductory *behold!* or *lo!* Thus with boldness God is commanded to look; the particle *na'* is precative (*we pray thee*). The command is that God pay heed and give consideration to the fact that those who pray are His people, who stand to Him in a relationship of covenant. For this reason He is not to forget them, for He has made promises to them.

10 What is stated in this verse is probably to be understood as a second reason why God should not be angry forever. Note the contrast between *The cities of THY holiness* (i.e. *THY holy cities*) and *the house of OUR holiness* (i.e. *OUR holy house*) in verse 11. God is thus reminded that His holy cities are *a desert,* so it is

498

incumbent upon Him to reclaim them. These cities are not different parts of Jerusalem, but the cities of Judah, which belong to God's royal and holy kingdom. Zion and Jerusalem are singled out, for Jerusalem was the chief of all the holy cities. The final word, sh*emamah* (*desolation*), calls to mind the prophecy of chapter six.

Attention must be given to the force of the verbs. I cannot find warrant for rendering them by the future as Hahn does. Far more erroneous, however, is the common translation, *has become.* To express a present condition, Hebrew normally employs no verb. The forms of *hayah* (*to be*) that are found here may of course be rendered by the past, e.g., *Thy holy cities have been a desert* or *were a desert.* Inasmuch as the punishment mentioned is still continuing, however, it is difficult to see how this translation can be correct. Furthermore, this rendering suggests that the cities were once a desert but are no longer so, a position that is not in agreement with historical fact. It is perhaps best to render the verbs as present perfects, i.e., "Thy cities have been a desert, ... and still are such." We may translate in English by the present, *Thy cities are a desert.* For a long time Zion has been a desert and Jerusalem a desolation.

11 From cities to Jerusalem to the Temple, the prayer has step by step approached the heart of the tragic condition depicted. The people speak of the Temple with pride, for it was the place in which they could find the true glory of their lives and the beauty and adornment of their being, through the worship of God. Inasmuch as the Temple *has become a burning of fire,* i.e. has been burned by fire, God's people cannot worship Him in His holy house as their fathers had done. In fact, all the objects of their desire had *become a desolation.* The reference is probably to things associated with God's worship in the Temple; the first part of the verse would seem to support this view.

If the reference is to the historical burning of the Temple (cf. Jer. 52:13), then the passage is to be regarded as a prophecy of the future. On the other hand, the prophet may be using figures taken from Israel's history to express the tragic condition in which the whole worship of God among the people had fallen.

12 *These things* refers to the conditions just described, the holy cities and the Temple in ruins. "Is it for these things that thou wilt

steel Thyself so as to restrain Thyself from showing mercy?" Of the
three verbs, only the third is introduced by the conjunction. Keeping silence implies a refusal to hear the prayers of the suppliants.
God had throughout manifested goodness and love toward Israel;
will His present afflictions therefore continue? (cf. 49:15, 16; Ex.
34:6; Jer. 31:20). The questions are of course to be answered with
a decisive negative, but the answer is not given in this verse. At the
same time we must note that God's people must often be brought
to the place of such importunate prayer before He will hear them,
for when they pray so fervently as this they truly have a sense of
their sin and misery.

SPECIAL NOTE: THE TEXT OF ISAIAH 64:4/5

Rosenmüller comments, "*Locus obscurus, si quis alius, qui proinde
varie tentatus est ab interpretibus.*" Some modern interpreters propose
emendations. It is suggested that '*ôsēh* be emended to '*ôsēy* (*doers of*)
in accordance with the Greek and Old Latin. But these texts may
simply have understood the Hebrew in a collective sense and hence
rendered by the plural. The same may well be true of the Syr.
de-'ô-be-din. The Targ. is so free that at this point it is of little help
in determining the true text, "Set before thee are the works of our
righteous fathers, who rejoiced to do thy pleasure." Although in 1Q
the word is not fully legible, the singular ending may be clearly
discerned. Vulg. also renders by the singular, *facienti iustitiam.*

Secondly, the proposal is made to omit the 2 m. s. suffix from the
verb and then to read the simple pausal imperfect, *yizkōrû.* Again,
appeal is made to B μνησθήσονται and the Old Latin. 1Q clearly has the
suffix, however, and is supported by Vulg. *in viis tuis recordabuntur
tui,* and the Syr., *net-dak-rû-nok.* Even the Targ. seems to reflect
the suffix, "they were remembering thy fear" (*dkyryn ldhltk*). Saadia,
with his *yaḍ-ku-rû-na-ka,* clearly presupposes the suffix.

In the third place *BH* proposes to read for the fourth hemistich
the following: *beka mē'ôlām wannipšā',* "in thee from eternity (and)
we have sinned," i.e. "we have been rebellious against thee for a
while." Penna renders: "*contro di te da tempo, siamo stati ribelli.*" B
is of little help, reading simply διὰ τοῦτο ἐπλανήθημεν. Syr. has a
feminine suffix *behēn,* which would refer to *thy ways.* Again 1Q supports M, as does Vulg. *in ipsis fuimus semper et salvabimur.* In the
light of these facts there would seem to be no justifiable reason for
textual emendation in this verse.

1 I have been sought of those that asked not, I have been found by those that sought me not; I have said, Behold me, behold me, to a nation that was not called by my name.

2 I have spread out my hands all the day to a rebellious people, those going in a way that is not good, after their own thoughts.

3 The people angering me to my face continually; sacrificing in the gardens, and burning incense upon the bricks.

4 Who sit in the graves, and in the holes they will lodge; eating the flesh of swine, and the broth of filthy things is in their vessels.

5 Who say, Draw nigh unto thyself, come not near to me, for I am holy to thee. These are a smoke in my wrath, a fire burning all the day.

6 Behold! it is written before me. I will not be silent except I repay, and I will repay into their bosom.

7 Your iniquities and the iniquities of your fathers together, saith the LORD, for they have burned incense on the mountains, and on the hills blasphemed me; and I will measure their first work into their bosom.

1 God here speaks of the Gentiles, who, in contrast to the Jews, have received His grace even though they had not asked for it. The first verb is not only passive but also reflexive: *I permitted myself to be consulted,*[1] i.e. as one would consult an oracle. Such consultation resulted in an obtaining of the desired knowledge. This consultation was permitted to those who had not asked[2] nor inquired of Him. Those who had not sought after Him found Him nonetheless. In other words, God's free grace reached those who did not know Him and who made no effort to find Him. They in fact were found of Him. Isaiah's forceful language simply asserts

---

1 *niḏraští* — *Niphal tolerativum, I allowed myself to be inquired of.*

2 *lelō'* — i.e., "by them that did not ask." The demonstrative pronoun, which would here be the object of a preposition, is omitted.

the reality of sovereign and free grace given to sinners who deserve it not, and who have had no concern for it.

The strength of the revelation is brought out in the words *Behold me,* and the repetition lends emphasis. In thus speaking to the Gentiles, God calls their specific attention to Himself, assuring them of His presence and causing them to see who He is. Those addressed are identified as a nation upon whom God's Name has not been called. They have not been known as God's people, for they have not been so identified by Him in having His Name placed over them. Israel, of course, was called by the Name of the Lord; indeed, it was the only nation so called (43:7; Jer. 14:9). That the prophecy refers to the Gentiles is indicated by Paul's interpretation, in which he expressly and by way of contrast applies the second verse to the Jews (Rom. 10:20-21).

2 Verses 1 and 2 are a general answer to the question raised in the preceding chapter, namely, "Will there ever be an end to the divine wrath? Must God's own people forever suffer the hiding of His face?" By way of answer, God declares that He will indeed come in grace, but to a people who had not sought Him, i.e. the Gentiles. To the chosen people, however, which throughout their entire history had been *rebellious* (cf. 63:10), there was no hope. It is the truth that Christ later declared: "The kingdom of God shall be taken from you, and shall be given to a nation which shall bring forth fruit" (Matt. 21:43; cf. also Deut. 32:5, 6, 21).

Spreading out the hand is an action denoting God's love and willingness to receive His people. God performed this action not merely once, but *all the day,* a phrase that indicates the constancy of His desire for Israel; perhaps Pieper is correct in referring it to His covenant relationship with Israel. Israel, however, was rebellious, an epithet the prophet had earlier applied to the princes (1:23). Throughout its history the nation had lived in constant rebellion against the gracious overtures of its God (cf. Ex. 14:11; 16:2; 32:1ff., etc.). They went (a figure for a course of life) *in a way* (a manner of life) that was *not good*[3] (i.e. was morally evil). *Thoughts* refers not merely to the thoughts of the mind but also to wicked intentions and devices. These produced evil and brought their inventors to an evil end. "That which led them," remarks Delitzsch, "and which they followed, was not the will of God, but

---

[3] The article is omitted from *ṭōḇ* because of the negative.

selfish views and purposes, according to their own hearts' lusts; and yet Jehovah did not let them alone, but they were the constant thought and object of His love, which was ever seeking, alluring, and longing for their salvation."

3 The prophet now presents a detailed statement of the "way not good" and the "thoughts" just mentioned. This evil way is described by means of a series of participles, which modify *The people.* The first participle, *provoking me to anger,* is modified by an adverbial phrase, *upon my face,* and by an adverb, *always.* There has been no letup in the vexing of God. Furthermore, this was done not in secret but in open defiance of God (cf. 3:9; Job 1:11). It is as though the sinner actually beheld the face of God and before Him engaged in vexation; thus is the impudent boldness described.

The people were religious and engaged in religious exercises; but it was a religion of idolatry, abominable to the Lord. The second and third participles do not have the definite article. *Sacrificing in gardens* (cf. 1:29) evidently refers to a Canaanitish worship which had characterized the people ever since their entrance into Canaan. *Offering incense upon the bricks,* however, while evidently a type of idolatrous worship, is difficult because its precise significance is not understood. Some refer it to a Babylonian custom, because of the prevalence of bricks in Babylon; and others take it as indicating an altar, probably composed of bricks. That an idolatrous form of worship is intended there can be no doubt; its precise nature, however, is unknown.

4 The description is continued by two participial clauses, each of which is completed by a second clause of parallel nature. Each participle is introduced by the definite article. Whereas the verse obviously is a description of Israel's idolatrous practices, the precise significance of each term is difficult if not impossible to determine. To *sit in the tombs* and to *lodge* (spend the night) *in the guarded* or *secret places* probably has some reference, as Jerome pointed out, to the practice of incubation or consulting the dead,[4] a practice forbidden in Scripture (cf. Deut. 18:11; 1 Sam. 28:3; Isa. 57:9). Eating swine's flesh was forbidden in Leviticus 11:7ff. and

---

[4] The practice was widespread in the ancient world; cf. *Aeneid* vii.88-91, and Horace *Satires* i.8, 23-29.

Deuteronomy 14:8, for the swine was regarded as ritually impure. The precise reason, however, is not given in the Scriptures.

We may construe the last clause either *and the fragments of foul things are their vessels* or *the fragments of foul things are in their vessels.* According to Ezekiel 4:14; Leviticus 7:18 and 19:7, *piggul* indicates meat that levitically is unclean and rotten. The plural here is probably to be taken concretely, *rotten pieces.* This disgusting and revolting practice was evidently part of a pagan cultic usage. What a sickening contrast! Throughout their history the Lord, with outstretched arms of love, sought to bless Israel; but they, with their own wisdom, that wisdom which knew not God, turned to the practices herein mentioned. How deeply deceiving is the power of sin!

5 Those who partake of the filthy practices just set forth are now introduced as speaking. They arrogate to themselves a certain superiority, believing that through their practices they have become *holy* (i.e. set apart from others). The first expression means literally, *Draw near unto thyself,* i.e. "Keep apart from me." This command is uttered by the idolatrous Jews not to those who had remained faithful to God, but to God Himself. To give fullness to the command it is then stated obversely, *do not draw near to me.* At the ratification of the covenant at Sinai Yahweh had come down from heaven (cf. Ex. 3:8, 9), His holy dwelling, to take up His abode in the midst of His people. Unbelieving Israel no longer desires this nearness of Yahweh, its God, but in effect is telling Him to break the covenant relationship (i.e. in effect to deny Himself) and to go back to heaven from whence He came.

Israel gives a reason, which may be paraphrased: *I am holy with respect to thee.* One recoils from the depravity expressed in these words, for they plainly imply a contrast between God and the depraved nation. The nation is holy, i.e. set apart (see Vol. I, p. 242, note 19). Their idolatrous practices have set them apart from God, so that to them He is profane and they holy, and hence unapproachable. Iniquity always justifies itself; it is the holy, the unapproachable, the thing set apart; God, on the other hand, is profane and common. In reality, Israel hated the holiness God had demanded. The holiness, the mere being set apart, that the ancient world believed in superstitiously, was no substitute for the true holiness demanded by the One who alone is holy. How clearly these words express the fact that sin depraves, perverts, and deceives.

God's comment is succinctly given in the final half of the verse. *These* is probably used in a depreciatory sense. The thought is not that these disturb God as smoke in a man's nostrils disturbs him, but rather that these have caused the wrath and anger of God to burn as smoke and as a continuously burning fire (cf. Jer. 17:4). Smoke and fire then are concomitant figures of God's avenging wrath, which is now burning and consuming.

6 This and the seventh verse, as Pieper observes, serve as an Amen to the preceding discourse. The introductory particle *hinneh* (*Behold!*) points to the magnitude and also to the certainty of what is to be predicted (Alexander). There are differences of opinion as to what is *written before* God, but probably the reference is to the sinful action of the people. Inasmuch as this is written before Him, He will not keep silence, etc. There is a book of God in which the deeds of men are written. Possibly, there may also be reflection upon the fact that judges wrote out their cases. Whatever be the basis of the figure, its point is to show that the actions of the people are clearly known to God. *I will not keep silence* reflects upon "wilt thou keep silence" in 64:12. Instead of keeping silence, God has recompensed. It seems best to adhere to the strict order of the tenses, thus: *I will not keep silence, but* (instead) *I have recompensed, and I will recompense even unto the bosom.* There will be no keeping silence until God has recompensed; and that He has already done, and will do to the fullest. The recompense will be to such an extent that it will return even to the bosom of the person involved. As Boaz measured the barley into the lap of the garment covering the bosom (cf. Ruth 3:15), so God will exact retribution.

7 This verse presents the carrying out of the recompense. Because of the change of possessive suffix, the words *Your iniquities, etc.* are not to be taken as the object of *I will recompense* in verse 6, but of another *I will recompense* understood. It may be that the change of suffix is due to the fact that in verse 6 the prophet is describing the descendants of the present sinful generation, but more likely this is one of those enallages of number so characteristic of Isaiah. From the objective tone, the Lord now addresses the people directly. *Your iniquities and the iniquities of your fathers—*

The nature of these iniquities is set forth in the idolatrous practices of burning incense upon the mountains and blaspheming God upon the hills. Note the chiastic form of the language. The word *'asher* is best taken as a causative particle (*for*) rather than as a relative. The idolatrous actions herein mentioned were characteristic of the preexilic period (cf. 57:7; Hos. 4:13; Jer. 2:20; 3:6ff.; 17:2, etc.).

In the final clause there is difficulty as to the significance of *ri'shonah* (*first*). It may be taken in the sense *the first*, i.e. the first work, or it may be taken adverbially, *first*. The recompense they deserve will be measured out to them. The punishment is sure.

8 Thus saith the LORD, As when the new wine is found in the cluster, and one says, Destroy it not for a blessing is in it: so will I do for the sake of my servants, not to destroy the whole.

9 And I will bring out from Jacob a seed, and from Judah an heir of my mountains; and my chosen ones shall inherit it, and my servants shall dwell there.

10 And Sharon shall become a fold of flocks and the Valley of Achor a lair of herds, for my people who have sought me.

11 And ye, forsakers of the LORD, who forget my holy mountain; who prepare for Fortune a table and who fill for Fate a mingled draught.

12 And I number you to the sword, and all of you shall bow to the slaughter, because I called and ye did not answer, I spake and ye did not hear; and ye did that which was evil in my eyes, and that in which I delighted not ye have chosen.

13 Therefore, thus saith the Lord GOD: Behold! my servants shall eat, and ye shall be hungry, behold! my servants shall drink, and ye shall be thirsty; behold! my servants shall rejoice, and ye shall be ashamed!

14 Behold! my servants shall shout from goodness of heart; and ye shall cry from grief of heart, and from brokenness of spirit ye shall howl.

15 And ye shall leave your name for an oath to my chosen ones, and the Lord GOD will slay thee; and his servants he shall call by another name.

16 So that the one blessing himself in the earth shall bless himself by the God of truth, and the one swearing in the earth shall swear by the God of truth; because the former troubles are forgotten, and because they are hidden from mine eyes.

8 By means of the first clause a new turn in the thought is introduced. God will indeed not spare the wicked nation, but will save the remnant. The prophet introduces this truth by means of a comparison. We would render *ka'aher* by *As when*, for the purpose is to present what occurs under certain circumstances. *Tirosh* is actually *must,* or *new, fresh wine;* it would seem that the word is used proleptically, as though to say, "As wine comes from the cluster of grapes, etc." It is also possible that the word refers to the original state of the juice in the grape.

Why should anyone say, *Do not destroy it!* if the cluster consists of good grapes and if juice is found therein? Would it not seem that this was the very time when the cluster should be destroyed? Isaiah, however, paints in general strokes, and we must assume that the good cluster in which the juice is found[5] stands out against the background of other clusters in which no juice is present. For the sake of the one good cluster, then, the others and primarily this one good cluster (note that the verbal suffix refers to *'eshkol, cluster*) are not to be destroyed. Whether the words *Do not destroy* are a reflection upon a vintage song[6] is difficult to determine. In the cluster there is a *blessing,* for it has been blessed by God and brings blessing for man, and so should not be destroyed. For the sake of God's servants, who serve Him faithfully, He will not destroy all (i.e. the whole nation; cf. Matt. 13:29; 1 Kings 19; Rom. 9). In the destruction of judgment the wicked will be punished, but the remnant will be saved and will call upon His Name.

9 This verse shows how God will carry out His promise ("so will I do"). The first verb is introduced by *waw* consecutive and follows the imperfect "I will do" of the preceding verse. Emphasis falls upon the increase of the people. Were God not to act to save the nation and bring from it a seed, there could be no seed. The seed refers not to contemporaries but to descendants, and the meaning is that from the present nation God *will bring forth* (lit., *cause to go forth*) *from Jacob* (a designation of the people in bondage) *a seed,* and *from Judah* (the southern kingdom) one who will inherit God's *mountains* (i.e. the mountainous land of Palestine). It was from Judah that the future ruler should come (cf. Mic. 5:2). The *chosen ones* are those whom God has chosen to

---

5 יִמְצָא — the imp. may express a general truth. Note, however, that it is continued by the perf. with *waw* consecutive.

6 So Marti; W. R. Smith. Cf. the headings for Ps. 57; 58; 59; 75; and cf. Isa. 16:10; Jer. 48:33, passages to which appeal is generally made.

be the heirs of eternal salvation; they will dwell in the land. The final word, *shammah* (lit., *to there, thither*), implies motion toward. Thus, the true heirs have come to the land and there find their eternal home. Due stress must be given to the use of the words for *inherit* in this verse. Those who will finally dwell in the land are its true heirs; it comes to them by legal and rightful inheritance.

What Isaiah is predicting is not a physical return of the Jews to Palestine, for the seed is to consist not merely of Jews but also of Gentiles (cf. v. 1). The geographical figures are symbols of the heavenly Canaan. God's purpose was to perpetuate the old theocracy not in the empirical nation of Israel itself but in the believing remnant of that nation which turned to Christ, ". . . and which, enlarged by the accession of the gentiles, is identical in character and rights with the church of the old dispensation, the heir to all its promises . . ." (Alexander). Believers are now in the heavenlies; and when the Lord returns in power and glory, then they will realize the fullness of the promises and blessings as now they cannot do.

10 Calvin well brings out the force of this verse: "Although, in consequence of the banishment of her inhabitants into a distant country, she shall be forsaken and desolate, yet she shall at length be inhabited, so as to abound in flocks and herds, and have lands that are fertile and that are fit for pasture, and supply abundantly everything that is necessary for the food and support of men." Two extremities of the land are mentioned, Sharon and Achor, the west and the east. *Sharon* was the fertile plain extending from Carmel south to Jaffa (cf. 33:9; 35:2). *The Valley of Achor* was named after the episode of Achan (Josh. 7:24ff.; cf. Hos. 2:15). Beautiful, fertile Sharon will become (lit., *will be for*) *a home of flocks*. Isaiah singles out one particular type of prosperity, that so well known to Palestinians, the raising of flocks and cattle. Perhaps we cannot give specific reasons why these two places are mentioned, and Alexander is probably correct in his comments: "For these or other reasons Sharon and Achor are here mentioned, in Isaiah's characteristic manner, as samples of the whole land, or its pastures, just as flocks and herds are used as images of industry and wealth, derived from the habits of the patriarchal age." The ones to enjoy these blessings are God's *people who have sought* Him. The final verb reflects upon the first verb of the chapter. All God's redeemed have sought Him, for He has made them willing and able.

11 Isaiah now returns to those who have forsaken the Lord, addressing them with the emphatic pronoun, *But ye*. The remainder of the verse, however, is not an address, but a description of the apostates. Not to be overlooked is the disjunctive and emphatic force of the conjunction and pronoun. Idolatry is mentioned as the manner in which these people forsake the Lord. They do not remember His holy mountain, Zion, where He dwells in the Temple, but rather seek the high places and valleys of their own delight. Perhaps the word *holy* serves to designate the true nature of God's dwelling place in sharp contrast to the idolatrous practices in which the people engage.

"Preparing a table" refers to the preparation of a meal, and has generally been identified, probably correctly, with the Latin *lectisternium* (i.e. a feast offered to the gods; cf. Livy v.13; xxi.62). The Latin word refers to the spreading of a bed in order that the gods might be served. Possibly the Hebrew word translated *prepare* or *spread*[7] has a similar reference. The second phrase refers to the pouring of a libation of wine, lit., *who are filling a mixed drink*. Isaiah does not mean that they prepare a table only for Gad and pour a libation only for M°ni, but rather that both for Gad and M°ni they do both these things. If the two words *Gad* and *M°ni* are to be taken as the names of deities, Gad refers to the god *Fortune*,[8] the Tyche of Greek mythology, whereas M°ni, which stands for *Fate* or *Destiny*, may possibly have a connection with the goddess Manat of Arabian mythology. The overruling providence of the sovereign Yahweh of hosts has been exchanged for devotion to the cults of fortune and fate.

12 With the first word (*manithi*) there is a word play on the name of the divinity in the preceding verse, M°ni. It is not necessary, and in fact it is even questionable, to construe this verse as an apodosis to the preceding; hence the introductory conjunction may be the weak *waw*. The verb may be translated by the past or the present, *And I number* or *And I have numbered*. God's

---

7 *ha'ōreḳîm* — note the unusual pointing of the article before *Ayin*.

8 The name seems to be maintained in names such as Baal-gad (Josh. 11:17; 12:7; 13:5) and Migdal-gad (Josh. 15:37). Muilenburg (*IB*) cites references to extrabiblical literature.

purpose in numbering was to single the people out, as it were, one by one, that they might be slain by the sword. Isaiah had earlier spoken of the sword (1:20) as the instrument by which the people would be devoured. Perhaps there is an intended contrast between spreading out the tables for meals and bowing down to be slaughtered.[9] No longer would the nation of the Jews be the true Israel of God, but from this time forth, when the excision had been made, the Israel of God would be a new body, composed both of Jews, the seed to go forth, and of Gentiles, the people that had not sought God.

That God is abundantly justified in His action is seen in that when He called to the people through the overtures of His goodness, they did not even trouble to respond. When He spoke they *did not hear* (i.e. *heed*) what He said. Be it noted that God approached the people by means of words, i.e. by propositional revelation. Rather than obedience, they did (not once but continuously) that thing which He regarded as evil and chose those things which He did not delight in. They had a free will to choose, and they chose within the capacity of their nature; they chose the evil. For the thought of this verse note also the words of the New Testament in Matthew 23:37; 22:7; Luke 19:27 and Acts 13:46.

13 *Therefore* refers to the preceding word of promise and judgment. Inasmuch as the things just announced are true, therefore God speaks, describing the different portions that await His servants and the apostate nation, which he addresses as *ye*. Three contrasts follow in this verse, each of which is introduced by *behold!* Here the true servants of God, His Israel, are distinguished from the empirical nation to which He speaks. Those who believe are to enjoy supreme happiness, whereas the apostate will obtain a portion of misery. The word *'adonai,* signifying God's power and sovereignty, precedes the divine Name, Yahweh, to show that the covenant God has the power to carry out both His promises and His judgments. Eating, drinking, and rejoicing characterize the blessings God's servants will receive. Isaiah refers not to physical eating and drinking, but uses these terms, which signify the satisfaction of bodily needs, as symbols of the fact that man's spiritual needs will be abundantly supplied so that man may rejoice in his

---

9 I.e. *'rk* and *kr'.*

510

God forever. Those, however, who have been disobedient will receive the opposite of what comes to God's servants. They will hunger, for their needs will in no way be satisfied; they will thirst, for the water of life will be withheld from them; and they will be ashamed, for they have done the foolish thing of disobeying God's calls and words. The Jewish nation and the elect people can no longer be considered identical; the tragic subsequent history of the Jewish nation is that of a people that does not have its God. Before the final peal of judgment sounds, ought not we who are the Israel of God make every effort to reach the Jew with the bread of heaven, the water of life, and the joy of the Gospel?

14 The contrast is continued. In each of these contrasts, the words *my servants* and *ye* form a *casus pendens* and have emphatic force. *Gladness* (lit., *goodness*) *of heart* suggests the supreme joy that reigns in the heart so overcome that it breaks forth into shouting. *Grief of heart* (i.e. *anguish, pain*) will cause the apostates to cry out. This second clause is strengthened by the addition of the parallel *brokenness of spirit* (cf. 61:1 and Ps. 51:7). Desperate despair will overtake those who have rejected the promises of hope. It will bring forth not merely a cry but actual wailing and howling.[10]

15 The name of the nation of unbelievers and the name of God's servants is to be changed.[11] Continuing the address to the nation, God declares that they will leave their name for (i.e. their name will be remembered as) *an oath* (i.e. a curse) for God's *chosen ones*. Generally, these words are taken to mean that the name of the nation will be used by the chosen ones as a formula of cursing, so that they may wish that others would be cursed as was the nation, i.e. nothing worse could be wished for others than what has come to the Jewish nation. Some (e.g. Pieper) think that the name is rather an object of cursing, so that as often as the elect think upon the name of the apostate nation, they will curse it. Again, it may be that the name is left for the elect so that they will see and understand that the historical nation of Israel has become a curse. Perhaps the first of these interpretations is correct; if the elect should ever have to employ a curse, there would be justification for so

---

10 *teyēlīlū* — the preformative has been added to the contracted form.
11 1Q gives only 15a, following *yhwh* with *tmyd ygr'*. B κληθήσεται; S Aq καλεσει.

doing, as those to be cursed would deserve it (cf. Jer. 29:22; also Zech. 3:2). In such a case there would be no evil or malevolence, but simply the expression of the truth that the ones to be cursed deserved what was to come to them.

There is significance in the words *my chosen ones,* for now it is clearly shown that the empirical nation as such is not synonymous with God's elect. Addressing the nation now in the singular (as a collective or ideal person), the prophet states that the Lord God (again, the epithet *'adonai,* which calls attention to God's sovereignty, precedes the covenant Name) will slay the Jewish nation as such. In the light of this express statement, what scriptural warrant is there for expecting a future resurrection of this nation?

There will also be a change with respect to God's servant in that He will call them (note the divine initiative) *by another name* (cf. Rev. 2:17). Basically this means that there will be a complete change of character and nature. There will no longer be the old Israel but it will become the new Israel of God. This passage probably parallels 62:2-4, where the new name is given as *hephtzi-vah* ("my delight is in her").

16 This verse shows what the consequences of the change of names will be, in that it refers to the actions of those who remain upon the earth, and are not destroyed in judgment. Perhaps too there is an implied contrast between the earth and Judah. Whenever one blesses himself he will do so *by the God of truth* (lit., the God of Amen). The introductory *'asher* is best taken in the sense *So that,* for what is here described is a result of what was stated in verse 15. He who swears is to swear by the same God. He is the God of truth, for in the carrying out of all His promises of blessing and threatenings of judgment, He has been successful and has shown that what He has spoken is true (cf. 2 Cor. 1:20; Rev. 3:14).

That He is the God of truth appears in that the *former distresses* the people suffered have been *forgotten* (a strong expression for stating their complete removal). Furthermore, they have been *hidden* from before God's eyes, so that He no longer sees them. The distresses are more than misfortunes; they are the result of the nation's sins. As there is a removal of the reason for punishing sin, the distresses that sin causes will be removed also.

17 For behold! I am about to create new heavens and a new earth; and the former things shall not be remembered, and they shall not come up upon the heart.

18 But rejoice and be glad unto eternity in that which I am about to create; for I am about to create Jerusalem a joy, and her people a rejoicing.

19 And I shall be glad in Jerusalem and I shall rejoice in my people; and there shall no longer be heard in her the voice of weeping and the voice of a cry.

20 There shall be no more from there an infant of days, and an old man who shall not fulfill his days; for the child a hundred years old shall die, and the sinner a hundred years old shall be accursed.

21 And they shall build houses and dwell; and they shall plant vineyards, and eat their fruit.

22 They shall not build and another inhabit, they shall not plant and another eat; for as the days of a tree shall be the days of my people, and the work of their hands my chosen ones shall use to the full.

23 They shall not labor in vain, and they shall not bring forth for terror; for the seed of the blessed of the Lord are they, and their offspring with them.

24 And it shall be, before they call, and I shall answer; while they are yet speaking, and I shall hear.

25 The wolf and the lamb shall feed as one, and the lion like the ox shall eat straw, and the serpent dust for his food. They shall not hurt and they shall not destroy in all my holy mountain, saith the Lord.

17 With grand solemnity Isaiah introduces the reason why the former distresses will be forgotten. The introductory *behold me!* directs the thought to God Himself, who is about to act. As often, the participle may have the sense of near futurity: *about to create*. Not without reason does the prophet use the word *bara'*, which had occurred in the first verse of Genesis. In the simple (*Qal*) stem it is used only with God as the subject; the material employed, if there be any, is never mentioned; the word implies effortlessness, and points to the production of something fundamentally new. What is to be announced is so revolutionary that it is the result of God's creative activity. That almighty power which was displayed at the original creation is again to be displayed in a new work of creation.

Again God creates heaven and earth, and they are *new*. In that they are new, they will so fully show forth the glory of God their creator, and so completely fulfill every need and desire of man the creature, that the former heavens and earth will no longer be remembered, nor will they even enter *upon the heart* of man.

Strictly speaking, the words *former things* refer to former heavens and earth. But heaven and earth are employed as figures to indicate a complete renovation or revolution in the existing course of affairs. With the advent of the Messiah the blessing to be revealed will in every sense be so great that it can be described only as the creation of a new heaven and a new earth. The reference, however, is not to be restricted to the first advent but includes the entire reign of Christ, including the second advent and the eternal state. Christ renews the world, and Hebrews speaks of it as the world to come (2:5). In passages such as 2 Corinthians 5:17 and Galatians 6:15, Paul shows how the new creation applies to believers; and Peter sets forth the hope of believers to receive this new heaven and earth (2 Pet. 3:15). In the concept of the prophet, time and eternity, the age of the New Testament and the eternal heaven, are not sharply distinguished; and believers are already in the heavenlies. Prominent in the prophecies of blessing to come is the idea of forgetfulness of the past (cf. Rev. 21).

18 Instead of the former things being remembered, the people are commanded (the first two verbs are imperative and need not be translated as future) [12] to *rejoice and be glad* forever on account of what God is about to create. In particular Jerusalem, the focal point of the new creation and of the kingdom of God, is to be created a rejoicing, and her people (those who truly belong to her) are to be created a joy. In this and the following verse the idea of joy is stressed, being expressed at least six times. To *create Jerusalem a joy* is to create her into that which is an object of joy. What is stated here is the same as that given in the preceding verse. The present Jerusalem will pass away, and at the center of God's kingdom there will be joy. Men will rejoice before God in His true worship.

19 Not only will God's people rejoice in that their distresses have passed, but God also will rejoice in them, for He need no longer grieve over them. Calvin appropriately remarks: "So great is

[12] The imperative expresses a distinct assurance or promise. Cf. GKC § 110 c.

his love toward us, that he delights in our prosperity not less than if he enjoyed it along with us." "In all their affliction He was afflicted," but also in all our joy He rejoices. *Jerusalem* and *my people* are synonymous. When this perfect joy appears there will no longer be heard in Jerusalem as at present the voice (i.e. the sound) of crying and the sound of a cry (cf. 25:8; 35:10; Rev. 7:17; 21:4).

20 The description now introduces particulars of the Messianic kingdom, stressing the longevity of those who will belong to that kingdom. *From there* may refer to Jerusalem, the thought being that *There will not be from there* (i.e. taken away from there by death) *a suckling*[13] *with respect to days*. Thus, death will not take away from there (i.e. from the Jerusalem of the Messianic age) one who is merely a suckling child as death is now wont to do. Nor will the elderly man who has not yet lived out the full span of life meted to him be taken away by death as is now the case.

In the second part of the verse the opposite truth is expressed. The youth who is one hundred years old[14] will die, i.e. when one dies at the age of one hundred, he shall be regarded as merely a youth, the implication being that he had yet far more life to live. Likewise, when death cuts off a sinful[15] man, it does so when he has lived a hundred years. Men will die, and death is a curse; and when that curse comes as a punishment for sin, as it does even to God's people, the sinner will be a hundred years old. Thus, one of the blessings of the new age is that of longevity. Basic to this promise is probably the conception already expressed in Genesis 6:3. The conditions of Paradise are to be restored, but the new age will surpass Paradise.

21 In the law it had been prophesied that due to the nation's disobedience it would not be able to enjoy the houses it had built nor the fruit of its labors (cf. Deut. 28:30; cf. also Zeph. 1:13 and Mic. 6:15). In the new age, however, the very opposite will prevail. Long had Israel suffered from the invasions of outsiders; but now they will themselves be able to build their houses and to dwell in them without interruption, and they will also be able to eat the

---

13 עוּל — *sucking child, suckling.* B ἄωρος· Aq βρέφος; S νήπιον; T νεωτερος.
14 Lit., *son of a hundred years; ben (son)* serves as a circumstantial clause.
15 The participle is pointed with *Segol* as though from a *Lamed-He* verb.

grapes they themselves have planted. It is a picture of tranquility, of a man laboring and enjoying the fruit of his labors. The blessing of labor characterizes the Messianic age.

22 Isaiah strengthens the promise through a denial of its opposite. The people will not build houses that others will thereafter enjoy, while they themselves are carried away by death; nor will they plant vineyards that will be enjoyed by others after they themselves have been taken away (cf. 62:8, 9). The comparison with *the days of a tree* seems to be based upon the fact that to the Palestinian the tree was a symbol of permanence and endurance. Isaiah does not necessarily mean that just as a tree lives for many days, so also will the people, but rather that their life will have the permanence of a tree (cf. Ps. 1:3; Jer. 17:1-8). Furthermore, God's *chosen ones* will enjoy *to the full* the work that their own hands have performed.

23 Verse 23 sums up 21 and 22 in negative manner. The labor the people will expend will not be *for vanity* (i.e. *in vain;* cf. 49:4). One result of the fall is that labor is often in vain; in the Messianic kingdom, men will labor for God and hence will see the produce of their efforts. Nor will they *bring forth for terror*, i.e. at a time when there is great fear and the children will be the objects of extreme solicitation and concern, the opposite of the right time to which men look forward with hope and expectation (cf. Lev. 26:16; Ps. 78:33; Jer. 15:8). The time of bearing children will be one of joy and blessing.

Isaiah gives a reason in the concluding half of the verse. They are a seed consisting of those whom God has blessed. *Seed* may be taken in the sense of generation, but it may also mean descendants. If this latter is correct the thought is that they are descended from those whom God has blessed. With them, in that they have not been lost through premature death, are *their offspring* (cf. Job 21:8). Thus, the redeemed with their offspring live together in blessedness, for they are the seed of blessed ones.

24 In chapter sixty-four the people had complained that God did not hear them when they cried out unto Him. In the Messianic age, however, He will abundantly hear, for as Calvin says, God's hearing those that call upon Him "is the most valuable fruit of faith." Isaiah introduces the promise with *And it shall be,* which

stresses futurity and presents a further fact of blessedness that will
characterize the kingdom. God will answer when the people have
not yet called upon Him. It is best to render *terem* as *not yet*.[16]
Stress falls upon *I*, so that we have, *not yet will they call, and I will
answer*. What is prominent is the fact of God's readiness to answer
prayer, for He has a love and concern over His own that they
cannot begin to appreciate. In fact, while the people are yet
speaking God will hear, in the sense of hearing favorably and
answering (cf. Matt. 6:8 and Isa. 30:19; 58:9; Ps. 145:18, 19).
What greater privilege than to have a God whose love is so great
that He answers before one calls to Him!

25 In a beautiful manner the prophet concludes the prophecy
of future blessing by repeating a prophecy he had earlier employed
in 11:6-9, to the effect that all hurtful things should cease in God's
holy hill. The *wolf* (in Hebrew the word is anarthrous) and the
tender young *lamb* will pasture *as one*, a stronger rendering than
together; so close will they be that they will be as one animal. The
following may be translated either *and the lion like the ox will eat
straw, and as for the serpent, dust is his food,* or *and the lion like
the ox will eat straw, and the serpent* (will eat) *dust for his
food*.[17] For the significance of these figures see the exposition of
11:6-9. Here is no mere picture of a golden age such as is found in
Hesiod (*Works and Days* 90-92) or in Vergil (*Eclogues* iv.8ff.),
nor is it a visionary dream of utopia. Rather, the prophet calls
attention to God's *holy mountain,* the place where He dwells with
His people and where a perfect peace is to be found. The promise
is strengthened by the final *saith the Lord,* and with this word
Lord the chapter closes.

---

[16] טרם followed by the imp. may express the future rather than the past;
before they call, i.e. *they have not yet called.*

[17] *Serpent* on this construction is a *casus pendens.* B ὄφις δὲ γῆν ὡς ἄρτον.

1 Thus saith the Lord, The heavens are my throne, and the earth my footstool; what is the house that ye will build for me, and what is the place of my rest?

2 And all these my hand hath made, and all these were, saith the Lord; and to this one will I look, to the afflicted and contrite in spirit and trembling at my word.

3 Slaying the ox, smiting a man; sacrificing the sheep, breaking a dog's neck; offering an oblation, the blood of a swine; making a memorial of incense, blessing vanity. Also they have chosen their ways, and in their abominations has their soul delighted.

4 I will also choose their wanton dealings, their fear I will bring upon them; because I called, and there was none answering, I spake and they did not hear. And they did evil in my eyes, and that in which I did not delight they chose.

1 With the asseverative *Thus saith Yahweh* the last prophecy begins, and immediately points us to the immensity of God. God is so great that even the heaven of heavens cannot contain Him (1 Kings 8:27). With the figure of heaven as God's *throne* and the earth as His *footstool*,[1] the prophet is asserting that God is King of all and rules over all, and that all creation (heaven and earth; cf. Gen. 1:1) is subject to Him. Inasmuch as God is thus King over all, *what is this house* that these disobedient ones will build for Him? The interrogative *'ey-zeh* (best rendered *what?*) is somewhat depreciative. This is not a condemnation of earthly temples as such, but a condemnation of the idea that God can be confined to and is satisfied with such an abode. Solomon had built his Temple for the Lord, but in doing so was well aware that God was not confined to an earthly building, and that only in a symbolical sense could one speak of the Temple as the dwelling of God. The rebellious Jews believed that they might construct the Temple as a place of rest for Yahweh. In that Temple, however, He would have

[1] Cf. Ug. *hdm*; Egy. *hdm.w*.

no place of rest nor would it be His sanctuary. Those who would build a house influenced by such conceptions were seeking to render the infinite finite, the eternal temporal, and the Creator a mere creature.

The last two words should probably be rendered, *a place,*[2] *even my resting place.* Here is no denial that God would have a house or a resting place, but simply the denial that any house that apostates think they can build for God, if not accompanied by true devotion such as was characteristic of Solomon, is a house or place of rest at all.

The language is reminiscent of the remainder of the second part of Isaiah. He who had prophesied the exile and return sees through the Spirit of prophecy that the unconverted, disobedient people having come into their land again are interested in the externalities of Temple worship. Their sacrifices and offerings, however, are heathenish and idolatrous. The true Creator cannot endure such worship.

2 In a certain sense the great temple of the universe is itself disparaged, for the Lord declares that His hand (i.e. His power) has made it. *All these* suggests all that is contained in heaven and earth. The phrase *and they were* calls to mind the oft repeated *and it was* of the first chapter of Genesis. Inasmuch as His hand has brought into existence heaven and earth, those who think that a mere earthly temple would be a pleasing place of rest for Him are haughty in spirit and heart, for they have shown themselves disobedient to Him. There is, however, one unto whom the Lord will look with affection and favor, namely the afflicted (not through outward afflictions but through a broken heart), the contrite[3] in spirit (cf. 57:15; 61:1), the one who trembles at God's word. Wherever such men are found, God looks with favor. He, however, whose whole concern is with the externalities of religion is not such a person; but when a man has seen God as the truly infinite One, then his own heart is abased.

3 Among those who wished to build an earthly Temple, however, there were none trembling at God's word; rather, they

---

[2] It may be, however, that we have here an absolute before the genitive. Vulg. renders 1b, *Qual est ista domus, quem aedificabitis mihi? et quis est iste locus quietis meae?*

[3] נכה — *smitten, stricken,* here *contrite;* cf. 2 Sam. 4:4; 9:3. 1Q reads *wnk'y.*

brought sacrifices that were abominations. If there is any historical reference, it is to those who, having returned from exile, desired to serve God by means of their own appointment. The reference may be in part to some who built the second Temple, but more fully it is to those who built Herod's temple and continued offering the sacrifices even after the one true Sacrifice had been offered. John 12:38 expressly applies Isaiah 53:1 to the unbelief of the Pharisees.

Of particular interest is the manner in which the prophet condemns the sacrificers. He employs four similarly constructed phrases, each consisting of two parts, the first of which in each instance refers to a legitimate sacrifice of the Mosaic law, and the second to an action contrary to that law. Thus: *slaying the ox, smiting a man*.[4] Apparently the thought is that he who slays an ox (for sacrifice) is in God's sight like one who slays a man.[5]

Are these phrases then condemnations of the Mosaic law, and of the Temple sacrifices? This has been affirmed by some; but the meaning actually is that all sacrifice is abominated by God if offered in the wrong spirit (cf. comments on 1:12ff.). *Slaying the ox, smiting a man*—The ox represented an animal sacrifice, and the participle *slaying* is applied to sacrificial slaughter under the law.[6] To slay an ox as a sacrifice when the accompanying spirit of devotion was absent was no act of faith but an act of murder, just like the smiting of a man. *sacrificing the sheep, breaking a dog's neck*—A legitimate animal sacrifice, if done without faith, is like the breaking of a dog's neck, for the dog was regarded as unclean (cf. Matt. 7:6 and 2 Pet. 2:22). According to the Mosaic law (Ex. 13:13; Deut. 21:4), when an unclean animal was not redeemed from consecration to the Lord, its neck was broken. Thus, the sacrifice has lost all its significance, and become like the breaking of the neck of an unredeemed, unclean animal. *causing to go up an offering, the blood of a swine*—The word *minḥah* signifies the unbloody offering, but now it is swine's blood. Note that there is no participle with the second part of this comparison; the abruptness of the expression serves to point out how abominable was the offering of these sacrificers. *making incense a memorial, blessing vanity*—Underlying this expression was the idea that the incense ascended from the altar and reminded God of the offerer. Alexan-

---

[4] 1Q inserts the preposition *kmkh*. Note the definite article with *šôr* but not with *'iš*.

[5] It is possible that the reference is to human sacrifice.

[6] Cf. Gen. 4:15; Ex. 2:12; Josh. 20:5; 1 Sam. 17:26.

der appeals to Acts 10:4 and points out that the words used there, *for a memorial* (εἰς μνημόσυνον), are used in Codex Vaticanus in translating the present verse. The word is probably connected with the *'azkarah*, the memorial offering of Leviticus 24:7. Instead of the incense reminding God of the worshipper so that He might hear and accept him, the worshipper in reality was blessing vanity; his act was meaningless.

For this abomination there was no excuse, for those who so sacrifice have themselves chosen their ways and find their delight in what they are doing. Not through ignorance have they turned to this way but through their own willful desire. And this is where man's free will leads him. The sinner chooses to delight in what God abominates.

4 The words *Even I* with which this verse begins are correlative to *Even they* in verse 3b. "Even as they on their part chose their own ways and their abominations, so I on my part will choose their wanton dealings, i.e. as the cause of their destruction; and their fears (i.e. those things that they feared) I will bring to them (i.e. visit upon them)." God, who is in supreme control, will choose those wanton dealings of the nation in order thereby to bring about its destruction. The objects that the people feared will be made realities, in that the fear in all its horror will be realized.

God's action, however, is not capricious. Like the people, He too has a complaint. They complained that He would not hear; now He complains that when He called there was no one answering and when He spoke they did not hear. Furthermore, they did not hear because they chose to engage in wicked deeds. What He did not delight in, *they chose*. Their punishment and abandonment is well deserved. Caprice may have characterized their doings, but it is wholly absent from what God does.

5 Hear the word of the LORD, ye that tremble at his word: Your brethren say, those hating you and casting you out for my name's sake, The LORD will be glorified, and we shall look at your joy; and they shall be ashamed.
6 A voice of uproar from the city! A voice from the Temple! The voice of the LORD, rendering requital to his enemies.
7 Before she travailed, she brought forth; before her pain came she was delivered of a male.
8 Who hath heard like this? Who hath seen such things? Shall a land be brought forth in one day, or shall a nation be born

at once? For Zion hath travailed, she hath also brought forth her children.

9 Shall I bring to the birth and not cause to bring forth? saith the LORD. Or, am I the one causing to bring forth, and shall I shut up? saith thy God.

5 From now on the Lord turns to His chosen ones alone to comfort them. If the apostates are mentioned it is only in passing, and only in the third person. To the chosen ones in whom the true remnant will be perpetuated God gives the comforting assurance that, even though their brethren, the unbelieving nation, should hate them and cast them out, claiming to do this for the Lord's glory, their hatred would not prevail and they will be filled with shame.

As in his earlier prophecy (1:2), Isaiah again commands his hearers to *Hear the word of the Lord*. This command lends assurance and certainty, for the promise to follow has been spoken by God. Those who tremble at God's word are not like those who turn unto their own ways, but rather with reverential and fearful expectation they turn to that word as truly spoken of God. The reference is not to Isaiah's own contemporaries, but to that godly remnant in the future which will survive when the apostate nation is rejected.

Those who hate the godly are identified as *Your brethren*, a designation Paul used in Acts 22:1, which does not identify them as brethren in the Lord but simply as brethren according to the flesh, members of the same nation. "These will hate you and all who like you tremble at God's words" (cf. Matt. 10:22; John 15:18; 17:14; 1 Thess. 2:14). The enemies of the godly are also described as those who are *casting you out*. Here the thought is simply that of casting out or banishing, although the word soon comes to have the technical connotation of excommunication (cf. Matt. 18:17; John 16:2 and the talmudic usages). The apostates cannot tolerate the righteous and want nothing to do with them. Is not the consistent Bible-believing Christian an object of ridicule and reproach on the part of the organized Church today? So will it ever be. This is *for my name's sake*, i.e., "because you have been true to My Name" (cf. Matt. 24:10). Hahn construes these words with what follows, but a better sense is obtained if we construe them with the preceding.

In thus casting the godly out, the apostates have said, *Yahweh will be glorified, and we shall see your rejoicing*. These two clauses are dependent upon the initial *Your brethren will say*. Such words are to be understood as ironical and mocking (cf. 5:19), as though to say, "We are casting you out; but you worship Yahweh, so let Him be honored that we may see your rejoicing for His sake." Such a mocking of the sufferings of the righteous is the very depth of wickedness itself.

The conjunction before *they* in the last clause is disjunctive, and may be rendered *but*; *they* is emphatic. Rather than see the rejoicing of the godly, they who thus speak in irony *will be ashamed* or *confounded* when they learn what the outcome of events will be. Herein is comfort for the true believer. The opposition of ecclesiastics who have renounced the faith cannot in the end triumph, but will only lead to confusion; those who tremble at God's word will indeed possess rejoicing, for they will have the favor of their Lord.

6 Having in general terms stated that the enemies of God would be confounded, the prophet now proceeds to describe the judgment in greater detail. The enemies are those just mentioned, the disobedient nation that has cast out the true seed. The threefold *qol* (*voice*) is used as an interjection as in 40:3. What is heard is a *sha'on* (*tumult*), a word that suggests the tumult of war and the noise of battles. It is most appropriate to indicate that the wrathful judgment of God is about to break forth upon His enemies. This noise of a tumult comes from the very city of Jerusalem and even more particularly from the Temple itself, the dwelling place of the true God. As he had earlier done, Isaiah again designates the Temple as *heykal* (cf. 6:2). It is the promised day of vengeance of God, who is about to complete the requital of His enemies. From that city in which He would perform His great act of redemption, God thunders forth in judgment to destroy His enemies.

7 The unnamed subject of this verse must be Zion herself, and the purpose is to show that there will come a great increase to the Church of God. This increase will be sudden and unexpected, which fact is presented by means of a description of a woman bringing forth a male child. The language is succinct; *before she travails*,[7] she has borne. In fact, even before a pain has come to

---

7 *tāḥil* — imp. in the protasis, the apodosis containing the instantaneous perf., which expresses the sudden certainty of the result accompanying the action of the protasis. Cf. *TT*, p. 176.

her, she has caused a man child to be delivered (lit., *to escape, to slip out*).[8] Thus, the old order passes away, the ancient nation will perish and the Zion of Old Testament times disappear; but from that old Zion there will suddenly come forth a seed, the Gentiles who will enter the household of faith (cf. Luke 24:47; Acts 3:26; 13:46; 18:6; Rom. 1:16; 2:10 and note in particular Acts 15:1ff.). The ideal Zion of course does not perish; but when the apostasy of Israel according to the flesh would seem to have brought about her destruction, she appears vigorously alive in the bringing in of the Gentiles.

8 By means of a question the prophet shows the uniqueness of the event just described. The questions imply a negative answer, namely, "No one has ever heard anything like this and no one has ever seen anything like these, for these things are not like the ordinary course of nature." What takes place in Zion is due to the supernatural working of God. Since the time of the curse (Gen. 3:16), the mother suffered in childbirth. This birth, however, is an exception, for it is not a natural birth, but rather one the like of which has never been known. *A land*, i.e. the men that inhabit the land, will be *brought forth in one day; a nation* will be *born at one stroke. Zion has travailed and brought forth.* There is no contradiction with what the previous verse has said, for the purpose is simply to show that Zion is pictured as a woman who has already travailed and so has brought forth. The reference is to the shortness of time needed for the birth.

9 The certainty of the events described is further set forth by means of questions, which suggest that God, having begun a work, will see it completed. *Shall I bring to the birth,* asks the Lord; lit., *shall I cause to break,* and then stop the process without bringing forth? Such an action might have caused the death of the mother, but that is not the predominant thought here. Rather it is that God, having begun a good work, will fulfill it, for He is its Author and Finisher. The truth is certified by the words *saith the Lord.*

By means of further questions the same thought is again expressed. God will not cause to bring forth and then shut up or restrain[9] so that there can be no birth. Again, this truth is

---

[8] The perf. (*Hiphil*) with *waw* consecutive in an apodosis after *ṭerem*.

[9] The perf. with *waw* consecutive is here interrogative. The *Tiphḥa* gives a minor pausal force to the word.

certified by the statement *saith thy God*; and in the possessive *thy* lies the tender indication that Zion's own God speaks. The true Zion will continue; the apostate nation will disappear; but from Zion the New Testament Church will surely come forth, for God, having begun, will not interrupt or change His purposes.

10 Be glad with Jerusalem and rejoice in her, all who love her; rejoice with her a rejoicing, all who are mourning concerning her.

11 To the end ye may suck and be satisfied with the breast of her consolations, that ye may drain out and delight yourselves from the abundance of her glory.

12 For thus saith the LORD, Behold! I am about to stretch unto her peace like a river, and like an overflowing stream the glory of the nations; and ye shall suck: on the side ye shall be borne, and on the knees ye shall be fondled.

13 Like a man whom his mother comforts, so will I comfort you and in Jerusalem shall ye be comforted.

14 And ye shall see, and your heart shall rejoice, and your bones like grass shall sprout; and the hand of the LORD shall be known to his servants, and he shall be indignant at his enemies.

10 By means of a command addressed to the remnant who love Jerusalem and mourn for her, Isaiah prophesies the glorious blessing to come. The two words *śimḥu* and *gilu* are practical synonyms, each meaning *rejoice* or *be joyful*. *In her* is probably to be taken in the sense of *with respect to her*, or *because of her*. Jerusalem is then the object of joy. It is also possible to take the words locally, implying that the rejoicing is to take place within the city. Jerusalem is pictured as rejoicing, and those who love her are to joy with her. Those who truly love Jerusalem, love the Lord, have repented of their own sins, and strive daily to be obedient to His gracious commands. The address is definitely not to the entire nation of Jews, but only to the remnant, the elect according to grace.

In the second half of the verse the cognate accusative is forceful; *joy with her in respect to a joying, etc.* Here the address is to those *who are mourning on account of her*. Those who love Zion also mourn for her when they behold the desolations and depredations that she must undergo. Whereas these words are immediately addressed to the true remnant from which the Israel of God will spring, and not to the unbelieving Jewish nation, the principle herein embodied is valid for all times. In all ages there will be those in the Church who love and mourn for her when they see the inroads unbelief, indifference, and immorality have made within her. Their cry goes up, "How long?" God knows their mourning and ever comforts them with the command, "Rejoice in Jerusalem." Nor is this any idle command. For if the future of the Church depended upon man, there would be cause for mourning but none for rejoicing; inasmuch, however, as the future of the Church depends upon the covenant God, those who mourn may indeed joy in the Church of the living God, the pillar and ground of the truth, for God Himself is in the midst of her.

11 Those who mourn over Jerusalem are to rejoice that they may partake of the abundant joy she has to offer. Isaiah continues the figure of the mother who nourishes her beloved children to satiety. Indeed, the two pairs of verbs may be construed as hendiadys, *suck to satiety* and *drain out with delight*. Thus, the prophet presents the beautiful figure of the mourners as a child sucking contentedly the breast of the mother and receiving an abundant satisfaction therefrom. *Breast of her consolations* means simply the breast from which she consoles her mourning children.

In the second half of the verse there is a parallel purpose clause, which expresses the same truth in a slightly different manner. Here it speaks of draining out and enjoying oneself from the abundance[10] of her glory, i.e. all her rich and wondrous consolation and satisfaction, which can be found nowhere else. Indeed, it is only in the Church of Jesus Christ that such abundance of comfort and consolation may be found. This is not because the Church in itself has any power so to bestow blessing, but because the Lord is with His Church; and it is from Him that these blessings come to His people. "Lo! I am with you alway, even unto the end of the world" (Matt. 28:20).

12 With the word *For* the prophet introduces the reason for what he has just stated. God is about to stretch out over Jerusalem *peace like a river*. The figure is that of an onrushing river, never dwindling in its supply of water, but without interruption rushing on and spreading out widely. Thus God will bring *peace*, i.e.

---

10 זיז —*abundance, fullness.* Cf. Ar. *zíza, udder.* The root probably means *to be abundant*; cf. Akk. *zizu, udder*; Ug. *zd, breast.*

11 Note the emphatic position of *šālôm* at the end of the clause.

abundant prosperity and welfare, unto Zion. By peace[11] she will, as it were, be inundated. Furthermore, *the glory of the nations* (i.e. all in which they could boast) will be brought to Zion as *an overflowing stream.* The figure is probably that of a wadi, which, filled with water, becomes a mighty torrent, carrying everything in its wake. Thus, the mighty blessings to come to Zion are brought to her of her Lord. The figure also points out the spiritual conquest Zion will have over the nations in that God will bring the Gentiles like an overflowing stream unto her (cf. 9:7; 48:18; 52:7; 54:13; 57:19; 60:17). Isaiah introduces this remarkable prophecy with *Behold!* thus calling attention to its uniqueness. In succinct manner he states the result of God's action: *ye shall suck,* i.e. they shall enjoy to the full the peace and the glory of the nations that God will bring in.

The two final clauses composing the second half of the verse are amplifications of the single statement *ye shall suck.* The figure is that of a mother who carries the child on her side (cf. 60:4) and who fondles[12] the child upon her knees. The greatest love will be shown to the remnant, for as a mother expends her love upon her child, so also will the Lord love His redeemed children.

13 Isaiah changes the figure. Not only as children sucking the mother's breast does God comfort His people, but also as a mother comforts her grown son. Although indefinite, the word *man* is emphatic. It is important also to note that *ka'asher* (*Even as*) is broken up into *as* (*k*) and *which* (*'asher*).[13] There is no need to detract from the full significance of *'ish* (*man*), for a full-grown man is often in need of a mother's comfort. Pieper asserts that the heartache of a grown man is the deepest and hardest on earth. Isaac brought his bride Rebekah unto his mother Sarah (Gen. 24:67), Micah received a blessing from his mother (Judg. 17:2), and Bathsheba gave advice to Solomon (1 Kings 2:19, 20). Alexander calls attention to the affection in the *Iliad* between Thetis and Achilles. The mother's love for her offspring remains firm throughout life and thus forms a natural comparison for the divine comfort (cf. 40:1). In the final clause the matter is defined somewhat: *in Jerusalem shall ye be comforted.* Not in the physical boundaries

---

12 *tešo'ošā'û — Polpal, ye shall be fondled.* 1Q *tšt'š'w.*

13 *'ašer* is added because special stress is laid upon the indefinite *'iš;* generally, after an indefinite noun the relative is omitted as in Arabic.

of the city, but in the Jerusalem of God, His Church, will God's people be comforted.

14 This verse gives an assurance that those addressed will themselves experience the blessings of the new Jerusalem. The reference then cannot be to Isaiah's own contemporaries nor to those who returned from the exile in Babylon, but only to those who as the true Israel of God sprang from the old Israel, which had to pass away. If we seek to identify them more fully, they were those who lived at the time of Christ and longed to see the desire of nations. These would *see* (in the sense of *experience*) and would *rejoice*. That is, when they saw, their heart would leap with joy (such seems to be the force of the original). The *heart* is regarded as the seat of the emotions, and the thought is that they would be so overcome when they beheld the fulfillment of the prophecy that they themselves would leap in joy. Such a sight would bring new vigor to the *bones,* which are described as sprouting *like grass* (cf. 27:6; 58:11). Then *the hand of the Lord shall be known,* in that it will be practically recognized that the cause of this happening is the power of God. At His enemies, however, God will have indignation. In keeping with the consistent representation of the Old Testament, the prophet announces a concomitant judgment and salvation.

15 For behold! the Lord will come in the fire, and like a whirl-wind are his chariots; to appease in fury his anger, and his rebuke in flames of fire.

16 For by fire will the Lord strive, and by his sword with all flesh; and multiplied are the slain of the Lord.

17 Those sanctifying themselves and cleansing themselves to the gardens after one in the midst, eaters of the flesh of swine, and detestation, and the mouse: together they shall come to an end, saith the Lord.

18 And I—their works and their thoughts—it is come, to gather all the nations and the tongues; and they shall come and see my glory.

19 And I will place among them a sign, and I will send of them escaped ones to the nations, Tarshish, Pul and Lud, drawers of the bow, Tubal and Javan; the distant isles, which have not heard my fame and have not seen my glory, and they shall declare my glory among the nations.

20 And they shall bring all your brethren from all nations, an oblation to the Lord, with horses, and with chariot, and with

litters, and with mules, and with dromedaries, on my holy mountain Jerusalem, saith the LORD; as the children of Israel bring the oblation in a clean vessel to the house of the LORD.

21 And also of them will I take for the priests, for the Levites, saith the LORD.

22 For even as the new heavens and the new earth which I am making are standing before, saith the LORD, so will stand your seed and your name.

23 And it shall be that from new moon to new moon, and from sabbath to sabbath, all flesh shall come to do obeisance before me, saith the LORD.

24 And they shall go forth and gaze upon the carcasses of the men who revolted from me; for their worm shall not die and their fire shall not be quenched, and they shall be a horror to all flesh.

15 Isaiah proceeds to amplify the statement just made concerning judgment. In fact he brings together in one prophecy the two great thoughts of his preaching, judgment for the apostates and final glory and salvation for the true remnant. Yet what is particularly to be noted in this final prophecy is the stress upon the sending out of the Gospel to the heathen. With the introductory *ki* (*For*) the reason for the preceding assertion is given, and *behold!* calls attention to its tremendous significance. Actually, *Lord* forms a *casus pendens*, and the statement made concerning Him is that *in the fire* (i.e. surrounded therewith; cf. 29:6; 30:27, 30) He *will come*. This coming is for punitive judgment. *His chariots* (for He appears, as it were, here and there to carry out His purposes) are *like the whirlwind.* Jeremiah applies the same figure to the Chaldeans (4:13). As the whirlwind sweeps briskly across the open desert, so His chariots are here and there to accomplish His purposes.

In the second half of the verse the purpose of the Lord's appearance is stated, *to cause to return with burning anger his wrath,* i.e. *to recompense* or *to appease* His anger by means of wrath. God's anger has been aroused because of the nation's sins. This anger must be recompensed, and the manner in which this will be done is through the outpouring of God's wrath upon the sinner. In the Bible the rebuke of God is often mentioned in connection with His wrath (cf. 17:13; 51:20; 54:9). We may consider this rebuke as the display of that wrath, which will appear in the judgment flames of

529

fire. The use of fire implies its all-consuming power and the complete destruction of God's enemies.

16 The introductory *ki* (*For*) is explicative of how the judgment is to be carried out, namely through *fire* and *sword*. Perhaps it is justifiable to say that in the world of nature God judges through fire and in history through the sword, but too sharp a distinction must not be made. Not to be overlooked is the reflexive force of the *Niphal* verb, *he enters for himself into controversy*, or *strives for himself*. Fire symbolizes the all-consuming judgment, and the sword is a symbol of the divine vengeance. It is by means of fire that the Lord will *strive*, and *with his sword* (will He contend) *with all flesh,* with the result that those whom He slays will be many. *All flesh* is here not to be taken in a universal sense, as, for example, Smart does, but is defined by the following verse. It stands for those of the Jewish nation, the great majority, who have abandoned the Lord for the service of idols. The verse pictures the judgment to fall upon the Jewish nation at the time of Christ, with all the actual tragic consequences of that judgment in the sufferings that befell the Jews until the destruction of the Temple in A.D. 70. It is this of which our Lord speaks in Matthew 24:22 (note His usage of the words πᾶσα σάρξ, *all flesh*).

17 This verse identifies those just described as the slain of Yahweh. The order of words reflects upon 65:3ff.; and those herein described are to be identified with the same class of idolaters mentioned in the latter passage, as is shown by the reference in both passages to the gardens and the swine's flesh. The two participles with which the verse begins are actually technical terms for the Mosaic ritual, but here are applied to the service of heathen rites (cf. Gen. 35:2; Ex. 19:22; Num. 8:7; 11:18). In cleansing themselves, the people became sanctified. That action which should lead to holiness before the one true God is turned into a preparation for the service of the devil. It is a preparation *unto* (i.e. *for*) *the gardens* where the idolatrous rites are to be carried out (cf. 57:5).

We may render the following words, which constitute the principal difficulty of the verse, *after one*[14] *in the midst*. What the precise significance is, it is difficult to tell. Both the *Qᵉre* and the

14 Some think the reference is to the god Hadad.

first Qumran Scroll take the word *one* as feminine. Is the reference then to a particular rite that is celebrated in the midst of the participants? At any rate, the abominable practices that accompany the rite are clearly stated: *those who eat the flesh of swine* (cf. the comments on 65:4), *the detestable thing* (probably a general term referring to unclean animals; cf. e.g. Lev. 11:41-43), and *the mouse* (cf. Lev. 11:29ff.). Their cultus expressed itself in an impure rite in their midst instead of being directed to the God above them who reigns on high.

In a short concluding clause it is stated that *together they shall come to an end*; and this is strengthened by the words *saith the Lord*. On this glorious word the verse closes. We have been lifted from the midst of the abominable and detestable ones to the clean purity of *the Lord*.

18 By the conjunction this sentence is connected to the preceding. The pronoun *I* is emphatic and disjunctive, calling attention to God in distinction from those who sanctify and purify themselves for idolatry. At the same time, it is best to construe it as a *casus pendens*, and to render as follows: *And I—their deeds and their thoughts—it has come, etc.* The deeds and thoughts (i.e. the evil intentions and devices of the apostates) express the entirety of their personalities. The thought is that "inasmuch as I know their thoughts and deeds, the time is coming that I will gather, etc." *Tongues* is used as a designation of nations, with respect to the fact that they differ from one another by the languages they speak (Gen. 10:5, 20, 31).

With a thought reminiscent of 2:2-4 Isaiah declares that *they* (i.e. the nations and languages) *will come and see* the Lord's *glory*. In his inaugural vision he himself had beheld the glory of the Lord, and now he can triumphantly declare that all nations will also behold it. Perhaps Matthew 24:31 reflects upon this passage (note the usage of ἐπισυνάξουσιν, *they will gather*). His glory had been particularly displayed in the judgment of the disobedient nation. In their place there will be the true Israel, which will include the Gentiles who have come to the Lord.

19 The fundamental exegetical question in this verse is the reference of the suffix in *bahem (among them)*. Smart and others refer it to the nations, and then assume that the verse is hopelessly confused, because survivors from the nations that are gathered are

sent as messengers to nations that have not yet seen God's glory. It
is not necessary, however, thus to refer the suffix. In fact the
context demands that the reference be to the Jews described in
verse 17 and of whose deeds and devices mention is made in verse
18. It is difficult to think that Isaiah intended to assert that God
would assemble *all* nations and then that those who had escaped
from them would be sent to *all* nations.

A *sign* in biblical thought need not necessarily be a miracle or
wonder; but inasmuch as the precise language here employed is
also used in Exodus 10:2 and Psalm 78:43 of a miracle, it is
probable that we are to understand this particular sign as partaking of the nature of the miraculous, although it is far more than
the performance of one individual miracle. In the light of the
context we must interpret this of the whole wondrous series of
events that occurred when the ancient Jewish nation was cast off
and the Church of Jesus Christ founded. To paraphrase: "Well do
I know the nature of the Jewish nation. Their deeds and their
devices are not unknown to Me; hence the time has come when I
shall in their place gather together the nations. In order to accomplish this I shall send out survivors of the judgment upon Israel
who will proclaim My greatness and saving power among those
nations which have never yet heard My Name nor seen My glory."
Hence, the suffix in *mehem* (*from them*) refers to the disobedient
Jewish nation; whereas this nation will perish, yet there will be
survivors (*p^eleyṭim*). Thus Peter, himself a survivor, pleads with
his hearers to escape from that crooked (σκολιᾶς) generation
(Acts 2:40). Included in this sign was the wonderful work of
converting some Jews from their enmity to God to acceptance of
the newly appeared Messiah; among these of course were the
apostles. But the sign includes more; it involves the bringing to an
end of the disobedient nation, the coming to earth of the Messiah,
whose appearance and work were enveloped with the supernatural
(cf. "Jesus of Nazareth, a man attested to you by God with miracles and wonders and signs which God did through him in your
midst" [Acts 2:22]). In one of those fine statements that characterize his commentary, Alexander remarks: "That there will not be
hereafter an analogous display of divine power in the further
execution of this promise, cannot be proved and need not be
affirmed; but if there never should be, it will still have had a
glorious fulfilment in a series of events compared with which the

restoration of the Jewish people to the land of Canaan is of little moment."

As examples of those distant nations that have not heard God's fame nor seen His glory, the prophet mentions several. For *Tarshish*, see the comments on 2:16. *Pul* is not mentioned elsewhere in the Bible; if we follow Codex Vaticanus and read Phoud, i.e. Put, we find this land mentioned in Genesis 10:6, and in Assyrian and Egyptian sources.[15] Both Put and *Lud* were regions along the African coast of the Red Sea. In the Hebrew text an epithet is appended to Put and Lud, namely *drawers of the bow,* emphasis thus being given to their warlike character. *Tubal* appears in Genesis 10:2 and Ezekiel 27:13 along with *Javan* and Meshech; Tubal and Meshech are mentioned in Ezekiel 32:26; 38:2, 3 and 39:1. *Tubal* probably refers to the Tibarenoi in northeast Asia Minor, and *Javan* to Greece (cf. Gen. 10:2; Dan. 8:21; Zech. 9:13). *The distant isles* are those of the Mediterranean Sea. The line of nations mentioned runs from west to east along the southern boundary and from east to west along the northern. Thus, these examples serve the purpose of indicating the universality of the proclamation. *My fame* refers to what has been heard concerning Him. Inasmuch as these nations to whom the messengers were to be sent had lain in the darkness and ignorance of heathendom and were bound with error's chains, they could not have heard of the sovereign Lord nor have seen His remarkable glory. How different from that nation which had heard of God's fame and seen His glory and yet had turned to the abominations of idolatry!

In the concluding clause the nature of biblical and missionary preaching is set forth with remarkable clarity; it is the making known among the nations of God's glory. This is accomplished by the faithful preaching of the Gospel, the whole counsel of God. Thus, the primary aim in missionary and in all preaching is not the betterment of the hearer but the glory of God. When this aim is lost from sight, the work of the Church fails. When the glory of God is made known, all these other things are added unto us; man receives his highest blessing and well-being when God is glorified.

20 This verse is to be considered as continuing the narrative; hence the subject of the first verb, *they shall bring,* is best taken as the survivors mentioned in the preceding verse. It is the task of

15 Akk. *Pûṭa*; Egy. *Punt.*

these to make known the glory of God and to bring an offering. The prophet employs a beautiful expression in speaking of the Gentile converts as *your brethren*. Nor must we overlook the force of *all*. None of the elect, whether from the Jews according to the flesh or from among the Gentiles, will be left behind. Through the preachers of the Gospel God will bring them all to Himself. Here is efficacious grace at work through the outward call that God offers to the world in the preaching of the truth. All true believers, and only true believers, whether Jew or Gentile, are also brothers in Christ. These brethren are characterized as an *offering* (*minhah*), a word that designates a nonbloody offering. It is a technical term of the Mosaic ritual and possibly is mentioned here purposely, in order to avoid any thought of the cruelty that may have been involved in the bloody offerings, and also as a contrast to the cultic practices mentioned in verse 17. In what sense, however, may the Gentile brethren be characterized as an offering? Perhaps Vitringa's suggestion is of merit, namely that the early Gentile converts were the firstfruits of the wondrous harvest brought in through the preaching of the Gospel to the Mediterranean world of the first century of our era.

In picturesque language the prophet describes how this oblation is to be brought, and mentions the animals upon which it is to be carried, namely *horses, chariot, litters* (covered wagons), *and with mules and with dromedaries.*[16] The great influx will come to God's *holy mountain*, to *Jerusalem*. The thought is the same as in 2:2-4. It is not merely to Jerusalem that the nations will come, but in particular to the holy mount, for here the God of glory is to be found; as in 2:2-4, so also here, the reference is not to the physical Jerusalem but to the spiritual Jerusalem, the Church of the glorious God. This truth is attested by the statement *saith the Lord*.

In the second half of the verse Isaiah compares the future (from his standpoint) oblation that the survivors will bring with the present pure offerings in the Temple. As the Israelites of Isaiah's day were accustomed to bring to the Temple a *minhah* in ceremonially pure vessels, and hence an offering legitimate and acceptable, so in the future the survivors will, through the making known of God's glory, bring a legitimate offering, namely the Gentiles.

16 *kirkārôt* — *dromedaries*, from *kārar*, "repeat," "whirl about"; evidently their name was suggested by the constant swaying, circular movement of their hump.

21 Not only will the Gentiles be brought into the household of faith, but also God will appoint them to the highest offices of ministry in His kingdom. Under the law only one tribe was admitted to the priesthood, and the Gentiles not only could not offer sacrifices, but were not even permitted access to the Temple. Under the Gospel, however, all without distinction are admitted to Zion. Isaiah mentions *priests* and *Levites,* prefixing to both words the definite article; yet he apparently does not make a distinction between them, and probably mentions both words simply for the sake of completeness. The beautiful truth herein expressed is that not only will the escaped of the judgment upon the Jewish nation be used of God as apostles to bring into the household of faith their brethren from among the Gentiles, but also these Gentile converts themselves will be chosen by God, taken especially by Him, for the purpose of serving as priests and Levites, i.e. as ministers to serve Him in the preaching of the Gospel. Calvin aptly appeals to Luke and Timothy and others of the same class, who "offered spiritual sacrifices to God by the Gospel."

22 With this verse the prophet makes known the foundation for the entire preceding line of thought. By *your seed* and *your name* he has in mind the spiritual Israel of which he has been speaking. *Seed* refers to the descendants of the people of God, who form the subject of this address. Their perpetuity is to be assured. *Name* indicates reputation; forever the Church will be recognized as the people whom God has chosen to be His own. To assure God's people of this perpetuity and constant recognition God institutes a comparison with the new heavens and the new earth. As God originally created the heavens and the earth, so now He is going to make (the participle suggests near futurity) *new heavens* and a *new earth,* which will stand before Him (i.e. under His constant care and protection; cf. 48:19; 53:2). The old Israel will pass away; but from it there will spring the remnant that has survived the judgment, and together with it will be a great influx of Gentiles, all of which will form the true Israel of God under the new dispensation. In the old dispensation this Israel of God (the Church) had been practically identical with the literal nation, but in the new the Gentiles "should be fellow heirs, and of the same body, and partakers of his promise in Christ by the gospel, . . . to the intent that now unto the principalities and powers in heavenly

places might be known by the church the manifold wisdom of God
. . ." (Eph. 3:6, 10). The promise is strengthened by *saith the Lord*.

23 The introductory words *And it shall be* are emphatic; they
do not particularly introduce a necessary consequence of what has
just been stated, but rather present a concomitant fact. They are to
be construed with *all flesh shall come*, so that the thought is: "And
there shall come to pass the fact that all flesh shall come to
worship, etc." The glorious fact to be announced is that all flesh
will come to worship before God. *All flesh* is to be taken, as the
context demands, in the sense of all people that belong to the new
kingdom, inhabitants of the new heavens and the new earth; it is
another designation of the redeemed, used somewhat in the sense
of "the world" in John 3:16. *Before me* calls to mind the identical
expression in the first commandment; the worship of the redeemed
world will be directed to God alone and will be conducted in His
very presence.

Isaiah spoke as a prophet of the Old Testament dispensation,
and employing the language that belonged to that dispensation he
prefigured the spiritual truth of the new economy. Hence the
words *new moon* and *sabbath*, chosen as examples of true worship,
are to be understood as teaching that the worship will be one
perfectly in accord with God's commands (cf. 56:6). A literal
rendering is: *from the abundance of new moon in its new moon
and from the abundance of sabbath in its sabbath*, i.e., "as often as
the new moon comes in its new moon (in its own time) and as
often as the sabbath comes in its sabbath (in its own time)."
Whenever the new moon appears and the sabbath, then the people
will bow down before the Lord. The worship, in other words, will
be in accordance with and in observance of the prescribed seasons
of the Old Testament dispensation. Using these figures the prophet
teaches that there will be a faithful, regular, legitimate worship of
God on the part of all flesh in the new dispensation when the new
heavens and the new earth are in existence.

24 We are to construe the first two verbs as expressing actions
concomitant with "they will come" in the preceding verse; and the
subject of the three verbs is the same, namely the true believers.
The thought is that as often as they go out (from Jerusalem) they
will see. Perhaps the reference is to a going out from Jerusalem to
return home after having worshipped God, but of this one cannot

be sure. There is no warrant for rendering "they will see with pleasure," and certainly none for Smart's comment that they will look "gloatingly" on the dead bodies of the damned. The sight, however, will remind them and should ever remind us of the greatness of our redemption and of the terrible punishment from which we have been saved by Christ. Those whom they behold are described as the ones who transgress against God. Despite all the pleadings and warnings of His prophets, they broke His laws, preferring the abomination of idolatry to obedience to God's commands. These are the natural children of Matthew 8:12.

The place of torment is evidently the valley of the sons of Hinnom, or Gehenna (cf. Jer. 7:32ff.), which lies south of Jerusalem, running in a southeasterly direction. The *worm* that gnaws at the body does not die. It is said to be *their worm*, as though it is their own, belonging to them as their due. Likewise, *their fire*, which burns constantly in Gehenna to consume the refuse, burns these bodies but is not quenched. The result is that it is an abhorrence to *all flesh* that beholds it. Thus, the wicked ones of Israel are cast out and perish eternally, and the tragic and terrible consequences of transgression are brought before our eyes.

It is on no unworthy note that the prophet closes his book. On two previous occasions, closing each section of this latter part of the book, he had asserted that the wicked had no peace; and now, at the very end, he again states the same truth. Whereas the reference in the first instance is to those of ancient Israel, they who are Jews according to the flesh, it must be remembered that this sad fate will be shared by all who have transgressed against God. That such is not our fate is due only to the fact that the blessed Servant of the Lord was wounded for our transgressions and bruised for our iniquities. To His Name be praise and honor and glory for ever and ever.

Appendix I

THE AUTHORSHIP OF ISAIAH

The present commentary has been written upon the assumption that the Scriptures of the Old and New Testament are the revelation of the ever living and true God. In adopting this position, therefore, the commentary has gone contrary to the prevailing views of Scripture and in particular to what is commonly designated "form criticism." In order to discuss the question of the authorship of the prophecy, we proceed upon the assumption that it is God's Holy Word.

The prophets were men raised up of God, who declared His word to the nation. They were men of their own time, but they spoke as they were moved by the Spirit of God. For this reason we may expect to find in their messages the predictive element. We heartily reject the view that the prophets were merely men of their own time who spoke only to their own contemporaries and who did not receive special supernatural communications from God. It is for this reason that we highly value the witness of the Scripture on questions of authorship.

That the eighth-century Isaiah was the author of the entire prophecy bearing his name appears from the following considerations:

(1) The only name that has ever been attached to the book of Isaiah, either to the whole book or to any part thereof, is the name of Isaiah the son of Amoz. An almost unanimous tradition has supported the claim of this heading. Among the Jews, Moses ibn Gekatilyah of Cordoba, Spain (c. A.D. 1100) and Ibn Ezra (1092-1167) expressed doubts about the authorship of the second part of the prophecy. In the Christian Church, however, until the rise of rationalism, this tradition was not denied.

(2) The earliest appearance of this tradition of Isaianic authorship is found in Ecclesiasticus, from the second century B.C. The manner in which the writer uses the book of Isaiah makes clear that the tradition of Isaianic authorship was well established long before his time (cf. *Who Wrote Isaiah?* p. 27).

(3) The evidence of the first Qumran Scroll is of supreme importance. This manuscript comes from about 125 B.C. and is a clear witness to the unity of the prophecy. In this manuscript, chapter 39 concludes just one line from the bottom of the column, leaving a space for about seven letters. Chapter 40 begins on the last line of the column and without any special indentation. There was no thought of any break at this point. Furthermore, it is evident to any careful student that this manuscript was copied from an earlier one. Taking together, therefore, the evidence both of Ecclesiasticus and the Qumran Scroll, we are on safe ground if we assert that in the third century B.C. the tradition of Isaianic authorship was well established, and the book of Isaiah existed in that century in the form in which we have it today.

(4) If then the tradition of Isaianic authorship is so early, we may legitimately ask what hapened to the identity of the supposed "second" Isaiah. How did all trace of him come to be lost in so short a period of time? This question is particularly significant, inasmuch as we are told that the author of chapters 40–55 was the greatest of all Israel's prophets, a man who towered high above others. From these chapters themselves, however, we can learn nothing about the personality of this particular "author." How are we to explain this phenomenon? Literary criticism has been remarkably silent with respect to this question.

(5) Not only is it impossible to explain the complete oblivion both of the author's personality and of his history, but we must furthermore explain, if these latter chapters are not the work of Isaiah, the son of Amoz, how Isaiah's name came to be attached to them. For the eighth-century Isaiah is not regarded by the negative critics as one of the greatest of the prophets. Certainly, if we are to believe "criticism" he is not to be compared with the great "second" Isaiah of the exile. How then did it come about that all trace of this greater prophet was completely lost and the name of Isaiah came to be attached to the entire prophecy? It is sometimes argued that the name of Isaiah is not found in the latter part of the book. That is true, but neither is the name of anyone else found there as author.

(6) The tradition of Isaianic authorship comes to its strongest and most noble expression in the inerrant and infallible New Testament, which is the very Word of the living God. If the New Testament ascribes Isaianic authorship to the book, the question is settled. And as to the attitude of the New Testament there can be no question. For the most part the New Testament, rather than speaking about a book, stresses the activity of the individual prophet himself. This fact nullifies the idea that the New Testament is not concerned to identify the author of the prophecy. It is a

grossly mistaken notion that in ancient times the question of authorship was of no concern. Let the reader, therefore, carefully consider the following New Testament passages: Matthew 3:3; 8:17; 12:17; 13:14; 15:7; Mark 1:2; 7:6; Luke 3:4; 4:17; John 1:23; 12:38, 39, 41; Acts 8:28, 30, 32, 33; 28:25; Romans 9:27, 29 (note the many allusions to Isaiah in both Romans 9 and 10); 10:16, 20. (Cf. *Who Wrote Isaiah?* pp. 9-14 and *Introduction to the Old Testament*, pp. 199-222.)

(7) That the tradition of Isaianic authorship is correct and that the book is a unit may be seen from a brief survey of its theme.

CHAPTERS 1-39

With chapter 1 the prophet sets forth in germ form the message he intends later to develop, namely, the sinfulness of God's people, the gracious and tender appeals of the Lord, the certainty of judgment to come, and the blessedness of the coming salvation. Introducing each of these themes, the Lord appears as speaking.

Chapters 2-5 apparently consist of the prophet's earliest messages; 2-4 constitute a unit which begins and closes with a proclamation of peace, and thus introduces the basic theme of the prophecy. This peace will come from God when men learn His ways and are taught of Him. Following this description the prophet appeals to Judah to walk in the light of the Lord and characterizes the condition that has come upon his nation. The present evil situation will not continue, for a day belonging to the Lord of hosts, the day of judgment, will come upon all in which man places his trust. The prophet then points out (chap. 3) that a proximate judgment will come, and describes the wicked conduct of the nation, in particular the haughty demeanor of the women. Then once again Isaiah turns to the subject of peace, but now advances a step, pointing out that peace is centered in an individual, the Sprout of the Lord. This is the first definite Messianic reference in the prophecy (4:2).

Chapter 5 serves as a transition from the preceding to the prophet's introduction of himself in the following chapter. Beginning with a parable, Isaiah points out that although God has done everything for His people, they in their turn have become worthless in that they have rejected Him. This is followed by an analysis of Judah's sins and also by a reintroduction of the subject of the judgment to come. Just as Isaiah had concluded the preceding chapter with an advance over the description of peace given in chapter 2, so now he proceeds a step in advance of previous descriptions of judgment, tying up the judgment with the coming of a hostile army. Thus for the first time Assyria is introduced in the prophecy, and we are now prepared to turn from the prophet's basic message to an introduction to the man himself.

In chapter 6 Isaiah gives this introduction, and by the content of the message (namely that he is to preach Judah callous) prepares for the Messianic section to follow. Immediately we learn the truth God had revealed to the prophet, namely that his words would fall on deaf ears and that the hearers would be hard of heart. Before Judah lay the threat of Assyria. The world power was rising fast and overshadowing everything that stood before it. Judah's king, Ahaz, was willing to turn to Assyria to find protection from a danger that he thought was posed by Syria and Ephraim. This would have meant a complete abandonment of the promises of God, for had Assyria been successful in engulfing Judah, as she had engulfed so many other countries, the Davidic dynasty would have disappeared, and the Christ would not have been born. It is for this reason that the prophet must approach Ahaz and warn him that there is nothing to fear, and that he must place his confidence in God. By way of encouragement, Isaiah announces the birth of the true king who will bring deliverance to His people. It is when this prophecy is set over against the background of Assyria and its claims that we realize that in offering hope, Isaiah is pointing to no mere earthly king, but to the Messiah alone, who can bring a genuine deliverance to His people. Ahaz, however, does not believe God's promises and appeals to Assyria. Isaiah points out that as a result desolation will come to the nation. In poignant language he indicates that the enemy like a great bird of prey will spread out its wings over the whole land that belongs to Immanuel. At this time there can be only one remedy, confidence in what God through His prophets has promised. For, although darkness will cover the land, the people that dwelt in darkness have seen a great light.

Thus Isaiah proceeds to speak further concerning the king whose birth he had announced to Ahaz. In language of unsurpassing majesty and strength he describes this king, identifying him as Wonderful Counsellor, and Mighty God, and speaking of the wondrous growth and increase of his kingdom. The people, however, do not want this king, and continue in their sinful ways. Punishment, therefore, must come, for "wickedness burneth as the fire and devoureth the briers and thorns" (9:18).

God will use as an instrument in this punishment the enemy Assyria. Assyria had thought that in its own power it would build a worldwide empire. It was confident that it could do what it willed, and Judah and its idols (i.e. the true God) would be taken by Assyria and treated by it as other nations and their idols had been. Actually, however, As-

syria was but a tool in God's hand. In vivid strokes Isaiah describes Assyria's march toward Jerusalem but shows that in the crucial moment
God will cut off its power. Judah, however, will not be destroyed as
Assyria had desired, but out of it there will come the Messiah, as the
sovereign God had promised. His reign will be unlike that of any earthly
king, for he will rule in righteousness, and peace over all the world will
be the result of his reign. Instead of perishing Judah will deal valiantly.
As a result the prophet breaks out in praise to the God of his salvation.
With chapter 12 Isaiah brings to a close his little book of Messianic
prophecies. He has now laid the foundation for what is to follow.

Having laid the groundwork Isaiah may now turn to a consideration of
the nations that have manifested themselves as God's enemies and determined to destroy His people. It is Babylon (the head of gold of Daniel's
colossus) that most deeply represents the spirit of hostility to the carrying
out of God's purposes of salvation in the world. Hence, Isaiah begins with
a burden of Babylon. That God's own people need not fall into deep
dismay, he points out that like Sodom and Gomorrah, Babylon will be
overthrown, and will become a place of desolation forever. In particular
the Babylonian king, who represents the spirit of man in defiance of God,
will be overthrown. He had sought to ascend the heights of heaven; he
shall be brought to the bottom of the pit. As Babylon would certainly be
overcome so also would Philistia, a contemporary enemy of Judah; and
so also would Assyria, which was in Isaiah's day harassing Judah. As
these enemies on the other hand would be overcome, so also would the
heart of the enemy Babylon.

The rise of Assyria results in the downfall of other nations, and the
prophet points out how this is so. Moab howls in anguish, for its land
is filled with tumult and confusion. Deliverance for Moab is to be found
in the house of David. Damascus has also perished; it had once been a
city, now it is a heap. Damascus, Aroer, Ephraim all feel the hand of
the conqueror. Even distant Ethiopia is in deep agitation, like the flutter-
ing of insects, for on the horizon is the enemy.

Egypt will feel the judgment of God and will fall into internal confusion as a result. Yet in the day to come there will be an altar in Egypt and
there will be a returning to the Lord, the God of Judah. Egypt, Assyria,
and Israel will be a threefold blessing unto the Lord.

As a manifestation of the judgment just announced Isaiah introduces
a historical situation. By means of a symbolical action he teaches that
the Egyptian kingdom will fall and be carried away by the Assyrians.
Hence, the Judahites will fear those countries in which they had falsely
trusted.

The enemy army is like storms that come from the Negeb; and this enemy will overcome Babylonia, a fact that produces deep emotion upon Isaiah. Babylon, however, unconcerned, revels in her luxury. Isaiah is commissioned to station a watchman who will report about Babylon, and who declares that Babylon has fallen.

The prophet proceeds to show in short strokes how the power of the Mesopotamian empire has overshadowed the world. Dumah is in night, and Arabia is overrun. Jerusalem also is an object of the enemy's designs, for like the first three places mentioned, it had looked to the arm of flesh. These destructions have occurred because the Lord of hosts has a day of confusion and trampling and perplexity. Judah has made preparations but has not sought the Lord. Hence, judgment must come. As a specific example of the self-centered life of the nation, Shebna, the steward, is mentioned.

The oracles against the nontheocratic nations—and Judah was acting like one of them—fittingly conclude with Tyre. Beginning with Babylon, the center of land power, they conclude with Tyre, the center of sea power. Judgment will come but the grace of God will conquer, and even the enemies of God will support His kingdom. Step by step the prophet is preparing for the universalism of chapters 40ff. By means of a remarkable conclusion Isaiah unites into one all the enemies of God's people which he had previously considered individually. Thus he speaks of a judgment that will extend over the entire covenant-breaking earth. Yet there will also come a worldwide salvation. Moab is singled out as an example of a heathen nation that will feel God's punishment, and a remnant saved from the four quarters of the earth is said to praise God. Here Isaiah presents the explanation and conclusion and draws into their true and abiding unity the differing strands of thought that had been revealed to him up to this point. For this reason we find the intermingling emphasis upon judgment and salvation.

With chapter 28 Isaiah introduces his second major division of the second part of the prophecy, which revolves about a historical point (the invasion of Sennacherib and the reign of Hezekiah), and he prepares for it by speaking of woe and disaster. Six chapters are introduced with the word "woe." Now that Assyria's help had been sought, Assyria has come, and there were those who would turn to Egypt for deliverance. Against such a foolish policy Isaiah must warn. Samaria is to be destroyed; Ariel is ripe for destruction, and her sins are vividly described. Yet God's promises will abide, and the people are informed of the Messianic king.

As he had given to the previous section a particular conclusion, so likewise does he conclude this section. In two chapters he announces judgment and blessing; and as in the preceding conclusion he had singled out Moab as an example of a Gentile nation to be punished, so now he selects Edom. Then in language of striking beauty he prepares the way for the glorious prophecies of chapters 40ff. A short table will exhibit the manner in which (in 1–35) Isaiah prepares for the latter part of his book.

THE BACKGROUND: Rise of the universal empire

      THE MESSIAH (7:14 and the subsequent Messianic prophecies
                     based upon this section)
THE NATIONS

AHAZ

A. The overspreading power of the universal empire
    BABYLON will fall
               (Moab, Damascus, Jacob, Ethiopia, Egypt, the historical
               Babylon, Dumah, Arabia, Jerusalem, Tyre)
    CONCLUSION: Judgment (Moab) and salvation

HEZEKIAH

B. The Book of Woes. Samaria, David's city, Egypt a poor ally
    CONCLUSION: Judgment (Edom) and salvation

It will be seen that, although uttered during the period of Assyrian supremacy, these chapters are clearly preparatory. Babylon is mentioned, and a universal outlook presented. What is to be the result of Ahaz' turning to Assyria for help?

By way of preparation for the answer, a bridge is introduced which connects 1–35 with 40–66. This bridge consists of 36–39, which again is divided into two parts. Chapters 36 and 37 relate the invasion of Sennacherib and thus point back to the Assyrian period, whereas in chapters 38 and 39 Isaiah deals with the sickness of Hezekiah and the Babylonian envoys of Merodach-baladan, pointing forward to the Babylonian period. Thus the two are tied together. The closing verses of chapter 39 in particular prepare for the captivity in Babylon (cf. 39:6, 7). The chapter then closes on a sad note. In Hezekiah's days there will be peace, but the threat of exile to Babylon hangs overhead.

Chapter 40 fits in beautifully with the mood created by 39. If it is divorced from the preceding it is left hanging in the air. 1–39 have prepared, stage by stage, for the message of 40–66; and in turn 40–66 are the unfolding of and answer to the questions raised in 1–39. This fact is a strong argument for the unity of the entire book. Separate 40–66 from the preceding, and we are really in entire ignorance concerning its origin and nature. As pointed out in the exposition, the threefold division of these chapters is immediately introduced. A brief glance at this division will make clear how beautifully the prophet has arranged this section.

CHAPTERS 40–66

40:1-11 The Prologue

I. *40:12–48:22.* The deliverance to be performed is so great that only God can accomplish it. Hence, by rhetorical questions the prophet directs the thought to a contemplation of God's greatness. It is God alone who raises up a conqueror and deliverer from the east. The reason is that Israel is God's servant whom He has chosen and not rejected. Hence, their enemies will be confounded; and the idols, whom God challenges, are works of naught.

A greater than Cyrus, however, will come to bring judgment to the entire earth, and deliver those who are in spiritual bondage. His appearance is in the hands of the Lord, who exercises sovereign power over all things, and as a man of wars prevails over His enemies. Hence, God utters words of comfort to His oppressed people, promising to bring them back to Himself. Jerusalem will be rebuilt, for God will raise up Cyrus as a shepherd. Cyrus will be successful, for the Lord will support him. The nations and their idols will be confounded, but Israel will be saved with an everlasting salvation. Only in the Lord are righteousness and salvation to be found. Bel and Nebo, the idols of the enemy nation, instead of taking Israel captive will themselves go into captivity. The great power of Babylon will be destroyed. Redemption has come to God's people, but there is no peace to the wicked.

II. *49:1–57:21.* The mysterious personage, God's servant, introduced in chapter 42, appears here as soliloquizing. He is the heart and center of this portion of the prophecy, for he brings the wondrous deliverance of which the prophet has just spoken. Yet Zion thinks that her God has forsaken her, not realizing that He has graven her on the palms of His hands. There is no evidence that God has divorced her. God challenges her to produce a divorce paper. It is her sins, rather, that have caused her to be put away. The servant is prepared to deliver her, despite the suffering that he must undergo. If Israel is to seek deliverance, then, let her look unto the Lord who formed her and depart from the midst of her dispersion. God's servant, whom men unjustly regarded as punished for his own sins, will, by means of a vicarious satisfaction to God, deliver his people from their sins, bearing their iniquities and justifying them.

Hence, they are to sing, for there will be a great increase of the Church. Men who thirst are to drink the life-giving waters and to seek the Lord while He may be found. The redeemed are to be obedient to God, and this obedience is to be exemplified in the keeping of the sabbath. Among the people of God, national and personal distinctions are to be abandoned; and all who truly repent will receive God's favor. Those who persist in their sins, however, will find no peace.

III. *58:1–66:24.* Isaiah now brings to the fore a truth for which he has been preparing. Israel as a political nation is to be rejected. Its worship of God is hypocritical and not acceptable. This rejection is not due to the Lord's inability to save, but to Israel's own sins. That the nation Israel is to perish, however, does not mean that God has abandoned His promises. The true Israel of God, the Church, is to receive a glorious and blessed change. She will be freed from national and local bonds and will be strengthened by all the nations.

This change is to be brought about by the servant, who brings restoration to a destroyed world. Zion's righteousness will thus be recognized by all the earth. Many will come unto Zion; but God, coming from Edom, has triumphed valiantly over Zion's enemies. Although the external Israel will perish, the true Israel will endure. No longer will the Lord abide in a Temple made by hands but in the heart of the humble believer. The old order, including its sacrifices, will pass away. Israel will grow as her members are brought in from all over the earth. The rebellious and apostate Israel, however, will be but carcasses, whose worm does not die and whose fire will not be quenched, a horror to all flesh.

(8) As may be seen from section (7), the position of chapters 36–39 is of particular significance, in that they point back to the Assyrian period and also forward to the exile. They thus effectively tie together the two parts of the prophecy. (Cf. also Franz Delitzsch, *"Schlussbemerkungen, Aechtheit der c. 40–66 und der verwandten Weiss,"* especially pp. 393-395, an Appendix to the commentary of Moritz Drechsler, Stuttgart, 1845; Berlin, 1851.)

(9) The prophecy concerning Cyrus is the basic stumbling block for acceptance of Isaiah's authorship. How, it is asked, could a prophet have predicted the name of an individual who would live some hundred and sixty years after his time? For those who believe in predictive prophecy, there is no problem; and we heartily concur with the words of Windischmann (quoted in Delitzsch, Vol. II, p. 138), "No one who believes in a living, personal, omniscient God, and in the possibility of His revealing future events, will ever deny that He possesses the power to foretell the

name of a future monarch." The name of Josiah was also predicted three hundred years before his birth (cf. 1 Kings 13:2). See the comments on the Cyrus prophecy for its significance. Were it uttered by a contemporary, it is difficult to understand; were it uttered by someone living long before, it fits in beautifully with the whole picture of Isaiah's thought.

(10) As may be seen from section (7), the second part of the prophecy, chapters 40–66, was in a state of continual formation during the writing of chapters 1–39. In these earlier chapters the prophet, step by step, was preparing for the great thoughts to which he was to give such eloquent expression in the later chapters. In this connection one may note, for example, the development of the idea of the captivity. In the earlier chapters the captivity was first presented in very general terms, then it became clear that an army would take the people captive. This army was headed by Assyria; and finally, Babylon herself appears as the power that will take the people into exile. Thus we are brought to the very threshold of chapters 40–66.

(11) In connection with the thought that an integral relationship is sustained between chapters 40–66 on the one hand and the earlier chapters on the other, we may note that the references to Babylon in the earlier prophecies form a preparation for 40–66. If Isaiah could speak of Babylon in these earlier messages, why could he not do so later? (Cf. *Who Wrote Isaiah?* pp. 41-43.)

(12) There are reflections upon Isaiah 40–66 in later prophecies, a fact that conclusively demonstrates that these chapters cannot come from the time of the exile. I have worked out this argument in detail in "Isaiah 34 and Its Position in the Prophecy" (*WThJ*, Vol. 27, No. 2, May 1965, pp. 93-114). Let the reader make the following comparisons:

Jeremiah		with	Isaiah	
	13:18-26	"		47:1-3
	48:18	"		47:1
	31:12	"		58:11
	31:13	"		61:3
	31:22	"		43:19
	31:34	"		54:13
	31:36	"		54:10
	5:25	"		59:2
	13:16	"		59:9-11
	50:8 and 51:45	"		48:20
	17:1	"		64:8
	18:6	"		65:6
	2:25	"		57:10

In particular it should be noted that Jeremiah uses earlier prophecies possibly more than any other of the writing prophets. To avoid the force of the argument critics are compelled to deny these sections to Jeremiah.

(13) A word should be said concerning the style in the two portions of Isaiah. It is true that there are divergences. The grand majesty of the sweeping style of chapters 40–49 is almost unique, but for this there is a reason. The subject matter requires such a style. If Isaiah as an old man wrote these chapters, we can well understand how over the years, as he had matured and his insight into divine revelation had grown, so also would his manner of expression change. With age there would come depth of understanding, breadth of vision, and an ability to express oneself in various ways. Surely the presence of a divergence of style in itself does not demand diversity of authorship. If it does, then we cannot believe that Sennacherib wrote his own accounts of his campaigns and also the building inscription that is found at their conclusion. On the other hand it is not justifiable to magnify the divergences of style that appear in Isaiah. That the same hand is at work throughout is seen from the following considerations.

The vocabulary of the book is obviously that which belongs to one writer. This has been demonstrated beyond the shadow of a doubt in the excellent work of Mrs. Rachel Margalioth (*The Indivisible Isaiah*, New York, 1964), which contains an almost exhaustive study of Isaiah's vocabulary. In the previous exposition we have often called attention to the manner in which a word in the first part of Isaiah is also found in the second. Not only, however, are similar words found in both sections of the prophecy, but also these words often appear in certain combinations that are peculiar to Isaiah. This phenomenon occurs so often that its force is overpowering. Let anyone who questions the Isaianic authorship of the entire prophecy work through Mrs. Margalioth's volume; he will be amazed at the strength of the evidence.

In presenting the above considerations we have been somewhat sketchy. This is partly due to lack of space and also to the fact that in *Who Wrote Isaiah?* we have set these arguments forth in greater detail. The above considerations, however, far outweigh the few points that have been urged in opposition to the Isaianic authorship. It must be remembered that such points are based upon a certain view of the Old Testament prophecy, a view we are unable to accept. Belief in the unity of authorship is usually bound up with belief that the prophecy is a supernatural revelation from God, a fact that can be explained upon the basis of the witness of the New Testament. The position that the prophecy is the work of more than one author flies counter to the express teaching of the

New Testament. This in itself is sufficient to reject it. And when this New Testament witness is supported by an immense amount of secondary cumulative witness, the case for the Isaianic authorship of the prophecy seems unanswerable.

Appendix II

"THY GOD REIGNETH"

In recent times the question of divine kingship in Israel has occupied a prominent place in scholarly discussion. That such an emphasis should follow a form-critical approach to the Old Testament is understandable, for if divine kingship was found among Israel's neighbors, the adherents of this position would ask whether it should not also have been present in Israel. One of the first, therefore, to discuss the question was Hugo Gressmann (*Der Ursprung der israelitisch-jüdische Eschatologie*, Göttingen, 1905, pp. 294ff.; cf. also A. F. von Gall, cited below in bibliography), who maintains that a number of Psalms began with the words "Yahweh has become king," which express the fact that Yahweh has seized the rule of the world.

It was Sigmund Mowinckel who really brought the idea to prominence. He held that the phrase "Yahweh has become king" pointed to something new and expressed a kingship that was universal. This kingship was based upon the creation, in which Yahweh emerges triumphant over other gods, upon judgment, and upon the creation of Israel by election and covenant. The phrase is closely related to the New Year festival of enthronement, and serves for the salute to Yahweh as the enthroned king.

There are two points in particular that call for discussion: (a) Does the phrase in the Psalms (*yhwh mālāk*) mean "Yahweh reigns" or "Yahweh has become king"; and (b) is the phrase in Isaiah 52:7 (*mālak 'elōhāyik*) in any sense to be connected with an annual festival of enthronement?

A number of recent scholars, including Gerhard von Rad, Artur Weiser, Hans Joachim Kraus, and to some extent Otto Eissfeldt, believe that the words in Psalms should be translated "Yahweh has become king," and so Isaiah 52:7 would be rendered "Thy God has become king." Those who thus translate wish to do justice to the perfect form of the verb. At the same time it cannot be insisted that the perfect demands such a translation. It is possible to translate by the present (cf. the perfects in

Gen. 14:22; 1 Sam. 17:10; 2 Sam 16:4; 17:11; 19:30; 1 Kings 1:35 and 2 Chron. 2:12, and cf. Driver, *TT*, p. 15, No. 10). The distinction between "Yahweh has become king" and "Yahweh is now reigning" (with the implication that the reign has recently begun) is indeed fine.

If we may employ form criticism (and a legitimate use thereof is not to be rejected) we may say that the phrase in Isaiah is a statement in the 3rd person which speaks about Yahweh and is not directly addressed to him. The Germans call this an *Er-Bericht*. Such "He-accounts" are said to be acclamations or proclamations concerning God.

Appeal may be made to the Babylonian *Marduk-ma šarru* (*Enuma Elish*, 4:28), "Marduk is king." The cry this nominal sentence expresses refers to the fact that Marduk is king; he is revealed as already king. The Egyptian phrase *'ḥ' m ḥkз* ("he stands as ruler") is of similar import. It is in the 3rd person and relates something concerning Horus. In none of these instances do we have an enthronement cry.

D. Michel, in his thorough study, maintains that there is a shade of difference between *Yahweh mālāk* and *mālak Yahweh*. The first states a fact concerning Yahweh, namely that He is one who exercises kingship. The second stresses the ruling; it is kingship that Yahweh exercises.

Perhaps it is not possible to prove beyond the shadow of a doubt that one of these interpretations is correct as over against the other. It should be noted, however, that Isaiah's purpose is to show that, in contrast to the dead gods of the nations, Israel's God is living and reigning. Even if one insists upon the rendering, "Thy God has become king," this does not suggest that Yahweh has just ascended the throne and begun to reign. Rather, the message of peace and salvation is simply that, instead of being hidden and impotent as Israel had wrongly believed, their God is reigning. The context would certainly seem to favor the translation "Thy God reigneth."

There would probably be little zeal for translating "Thy God has become king," were it not for the desire to see in these words evidence for an act of enthronement. Inasmuch as—if we may still continue the role of a form critic—this phrase is not in the 2nd person, it has nothing to do with the actual act of becoming king; and if the phrase does not refer to some definite historical act of enthronement, there is no point in so rendering it. Lipinski tries to find such a historical act in the fact that through the liberation of the captives Yahweh has become king. This, however, is to read into the text what is not present (cf. the discussion of 51:11; 52:9 and the general interpretation).

The context, therefore, favors the rendering "Thy God reigneth." The prophet is not asserting that Israel's God has just ascended the throne, but is proclaiming the far grander, truly dynamic fact that Israel's God does reign. What a remarkable declaration this is! The gods of the heathen could neither declare the past nor predict the future. Dead idols, they had no power. Israel's God, however, was alive and He was sovereign. This is the truth the context demands.

Secondly, there is not the slightest evidence that an annual enthronement festival was ever held in Israel or that this phrase is in any sense connected with such a festival (cf. Vol. I, pp. 494ff.). As Odendaal well remarks: "The idea of a cultic annually renewed enthronement of Yahweh, however, can be excluded as a view superimposed over the facts" (p. 82; see bibliography). In the enthronement of an earthly king or a deity, power was given or bestowed by another. None, however, can give power to Yahweh or invest Him with the kingship. Hence, we are compelled to reject the view that the phrase "Thy God reigneth" has any reference to an enthronement festival.

BIBLIOGRAPHY

A. Alt, "Gedanken über das Königtum Jahwes," *Kleine Schriften zur Geschichte des Volkes Israel*, Vol. I, Munich, 1953.

K. H. Bernhardt, *Das Problem der altorientalischen Königsideologie im Alten Testament*, Supplements to *VT*, Vol. 8, 1961.

Otto Eissfeldt, "Jahwe als König," *Kleine Schriften*, Vol. I, Tübingen, 1962, pp. 174ff.

A. F. von Gall, "Die Herkunft der Bezeichnung Jahwes als König," Beihefte zur *ZAW*, No. 27, 1914, pp. 145-160.

J. Gray, "The Hebrew Conception of the Kingship of God: its origin and development," *VT*, Vol. 6, 1956, pp. 268-285. "The Kingship of God in the Prophets and Psalms," *VT*, Vol. 11, 1961, pp. 1-29.

A. S. Kapelrud, "Nochmals Jahwä mālāk," *VT*, Vol. 13, 1963, pp. 229-231.

Ludwig Köhler, "Jahwäh mālāk," *VT*, Vol. 3, 1953, pp. 188-189.

M. J. Lagrange, "Le Regne de Dieu dans l'Ancien Testament," *RB*, Vol. 5, 1908, pp. 36-61.

E. Lipinski, "Yahweh mālāk," *Biblica*, Vol. 44, 1963, pp. 405-460.

D. Michel, "Studien zu den sogenannten Thronbesteigungspsalmen," *VT*, Vol. 6, 1956, pp. 40-68.

S. Mowinckel, *Psalmenstudien*, II, Amsterdam, 1961, pp. 3-340.

Dirk Hermanus Odendaal, *The Eschatological Expectation of Isaiah 40–66 With Special Reference to Israel and the Nations*, unpublished doctoral dissertation, Westminster Theological Seminary, 1966.

J. Ridderbos, "Jähweh Malak," *VT*, Vol. 4, 1954, pp. 87-89.

Bibliography

Abarbanel, Don Isaac; also Abravanel; cf. Rosenmüller.
Abulfeda; cf. H. O. Fleischer, *Historia anteislamica arabice edidit, versione latina auxit.* Lipsia, 1831.
Albright, William F., *Archeology and the Religion of Israel.* 1942.
Alexander, Joseph Addison, *Commentary on the Prophecies of Isaiah.* 1846. Grand Rapids, 1953.
Allis, Oswald T., *Prophecy and the Church.* Philadelphia, 1943.
————, "The Transcendence of Jehovah God of Israel," *Biblical and Theological Studies,* 1912.
Alt, Albrecht, "Ägyptisch-ugaritisches," *Archiv für Orientforschung,* 15, 1951.
————, "Galiläische Probleme," *Palästinajahrbuch,* 1937.
————, *Kleine Schriften,* II. Munchen, 1953.
————, "Menschen ohne Namen," *Archiv Orientální,* 18, 1950.
Amarna Text. J. Knudtzon, *Die El-Amarna Tafeln.* Aalen, 1964.
Amr el-Quais, *Moallaka;* cf. W. Ahlwardt, *The Divans of the Six Ancient Arabic Poets.* London, 1870.
Anderson, Robert T., "Was Isaiah a Scribe?" *JBL,* 79, 1960.
Annals of Mursilis, text in Sturtevant and Bechtel, *A Hittite Chrestomathy.* Philadelphia, 1935.
Anspacher, Abraham S., *Tilgath Pileser III.* New York, 1912.
Arias Montanus, Benito, *Polyglot Antwerp,* 1569-1573.

Baedeker, *A Handbook of Palestine and Syria.* 1912.
Barnes, A., *Notes on Isaiah.* New York, 1840.
Bea, A., "Ras Samra und das Alte Testament," *Biblica,* 19, 1938.
Béguerie, *La Vocation d'Isaiae,* Études sur les prophètes d'Israel. Paris, 1954.
Behr, J. W., *The Writings of Deutero-Isaiah and the Neo-Babylonian Inscriptions.* Pretoria, Ill., 1937.
Bentzen, Aage, *King and Messiah.* London, 1955.
Berry, G. R., "Messianic Predictions," *JBL,* 45, 1926.
Bewer, Julius A., *The Literature of the Old Testament.* New York, 1940.
Biblia sacra iuxta versionem simplicem quae dicitur Peschitta, II. Beirut, 1951.
Bijbel in Nieuwe Vertaling. Kampen, 1952.
Birkeland, H., *Zum Hebräischen Traditionswesen.* Oslo, 1938.
Blank, Sheldon H., *Prophetic Faith in Isaiah.* New York, 1958.
Böhl, Franz, *Nieuwjaarsfest en Konigsdag in Babylon en Israel.* 1927.
Boutflower, C., *Journal of the Transactions of the Victoria Institute,* 1928.
Breasted, J. H., *Ancient Records of Egypt,* Vol. II.
Bright, John, *A History of Israel.* Philadelphia, 1959.
Briggs, Charles A., *Messianic Prophecy.* New York, 1886.
Brockelmann, *Hebräische Syntax.* Neukirchen, 1956.
Bruno, D. Arvid, *Jesaja, eine rhythmische und textkritische Untersuchung.* Stockholm, 1953.
Bultema, Harry, *Practische Commentaar op Jesaja.* Muskegon, 1923.

Burrows, M., Trevor, J. C., Brownlee, W. H., *The Dead Sea Scrolls of St. Mark's Monastery*, I, *The Isaiah Manuscript and the Habakkuk Commentary*. New Haven, 1950.

Calvin, *Commentarii in Isaiam prophetam*. Geneva, 1570. E. T. Grand Rapids, 1850.
Campbell, Roderick, *Israel and the Covenant*. Philadelphia, 1954.
Cappellus, Ludwig, *Critica Sacra*. 1650.
Caspari, Carl Paul, *Jesajanische Studien*. Leipzig, 1843.
Castellio, Sebastian, *Biblia Sacra*. 1531. Frankfurt, 1669.
Ceriani, A. *Translatio syra Pescitto Veteris Testamenti*. Milan, 1876.
Chafer, Lewis S., *Systematic Theology*. Dallas, 1947-48.
Cheyne, T. K., *The Prophecies of Isaiah*, I. 1868. New York, 1888.
Childs, B. S., *Myth and Reality in the Old Testament*. Naperville, 1960.
Chrysostom, *Hermeneia*, in Migne, *Patrologia*.
Churgin, P., *Targum Jonathan to the Prophets*. New Haven, 1927.
Cocceius, Johannes, *Opera Omnia Theologica*. Amstelodami, 1701.
Condamin, Albert, *Le Livre d'Isaie*. Paris, 1905.
Contenau, G., *La civilisation phénicienne*. 1928.
Cooke, G. A., *A Textbook of North Semitic Inscriptions*. Oxford, 1903.
Cordero, M. Garcia, "El Santo de Israel," *Mélanges Bibliques rédigés en l'honneur d'André Robert*. Paris, 1957.

Dalman, Gustav, *Jerusalem und seine Gelände*. Gütersloh, 1930.
Dathe, Johann August, *Opuscula*, ed. E. F. Rosenmüller. Lipsiae, 1796.
DeBoer, P. A. H., *Second-Isaiah's Message*. Leiden, 1956.
De Fraine, *L'aspect religieux de la royaute israelite*. Rome, 1954.
de Leeuw, V., *De Ebed Jahweh-Profetieen*. Assen, 1956.
Delekat, L., "Die Peschitta zu Jesaja zwischen Targum und Septuaginta," *Biblica*, 38, 1957.
Delitzsch, Franz, *Biblical Commentary on the Prophecies of Isaiah*. 1866. Grand Rapids, 1949.
Dhorme, E., *L'evolution religieuse d'Israel*. Bruxelles, 1937.
Dillmann, August, *Das Prophet Jesaia*. Leipzig, 1890.
Diringer, *Le Iscrizioni Antico-Ebraiche Palestinesi*. Firenze, 1934.
Döderlein, Christoph, *Esaias*. Altsofi, 1825.
Drechsler, Moritz, *Der Prophet Jesaja*. Stuttgart, 1849.
Driver, G. R., *Canaanite Myths and Legends*. 1956.
————, *Von Ugarit nach Qumran*. 1958.
Driver, S. R., *Isaiah, His Life and Times*. New York.
————, *A Treatise on the Use of Tenses in Hebrew*. 1892.
Duhm, Bernhard, *Das Buch Jesaia*. 1892. Göttingen, 1922.
Dussaud, R., *Des religions de Babylonie et d'Assyrie*. Paris, 1945.

Eaton, J., "The Origin of the Book of Isaiah," *VT*, 9, 1959.
Edelkoort, A. H., *De Christusverwachting in het Oude Testament*. Wageningen, 1941.
Eichhorn, Johann G., *Die hebräische Propheten*. Göttingen, 1819.
Eissfeldt, O., *Baal Zaphon, Zeus Kasios und der Durchzug der Israeliten durchs Meer*. Halle, 1932.

BIBLIOGRAPHY

Eitan, I., "A Contribution to Isaiah Exegesis," *HUCA*, 12-13, 1937-38.

Elliger, Karl, *Deuterojesaja in seinem Verhältnis zu Tritojesaja.* Stuttgart, 1933.

——, *Die Einheit des Tritojesaja.* Stuttgart, 1928.

Engnell, Ivan, *The Call of Isaiah.* Uppsala and Leipzig, 1949.

——, *Studies in Divine Kingship in the Ancient Near East.* Uppsala, 1943.

——, "Till frågan om Ebed.Jahve-sångerna och den lidande Messias hos 'Deuterojesaja,'" *Svensk Exegetisk Årsbok*, 10, 1945; E.T. in *Bulletin of the John Rylands Library*, 31, 1948.

Erman, A., *The Religion of the Egyptians.*

Euting, Julius, *Sinaitische Inschriften.* Berlin, 1901.

Ewald, H., *Die Propheten des alten Bundes erklärt.* Stuttgart, 1840-41.

Fahlgren, K. H., *Nahestehende und entgegengesetzte Begriffe im Alten Testament.* Uppsala, 1932.

Feldmann, Franz, *Das Buch Isaias*, I, II. Münster, 1926.

Finkelstein, Louis, *The Commentary of David Kimchi on Isaiah.* 1926.

Fischer, Johann, *Das Buch Isaias.* Bonn, I, 1937, II, 1939.

Frankfort, Henri, *Kingship and the Gods.* Chicago, 1948.

Friedrichsen, A., *Hagios-Qadosh.* Oslo, 1916.

Frost, S. B., *Old Testament Apocalyptic.* 1952.

Fullerton, K., "Studies in Isaiah," *JBL*, 38, 1919.

Gadd, C. J., *Ideas of the Divine Rule in the Ancient East.* 1948.

Galling, Kurt, *Textbook zur Geschichte Israels.* Tübingen, 1950.

Gesenius, Wilhelm, *Der Prophet Jesaia.* Leipzig, 1820, 1821.

Gesenius, Kautzsch, Cowley, *Hebrew Grammar.* Oxford, 1910.

Gill, John, *Body of Divinity.* 1771. Grand Rapids, 1951.

Ginsburg, C. D., *Prophetae posteriores.* London, 1911.

Goetze, A., "The So-Called Intensive of the Semitic Language," *JAOS*, 62, 1942.

Gordon, C. H., *Ugaritic Literature.* 1947.

——, *Ugaritic Manual.* 1955.

——, *Ugaritic Textbook.* 1965.

Gray, G. B., "Kingship of God in Prophets and Psalms," *VT*, 11, 1961.

——, *The Prophecy of Isaiah.* Edinburgh, 1926.

Green, *Hebrew Grammar.* New York, 1898.

Greenberg, "Text of the Hebrew Bible," *JAOS*, Vol. 76, No. 3, 1956.

Grelot, P., "La denière étape de la redaction sacerdotale," *VT*, 6, 1956.

Gressmann, *Altorientalische Texte zum Alten Testament.* 1909.

——, *Der Ursprung der israelitisch-jüdische Eschatologie.* Göttingen, 1905.

Grotius, Hugo, *Annotata ad Vetus Testamentum.* 1644.

Guillaume, A., "The Dead Sea Scrolls of Isaiah," *JBL*, 76, 1957.

Gunkel, Herman, *Die Schriften des Alten Testaments*, 2. Abteilung, 2. Band. 1921, 1925.

Haller, Max, *Die Schriften des Alten Testaments*, II, 3. Göttingen, 1914.

Hanel, J., *Die Religion der Heiligkeit.* Gütersloh, 1931.

Hattusilis, *Apology;* cf. Sturtevant and Bechtel, *Hittite Chrestomathy.* Philadelphia, 1935.

Heidel, W. A., *The Day of Jahweh.* New York, 1929.

Held, Moshe, *Studies and Essays in Honor of Abraham A. Newman.* 1962.
Henderson, Ebenezer, *The Book of the Prophet Isaiah.* 1840. London, 1857.
Herzfeld, E., *Altpersische Inschriften.* 1938.
Hillers, *Treaty-Curses and the Old Testament Prophets.* Rome, 1964.
Hitti, P. K., *History of Syria.* New York, 1951.
Hitzig, Ferdinand, *Der Prophet Jesaja.* Heidelberg, 1833.
Hölscher, G., *Die Profeten.* Leipzig, 1914.
————, *Geschichte der israelitischen und jüdischen Religion.* 1922.
————, *Die Ursprünge der jüdischen Eschatologie.* Giessen, 1925.
Holwerda, B., *De Wijsheid die Behoudt.* 1957.
Honor, L., *Sennacherib's Invasion of Palestine.* 1926.
Hoonacker, A. Van, *Het Boek Isaias.* Brugge, 1932.
Huffmon, Herbert, "The Covenant Lawsuit in the Prophets," *JBL,* 78, 1959.
Hummel, Horace, "Enclitic Mem in Early Northwest Semitic, Epecially Hebrew," *JBL,* 76, 1957.
Hvidberg, "The Masseba and the Holy Seed," *Interpretationes (Mowinckel Festschrift).* Oslo, 1955.
Hyatt, James P., *Prophetic Religion.* New York, 1947.

Ibn Hisham, ed. Wüstenfeld, *Des Leben Mohammeds.*
Ilgen, Karl David, *Die Urkunden des jerusalemischen Tempelarchivs in ihrer Urgestalt, als Beitrag zur Berichtigung der Geschichte der Religion und Politik.* 1798.
Interpreter's Bible. New York, Nashville, 1952ff.
Itkonen, L., *Deuterojesaja [40-55] metrisch untersucht.* Helsinki, 1916.

Jacob, Edmond, *Theologie de l'Ancien Testament.* Neuchâtel, 1955.
Jastrow, *Hebrew-Babylonian Traditions.* 1914.
Jenni, "Das Wort 'ōlām im Alten Testament," *ZAW,* 65, 1953.
Jennings, F. C., *Studies in Isaiah.* New York, 1950.
Johnson, Aubrey R., *Sacral Kingship in Ancient Israel.* Cardiff, 1955.

Keizer, P., *De profeet Jesaja.* Kampen, 1947.
Keilschrifturkunden aus Boghazkeui, 1916, 1921.
Kennett, R. H., *Ancient Hebrew Social Life and Custom as Indicated in Law, Narrative and Metaphor.* 1933.
Kimchi, David; cf. L. Finkelstein.
Kissane, E. J., *The Book of Isaiah.* New York, 1926; Dublin; I, 1941, II, 1943.
Kittel, Gerhard, ed., *Theologisches Wörterbuch zum Neuen Testament.*
Kittel, Rudolf, *Biblia Hebraica,* 3rd ed. Stuttgart, 1937.
————, *Geschichte des Volkes Israels.* III, 1927.
Kline, Meredith, "The Intrusion and the Decalogue," *WThJ,* 16, Nov., 1953.
————, *Treaty of the Great King.* Grand Rapids, 1963.
Knight, George, *Deutero-Isaiah.* New York, 1965.
Knobel, August W., *Der Prophet Jesaja.* Leipzig, 1872.
Köhler and Baumgartner, *Lexicon in Veteris Testamenti Libros.* 1953.
Köhler, Ludwig, *Theologie des Alten Testaments.*
————, "Syntactica, II, III, IV," *VT,* 3, 1953.
König, Eduard, *Stylistik.*
————, *Syntax.*
————, *Das Buch Jesaja.* Gütersloh, 1926.

Koppe, J. B., 1779-81, editor of Lowth's commentary on Isaiah.
Koran, ed. Mavlana Muhammed 'Ali. Lahore, 1951.
Kraus, Hans Joachim, *Psalmen.* Neukirchen, 1958.
Kroeker, Jakob, *Jesaia der Altere (Cap. 1-35).* Giessen, 1934.
Kuyper, L. J., "The Meaning of Isa. XL.6," *VT,* 13, 1963.

Lambert, W. G., "Three Unpublished Fragments of the Tukulti-Ninurta Epic," *Archiv für Orientforschung,* 1957.
Landsberger, Benno, *Sam'al.* Ankara, 1948.
Lindblom, *Prophecy in Ancient Israel.* Oxford, 1962.
————, *The Servant Songs in Deutero-Isaiah.* Lund, 1951.
Lindhagen, C., *The Servant Motif in the Old Testament.* Uppsala, 1950.
Löw, I., *Die Flora der Juden,* I-IV, 1924-34.
Löwth, Robert, *Isaia.* London, 1779.
Luckenbill, D. D., *The Annals of Sennacherib.* Chicago, 1924.
————, *Ancient Records of Babylonia and Assyria.* Chicago, 1926.
Ludwig, Emil, *The Nile.* New York, 1937.
Luther, *Luthers Werke, Deutsche Bibel,* II. Band, I. Hälfte. 1528. Weimar, 1960.
Luzzatto, Samuel David, *Il Propheta Isaia volgarizzato e commentato ad uso degl'Israeliti.* Padova, 1855.

Macadam, M. F. L., *The Temples of Kawa.* London, 1949.
Margalioth, R., *The Indivisible Isaiah.* New York, 1964.
Marti, Karl, *Das Buch Jesaja.* Tübingen, 1900.
Maurer, *Commentarius in Vetus Testamentum,* I. Lipsiae, 1835.
McClain, Alva J., *The Greatness of the Kingdom.* 1959.
Meyer, Ernst, *Der Prophet Jesaja.* Pforzheim, 1850.
Michaelis, J. H., Halle Bible with annotations, 1720.
Moallaka, see Amr 'l-Quais.
Möller, Wilhelm, *Die messianische Erwartung der vorexilischen Propheten.* Gütersloh, 1906.
Mowinckel, Sigmund, *He That Cometh.* Nashville, 1954.
————, *Jesaja Disciplinen.* Oslo, 1926.
————, *Psalmenstudien II, Das Thronbesteigungsfest Jahwäs und der Ursprung der Eschatologie.* Christiana, 1922.
Munch, P. A., *The Expression bajjōm hāhū.* Oslo, 1936.
Murray, J., *Romans, NICNT.* Grand Rapids, 1959.
Musil, Alois, *The Northern Hegaz.* New York, 1926.

Nägelsbach, Carl W. E., *Der Prophet Jesaja.* Leipzig, 1877.
North, C. R., *The Second Isaiah.* London, 1964.
————, *The Suffering Servant in Deutero-Isaiah.* London, 1956.
Noth, M., *History of Israel.* London, 1958.
————, *The Old Testament World.* Philadelphia, 1966.
Nöttscher, F., "Entbehrliche Hapaxlegomena in Jesaia," *VT,* 1951.
Nyberg, H. S., *Hebreisk Grammatik.* Uppsala, 1952.

Oesterley, W. O. E., *The Doctrine of the Last Things.* London, 1909.
Oppenheim, A. Leo, "Assyriological Gleanings," *BASOR,* No. 103.
Orelli, Konrad von, *The Prophecies of Isaiah.* Edinburgh, 1899.

Orlinsky, Harry M., "Studies V," *Israel Exploration Journal*, 4, 1954.
————, "The Treatment of Anthropomorphisms and Anthropopathisms in the Septuagint of Isaiah," *HUCA*, 27, 1956.
Ottley, R. R., *The Book of Isaiah According to the Septuagint*. I, 1904, II, 1906.

Palache, J. L., *The Ebed-Jahweh Enigma in Pseudo-Isaiah*. Amsterdam, 1934.
Pallas, Svend Aage, *The Babylonian 'akitu' Festival*. Kφbenhavn, 1926.
Pap, L. I., *Das israelitische Neujahrsfest*. Kampen, 1933.
Paulus, Heinrich Eberhard Gottlob, *Philologische Clavis über das Alte Testament*. Jena, 1793.
Pedersen, J., *Israel*, I, II. London, 1926, 1947.
Penna, Angelo, *Isaia* (La Sacra Biblia). Torino, Roma, 1958.
Pentecost, J. Dwight, *Things to Come*. 1958.
Perles, *Analecten zum Alten Testament*, 2 vols.
Pfeiffer, *Introduction to the Old Testament*. New York, 1948.
Poidebard, A., *Un grand port disparu: Tyr*. 1939.
Poole, M., *Annotations Upon the Holy Bible*. London, 1688.
Pope, Marvin, "Isaiah 34 in Relation to Isaiah 35; 40-66," *JBL*, 71, 1952.
Pritchard, James, *Ancient Near Eastern Texts*. Princeton University, 1950.
Procksch, Otto, *Theologie des Alten Testaments*. Gütersloh, 1950.

Rahlfs, A., *Septuaginta*, II. Stuttgart, 1935.
Ranke, H., *Die aegyptischen Personennamen*. 1935.
Reichel, Carl Rudolf, *Der Prophet Jesaias*. Leipzig and Görlitz, 1755-1759.
Reider, J., "Etymological Studies in Biblical Hebrew," *VT*, 2, 1952.
Ridderbos, J., *Jesaja in Het Godswoord des Profeten*, 1932.
————, "Jahwäh malak," *VT*, 4, 1954.
Ringgren, Helmer, *The Prophetical Consciousness of Holiness*. Uppsala, 1948.
————, *Word and Wisdom*, 1947.
————, *Messias Konungen*. Uppsala, 1954.
Robinson, *Studies in Old Testament Prophecy*. 1950.
Rosenmüller, E. F., *Scholia in Vetus Testamentum*. Lipsiae, 1791-93.
Rost, P., *Die Keilschrifttexte Tiglatpilesers*, III. Leipzig, 1893.
Rowlands, E. R., "The Targum and the Peshitta Version of the Book of Isaiah," *VT*, 9, 1959.
Rowley, H. H., *The Biblical Doctrine of Election*. Naperville, 1950.
————, *The Faith of Israel*. 1956.
————, *The Servant of the Lord*. Oxford, 1965.
————, *The Relevance of Apocalyptic*. London, 1944.
————, *The Zadokite Fragments and the Dead Sea Scrolls*. Oxford, 1952.
Rudolph, Wilhelm, "Jesaja 23, 1-14," *Festschrift Friedrich Baumgärtel*. Erlangen, 1959.
————, "Jesaja 24–27," *Beiträge zur Wissenschaft vom Alten Testament*. Leipzig, 1908.

Saadia; see Gesenius' commentary for Saadia's exposition. Cf. also S. Landauer, *Kitab al-Amanat*. Leiden, 1880.
Sabatier, P., *Bibliorum sacrorum latinae versiones antiquae*, II. Paris, 1751.
Saggs, H. W. F., "The Nimrud Letters," *Iraq*, Vol. 21, Part 2, Autumn 1959.
Schilling, S. Paul, *Isaiah Speaks*. New York, 1958-59.

BIBLIOGRAPHY

Schmidt, Hans, *Die Schriften des Alten Testaments*. 1921, 1925.
————, *Die Thronfart Jahves*. Tübingen, 1927.
Schmidt, Sebastian, *Commentarius super illustres prophetias Jesaeae*. Hamburgi, 1702.
Schräder, *Die Keilschriften und das Alte Testament*. 1883, 1903.
Seeligmann, I. J., *The Septuagint Version of Isaiah*. Leiden, 1946.
Sellin, E., *Israelitische-jüdische Religionsgeschichte*. Leipzig, 1933.
————, *Serubbabel*. Leipzig, 1898.
————, *Studien zur Entstehungsgeschichte des jüdischen Gemeinde nach dem babylonischen Exil*. Leipzig, 1901.
Skinner, J., "Isaiah," *Cambridge Bible*. Cambridge, 1925.
Smart, James D., *History and Theology in Second Isaiah*. Philadelphia, 1965.
Smend, R., and A. Socin, *Die Inschrift des Königs Mesa von Moab*.
Smith, George Adam, *The Book of Isaiah*. New York; I, 1888, II, 1890.
Snaith, N. H., "The Exegesis of Isaiah XL. 5, 6," *ExT*, 52, 1941.
Stamm, J. J., "Ein Vierteljahrhundert Psalmenforschung," *Theologisches Rundschau*, 23, 1955.
Steinmann, J., *La Prophète Isaïe*. Paris, 1950.
Stenning, J. F., *The Targum of Isaiah*. Oxford, 1949.
Strachey, Edward, *Hebrew Politics in the Times of Sargon and Sennacherib*. London, 1853.
Stummer, F., *Einführung in die lateinische Bibel*. Paderborn, 1928.
————, "Einige Keilschriftliche Parallelen zu Jes. 40–66," *JBL*, 45, 1926.
Sukenik, Eleazer, *Otzar Hammegilloth haggenuzoth*. Jerusalem, 1954.

Tadmor, H., "The Campaigns of Sargon II of Assur: A Chronological-Historical Study," *Journal of Cuneiform Studies*, 12, 1958.
Talmon, S., *Annual of the Swedish Theological Institute*, 1, 1962.
Targum; see Stenning, J. F.
Thiele, Edwin F., *The Mysterious Numbers of the Hebrew Kings*. Grand Rapids, 1965.
Thomas, D. Winton, *Documents from Old Testament Times*. 1958.
Torrey, C. C., *The Second Isaiah*. Edinburgh, 1928.
Trapp, John, *Commentary on the Old and New Testaments*. London, 1867.

Umbreit, F. W. C., *Jesaja*. 1841.

Van der Flier, A., *De Profeet Jesaja*. Zust, 1931.
Van Dorssen, J. C., *De Derivata van de stam 'mn in het Hebreeuwsch van het Oude Testament*. Amsterdam, 1951.
Van Imschoot, *Theologie de l'Ancien Testament*. Tournai, 1954.
Van Til, Cornelius, *The Defense of the Faith*. Philadelphia, 1955.
Van Zyl, A. H., "Isaiah 24–27; Their Date of Origin," in *New Light on Some Old Testament Problems. Papers read at 5th meeting of Die O. T. Werkgemeenskap in Suid-Afrika*, 1962.
Varenius, August, *Commentarium in Isaiam*, Pars I-III. Rostochi, 1673.
Verhoef, P., *Die Dag van die Here*. Den Haag, 1956.
Vincent, *Jerusalem de L'Ancien Testament*. Paris, 1954.
————, "La notion biblique du haut-lien," *RB*, Vol. 55, 1948.
Vischer, *Die Immanuel Botschaft im Rahmen des königlichen Zionsfestes*. Zollikon-Zürich, 1955.

Vitringa, Campegius, *Commentarius in librum propheticum Jesaiae.* Leavadre, 1724.

Volz, Paul, *Das Neujahrsfest Jahwes.* Tübingen, 1912.

————, *Jesaja II.*

Von Rad, Gerhard, *Old Testament Theology,* 2 vols. New York, 1962, 1966.

————, "The Origin of the Concept of the Day of Yahweh," *JSS,* 4, April, 1959.

Vos, Geerhardus, *Biblical Theology.* Grand Rapids, 1954.

Vriezen, Th. C., *Hoofdlijnen der Theologie van het Oude Testament.* Wageningen, 1954.

Wade, G. W., *Old Testament History.* New York, 1908.

Weinfeld, M., "Cult Centralization in Israel in the Light of a Neo-Babylonian Analogy," *JNES,* Vol. 23, No. 3.

Weiser, Artur, *Einleitung in das Alte Testament.* Göttingen, 1949.

Welch, Adam, *Kings and Prophets of Israel.* London, 1953.

Westermann, C., *Grundformen prophetischer Rede.* 1960.

Winckler, H., *Die Keilschrifttexte Sargons.* Leipzig, 1889.

Whitcomb, J. C., Jr., *Darius the Mede.* Grand Rapids, 1960.

Widengren, George, *Religion och Bibel,* II, 1943.

Wilson, Robert Dick, *A Scientific Investigation of the Old Testament.* Chicago, 1959.

Wiseman, Donald J., *Chronicles of the Babylonian King.* London, 1956.

————, "Secular Records in Confirmation of the Scriptures," *Victorian Institute,* 1954.

————, *Vassal Treaties of Esarhaddon.* London, 1958.

Wright, G. E., *Biblical Archaeology.* Philadelphia, London, 1957.

————, *Isaiah.* Richmond, Va., 1964.

Wright, William, *Arabic Grammar.* Cambridge, 1967.

Young, E. J., *Introduction to the Old Testament.* Grand Rapids, 1958.

————, *My Servants the Prophets.* Grand Rapids, 1954.

————, *The Study of Old Testament Theology Today.* London, 1958-59.

————, *Studies in Isaiah.* Grand Rapids, 1954.

————, *Thy Word Is Truth.* Grand Rapids, 1957.

————, *Who Wrote Isaiah?* Grand Rapids, 1958.

————, "Adverbial *u* in Semitic," *WThJ,* 13, May, 1951.

————, "Isaiah 34 and Its Position in the Prophecy," *WThJ,* Vol. 27, No. 2, 1965.

Ziegler, J., *Isaias* (Septuaginta Vetus Testamentum graecum). Göttingen, 1939.

Zwingli, *Zwingli's Sämtliche Werke,* 14. Zürich, 1959.

Index of Scripture

Index of Persons

Index of Authors

579